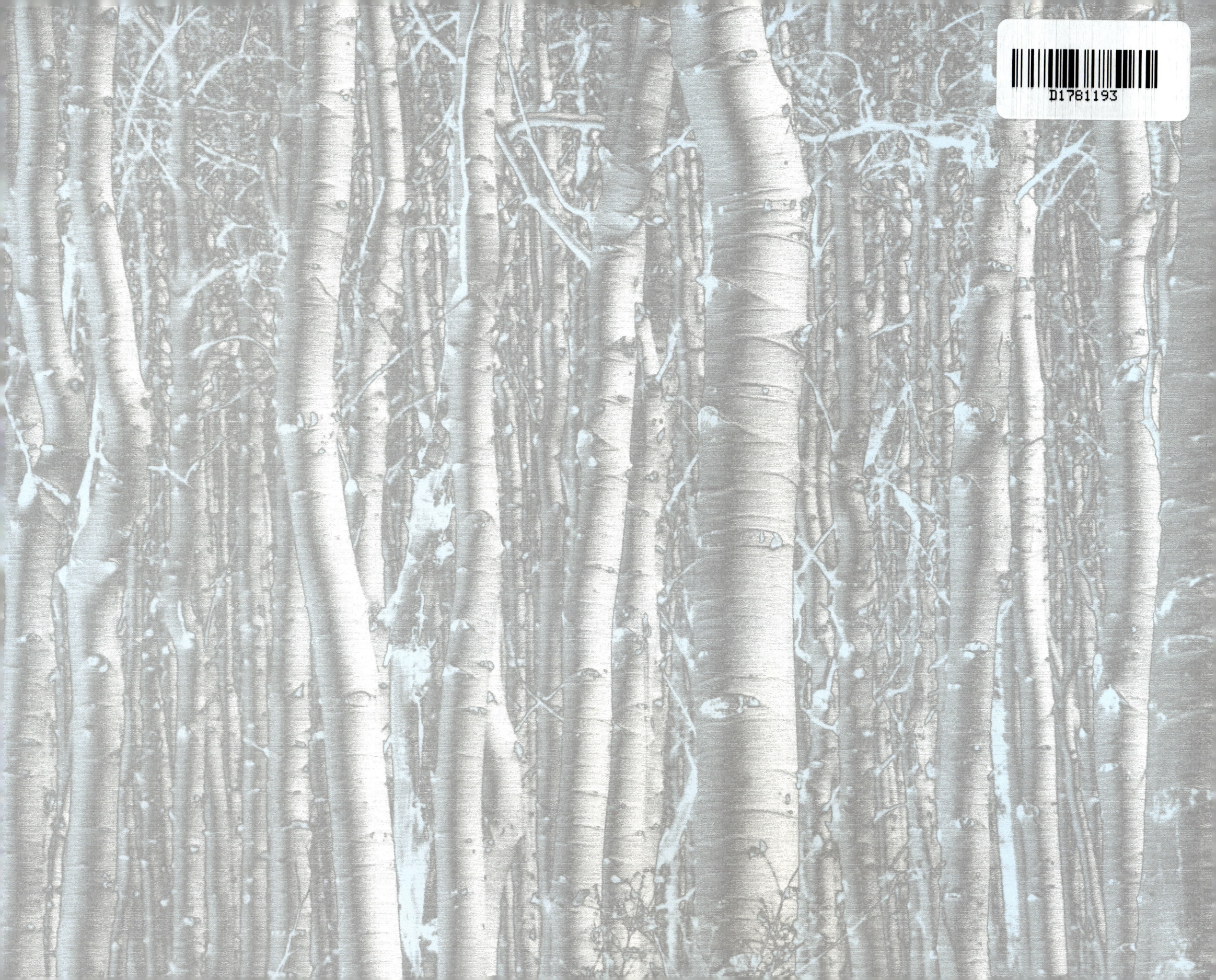

DREAM HOMES
COLORADO

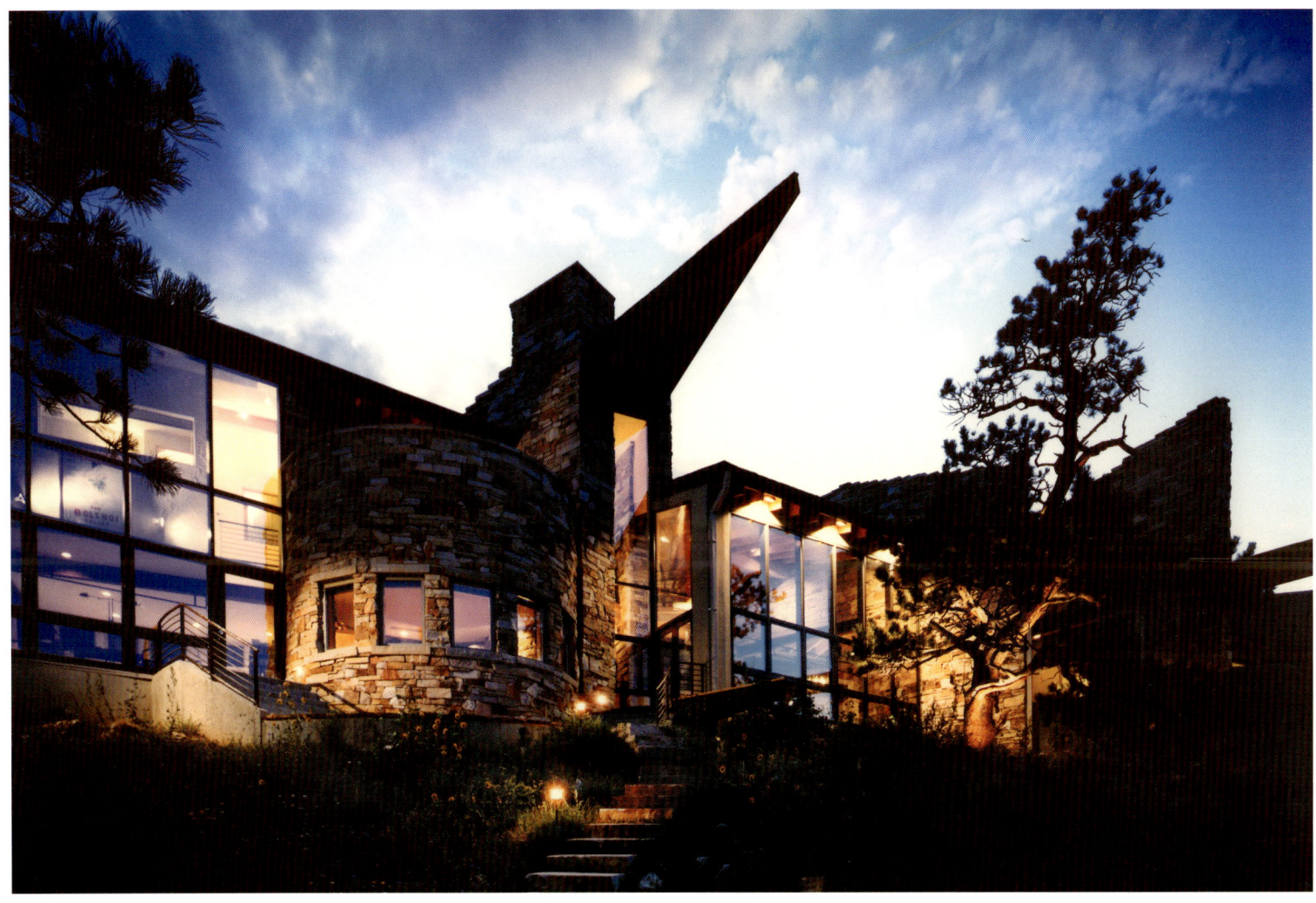

AN EXCLUSIVE SHOWCASE OF COLORADO'S FINEST ARCHITECTS, DESIGNERS AND BUILDERS

Published by

PANACHE
PARTNERS LLC

PANACHE PARTNERS LLC
13747 Montfort Drive, Suite 100
Dallas, Texas 75240
972.661.9884
972.661.2743
www.panache.com

Publishers: Brian G. Carabet and John A. Shand
Executive Publisher: Steve Darocy
Regional Publishers: Tom Fischer & Elizabeth Fischer
Editor: Beth Gionta
Art Director: Michele Cunningham-Scott

Copyright © 2006 by Panache Partners, LLC
All rights reserved.

No part of this book may be reproduced or transmitted in any form or by any means, electronic or mechanical, including photocopying, recording, or by any information storage or retrieval system, except brief excerpts for the purpose of review, without written permission of the publisher.

All images in this book have been reproduced with the knowledge and prior consent of the architects, home designers and custom builders concerned and no responsibility is accepted by the producer, publisher, or printer for any infringement of copyright or otherwise arising from the contents of this publication. Every effort has been made to ensure that credits accurately comply with the information supplied.

Printed in China

Distributed by Gibbs Smith, Publisher
800.748.5439

PUBLISHER'S DATA

Dream Homes of Colorado

Library of Congress Control Number: 2006930749

ISBN 13: 978-1-933415-31-4
ISBN 10: 1-933415-31-2

First Printing 2006

10 9 8 7 6 5 4 3 2 1

Previous Page: Barrett Studio Architects
See page 35   *Photograph by Wayne Thom*

This Page: Malibu Homes, Inc. and Woodley Architectural Group
See pages 123 and 201   *Photograph by Jeffrey Aron*

This publication is intended to showcase the work of extremely talented architects, home designers and custom builders. The Publisher does not require, warrant, endorse, or verify any professional accreditations, educational backgrounds or professional affiliations of the individuals or firms included herein. All copy and photography published herein has been reviewed and approved as free of any usage fees or rights and accurate by the individuals and/or firms included herein.

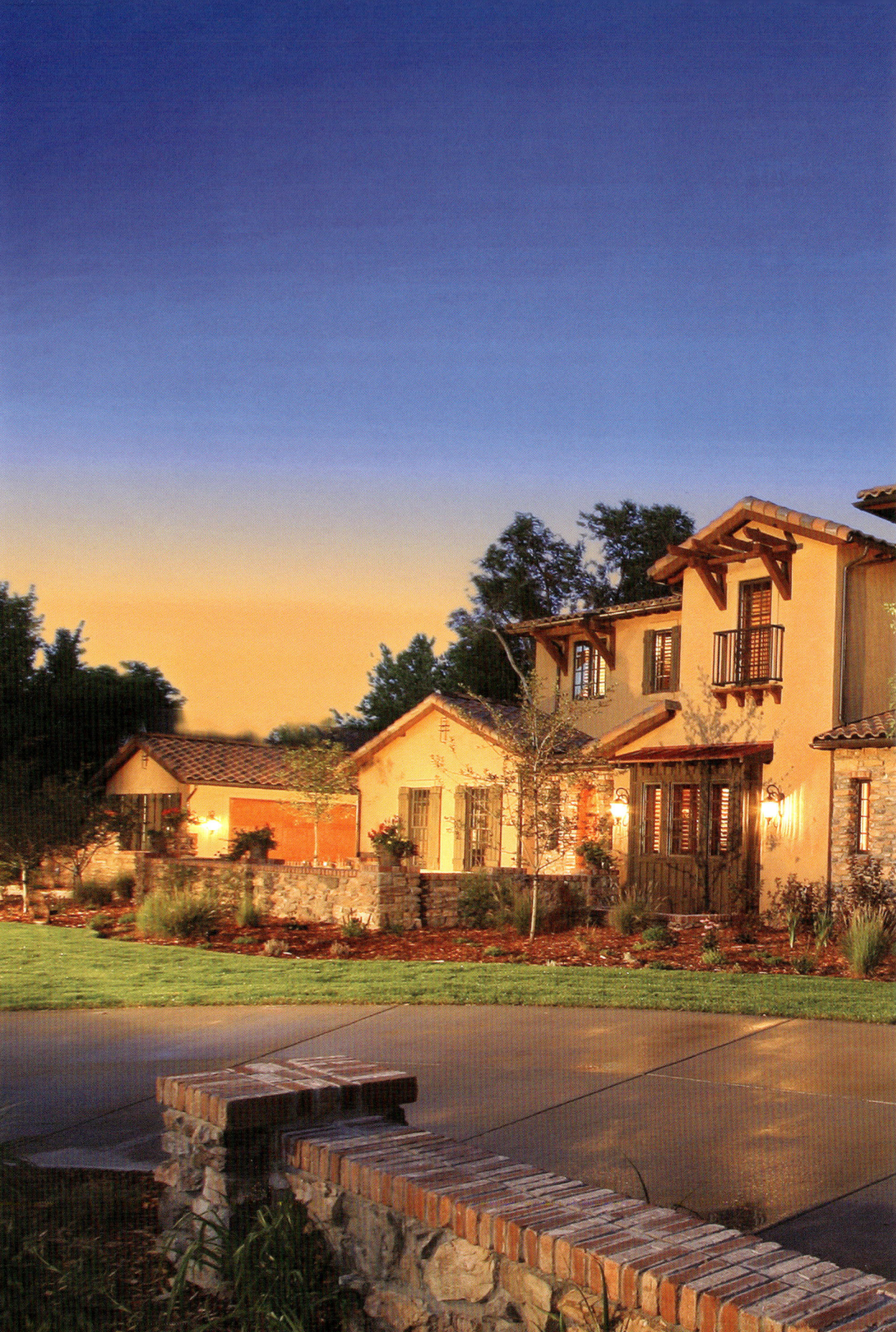

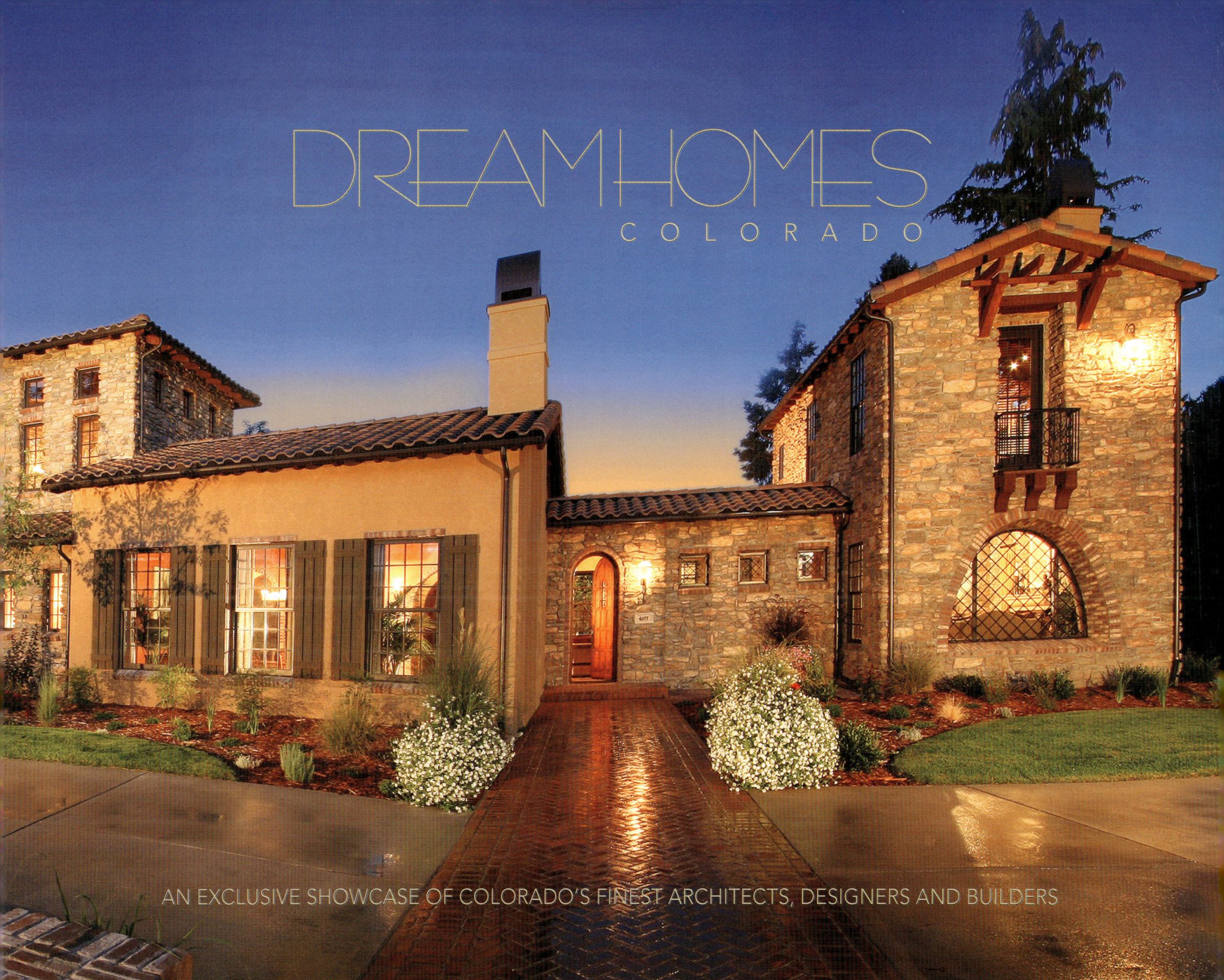

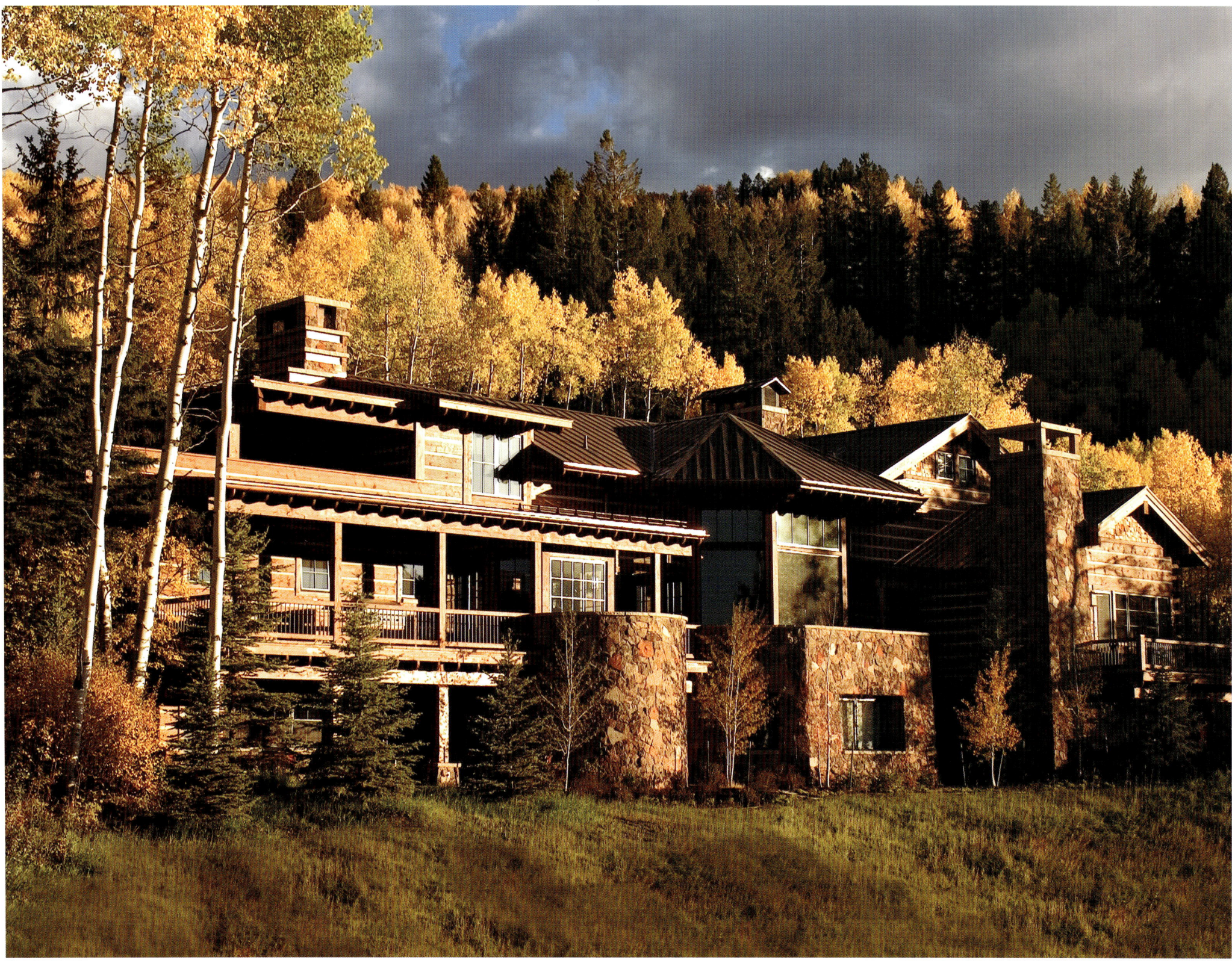

INTRODUCTION

Colorado is a place where many have dreamed of living. Teddy Roosevelt described Colorado by saying that "the scenery bankrupts the English language." Colorado is defined by its landscape. For most of us in this great state, the mountains are either surrounding you or are visible on the horizon. Colorado is a rich and varied land that features a healthy mix of outdoor adventures and culture combined with the charm of the Old West.

It is this magnificent scenery, activity and charm which drives the exceptional architecture and design in Colorado. This setting has resulted in the complexity of the Mountain West Vernacular and the often-times refreshing and pragmatic design responses to its climate and available materials. The old and the new, the rustic and the sophisticated, the wild and the refined–all of these experiences exist in Colorado. From the European-styled mansions in the Front Range, to the timber and stone retreats in the mountains, to the corrugated steel ranch houses in the valleys, to the contemporary designs found throughout Colorado–each home is designed with the landscape and culture in mind.

With the Rocky Mountains as the backdrop, the pages that follow feature some truly inspirational homes that express the timeless architecture and vision of the talented architects, designers and builders who have created them. Some common themes we heard throughout our discussions with these gifted individuals is a design and construction philosophy of listening to their clients and allowing their desires and lifestyle to drive the project while respecting the surrounding landscape in an environmentally sound and energy efficient approach. Colorado is a Dream Home destination because of the breathtaking views and Old West charm. It is evident that the architects, designers and builders presented in this book respect these elements.

Our thanks to everyone who has been a part of this journey and made it a great adventure. Many thanks to our production team for your tireless efforts in making this book all that it is. We would like to personally express our sincere thoughts and condolences to the family, friends and colleagues of David Gibson. Gibson Architects truly represents the timeless architecture and respect for the environment that makes Colorado a Dream Home destination.

Warmest Regards,

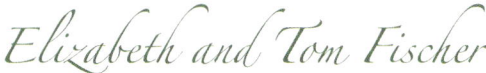
Elizabeth and Tom Fischer

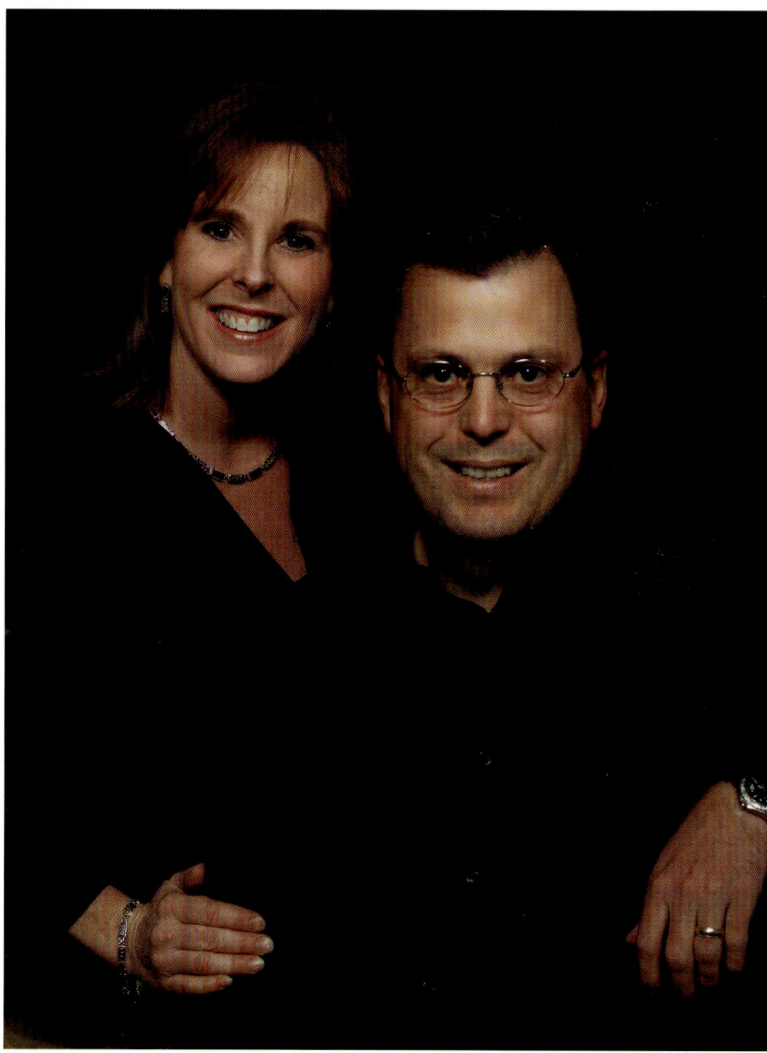

ARCHITECT Glen Rappaport, Black Shack Office, LLC: Page 41

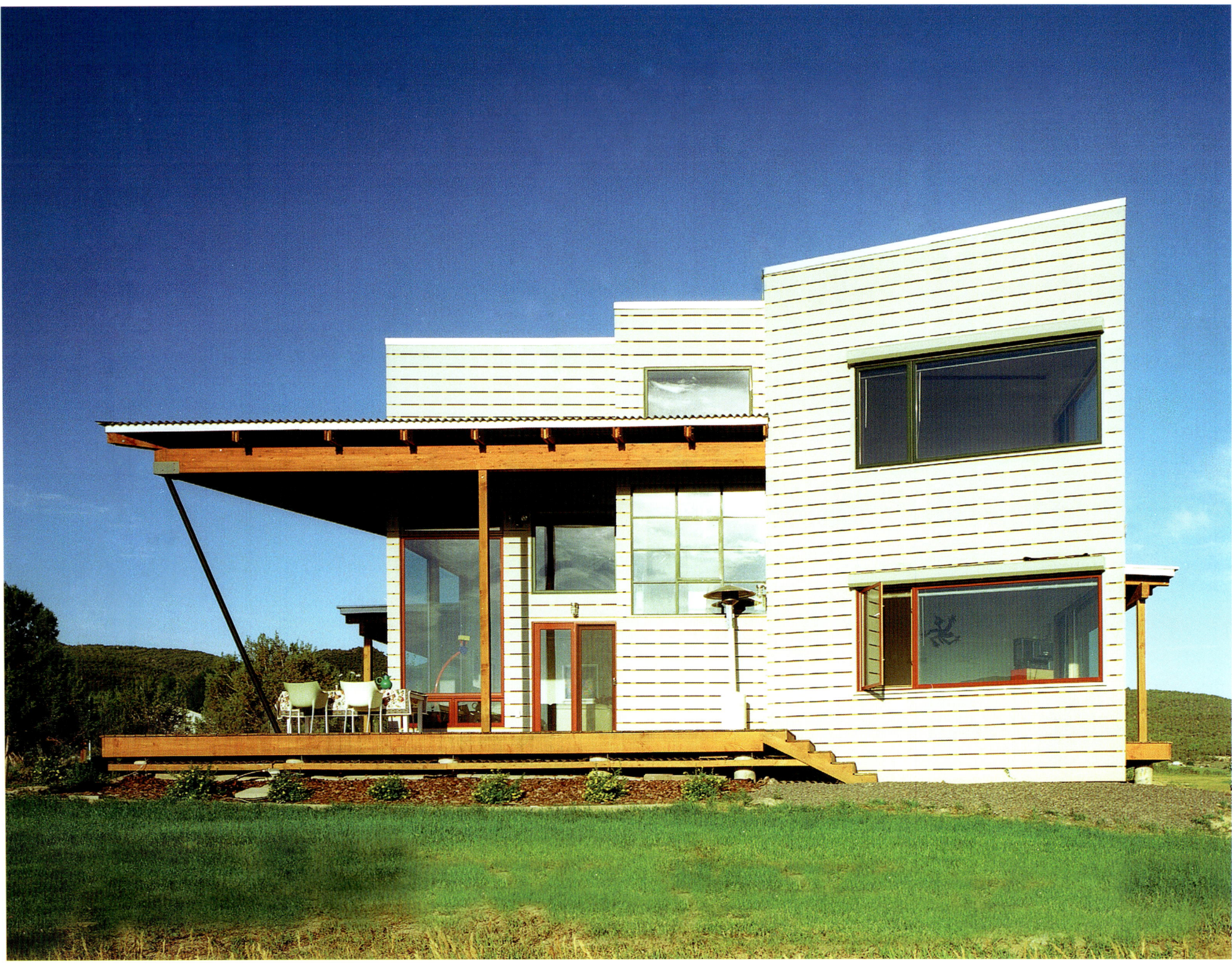

TABLE OF CONTENTS

ART - D.H. RUGGLES & ASSOCIATES 11
DON H. RUGGLES

ALLEN-GUERRA DESIGN-BUILD, INC 17
SUZANNE ALLEN-GUERRA & ETHAN GUERRA

ARAPAHOE ARCHITECTS P.C. 23
BOBBY CRAIG

ARCH 11 & HAMMERWELL INC. 27
E.J. MEADE, JAMES TREWITT & RICHARD SANDS

ARCHITECTUREDENVER 33
STEVE CHUCOVICH

BARRETT STUDIO ARCHITECTS 35
DAVID BARRETT

BLACK SHACK OFFICE, LLC 41
GLENN RAPPAPORT

BVZ ARCHITECTS & DAVID WILLIAMS HOMES 45
GARY BROTHERS, JIM VANDERVORSTE & DAVID WILLIAMS

CHARLES CUNNIFFE ARCHITECTS 51
CHARLES CUNNIFFE

CUSTOM MOUNTAIN ARCHITECTS 55
JON GUNSON

DIAMOND HOMES, INC. 61
EDWARD DIAMOND & STEVEN DIAMOND

ELIZABETH WRIGHT INGRAHAM ARCHITECTS 65
ELIZABETH WRIGHT INGRAHAM

FINHOLM ARCHITECTS & FW INTERIOR DESIGN GROUP 67
DAVID FINHOLM & KAREN WHITE

FRITZLEN PIERCE ARCHITECTS 71
LYNN FRITZLEN & WILLIAM PIERCE

GIBSON ARCHITECTS, LLC 75
DAVID GIBSON

HAGMAN ARCHITECTS 81
TIM HAGMAN

HARRISON CUSTOM BUILDERS, LTD. 85
LYNN & PAM HARRISON

HARRY TEAGUE ARCHITECTS 91
HARRY TEAGUE

JACK WILKIE BUILDER, INC. 93
JACK WILKIE

JEFFREY K. ABRAMS ARCHITECT P.C. 99
JEFFREY K. ABRAMS

JVL ASSOCIATES 103
LAYNE BENNETT

KH WEBB ARCHITECTS P.C. 107
KYLE H. WEBB

KNUDSON GLOSS ARCHITECTS 111
JOHN KNUDSON, JERRY GLOSS, PAUL MAHONY & MARTY BEAUCHAMP

LIPKIN WARNER DESIGN & PLANNING 117
MICHAEL LIPKIN & DAVID WARNER

MALIBU HOMES, INC. 123
GLEN ZAHORKA

MICHAEL HAZARD ASSOCIATES 127
MICHAEL HAZARD

MICHAEL KNORR & ASSOCIATES 133
MICHAEL KNORR

MORTER ARCHITECTS 137
JAMES R. MORTER

NEDBO CONSTRUCTION 143
ROLAND KJESBO

NO NAME ARCHITECTS 147
DAVE ARGO

POSS ARCHITECTURE + PLANNING 153
*BILL POSS, CHRIS RIDINGS, LES ROSENSTEIN
KIM WEIL & ANDY WISNOSKI*

RENO SMITH ARCHITECTS, LLC 159
AUGIE RENO & SCOTT SMITH

RMT ARCHITECTS 163
HARVEY ROBERTSON, PAUL MILLER & JEFFREY TERRELL

SATTLER HOMES, INC. 169
THOMAS W. SATTLER

SEARS BARRETT ARCHITECTS 173
SEARS BARRETT

SHEPHERD RESOURCES, INC./AIA 177
DOUGLAS MILLER DECHANT

T. MICHAEL MANCHESTER & ASSOCIATES, INC. 183
T. MICHAEL MANCHESTER

TKP ARCHITECTS, PC 189
KAREN KEATING & PAUL DEARDORFF

THE ERNEMANN GROUP ARCHITECTS 193
MICHAEL ERNEMANN

WODEHOUSE AUGELLO BUILDERS 197
RICHARD WODEHOUSE & MICHAEL AUGELLO

WOODLEY ARCHITECTURAL GROUP 201
MICHAEL WOODLEY

COLORADO PRESERVATION 205

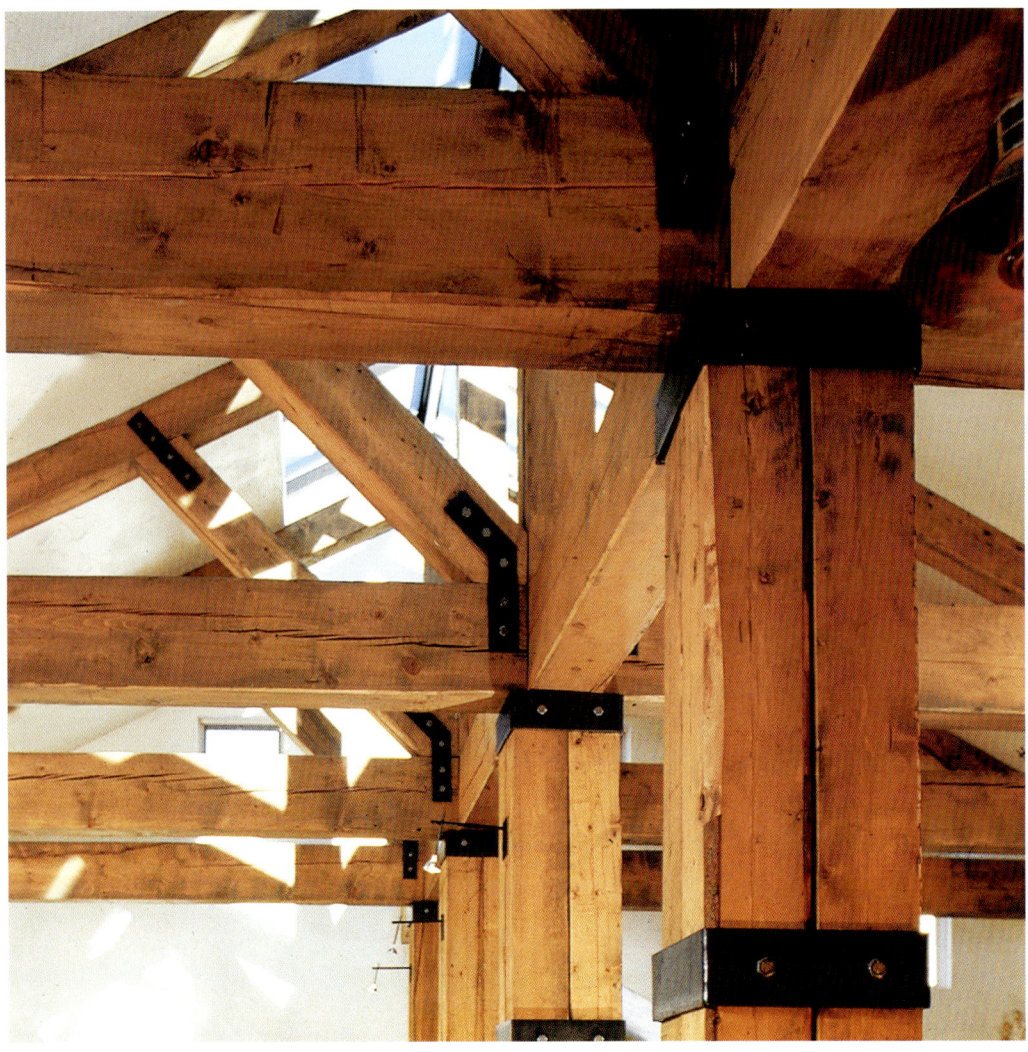

Shepherd Resources, INC./AIA: Page 177

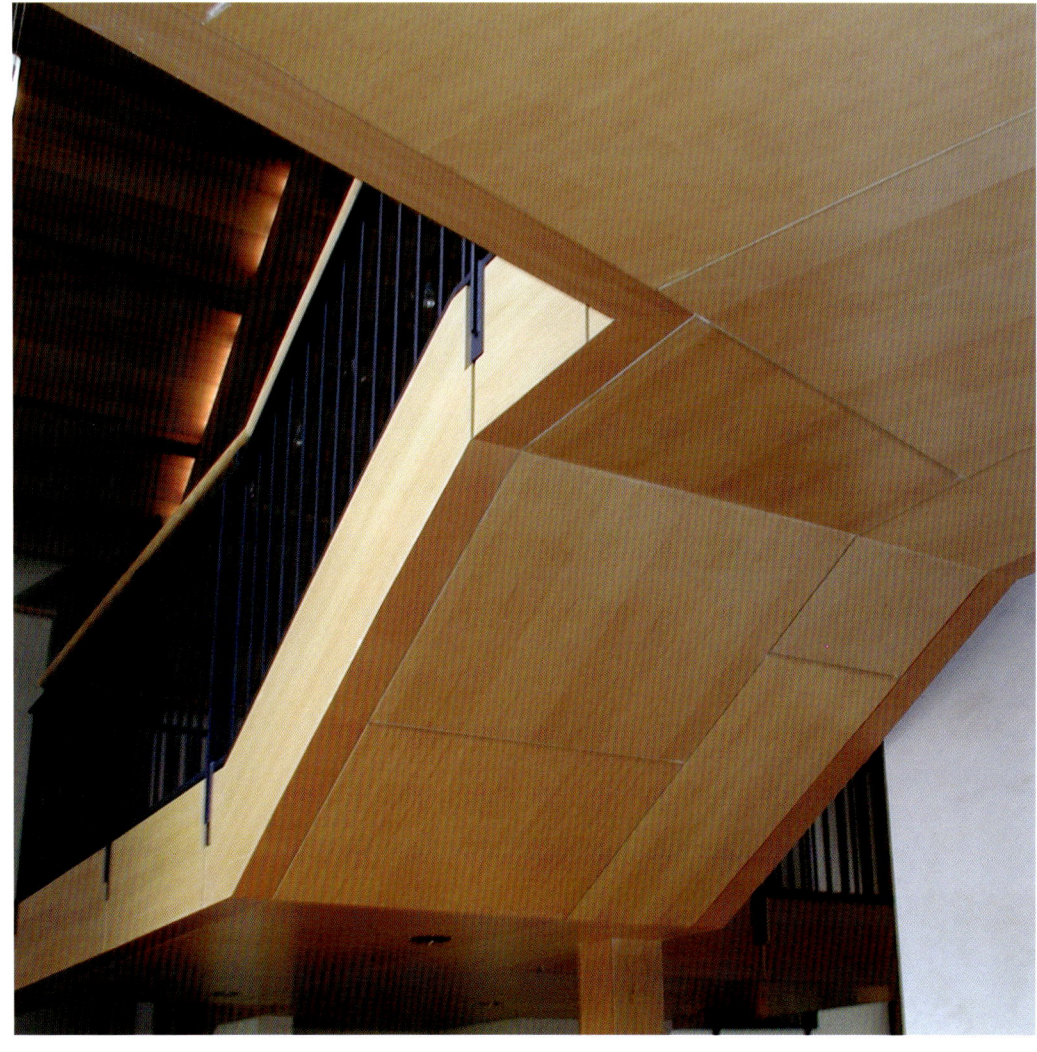

Arch 11/ Hammerwell Inc.: Page 27

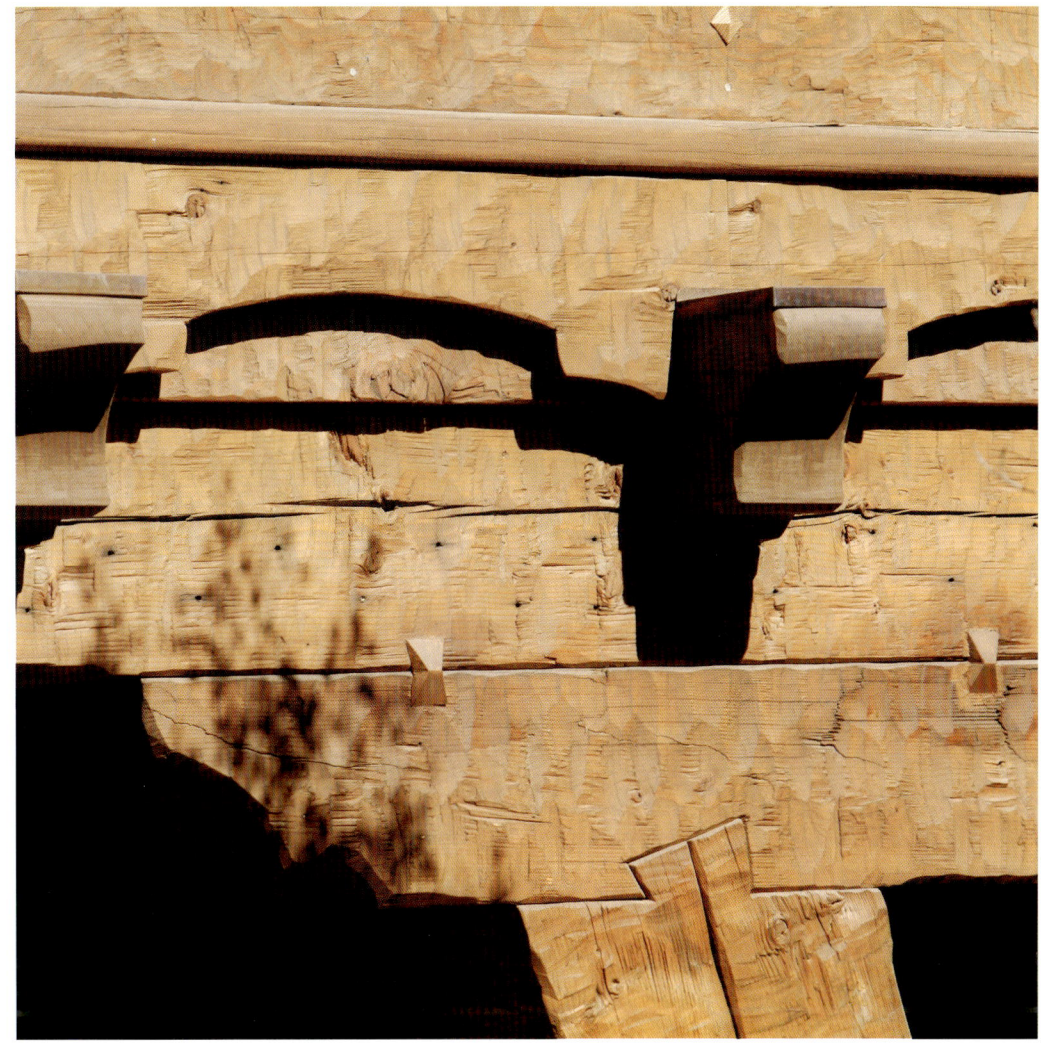

Shepherd Resources, INC./AIA: Page 177

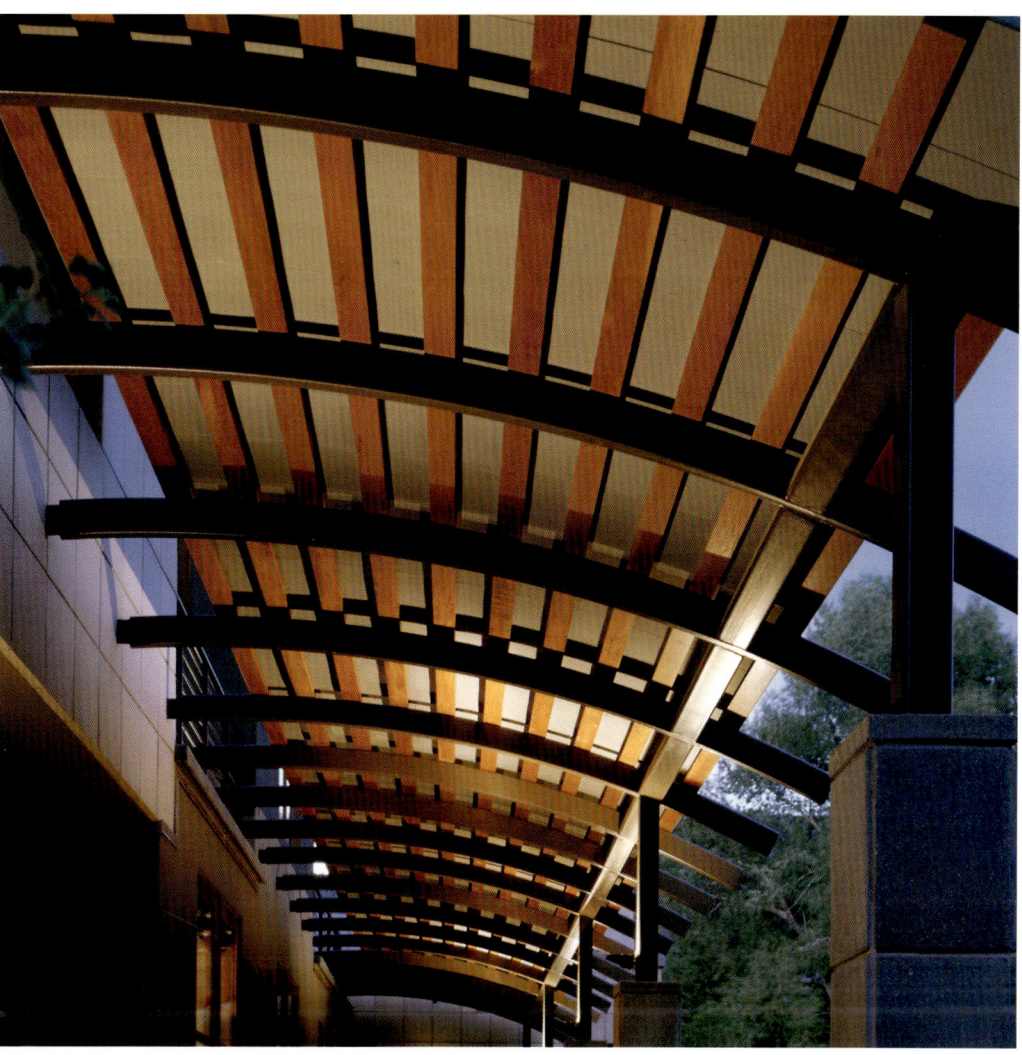

Jack Wilkie Builder, Inc. and Lipkin Warner Design & Planning: Pages 93 and 117

COLORADO

AN EXCLUSIVE SHOWCASE OF COLORADO'S FINEST ARCHITECTS AND BUILDERS

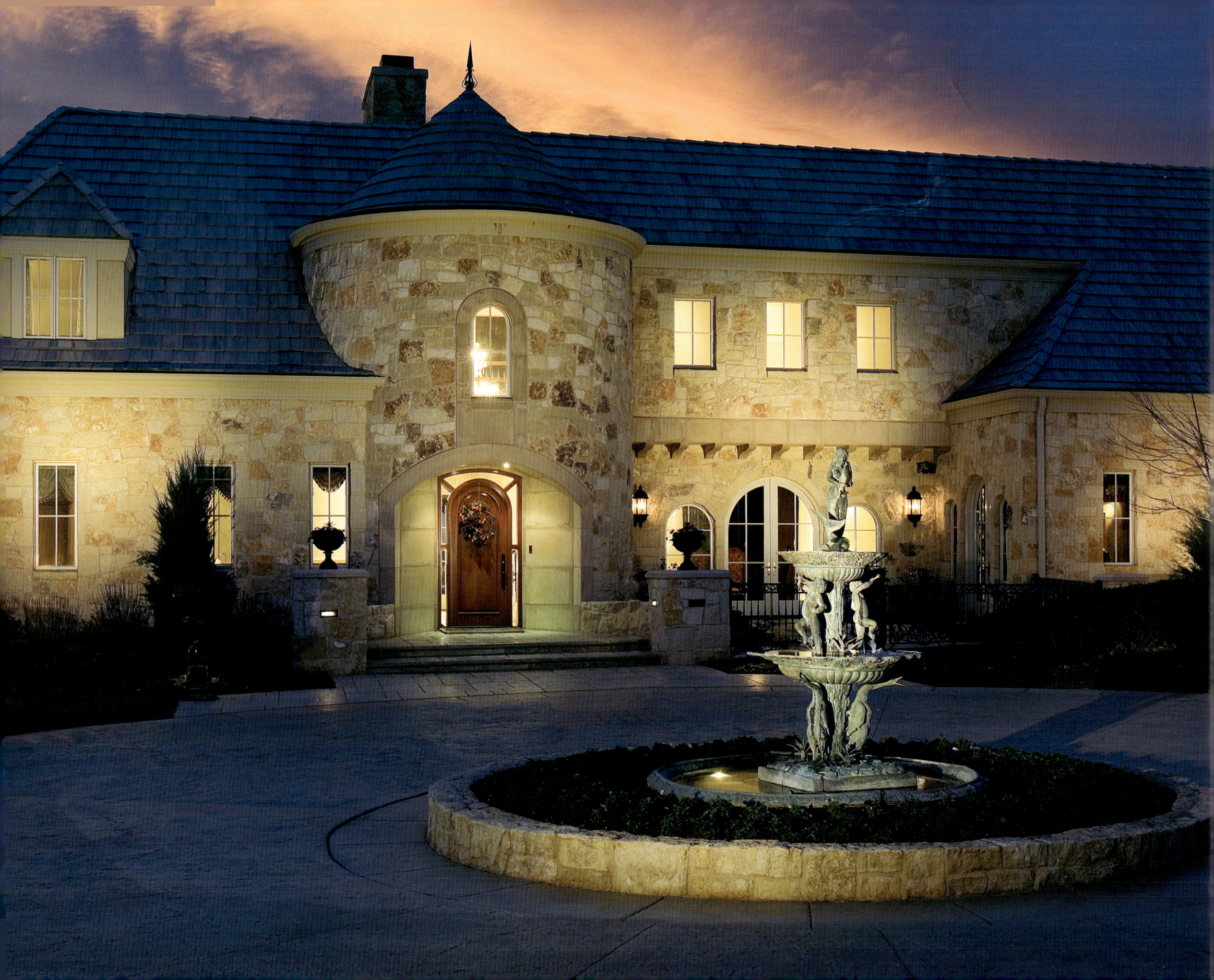

DON H. RUGGLES

ART - D.H. RUGGLES & ASSOCIATES

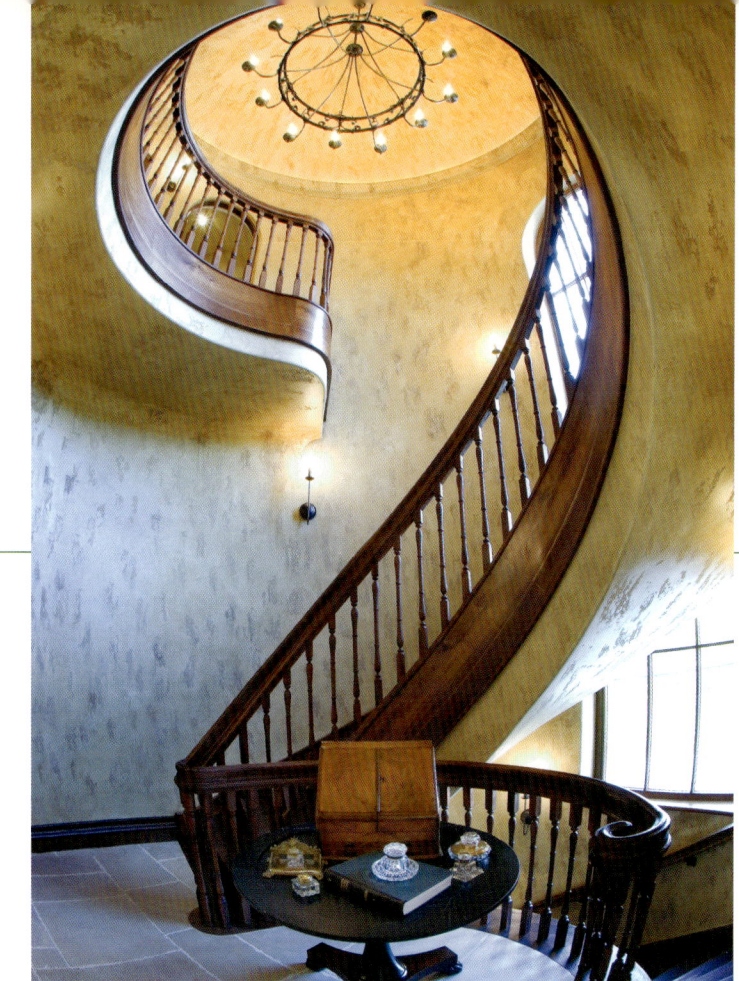

A sense of serene elegance coupled with the assurance of well-organized architectural plans defines the Don Ruggles approach. His firm, founded in 1970, builds on traditional architectural forms to respond to clients' needs in a most authentic way. D.H. Ruggles clients can expect to live in beautifully detailed and proportioned homes that reflect a feeling of composure and balance and look to historic styles to establish mood and tone.

Don's affinity for traditional styles such as Tudor, French Manor, English Country, Mediterranean, Tuscan and Santa Fe, is linked to his extensive travels and to his own family history. The Ruggles family left England for pre-Revolutionary War Boston, and helped to finance Jamestown. One ancestor sheltered Paul Revere in Cambridge. Moving westward, branches of the family eventually settled in Tulsa, where a 10-year-old Don compiled a list of favorite homes he could view as he rode by on his bicycle. Growing up amid these stately houses, many built with oil money, has influenced Don's life and his architectural practice.

In 1973, Don graduated with a B.A. in architecture from the University of Oklahoma where he was a member of the Architecture Honor Fraternity, Tau Sigma Delta. After graduation, he lived in Versailles, with secondary study sites in Nice, Loire Valley and Paris, where he studied historic innovations in structural logic of the 20th century. Don also conducted extensive research relating to contemporary architecture at the Le Corbusier Foundation in Paris. His passionate interest in architecture has fueled independent studies around the world including extensive research in Mayan architecture at the University of Mexico, studies of historical and contemporary Japanese architecture, building technologies and manufacturing methods at such sites as Tokyo and Osaka, and a Rome-based Italian foray for in-depth study of Renaissance, Baroque and late-Baroque design. Further studies in the British Isles, Scandinavia, Barcelona and throughout the continental U.S. to explore regional American architecture have served to infuse Don's work with a sense of meaning and historic references. The combination of rusticated beauty and gracefulness which he experienced in Europe has been translated as

ABOVE:
The elegant sweep of this entry hall stair gives this home a sense of grace and composure.
Photograph by Jim Scholz

FACING PAGE:
The entry to a French Manor-style home sets a mood of beauty and strength.
Photograph by Jim Scholz

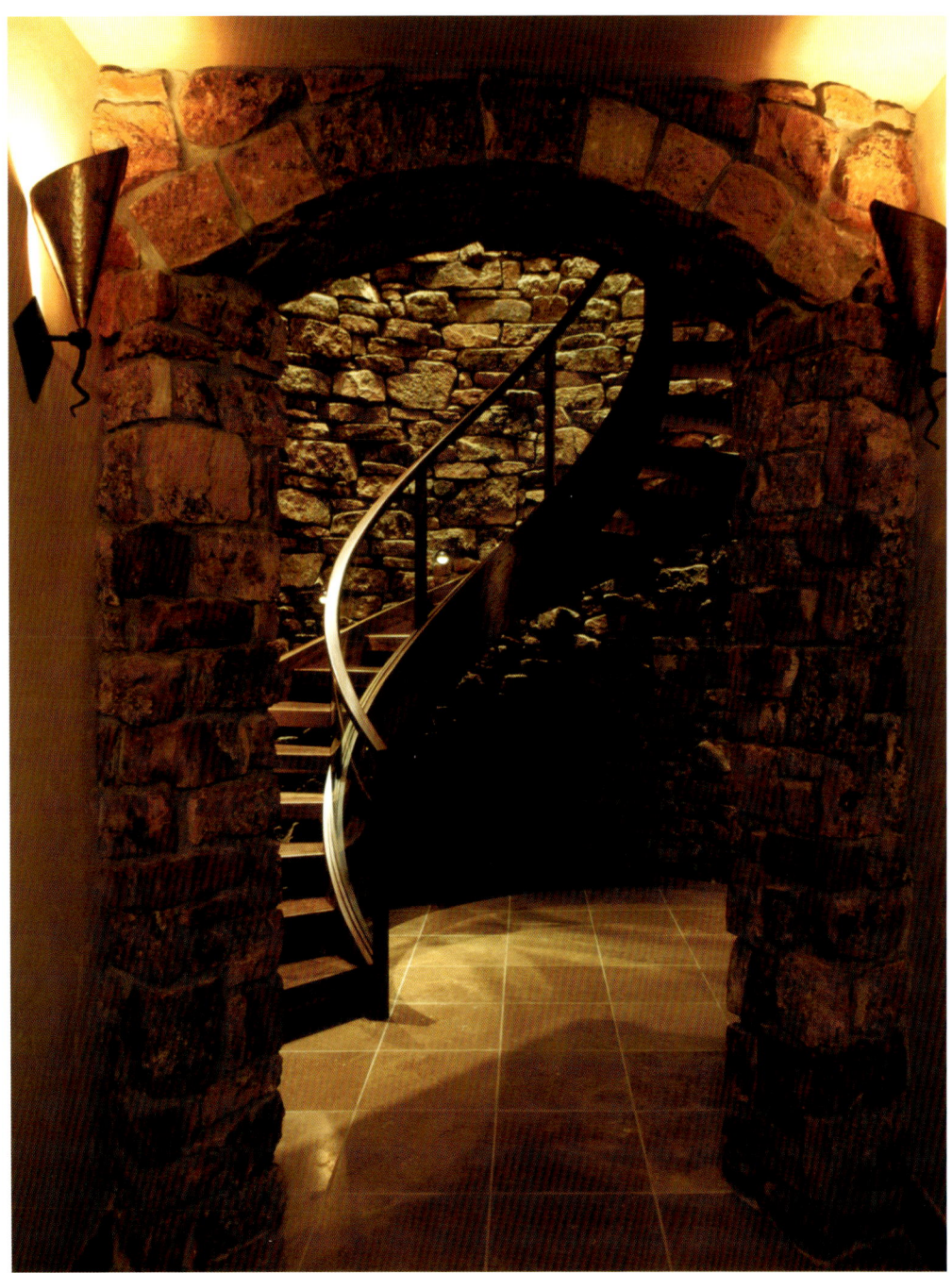
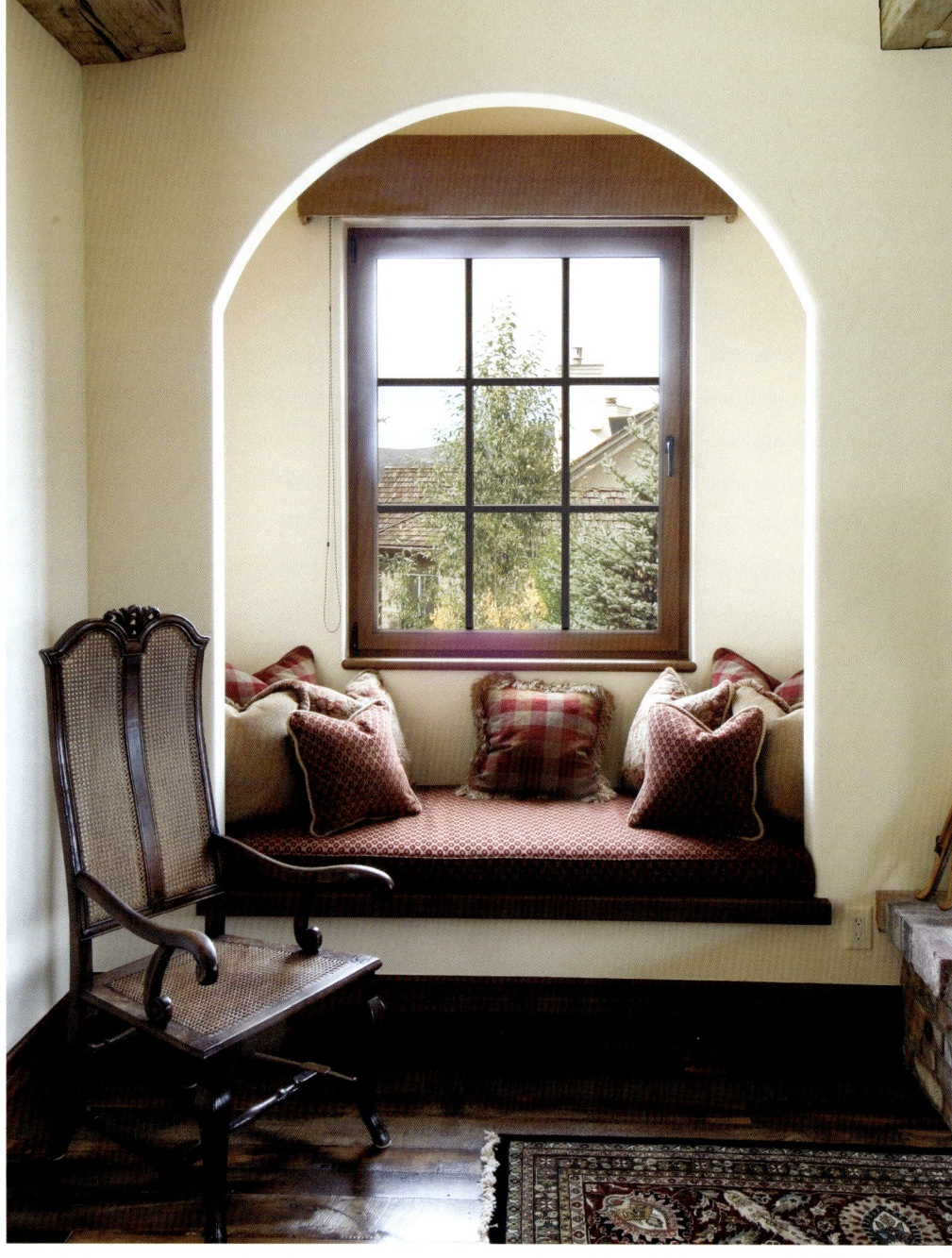

ABOVE LEFT:
An ancient stone Kiua shelters the stair of this contemporary home.
Photograph by Karen Enenkel-Coutu

ABOVE RIGHT:
A quiet nook allows for reading and mountain viewing.
Photograph by Jim Scholz

FACING PAGE:
A grand loggia echoes the rhythms of the distant horizon at sunrise.
Photograph by Jim Scholz

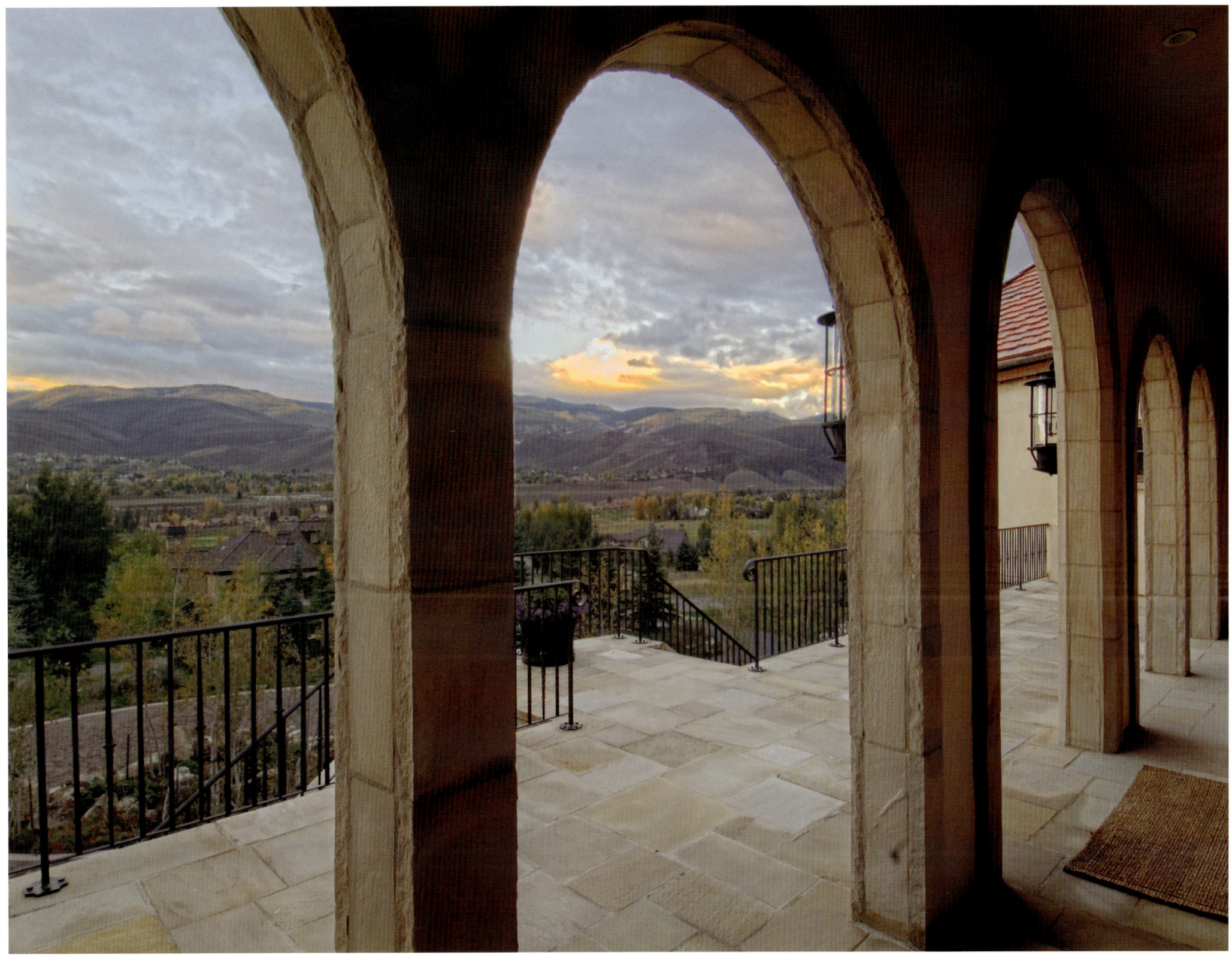

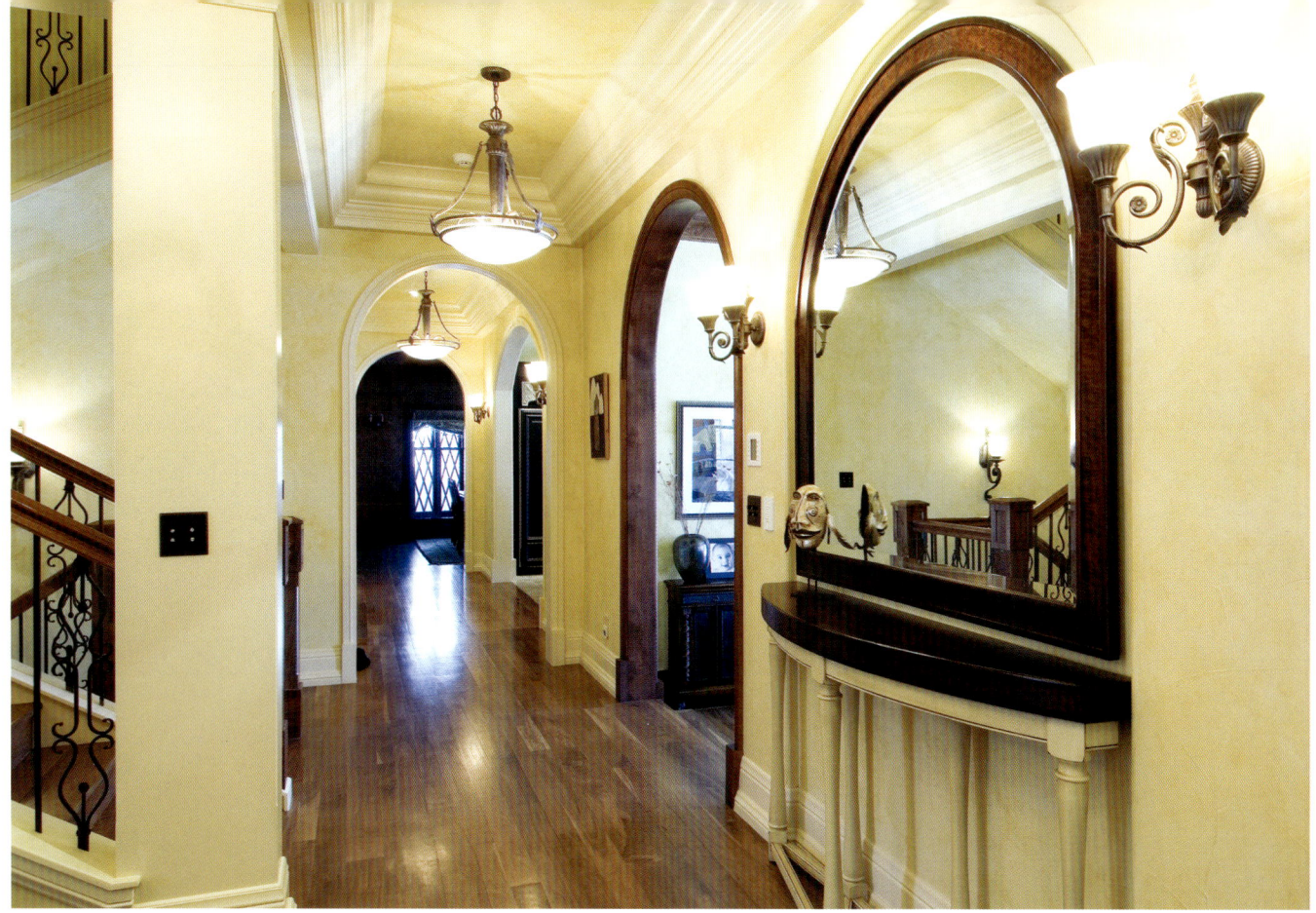

a hallmark in many D.H. Ruggles homes, throughout 15 states including Colorado. It's about simple, rich shapes, an assemblage of ideas evolving with different symmetries combined into one unit. Don uses those ideas to give his houses an immediate sense of history, shifting materials from one portion to another, perhaps rotating a wing off the grid to create small subtle shifts filled with life and energy.

These traditional concepts adapt very well to Denver, a forward thinking and energetic area. With such variable weather conditions, the importance of an exterior wall in a home takes on a lot of significance, for example.

These historic forms provide a strong sense of protection and shelter here, and the weight and thickness of their original walls translate nicely into every style of home designed by D.H. Ruggles. Don and the D.H. Ruggles staff work closely with clients to define personal style, crafting each home, and its interior flow to accommodate every lifestyle from a formal composed family to a family that likes to open the house to frequent neighborhood visitors. Clients often sketch along with Don to combine historical forms with current lifestyle requirements such as large kitchens, media rooms, gyms, and homework rooms with multiple computers. The process includes a client wish list and clients are gently prodded to acknowledge subconscious items, perhaps a rear porch from childhood that can be woven into the fabric of the house. The ultimate goal is that clients take emotional as well as physical ownership of their homes."Each time I travel I bring back subconscious images that go into my mind's 'databank,'" Don says. "Colorado is a good palette for that. My clients have the benefit of years of my travel and research, and they have access to it. We give them everything we have."

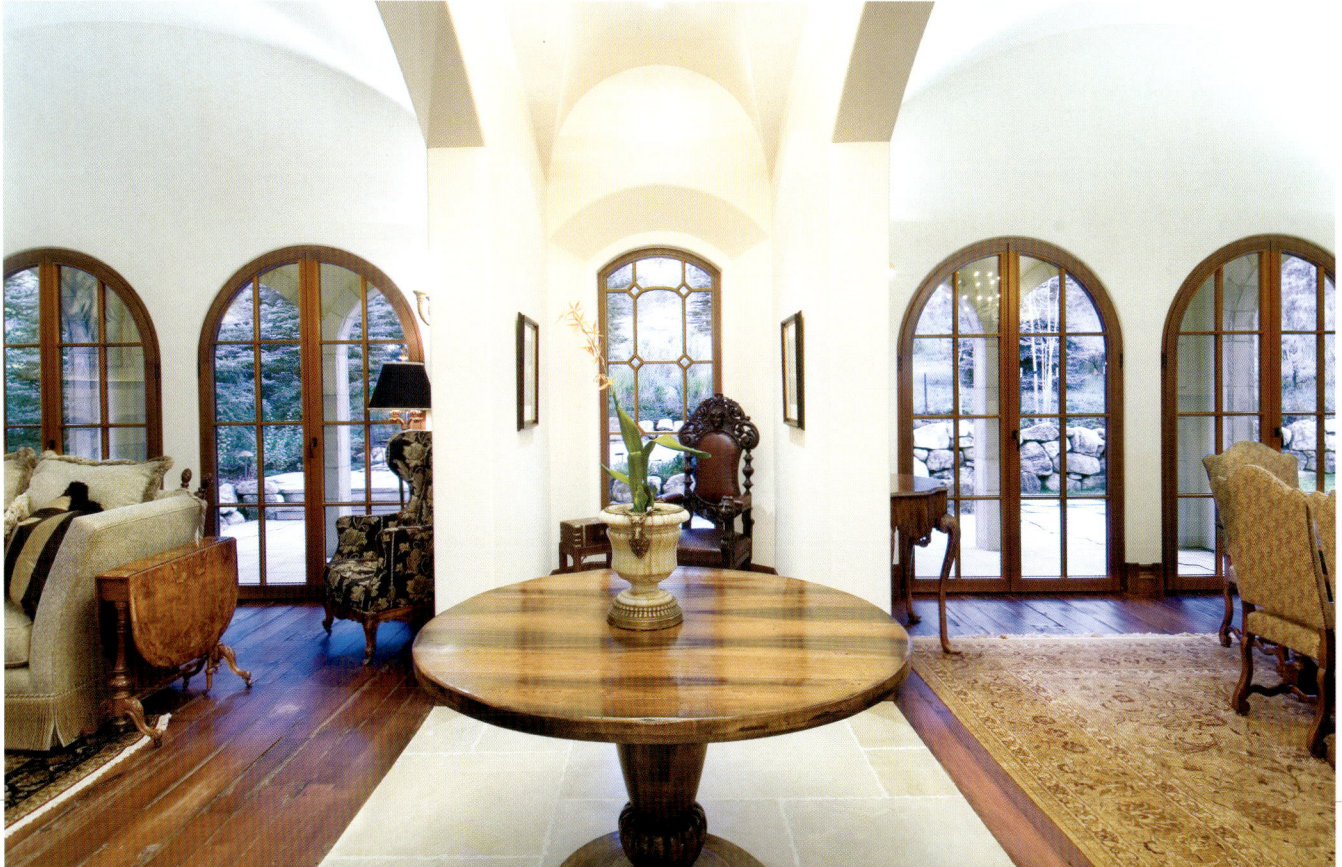

TOP LEFT:
Plaster, hardwood and arches combine to form this beautiful Tuscan interior.
Photograph by Jim Scholz

BOTTOM LEFT:
Groin vaults cascade over this living room to quiet the space while the arches flow to a rear court.
Photograph by Jim Scholz

FACING PAGE TOP:
The sweeping views of this hearth room are offset by a sense of warmth and comfort.
Photograph by Jim Scholz

FACING PAGE BOTTOM:
The depth of wood and the strength of granite are woven into a Tuscan style kitchen.
Photograph by Jim Scholz

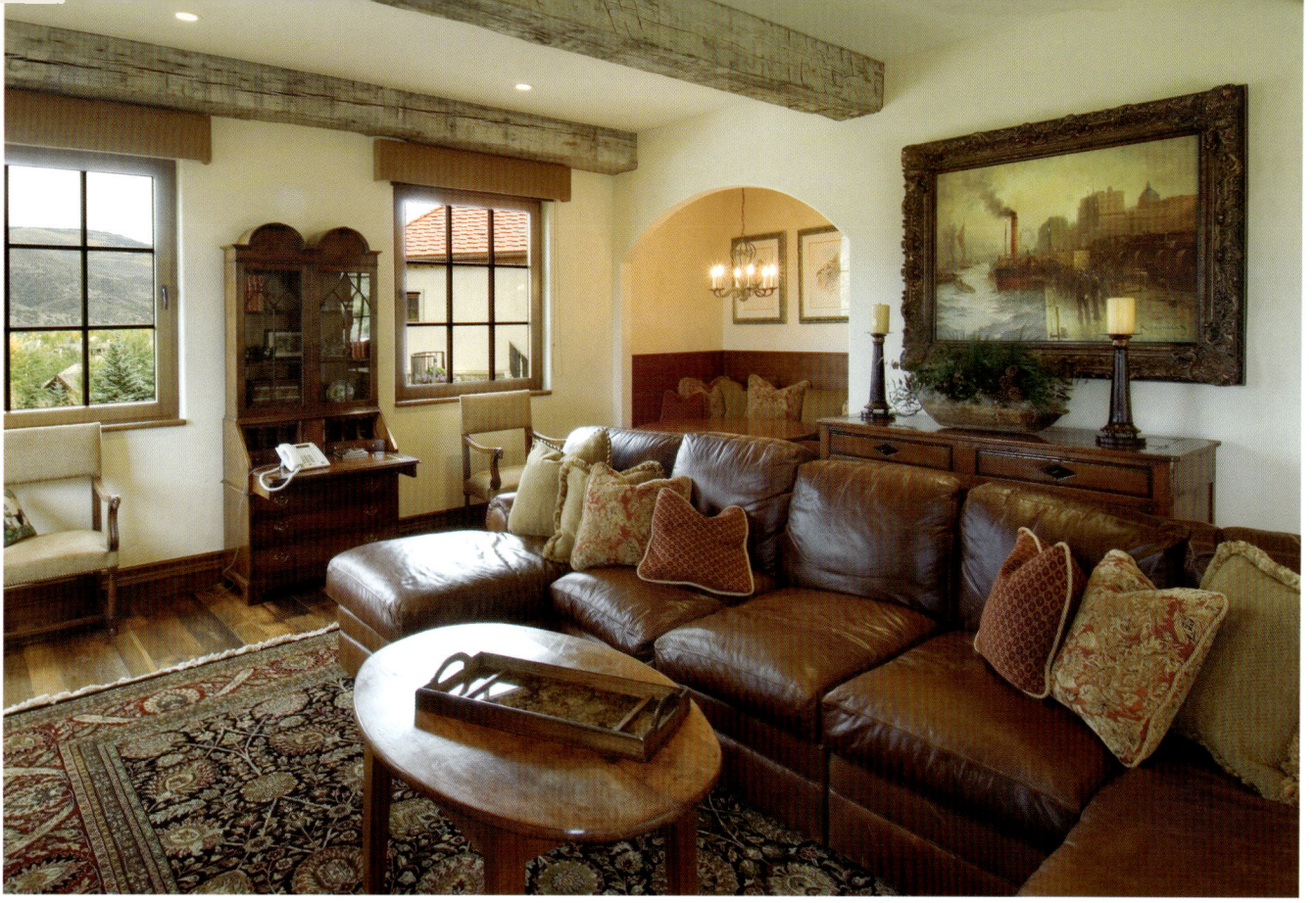

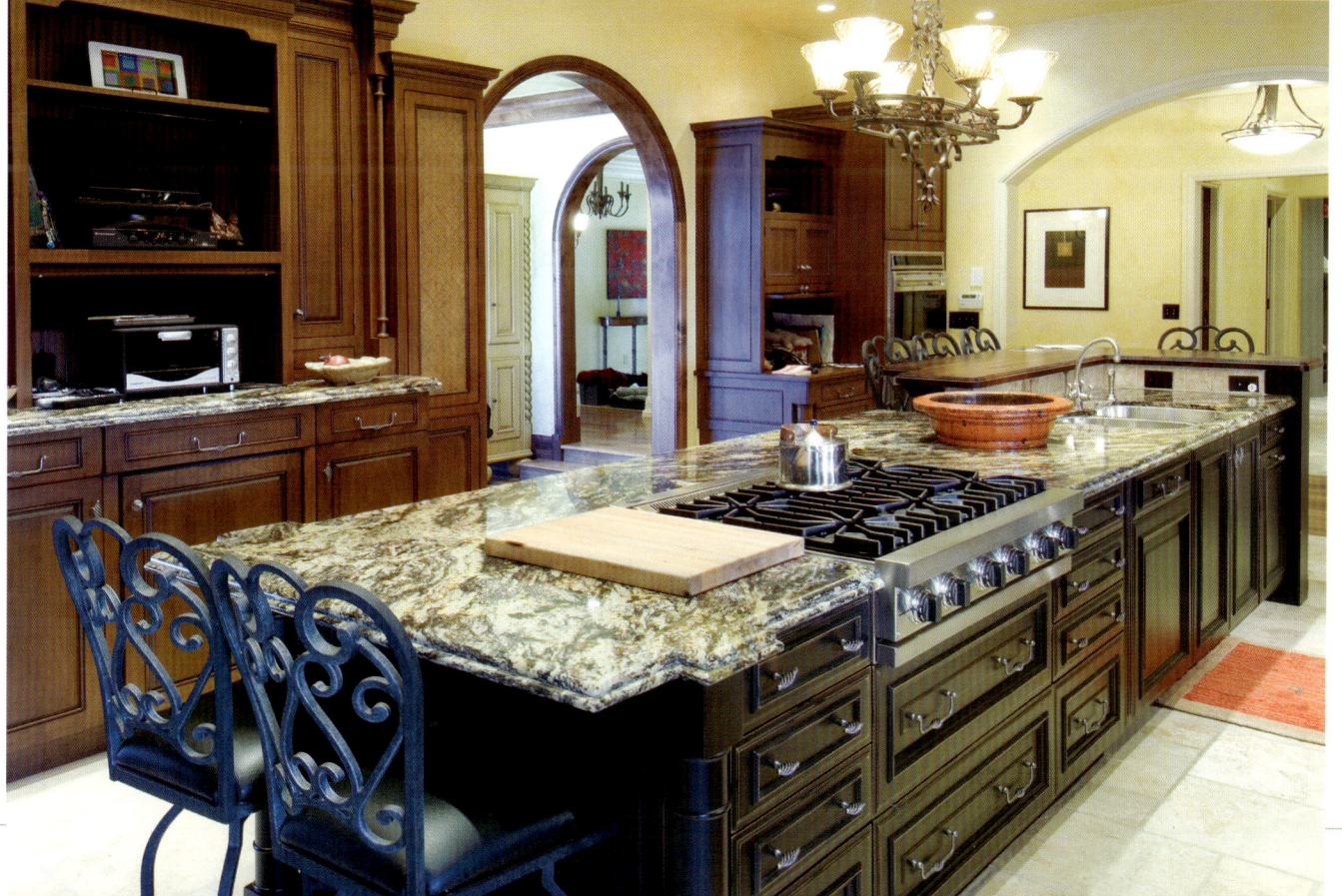

Q&A
more about don...

ANY AWARDS OR SPECIAL RECOGNITION YOU WOULD LIKE MENTIONED? PLEASE SELECT A FEW FROM YOUR NUMEROUS AWARDS:
We were *Colorado Homes & Lifestyles* magazine's "Home of the Year" winner in 1991, 1996 and 2001.

WHAT BOOK ARE YOU READING NOW?
Nature of Order by Christopher Alexander.

WHAT IS THE MOST UNIQUE HOME WITH WHICH YOU ARE INVOLVED?
Baker Ranch, in Rapid City, South Dakota. It's a home designed to look like an old French village. The owner has collected antiques and architectural pieces for 10 years. It is truly a remarkable project.

NAME SOME THINGS MOST PEOPLE DON'T KNOW ABOUT YOU?
I'm interested in music theory and quantum physics. I also play classical piano.

WHO HAS HAD THE BIGGEST INFLUENCE ON YOUR CAREER?
My mother, father and wife.

ART - D.H. RUGGLES & ASSOCIATES
DON RUGGLES, AIA
3200 Cherry Creek South Drive #410
Denver, CO 80209-3246
303.355.2460
f: 303.355.2546

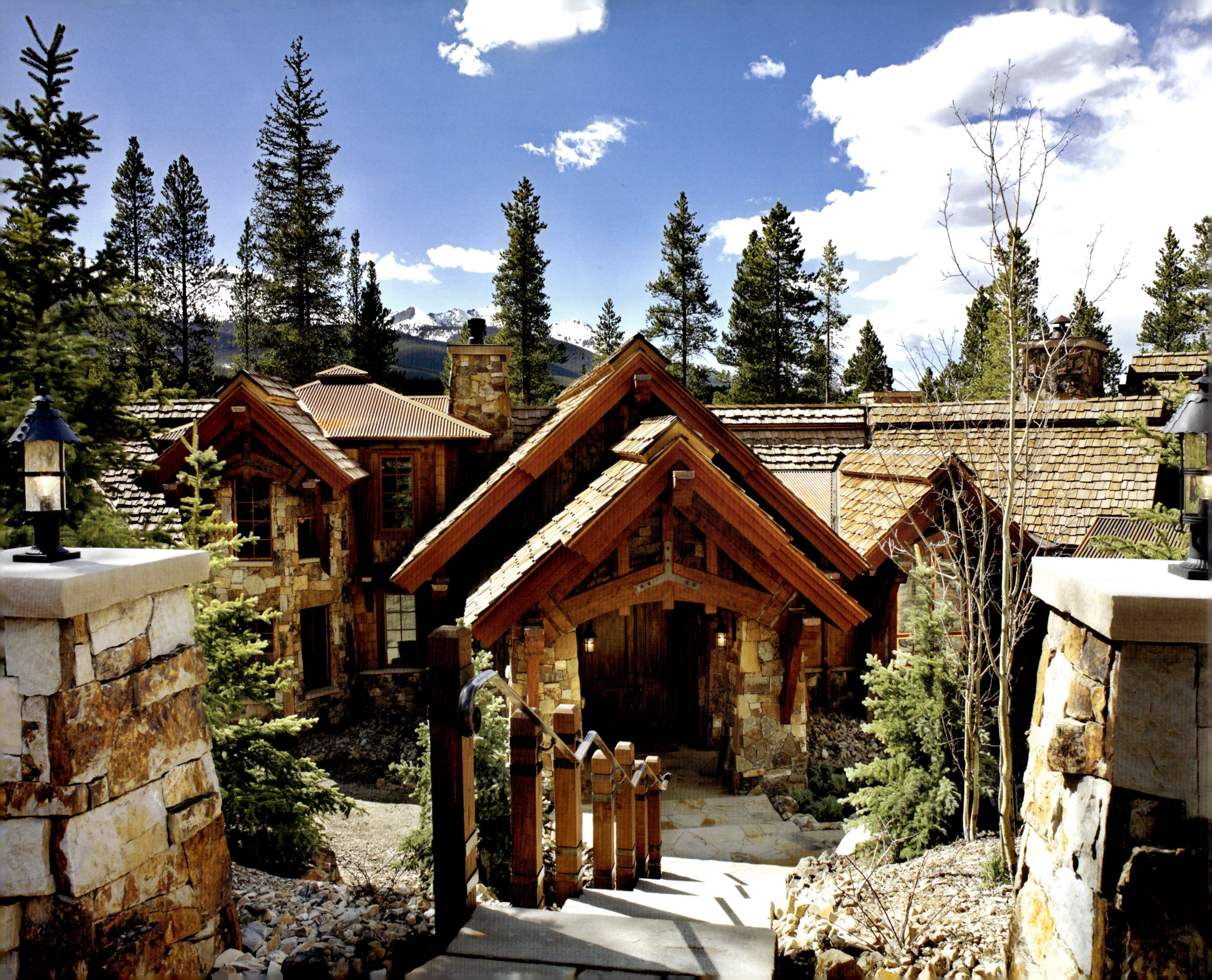

SUZANNE ALLEN-GUERRA
ETHAN GUERRA

ALLEN-GUERRA DESIGN-BUILD, INC

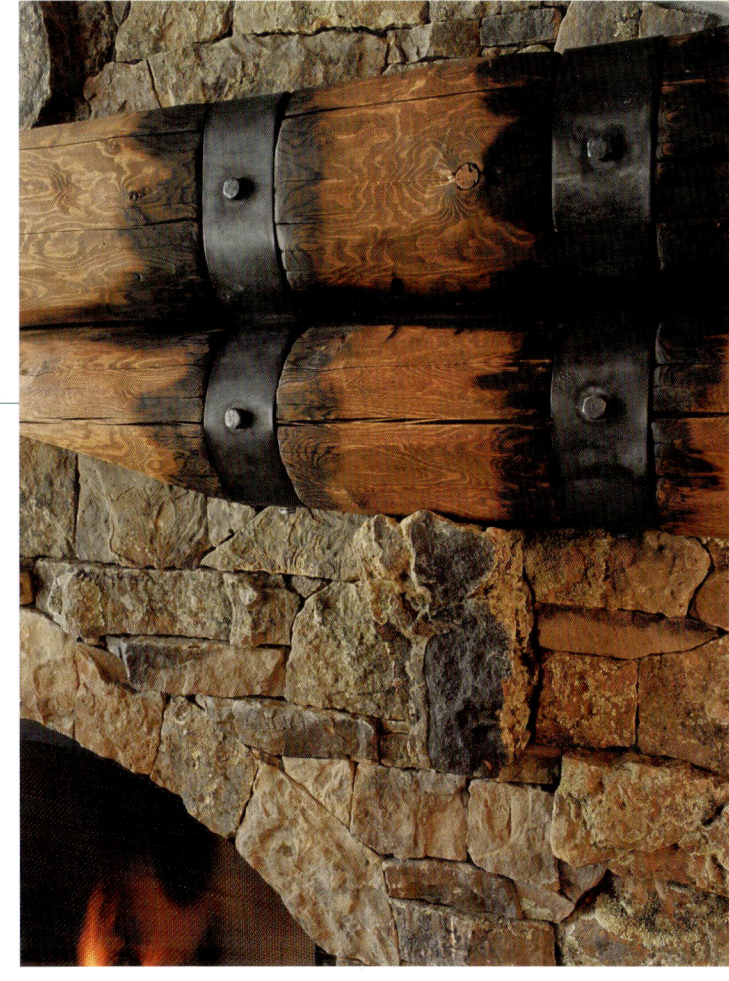

Suzanne Allen-Guerra and her husband and partner, Ethan Guerra, have owned their firm, Allen-Guerra Design-Build, Inc, in Breckenridge, Colorado, since 1997. Their firm has become widely known and respected for its commitment to excellence in architecture and construction, as well as its focus on details and the ability to listen to clients in order to turn their desires into built form.

Most important to Allen-Guerra Design-Build is designing and building timeless architecture. They strive to design and build homes that appear to have grown organically out of their respective sites and look like they could have been standing on the site for 10, 20 or even 100 years. Innovatively utilizing reclaimed or recycled materials is one of their keys to creating an ageless architectural style.

Allen-Guerra Design-Build is dedicated to designing and constructing buildings that conform to their landscape in an environmentally sound and energy efficient manner. Utilizing alternative materials, renewable energy sources and new construction methods, the team integrates environmentally sound solutions with any home design they approach. Their design philosophy of listening to their clients and allowing their desires and lifestyle to drive the project, along with tremendous attention to detail are what make Allen-Guerra Design-Build homes stand apart.

Suzanne receives immense gratification from her work. "The best part of owning a design-build firm is seeing your drawings and ideas come to fruition through the construction process. There's no greater compliment to my work than the return clients we constantly work with," she noted.

To Suzanne, a good design always has immaculate details, which is why she and her firm spend an incredible amount of time during the planning process on all their projects. She learned this design principle, as well as many others, from the work of Mary Elizabeth Colter, an outstanding

ABOVE:
Architecture can be found in the details. The steel brackets on this mantel were forged in place.
Photograph by Matthew Krane

FACING PAGE:
Built and designed by Allen-Guerra Design-Build, this Breckenridge home's distinctive combination of stone, copper, steel and cedar blends perfectly with the surrounding landscape.
Photograph by Ron Ruscio

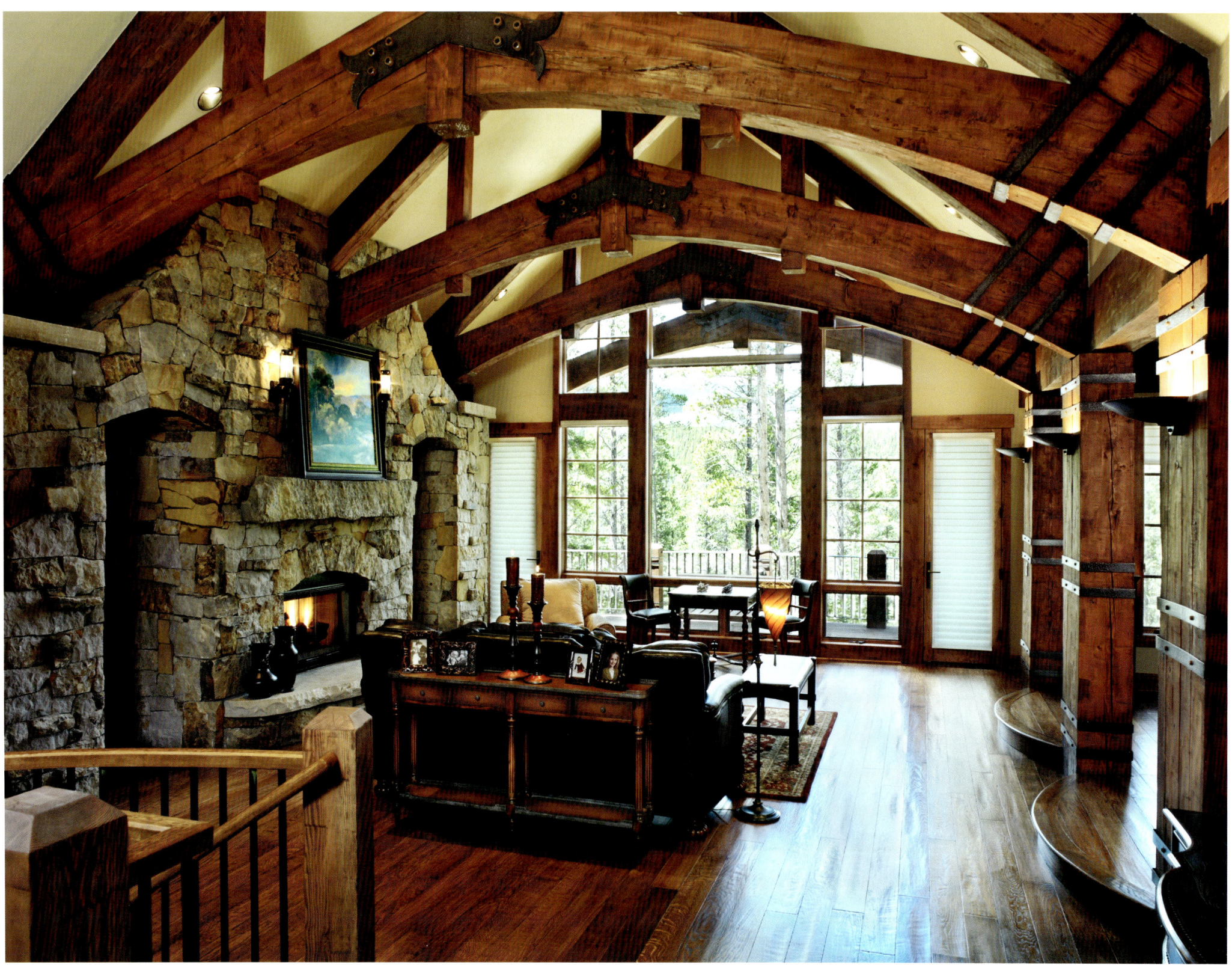

architect who has had a great influence upon Suzanne's work. In fact, much of Suzanne's architecture has been driven by the fact that she was awarded a grant from the American Institute of Architects, enabling her to travel and study Colter's work in great detail. She spent many hours studying the work of the turn-of-the-century architect, including many buildings along the Santa Fe Rail Road and in the Grand Canyon. Colter's timeless designs and buildings which seem to grow out of their landscape continue to inspire Suzanne to strive for the same qualities in all of her designs.

While a home is being built, no detail goes overlooked in an Allen-Guerra Design-Build project. During construction, Ethan has even gone as far as personally selecting and placing each individual boulder at the base of a home. The design-build process allows for artistic interpretations of ideas during construction.

The Allen-Guerra Design-Build team is composed of architects, designers, and general contractors with varied backgrounds. With each project, the team learns and utilizes new concepts and techniques. Each project presents Allen-Guerra Design-Build with an opportunity to try something different. "We feel that each home should have a unique identity which relates to our clients' way of life," Ethan commented.

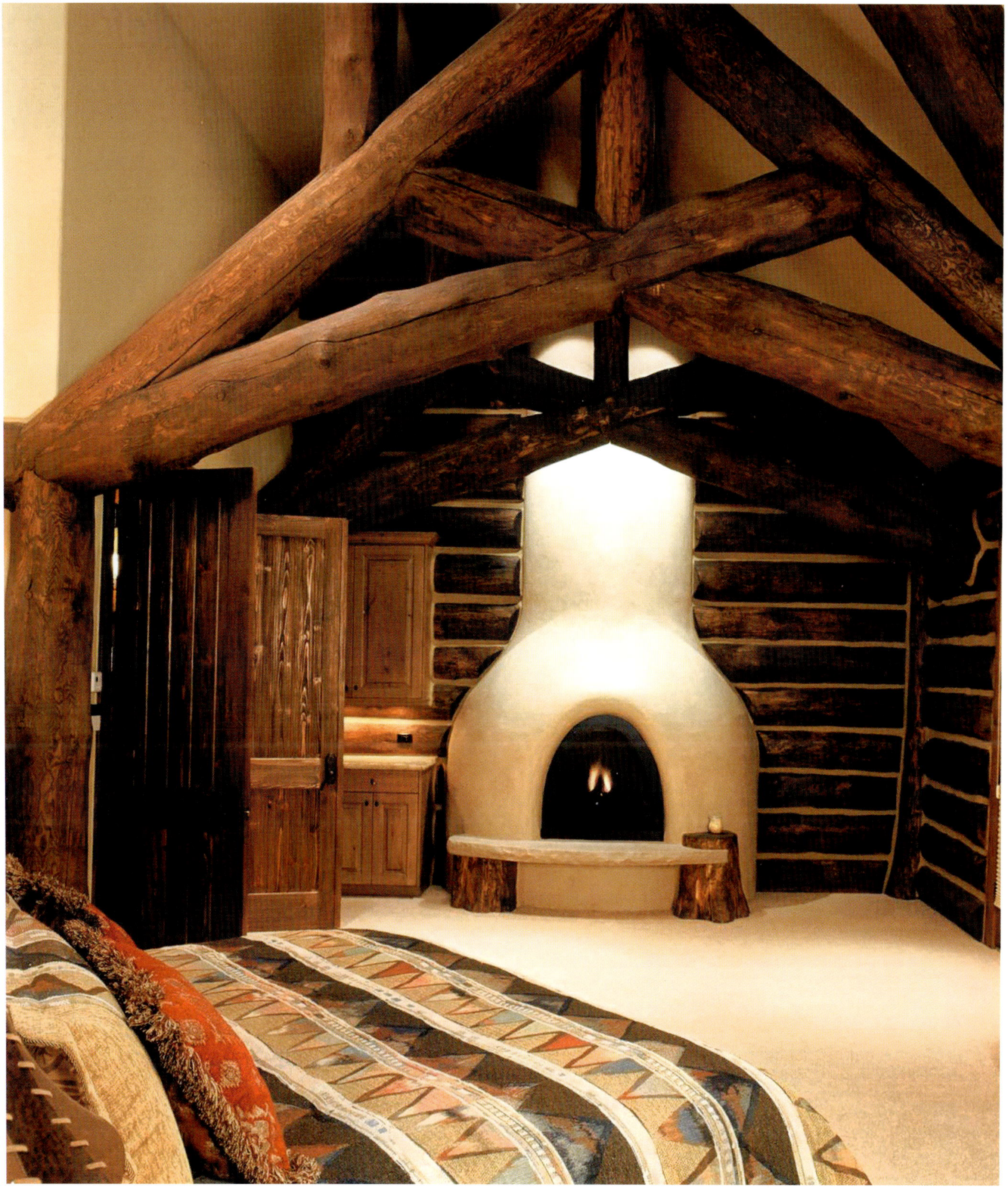

RIGHT:
This eclectic Silverthorne home combines elements of the rustic lodge and the Southwestern adobe.
Photograph by Matthew Krane

FACING PAGE:
The stone fireplace in this home designed by Suzanne Allen-Guerra provides a symbolic barrier between the public and private rooms on the main level.
Photograph by Ron Ruscio

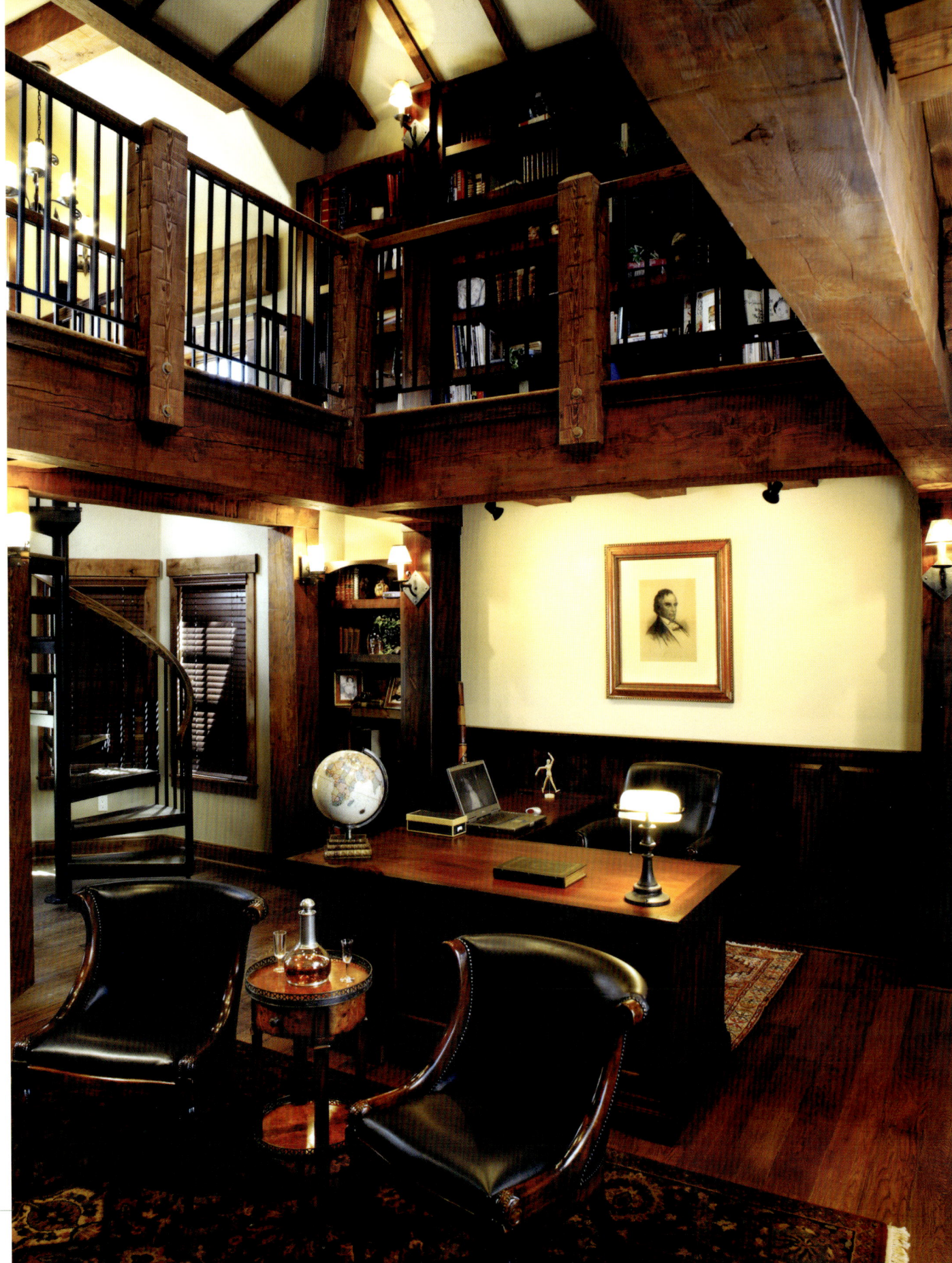

"Our creative and enthusiastic approach to the process of architecture keeps our clients excited about designing and constructing their new home," stated Fred Newcomer, a project manager at Allen-Guerra. He continued, "we are designing something so intimate, so personal, that the clients should always feel comfortable and free to express themselves." Everyone in the Allen-Guerra Design-Build team gets involved personally with each project. It is this commitment to their clients and their attention to detail that allows Allen-Guerra Design-Build to create the Art of Mountain Living.

LEFT:
Etchings of presidents adorn the walls of this classic library designed by Allen-Guerra Design-Build, Inc.
Photograph by Ron Ruscio

FACING PAGE:
The fireplace with bread warming capability, creates a cozy place to sit adjacent to the kitchen.
Photograph by Ron Ruscio

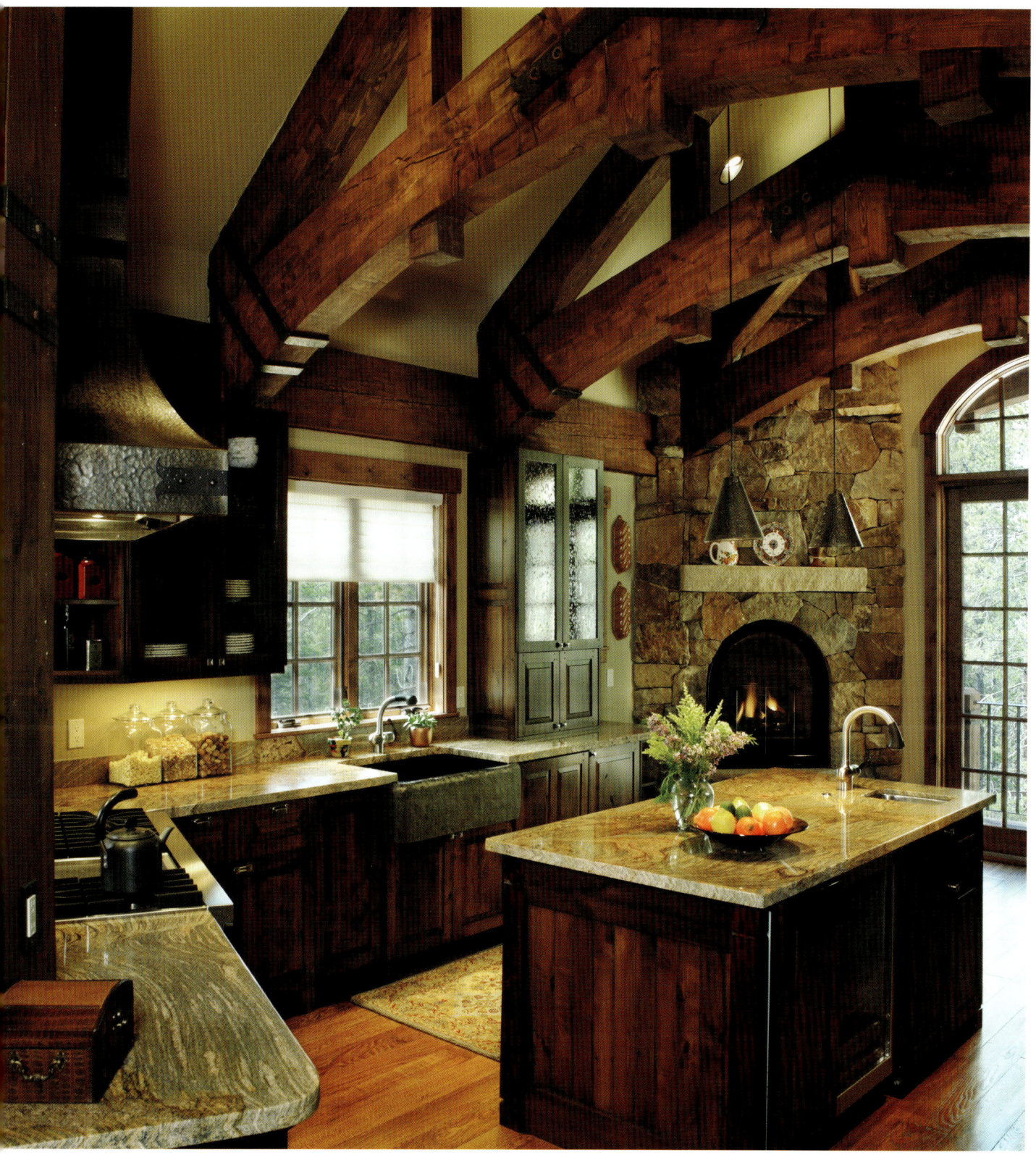

Q&A
more about suzanne...

NAME ONE THING MOST PEOPLE DON'T KNOW ABOUT YOU.
I studied architecture at the American University in Cairo, Egypt.

YOU CAN TELL I LIVE IN COLORADO BECAUSE I...
Love to ski!

YOU WOULDN'T KNOW IT, BUT MY FRIENDS WOULD TELL YOU I WAS...
A workaholic! I love my work and I spend my free time working on architecture or reading about architecture.

WHAT BOOK ARE YOU READING RIGHT NOW?
Architecture and Feminism by Coleman, Danze and Henderson.

WHO HAS HAD THE BIGGEST INFLUENCE ON YOUR CAREER?
The architect Mary Elizabeth Colter has inspired me because her structures have a timeless quality and that is what I strive for in my architecture.

WHAT IS THE MOST UNUSUAL DESIGN OR TECHINIQUE YOU'VE USED IN ONE OF YOUR PROJECTS?
We are currently designing a home in Breckenridge that utilizes several old buildings that were being torn down. This project has become an enormous design challenge!

ALLEN-GUERRA DESIGN-BUILD, INC
SUZANNE ALLEN-GUERRA
ETHAN GUERRA
1915 Airport Road, Suite 105
Breckenridge, CO 80424
970.453.7002
f: 970.453.7040
www.allen-guerra.com

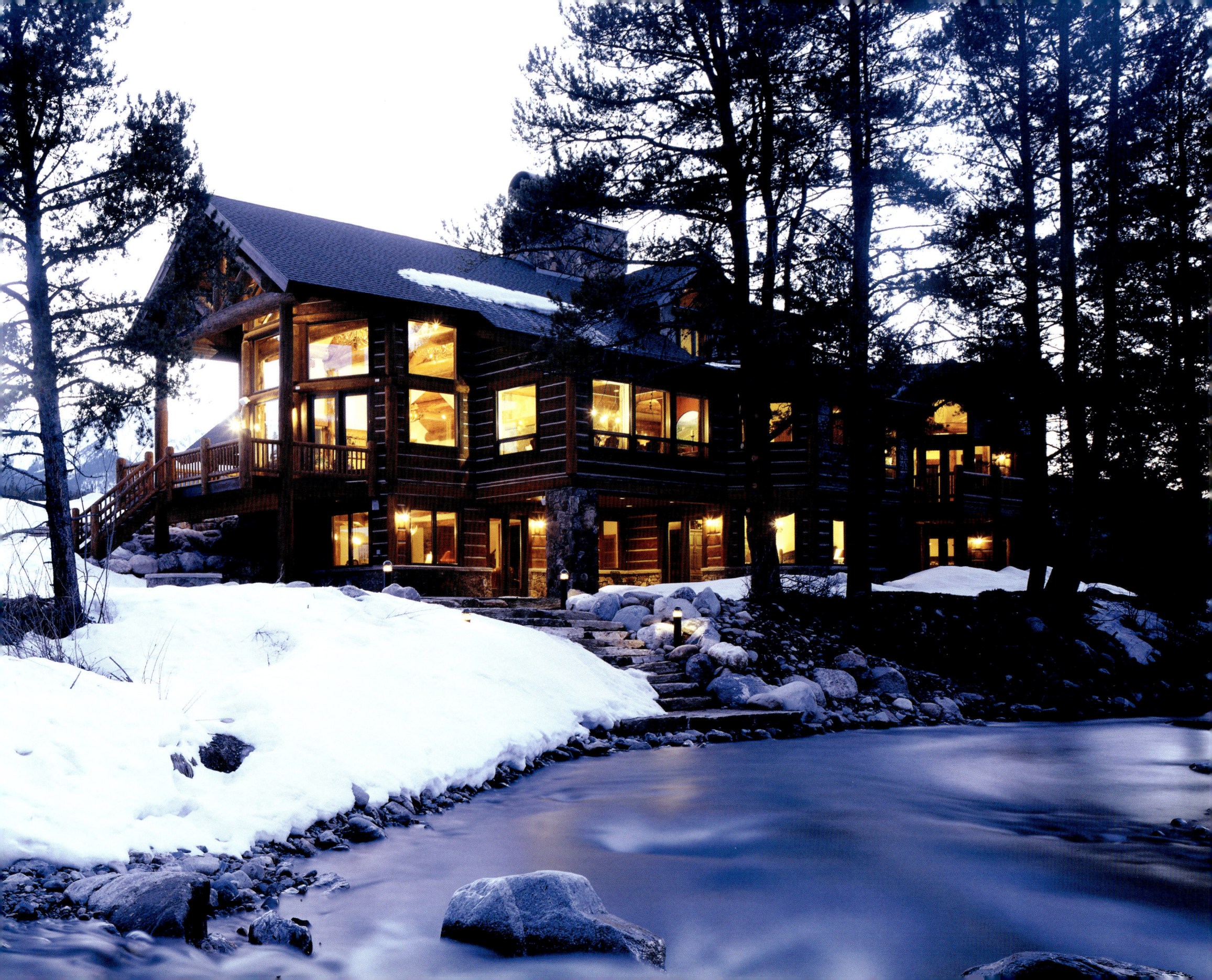

BOBBY CRAIG

ARAPAHOE ARCHITECTS P.C.

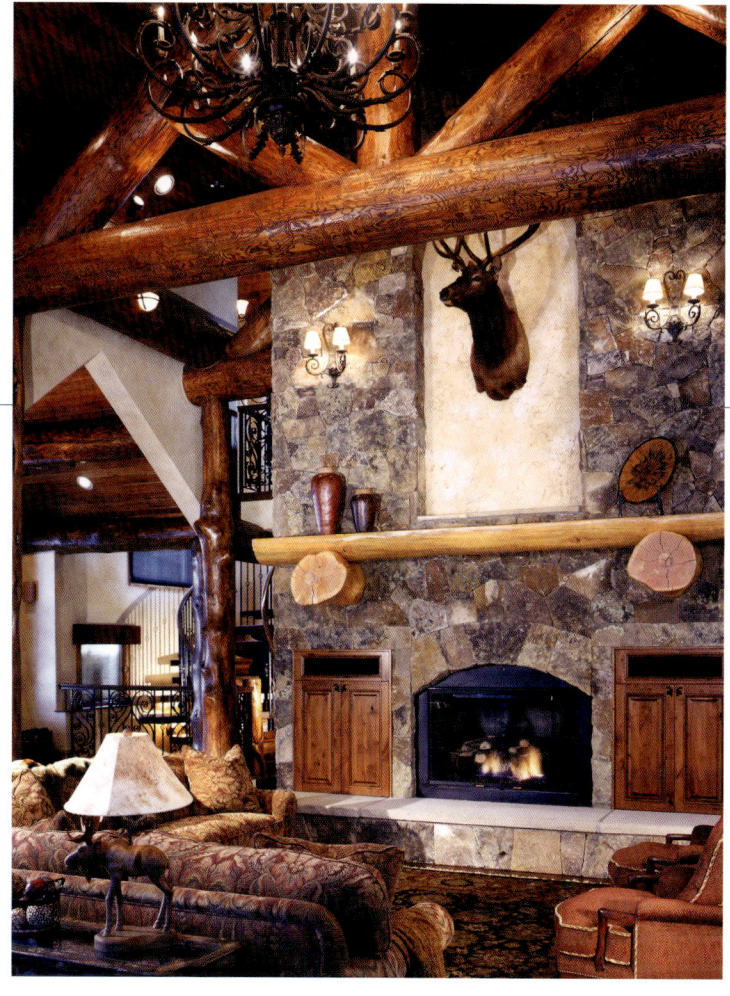

In 1990 Bobby Craig took what he believed was a ski sabbatical from the east coast to Breckenridge, Colorado. He fell in love with the beautiful mountain town and decided to make Colorado his home. Since founding Arapahoe Architects, P.C., Bobby's philosophy that great design transcends time has continued. Providing residential, commercial and historic restoration services, he creates timeless architecture that will be cherished by future generations.

Bobby completed the architecture program at the University of Virginia and was licensed in Washington D.C. where he gained experience designing traditional, Jefferson-influenced structures. Now he is fond of creating architecture in the extreme Colorado climate knowing that buildings must be able to withstand intense snow, extreme cold and brilliant sunlight.

Viewing each property as a complex sundial, Bobby strategically places windows throughout the home so that Colorado's abundant sunlight can be enjoyed in its purest form all day long. From every space, even laundry and powder rooms, residents can follow the sun as it moves through morning and afternoon hours. Bobby believes that light connects the interior with the exterior.

Many elements are factored into the design of a custom home: topography, solar orientation, views, number of rooms and budget. To create a pleasing solution which takes each of these aspects into account, Bobby keeps the client's dream foremost in his mind, never approaching a situation with preconceived notions.

ABOVE:
This traditional log joinery home is complemented with untraditional technological detail.
General contractor: Tony Harris.
Photograph by James Ray Spahn

FACING PAGE:
A fly fisherman's dream, this log home is just steps from the Blue River in Summit County, Colorado. Stunning views complete the mountain experience.
Photograph by James Ray Spahn

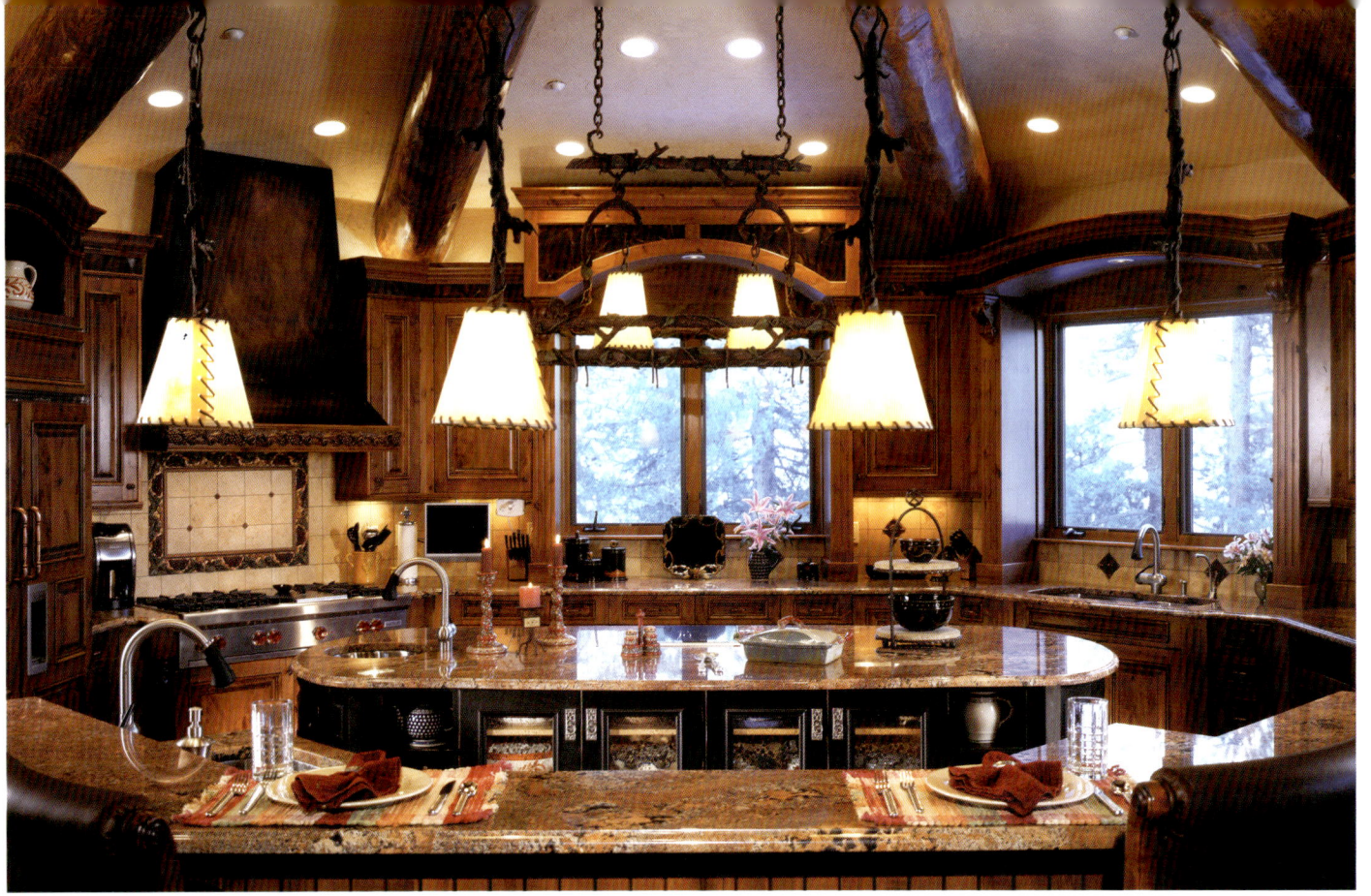

Montezuma, an old mining town at an elevation of 11,000 feet, provided the foundation for one of the firm's most unusual projects. In an avalanche zone, building activity and occupation is allowed only during summer months from May through November. Bobby and his team designed a unique solution by tucking the home into the hillside like an inverted ship's hull. The heavy timber, rock and concrete structure is designed to withstand an avalanche's impact.

With a wide variety of projects in their portfolio, Arapahoe Architects has designed timber, log and conventionally framed houses, each with their own uniqueness. The commonality of their impressive work is, "we don't dictate, we collaborate."

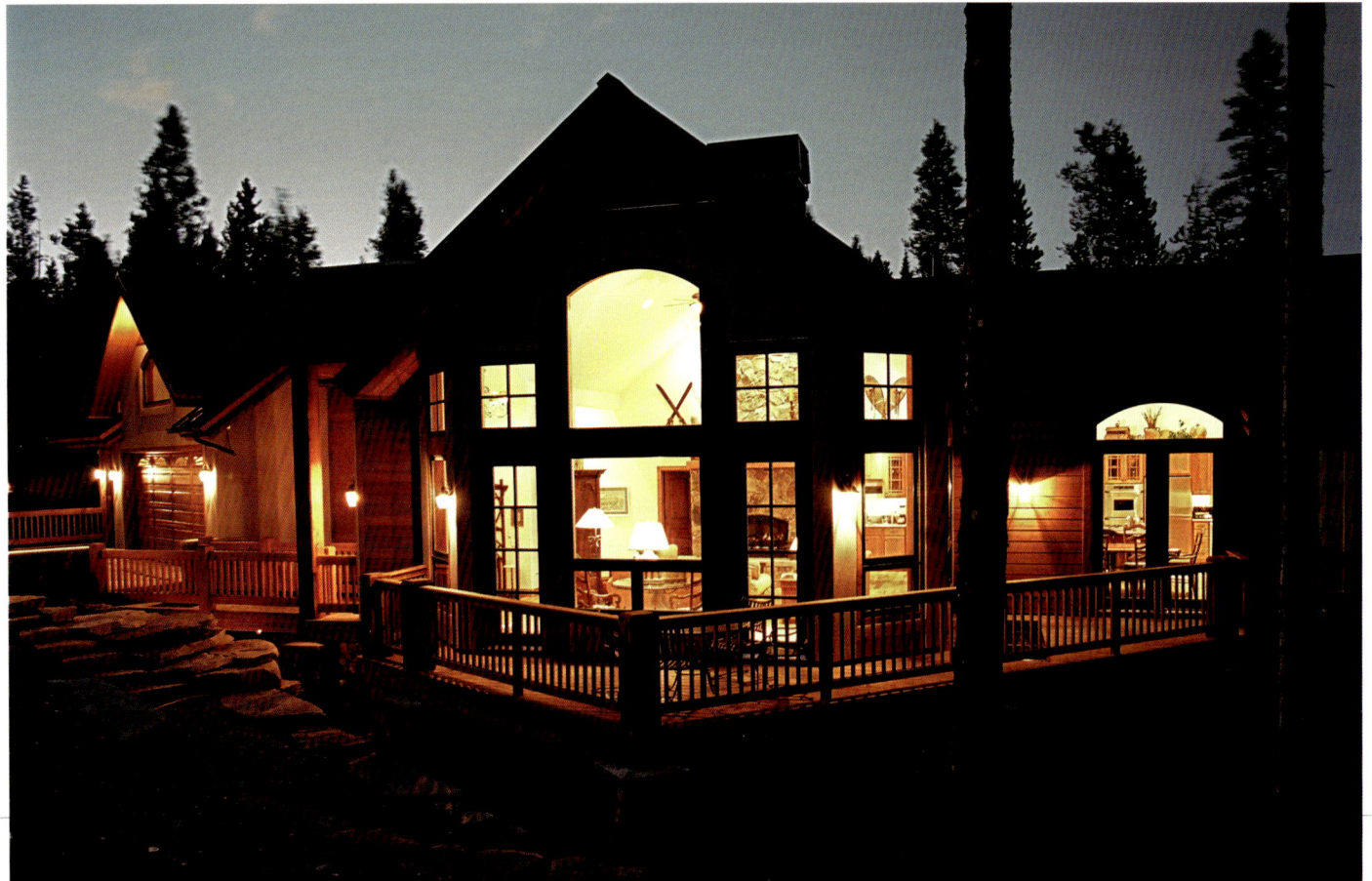

LEFT TOP:
An octagonal roof frames the kitchen's double island, as envisioned by designer Marcia Bauer. Windows overlook a bend in the Blue River.
Photograph by James Ray Spahn

LEFT BOTTOM:
Dusk settles over this residence that overlooks Beaver Run in Breckenridge, Colorado. Warm lighting and interiors offer a mountain haven.
Photograph by Gary Soles

FACING PAGE:
The Elk's Perspective: recycled mortise joinery with oak tenons form a traditional bent timber frame for this vacation home in Breckenridge, Colorado.
Photograph by Gary Soles

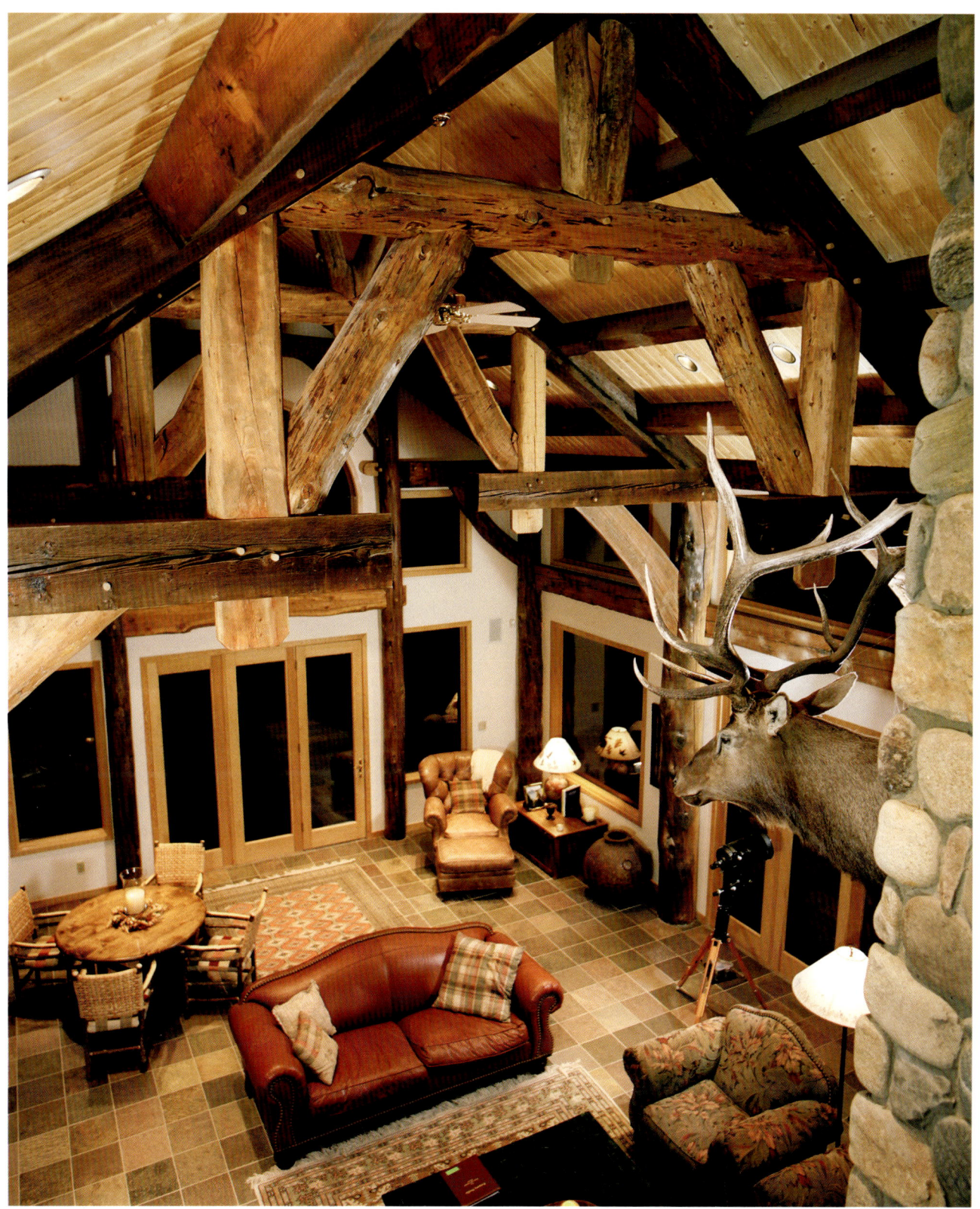

Q&A
more about bobby...

HOW WOULD YOUR FRIENDS DESCRIBE YOU?
People who know me best would say that I'm very easy going, and the laid back atmosphere of Colorado fits me perfectly.

WHAT IS YOUR FAVORITE EXAMPLE OF CLASSICAL ARCHITECTURE?
I've always been impressed with the logistics of the Florence Cathedral's dome and the manner in which someone solved a problem created 100 years earlier.

WHO INSPIRED YOU TO PURSUE ARCHITECTURE?
My older sister studied architecture and the prospect of designing things which would come to fruition on a grand scale really appealed to me.

WHAT IS THE MOST ENJOYABLE ASPECT OF DOING BUSINESS IN COLORADO?
Skiing. Breckenridge has fabulous slopes, so when I'm not drafting architecture, you can find me gliding down snowy mountains.

ARAPAHOE ARCHITECTS, P.C.
BOBBY CRAIG, AIA
322C North Main Street
Breckenridge, CO 80424
970.453.8474
www.arapahoearchitects.com

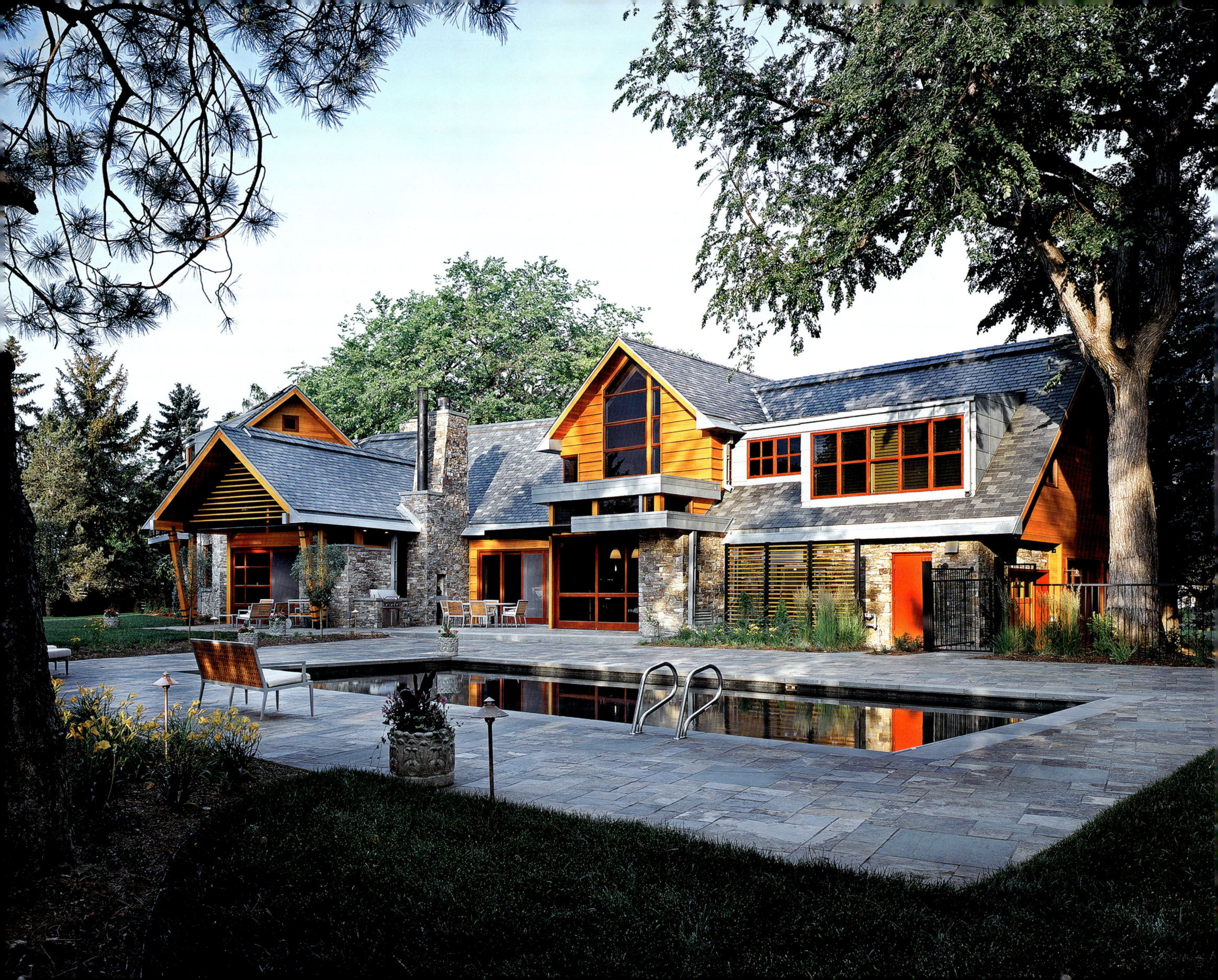

E.J. MEADE
JAMES TREWITT
RICHARD SANDS

ARCH 11
HAMMERWELL INC.

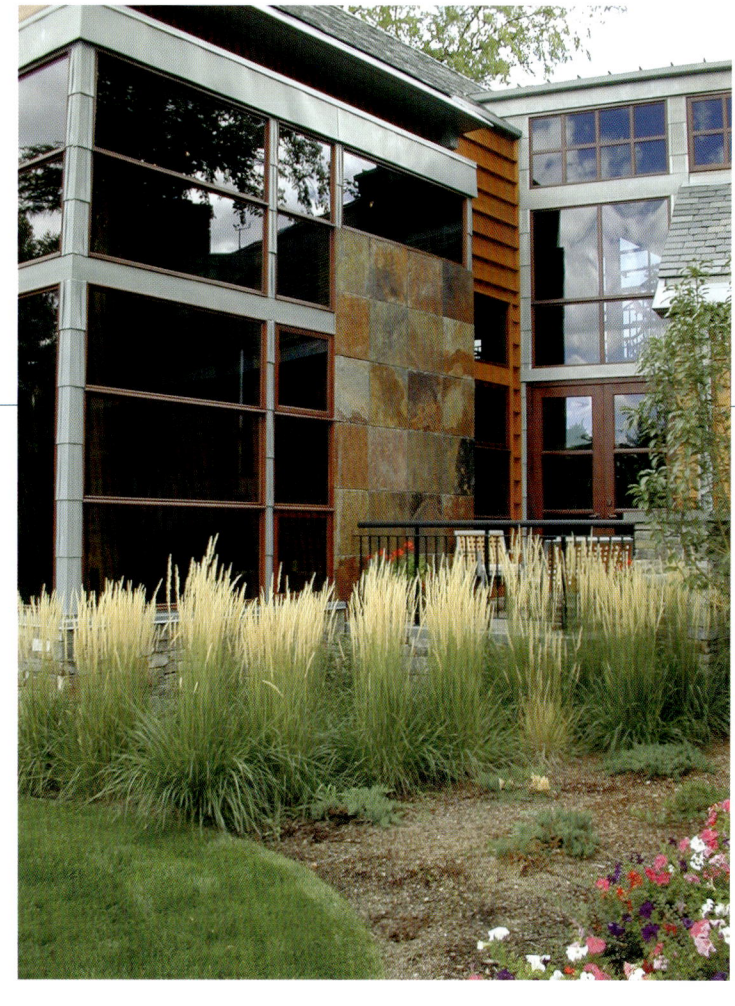

The simple act of glancing up at a sign at the perfect moment led Rich Sands, owner of Hammerwell Incorporated, to a design/build relationship that has flourished to the benefit of numerous clients. Sands had built high-end custom homes in California for almost two decades when he visited Boulder in 1996, purchased two lots, and went in search of an architect with whom he could foster a long-distance working relationship. Midway through a day of interviews with various firms, Rich paused for coffee, and by chance, noticed the nearby offices of the architecture and interior design studio, Arch 11. As if by instinct he strolled in, staying to chat for a serendipitous two hours, delighted to discover that Arch 11 principals E.J. Meade and James Trewitt held an abiding appreciation for the same aspects of design as he. So much confidence did he have in this new relationship that Rich relocated his business to Boulder and started these first two spec houses. Although both Hammerwell and Arch 11 work also with other architectural and construction partners, they collaborate frequently, when given a choice, pairing up for projects in Boulder County, Denver and mountain communities throughout Colorado.

A true design/build process begins at the outset and creates a single entity that delivers a project to the client. This close-knit relationship between architect and builder allows contiguous ownership in the process through each stage of project delivery and, through close communication, helps to tightly control costs and scheduling. In the end, it saves time and money for the client and guarantees the integrity of a design for which years of building experience help to clearly realize the architect's intent.

E.J., who grew up on the East Coast, received his B.A. from Colby College, studied architecture at the University of Washington and received a M.Arch from the University of Colorado, where he spent 12 years on the faculty as a senior design instructor. James completed his first professional degree in architecture from Louisiana Tech and his M.Arch from the University of Colorado where he taught furniture design and design studios. Both

ABOVE:
Zinc, slate and cypress siding compose a backdrop for ornamental grasses to dance in the Colorado breeze.
Photography by E.J. Meade, Arch 11

FACING PAGE:
Sited on three acres within the Denver city limits, this home—with its familiar typology and materials—cradles the backyard offering a private respite from the city bustle.
Photograph by Ron Forth, Ron Forth Photography

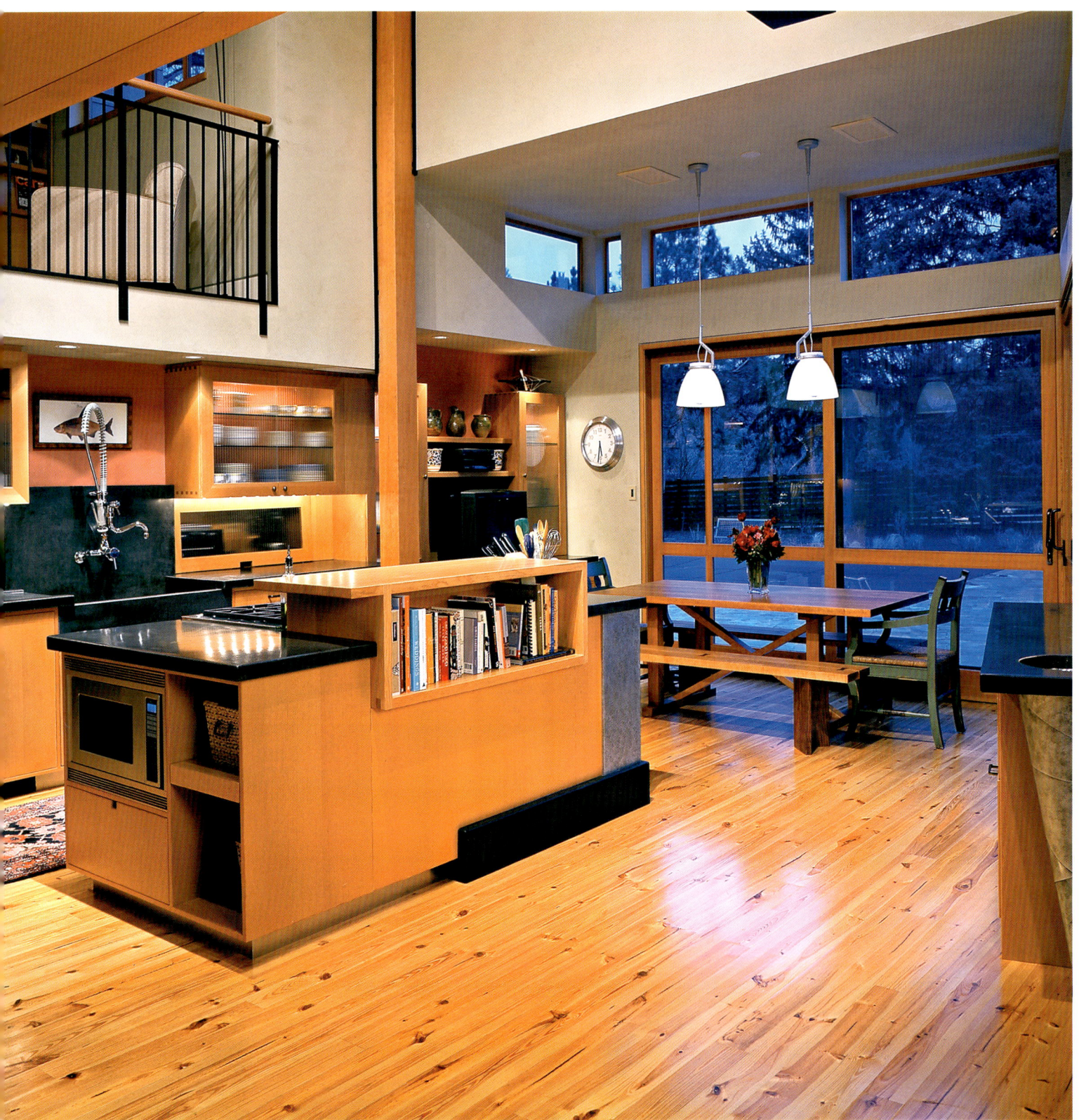

architects had significant carpentry and construction experience, E.J. in New England, James in Arkansas, before meeting while teaching at the University of Colorado and establishing Arch 11 in 1993.

The design/build custom homes they create with Hammerwell resonate with modern spatial sensibilities and technology in which walls subtly frame landscapes characterized by the uplift of the Front Range juxtaposed with the horizontality of the plains. Indoor and outdoor spaces frequently overlap forming outdoor rooms in these naturally Green homes, conceived to take full advantage of the region's outdoor-oriented climate.

No two alike, the Arch 11/Hammerwell homes are bound by the specifics of site and budget, with each of these facets studiously reviewed and treated as if they were the components of a tailor-made suit cut for the client, and that client alone. Modern refined materials meet primitive materials for a tactile contrast. What results is a haptic understanding of the roughness of stone against smooth wood, of the feel of galvanized metal and steel and of the earthy finish of exposed concrete floors and countertops.

LEFT:
Sliding glass walls allow a casual dining area to connect a working kitchen and a playful patio.
Photograph by Ron Forth, Ron Forth Photography

FACING PAGE LEFT:
Defined by an art wall, transparent sideboard and custom light fixture, the dining room mediates between kitchen and living spaces.
Photograph by Ron Forth, Ron Forth Photography

FACING PAGE RIGHT:
While asymmetrical windows cut playful openings in the gabled wall, the timber and steel framed structure reinforces a barn-like comfort for family room activities.
Photograph by Ron Forth, Ron Forth Photography

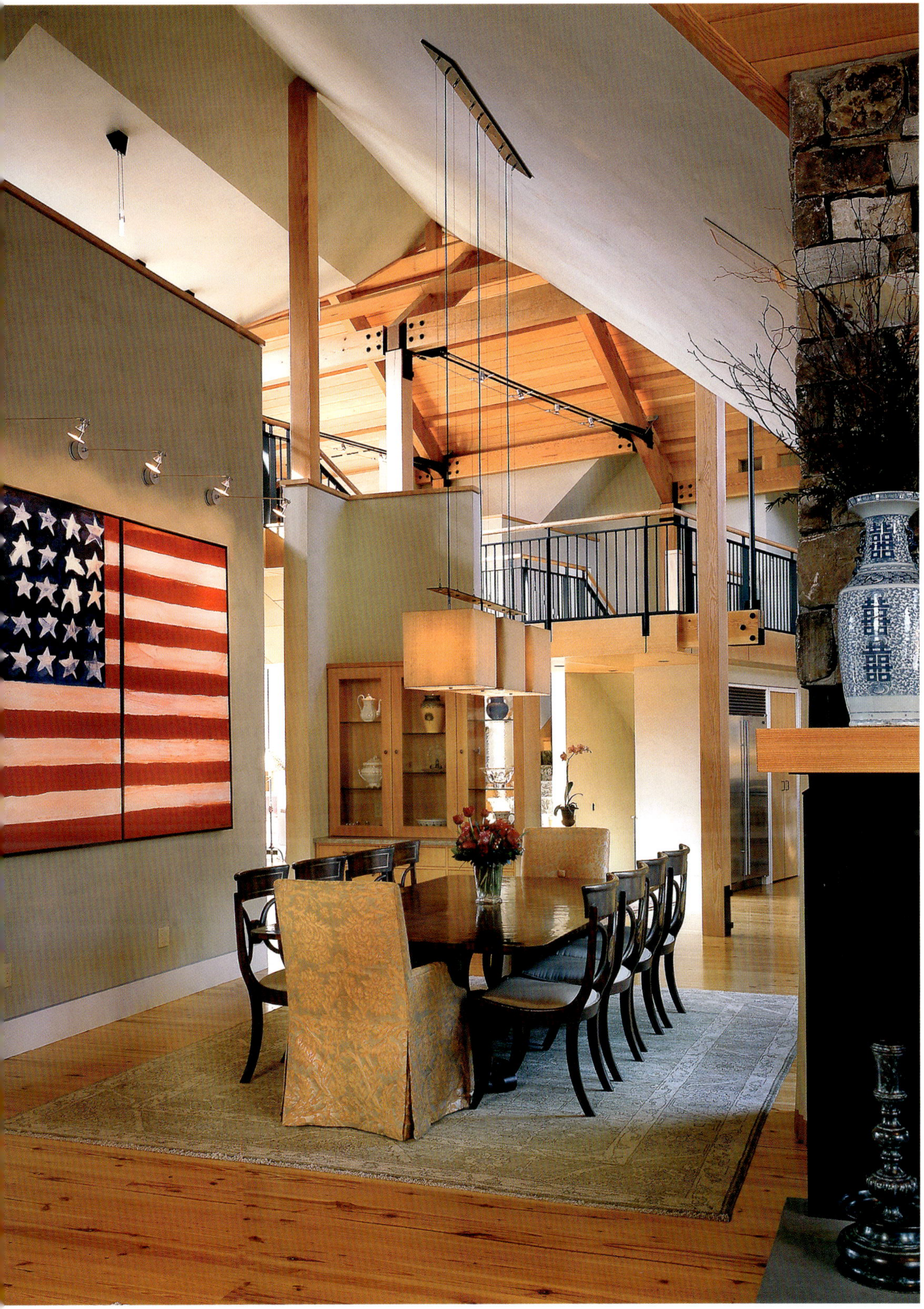

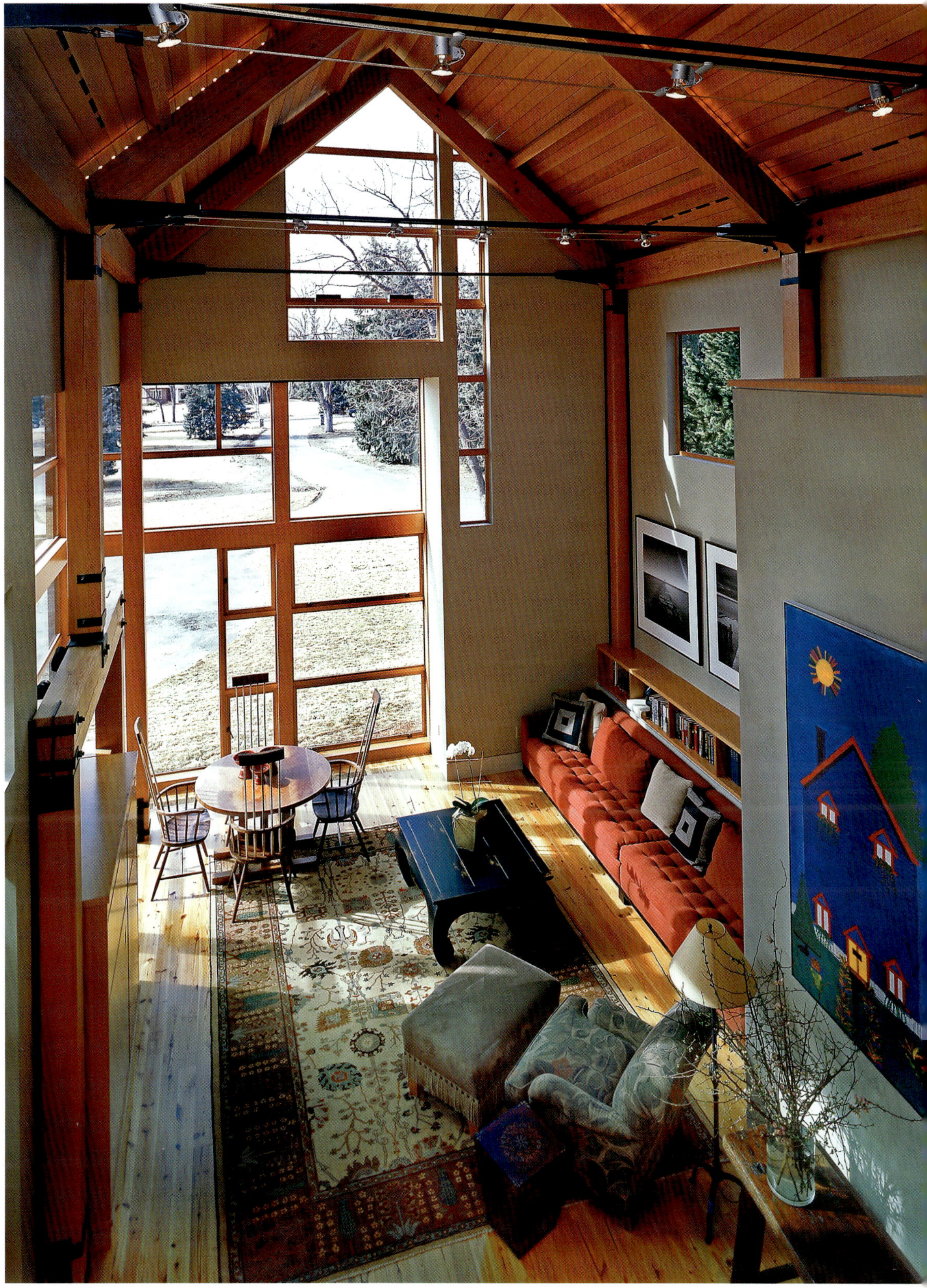

29

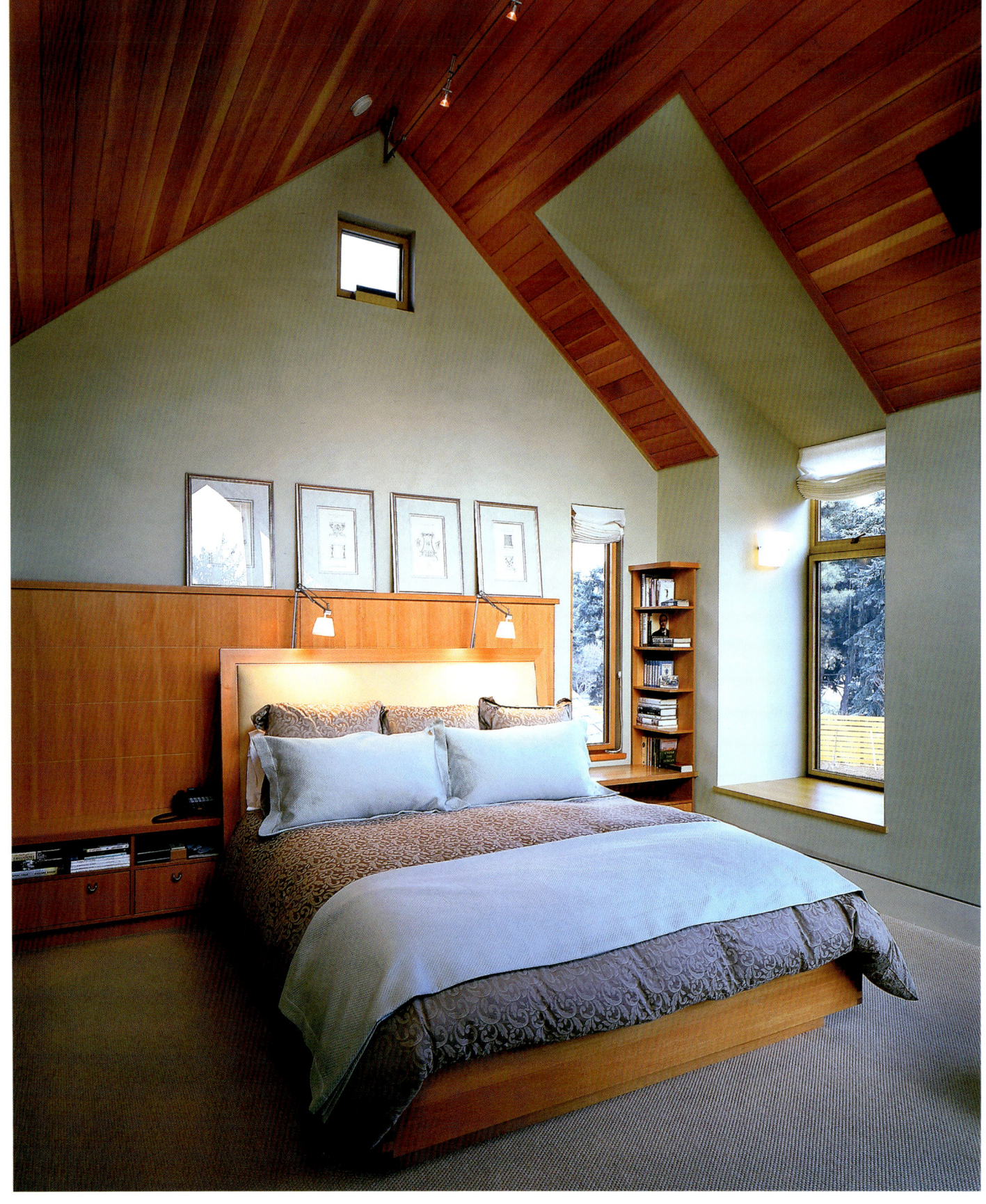

Layered spaces, broad porches, expansive glass, wood louvers, and exposed structural elements are design strategies favored by Arch 11. Site lines often are designed to take the eye through an architectural promenade akin to looking through a private space to reveal the landscape beyond. Arch 11/Hammerwell homes have meticulously detailed interiors integrated seamlessly with the shell of the house. The same hand, the same intent, carries through from the foundation to the roof, from exterior details to interior finishes, creating cohesiveness. Arch 11 designs and fabricates furniture, casework, custom sinks and fixtures, and works directly and closely with installers and craftspeople to ensure that each detail is client-specific.

"There is a Western vernacular that includes our mining and agrarian heritage, and we have at times addressed that, but we have a more critical response to topography, views, climate and the times in which we live," E.J. says. "Our homes are modern spaces that reveal the landscape and reference Western traditions."

LEFT:
The quiet of the master bedroom "cottage" is interrupted only by an overscaled window-seat that allows morning sun into this peaceful retreat. The bed and cabinetry are designed by Arch 11.
Photograph by Ron Forth, Ron Forth Photography

FACING PAGE:
Not just any old outbuilding, the pool house offers a complete materials palette of the main house in its simplest, distilled form. Screens of wood and a sliding door of steel and etched glass provide light and privacy for the bather.
Photograph by Brad Burch, Arch 11

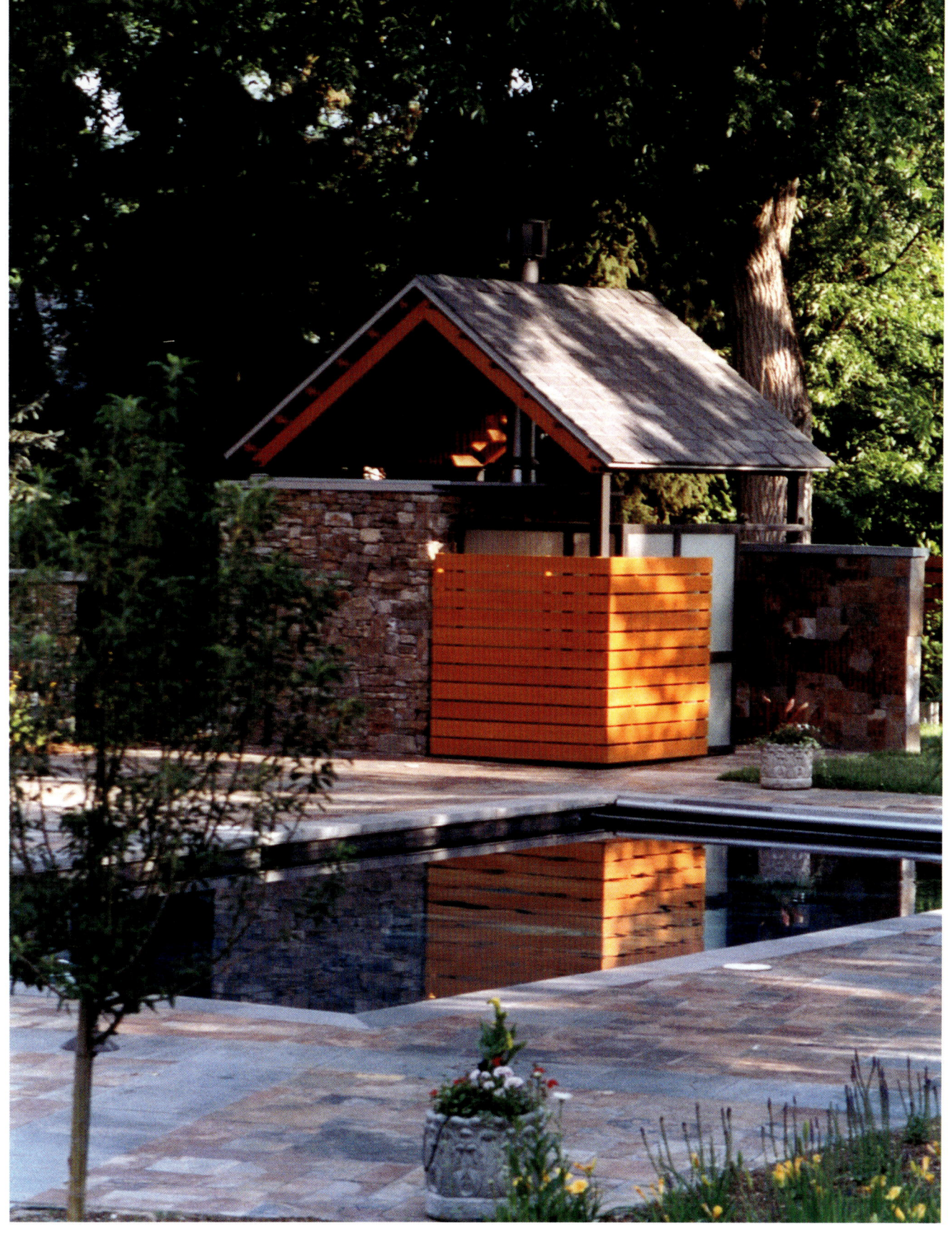

Q&A

more about rich...

WHAT IS A SINGLE THING YOU WOULD DO TO BRING A DULL HOUSE TO LIFE?
Remove some interior walls to open up spaces to each other.

PLEASE NAME ANY PROFESSIONAL ASSOCIATIONS OF WHICH YOU ARE A MEMBER.
Home Builders Association of Metro Denver, Sunset Western Home Alliance.

WHAT IS THE HIGHEST COMPLIMENT YOU HAVE RECEIVED PROFESSIONALLY?
Being introduced at an architectural symposium as a builder who has influenced housing styles in the Boulder area.

more about e.j. ...

IF YOU COULD ELIMINATE ONE STYLE FROM THE WORLD, WHAT WOULD IT BE?
Every revival period of the 19th century, nostalgic revival is like architectural Prozac.

WHO HAS HAD THE BIGGEST INFLUENCE ON YOUR CAREER?
Carlo Scarpa, a Venetian architect who artfully weaves modern space, detailing, and craft with the buildings of Venice allowing unexpected moments in which the old and new complement one another.

ANY AWARDS OR SPECIAL RECOGNITION YOU WOULD LIKE MENTIONED?
Among other national honors, James and E.J. both received the Emerging Impressions award from the Colorado AIA.

ARCH 11 INC.
E.J. MEADE
JAMES TREWITT
3100 Carbon Place
Suite 100
Boulder, CO 80301
303.546.6868
f: 303.443.3910
www.arch11.com

HAMMERWELL INC.
RICHARD SANDS
3100 Carbon Place
Suite 100A
Boulder, CO 80301
303.443.3430
f: 303.443.3431
www.hammerwell.com

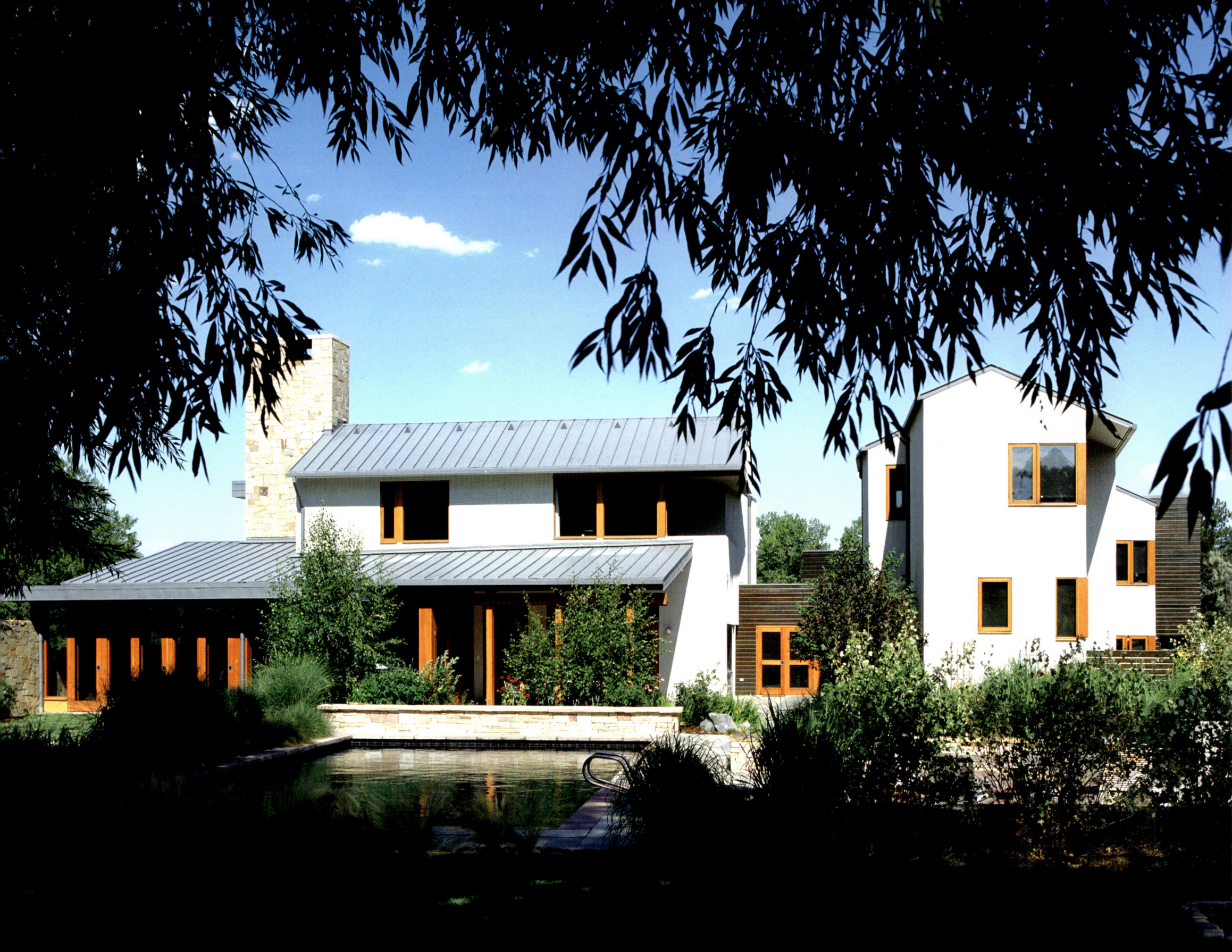

STEVE CHUCOVICH

ArchitectureDenver

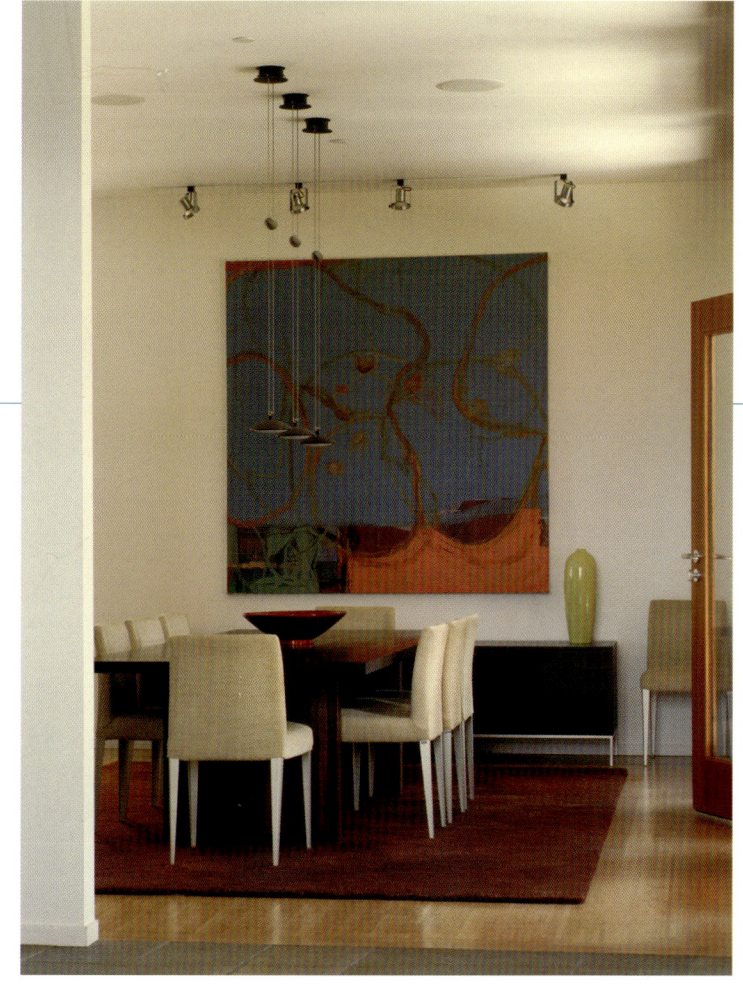

For Steve Chucovich, the design process flows from a stream of consciousness about how we live in contemporary society. Design principal of AchitectureDenver, Steve is a fourth generation Denver native with an abiding appreciation for the distinct qualities of mountain and prairie landscape and the built environment within. That reverence is evident in the way his work connects to that context, whether urban or rural.

The use of water, the modeling of light and the authentic colors and materials relating to the landscape are important elements in Steve's designs. Whether building at a 10,000-foot elevation, or designing for city dwellers and in tight urban spaces, concern for the context and the environment through design has high priority in the process.

Animating the architectural design, using sun and the landscape to wed interior and exterior is a goal in the homes Steve designs for a small, discerning clientele. He is intent on connecting the client to the senses we all experience, air, light, color, smell and touch; the collective human sensory response. In this way, Steve's work is defined as a sense of place and a connection to people as much as it is to the air and light, and the ability to see the vista offered by a particular setting.

"What intrigues me is Colorado's clear cleansing environment, the way you can smell the grass or the trees and the sharpness of the sunlight accentuating it all. This kind of clarity doesn't exist in other places, and our ability to create a place for someone to live here completes the whole cycle of human endeavor."

ABOVE:
A view of the dining room from the living room shows rich materials in the furniture and an extensive art collection.
Photograph by Emily Minton-Redfield

FACING PAGE:
The west garden elevation through the trees shows a real blend of contemporary form and traditional elements such as the chimney.
Photograph by Emily Minton-Redfield

ArchitectureDenver
STEVE CHUCOVICH
1855 Blake Street
Suite 100
Denver, CO 80202
303.893.1600
f: 303.893.5658

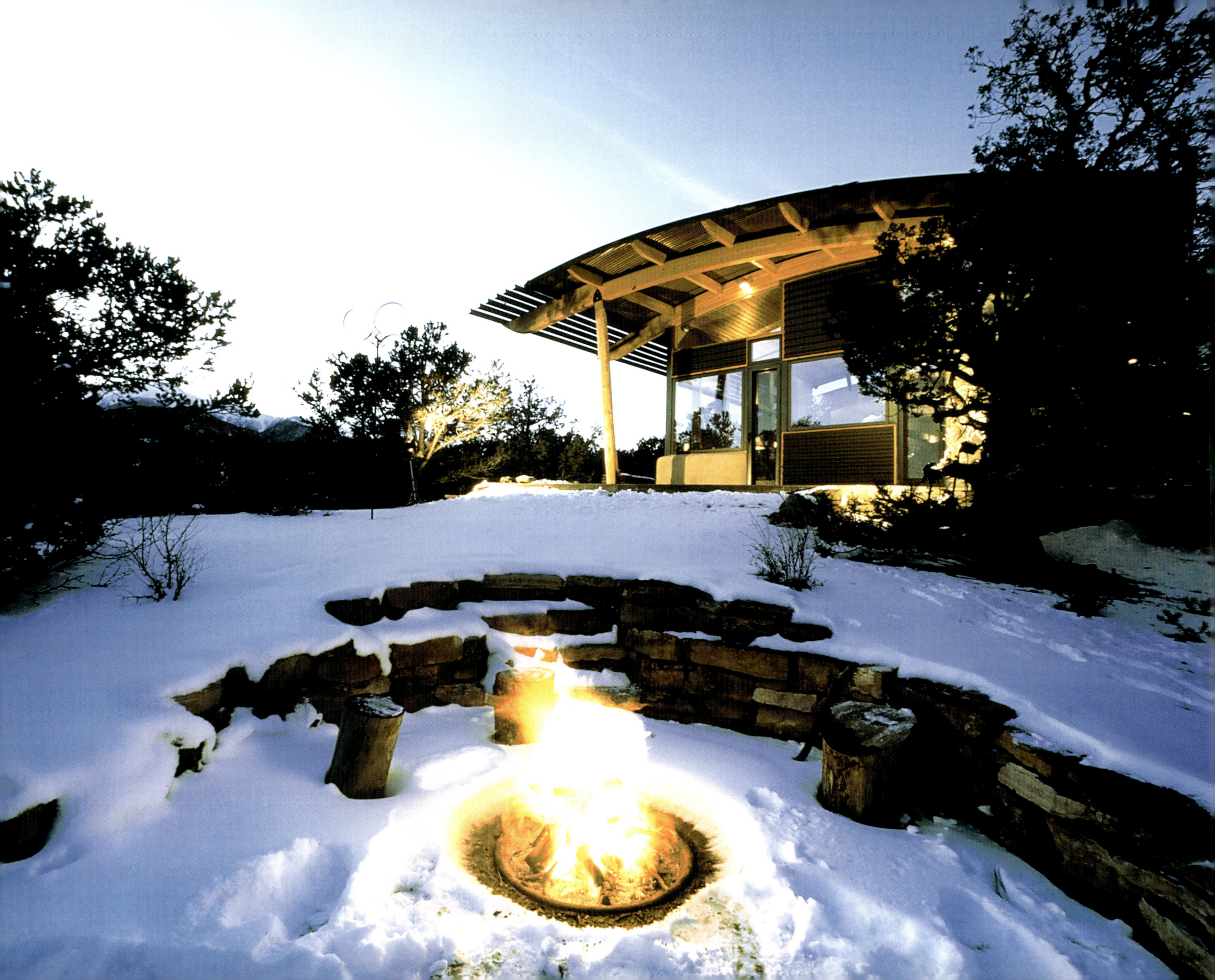

DAVID BARRETT

BARRETT STUDIO ARCHITECTS

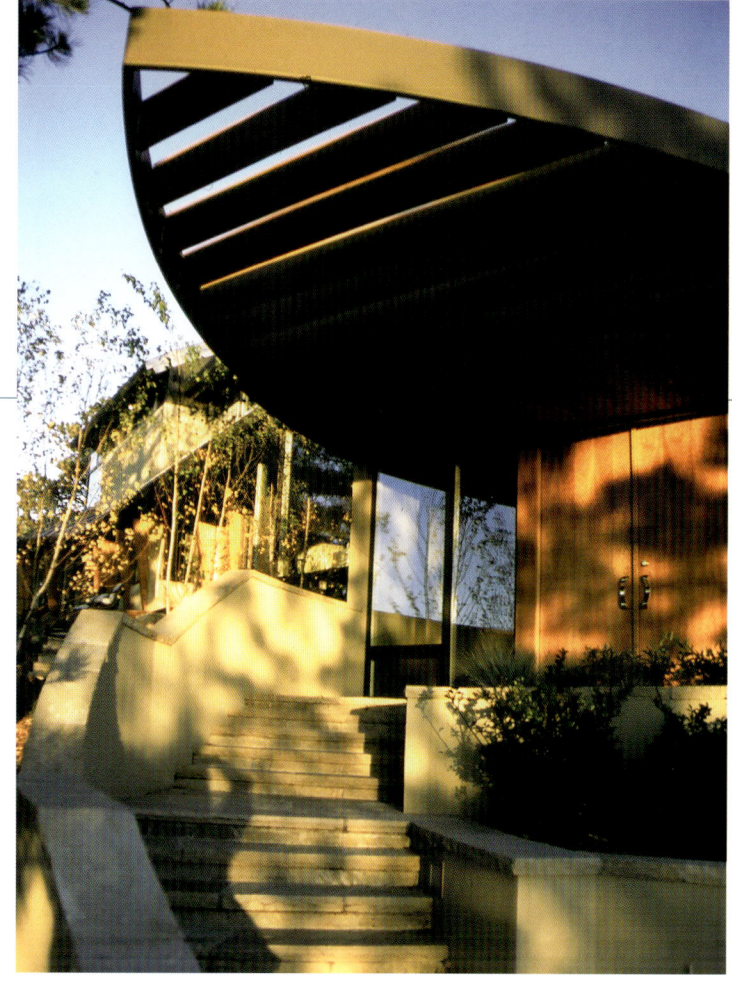

Homes are more than a structure of sticks and bricks: A home is an emotional collection of materials, memories, and images of comfort; those things that make us feel safe and comfortable. A home even has the power to move us, and if it does so it is due to the sense of connectivity impacting us on an emotional level. That's the philosophy behind Barrett Studio Architects, a place for architecture, interiors, and community design established over 30 years ago representing an assembly of passionate architects led by principal David Barrett, the 2002 AIA Colorado Architect of the Year. The Studio designs custom homes in such diverse locations as the unique climates of Colorado—mountainous regions, the dramatic high desert, wind swept plains, and urban oases—upstate New York, the tropics of Florida, and Koh Samui, Thailand.

Working within the belief that co-creation brings ideas to fruition, the studio is a balance of male and female architects & designers who contribute to every project, maintaining the excitement of making exceptional projects in collaboration with exceptional clients. From its inception, the Studio was driven by an environmental ethic advocating Green Building—such as solar energy, high efficiency systems, and alternative building materials—and by determining and respecting the climate's influence on architecture. David is committed to marrying design with a site that resonates with the client to arrive at a home that both meets programmatic needs and delights the senses.

Often, Barrett Studio Architects' designs reference nature in a kind of organic modernism that strives to create a living quality about a place. The designs may be inspired by a rockscape, a leaf, or by lenticular clouds hovering above the landscape. The Studio takes its cues from nature, with these inspirations giving the homes a timeless quality and a sense that they are connected to something larger. David has termed these patterns in nature that provide lessons in design "Ecomorphic Principles."

ABOVE:
A welcoming entry inspired by the humble leaf sets the ecological tone in this home.
Photograph by David Barrett

FACING PAGE:
A strawbale home in Salida exudes the warmth and welcome of a sustainable Colorado lifestyle.
Photograph by Graylon Wampler

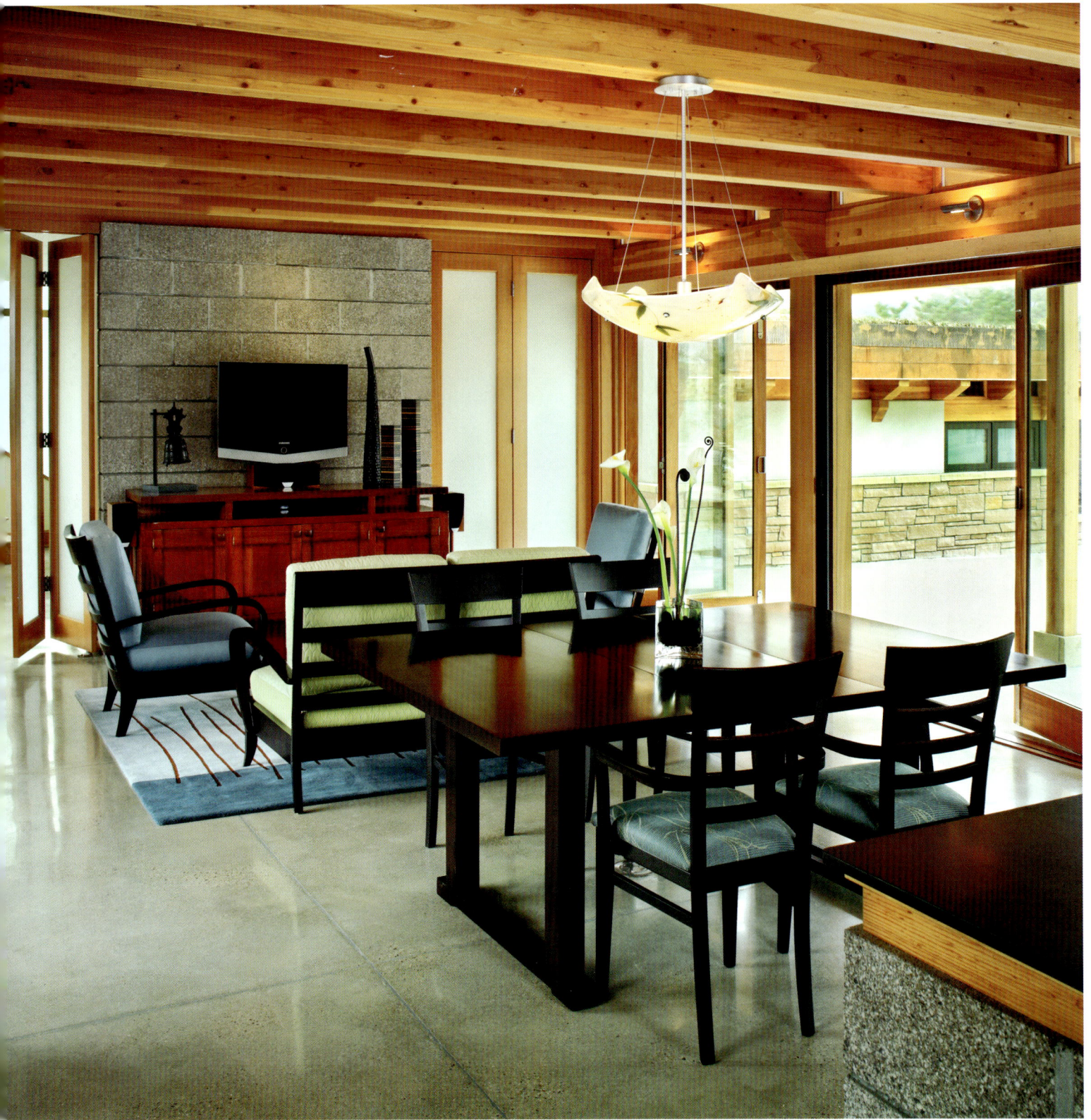

Barrett Studio Architects' clients include those with a wide range of custom home budgets and dreams. Projects are varied, ranging from renovations of small cabins and places of refuge to an elegant city loft or a spacious home in the mountains. Dream homes come in many sizes, shapes and colors, and the Studio's goal is to fulfill that aspiration responsibly and beautifully, including the creative use of available recycled materials to "Green the Dream" for smart clients with a value to preserving what they love.

A part of how we live in Colorado embodies a sense of freedom and space in a bright "big sky" place that is spirited and young in attitude, and this influences the Studio's architecture. It's evidenced in courtyard homes wrapped around an outside room and in the way each room in a house lives larger by extending to the courtyard and inviting indoor/outdoor living.

In this intense climate, with extreme temperatures and rock, in which soil freezes and thaws, experience and expertise join to inform the Studio's designs and to take advantage of nature's incredible gifts of distant views, sharp light, and solar warmth. These elements enhance an atmosphere of exciting architecture and help to balance the idea of what is modern, rational, and technically motivated with what is organic and of the hand. Wabi Sabi, the Japanese tradition of celebrating impermanence & imperfection, is an idea that the Studio often references in attempt to humanize the rational modernism that is in intrinsic part of our technological world. With this in mind, the Studio aims to create houses as custom works of art, but not so perfect that they are not comfortably livable.

"If you're going to create something unique, what you're doing is trying to uncover something deeper than data about the climate and the site," David says. "I often call it the poetic seed. It's the big idea, the DNA of a home. It is the intangible that gives soul to the tangible."

LEFT:
This meditation and recreation pavilion's integrated indoor/outdoor living space celebrates Colorado's glorious climate.
Photograph by Ron Ruscio

FACING PAGE:
Cues from indigenous structures and unique geologic formations shape this home.
Photograph by Wayne Thom

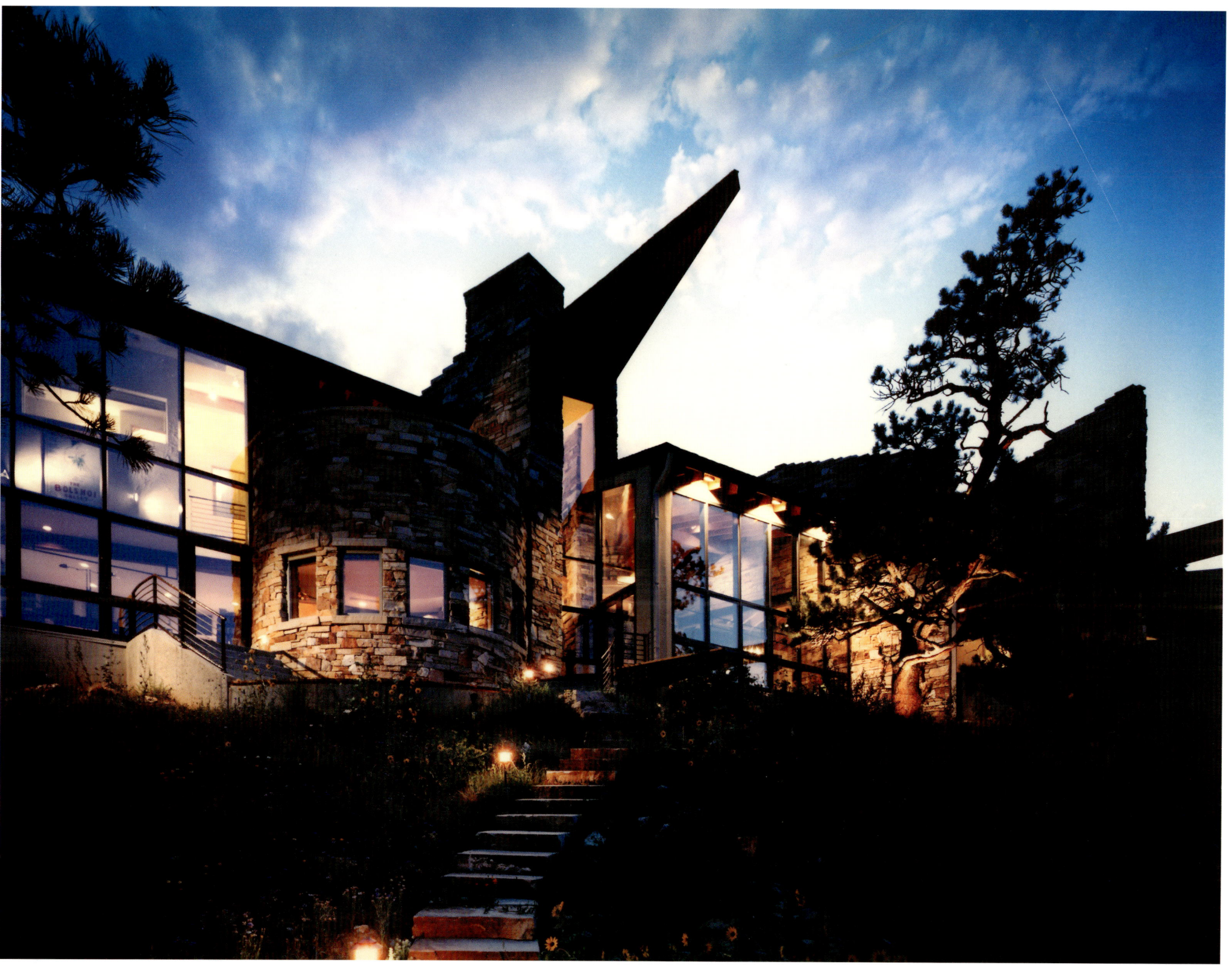

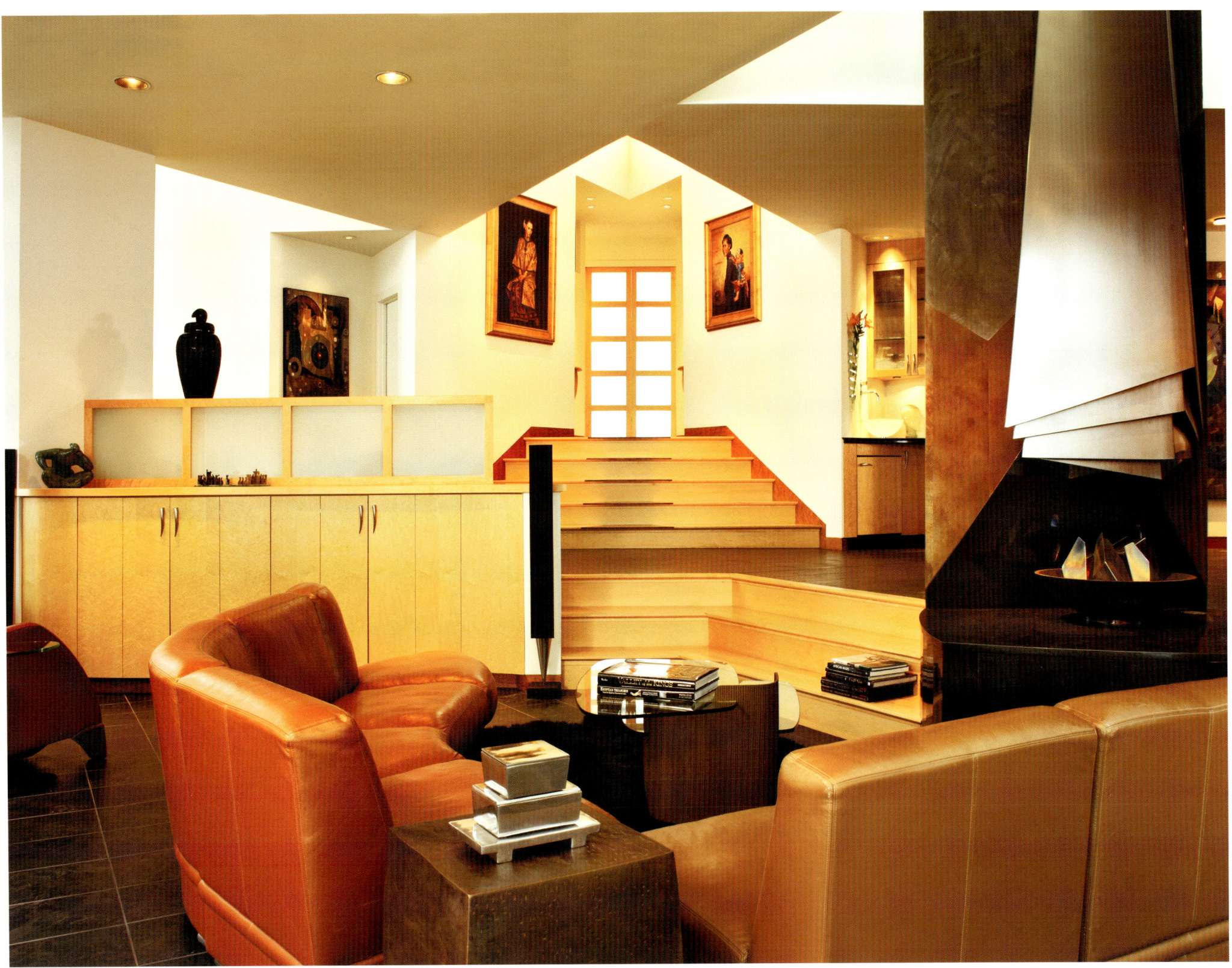

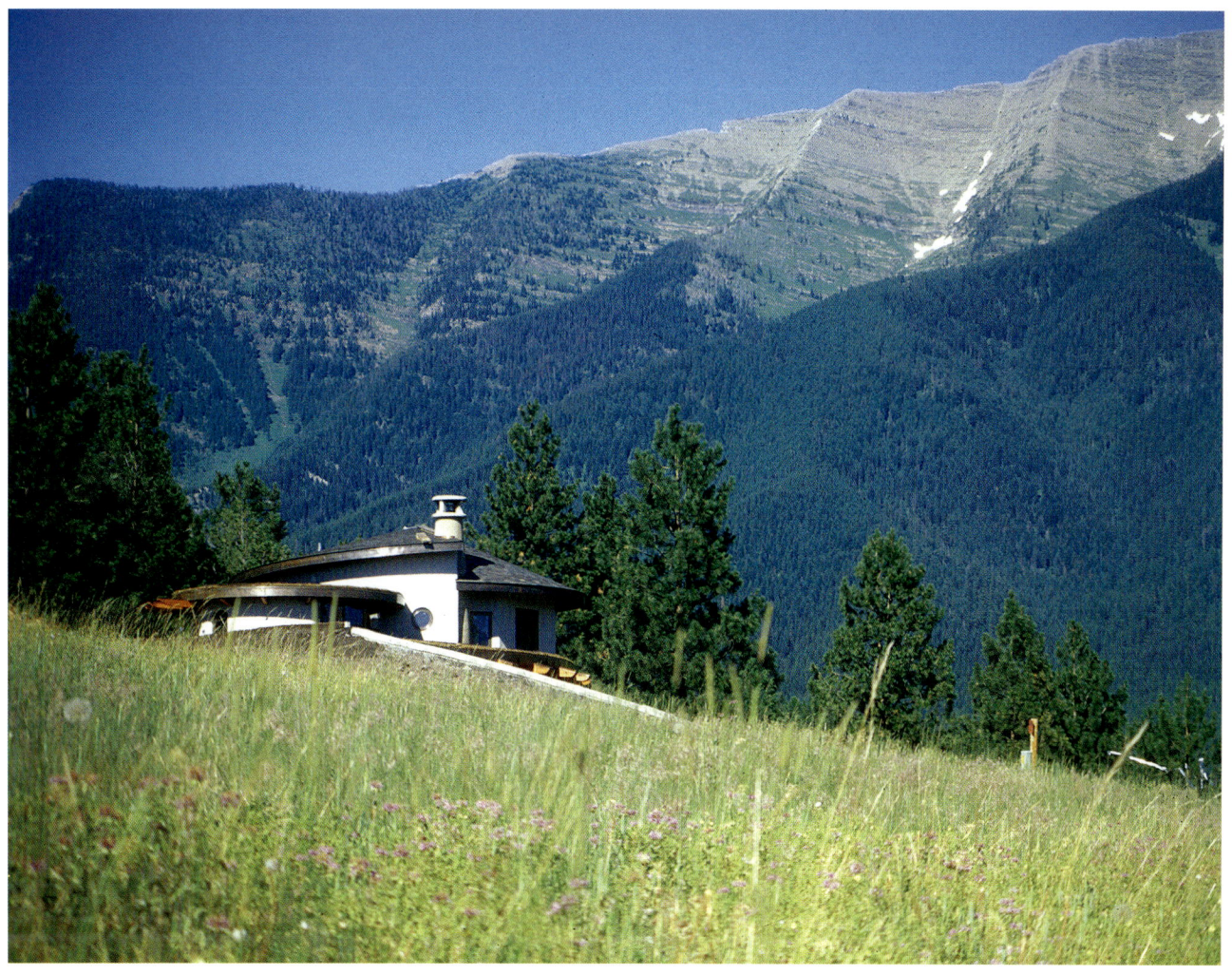

ABOVE & FACING PAGE:
A timeless blend of rugged mountain materials and modern form inform these unique homes.
Photograph by David Barrett (above)
Photograph by Ron Ruscio (facing page)

Q&A
more about david...

HOW LARGE IS YOUR STAFF? FEEL FREE TO NAME THEM, DESCRIBE THEIR POSITIONS OR TALK ABOUT THEIR INPUT, ETC.
Our intimate studio of 10 treats each project as a unique exploration within an open studio exchange. A Project Manager heads each team with the close involvement of David, allowing for an idea flow to maximize both efficiency and creative input through lifestyle analysis, site analysis, conceptual visualization, permit acquisition, design documentation and construction observation. An integral part of this participatory structure is the clients themselves, who are brought along through each decision in the design process. This allows for the mixing of our employees' creative and technical expertise with the clients dreams and needs to bring to bear their unique place for living.

WHAT ONE ELEMENT OF STYLE OR PHILOSOPHY HAVE YOU STUCK WITH FOR YEARS THAT STILL WORKS FOR YOU TODAY?
Spending time on the land on which a home will come to fruition. There is a knowledge, in fact, a relationship with the land that can only be known by experience. For this reason, we often camp on the land at the outset of the project.

WHO HAS HAD THE BIGGEST INFLUENCE ON YOUR CAREER?
I grew up in Western Pennsylvania not far from Fallingwater. I will never get over the feeling of that home's dialogue with the water, woods and rocks. For me, the bar was set!

WHAT IS THE MOST UNUSUAL/EXPENSIVE/DIFFICULT DESIGN OR TECHNIQUE YOU'VE USED IN ONE OF YOUR PROJECTS?
We love to use materials and structural systems that are from our cultural waste stream. These have included strawbale, rastra block, rammed earth, bamboo, and recycled timber. We also like to integrate solar systems as a sort of living skin for a building.

WHAT BOOK ARE YOU READING RIGHT NOW?
I try to keep a balance in my reading and to that end I am currently enjoying Tom Robbins' *Fierce Invalids Home from Hot Climates* and Paul Roberts' *The End of Oil: on the Edge of a Perilous New World*.

BARRETT STUDIO ARCHITECTS
DAVID BARRETT, AIA
1944 20th Street
Boulder, CO 80302
303.449.1141
f: 303.449.9320

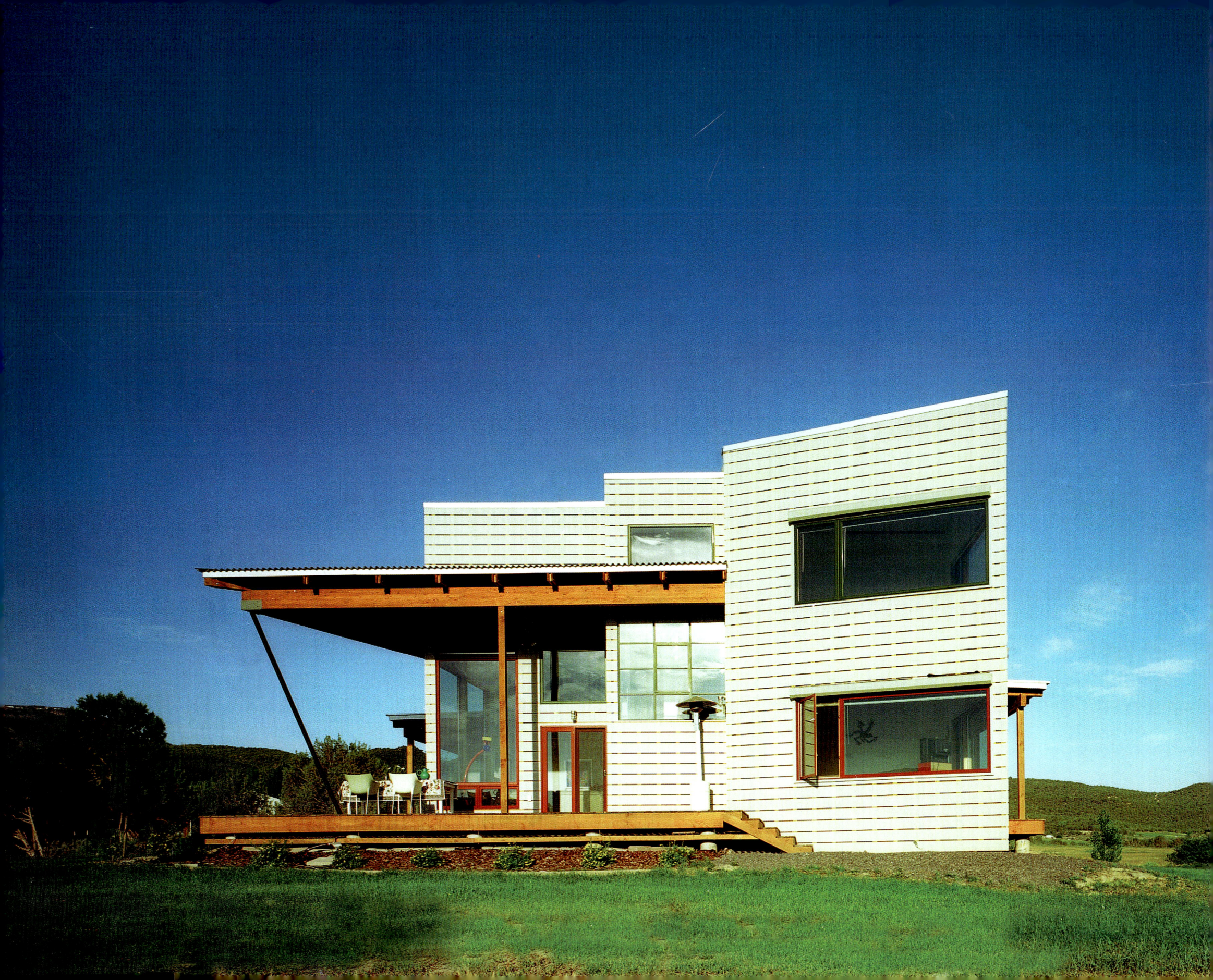

GLENN RAPPAPORT

BLACK SHACK OFFICE, LLC

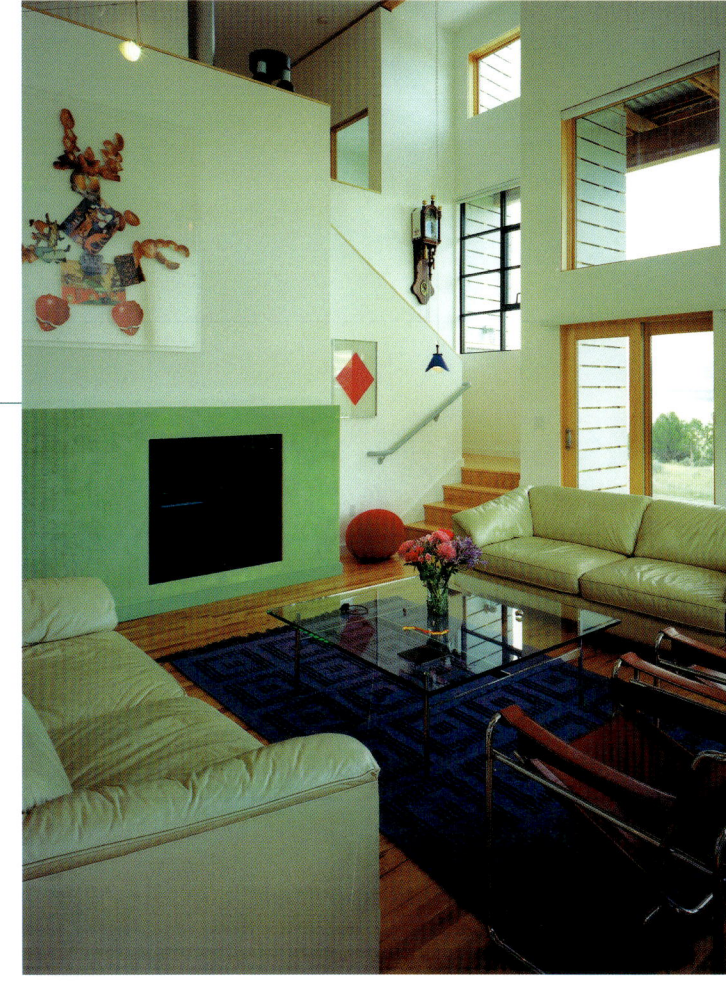

For Black Shack Office principal Glenn Rappaport, the decision to become an architect was a natural extension of his passion for art, the process of building, and his desire to form connections to places. Born in California, and after spending some time in Chicago and New York, he came to settle in Colorado's Roaring Fork Valley 35 years ago. Glenn opened his current office in 1990, naming it after the small alley coal shed that housed his original office. An advocate of what he called a kind of poetic functionalism, the melding of intellect and feeling, he believes that good architecture should be about inspiring us in our daily lives, and that by understanding light, proportion and the ideas of place making, the most ordinary pursuits can be elevated to special rituals. Where a client chooses to enjoy morning coffee, for instance, can be thought of as a departure point for the creation of a space comfortable for a single person, where the morning light becomes something to anticipate.

This dialogue between Glenn and his clients is the foundation of his practice, underpinning an architect/client relationship akin to making art together. His custom home design style, garnered from the essence of these conversations, embodies a contemporary American aesthetic. Black Shack Office typically uses simple materials in thoughtful and unusual ways in order to create something new and yet vaguely familiar.

As principal of his small practice, Glenn often works to assemble diverse project teams that are focused on a specific set of tasks and their execution, somewhat analogous to making a film. The Black Shack firm is close to a true design/build office in its approach, staying involved in a homebuilding project through to completion.

ABOVE:
Leendertsee Residence, Mesa, Colorado. View of Living area.
Photograph by Wayne Thom

FACING PAGE:
Leendertsee Residence, Mesa, Colorado. Exterior view.
Photograph by Wayne Thom

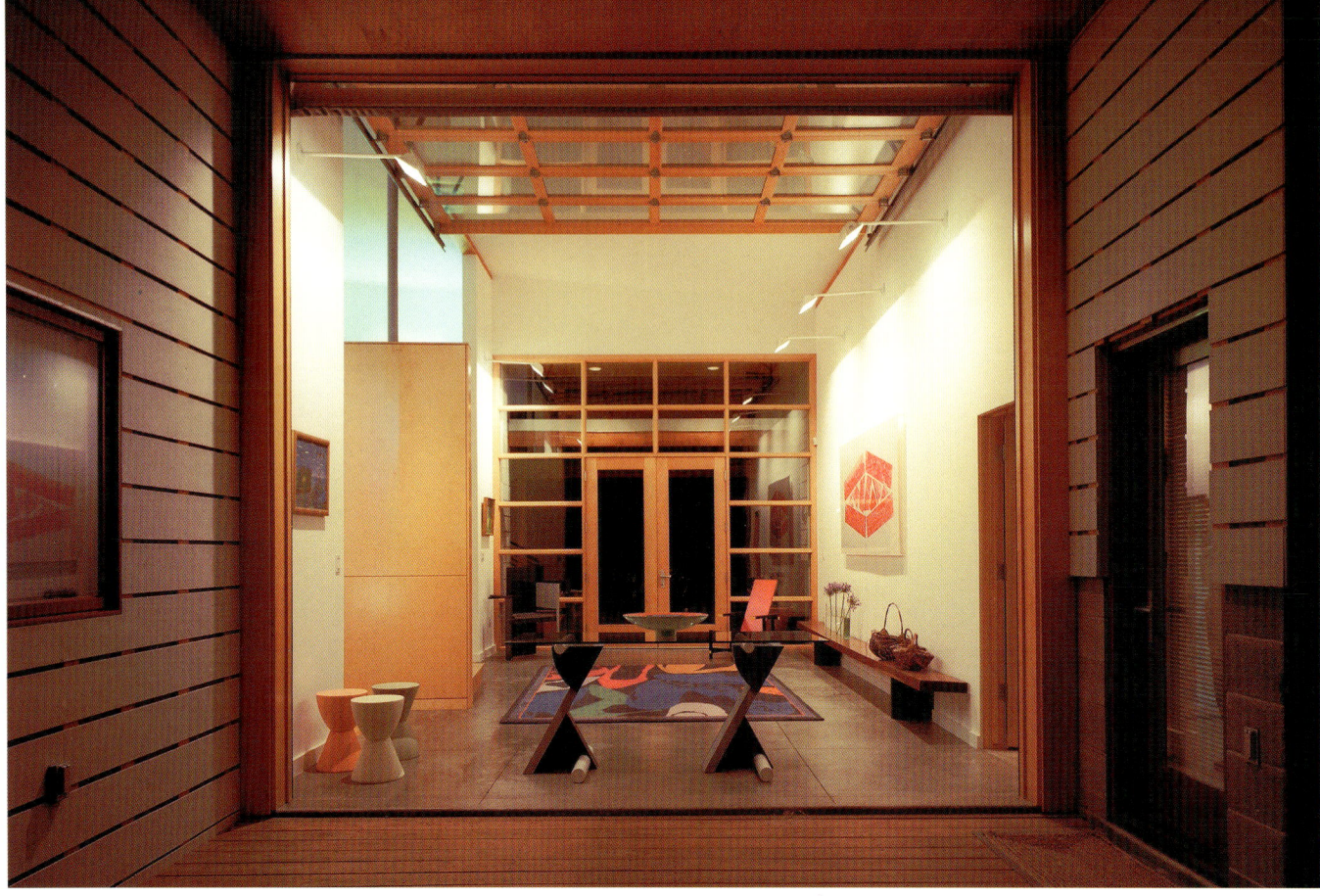

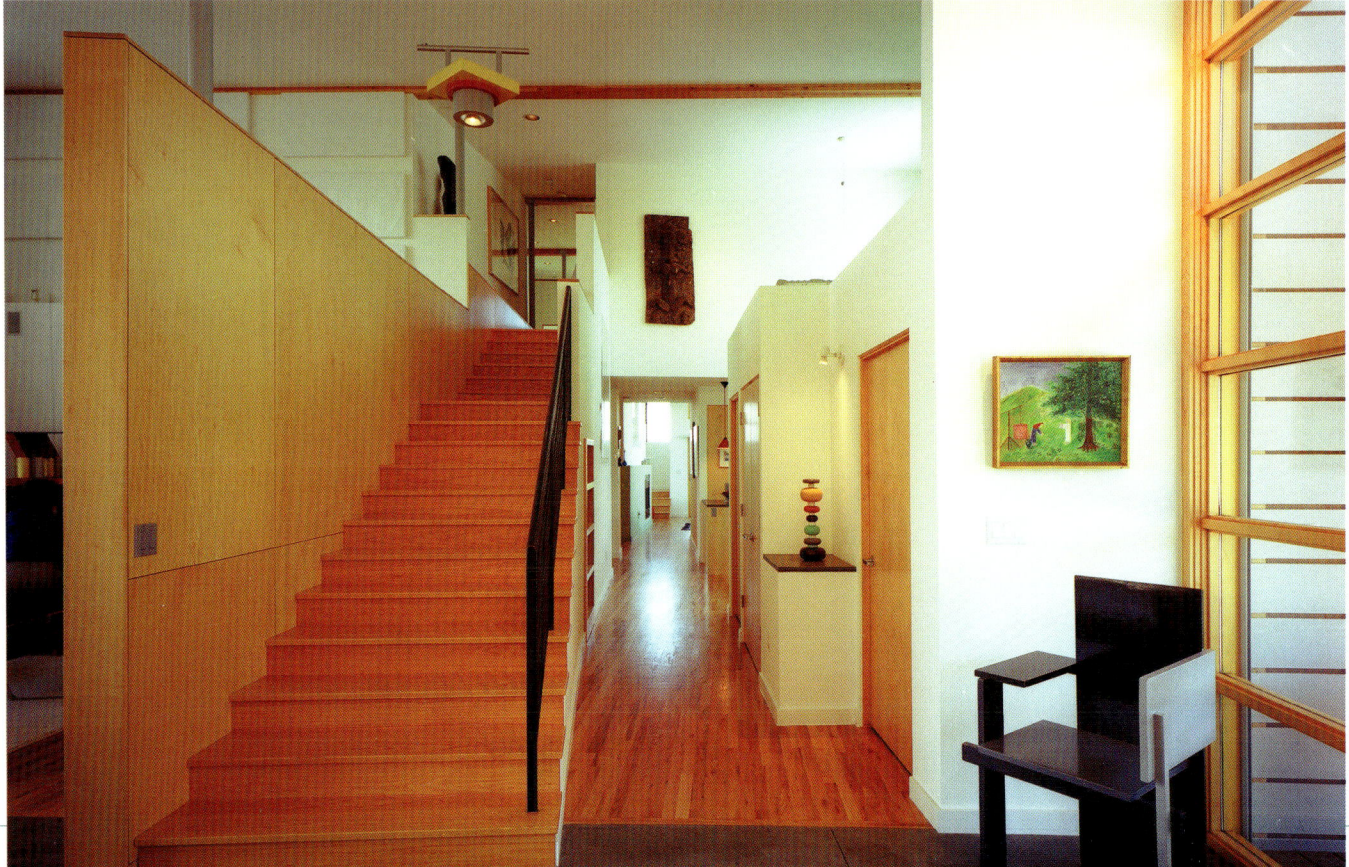

The Roaring Fork Valley has a unique microclimate in which the weather almost always sweeps in from the west and drops its moisture as it reaches the end of the valley in Aspen. This affords architects a tremendous opportunity in the planning of building sites and indoor/outdoor rooms. It is important for Black Shack Office to understand the issues of place in all of its projects, in order that they can rise to a level beyond building and become an honest extension of their clients' lives.

Everything Black Shack designs begins with a sense of the emotional as well as the physical. A house on a street in town might contribute to the overall urban scene by simply considering its dimension from the street, sidewalk, front yard gate and porch. In the mountains, a Black Shack project might encompass the home as well as an art studio or other outbuildings. By adding a large window to a garage, a view can be created to another building, so that if a client is using the garage for a project, that space becomes a place that exceeds its utilitarian function. If considered in a thoughtful way, the spaces between buildings can then become just as important as the enclosed and heated ones. In one project, Black Shack designed a master bedroom as a small cabin separated from the rest of the house.

"The client wanted to spend time in the landscape, and we tried to honor that," Glenn explains. "When you live in a place that's fairly remote, you need to be open to all kinds of things."

TOP LEFT:
Leendertsee Residence, Mesa, Colorado. Indoor/outdoor room.
Photograph by Wayne Thom

BOTTOM LEFT:
Leendertsee Residence, Mesa, Colorado. Main stair and hall.
Photograph by Wayne Thom

FACING PAGE TOP:
Leendertsee Residence, Mesa, Colorado. Evening view exterior/living.
Photograph by Wayne Thom

FACING PAGE BOTTOM:
Leendertsee Residence, Mesa, Colorado. Evening view of the exterior and entry.
Photograph by Wayne Thom

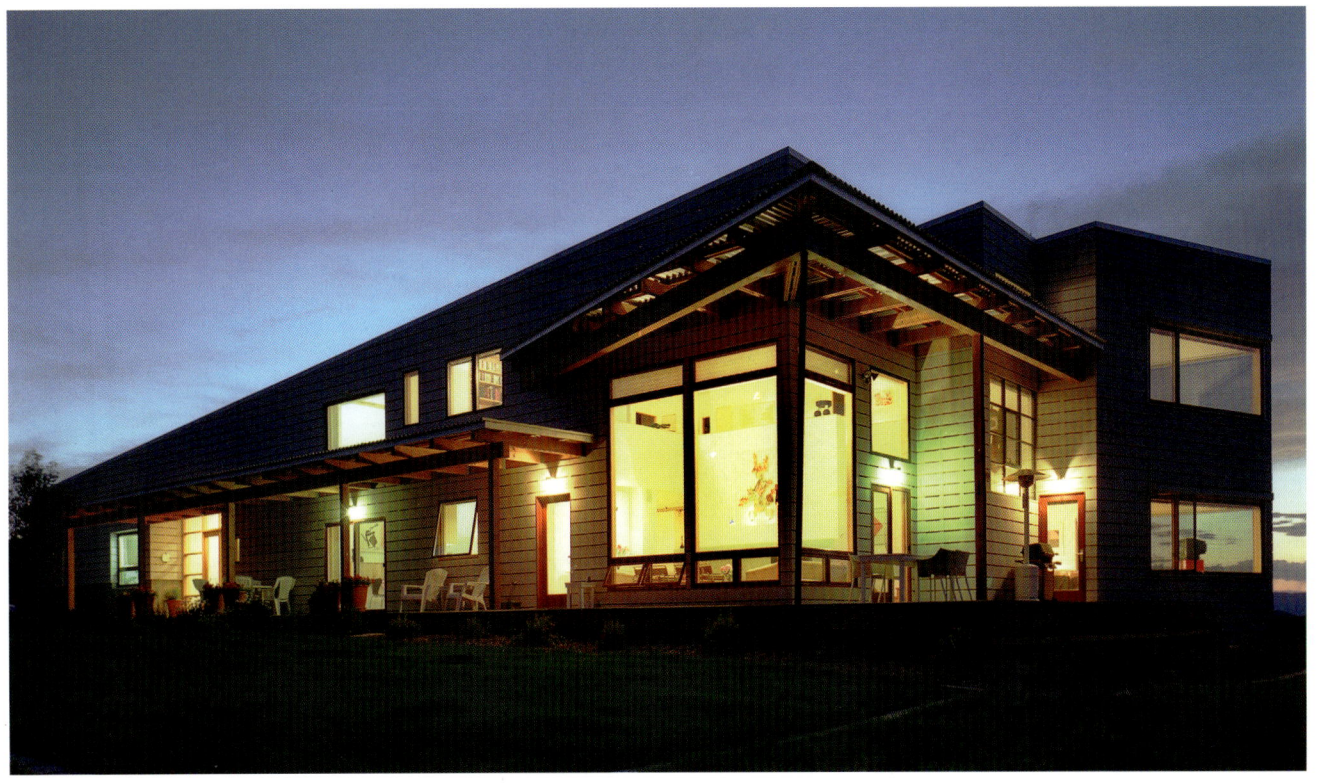

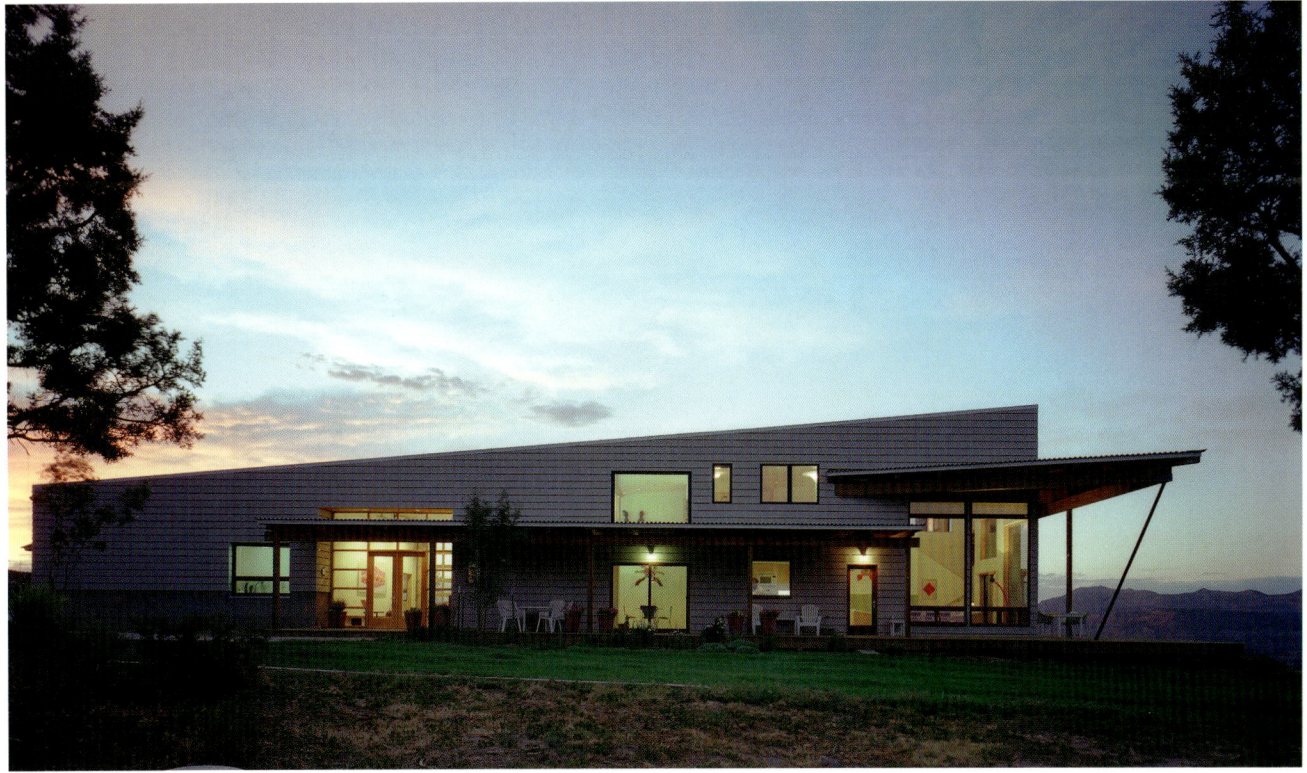

Q&A
more about glenn...

DESCRIBE YOUR DESIGN STYLE OR PREFERENCES.
Poetic Functionalism.

ANY AWARDS OR SPECIAL RECOGNITION YOU WOULD LIKE MENTIONED?
Black Shack Office has received a number of American Institute of Architects Honor Awards for residential and community-oriented work.

WHAT IS THE SINGLE THING YOU WOULD DO TO BRING A DULL HOUSE TO LIFE?
Fill it with flowers.

WHAT IS THE MOST UNIQUE/IMPRESSIVE/BEAUTIFUL HOME YOU'VE BEEN INVOLVED WITH? WHY?
Our home. We are raising four children and they love it. To us, it is small and beautiful.

BLACK SHACK OFFICE, LLC
GLENN RAPPAPORT
Box 1847
Basalt, CO 81621
970.927.0635
f: 970.927.0654
www.blackshackoffice.com

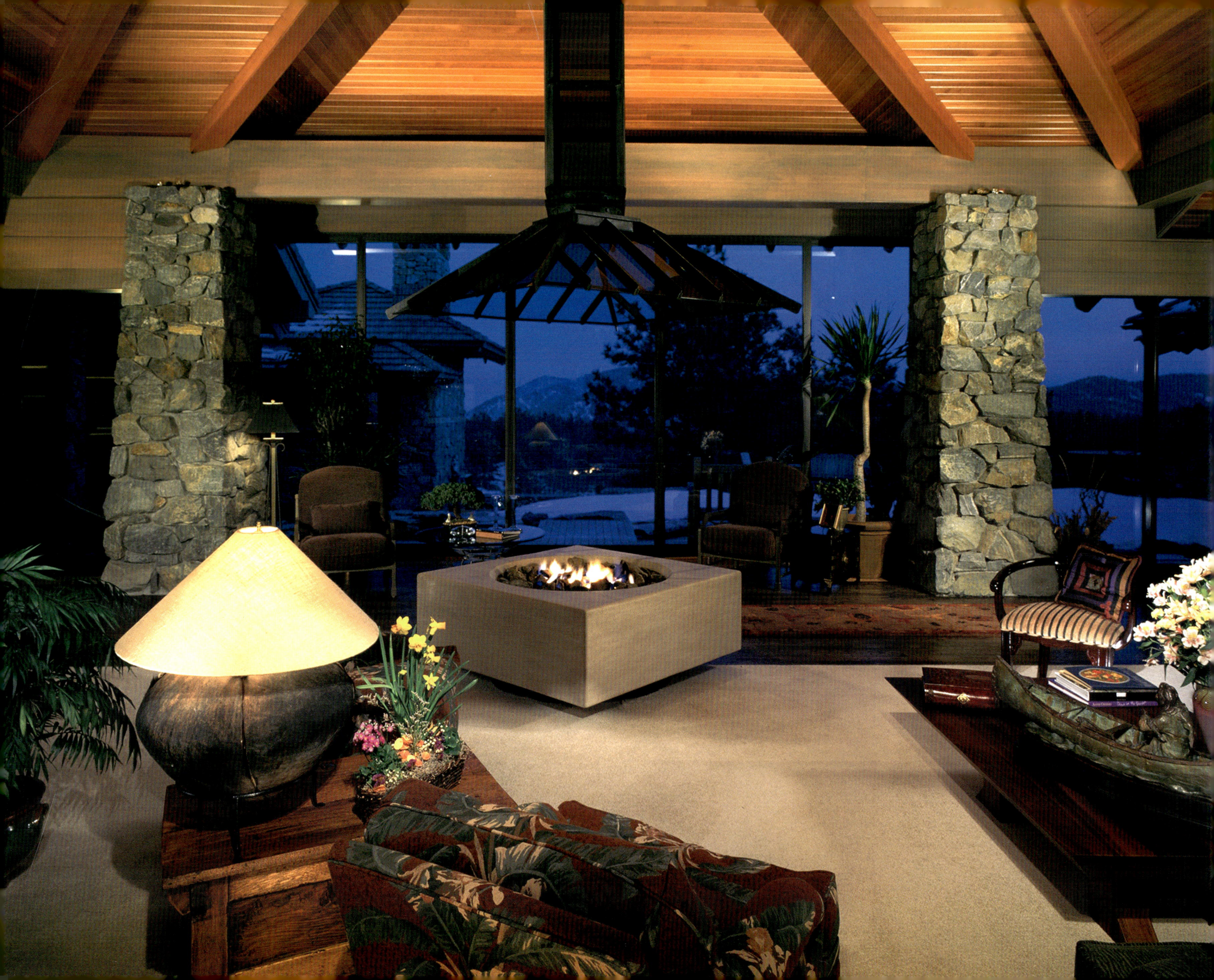

GARY BROTHERS
JIM VANDERVORSTE
DAVID WILLIAMS

BVZ ARCHITECTS
DAVID WILLIAMS HOMES

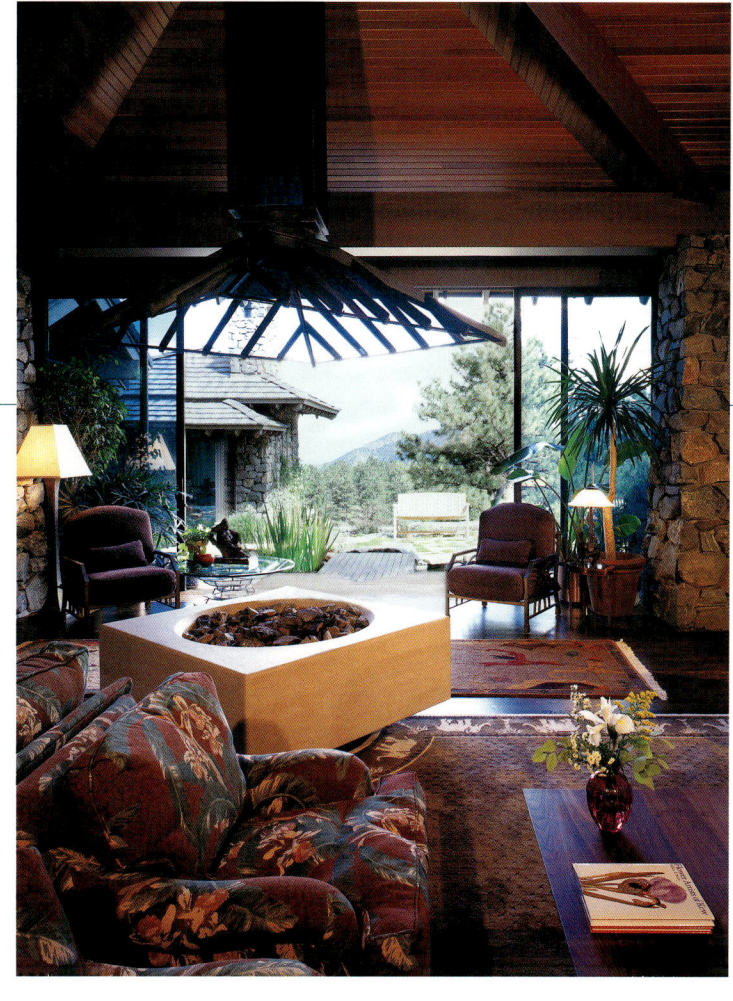

BVZ Architects has established a tradition of helping create special places for special people. With a solid commitment to strong design emphasis with timeless quality, the firm's goal is to help each client solve their building needs as efficiently and uniquely as possible. BVZ adopts a team approach, which has proven to work well in providing flexibility and the expertise necessary to effectively meet the different project needs of every client.

Teamwork is working together toward a common vision. It is the fuel that allows ordinary people to attain extraordinary results. The BVZ office is firmly committed to the concept that overall design is a team effort. The best value and most successful results are achieved when all team members: the owner, architects, engineers and contractors are working together toward the common goal of a well thought-out, distinctive, affordable and efficient project.

BVZ has had the good fortune of utilizing this team approach with David Williams Homes on one of their finest projects, the Kerr Gulch Home, located in Evergreen, Colorado. The team members included architects Gary Brothers, AIA and Jim VanderVorste, AIA, designer/artist Priscilla Baldwin, builder David Williams and designer of interiors, Micky Ackerman.

"On this project, the owner was an integral part of the design team, which typically doesn't happen. The energy and desire to be engaged in the process exuded from everyone involved made the project something very special. It was such an advantage to have the builder captive from the beginning; this was a pretty unique approach to the project and one of the main reasons it turned out as special as it did."

ABOVE:
On mild days, the glass wall opens wide to let the great room and garden spaces flow together.
Photograph by Michael Shopenn

FACING PAGE:
The stone fireplace and glass hood provide a warming focal point without blocking the view through the glass wall beyond.
Photograph by Willie Gibson

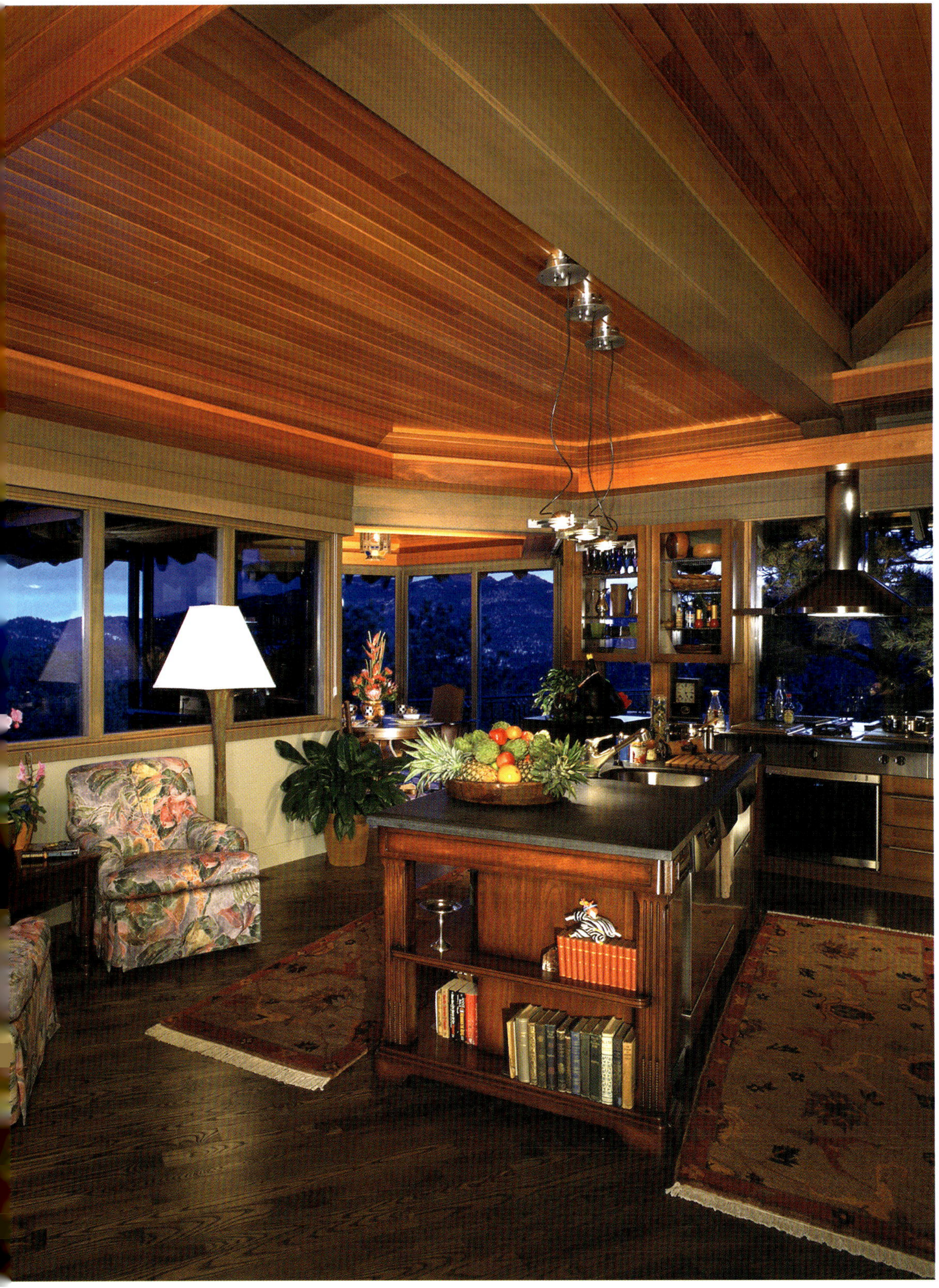

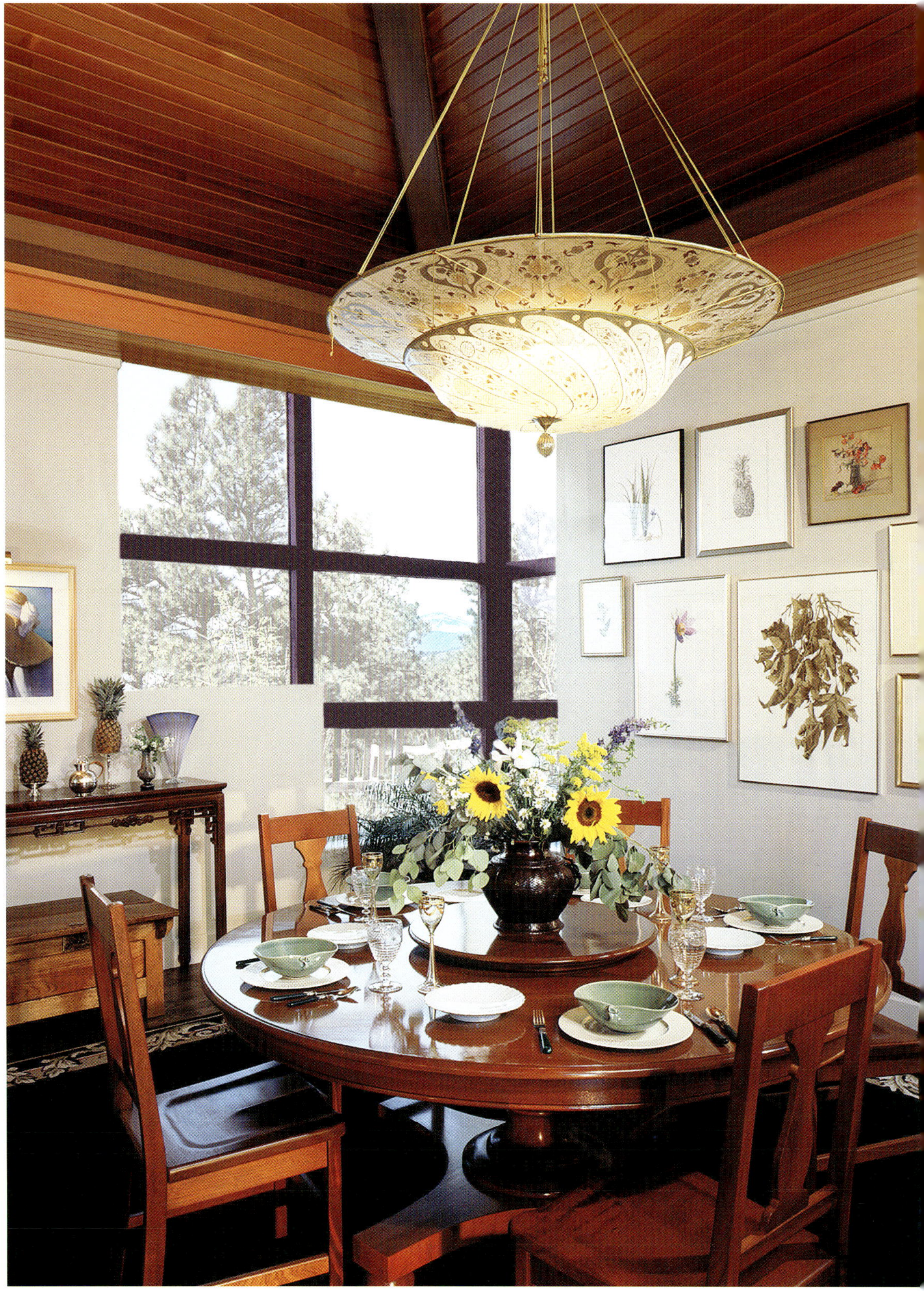

The simple fact about this union is that everyone brings real talent to the table. David Williams' expertise stems from his 29-year building career. Jim and Gary of BVZ have been working together for over 20 years as a cohesive unit, while at the same time, defining their own strengths. The owner of the Kerr Gulch Home came from a strong art background and had the ability to visualize the architects' and builders' ideas while adding her desires and personality.

The home sits on a unique site—a mountain site with extreme grade differential. Tucked into the hillside, the structure opens up on the downhill side around a very special courtyard approach which was developed into a pond and garden area. The owner is a master gardener and the team wanted that reflected in their home. The concept of the house was to enjoy the garden from every living area—this was the most difficult challenge they undertook. The other challenge was to keep the majority of living spaces on one level; a difficult task with the significant grade change. The whole team was extremely pleased when a two-foot grade change was accomplished throughout the house without any steps.

FACING PAGE LEFT:
Upper cabinets with glass doors and backs allow for an uninterrupted view to flow across the kitchen area without sacrificing usable storage.
Photograph by Willie Gibson

FACING PAGE RIGHT:
The dining room glass corner allows a borrowed view of Mt. Evans from adjacent spaces while retaining solid walls for inward focus and display of artwork.
Photograph by Michael Shopenn

RIGHT:
Links connecting the main spaces are ramped to allow the house to step up the sloped site.
Photograph by Willie Gibson

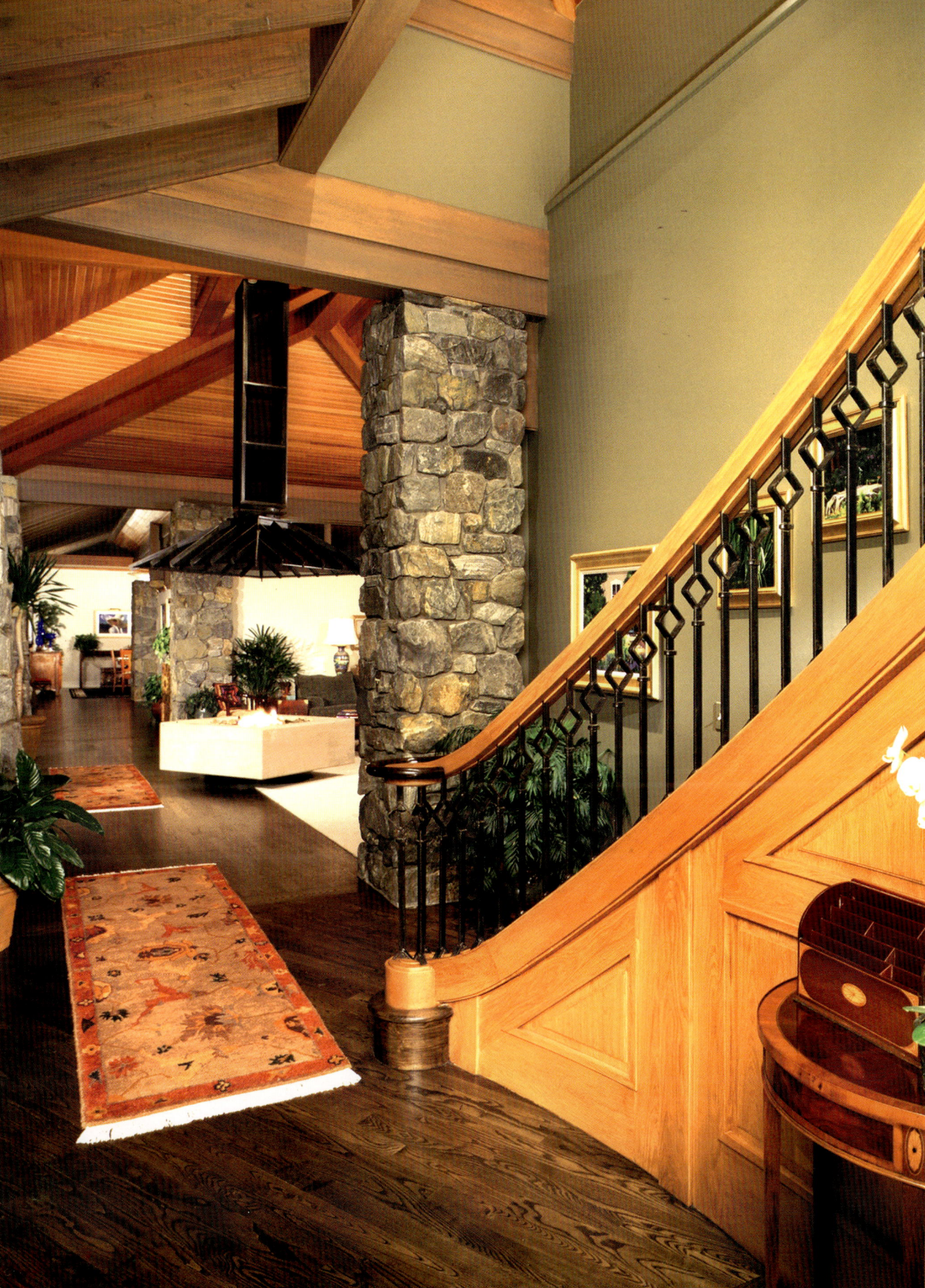

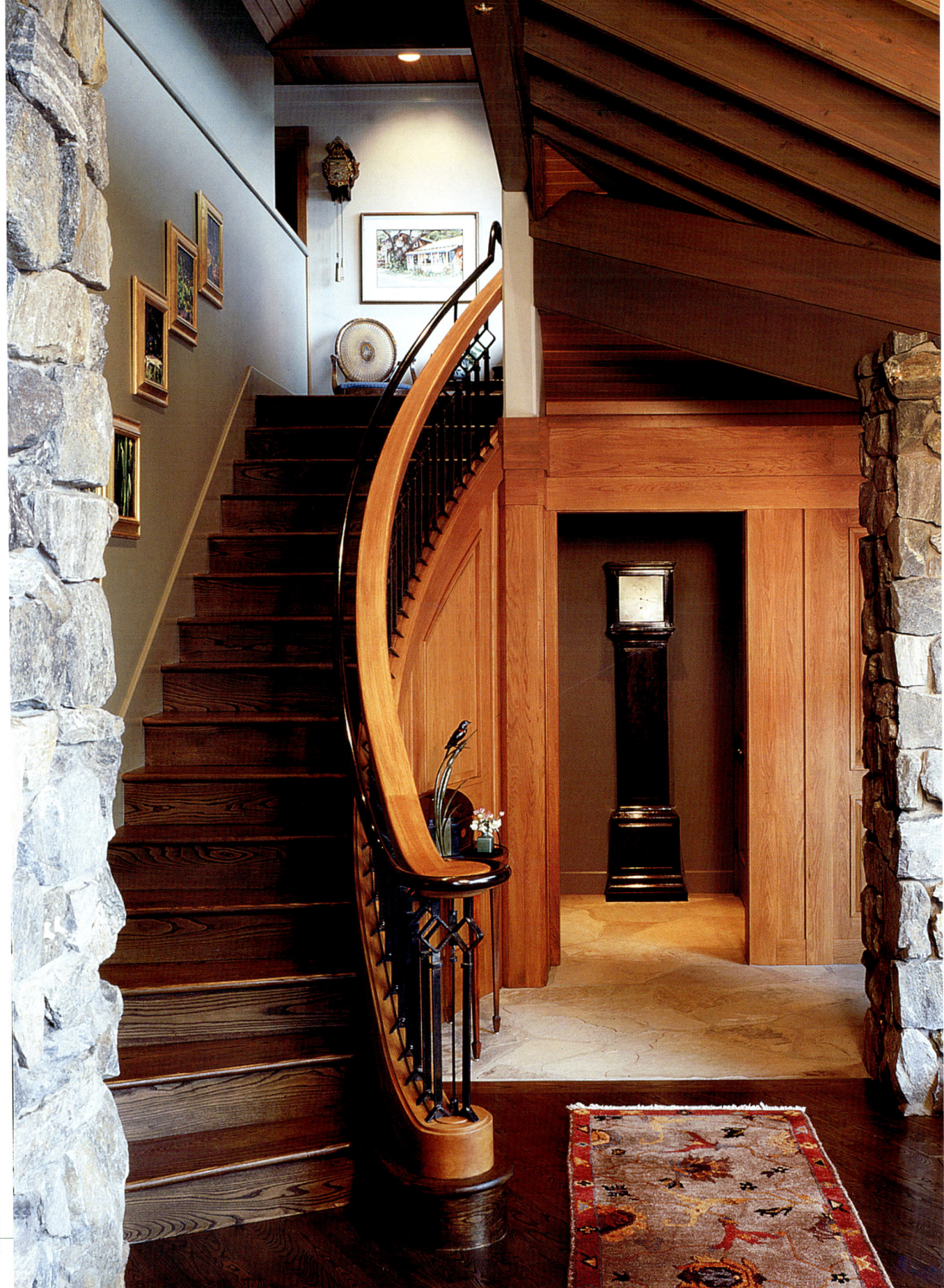

The Kerr Gulch Home was the first project that saw the marrying of BVZ and David Williams Homes, but 10 projects have since been cultivated between the pair. As this relationship between BVZ and David Williams Homes grows, so does their capability to create the perfect dream home.

The knowledge that they are creating people's dream homes is the most satisfying part of their jobs. The team very often has clients return to them for their second home; evidence that the quality of their work is affecting the quality of their clients' lives. Building and architecture isn't just a job to BVZ and David Williams Homes; it's a passion they enjoy each day.

LEFT:
Nested around a central garden, the three main living modules open to the tranquility of this space and the grandeur of the panoramic surroundings.
Photograph by Michael Shopenn

FACING PAGE:
The stairway, as in other detailing, is formed to avoid style stereotypes and to comfortably relate to both antique and contemporary family furnishings.
Photograph by Michael Shopenn

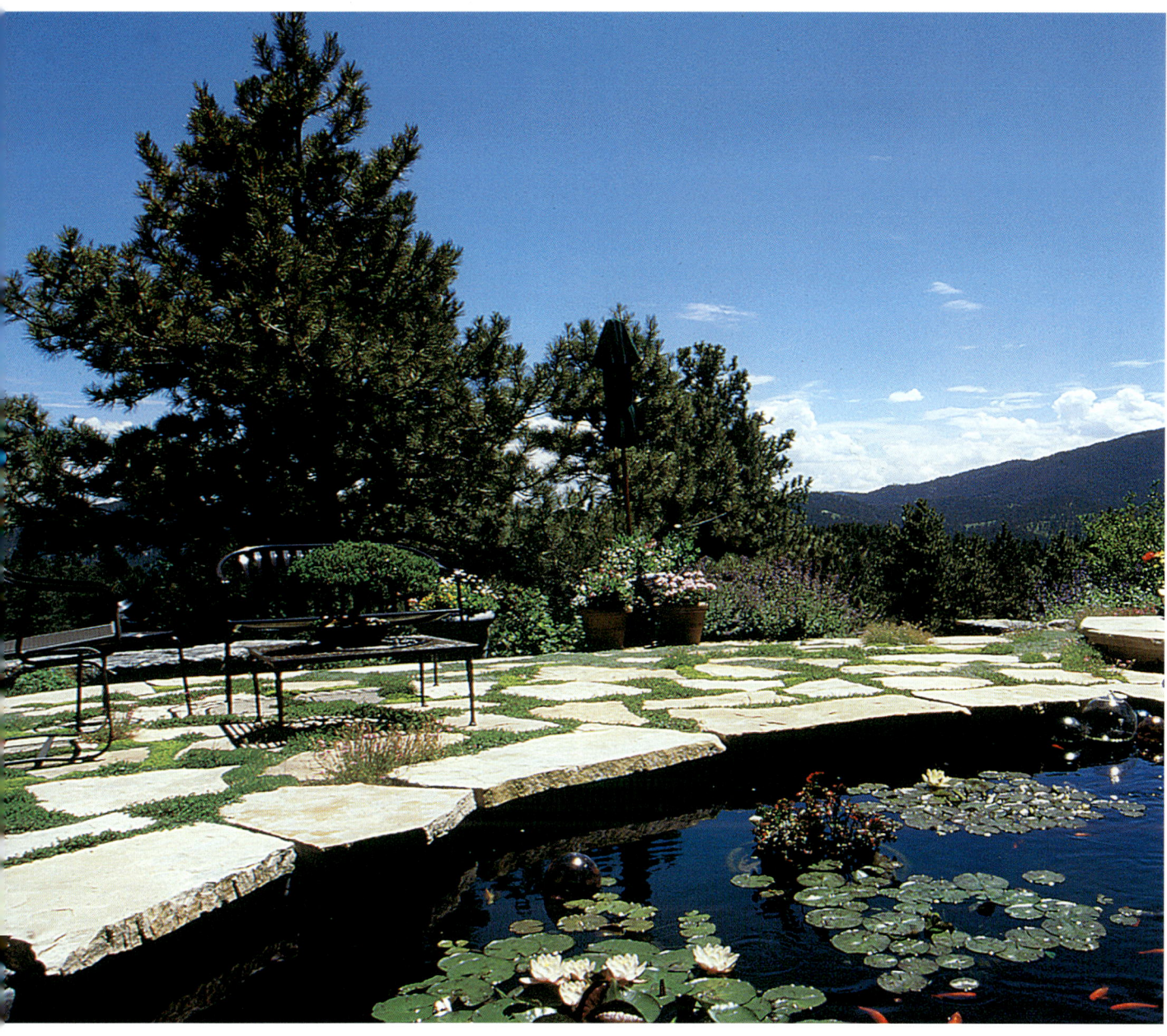

Q&A
more about gary & jim...

WHO HAS HAD THE MOST INFLUENCE ON YOUR CAREER?
Jim and I have had the opportunity to work with some very talented people over the years. We think they have all had a lasting impact, but the most significant was Hoby Wagener. An architect's work we have always enjoyed is Fay Jones, a student of Frank Lloyd Wright and an outstanding architect who gets very little credit. Much of his early work in Arkansas has coupled with the influence of working with Hoby to have a powerful effect on levels of details and how we view spaces.

WHAT ARE THE WORDS YOU PRACTICE BUSINESS BY?
"A good house speaks not just of the materials from which it is made, but of the intangible rhythms, spirits and dreams of people's lives." — Charles Moore

WHAT IS THE HIGHEST COMPLIMENT YOU HAVE RECEIVED PROFESSIONALLY?
The most rewarding words we have heard are a client telling us they would rather be at home than anywhere else.

WHAT IS THE MOST UNUSUAL DESIGN IN WHICH YOU HAVE BEEN INVOLVED?
We designed a stone fireplace that also featured a circular stone stairway leading to a glass enclosed observation deck. It was a very special place to be.

WHAT IS A SINGLE THING YOU WOULD DO TO BRING A DULL HOUSE TO LIFE?
Add daylight!

HAVE YOU RECEIVED ANY SPECIAL AWARDS OR RECOGNITION?
Yes, one of our most successful projects, the Kerr Gulch Home, was awarded "House of the Year" from the Homebuilder's Association. The design team, which includes the owner, has gone on to complete several additional projects including a home for the builder. In addition, we have also had the honor of being published several times over the years.

BVZ ARCHITECTS
GARY BROTHERS, AIA
JIM VANDERVORSTE, AIA
3445 Penrose Place #210
Boulder, CO 80301
303.442.0295
www.bvzarchitects.com

DAVID WILLIAMS HOMES
DAVID WILLIAMS
33208 Alta Vista Drive
Evergreen, CO 80439

PO Box 4269
Evergreen, CO 80439
303.674.1333

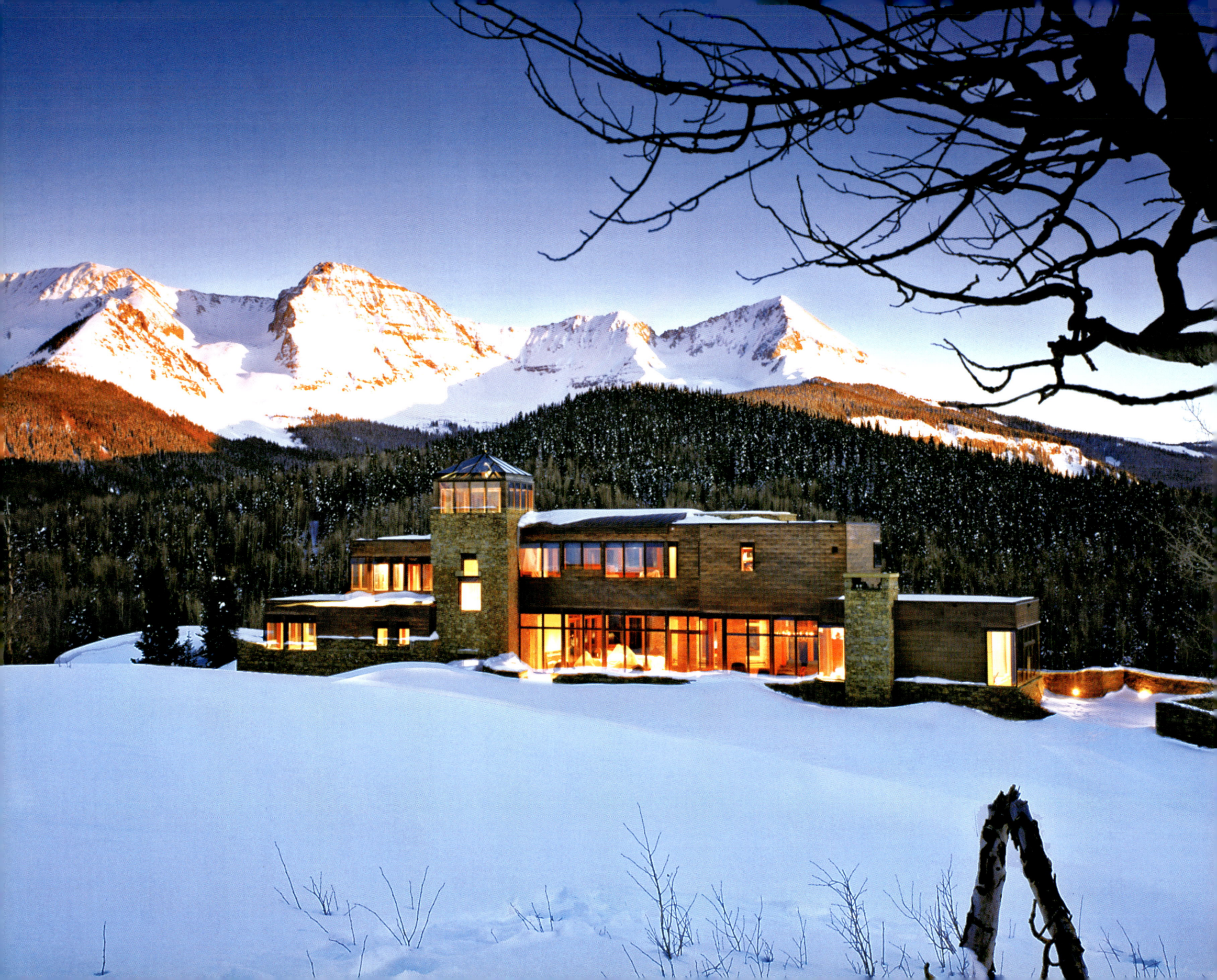

CHARLES CUNNIFFE

CHARLES CUNNIFFE ARCHITECTS

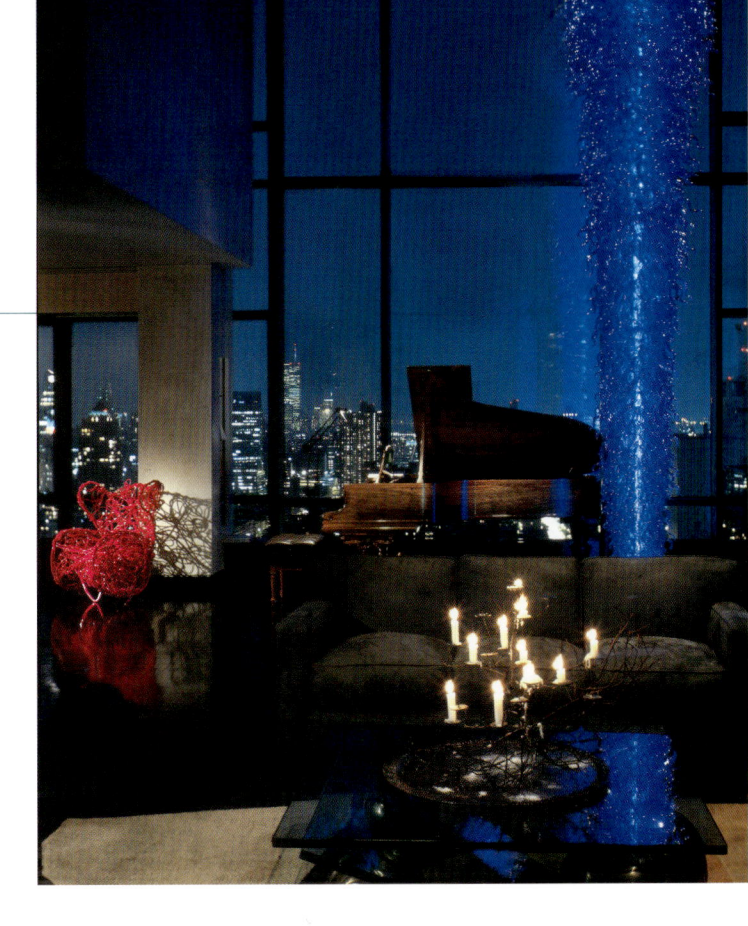

Charles Cunniffe founded Charles Cunniffe Architects in 1980. The firm offers comprehensive, integrated design services that honor the needs, vision and context of each of their clients. Charles was originally called to Aspen in 1979 to do the master plan and design work on the Hotel Jerome and as they say, the rest is history. Now with offices located in Aspen and Steamboat Springs, CCA has extensive experience in mountain regions and many other diverse and sensitive environments..

CCA approaches every project as a challenge to design buildings that fit gracefully into their context. Charles and his team pay careful attention to studying the site, the history of the site, the climatic conditions, and the client's needs. CCA considers themselves to be "place makers," designing appropriate architecture to suit each locale. Along with their passion for great design, the team also avidly pursues sustainability and employs the latest technological advances in each project. They are dedicated to a humanistic, socially responsible and technologically sophisticated vision of design.

The firm structure is geared to be competitive and effective for any size and scope of project with an emphasis on client satisfaction, quality service and excellent design. From major golf and resort planning, hotels and commercial projects, to single family residences and historic renovation, their commitment to excellence remains the underlying principle of their practice.

Charles is constantly contacted by clients who recognize each of his projects has a unique personality of its own. This personality is born through sensitivity to the client's interests and understanding context of each site, as well as the collaboration of the team members involved in the project.

ABOVE:
Palm Penthouse, New York City, New York.
Photograph by Philip Ennis

FACING PAGE:
Frazier Homestead, San Miguel County, Colorado.
Photograph by Ron Semrod

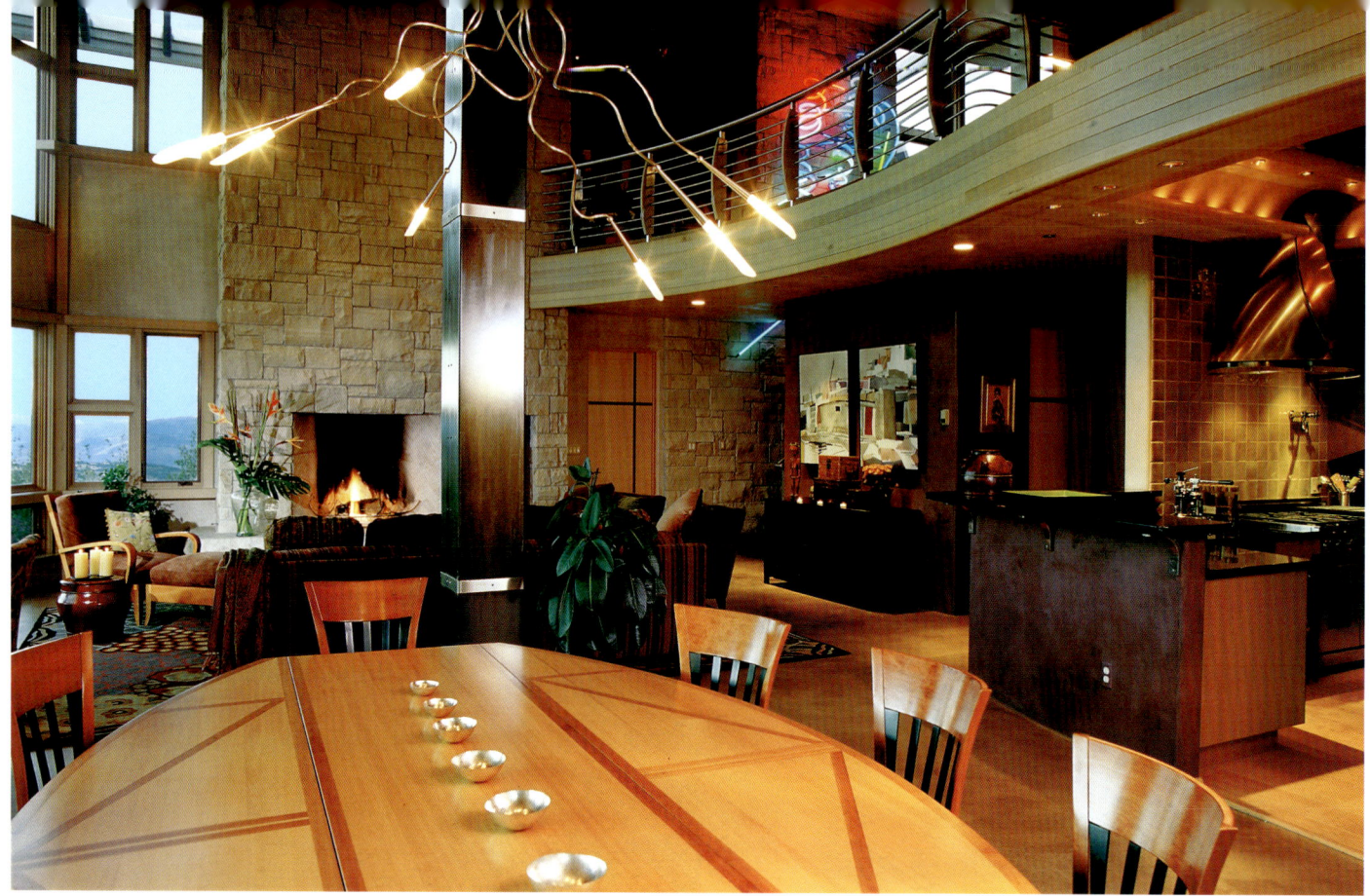

The hallmark of CCA's work is individuality; the firm doesn't have a formula and makes an effort to avoid repeating themselves in any project. The goal of each and every project is to create a new work of art in each instance. Using their studio-style creative design process, CCA makes it clear that good design isn't about buildings, it's about people.

With a global regionalism focus, CCA has created works of art in 17 countries and 29 states. "Working with people from all over the world is the most rewarding thing I do. I work with an extraordinarily talented staff and amazing clients. Many of my clients have become lifelong friends. It's so satisfying to know that when we create a home or building for them, we are contributing to their quality of life," said Charles. He continues to design structures for friends and clients across the globe, starting each project with fresh energy and an open mind, pursuing excellent results. We hope to leave behind a legacy of improving and enhancing the lives and communities we interact with.

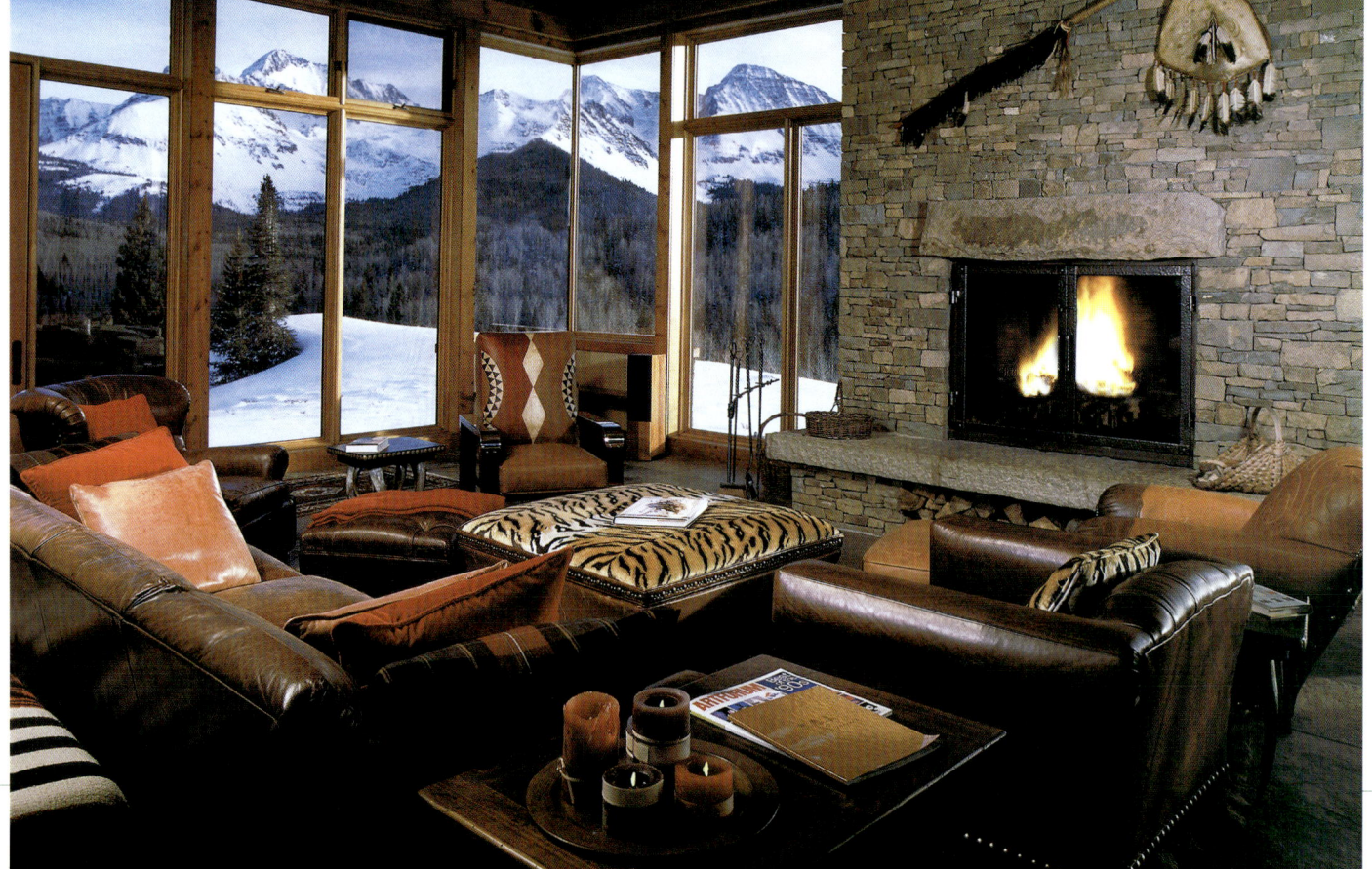

TOP LEFT:
Baker Residence, Park City, Utah–great room.
Photograph by Laurie Dickson

BOTTOM LEFT:
Frazier Homestead, San Miguel County, Colorado–living room.
Photograph by Ron Semrod

FACING PAGE:
Baker Residence, Park City, Utah.
Photograph by Laurie Dickson

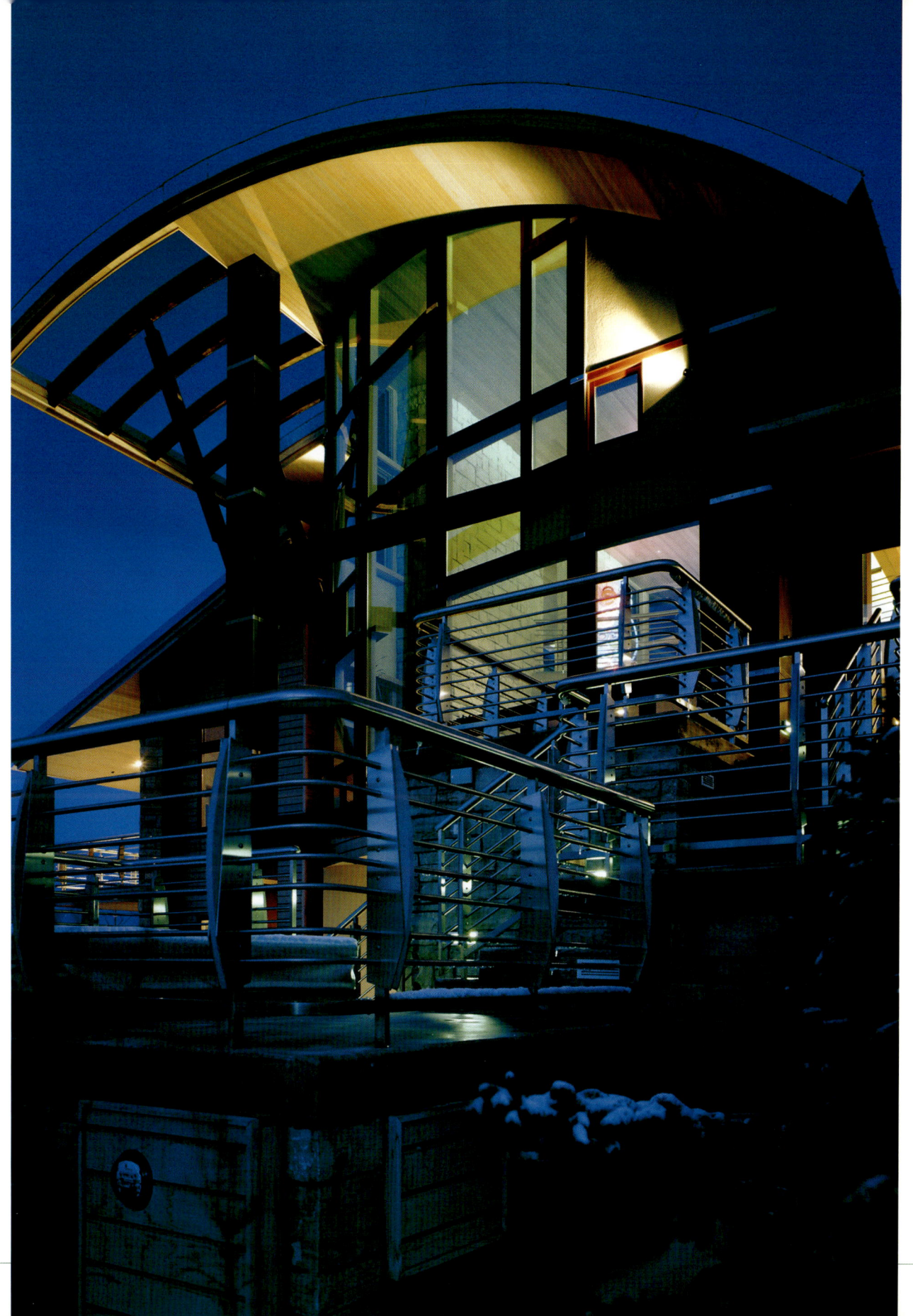

Q&A
more about charles...

WHAT PERSONAL INDULGENCE DO YOU SPEND THE MOST MONEY ON?
Adventure Travel to exotic places is one of my greatest passions. In the past year, I have traveled to 33 countries, many of them third-world. It is always mind expanding and educational, improving our work with a greater understanding of world history and our global environment.

WHAT COLOR BEST DESCRIBES YOU AND WHY?
Blue best describes me because it's like the sky—subtle and ever changing.

HAVE YOU BEEN PUBLISHED IN ANY NATIONAL OR REGIONAL PUBLICATIONS?
The firm and its work have been published in virtually all architecture, interior and trade magazines as well as in many books and textbooks.

WHAT SINGLE THING WOULD YOU DO TO BRING A DULL HOUSE TO LIFE?
The key to bringing life to any home is opening it up to nature and light.

CHARLES CUNNIFFE ARCHITECTS

CHARLES CUNNIFFE
610 East Hyman Avenue
Aspen, CO 81611
970.925.5590
f: 970.925.5076
www.cunniffe.com

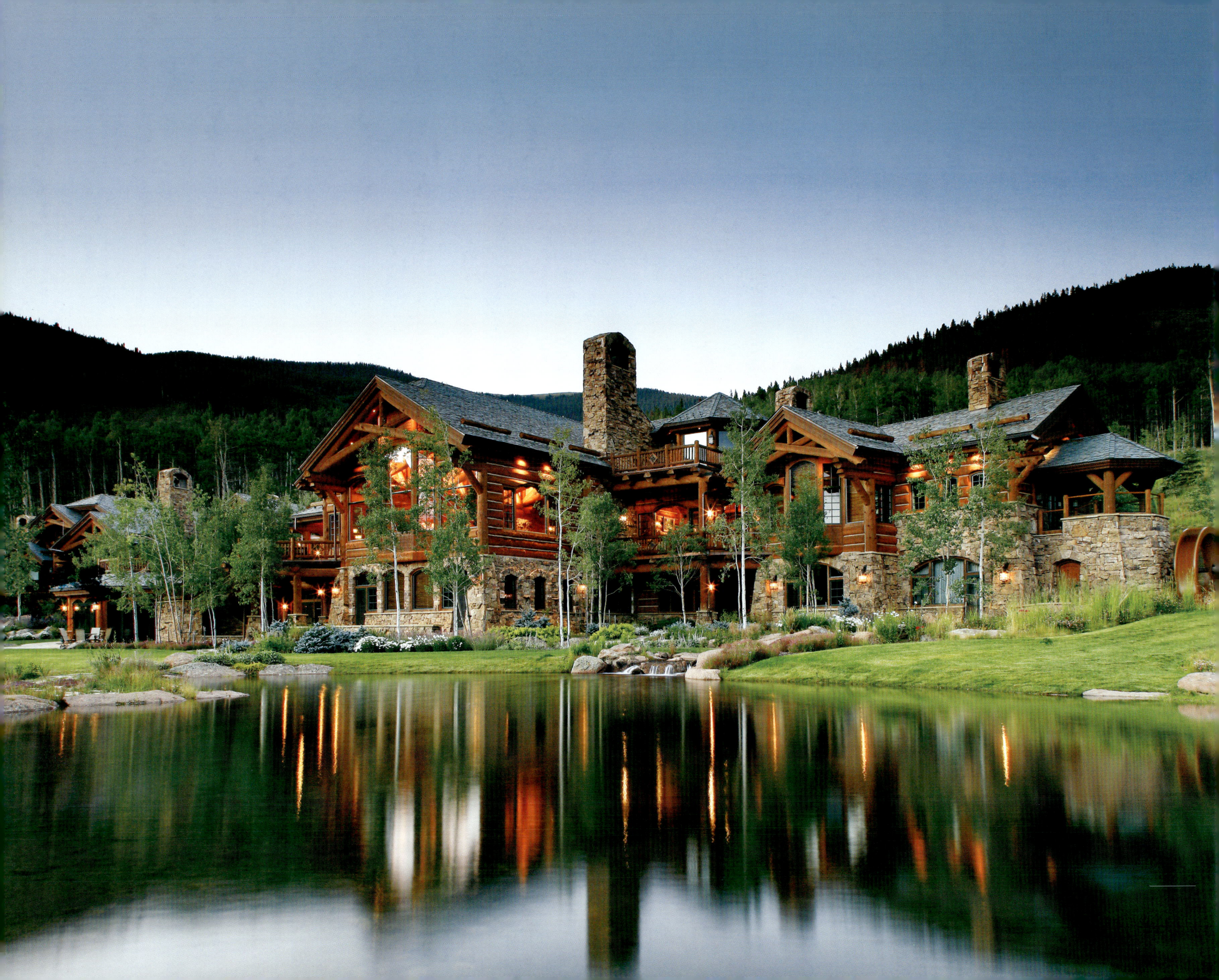

JON GUNSON

CUSTOM MOUNTAIN ARCHITECTS

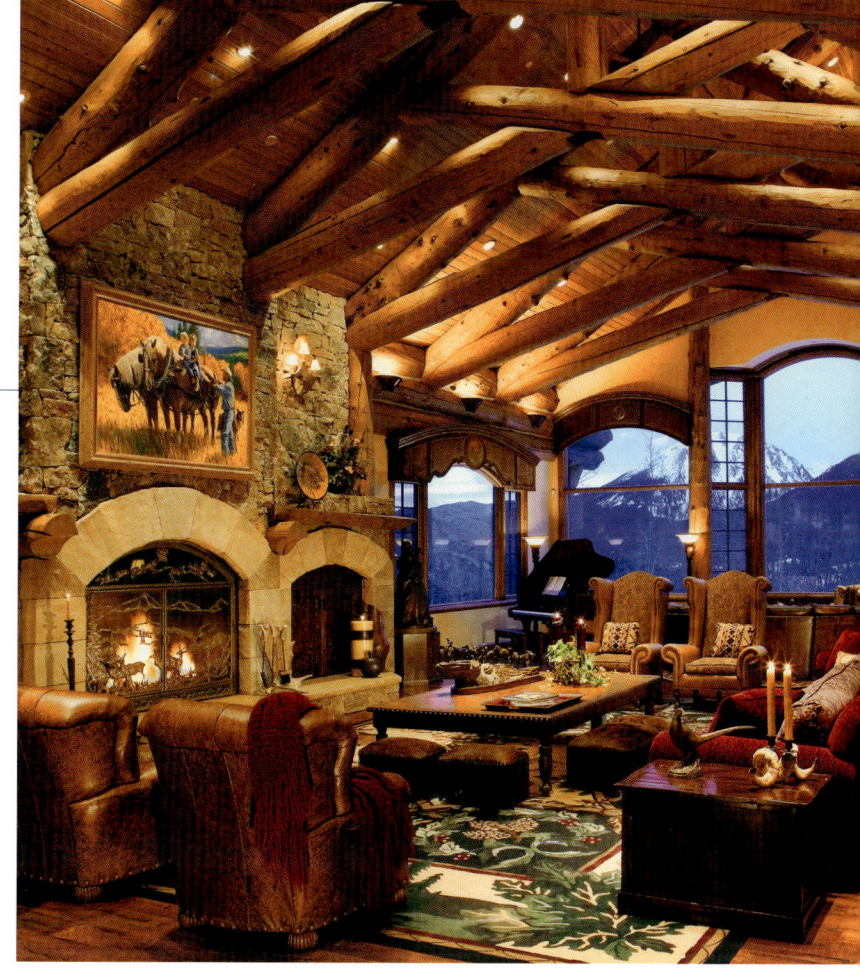

Never having heard the word "architect" as a child, Jon Gunson loved building club houses and tree houses throughout his neighborhood for his friends to enjoy. Everything clicked one day when his grade school art teacher introduced him to a book about Frank Lloyd Wright where a grown-up actually got paid to design beautiful homes. Raised in the Midwest, he loved the family vacations to Colorado and dreamed of someday combining his love of the mountains with his love of designing buildings.

After receiving his degree, Jon worked for architectural firms in Denver. But this wasn't close enough to the mountains so, in 1970, he moved to Breckenridge to establish his own company, Custom Mountain Architects. Over the years, with a team of five professionals, his firm has earned a reputation for quality, creativity and dedication to his clients. They specialize in designing beautiful homes in the Colorado Mountains, but Jon also loves designing ranch properties because of their unique western tradition, wide open land and endless possibilities.

Spending quality time with clients to have sincere discussions about their thoughts and dreams is very enjoyable for Jon. He wants to learn about his clients and their families, to gain a sense of their personalities and lifestyle in order to understand their functional needs and their aesthetic wishes. While many architects seem to focus only on the exterior appearance of a home, Custom Mountain Architects strives to create the clients' entire living environment, both interior and exterior, so that it works perfectly for their family's lifestyle as well as providing beautiful and exciting spaces.

Jon believes that, just as each client is unique and has special requirements for their home, the property they have purchased is also unique and has its own characteristics. Custom Mountain Architects analyzes each site to study its access, slope, vegetation, sun angles and views. Jon also wants

ABOVE:
The great room was also designed in the lodge tradition with glorious views and a massive fireplace. Yet it has smaller furniture groupings for friendly discussions or for reading in a cozy corner.
Photograph by Living Images

LEFT:
The owners pictured a home in the style of a historic mountain lodge as a gathering place for family and friends. We created the pond and a flowing stream to complete the tranquil setting.
Photograph by Todd Pierce

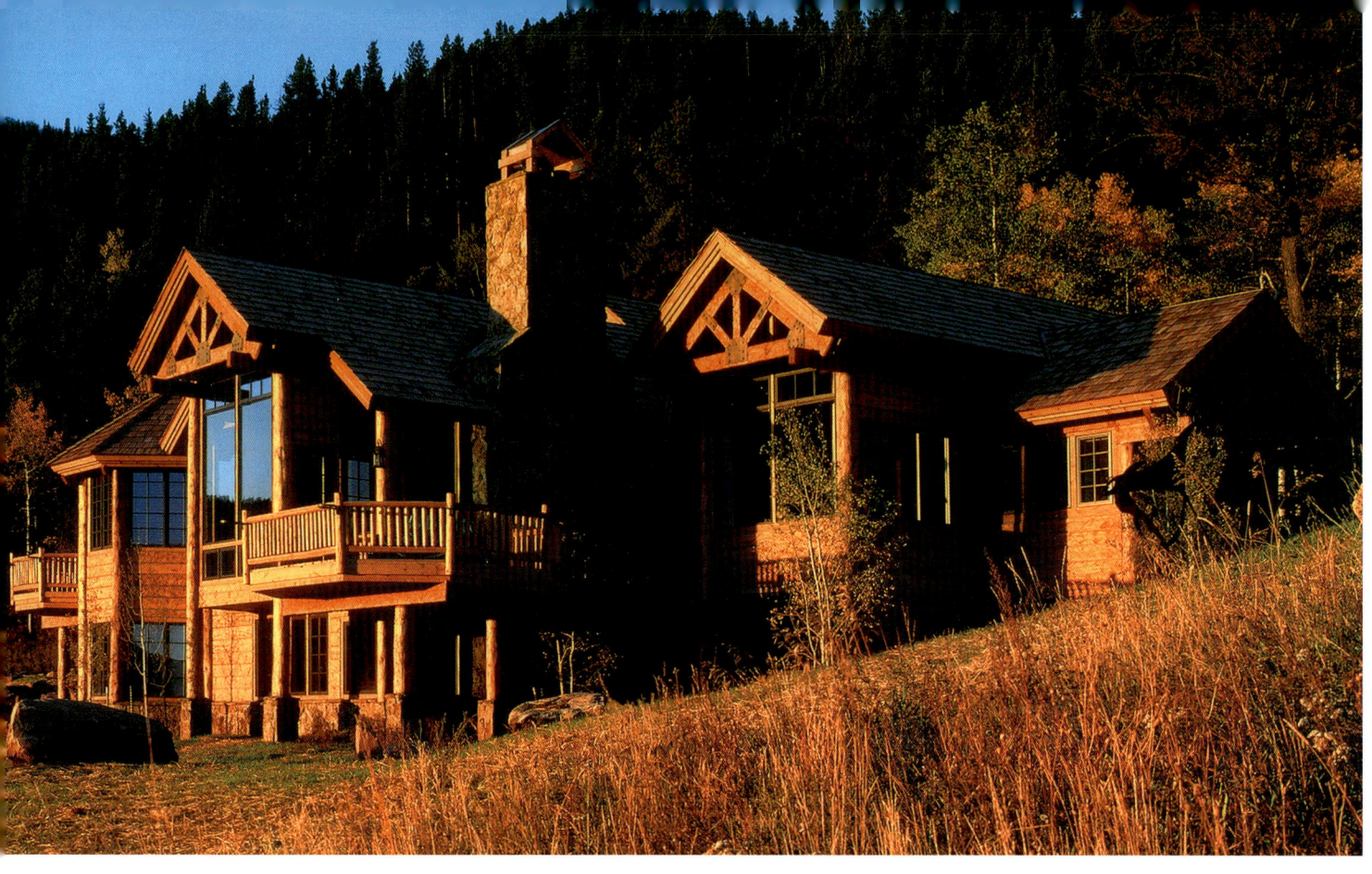

to understand why his clients have selected their property. Whether they love a view of the majestic mountains, or the sound of a flowing stream, or the simple solitude of the forest, he wants to make sure that the design truly reflects his clients' wishes. He analyzes whether they like morning sun or would prefer to sleep in, designing each space so that it welcomes the sun at the appropriate times or captures their favorite view. Through years of experience, Jon has learned that the best and most livable homes are those where the architect creatively blends what the client is asking for with what their property is asking for.

For the conceptual design, Custom Mountain Architects much prefers a pencil and paper over any kind of computer program, because sketching allows maximum freedom and a flow of creativity. With a pencil they can sketch ideas without rigid, defined lines, whereas a computer insists on the absolute. On every home, they like to explore many different design options to share with the client and get their input. This leads to more options for evaluation until the client decides when they have arrived at the perfect solution. Then, as plans become more finite, they transfer the design to the computer where precision is of utmost importance for the final construction plans and details.

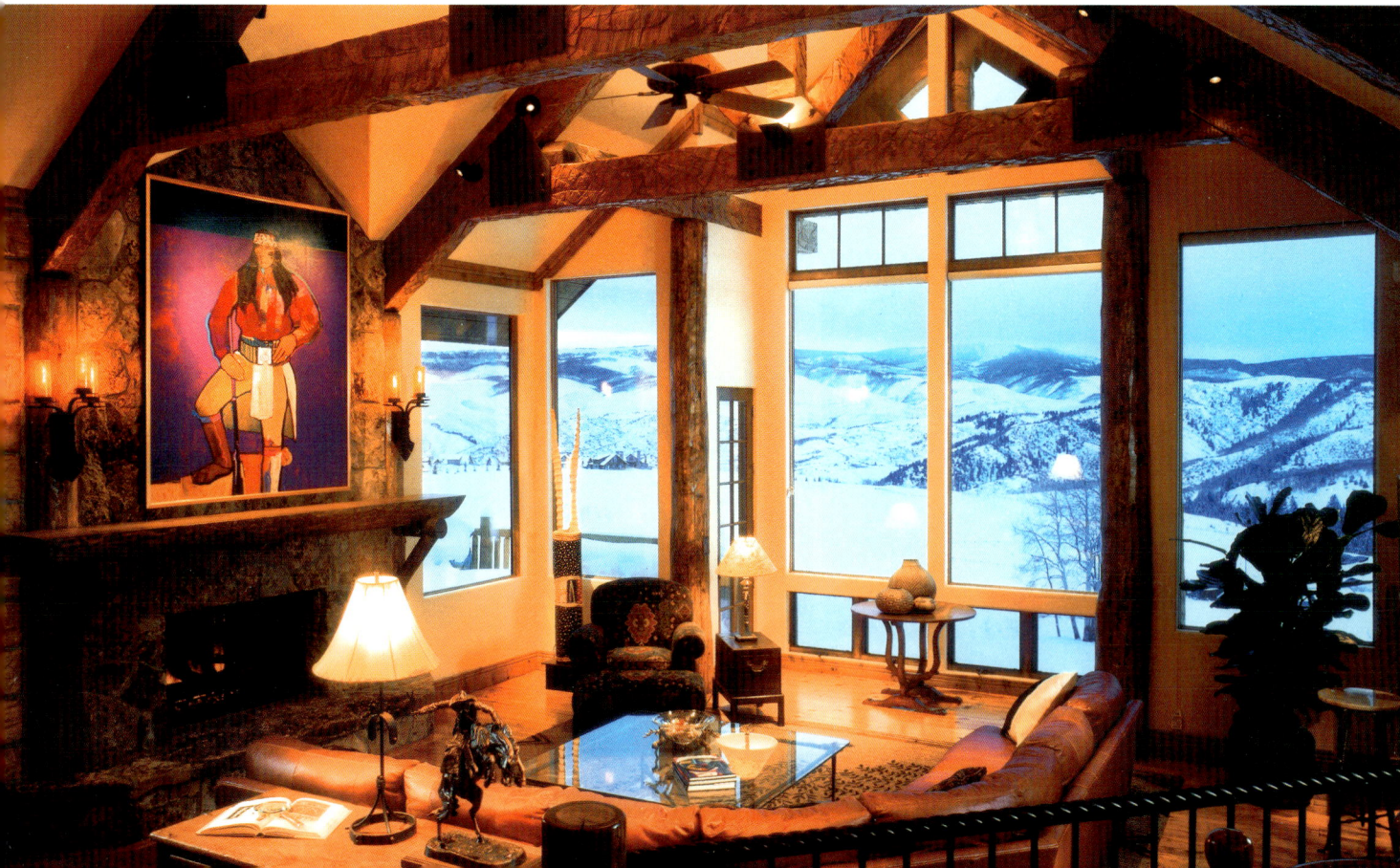

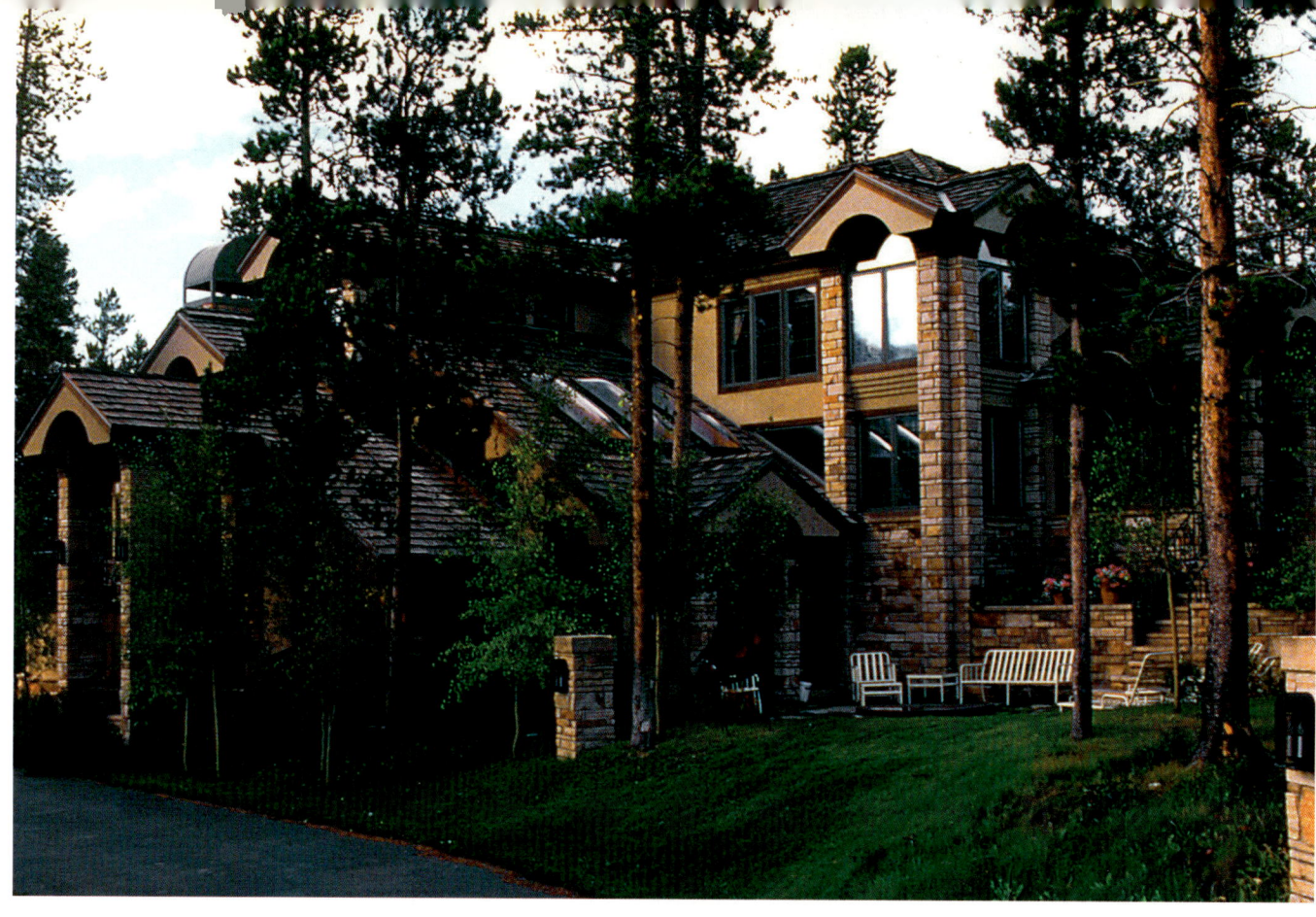

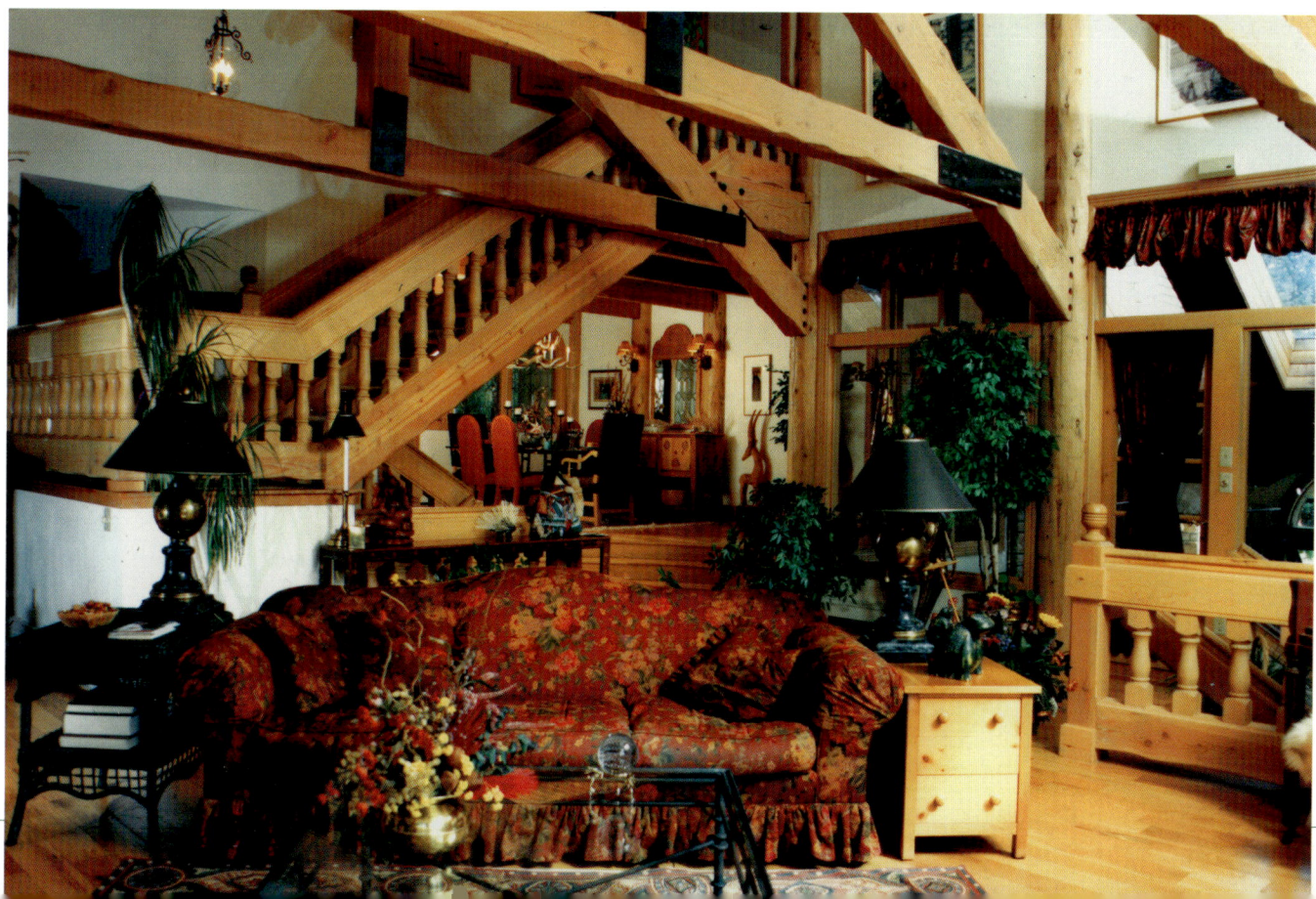

FACING PAGE TOP:
With an engineering background and a love for Colorado's mining heritage, the owners wanted to emphasize their home's structure with large, hand hewn beams, forged steel plates and rugged connections.
Photograph by Kenneth Redding

FACING PAGE BOTTOM:
For the owners' extensive art collection, we designed a specific wall space, recessed niche or pedestal for each unique piece. Then we added special lighting to enhance the art work and the roof trusses.
Photograph by Kenneth Redding

TOP RIGHT:
As a professional chef, the owner wanted a more traditional home with the simple elegance of the French countryside. A concession was made to add a few large windows to capture the irresistible view.
Photograph by Lynn Rice

BOTTOM RIGHT:
Refined but not ornate, the living room has an airy yet cozy feeling with the stair floating up to the master suite above. The wall of glass on the right overlooks a waterfall cascading into the lap pool below.
Photograph by Lynn Rice

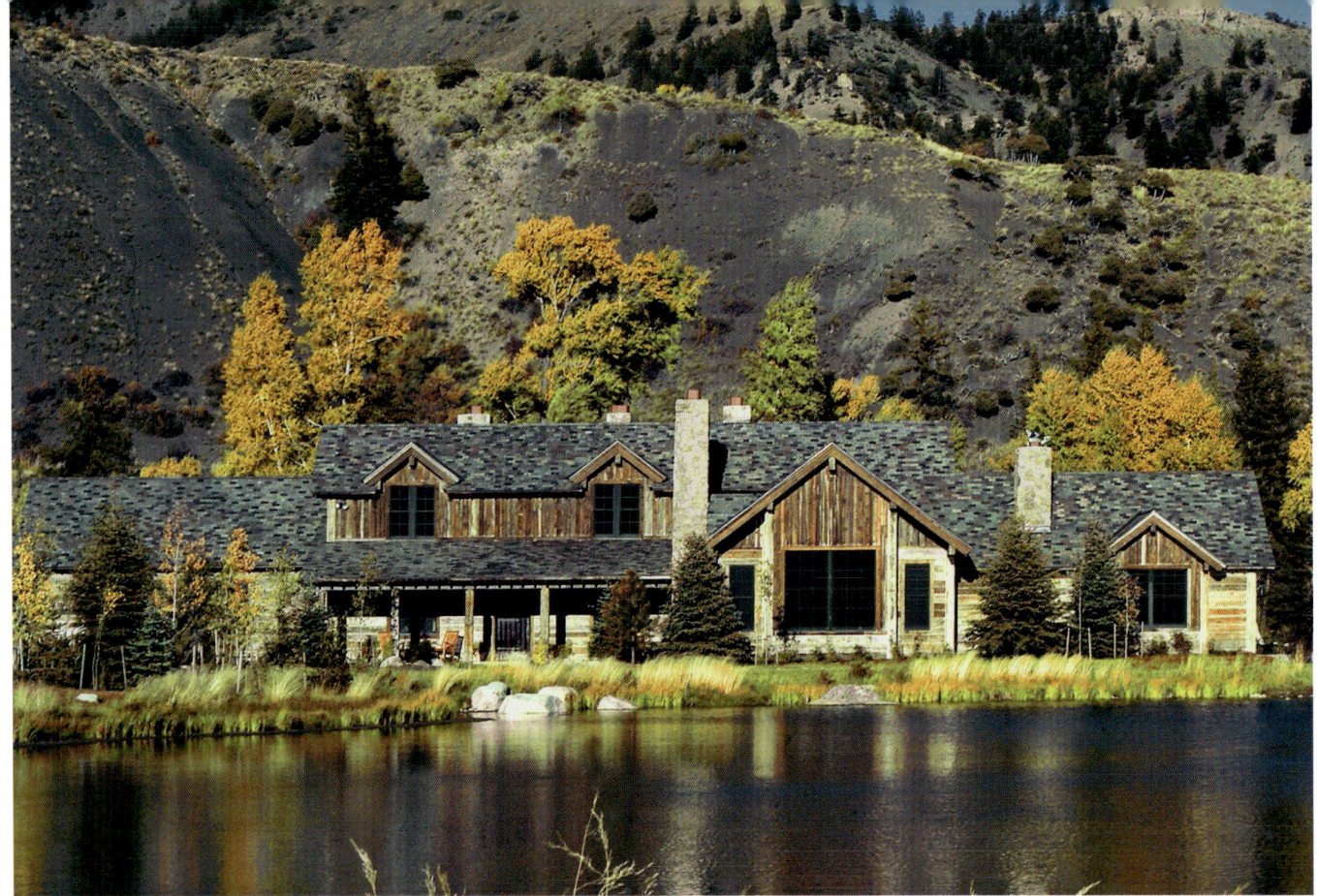

At the client's request, Custom Mountain Architects has designed homes in various styles from contemporary to traditional to mountain rustic, illustrating that they truly design with the philosophy that the style should be dictated by the client, and then carefully woven with their functional requirements and the site characteristics to create the perfect home. Although Jon endeavors not to have a defined style, admirers of his work notice a thread of continuity in everything he creates. Each of Jon's homes has extraordinary detailing, from custom doors to special lighting, unique fireplaces and artistic accents which enhance the design concept of each home and add a personal touch for the owners. Jon explains, "Every time I meet with a new client and walk a new site, I am thrilled to be starting a new creative journey."

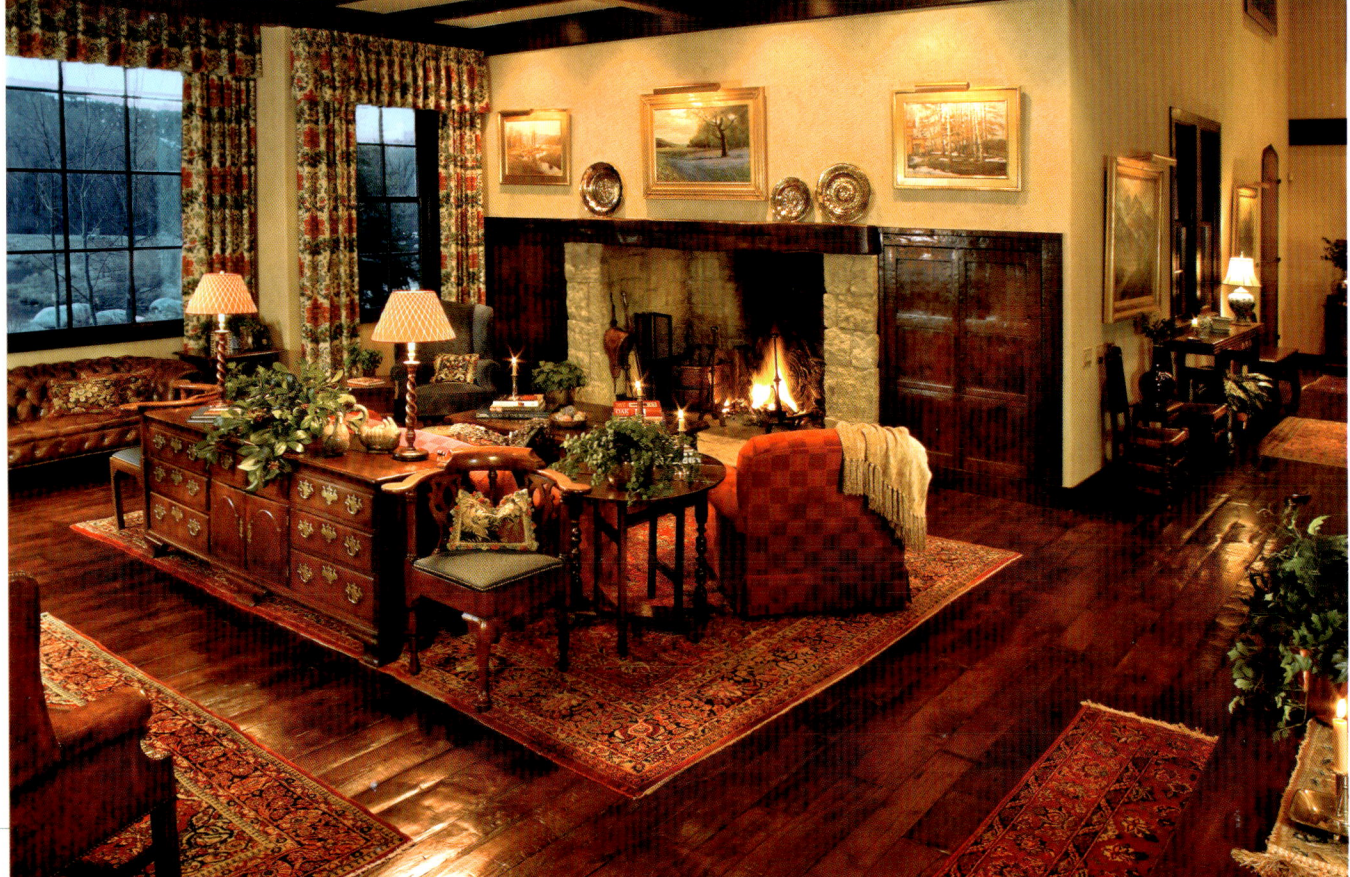

TOP LEFT:
For their ranch nestled on the banks of a river, the owners wanted a western interpretation of an English manor house. It should look as if it had been handmade by the original settlers a century before.
Photograph by Monika Hilleary

BOTTOM LEFT:
The living room features a 7-foot wide by 6-foot high traditional English fireplace. Simple wood details reflect a quality and craftsmanship worthy of the owners' collection of beautiful English antiques.
Photograph by Monika Hilleary

FACING PAGE TOP:
The multi-gabled roof line silhouettes the mountain range beyond. Wide, low angled eaves combine with steeply pitched log trusses as though the peaks are rising out of the valley below.
Photograph by Monika Hilleary

FACING PAGE BOTTOM:
To capture the expansive views, the living room is focused on one mountain while the master suite centers on another. The owners can lie in bed and look over their toes at the moonlit peaks.
Photograph by Monika Hilleary

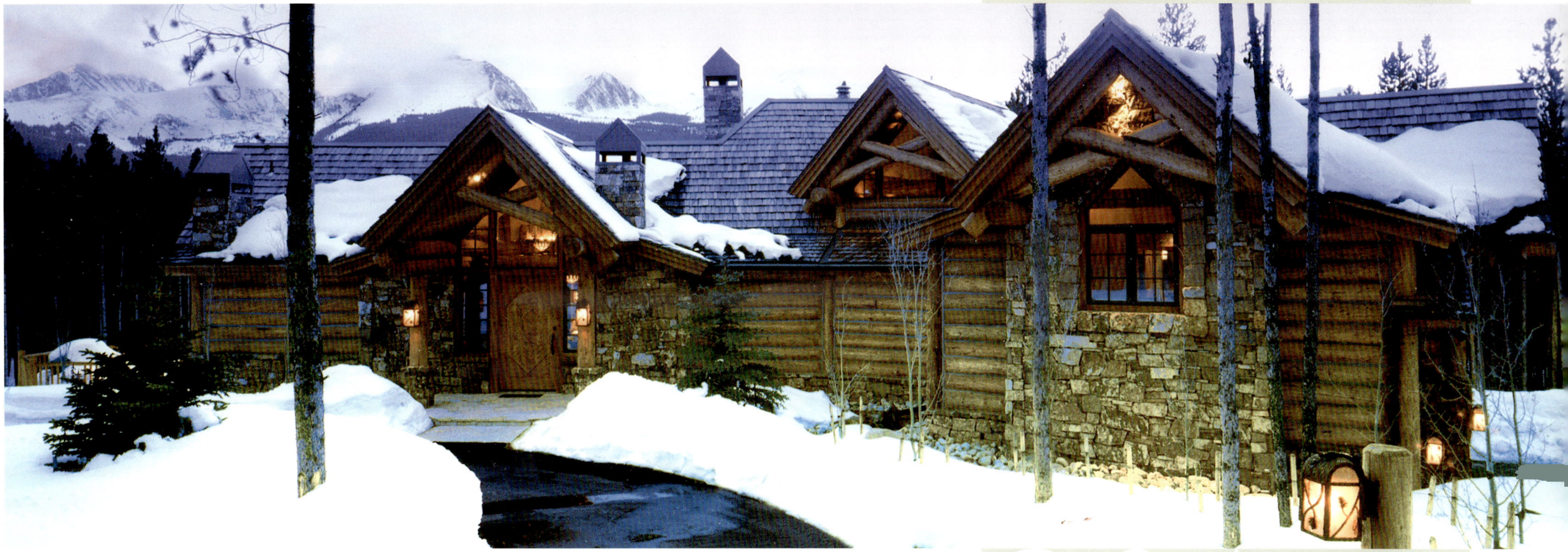

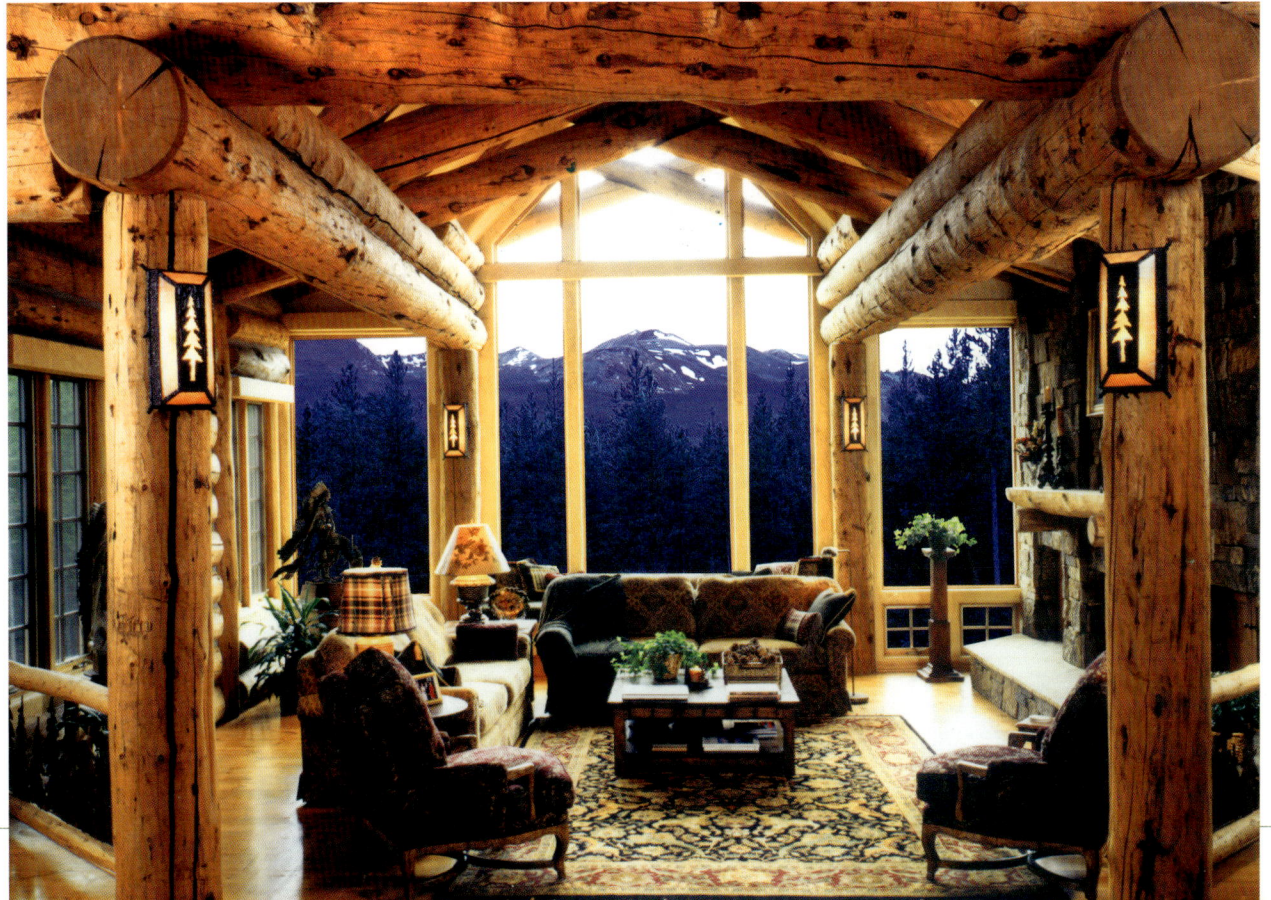

more about jon...

WHAT IS THE BEST PART OF BEING AN ARCHITECT?
I love designing custom homes because each client is different and each site is different so no two projects are ever alike. Plus I get to work with great clients who are excited about what we design for them. Yes, I get paid for doing what I love to do in the place I want to live, but please don't tell my clients (or my wife) that I enjoy it so much I would probably do it for free.

WHAT ONE PHILOSOPHY HAVE YOU STUCK WITH FOR YEARS THAT STILL WORKS FOR YOU TODAY?
My grandfather was a Swedish cabinet maker and a perfectionist who let me help in his shop, but only if the quality of my work was up to his stringent requirements. He would often state his philosophy which I still live by every day: "Excellence is the journey, perfection is the destination."

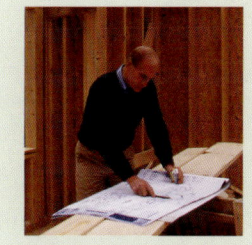

CUSTOM MOUNTAIN ARCHITECTS
JON GUNSON
PO Box 1490
Breckenridge, CO 80424
970.453.6657

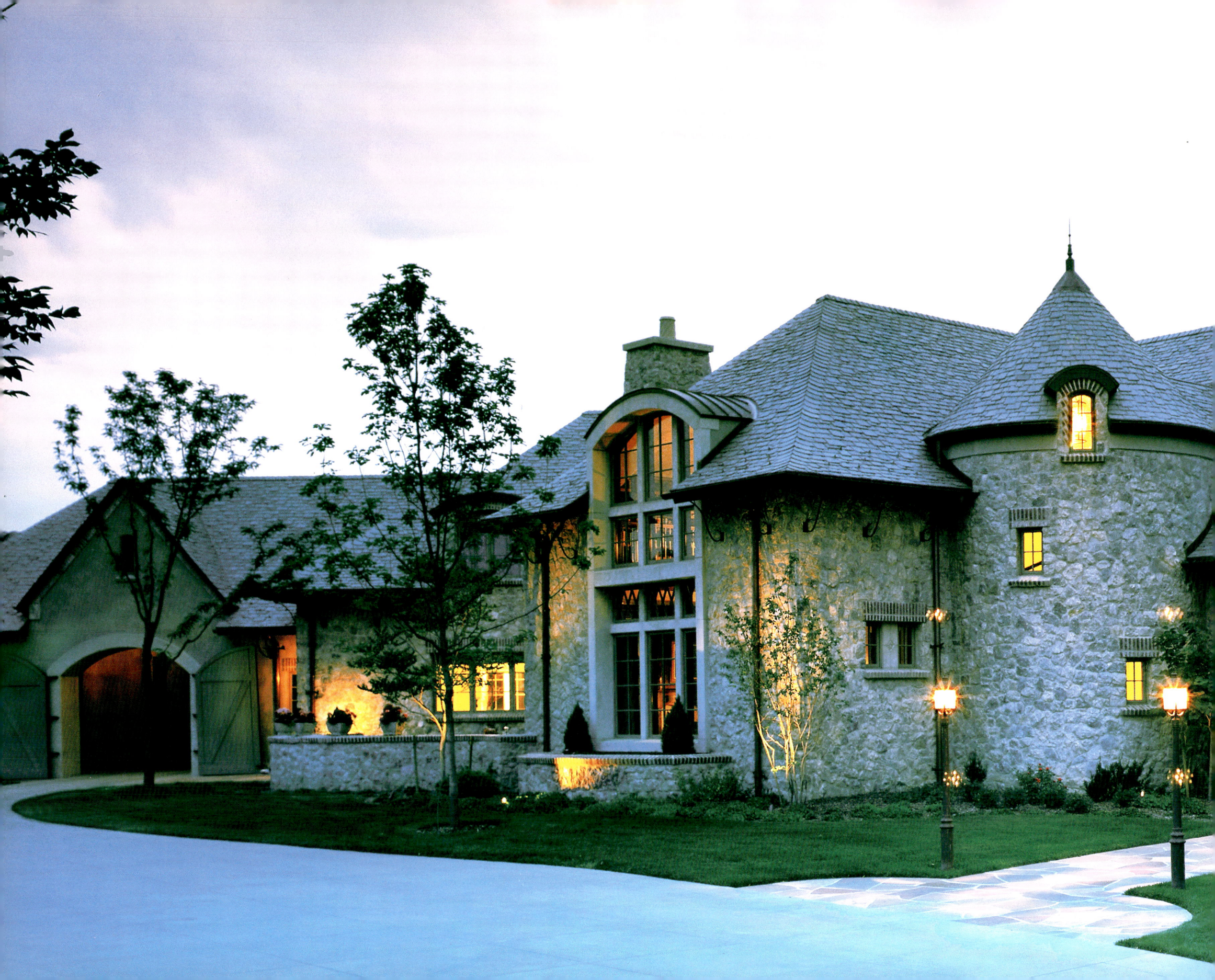

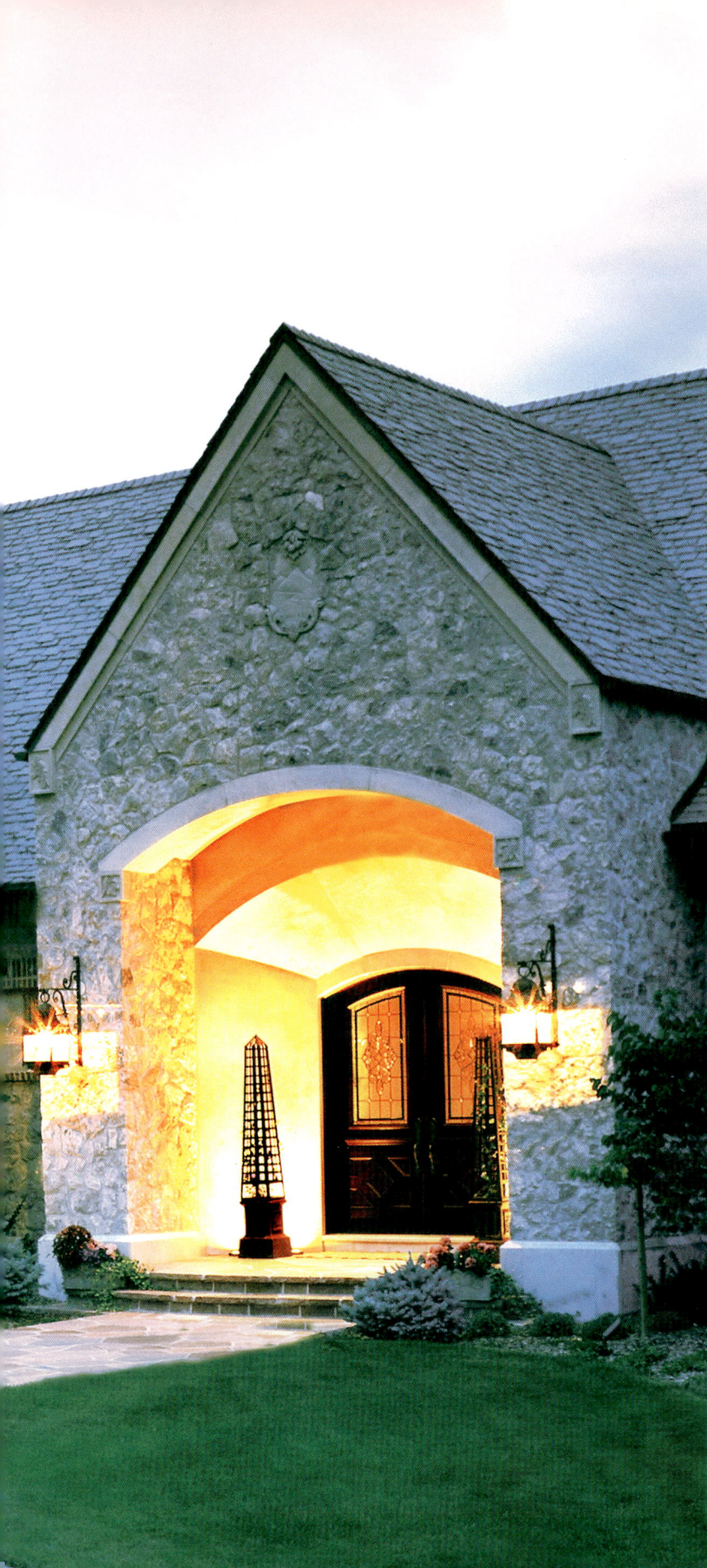

EDWARD DIAMOND
STEVEN DIAMOND

DIAMOND HOMES, INC.

Diamond Homes is a design/build firm specializing in constructing exquisite custom residences throughout Colorado. The Diamond family has been active in the homebuilding business since 1970. Owner Edward Diamond's passion for design and construction has been instilled in him through a lifetime of interaction and achievements in both trades.

Edward earned a B.B.A. from the University of Iowa with an emphasis in architecture, engineering, and business. He joined Diamond Homes in 1970 and became president in 1975. Steven Diamond, Edward's brother, joined the team in 1987. Steven graduated from the University of Colorado with a B.A. in economics and earned a master's degree in finance from Thunderbird. Brian Husmann, Edward's son-in-law, recently joined the company to lend his complementary legal and business skills.

Diamond Homes has a full complement of qualified professionals including the owners, architectural design group, sales staff, construction management team, and the administrative support staff.

Diamond Homes builds in Denver's finest neighborhoods and in some of Colorado's most exciting mountain communities. These fine neighborhoods include: Cherry Hills Village, Denver Country Club, Hilltop and The Polo Grounds. Examples of exquisite mountain homes and lodges can be found in Vail, Aspen, Snowmass, Breckenridge and Steamboat Springs.

LEFT:
The simplicity and strength of this French Country residence can be found in the multiple layers of detailing, from the finish limestone surrounds, soffit brackets and slate fan tail hip ridge.
Photograph by Monika Hilleary, LightDance Studio

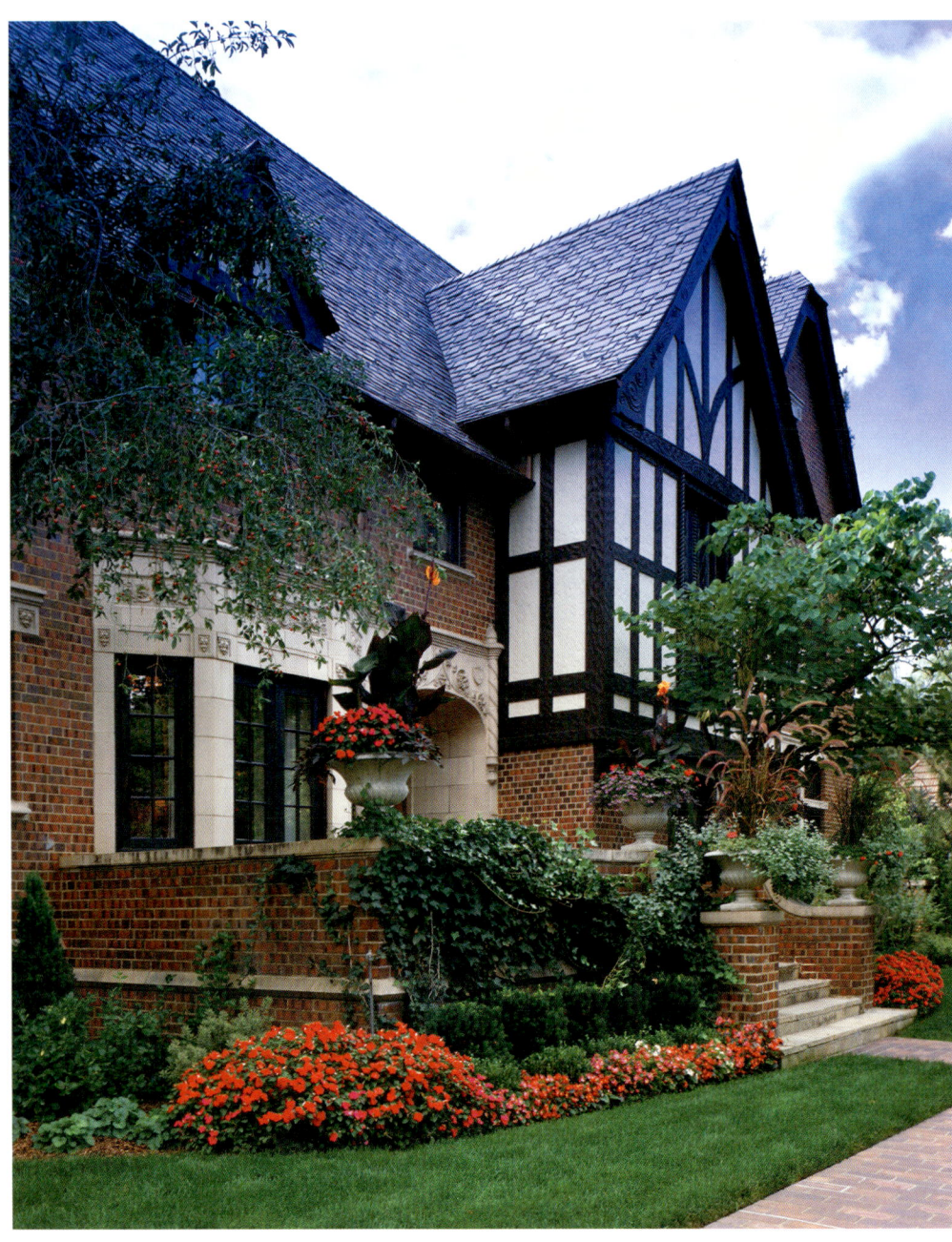
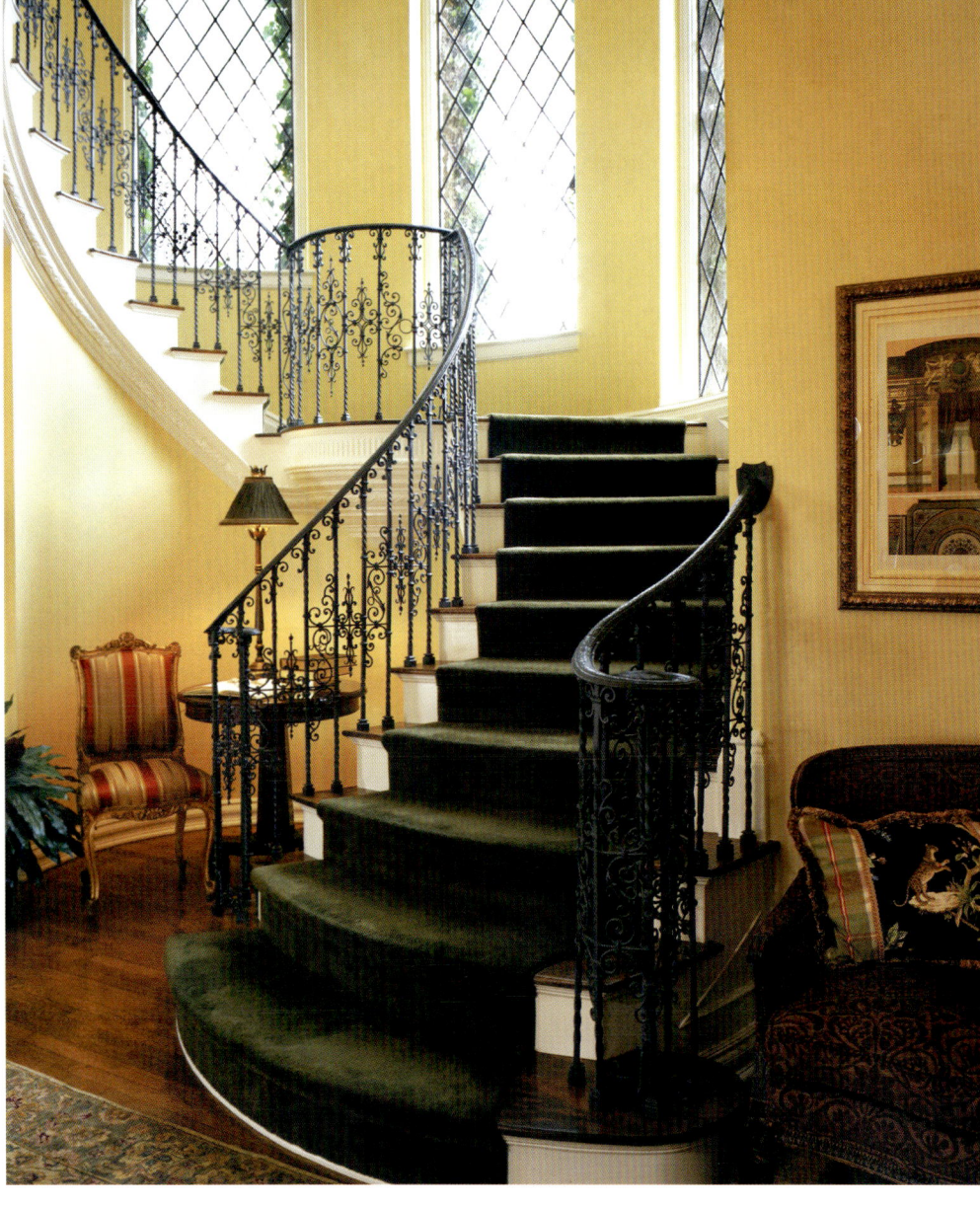

ABOVE LEFT:
The limestone detailing, rusticated woodwork, copper clad oak windows and textural slate roof with hidden valley and copper accessories lend themselves to this beautiful restored turn-of-the-century Tudor home.
Photograph by Monika Hilleary, LightDance Studio

ABOVE RIGHT:
Premoulded stair apron with wrought iron stair railing and lead glass windows allow the second floor to elegantly present itself to the main foyer and entry.
Photograph by Monika Hilleary, LightDance Studio

FACING PAGE:
Providing a stone and stucco veneer to denote the three uses of the home: private, public and service, helps to reduce the scale of this spacious residence.
Photograph by Monika Hilleary, LightDance Studio

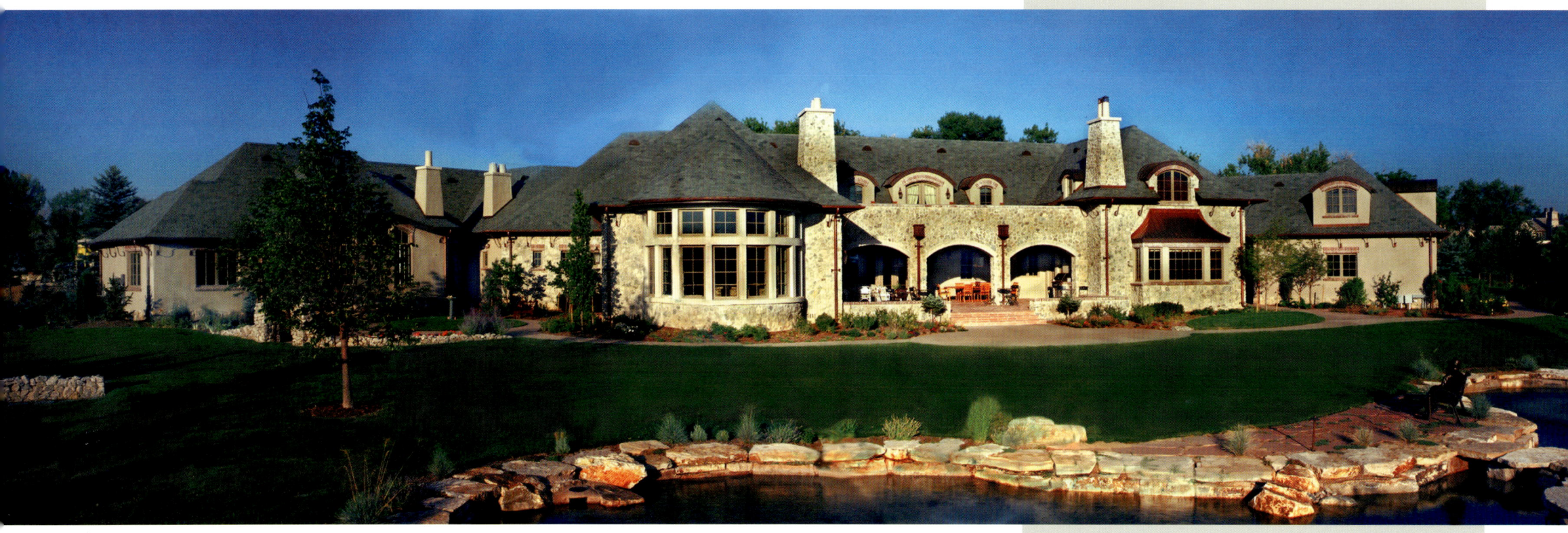

Committed leaders in the design/build field, Edward and Steven Diamond have assembled a team that brings the highest level of expertise to every aspect of custom home construction. Their attention to detail, knowledge of the industry, and unparalleled dedication to their clients have earned Diamond Homes its reputation as the premier builder of elegant custom homes.

Members of the staff at Diamond Homes are not only experts in the field of new home design and construction, they also excel in renovation and restoration. Whether it is a home addition, an upgrade to an existing room, or a complete home renovation, these talented and innovative experts are skilled at providing exceptional quality work with outstanding results. Great care and meticulous attention to detail are incorporated into each job, ensuring the client's ultimate satisfaction.

At Diamond Homes, the architectural and construction teams constantly strive to blend exquisite design, superior craftsmanship, and a client's personal desires and tastes to create an exceptional and beautiful home. This philosophy exemplifies Diamond Homes' dedication and commitment to excellence.

Q&A
more about edward...

WHY DO YOU TAKE SUCH GREAT PRIDE IN YOUR WORK?
In my immediate neighborhood I've worked intimately with dozens of clients. Houses are like old friends: both welcome you home, provide a refuge from the outside world, and offer a place to raise a family.

WHAT CHALLENGES DO YOU FIND MOST REWARDING?
My team and I appreciate the challenge of incorporating modern technology and the conveniences of 21st century living while preserving the beautiful historical features.

DIAMOND HOMES, INC.
EDWARD DIAMOND
STEVEN DIAMOND
3279 South Santa Fe Drive
Englewood, CO 80110
303.789.4451
f: 303.781.0826
www.diamondhomesinc.com

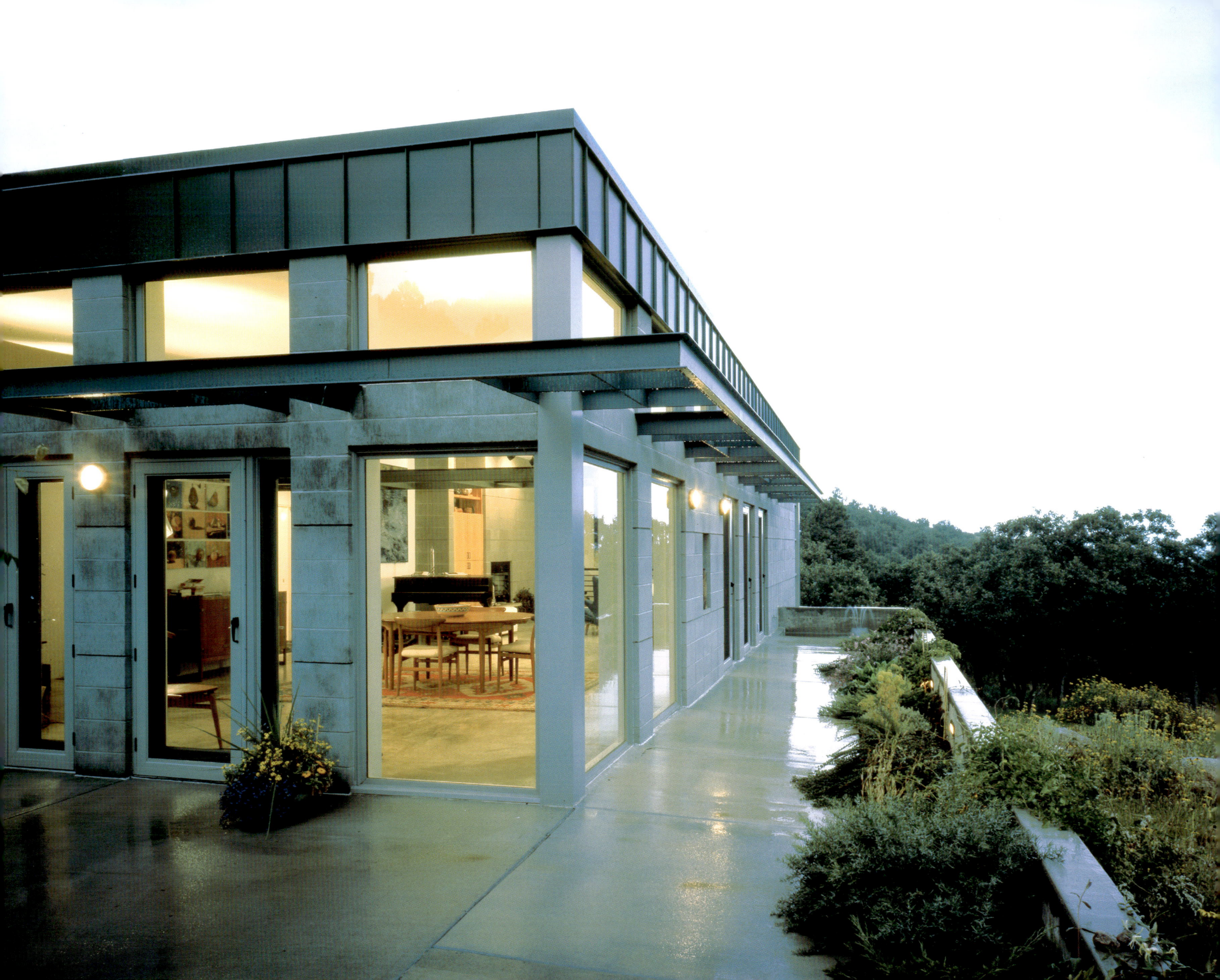

ELIZABETH WRIGHT INGRAHAM

ELIZABETH WRIGHT INGRAHAM ARCHITECTS

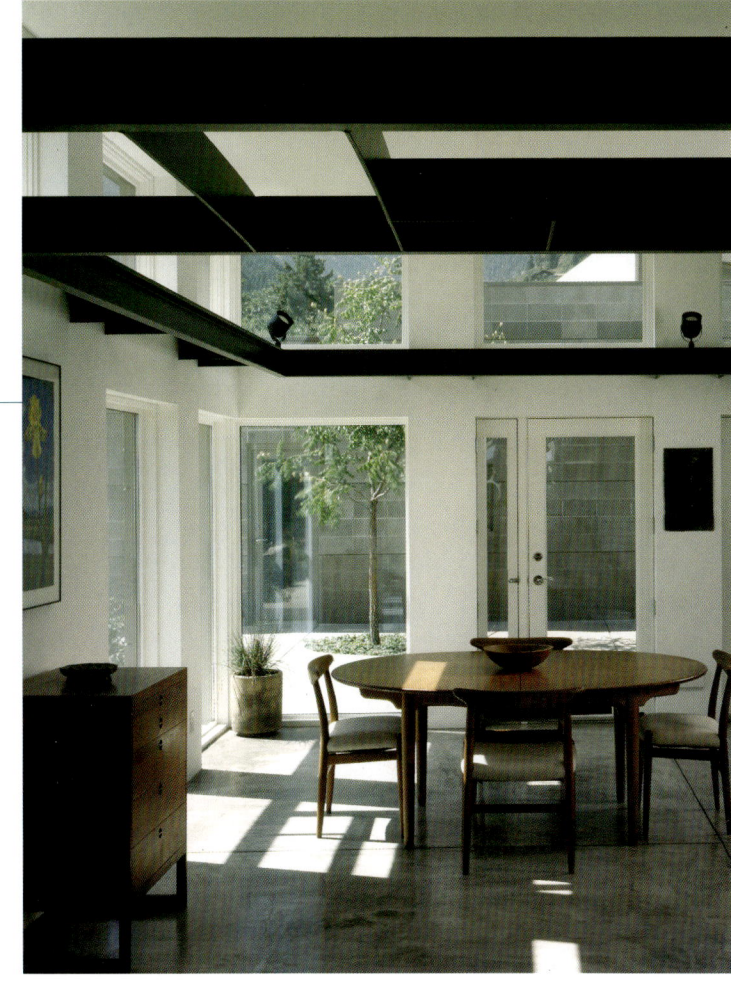

For Elizabeth Wright Ingraham, life is a fascinating ever-changing pattern. A practicing architect for more than 50 years, Elizabeth came to Colorado in 1952 with her husband, the late architect Gordon Ingraham. A solo practitioner since 1972, she has designed many homes and both public and private buildings in Colorado Springs, Pueblo, the Front Range foothill communities, and Colorado mountain towns.

Born into a family of architects–her grandfather was architect Frank Lloyd Wright, her father was architect John Lloyd Wright, inventor of "Lincoln Logs"–Elizabeth searched hard for her architectural vision. As a young person, she says she was a "rebel with a cause," as she developed her own vernacular when there were few women in the profession. She studied with Mies van der Rohe at the Illinois Institute of Technology in Chicago and at the University of California in Berkley. She received an honorary doctorate from the University of Colorado and has served on numerous boards and commissions.

Her clients are those individuals, firms and public institutions attracted to contemporary work. Keenly interested in science and the environment, Elizabeth founded the 640-acre Running Creek Field Station in Elbert County, Colorado. The institute was one of the first campuses in the United States to develop a graduate level core course in integrative studies for students from universities across the country. Elizabeth thinks that her broad palette of interests including education, politics and the arts has acted to stimulate her architectural work.

ABOVE & FACING PAGE:
"SOLAZ" Manitou Springs, Colorado.
Photographs by Ron Pollard, Denver

ELIZABETH WRIGHT INGRAHAM ARCHITECTS
ELIZABETH WRIGHT INGRAHAM, FAIA
111½ East Pikes Peak Avenue
Colorado Springs, CO 80903
www.ewrightingraham.com
719.633.7011
f: 719.630.1733

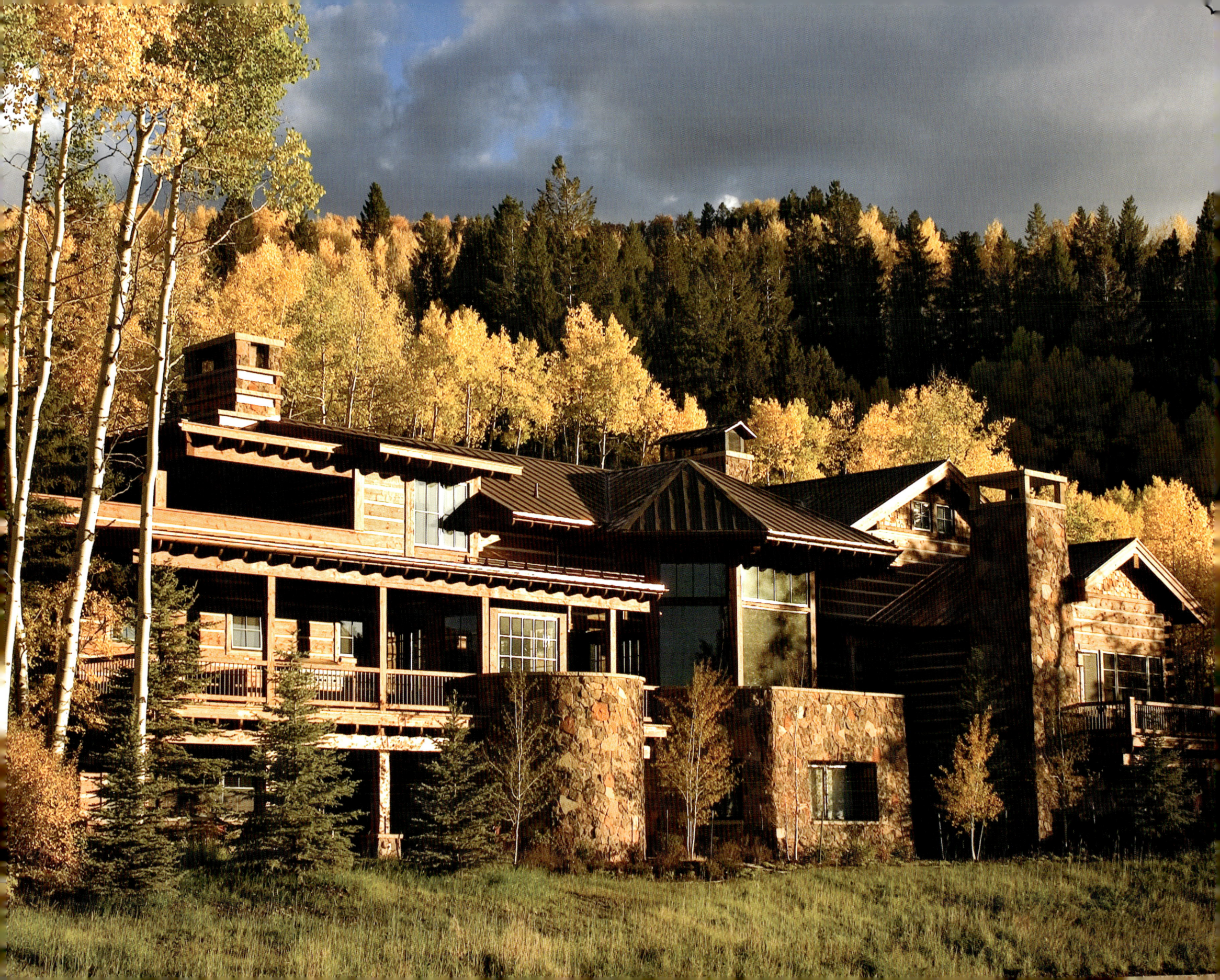

DAVID FINHOLM
KAREN WHITE

FINHOLM ARCHITECTS
FW INTERIOR DESIGN

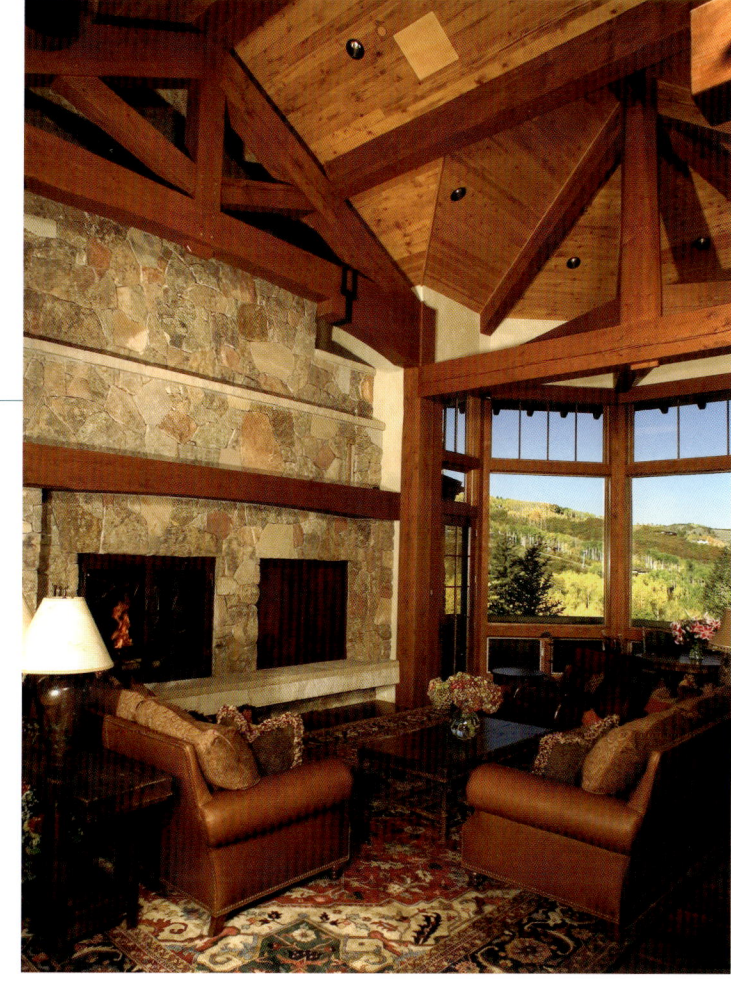

It's not easy to see where the talents of Karen S. White end and those of David Finholm begin. The luxurious homes they create in Aspen and around the country are marked by a seamless integration of her interior design and his architecture. David, an architect since 1970 and Principal of Finholm Architects, has partnered with Karen in the FW Interior Design Group since 1999. Their teamwork begins at the initial schematic stages of a project, giving the client a comprehensive and concise design package down to details such as furniture placement.

Affording clients the opportunity to express their personal tastes and styles with art and furnishings, in what might be their primary residence or a special retreat, is of great emphasis at the firm. Be it a cherished antique or that 100-year-old hutch with sentimental value, its place in the home is always defined from the beginning of the design process. Similarly, ample galleries are planned to house clients' art collections. Karen and David's close communication with clients, coupled with their experience and keen intuition, aids their clients in decision-making and ensures a successful and fulfilling project outcome.

Karen and David particularly enjoy the challenges of designing mountain homes. Most of these homes are secondary homes with components which are similar to the client's primary home, but each new residence has its own unique character based on the mountain lifestyle and environment. Stone and timbers all are part of the architecture that makes it work. Almost all structural wood used is garnered from reclaimed sources such as old barns and other structures around the country and the world, and is integrated into the home design. Dining tables from South African Jarrah wood railroad ties and billiard tables made from the wood of barns more than a century old now are in homes designed and built by Karen and David.

ABOVE:
The living area affords long-range pristine mountain views, and features a wood burning fireplace, and built-in TV cabinet. Custom ironwork adds interest to fireplace doors and structural timbers.
Photograph by Steve Mundinger

FACING PAGE:
The exterior finishes of the house include stone, timber siding with chinking, copper roofs and flashing.
Photograph by Steve Mundinger

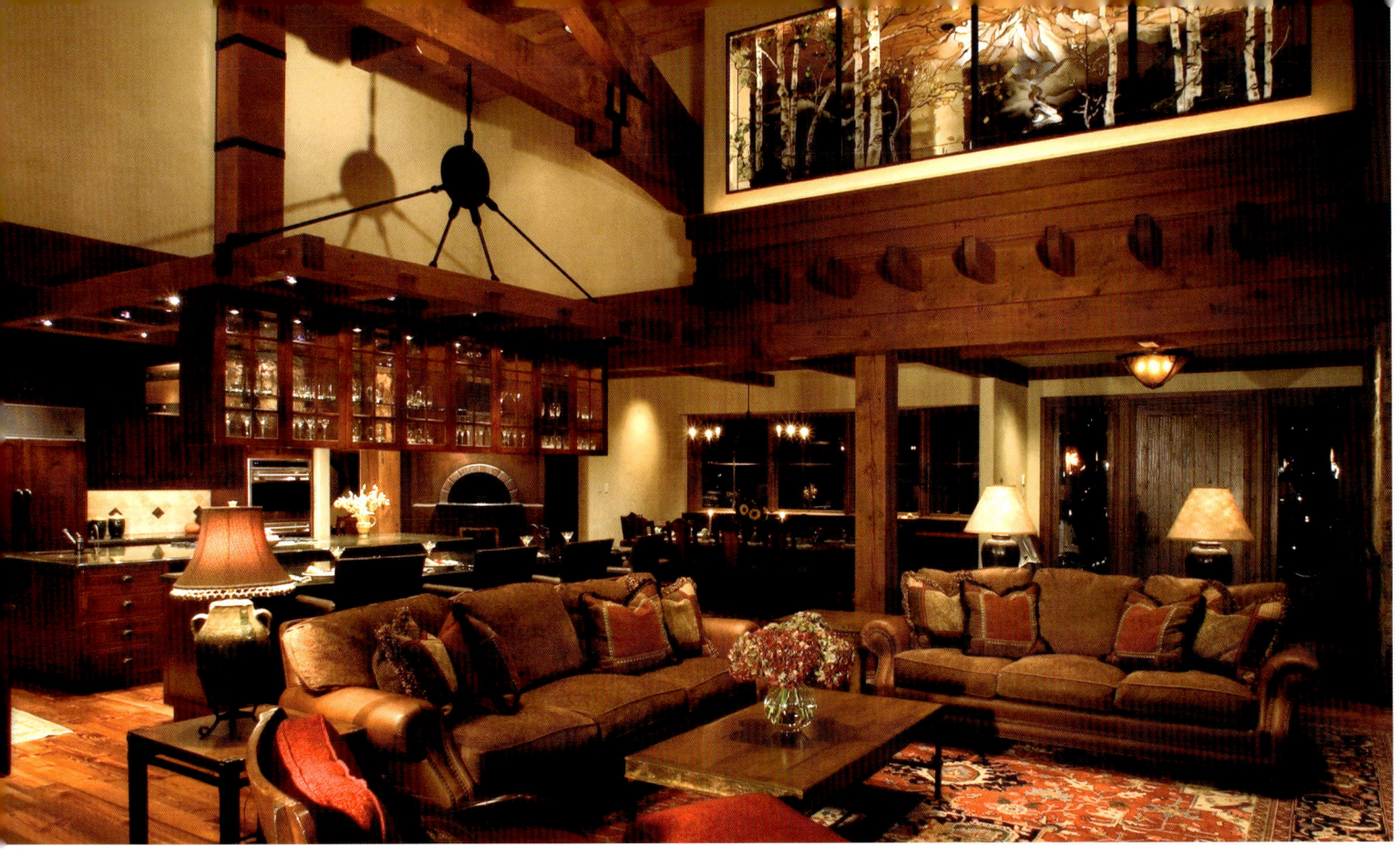

There's nothing of the internal elements that doesn't play a role in color choice. Lamps, fabrics, architectural and decorative fixtures are all part of the palette which is designed to complement the architecture. Karen's goal is to achieve harmony and create functional living environments specific to the client's personal taste.

David's architectural design always begins with a carefully integrated site plan incorporating carefully planned rooflines for snow protection and overhangs for sun protection. Weather-appropriated vehicular access also is carefully calculated and incorporated into the overall design.

"Scaling furnishings appropriately and choosing the right antiques, art and accessories brings together an intimate integrated feel and will ensure that the house stands the test of time," Karen says. "These homes are classic and timeless and they suit each client's reflection on living."

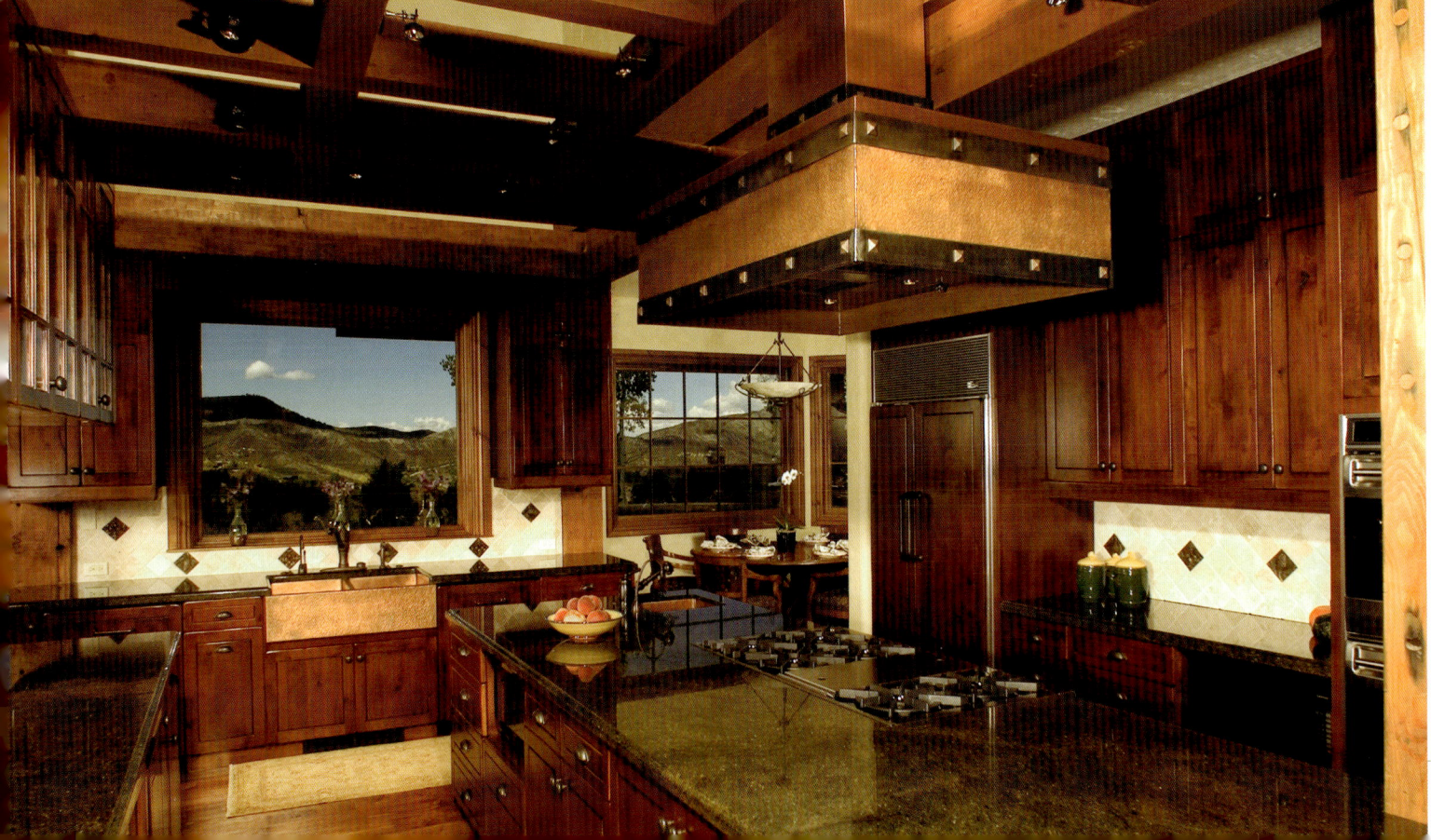

TOP LEFT:
Some of what the open floor plan hosts include custom art glass, a suspended trellis over the kitchen and a wood burning pizza oven.
Photograph by Steve Mundinger

BOTTOM LEFT:
Copper accents in the kitchen are the cook top hood and sink. A tiled motorized appliance garage nestles between the wall ovens and refrigerator.
Photograph by Steve Mundinger

FACING PAGE:
The outdoor room has the multipurpose use of fireplace seating, serving area for entertaining and full audio-visual capabilities.
Photograph by Steve Mundinger

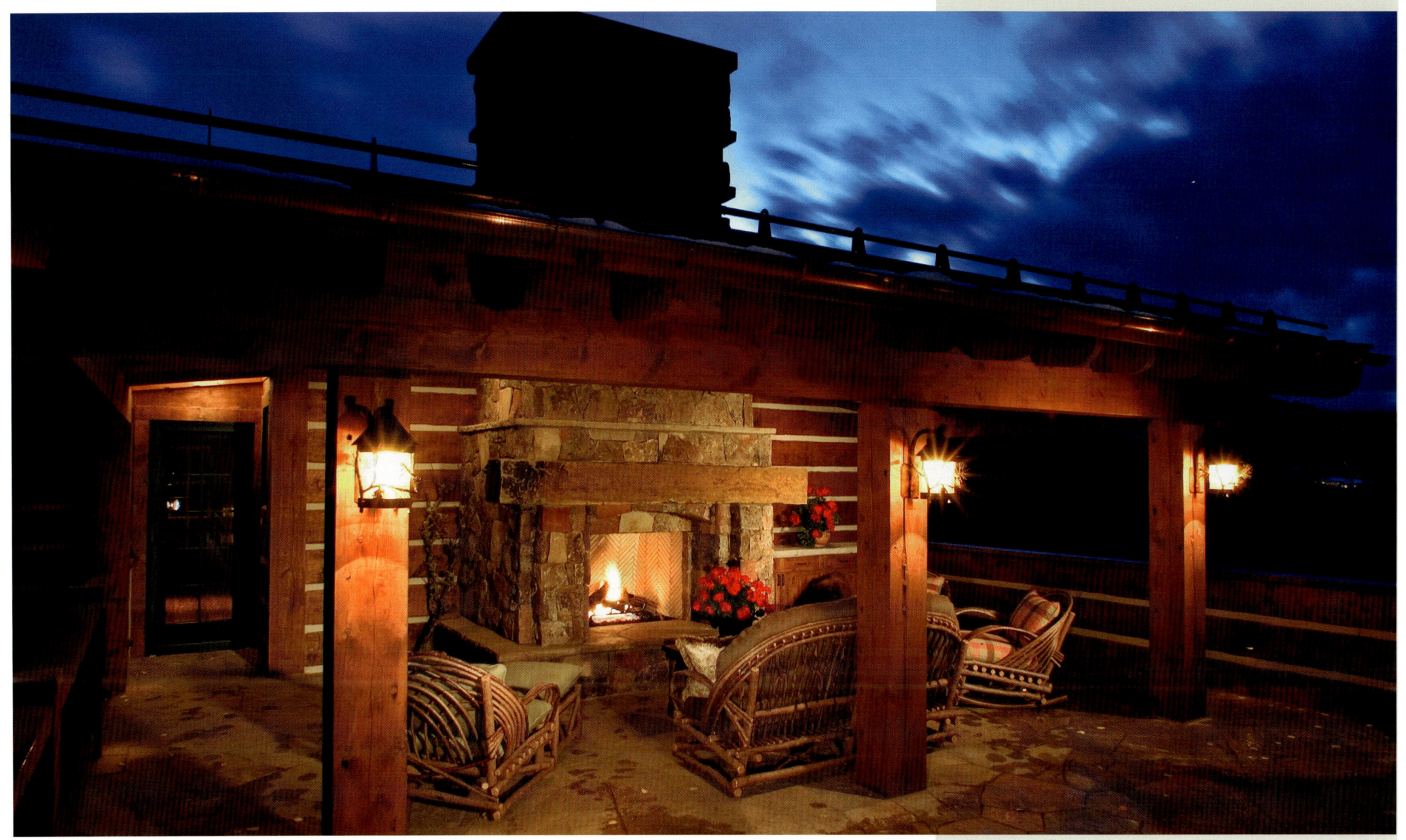

FINHOLM ARCHITECTS
FW INTERIOR DESIGN
DAVID FINHOLM, AIA
KAREN S. WHITE, ASID
111-L Aspen Business Center
Aspen, CO 81611
970.925.5713
f: 970.920.4471
www.finholmarchitects.com
www.fwinteriordesign.com

Q&A more about david & karen...

WHAT WOULD YOU LIKE TO MENTION ABOUT YOUR BUSINESS?
We are able to provide our services to the client from the early stages of architectural conception through to the furnishings. This allows us to give our clients a complete and uninterrupted design process whereby all elements integrate with one another achieving harmony and elegance.

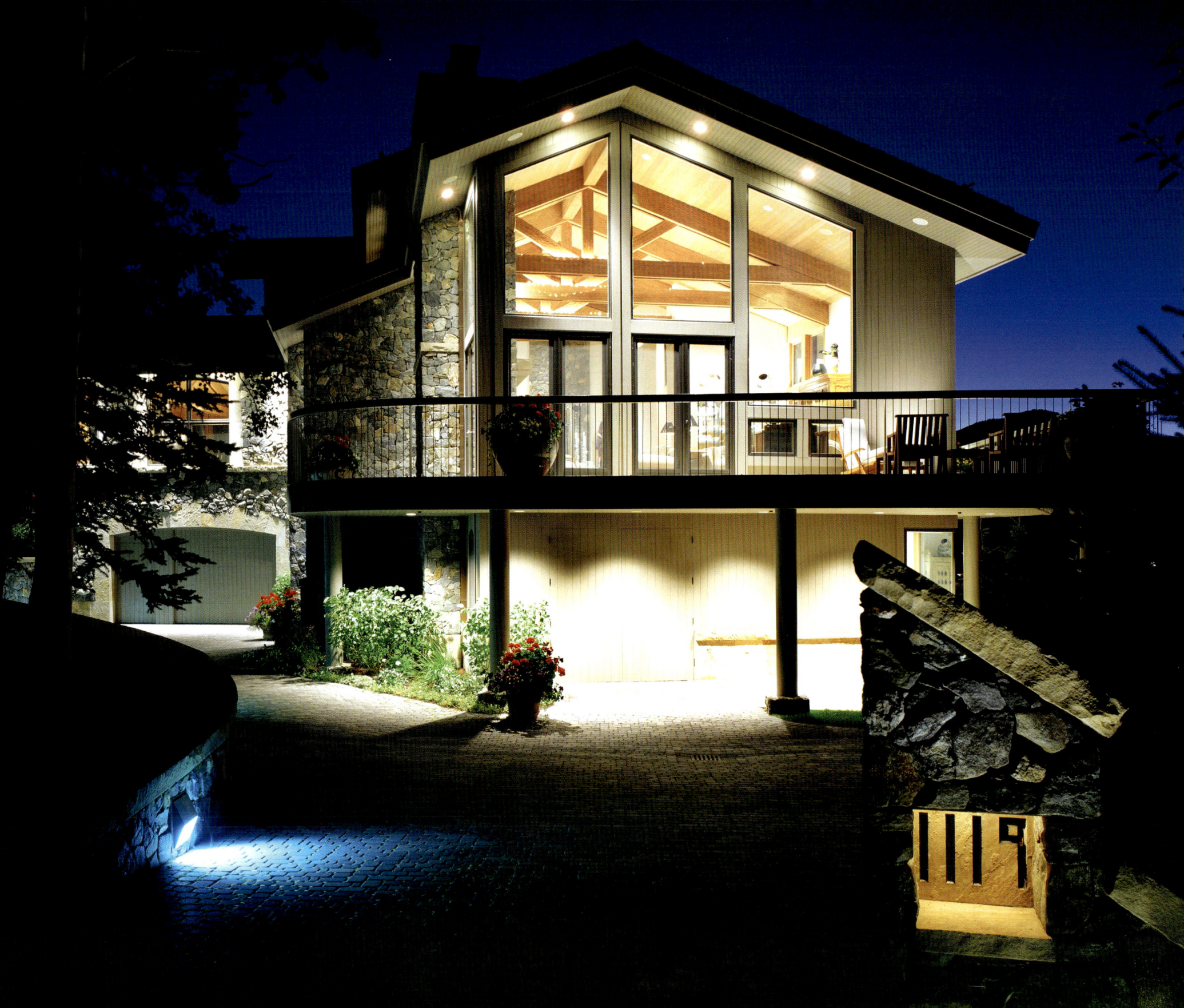

LYNN FRITZLEN
WILLIAM PIERCE

FRITZLEN PIERCE ARCHITECTS

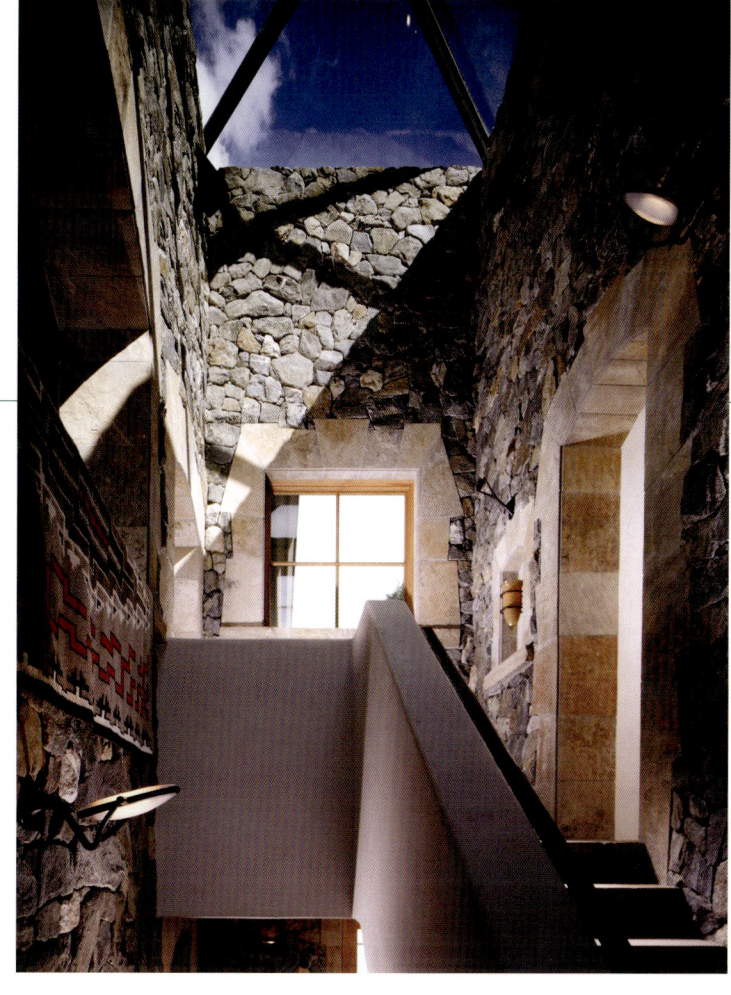

When Lynn Fritzlen and Bill Pierce launched their practice in 1980, both were long time residents of Vail. Bill came to Vail in 1974 to work for one of the community's original architects and Lynn moved from Kansas City with her family in the late 60s. Since the establishment of Fritzlen Pierce Architects they have designed numerous commercial and residential properties that speak to the unique mountain resort surroundings. They firmly believe that innovative designs spring from an in-depth understanding of the regional environment, great communication, mutual respect, and collaboration between designer and client.

Approaching each project with a fresh perspective, they draw on a variety of architectural genres and provide a comprehensive array of services from conceptual planning to interior architecture. Each project reflects the owner's preferences, but the firm's overall style combines the best of modern design and the warmth of Rocky Mountain resources.

Fritzlen Pierce utilizes a palette of textured exterior materials such as natural copper, rusticated stone, heavy timbers and Corten steel that patina well in the alpine climate. The partners pride themselves on being environmentally sensitive, creating spaces with minimal environmental impact by utilizing solar exposure, geothermal heat sources and high-efficiency heating and insulation systems.

The firm draws on historical references to create buildings that reflect their owner's preferences within the context of the applicable design guidelines. Vail is an upscale community and most of Fritzlen Pierce's clients are both well educated and discriminating in the discipline of architecture and design. Often they have experienced, firsthand, the joy of living with great design that fits their needs. The firm works on a good balance of new construction and renovation projects, always trying to make the best possible use of space. Steep sites incorporate interesting vertical circulation with stairs and even elevators for connecting upper and lower portions of the site.

ABOVE:
Throughout the day angled shadows and natural light graze the stone walls of this stairwell.
Photograph by David Marlow

FACING PAGE:
As day fades to twilight, transparency supplants mass and the residence begins to glow from within, revealing the rhythmic roof structure to the arriving visitor.
Photograph by David Marlow

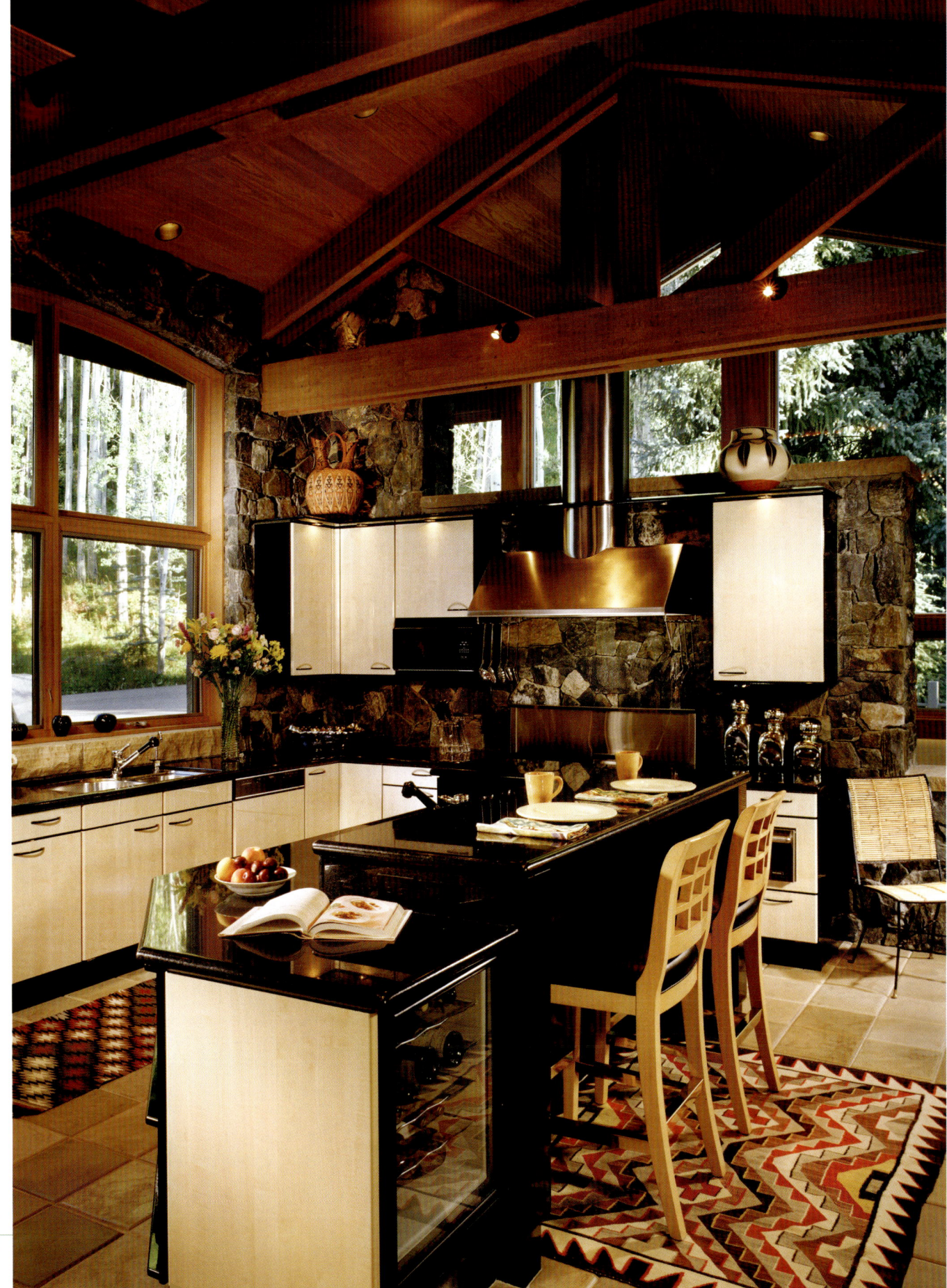

Bill and Lynn both decided to become architects in their teens. Bill's interest was first piqued by journals and periodicals. He became further fascinated when his parents commissioned a Colorado arachitect to design their home in Boulder because he was able to experience the process and enjoy the result. With the encouragement of her parents, Lynn decided to balance her passion for drawing and mathematics with a career in architecture. Lynn found inspiration from her father, an inventor, always on the cutting edge of technology.

To keep abreast of new ideas and avoid falling into provincialism, the firm actively participates in a national forum of architects that meets semi-annually to brainstorm business and design ideas. Involved in their immediate community, Lynn serves on the Denver Art Museum Design Council and both partners are appointed members of the Vail Design Review Board and Planning Commission. They have been widely published in *Colorado Homes and Lifestyles*, *Architecture and Design of the West*, *Stone World*, and *Mountain Home & Properties* in addition to receiving COBRA and AIA Colorado West Chapter Honor awards.

LEFT:
In this family living space the warmth of stone and timber fluently translate from the exterior to the interior.
Photograph by David Marlow

FACING PAGE TOP:
Interior stone walls contrast with extensive glazed openings to create a seamless flow between indoor and outdoor.
Photograph by David Marlow

FACING PAGE BOTTOM:
The stone clad main residence and clubhouse frame a playful yet comfortable, intimate pool and patio setting.
Photograph by David Marlow

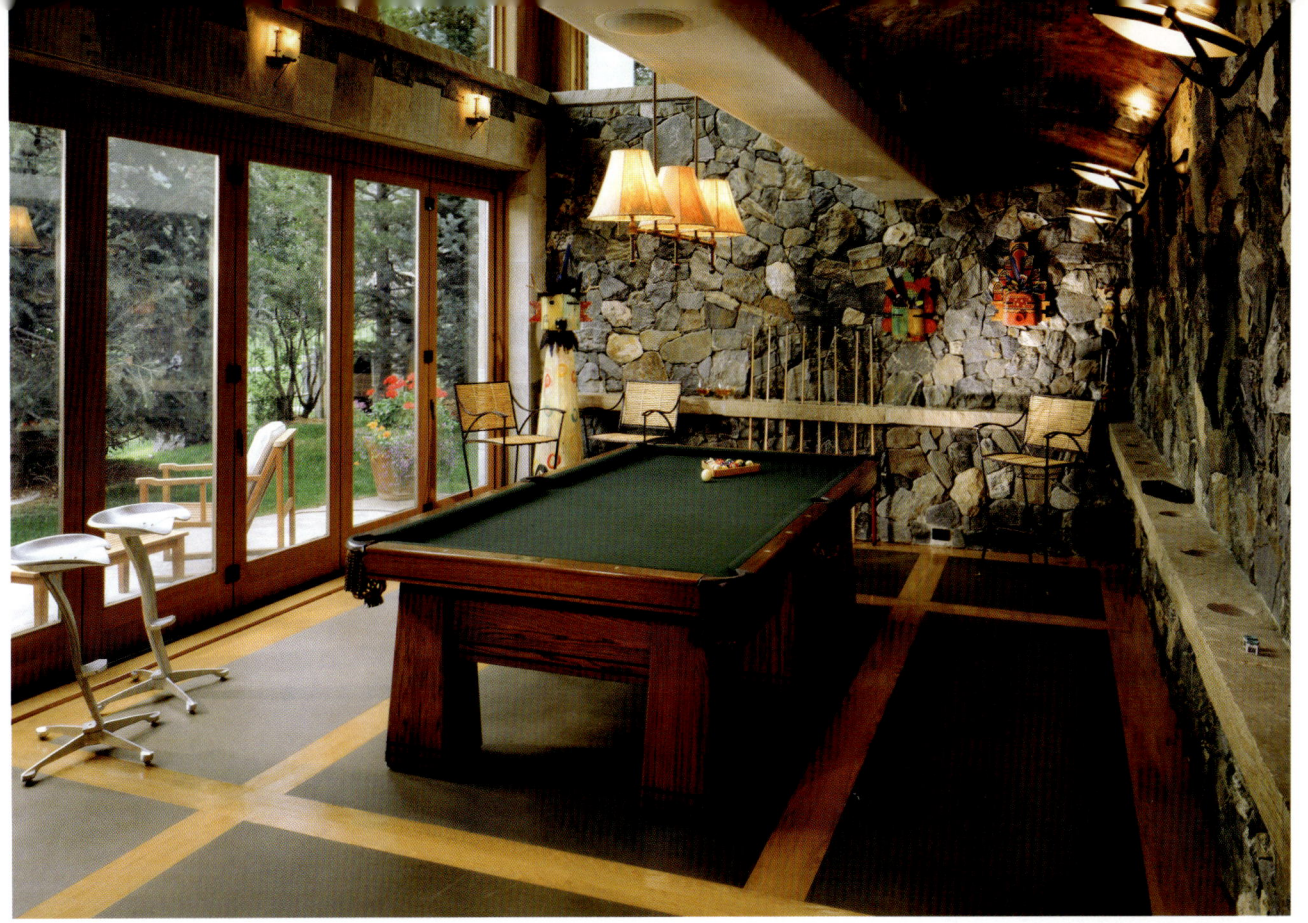

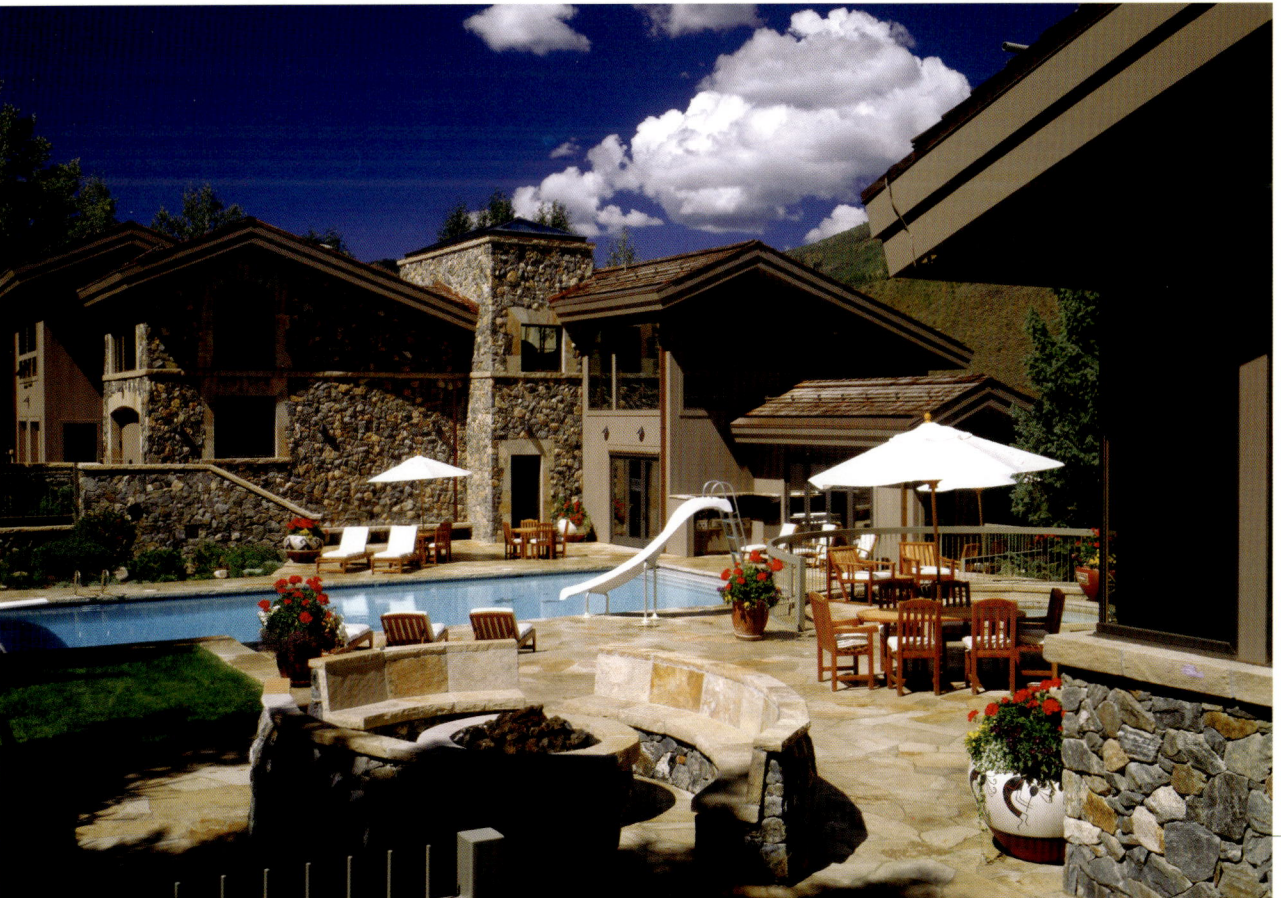

Q&A
more about lynn & bill...

WHAT IS A PARTICULARLY DIFFICULT TYPE OF PROJECT THAT FRITZLEN PIERCE ARCHITECTS HAS UNDERTAKEN?
Integrating handicap accessibility into mountain residences can be quite challenging but even more rewarding.

WHAT ARE THEIR FAVORITE BOOKS?
Lynn's favorite book is *The Rise of the Creative Class* by Richard Florida, while Bill enjoys Hunter S. Thompson's *The Curse of Lono*.

HOW WOULD LYNN BRING A DULL HOUSE TO LIFE?
We would create an arrival sequence that would take residents from the dominating natural environment to the more intimate scale of the built space. We would also introduce light, ensure that views are optimized, and then update the kitchen and bathrooms.

WHAT ASPECT OF BEING AN ARCHITECT DO THEY MOST ENJOY?
We appreciate the opportunity to interact with creative clients and colleagues from all over the country who share a common passion for architecture and design.

WHAT IS THE HIGHEST COMPLIMENT THAT THEY HAVE RECEIVED, PROFESSIONALLY?
Having a great percentage of return and referral clients is quite a compliment. One client said, "Dear Lynn . . . I want you to know that I would do it all again because of you and your associates. You made it so easy that I'd like to do it again right now. If I can ever be a reference, do not hesitate."

FRITZLEN PIERCE ARCHITECTS
LYNN FRITZLEN, AIA
WILLIAM PIERCE, AIA
1650 East Vail Valley Drive
Fallridge C-1
Vail, CO 81657
970.476.6342
f: 970.476.4901
www.vailarchitects.com

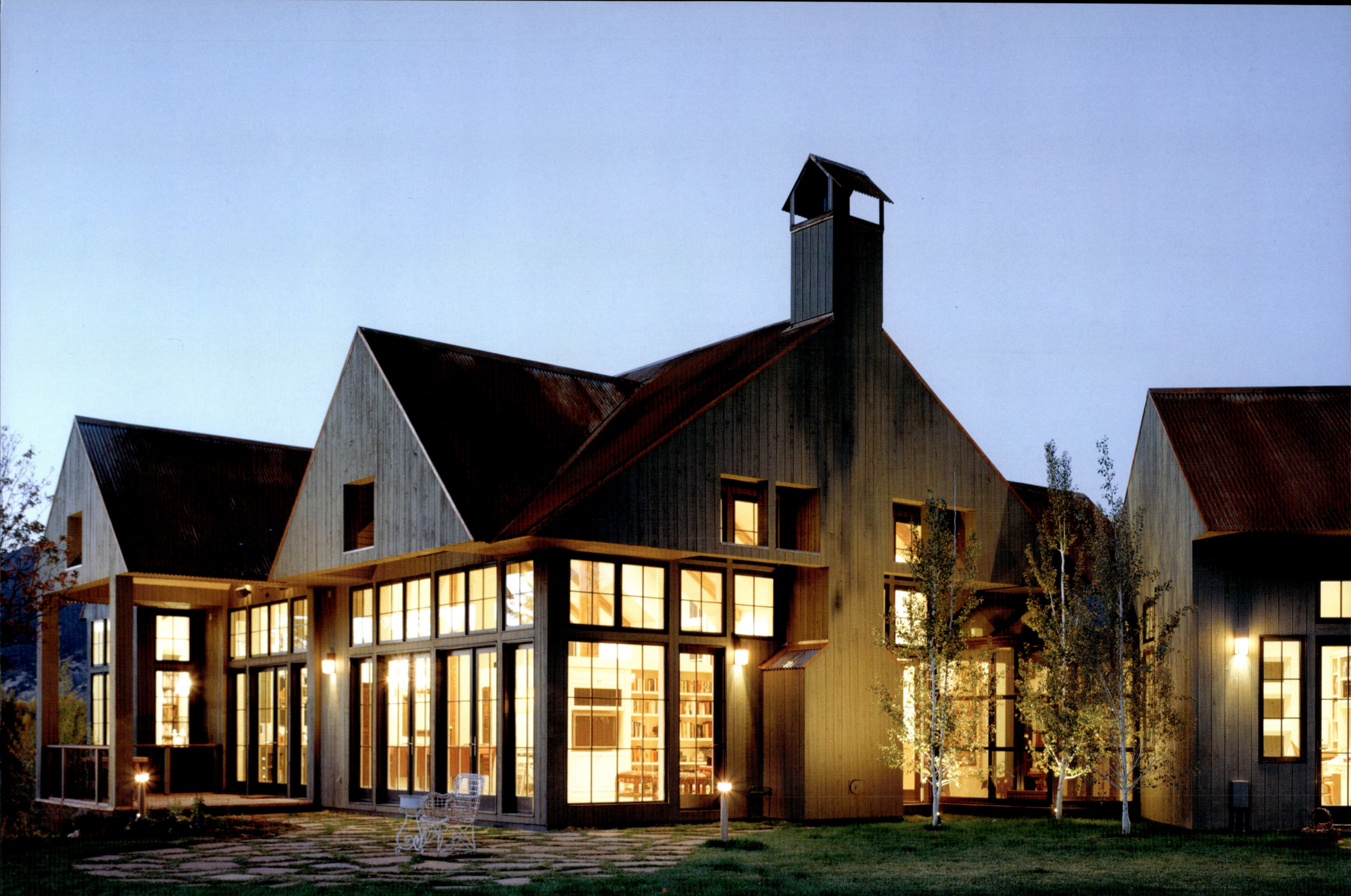

DAVID GIBSON

*IN MEMORIAM
1945-2006*

GIBSON ARCHITECTS, LLC

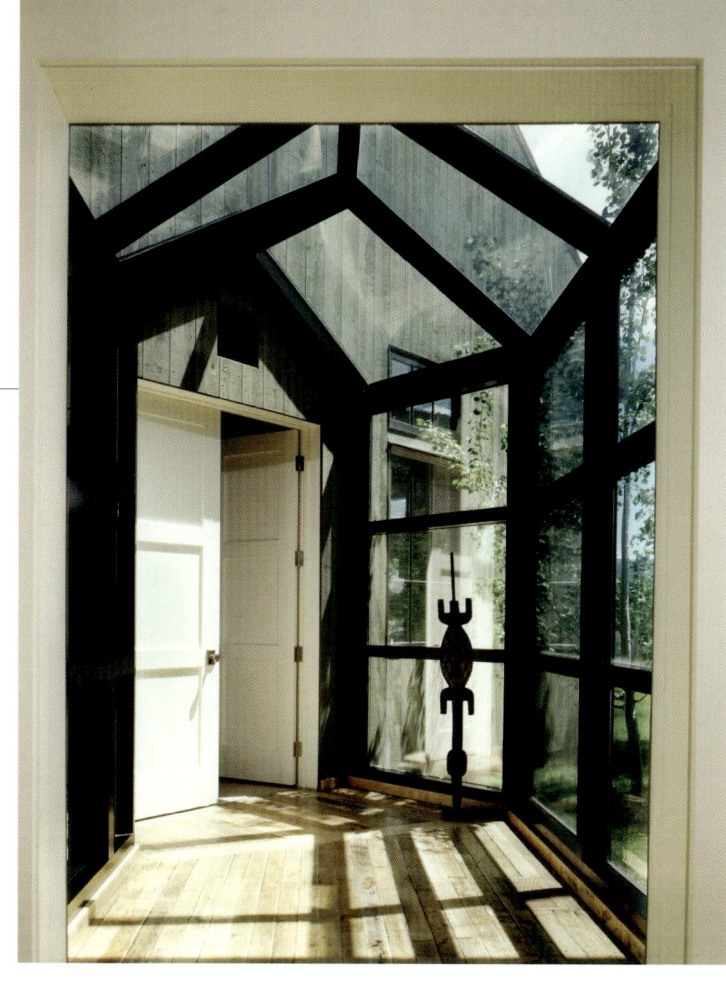

After graduating from Yale University, first with a BA, then with a master's degree in architecture in 1972, David Gibson headed west, drawn to Colorado by its stunning scenery and alpine environment. David always has enjoyed Aspen's stature as a "big little city."

Creating buildings that fit the landscape and take advantage of natural materials and generous day lighting is paired with the goals and dreams of GA clients in designing homes in Aspen, Telluride and throughout the West. GA's approach is an additive one; the design gains strength as ideas build upon each other. Egalitarian in nature, a team approach gives clients input into the design progression from the beginning.

In addition to David, the GA staff includes LEED certified project manager/designer Jamie Brewster, Associate AIA, who lends expertise in incorporating energy-saving and renewal resources as well as Green building techniques within the design phase. GA project manager/designer Michael Balser, working from GA's Telluride office, is particularly adroit in knowledge of construction and construction documentation, historic preservation and building at alpine elevations.

To this core come builders, craftsmen, and consultants who bring to the table additional layers of expertise. David, who as a student worked on design/build construction projects in Colorado and Connecticut, values the aptitude and experience of contractors and consultants in lighting, landscape design, interior design, and mechanical engineering, expanding the GA team with their specialized knowledge.

About 50 percent of GA designed projects are for second homes, many drawing from the rich vernacular ranching and mining traditions of the West. These architectural languages are expressed with strong materials such as exposed metal and large exposed timbers fitted with bolts and plates,

ABOVE:
The glass-enclosed link between the great room and master gives the experience of going "outside" and reentering the house.
Photograph by David O. Marlow

FACING PAGE:
At twilight the interior space casts a warm glow on the riverfront terrace, inviting one to come out and linger a few more minutes.
Photograph by David O. Marlow

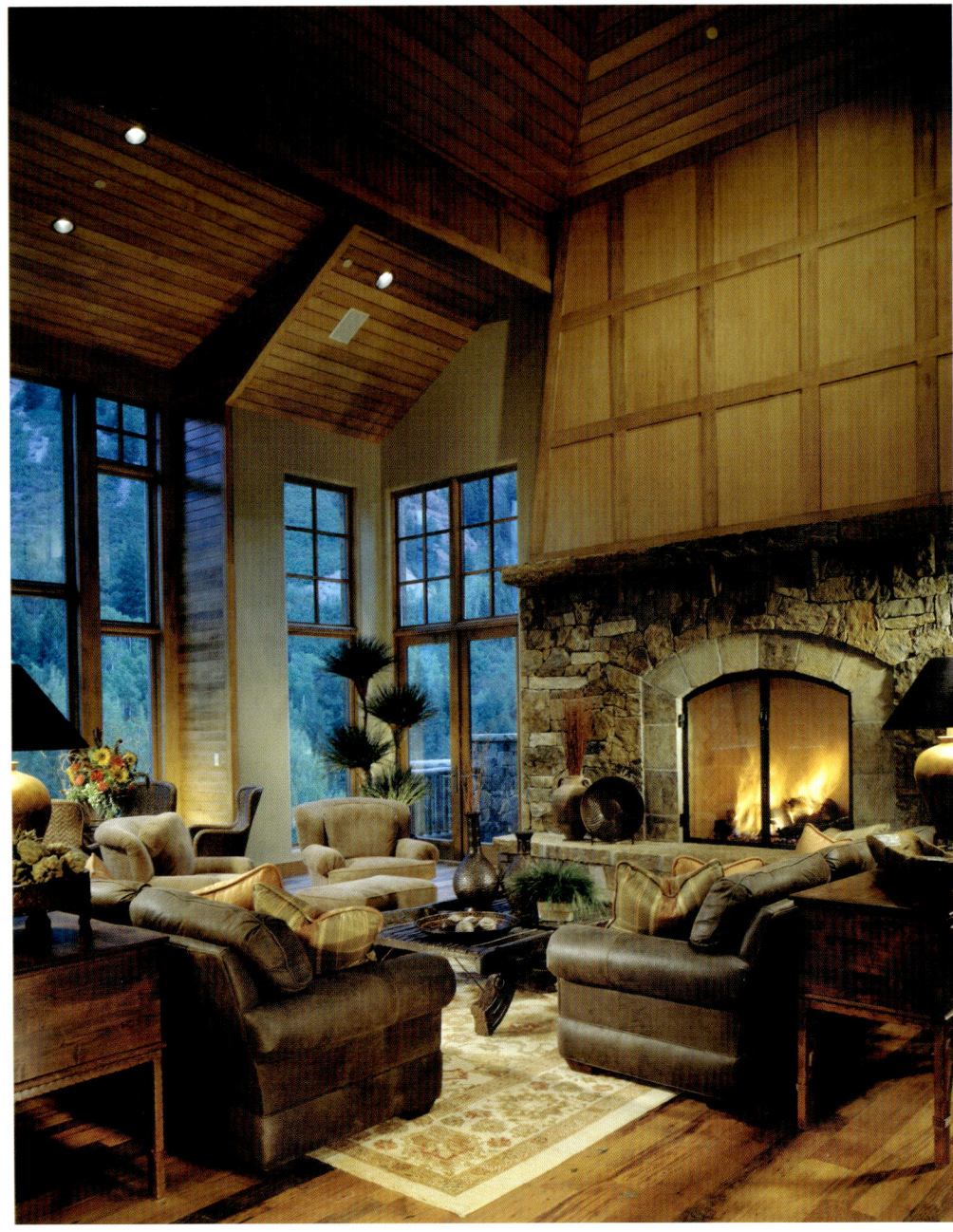
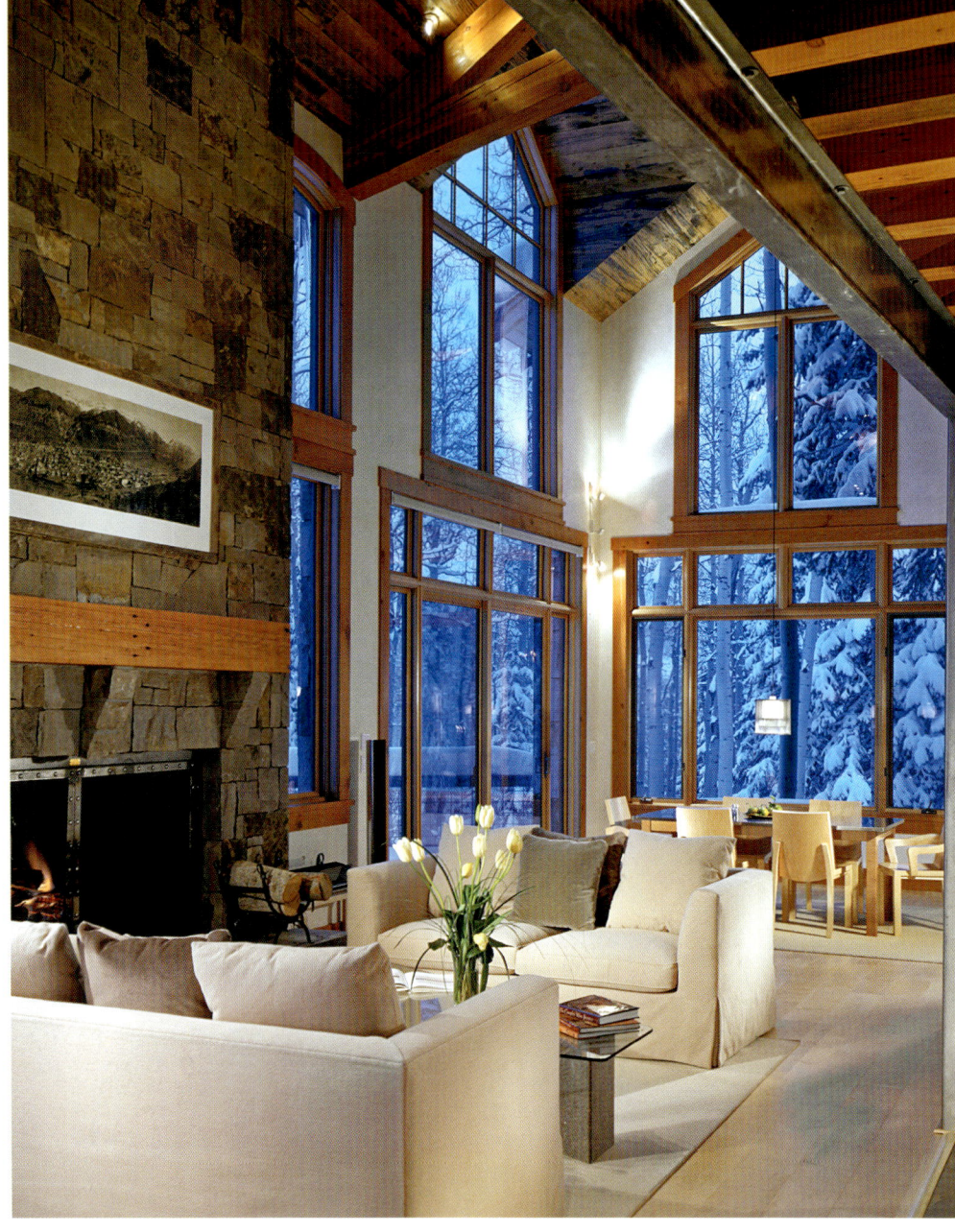

ABOVE LEFT:
The warmth of natural wood paneling (pine, maple, oak) sandstone, and comfy leather all come together in front of a warm fire.
Photograph by David O. Marlow

ABOVE RIGHT:
Tall windows capture the drama of tall trees, with sunlight filtering down through snow laden branches.
Photograph by David O. Marlow

FACING PAGE:
The warm alderwood paneling arrayed on each surface of the library creates a reposeful setting for conversation or a good book.
Photograph by David O. Marlow

lending a robust look. The iconography of the region's great historic lodges, with their ample timber-trussed great rooms and rough hewn stone fireplaces, also provides inspiration for GA designs.

Local materials from the Rockies, such as sandstone, with its palette ranging from charcoal to tans to reds, often figure into GA designs. To achieve the perfect palette GA has on occasion mixed five sources of stone to achieve a balance of reds, greens and eggplants. The result is akin to an impressionist painting with sparkle. Antique wood, imbued with color and character, also is found in GA homes. Old hickory, oak and chestnut woods are garnered from barns that are taken down along the east coast and in the Appalachians. From the Pacific Northwest comes a lot of first growth timber originally used in factories. Its straight grain is particularly pleasing to engineers and provides the overarching trusses and beams in major spaces.

Day lighting, another hallmark of GA design, takes on added significance in forest environments and on steep hillsides because the sun will set earlier on the north side of a hill or a deep valley. David and his staff make efforts to daylight every room in the home so lights are not needed during the day, enhancing clients' natural connection with the sky. Taller windows ensure that the stunning views of ridge tops are not lost and this technique also throws light deeper into a particular space.

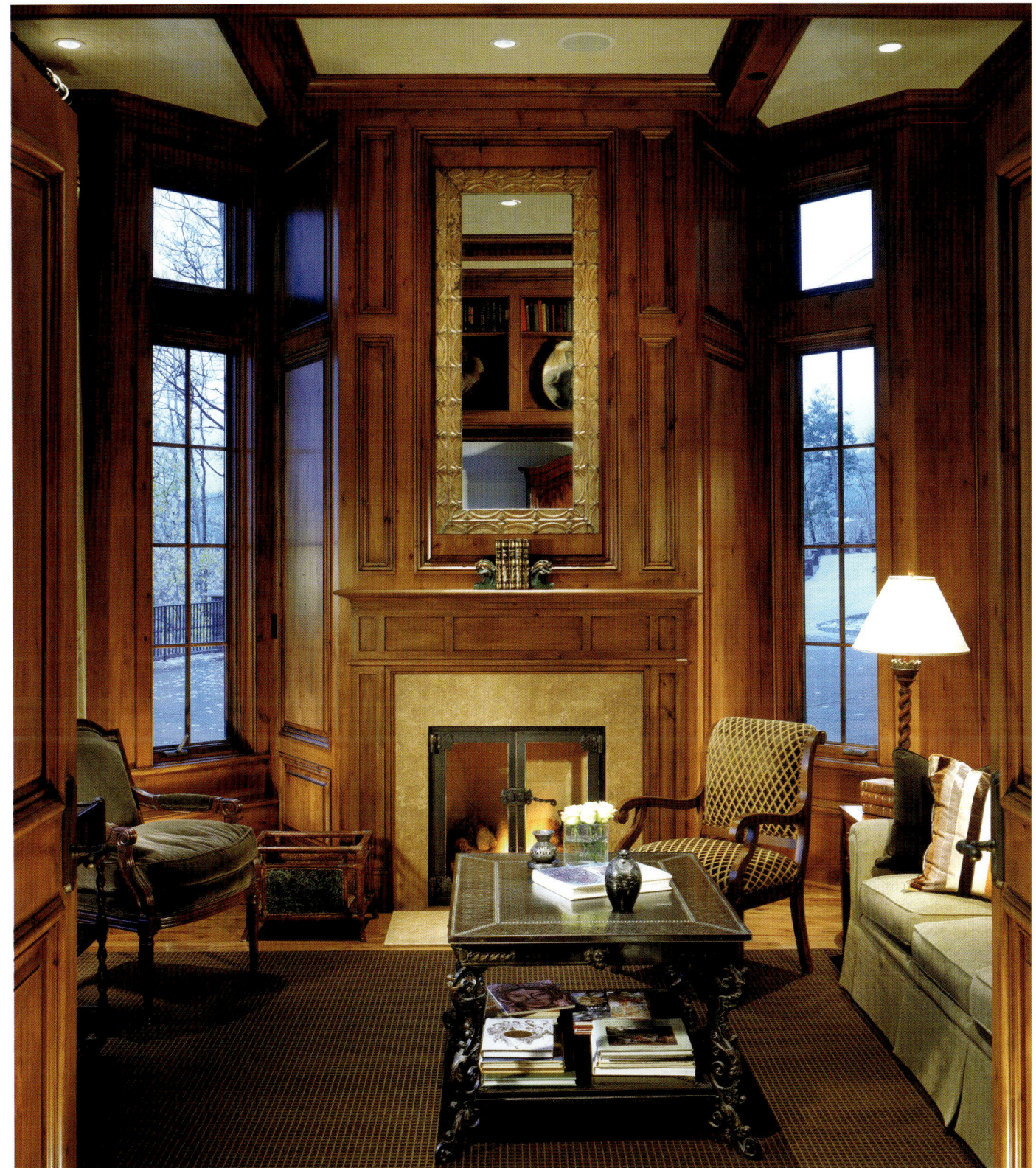

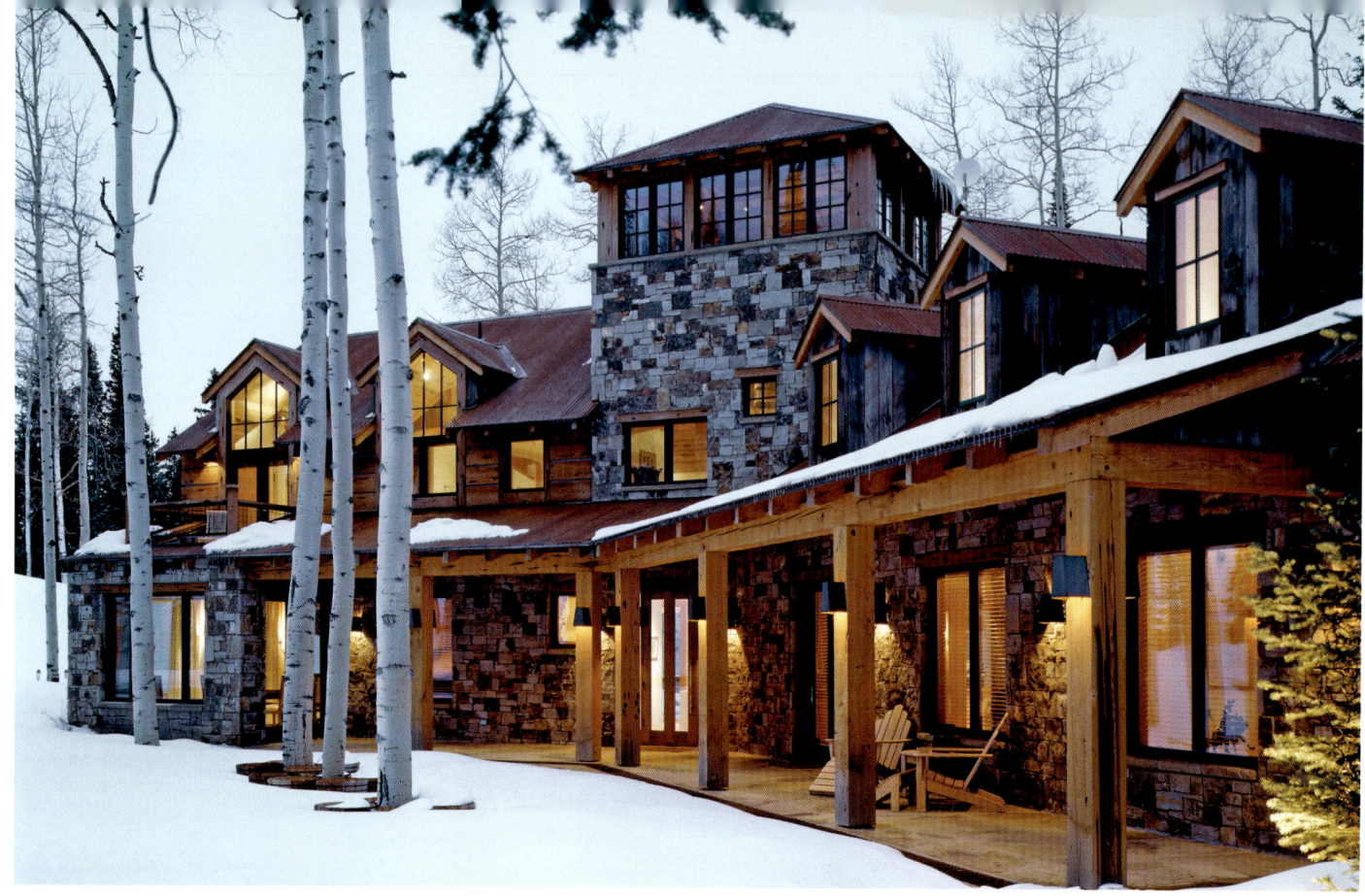

David, who became a pilot 10 years ago, often takes aerial photographs of GA rural building sites for analysis and for site design before the building design begins. "It's a great way to get around," he says. "You can't always get a feel for a place in one image, especially for large acreage, so aerial photography is a valuable design tool."

David Franklin Gibson achieved the life he had always dreamed of; one filled with a blissful balance of career, activities, hobbies and most importantly, family, that gave his life true meaning.

In July 2006, David left this life. He lived with his wife Kathleen and sons Jared and Colin in Aspen, Colorado. He also leaves behind his daughter Eren in New York City.

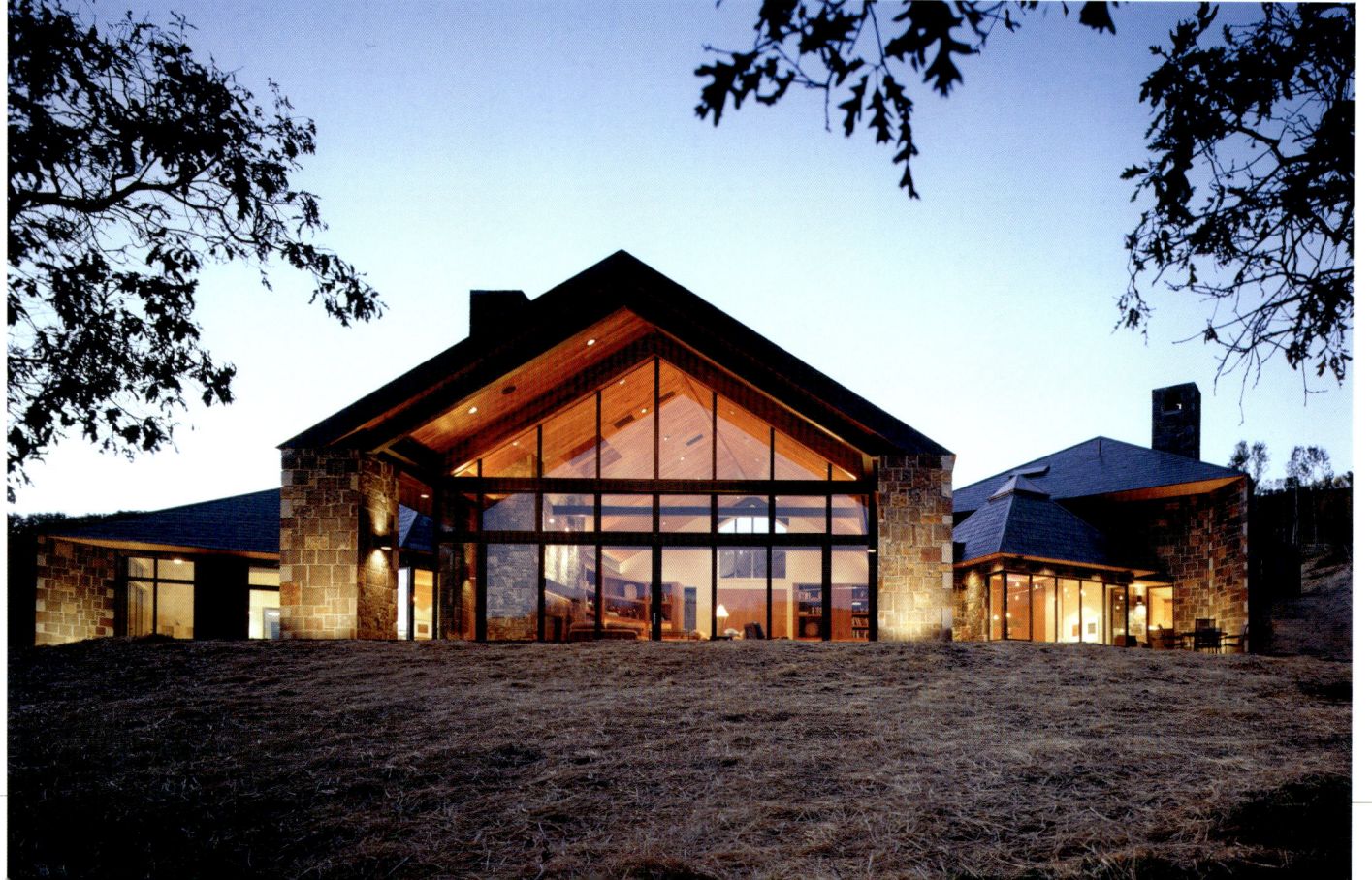

TOP LEFT:
The wraparound porch gives a welcoming greeting to this mountain lodge which serves as a retreat for three generations of extended family.
Photograph by David O. Marlow

BOTTOM LEFT:
Contemporary detailing, rich materials and quality of stunning transparency give a memorable experience.
Photograph by David O. Marlow

FACING PAGE:
Space flows unimpeded from the landscape, into the interior, and back out again.
Photograph by David O. Marlow

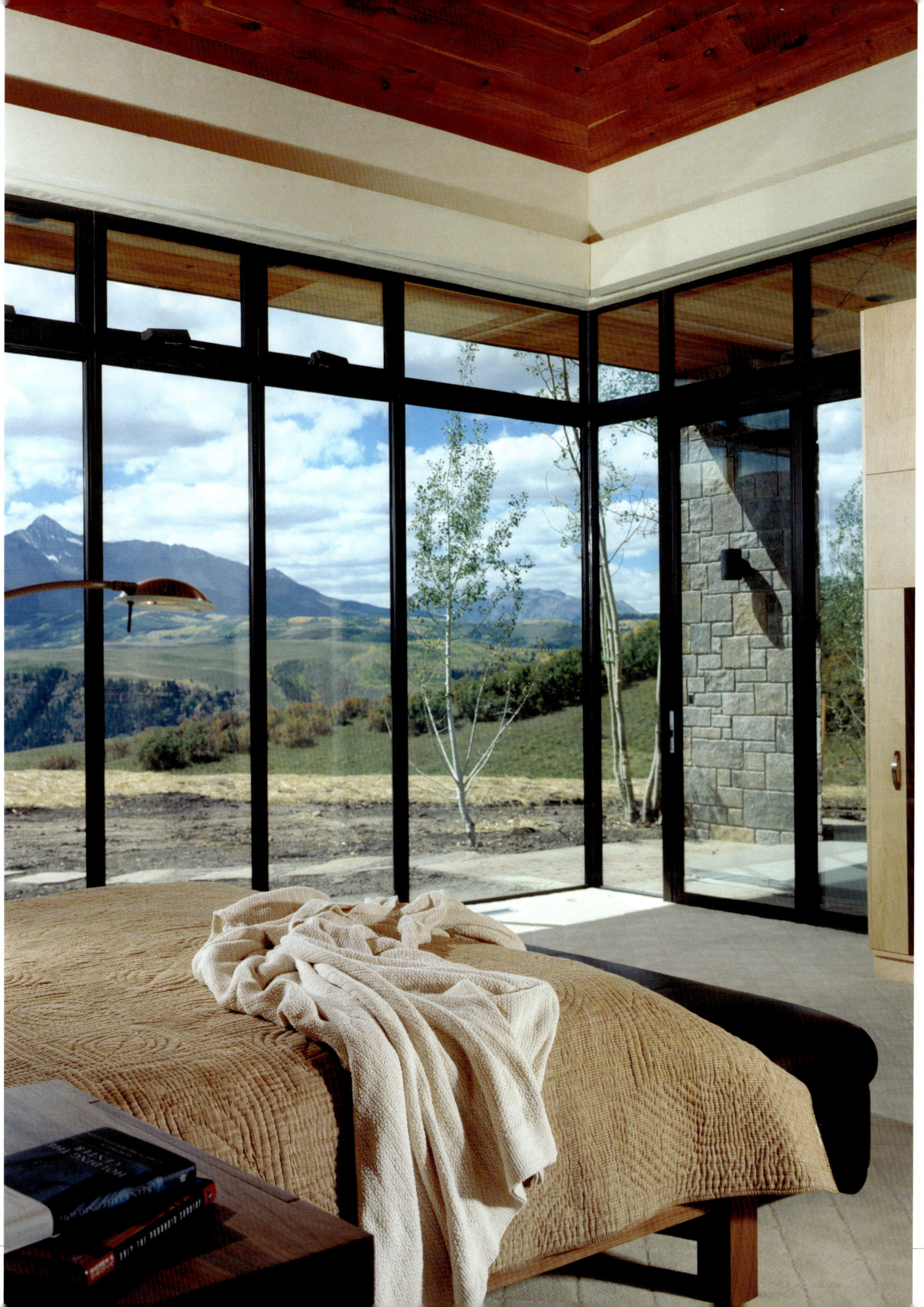

Q&A
more about david...

WHAT IS THE MOST UNIQUE AND IMPRESSIVE HOME YOU'VE BEEN INVOLVED WITH?
The Residence at Aldasoro Ranch, Telluride. It redefines "mountain contemporary" with its rich materials and clean detailing.

WHAT IS THE MOST UNUSUAL DESIGN OR TECHNIQUE YOU'VE USED IN ONE OF YOUR PROJECTS?
An indoor waterfall in a hotel penthouse.

HAVE YOU BEEN PUBLISHED IN ANY NATIONAL OR REGIONAL PUBLICATIONS?
Luxe, Sojourner, Mountain Homestyles, Landscape Architecture, and *My House Magazine*.

ANY AWARDS OR SPECIAL RECOGNITION YOU WOULD LIKE MENTIONED?
We've received 12 AIA awards from the Mountain Region, Colorado and Colorado West chapters and four honor awards from the Historic Preservation Commission of Aspen.

IF YOU COULD ELIMINATE ONE ARCHITECTURAL ELEMENT FROM THE WORLD, WHAT WOULD IT BE?
Storage buildings.

WHAT COLOR BEST DESCRIBES YOU AND WHY?
Rust. It occurs naturally and is non-glare and abundant.

YOU WOULDN'T KNOW IT BUT MY FRIENDS WOULD TELL YOU I WAS:
Modest.

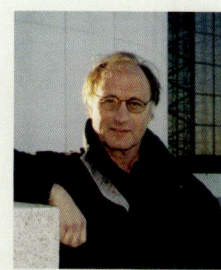

GIBSON ARCHITECTS, LLC
DAVID GIBSON, AIA
715 West Main Street. #203
Aspen, CO 81611
970.920.3007
f: 970.920.3103

Telluride office:
101 East Colorado Avenue 301
PO Box 278
Telluride, CO 81435
970.728.6607
f: 970.728.6658
www.gibson-architects.com

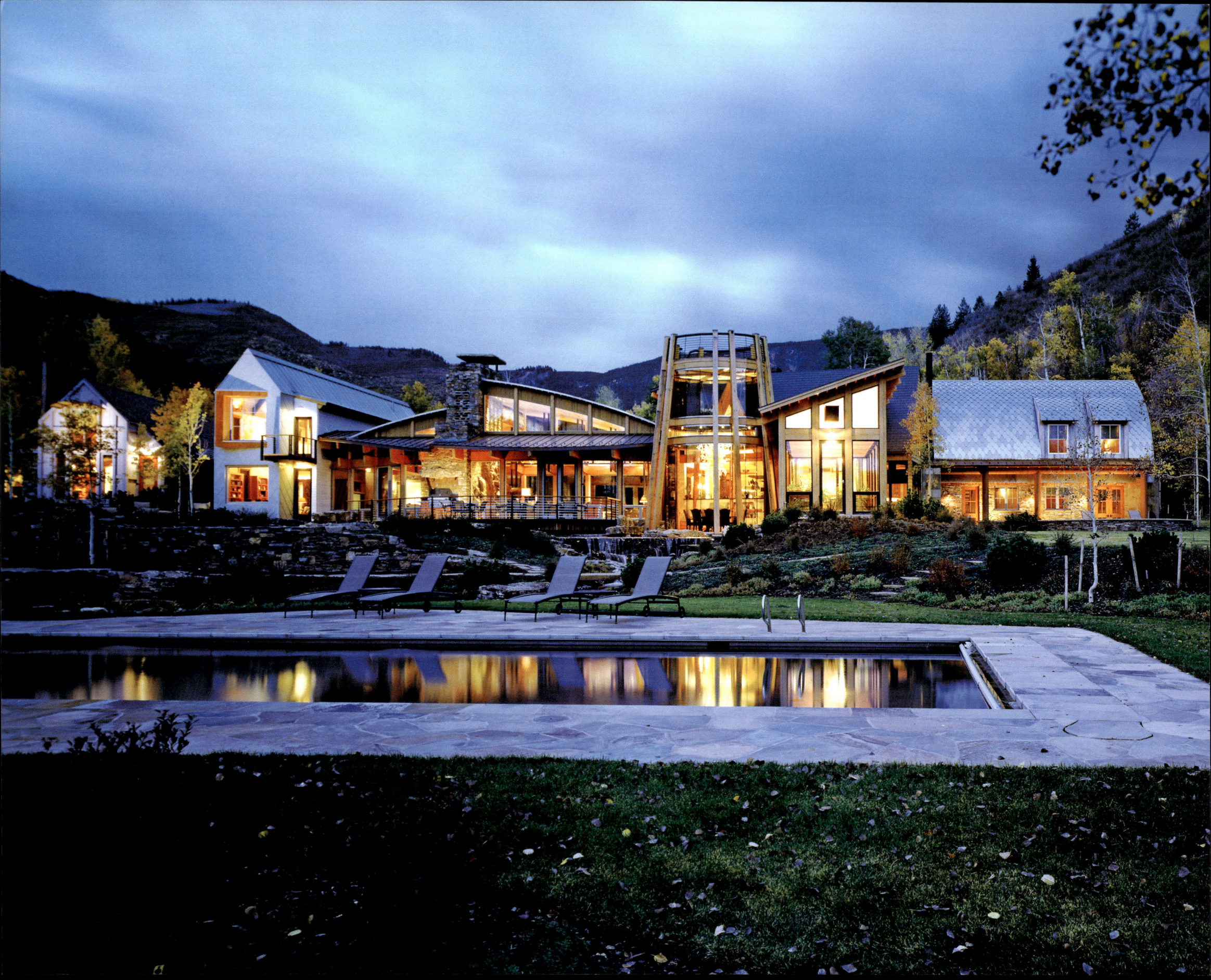

TIM HAGMAN
HAGMAN ARCHITECTS

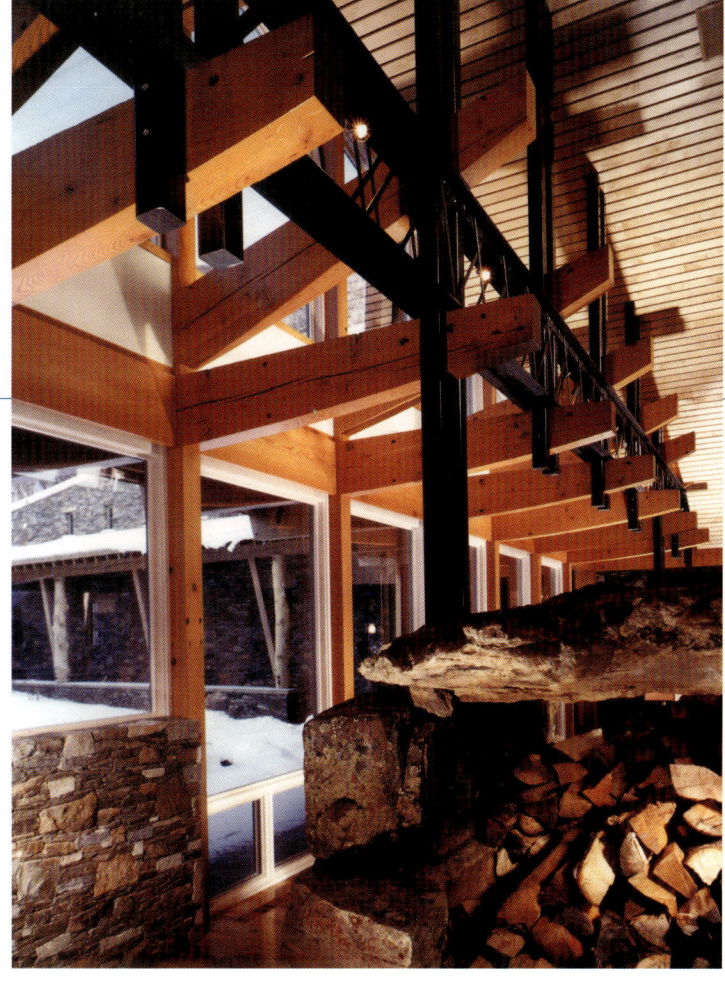

Tim Hagman founded Hagman Architects in the Roaring Fork Valley over 30 years ago. Since that time, he and his firm have worked on every kind of building possible in a mountain community. From residential to hotel and commercial, Tim and his team have seen and done it all. Over the years, their projects have run the gamut from 5,000 to 15,000-square-foot residential sites to much larger commercial sites.

After spending many years as a relatively large firm and focusing mostly on large commercial work, Tim had a desire to get back down to the roots where he started; environmentally responsible "Green" architecture. As the firm began to focus more and more on Green architecture, Aspen developed building standards that required Green building. Since that time, a lot of progress has been made toward making building environmentally conservative and sustainable. Designing and building Green, sustainable architecture is a now the platform of Hagman Architects and one from which they never stray. As a LEED accredited firm, they continually educate themselves in environmental and Green building design, employing and applying the latest technology available.

An integral part of the team, Tony Major has been with the firm since 1994, playing a large role in the design and execution of many projects. A Colorado native, he is passionate about fine design that is sustainable with Green bases; a goal that's aligned with the firm's. Like the rest of the team, he gets a great satisfaction out of projects which are conservation oriented. Kurt Carruth has also been an integral part of the team for nearly a decade. Through his appreciation and love for work, he has been responsible for many of the firm's finest projects. The entire staff at HA collaborates on all projects, with each member bringing a personal perspective to the design process.

ABOVE:
Recycled 100-year-old fir beams, steel trusses, indigenous stone walls and fireplace frame the interior/exterior connection of living space to garden.
Photograph by David O. Marlow

FACING PAGE:
A unique expression for each of the different spaces were gathered together, referencing regional historic buildings, while creating the feel of a rural compound.
Photography by David O. Marlow

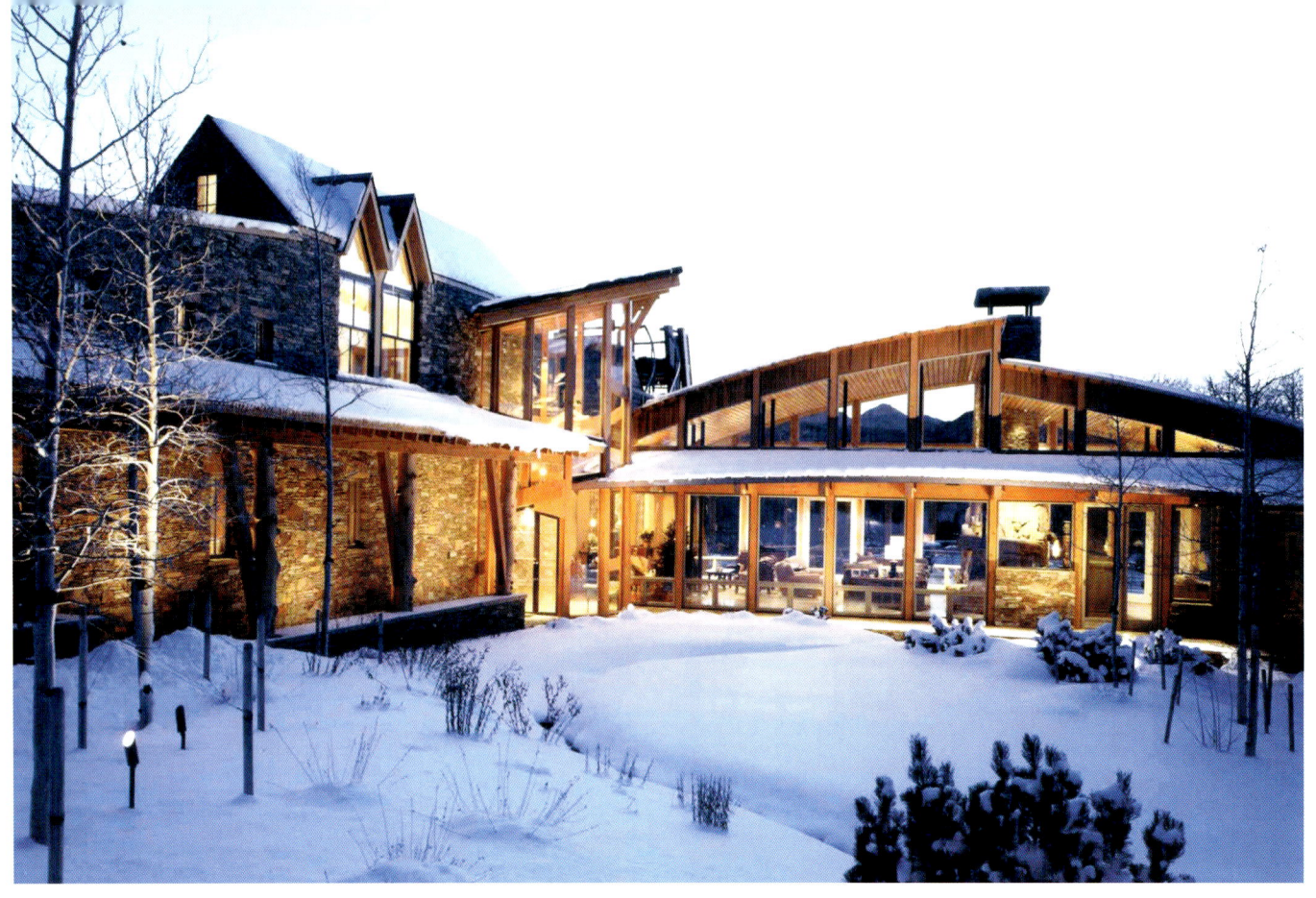

Tim and his team have a roster of projects that would amaze the finest architects. The firm recently completed the Aspen Recreation Center, an 80,000-square-foot facility with an ice rink, swimming pool and other amenities. And it sounds like a line from a fairy tale, but Tim has also built a house made of straw. Building the house out of this material lowered the cost of building the home by almost 60% and lowered the heating bills to 25% less than they would have been.

Over last three decades in Aspen, a state of the art in the community has been developed. Architects are building new things that haven't been built before. Hagman Architects is proud to be a part of this revolution. "One of the great things about working in this area is that the clientele, government and code required are very sophisticated. For years to come, this will only get better and better—that's very encouraging," said Tim.

Tim and his team utilize a dynamic and farsighted approach, creating art that is functional, unique and timeless. Using an open studio atmosphere, their clients are encouraged to freely participate in all aspects of the work. Distinctive and innovative detailing gives each of their projects a special sense of place. Winner of multiple Colorado West Chapter AIA awards, Hagman Architects is dedicated to bring their clients' visions to reality—all in a responsible way—"by recycling, using the sun and building Green."

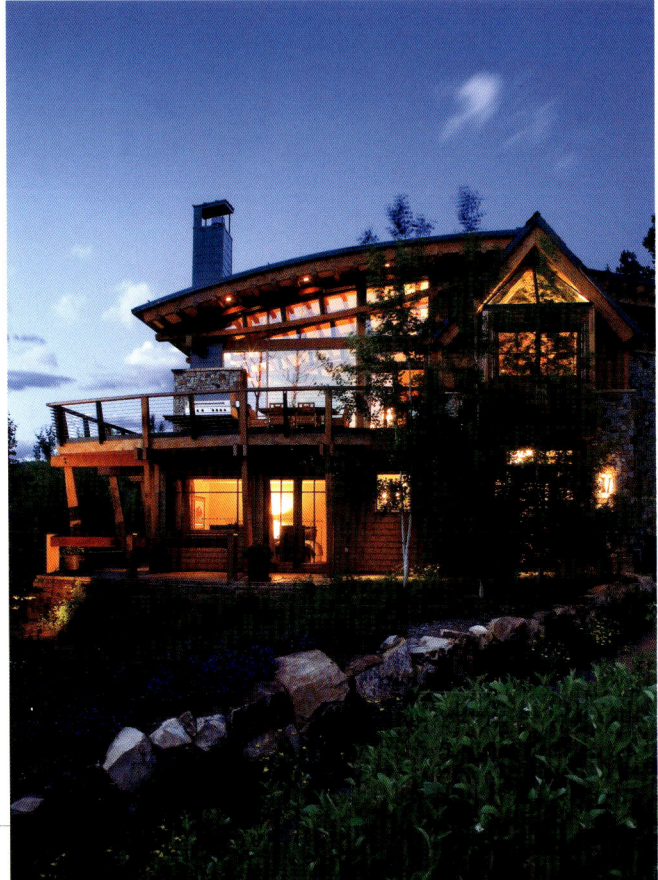
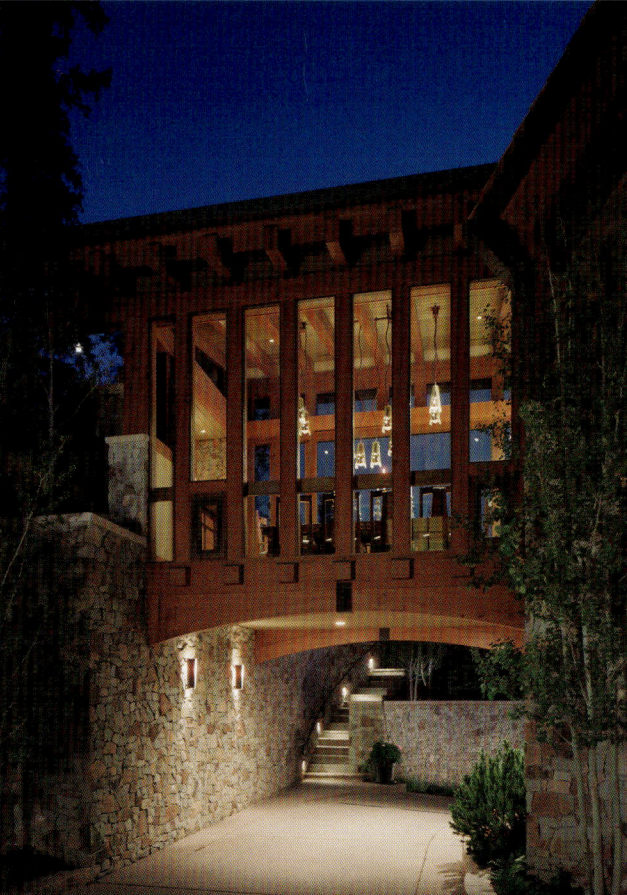

TOP:
Approaching the home under a covered walk, then through the entry tower, the living room then opens to natural landscaped areas on both sides.
Photograph by David O. Marlow

BOTTOM LEFT:
The gently arched room and deck embrace a contemporary open concept within classic mountain materials of fir and local granite.
Photograph by Robert Millman

BOTTOM RIGHT:
Entrance to the entry court is under the dining room of fir columns.
Photograph by Timothy Hursley

FACING PAGE TOP:
Western archetypes are brought together by a transparent, minimal living room connector.
Photograph by Robert Millman

FACING PAGE BOTTOM:
The living room incorporates the exterior fir and granite, opening to surrounding mountain views.
Photograph by Timothy Hursley

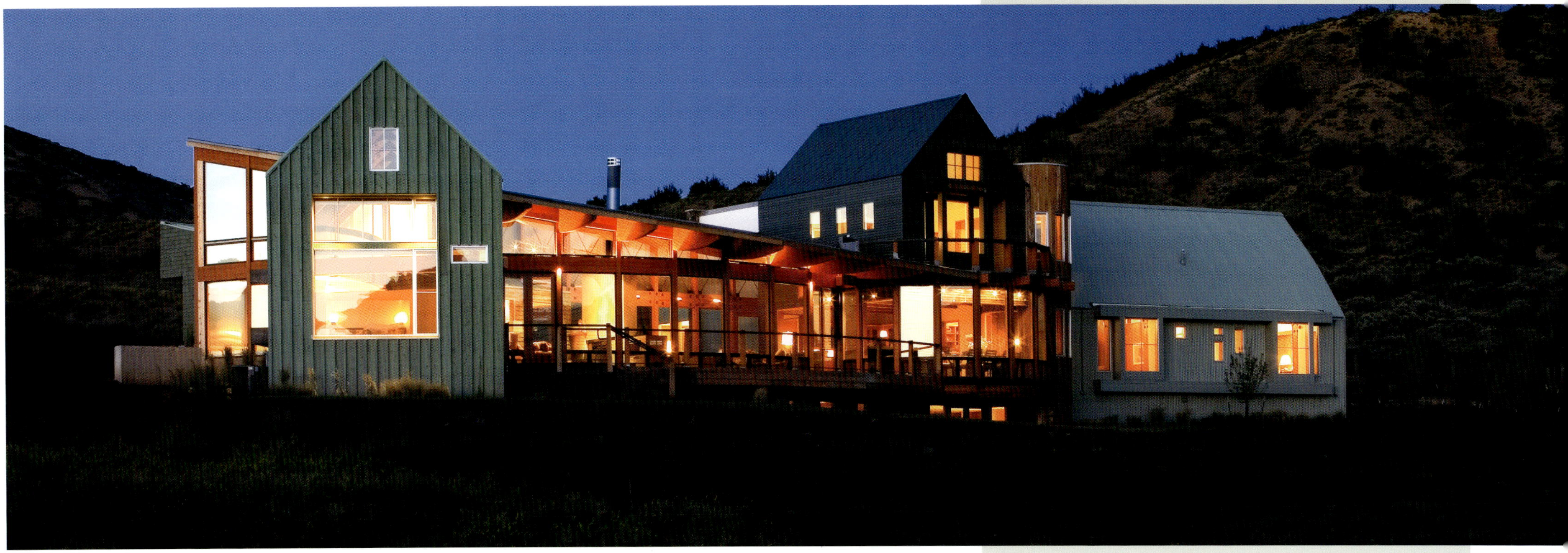

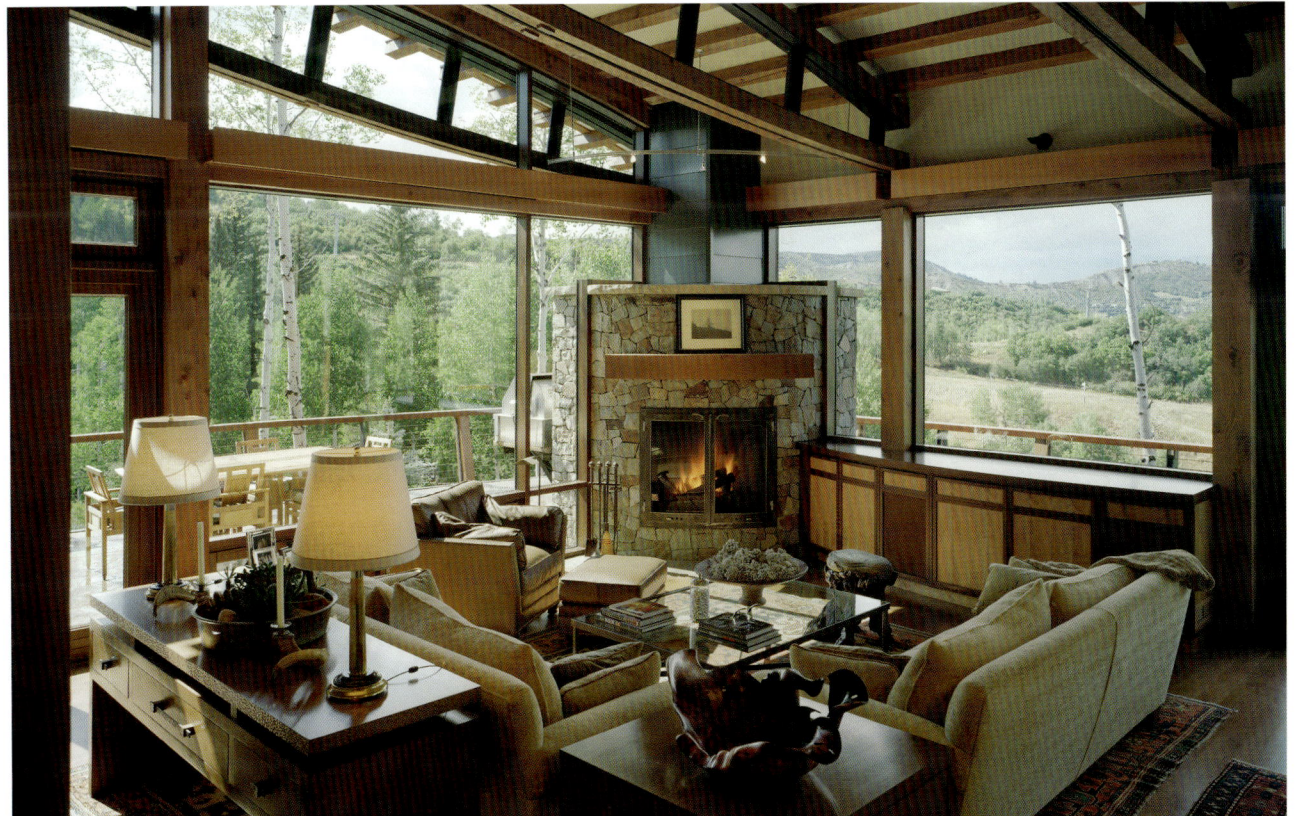

more about tim...

HAVE YOU BEEN PUBLISHED IN ANY NATIONAL OR REGIONAL PUBLICATIONS?
Our work has been presented in *SKI Magazine*, *Aspen Magazine*, *Mountain Living*, *My House Magazine* and *Luxe*, among others.

WHAT'S THE BEST PART OF BEING AN ARCHITECT?
Building people's dream homes with a sustainable, environmentally friendly process.

WHAT IS THE MOST IMPRESSIVE HOME YOU'VE BEEN INVOLVED WITH?
I am most impressed with homes I've built for people that have come to me with visions that aren't the traditional mountain mansion but cost and energy efficient homes to last their lifetime.

HAGMAN ARCHITECTS
TIM HAGMAN
104 Midland Avenue, Suite 201
Basalt, CO 81621
970.927.3822
f: 970.927.3899
www.hagmanarchitects.com

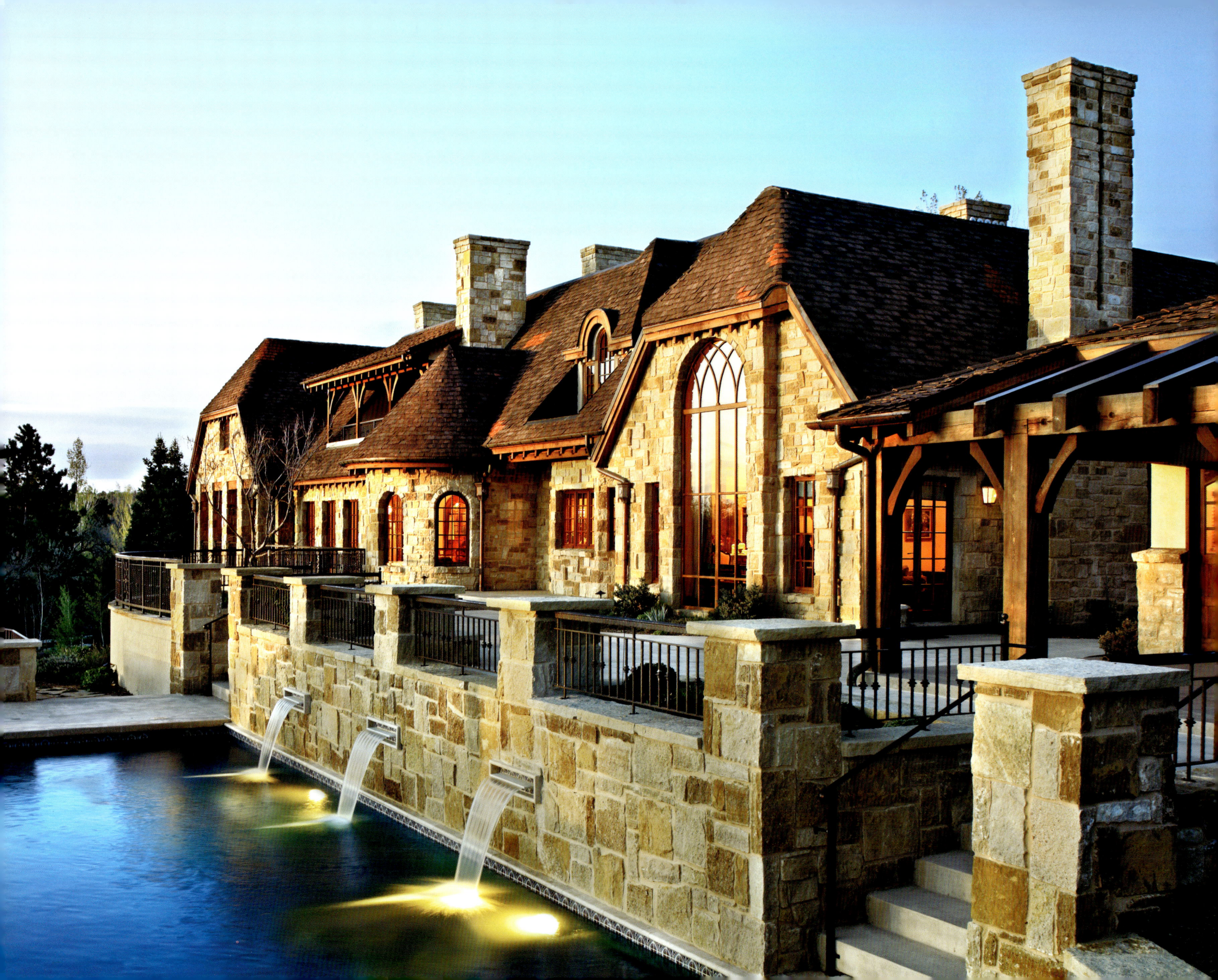

LYNN & PAM HARRISON

HARRISON CUSTOM BUILDERS, LTD.

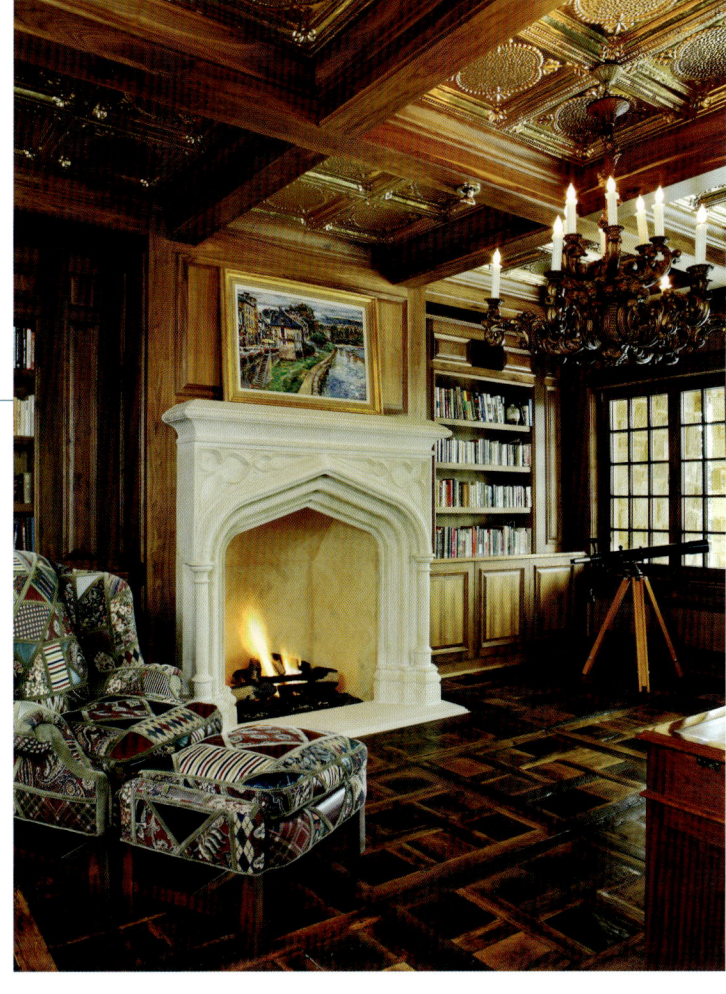

Harrison Custom Builders is a third-generation custom home-builder which has been crafting quality since 1955. Lynn Harrison carries on this unique 50-year family legacy passed down from his father, Aubrey Harrison. As a child, Lynn would go to work with his dad. It was during these formative years he learned the home-building trade that would come to be his life's work. After Aubrey's retirement in 1983, Lynn and his brother Rod began building exquisite luxury custom homes. Lynn and his wife, Pam, have built the company over the last several decades and the family business is now in its third generation. Lynn's son Scott and Scott's wife, Christie, are steadily continuing to move the company into its next 50 years. As a family-owned company, Harrison Custom Builders utilizes solid craftspeople and subcontractors with whom they have maintained relationships for over 23 years. With such a talented team, Lynn enjoys creating authentically Old World, European-style, elegant, historic feeling homes such as English Tudors, French Country Chateaus and Tuscan Villas which contain detailed craftsmanship and all the amenities of new, luxury custom homes. Lynn's team is often involved with exceptionally unique building projects. In the last several years they have enjoyed using reclaimed materials gathered from throughout the world, giving them the opportunity to marry authentic, historic materials in modern, luxury custom homes. Many of these works of art have been featured on the pages of *Colorado Homes and Lifestyles*, *LUX*E and *Professional Roofing* magazine.

These homes are among the most sought after properties in the community because Harrison Custom Builders and the "Harrison" brand are established and well-known in the high-end, custom home community of Colorado. Harrison is distinct in the building community—they offer consultative, personal service to each client. They build every home as if it were their own. Senior management spends time managing each building project on-site daily, not from a distant, far-removed executive office. As the owner of the company, Lynn serves as the master builder and personally supervises each custom home built. He believes that custom homeowners deserve personal service and direct access to the builder. As such, each

ABOVE:
Library with reclaimed flooring, immaculate craftsmanship and attention to detail.
Photograph by Ron Ruscio

FACING PAGE:
Unique, luxurious French Country home with Old World materials collected from around the world.
Photograph by Ron Ruscio

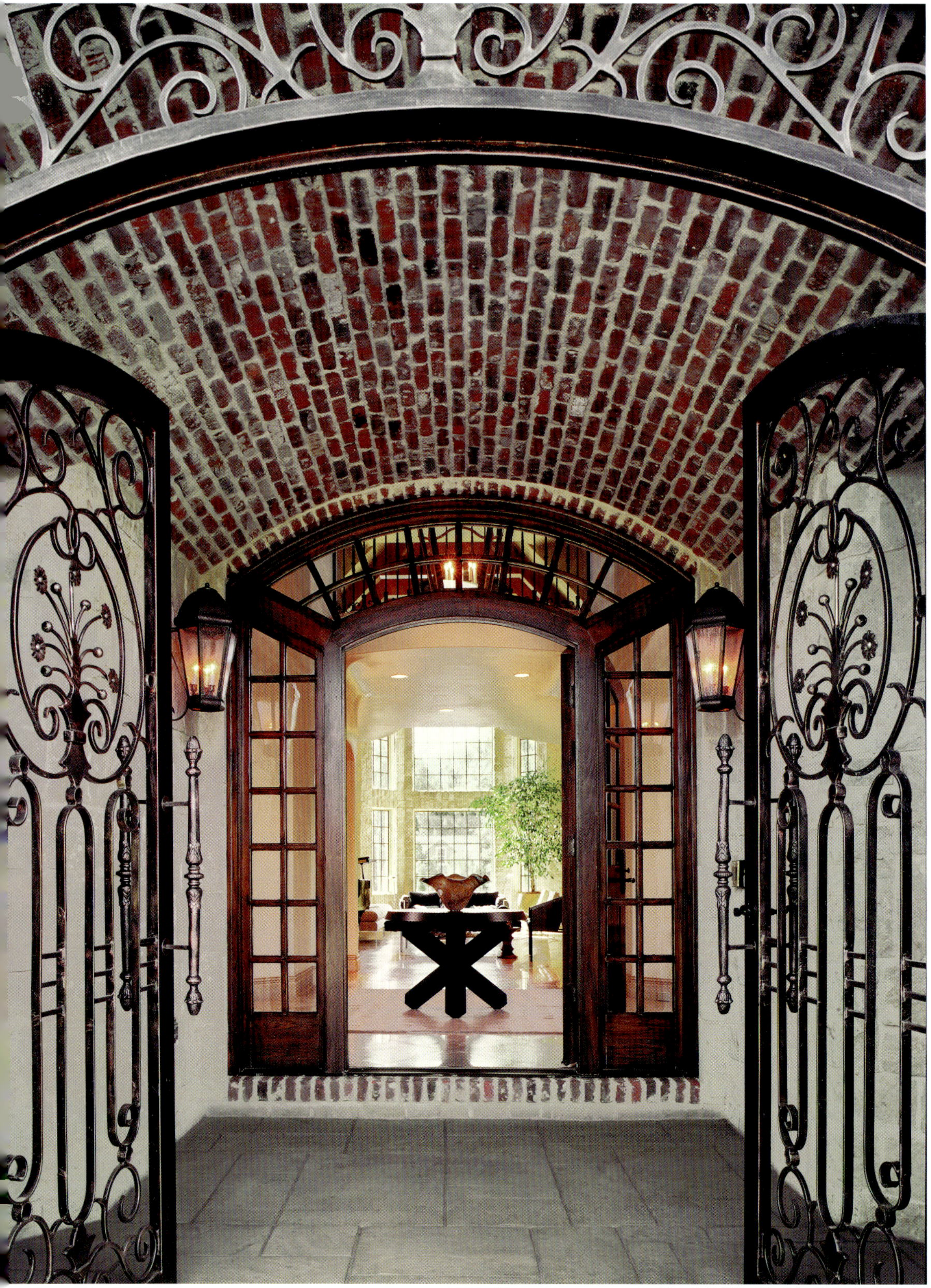

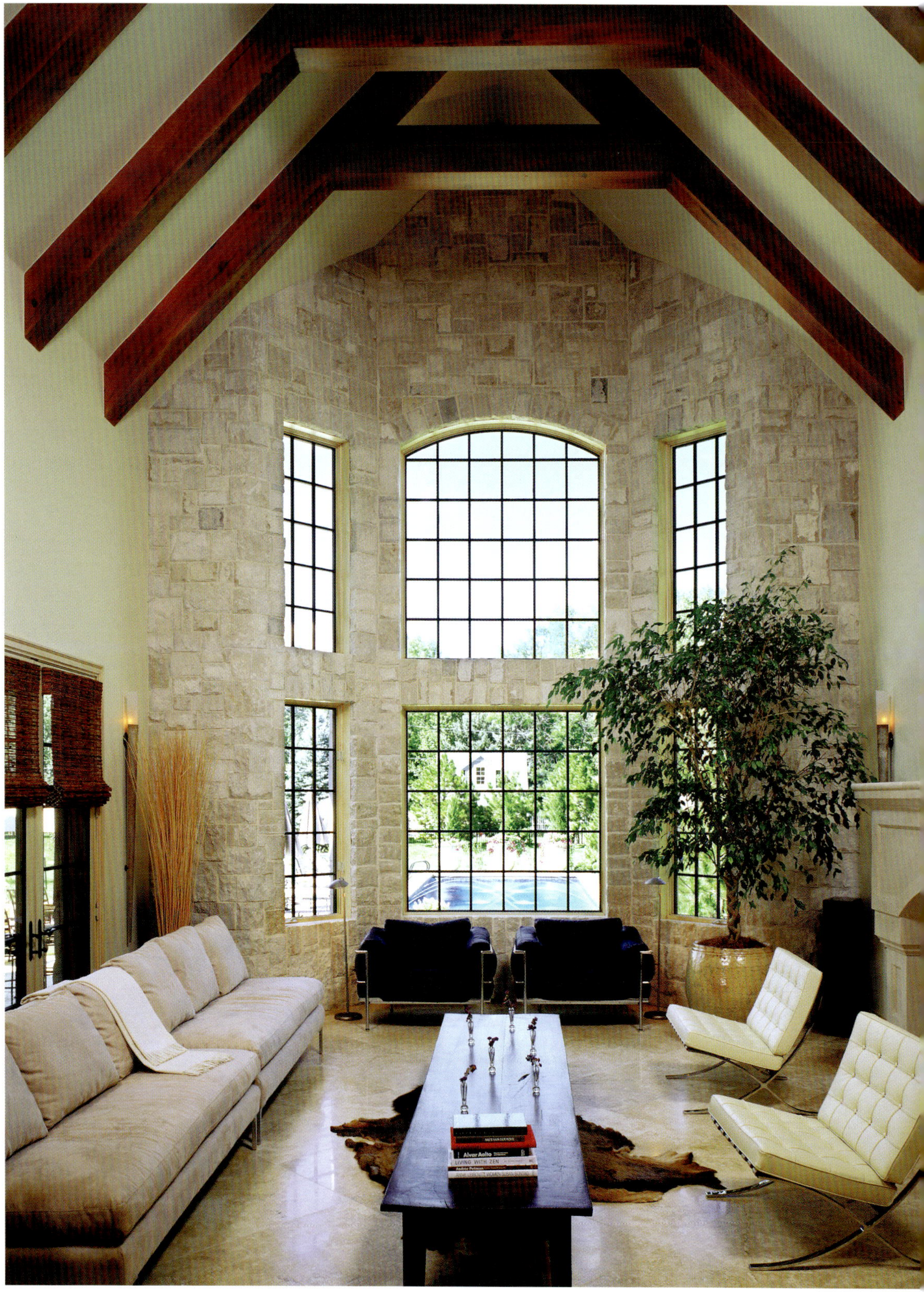

home built receives personal attention and expertise in every phase of the construction process—ranging from site selection to completion of the final punch list. The company offers this type of consultative, personal service by building only the quantity of custom homes that Lynn can personally supervise—a decision designed to keep quality at its best. The family's passionate dedication to detail shines in everything the Harrisons pursue—from their exquisite finish work to their safe, clean construction sites that minimize neighborhood disruption.

To Lynn, the best part of being a builder is taking inspiration from the beauty of the past, utilizing the creative process and manifesting elements of history in luxury custom homes. Because he is building the homes of people's dreams, his clients often can't believe that the process of building a dream home can be so smooth. Lynn and his team strive to come together with their clients and make everyone feel as comfortable as possible. A recent client reflecting on their home building experience stated: "there are no words to express our appreciation for the fabulous home you have built for us. The help, guidance, patience and professionalism you offered made the entire project a labor of love." To Harrison Custom Builders, there could be no greater compliment.

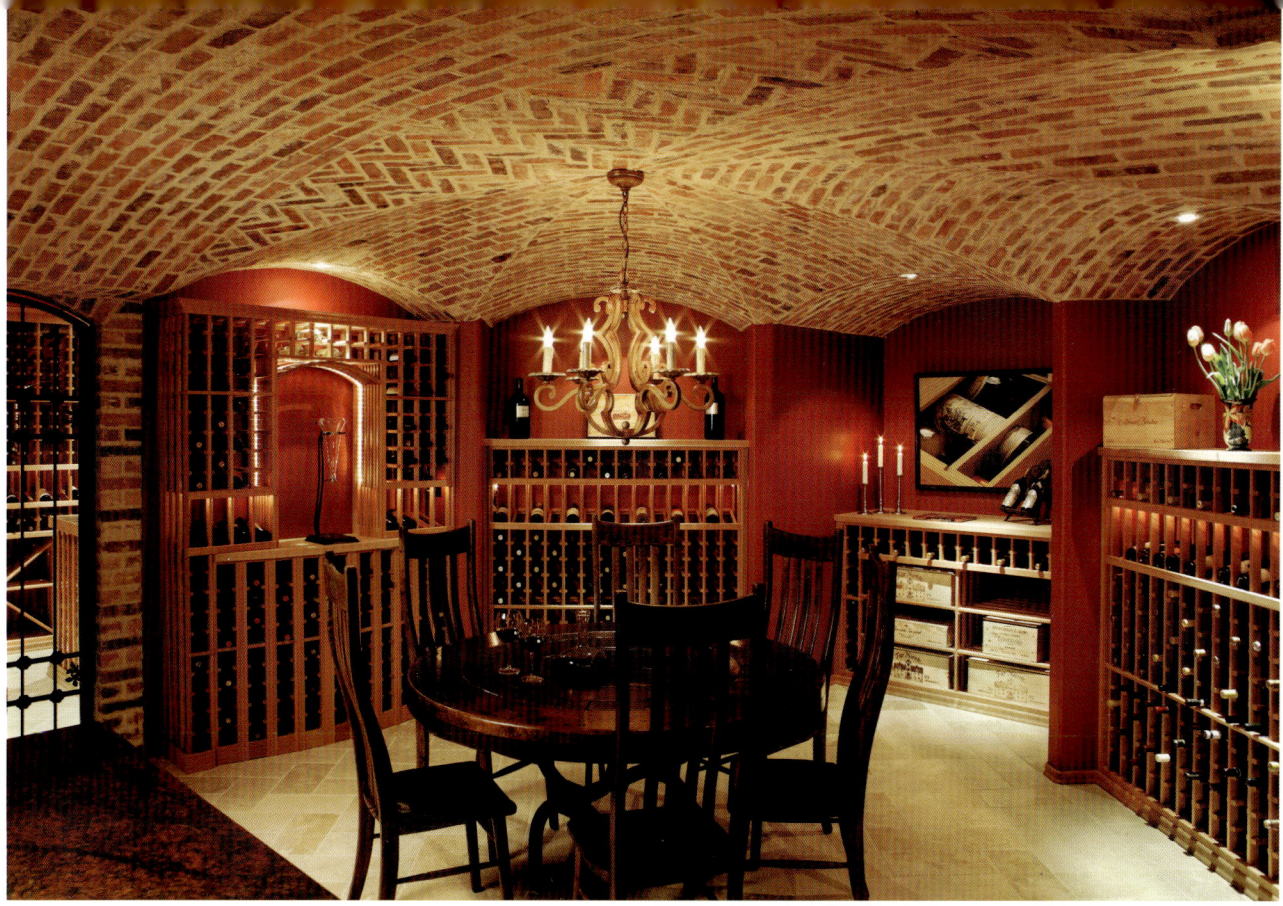

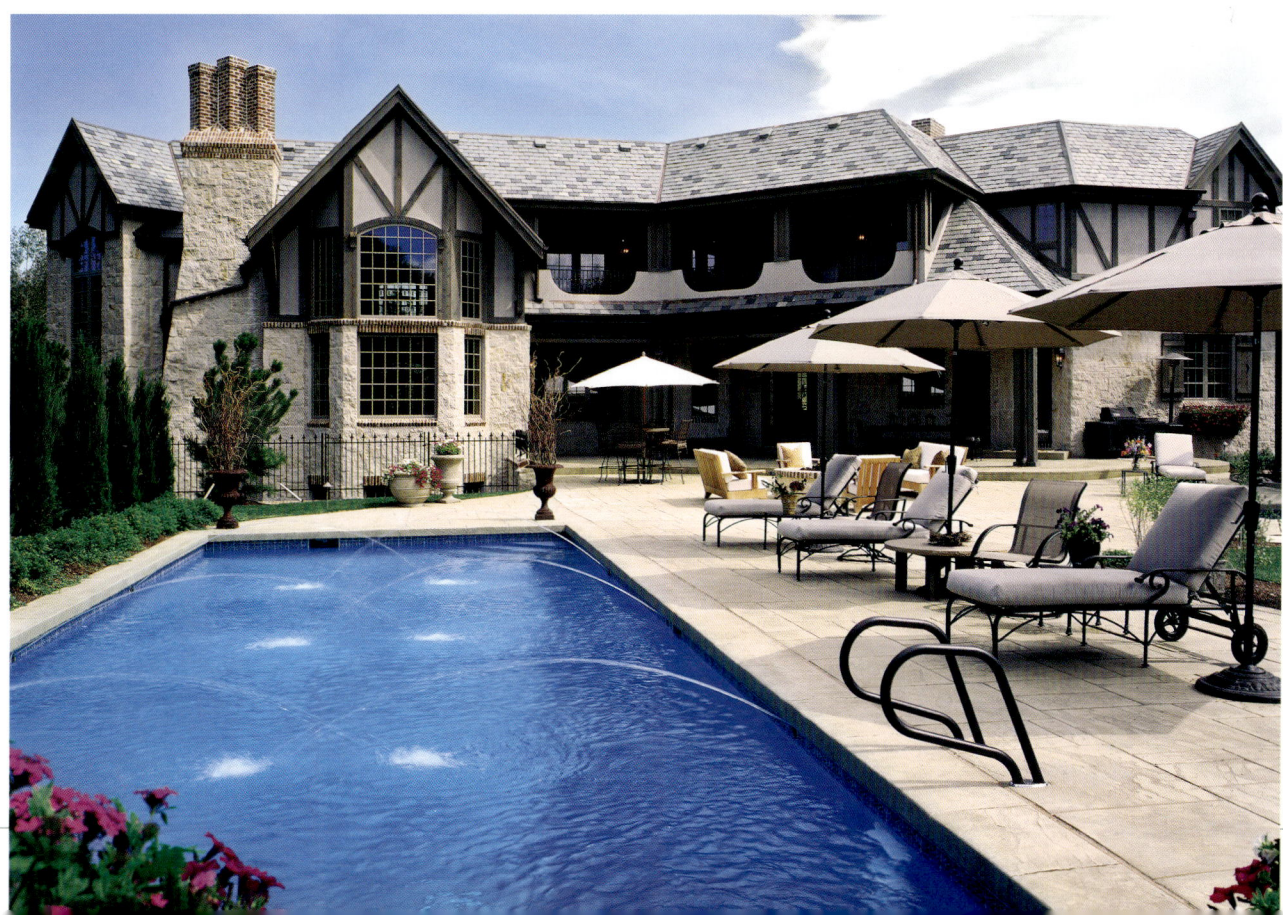

TOP RIGHT:
Intimate wine cellar, vault and tasting room with brick gothic ceiling detail.
Photograph by Ron Ruscio

BOTTOM RIGHT:
Old World English Tudor with modern, luxurious amenities.
Photograph by Ron Ruscio

FACING PAGE LEFT:
Welcoming and inviting barrel brick entry with custom iron work.
Photograph by Ron Ruscio

FACING PAGE RIGHT:
Old World materials in a beautiful Tudor with a French contemporary interior.
Photograph by Ron Ruscio

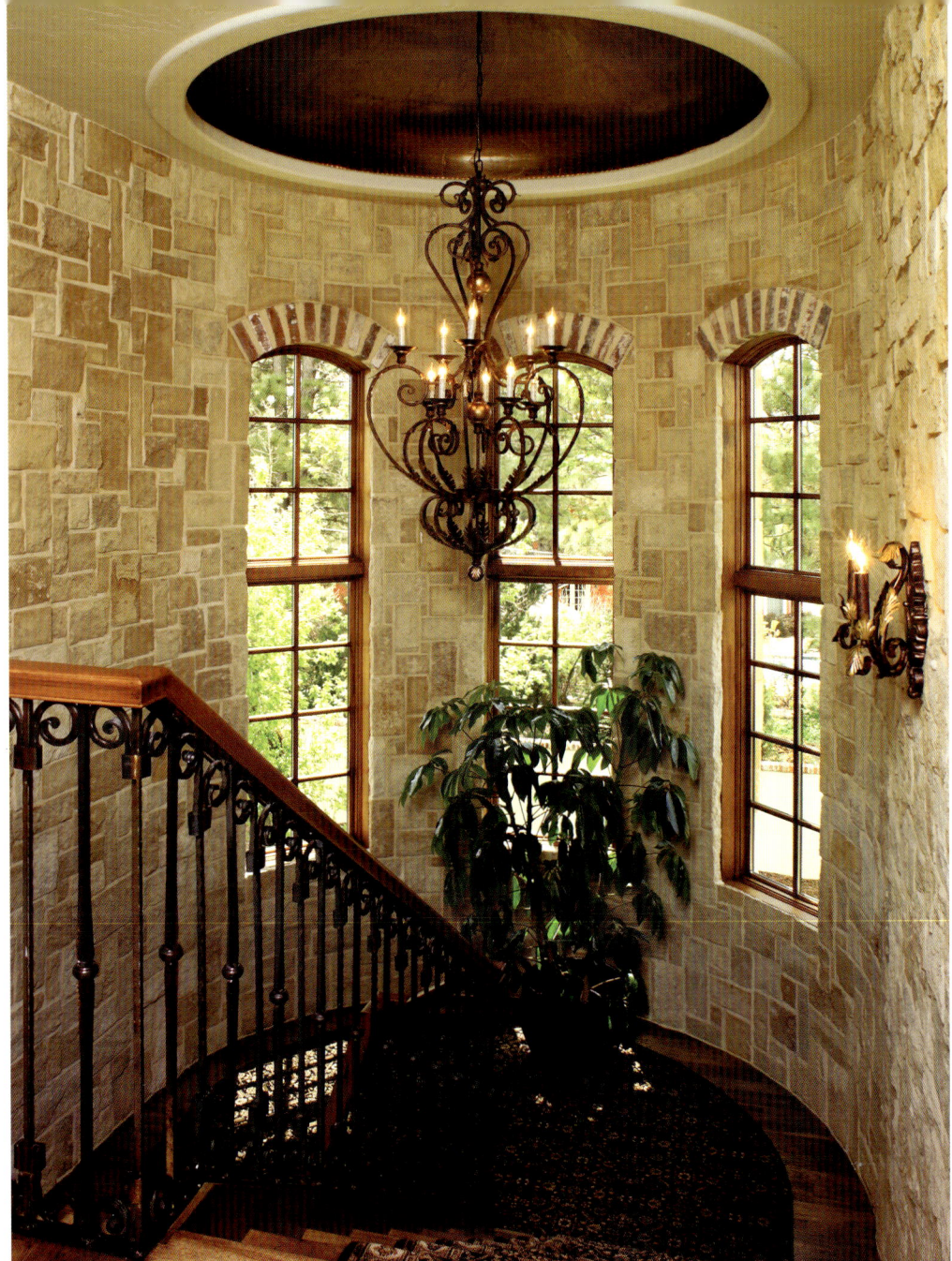
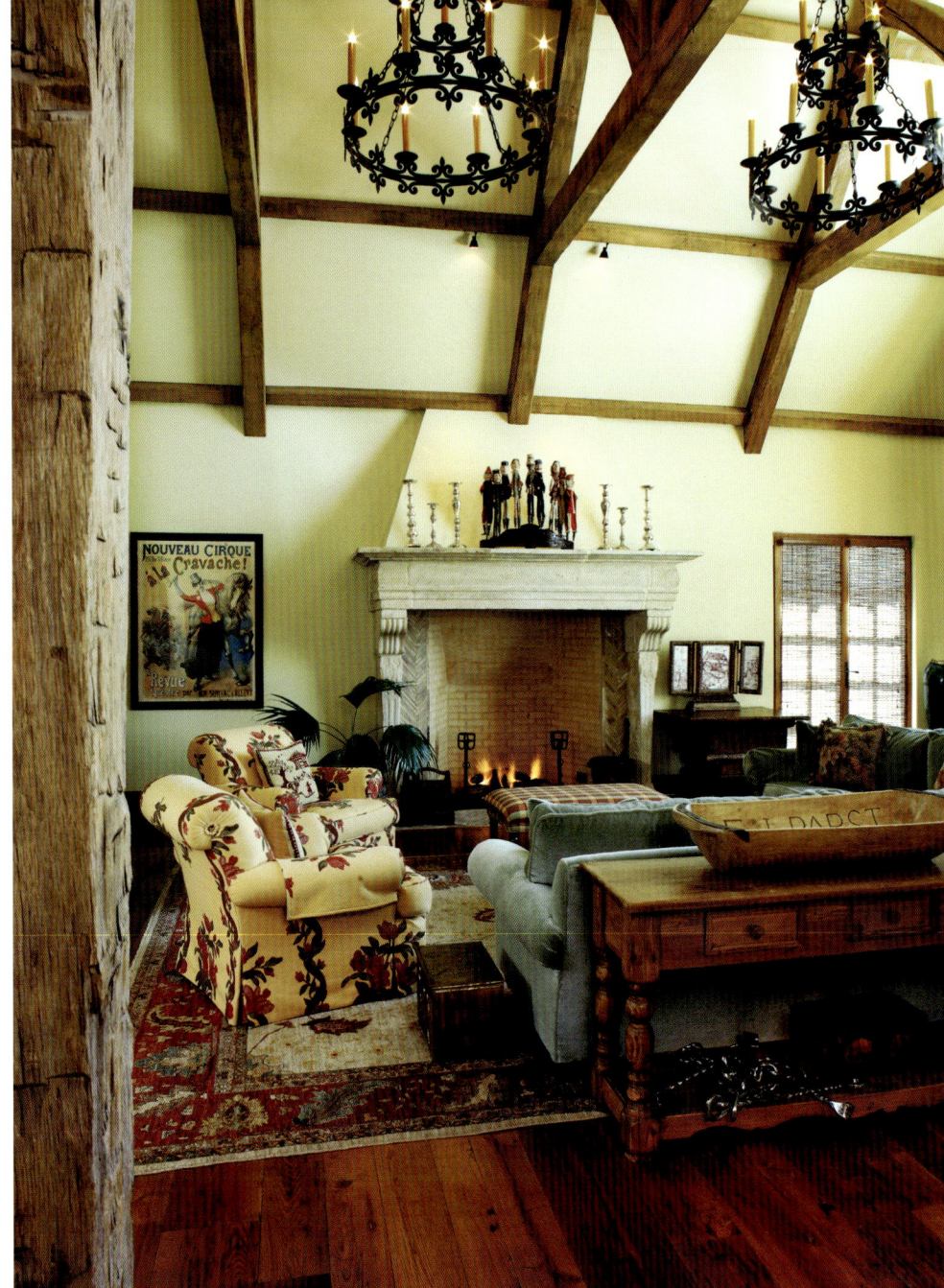

ABOVE LEFT:
Immaculate staircase with custom iron, stone walls, arched windows and domed chandelier.
Photograph by Ron Ruscio

ABOVE RIGHT:
Beamed great room with reclaimed materials and French architectural elements.
Photograph by Ron Ruscio

FACING PAGE TOP:
French Country chateau with Kansas limestone, an English roof and German windows.
Photograph by Ron Ruscio

FACING PAGE BOTTOM:
Kitchen blending old with new–two islands with top of the line appliances built in as furniture and imported, reclaimed materials.
Photograph by Ron Ruscio

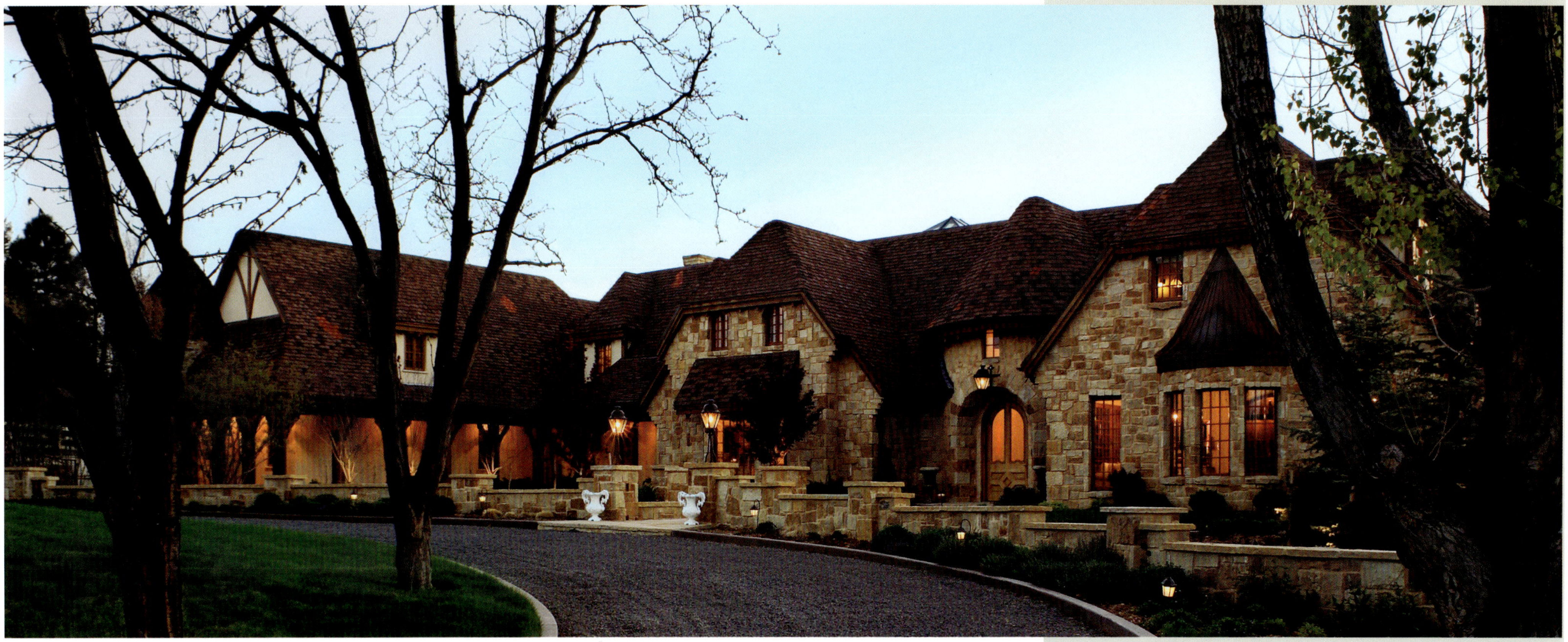

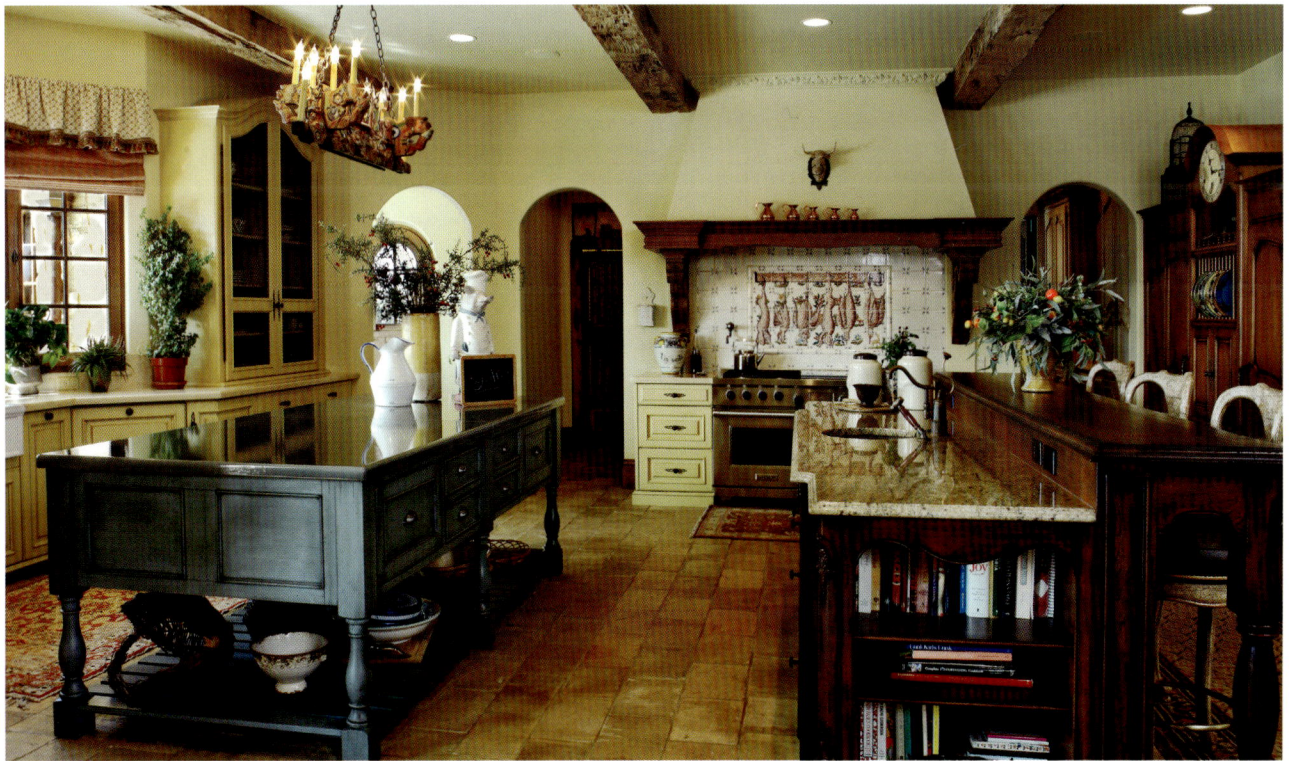

Q&A
more about lynn...

NAME ONE THING MOST PEOPLE DON'T KNOW ABOUT YOU?
In the 1970s, I was a professional race car driver. This experience benefited me in the custom home building business because it instilled in me a strong attention to detail, competitive spirit and appropriate risk taking.

WHAT ONE ELEMENT OF STYLE OR PHILOSOPHY HAVE YOU STUCK WITH FOR YEARS THAT STILL WORKS FOR YOU TODAY?
Timeless, European, Old World architecture never goes out of style.

HARRISON CUSTOM BUILDERS, LTD.
LYNN & PAM HARRISON
1500 West Thomas Avenue
Englewood, CO 80110
303.471.9543
f: 303.471.9544
www.harrisoncustombuilders.com

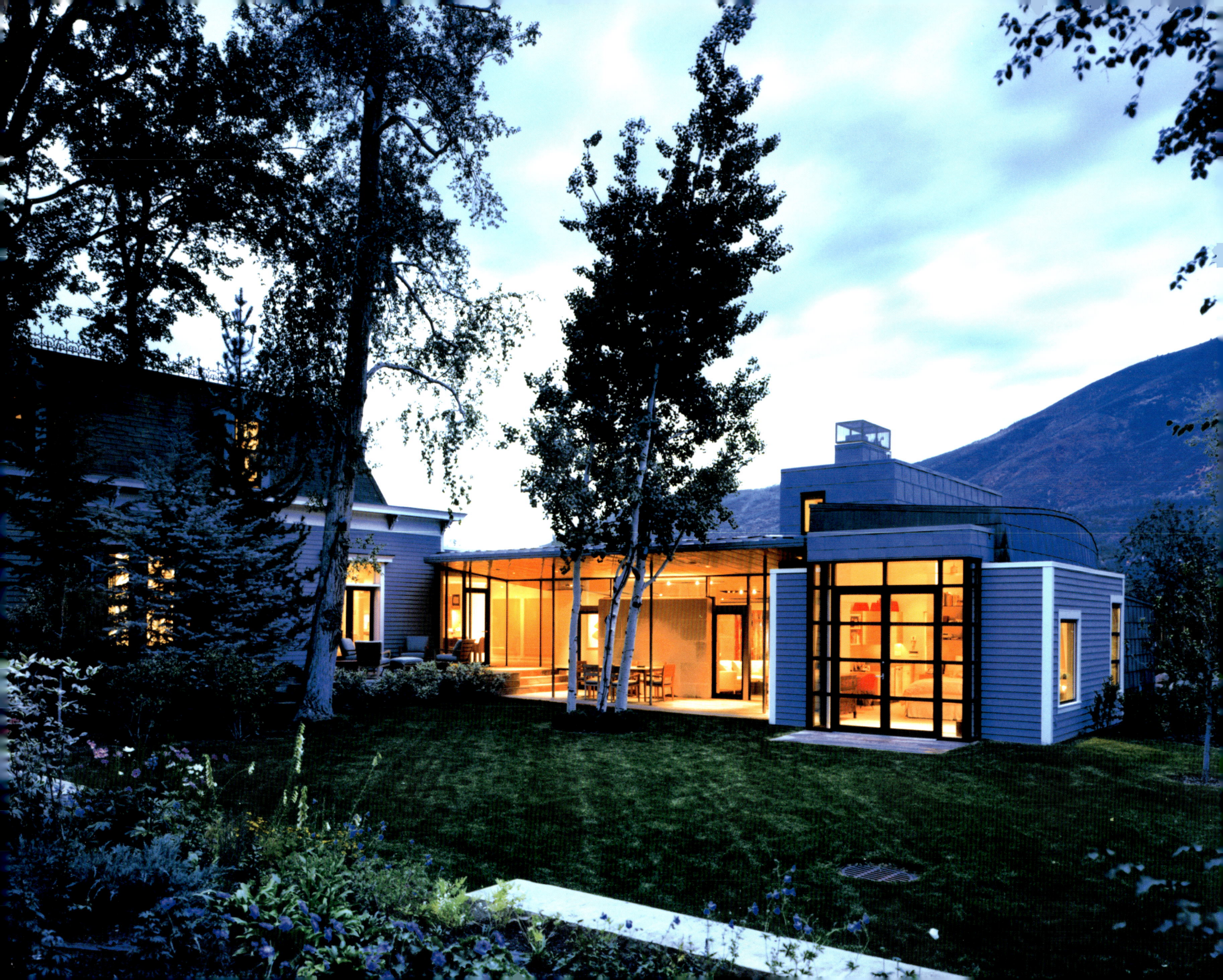

HARRY TEAGUE

HARRY TEAGUE ARCHITECTS

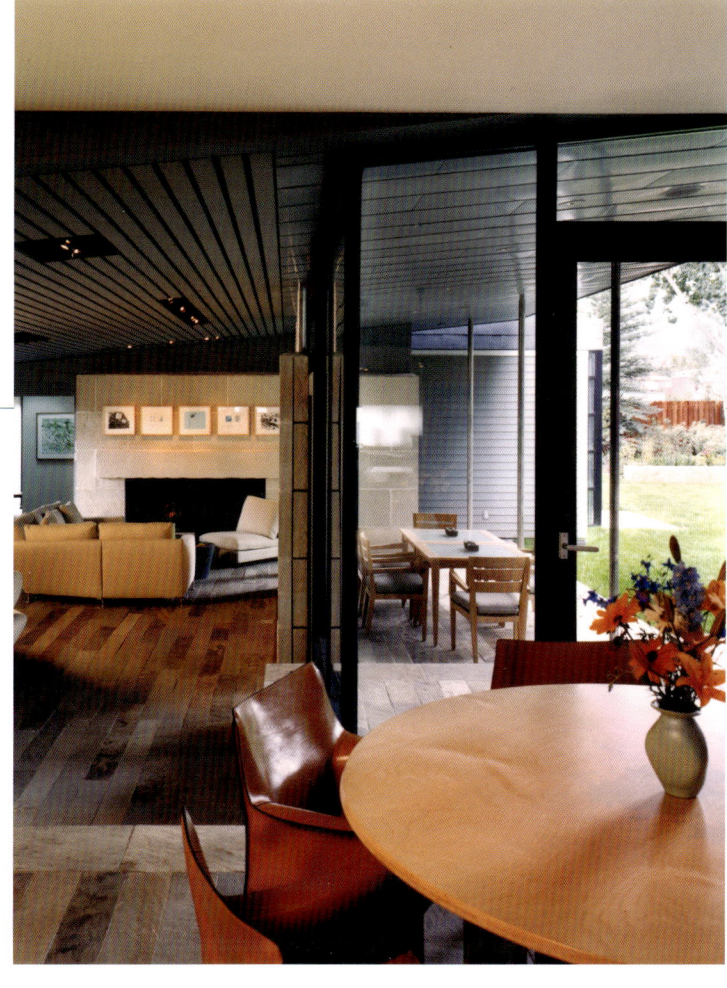

"Every house is a balance between practical needs and your dreams," says Aspen architect Harry Teague. Like an interpreter of dreams, he feels the architect must become a medium between the fantasies of a client's dreams and the realities of a physical building. The most successful houses then, are a result of the most poetic and thoughtful interpretation of these dreams combined with the most practical and ingenious solution to the practical problems.

When Harry first saw the West as an architecture student from the East Coast he was enthralled by the complexity of the Mountain West vernacular and its refreshing and rather pragmatic responses to the climate and available materials.

Among many of his own subsequent contributions to this vernacular is the introduction of rusty corrugated raw metal as a modern building material. Harry first noticed it on the sides and roof of the 90-year-old house of a high alpine sheep ranch and began to incorporate it into his own designs in 1980. The rich plumb-colored metal is now ubiquitous throughout the West and continues to be included in his own palette as a material that will improve with age.

"Often my buildings acknowledge the large scale of the western landscape by responding to the tensions of the geologic events that shaped it, such as when one valley crosses another. This creates a house with a more engaged, powerful presence," Harry says. "I like to take cues from geography and geology, not to make a house look like a rock, but to let the building have a conversation with its surroundings. We're never going to beat the mountains at their own game; our only choice is to become part of the great big overall fabric."

ABOVE:
A "transparent" gallery connects the new wing to the old, blurring the distinction between outside and in.
Photograph by Timothy Hursley

FACING PAGE:
A glass addition to a mining era Victorian opens up thehome to spectacular mountain views.
Photograph by Timothy Hursley

HARRY TEAGUE ARCHITECTS
HARRY TEAGUE, AIA
412 North Mill Street
Aspen, CO 81611
970.925.2556
f: 970.925.7981

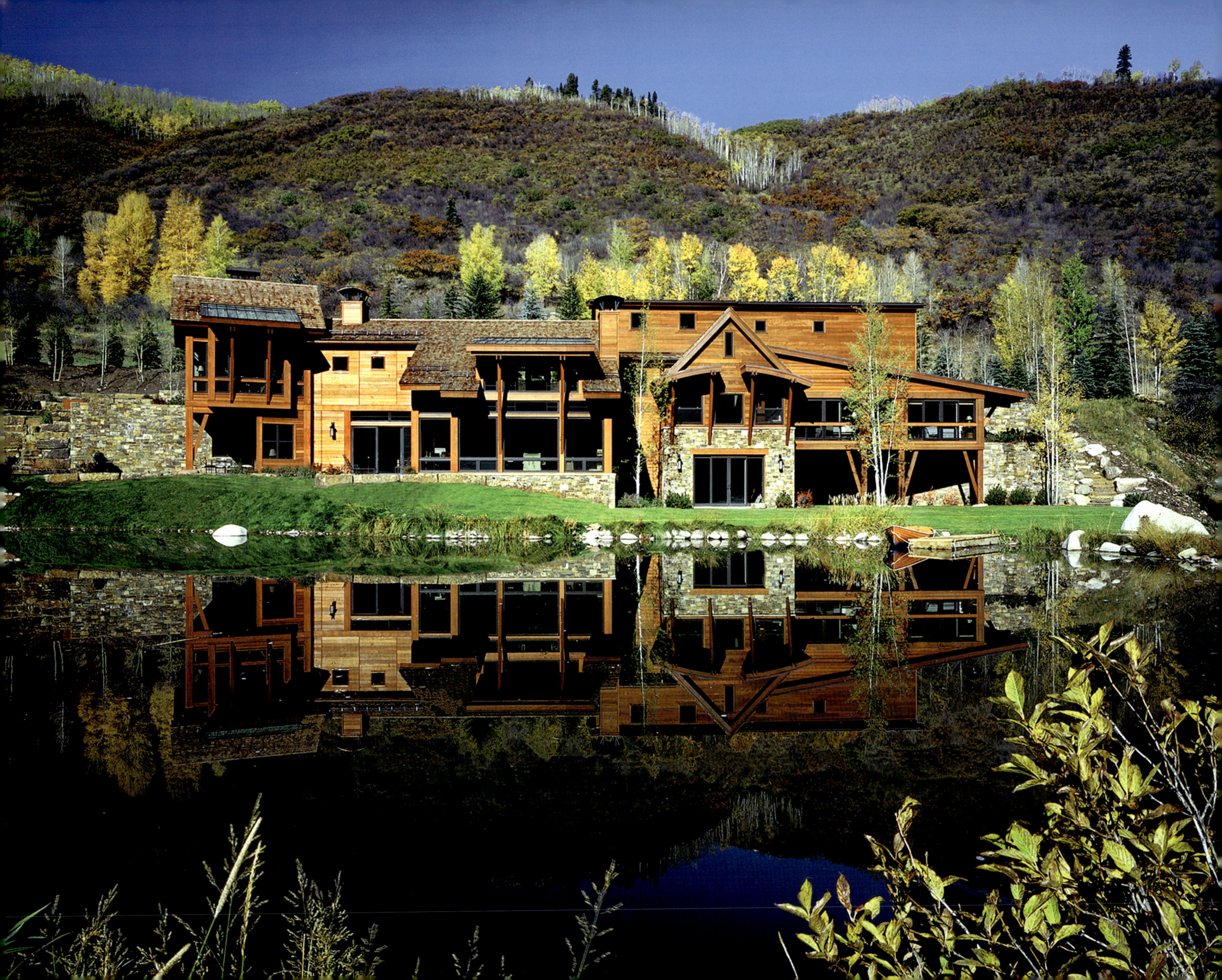

JACK WILKIE

JACK WILKIE BUILDER, INC.

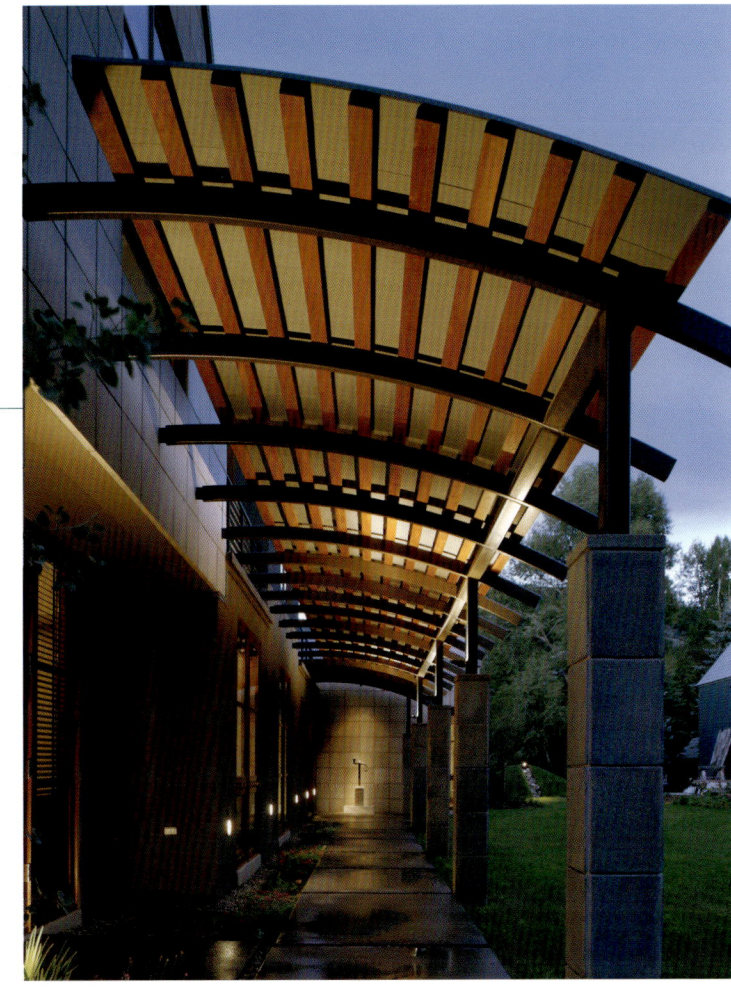

Although signature homes built by Jack Wilkie and his team at Jack Wilkie Builder, Inc. line the celebrated Roaring Fork Valley of Colorado's Rocky Mountains, the homes themselves are only a small part of what Jack has built during his 32 years in the Aspen area. Jack and his wife, Linda, have had the opportunity to forge long-lasting relationships with seasoned professionals such as architects, subcontractors, and talented craftsmen. In addition, the men and women of JWB have welcomed into their extended family numerous clients with whom they have become friends over the years.

Raised in New England, Jack migrated to Colorado to study engineering, and worked as a carpenter and a logger, experiences that imbued him with an understanding of home building from the ground up. The chance to work closely with an Aspen architect on the construction of a private residence in the exclusive Red Mountain area of Aspen propelled him into founding his own full-service building corporation in 1974, and Jack continued for the next six years to work in-house with the architect, using his design talents as well as his building skills to complete numerous custom homes including his own. The company still revolves around its original principles as a close-knit family corporation guided by integrity and communication with clients at every stage of the home building process.

Always the hands-on professional, directly involved in the daily operations of every JWB project, Jack is part of a team approach that includes the client, project managers, on-site supervisors and craftsmen. JWB is committed to offering its clients the information needed to make sound decisions that ultimately lead to a successful construction outcome. While Jack's emphasis on scheduling and planning helps to establish realistic completion goals, his dedication to the critical analysis and estimation of material and construction costs ensures that the client's design and budget requirements benefit from cost-effective solutions to any issue that may arise.

ABOVE:
Aspen West End.
Photograph by David Marlow

FACING PAGE:
Castle Creek near Aspen.
Photograph by Steve Mundinger

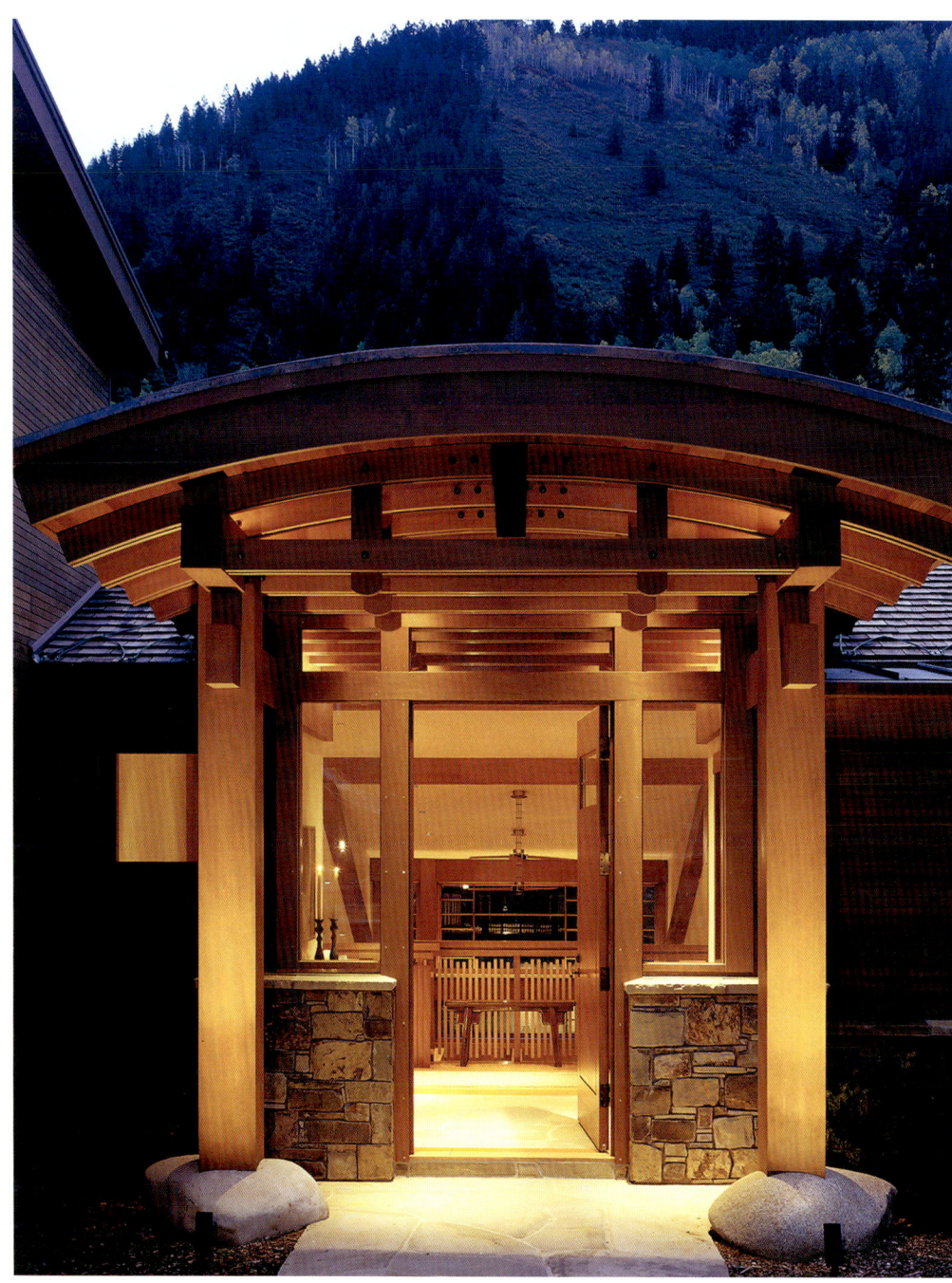
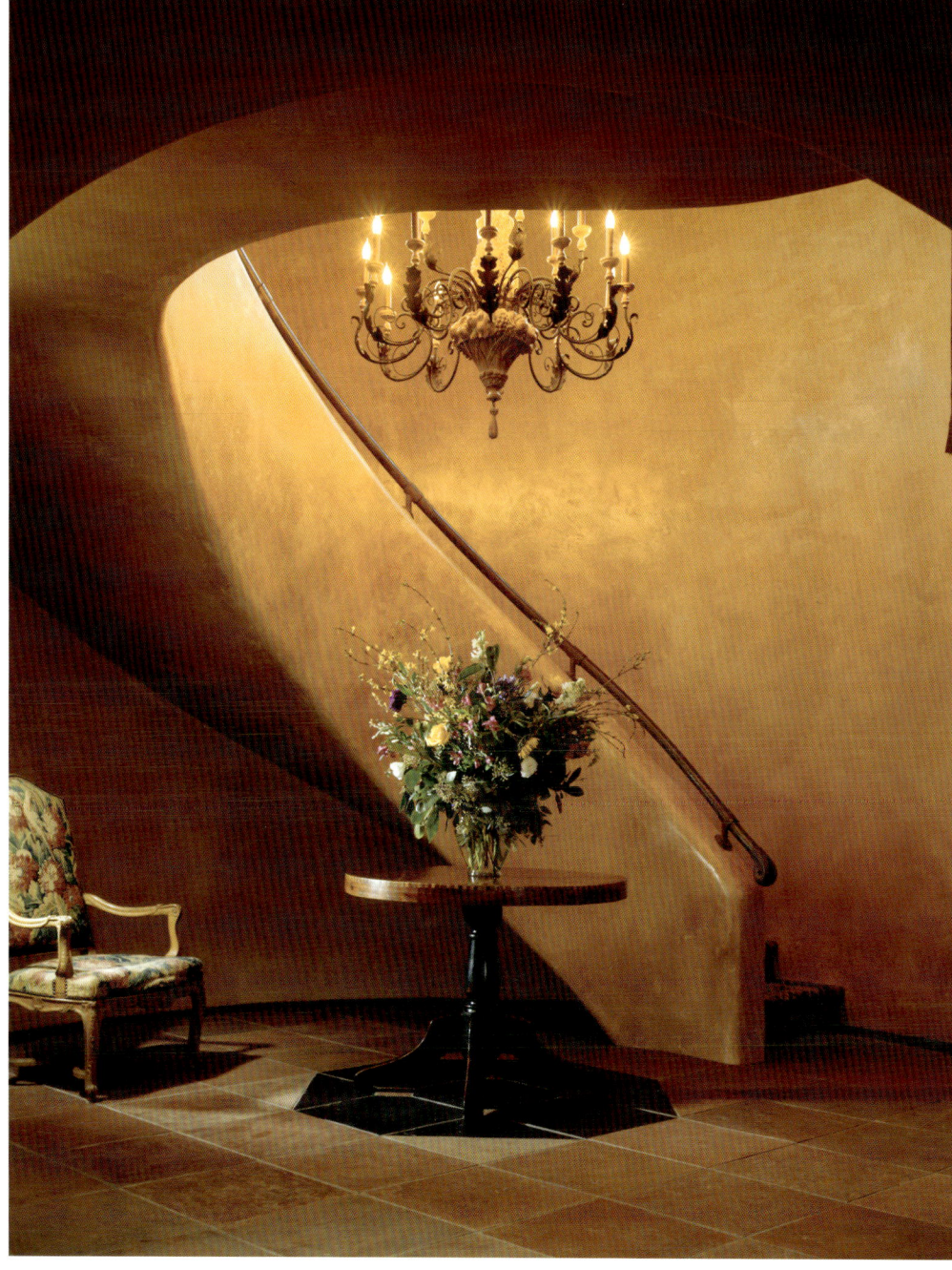

ABOVE LEFT:
Castle Creek near Aspen.
Photograph by Steve Mundigner

ABOVE RIGHT:
The Divide in Snowmass Village.
Photograph by David Marlow

FACING PAGE:
Wood Run in Snowmass Village slope side.
Photograph by Robert Shafer

The professionals at JWB value clients' dream home wishes and expectations. Whether working in conjunction with the client's architect or guiding the client in the selection of an architectural firm, Jack's team strives to remain true to the client's vision. This dedication is validated by the many clients for whom JWB has completed multiple projects, including multi-generational members of one family who put their faith in Jack to complete seven homes for them.

Jack's rigorous devotion to detail in management and construction processes translates into a deep a passion for the aesthetics seen in JWB custom homes, several of which have been featured in *Architectural Digest* and other publications. Designed by an array of sought-after architects, JWB's new and remodeling projects embrace a variety of styles from log-accented and elegant mountain rustic, to high-tech contemporary and European-influenced designs. Native woods such as clear fir, redwood or cedar, as well as stones from quarries all over the map, frequently accent the stunning architecture and contribute to a unique mountain style enhanced with contemporary flair. Hand-textured plaster and stone interiors, in conjunction with timber trusses and other accents such as forged iron, create and define a particular space, thus lending character to these distinctive dwellings.

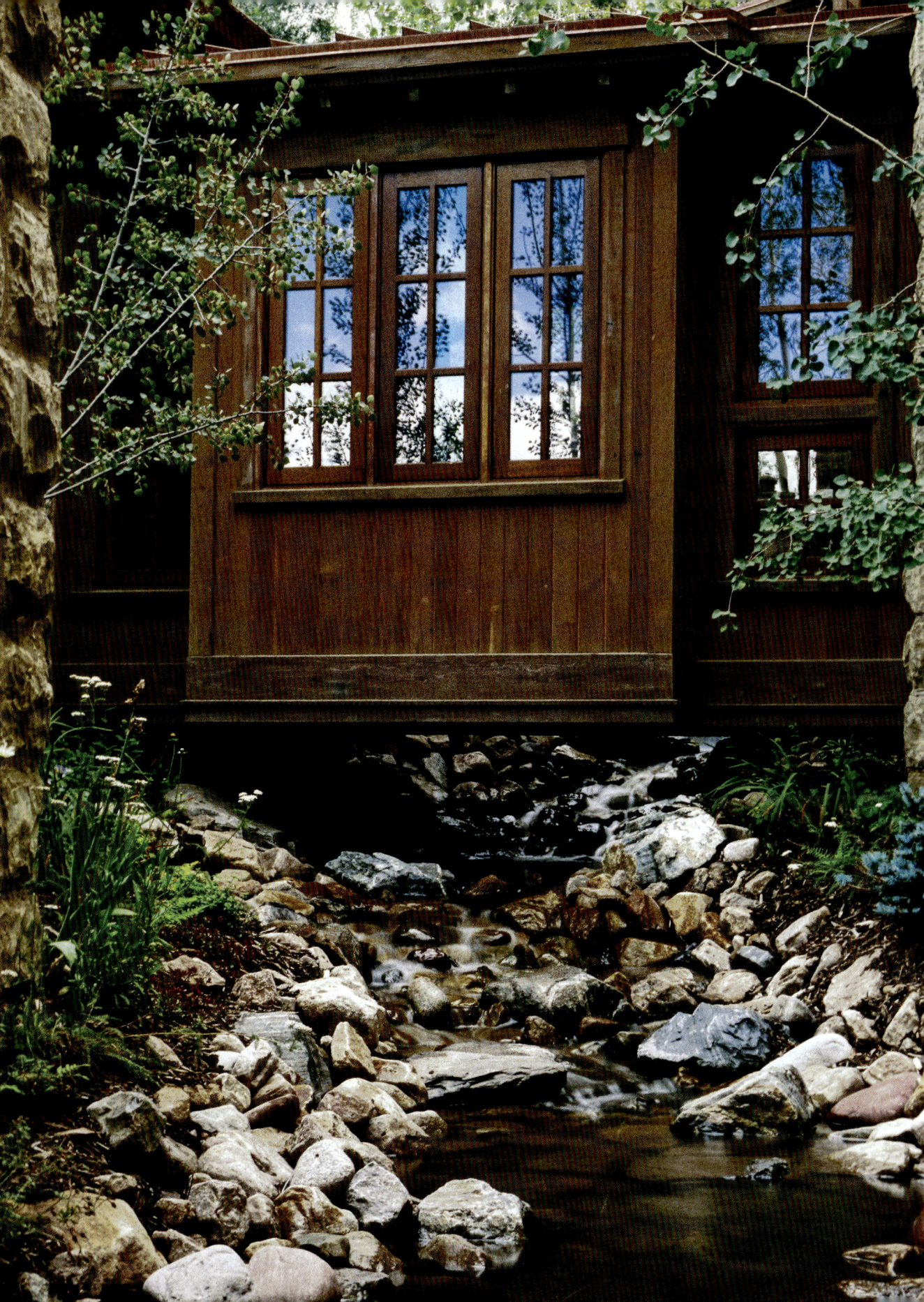

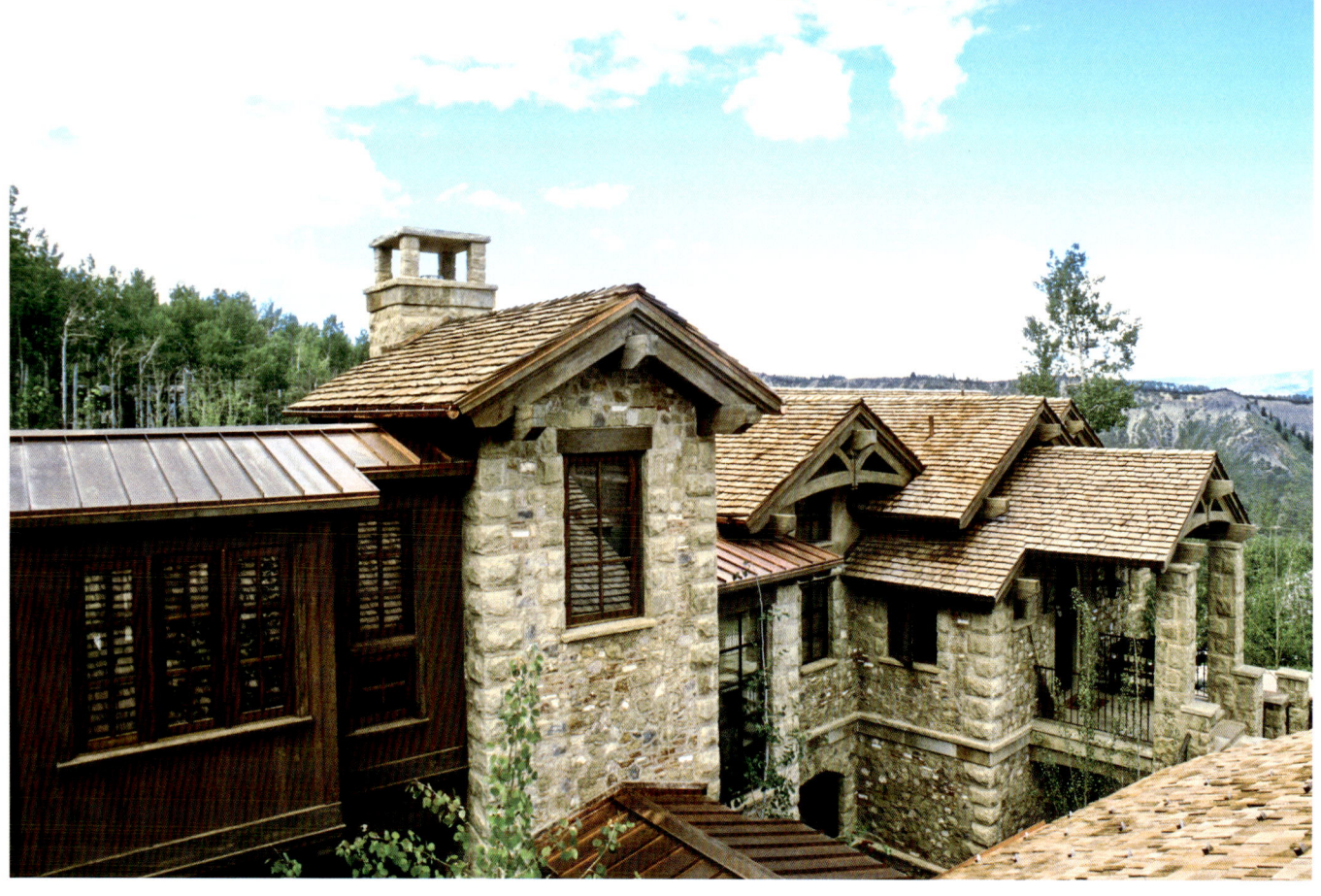

Another JWB hallmark is the abundant use of glass which opens these homes to the views of the mountain and river settings of the Roaring Fork Valley, views often more spectacular than the homeowners' imaginations. Custom crafted windows from Europe, Canada and the U.S., provide a distinctive method for setting a JWB home apart from any other. Millwork, cabinetry and stair systems are specialties of JWB's in-house craftsmen, offering clients unlimited selections of exotic woods, iron and glass for stair systems in circular, free-standing, open rise and rail system designs.

It's a treat to build in the Roaring Fork Valley, Jack acknowledges. "Many clients who've come to spend their lives here have become our close friends. It's always a great pleasure for us to revisit their dream homes and to see them enjoy what we've created as a team."

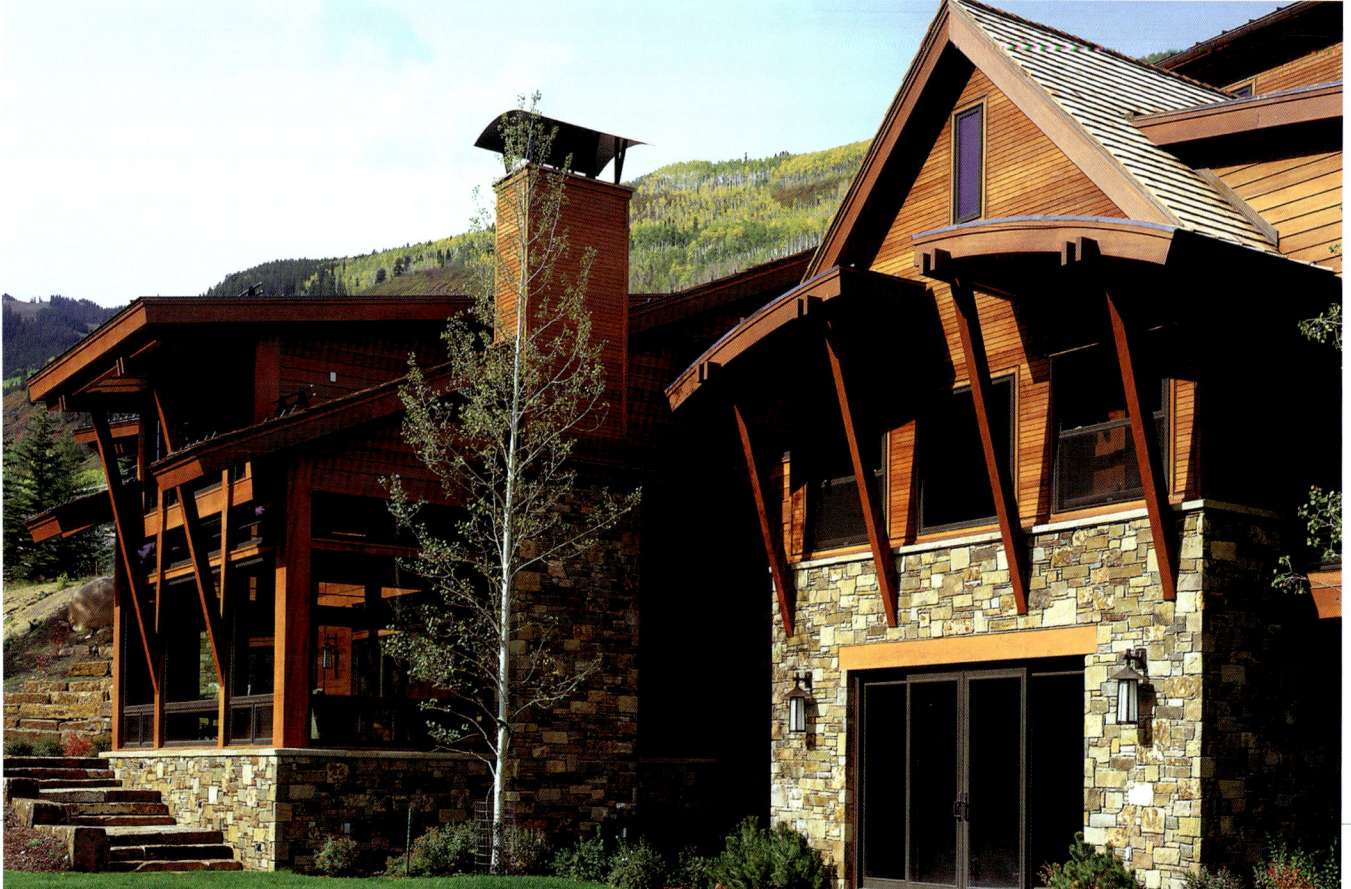

TOP LEFT:
Wood Run in Snowmass Village slope side.
Photograph by Robert Shafer

BOTTOM LEFT:
Castle Creek near Aspen.
Photograph by Steve Mundinger

FACING PAGE:
Aspen West End.
Photograph by David Marlow

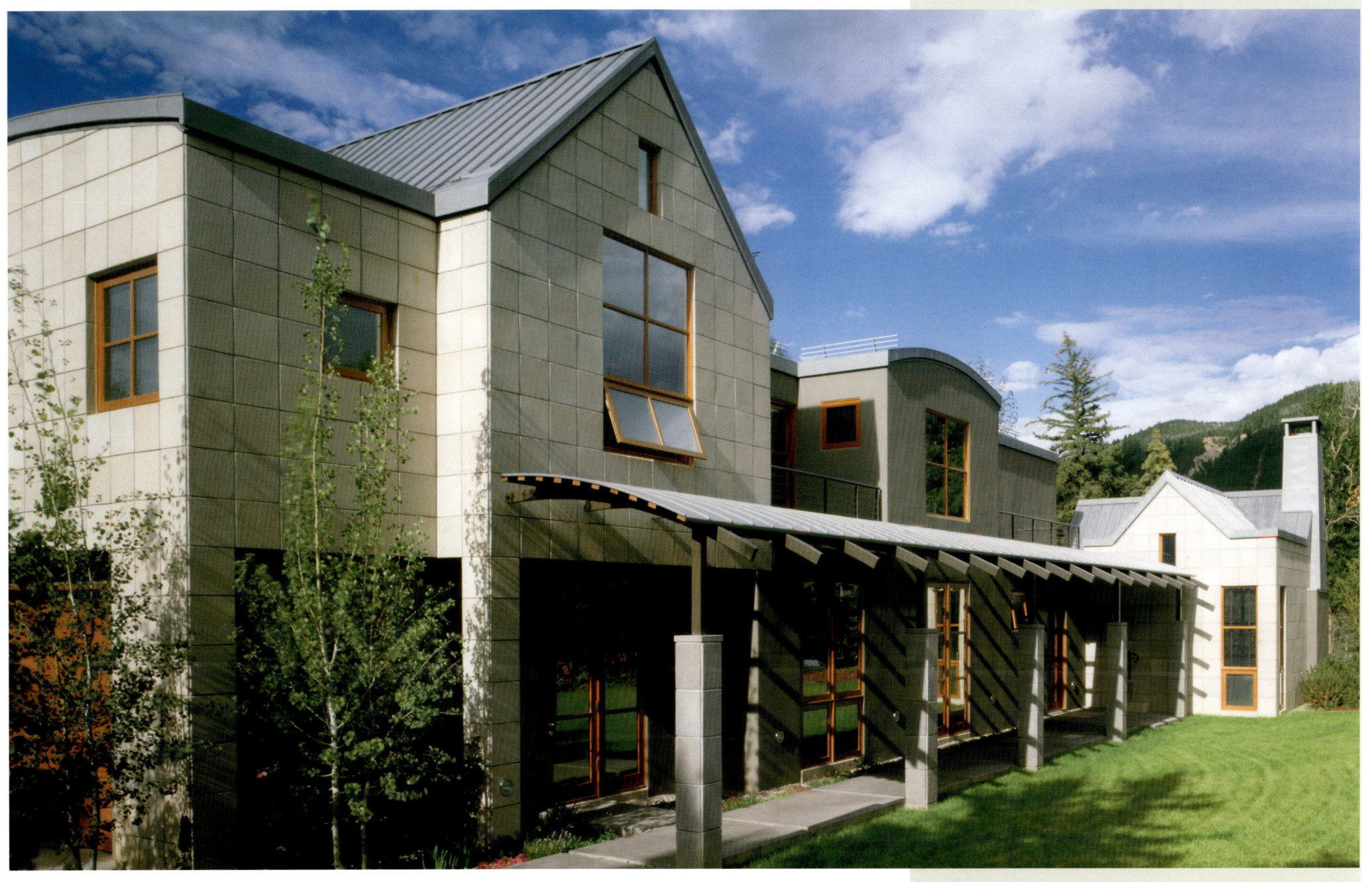

JACK WILKIE BUILDER, INC.
JACK WILKIE
0020 Sunset Drive, Suite 3
Basalt, CO 81621
970.927.4226
f: 970.927.4712
www.jwbinc.com

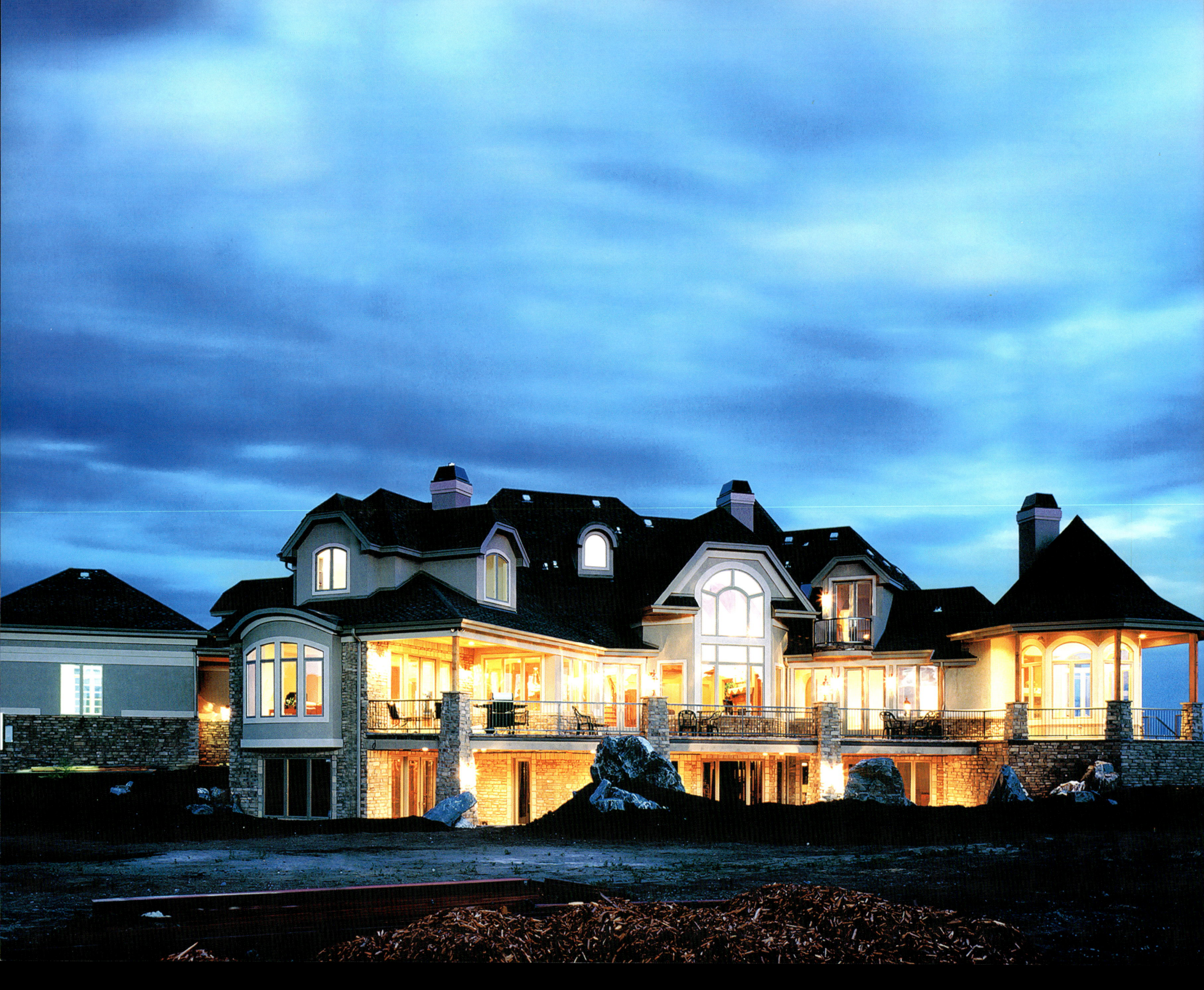

JEFFREY K. ABRAMS

JEFFREY K. ABRAMS ARCHITECT P.C.

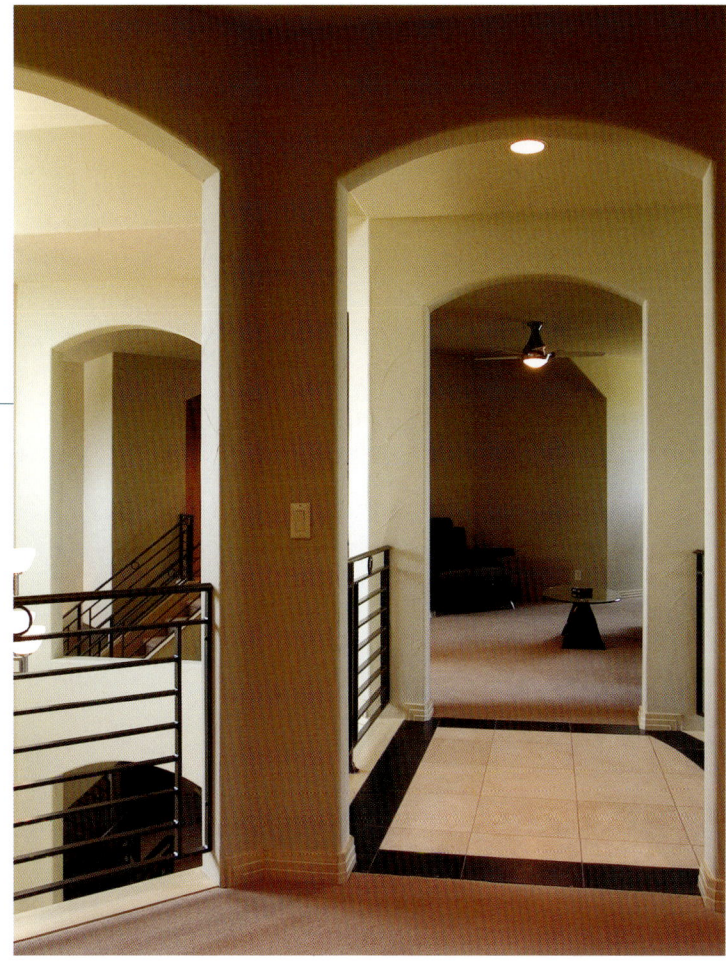

Jeff Abrams grew up in northern New Jersey, confident that if he studied architecture a world of related disciplines would take him down an artistic career path. He entered the Yale School of Architecture and fell in love with the renowned Paul Rudolph structure housing the school. The creative use of space and light in the building had him hooked on architecture.

Immediately after graduation in 1972, Jeff headed to Boulder, visions of mountains and streams he had visited still illuminated in his mind. After practicing at a couple of Denver and Boulder firms, Jeff joined the University of Colorado Planning Staff. In 1974, upon achieving architectural registration, he established his own firm designing and building cutting-edge custom residences. JKA's practice blossomed and the firm now designs for clients all along the Front Range and occasionally in the mountains.

The individuality of each client's agenda, their needs and desires, captivates Jeff and informs his design work even in the smallest remodels. Another essential piece of the JKA program is the property itself, land that has its own microclimate with a unique set of various topographic features, vegetation and views. Jeff often has risen to the challenge of creating viable and exciting solutions for sites that are "just about impossible to build on" such as a house on a long narrow lot for which JKA designed a series of linked spaces, thus giving all rooms direct access to the outdoor landscape.

After meeting with prospective clients to ensure there is good chemistry between architect and client, JKA prompts them to create an informed list elaborating their specific wishes for the home, such as how they project the location of certain spaces and their inter-relationship to each other. Since there aren't many available courses detailing the architect/client relationship, JKA encourages clients to ask meaningful questions about the firm's approach in the initial interview.

ABOVE:
This home, while a clean-cut traditional on the exterior is a tour de force of contemporary vertical and horizontal spaces linked through a series of truncated plaster arches.
Photograph by Don Murray Photography Inc.

FACING PAGE:
European-style custom residence for a maturing family of four, located close to the foothills of the Rockies west of Denver. The view from afar reminds one of a country château in France.
Photograph by Philip Wegener Photography

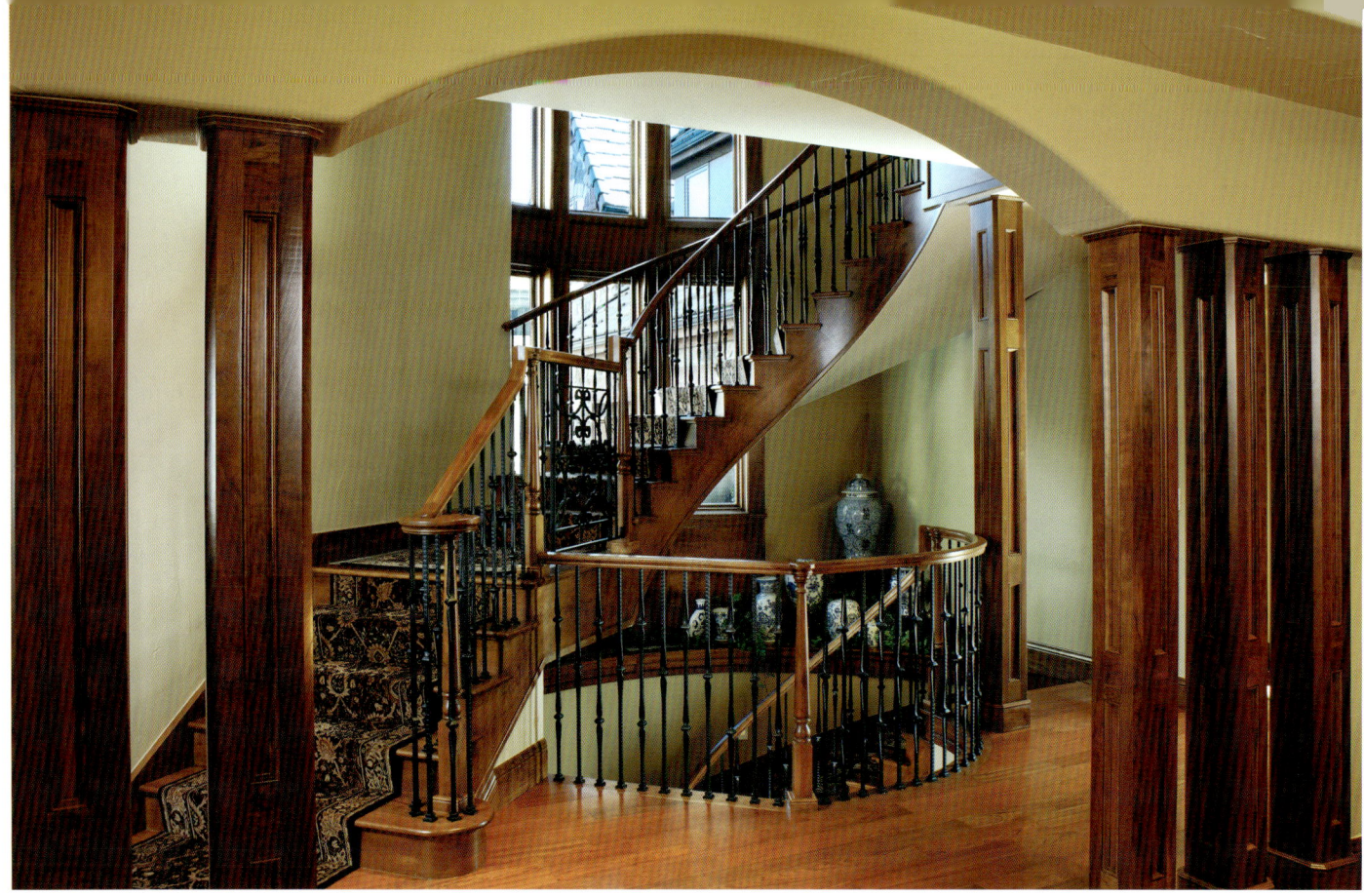

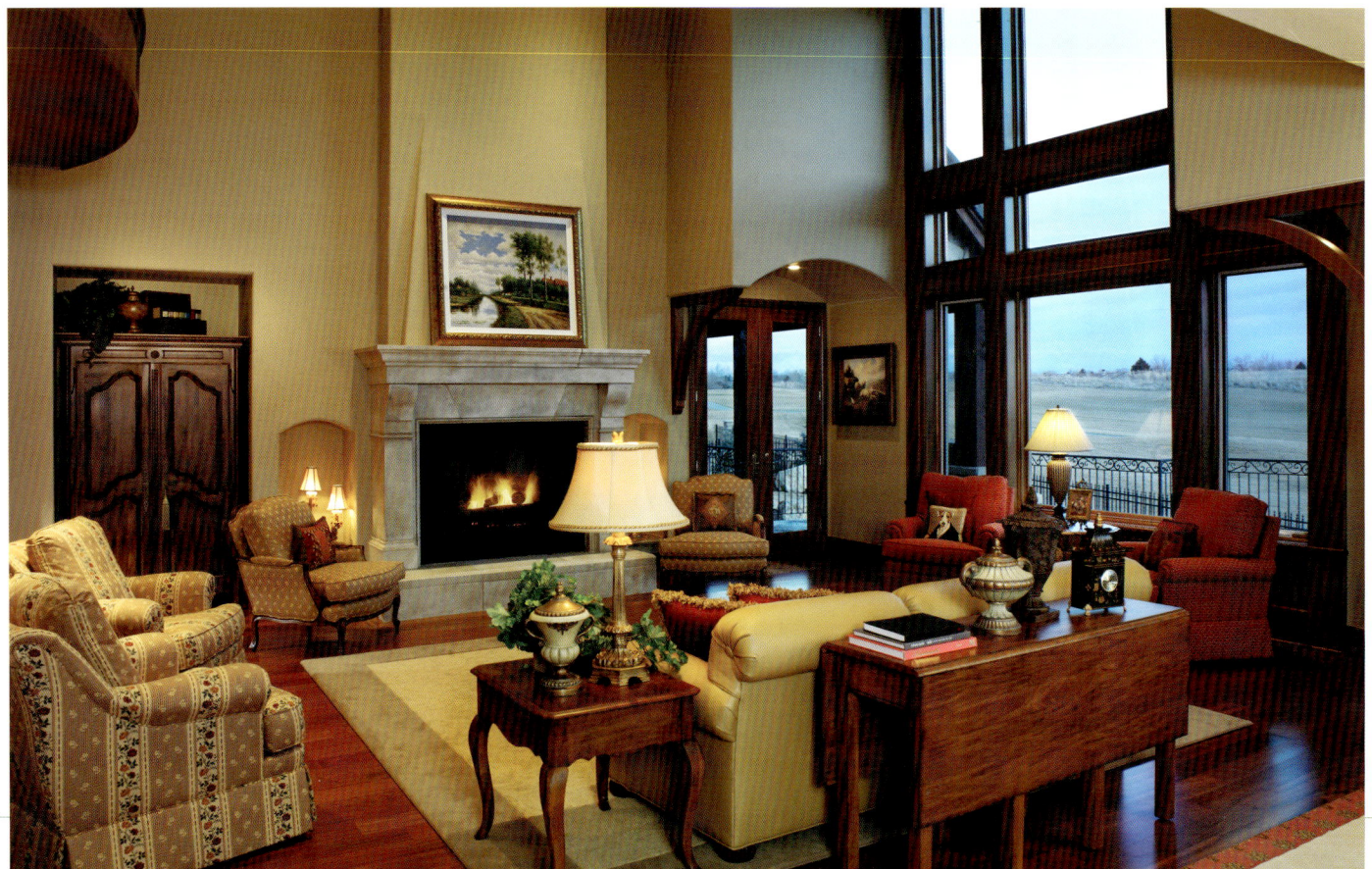

Jeff's experience in construction and design/build lends itself to an acute understanding of materials and the design of contemporary homes. Yet JKA just as often creates comfortable designs for a varied and discriminating clientele who favor more traditional styles such as Tudor, Shingle-style, Craftsmen, Normandy, Victorian, Country French, Mediterranean and Italianate.

"I like to design tasteful houses that sit in their environment in appropriate fashion and don't shout too loudly," Jeff says. "If they're out on the plains, we design them to stretch out, to nestle into the ground and settle into the low landscape with walls that reach out, and blur the difference between inside and out."

TOP LEFT:
The first view inside this dramatic traditional design invites one inside from the rush of natural light that cascades down and through the dynamic curved wood and iron staircase.
Photograph by Ron Ruscio photography

BOTTOM LEFT:
A most comfortable gathering room accented by the projecting curved balcony, limestone fireplace and golf course views.
Photograph by Ron Ruscio Photography

FACING PAGE TOP:
A traditional home in north Denver stretched out along a fairway to create views and plan flexibility. A large front porch and auto court anchor the plan at opposite ends.
Photographer: Jeff Abrams

FACING PAGE BOTTOM:
This comfortable Euro kitchen leads to outdoor "golf course" eating and pantries on the way to a formal dining room.
Photographer: Ron Ruscio Photography

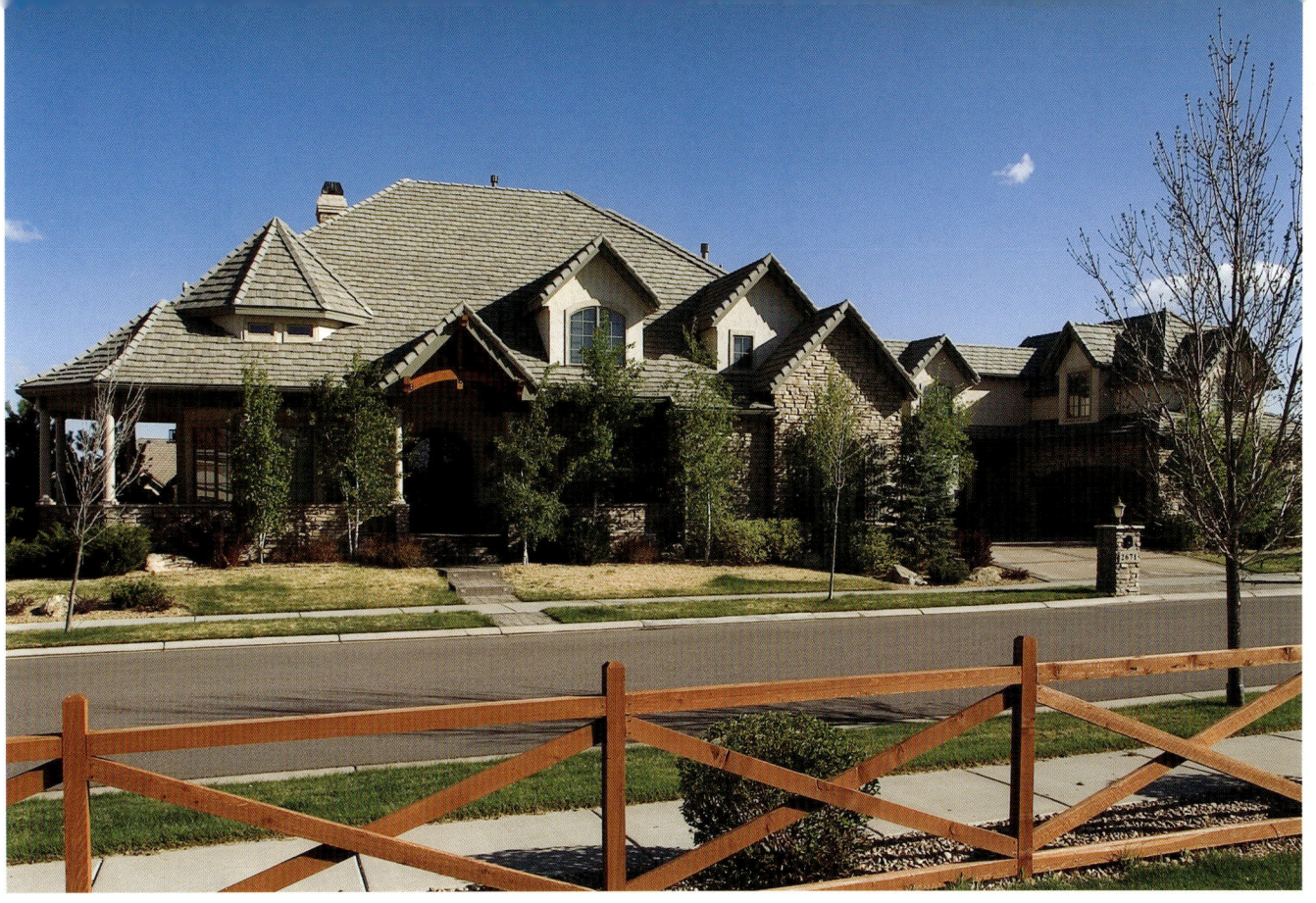

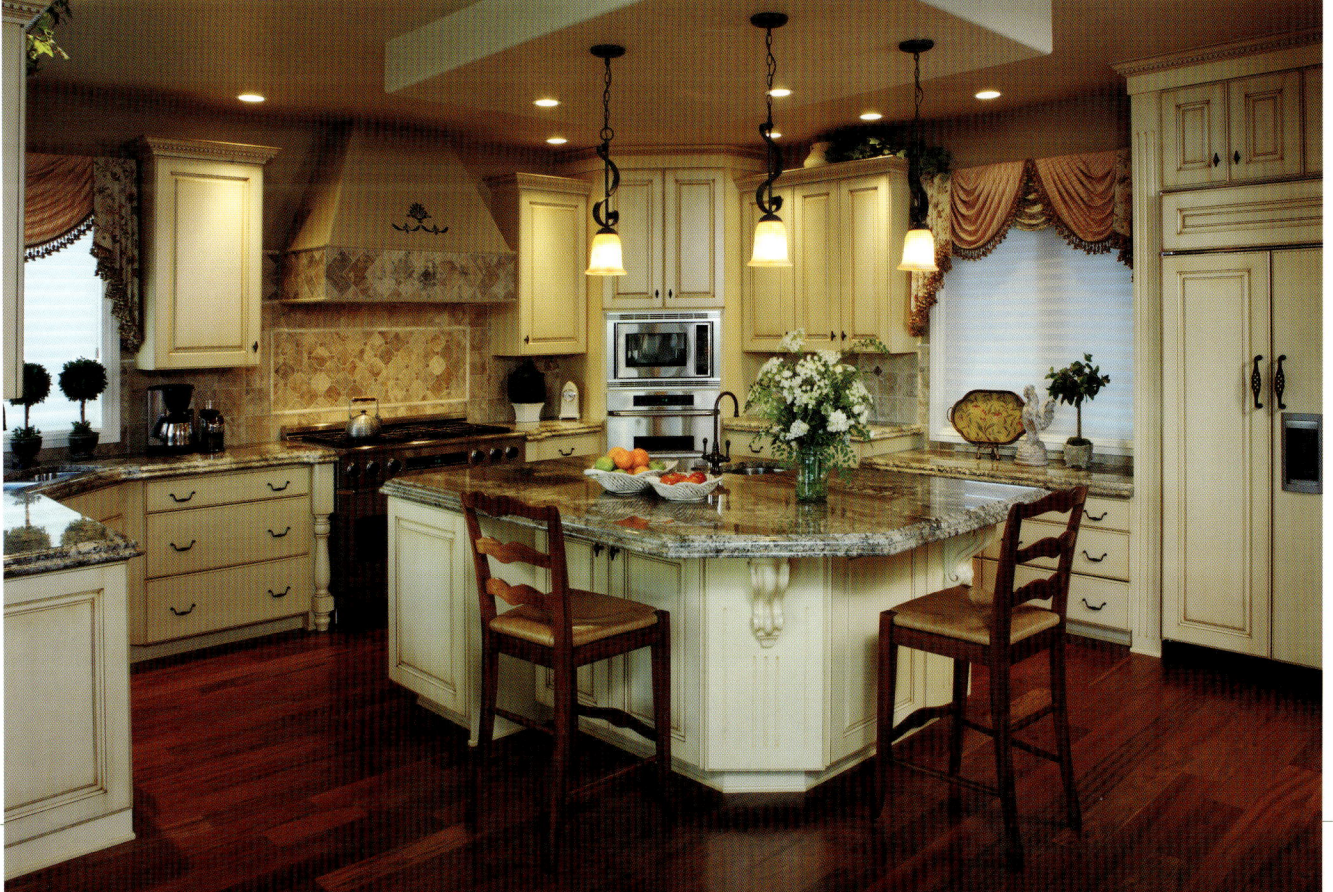

Q&A
more about jeffrey...

WHO HAS HAD THE BIGGEST INFLUENCE ON YOUR CAREER?
My Hungarian grandfather.

WHAT SIZE IS YOUR COMPANY?
In addition to me, there are two skilled and diligent architects, Melissa Baker and Maria Wells, a CAD-draftsman, and our administrative assistant, Betsy Cropley.

ANY ASSOCIATIONS OR MEMBERSHIPS YOU WOULD LIKE TO MENTION?
The National Association of Homebuilders, American Institute of Architects, The Boulder Chamber of Commerce, Boulder Flycasters and The University of Colorado Buff Club.

WHAT DESIGN TECHNIQUE DO YOU USE IN EACH OF YOUR PROJECTS?
We create buildings the old-fashioned way, in scale, allowing people to feel comfortable and have a sense of wonder. Our spaces are three-dimensional and tailored to fit people. All JKA residences take strong consideration of the human scale, shying away from overscaled innocuous spaces, so our homes have an air of the authentic.

WHAT IS THE HIGHEST COMPLIMENT YOU'VE RECEIVED PROFESSIONALLY?
Client's tell us our homes are so comfortable and our documentation and communication with builders comprehensive and complete.

NAME ONE THING PEOPLE DON'T KNOW ABOUT YOU.
I designed the world's first solar-heated church in Westminster, Colorado, in 1975.

JEFFREY K. ABRAMS ARCHITECT P.C.
JEFFREY K. ABRAMS, AIA
1526 Spruce Street
Suite 102
Boulder, CO 80302
303.440.5497
f: 303.442.0815
www.jkadesign.net

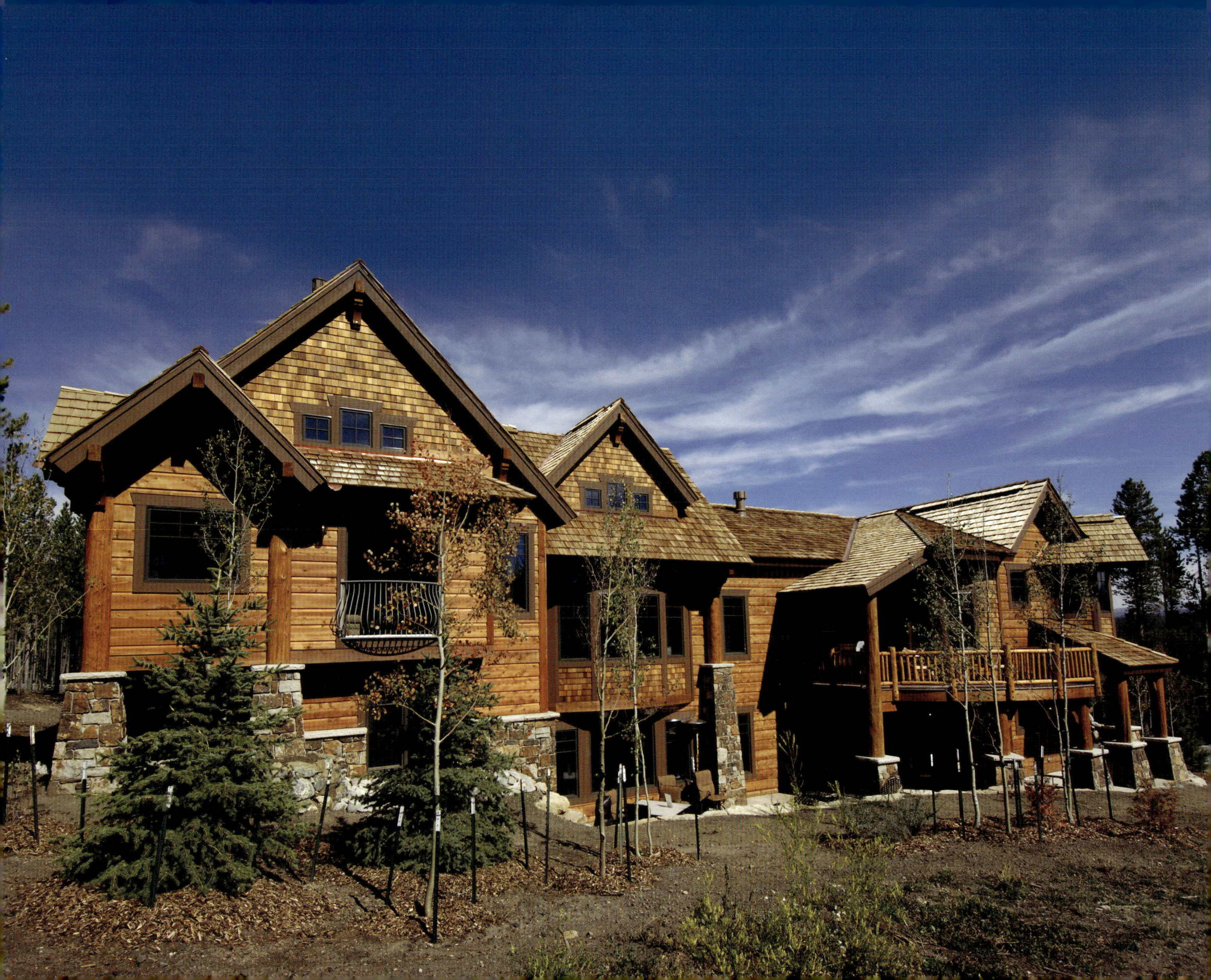

LAYNE BENNETT

JVL ASSOCIATES

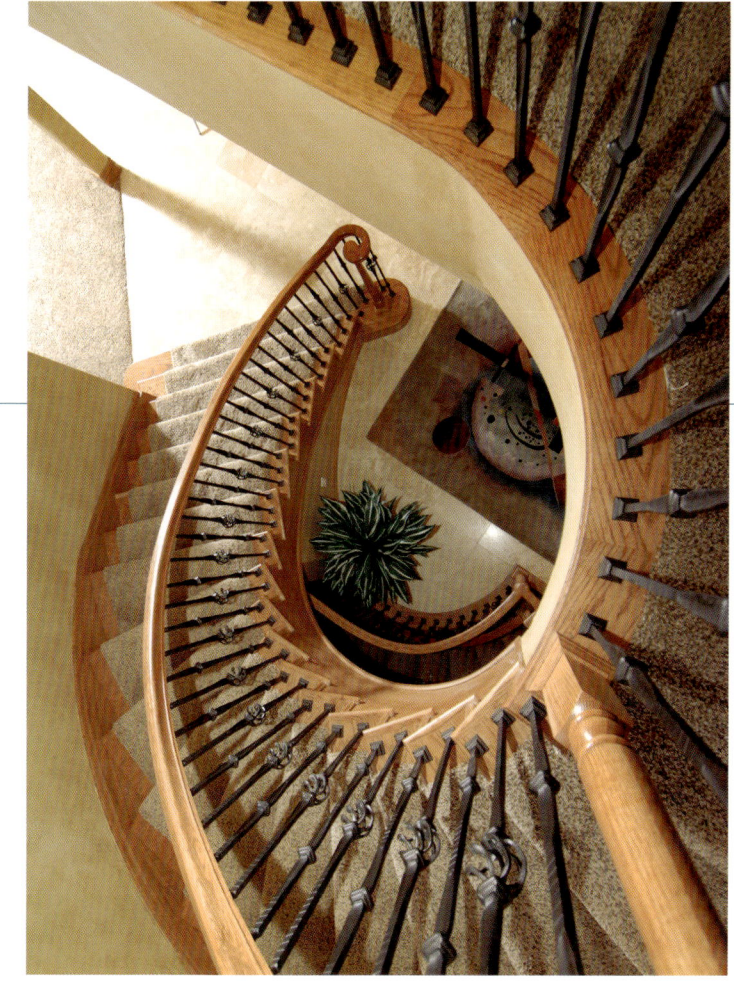

Layne Bennett's passion for designing and building beautiful homes began with his own childhood drawings of the farmhouses around him in southeastern Idaho. His detailed artwork, often depicting the imagined interiors of his rural world, served as a foundation for the keen eye that has made JVL a successful architecture and design firm.

After studying commercial art, Layne stayed in the West, drafting for a home builder in Utah. In 1984 he moved to Denver, and joined a large residential home builder as Senior Draftsman. The experience taught Layne the finer points of construction, and how all the essential elements for construction fit together, even down to counting the pieces of lumber for a flooring layout. Every detail was crucial.

A job transfer in 1987 took Layne to Southern California where he continued to design production homes. To make ends meet, Layne also moonlighted for a structural engineer as a draftsman, a move that led him into custom residential design and paved the way for his future. Layne returned to Colorado in 1993, setting in motion the events that led to the founding of JVL Associates later that year. Layne continued to draft by hand, working alone for the next two years, designing custom and production homes in the Denver area for various individuals and a few local builders.

A contract for a large residential project was the impetus for Layne to study and learn computer drafting and to begin to hire employees. JVL's current staff of nine draftsmen, business manager and accounting personnel work together to make every client's home design experience enjoyable. Layne designs custom and production homes throughout Colorado, and is making inroads into the surrounding Western states. A home, he believes, is so much more than its floor plan. It should work with and enhance its overall environment.

ABOVE:
Kramer Residence, Arvada, Colorado. Completed in spring 2005. View looking down through the main staircase.
Photograph by Michele Holland

FACING PAGE:
Nykaza House, Breckenridge, Colorado. Completed in 2005. Winner of seven awards in 2005 Summit County Parade of Homes, including "Best Overall Floor Plan" and "Best Exterior Design Elevation."
Photograph by Michele Holland

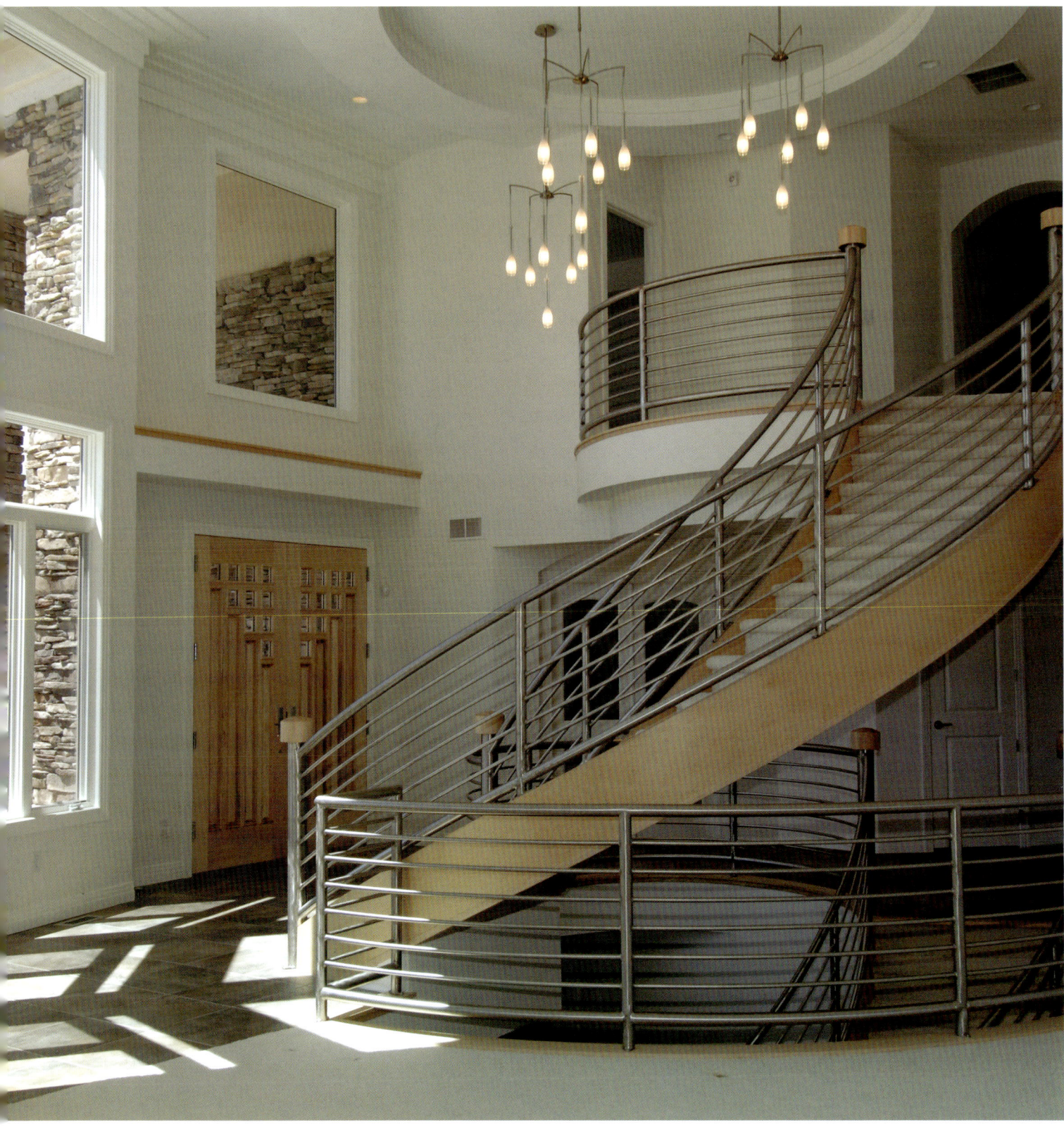

Open to the appreciation of many styles of design, Layne enjoys scouting Denver and its environs for examples of its historic and venerable architecture such as Victorian houses with East Coast influences, and California-style bungalows made popular during the early years of the 20th century. A touch of the farm vernacular, with which he is so familiar, might appear in JVL homes in a rural setting. In town, Layne believes homes should blend into the existing scale rather than overpower the neighborhood.

"Much of our local residential design seems to be influenced by a California style that is interesting both in design and in land usage." he says. "I would love to do a Mediterranean courtyard-style house since we have only about one month per year with bad weather. I love to design indoor/outdoor spaces and we're ready for more of that here."

LEFT:
Klympkow Residence, Parker, Colorado. View of the free floating main and basement stairs and entry.
Photograph by Michele Holland

FACING PAGE TOP:
Baker Residence, Arvada, Colorado. Streetscape.
Photograph by Michele Holland

FACING PAGE BOTTOM:
Kramer Residence, Arvada, Colorado. Formal living room with detail of beamed ceiling.
Photograph by Michele Holland

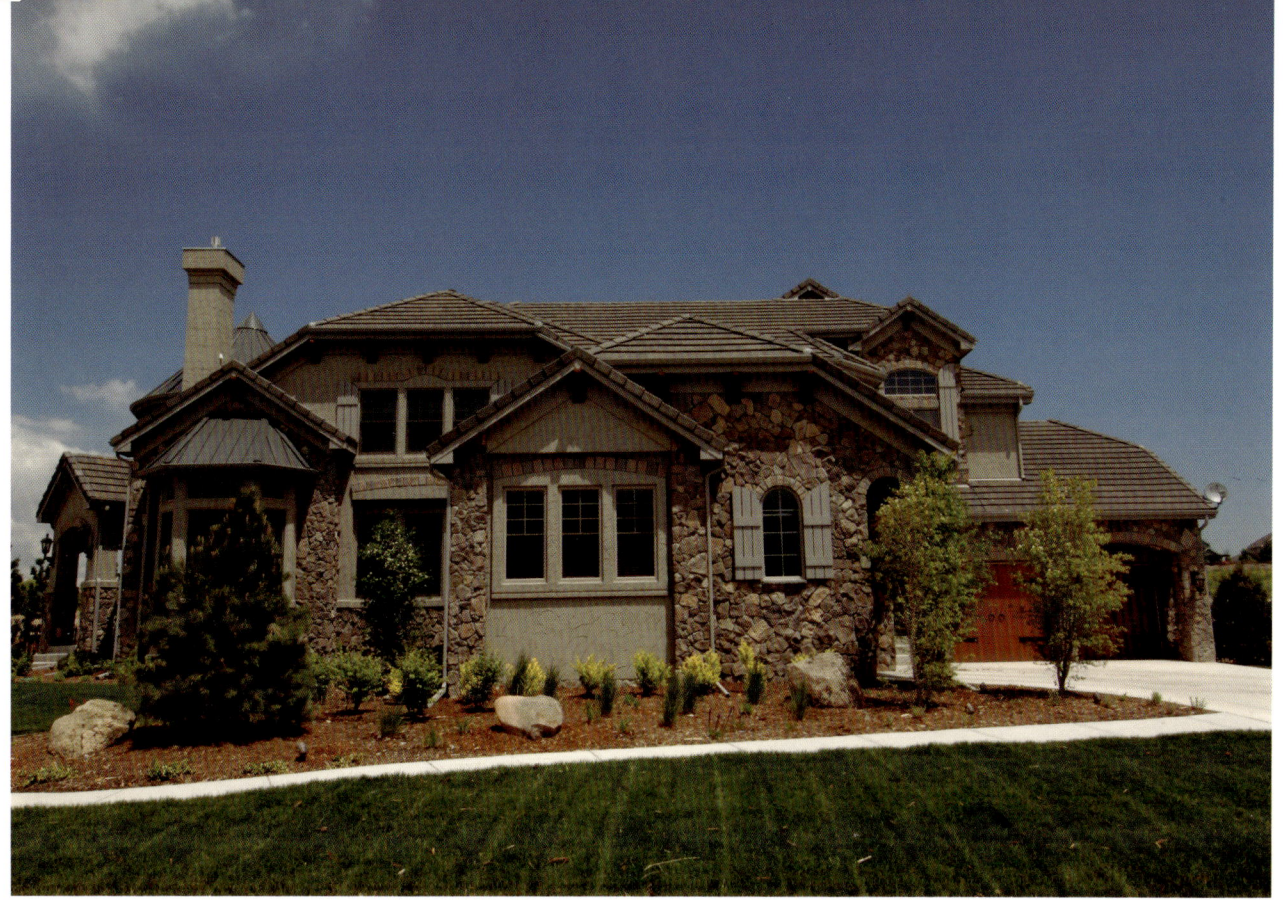

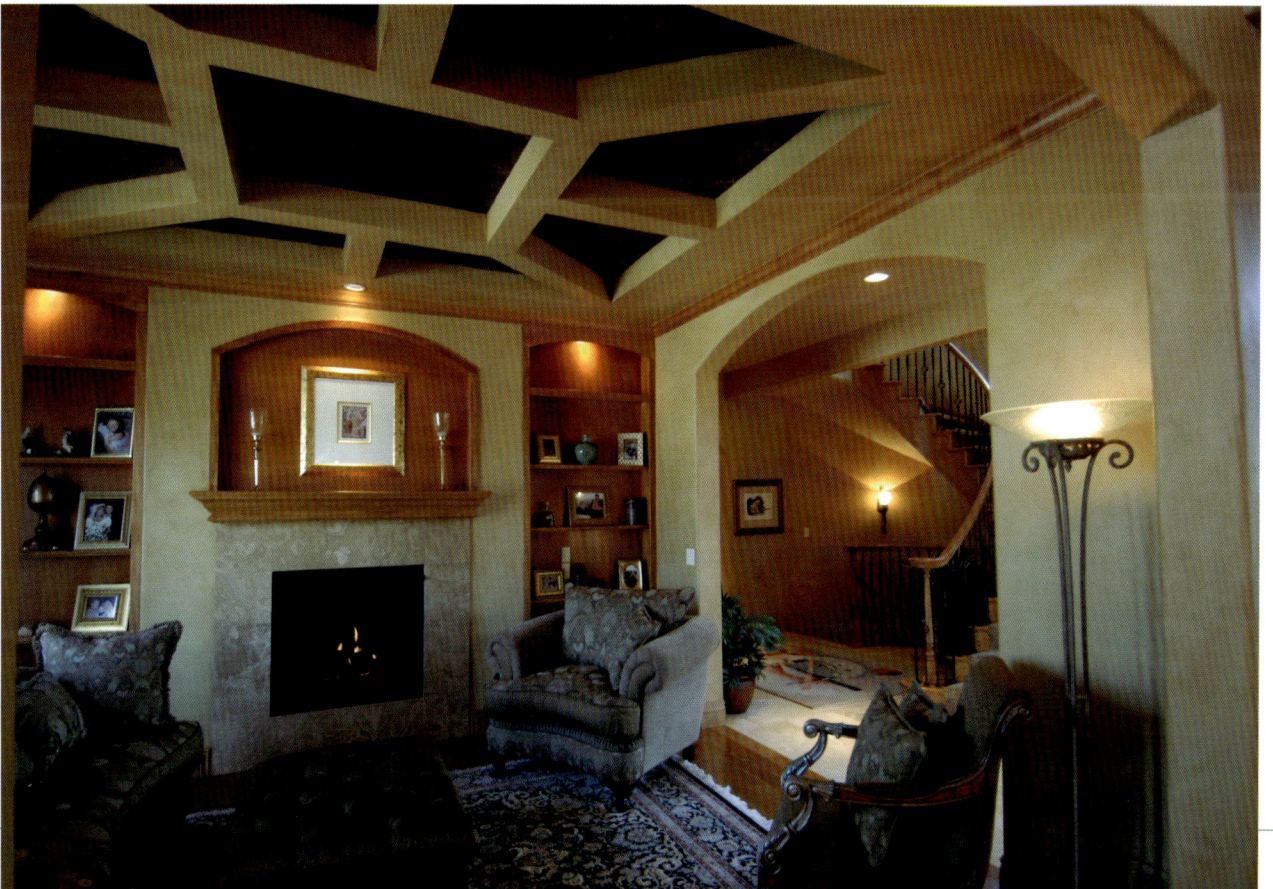

Q&A
more about layne...

WHO HAS HAD THE BIGGEST INFLUENCE ON YOUR CAREER?
Joel Hayes helped me to get started and continues to be my close friend and mentor. JVL stands for Joel and Vickie Hayes, and me. Joel and Vickie aren't my partners but they let me live and work out of their house after my move here from California. I was nearly broke, and job prospects were slim. Joel worked really hard to help me get work and help get my business started. I don't recall what he said or promised those potential clients, but all I had to do was draw as quickly as I could!

OF WHICH AWARDS ARE YOU MOST PROUD?
I designed a vacation home for a family of 13 in Breckenridge. The house was an entry in the 2005 Summit County Parade of Homes and won seven awards. This was a challenge due to the size of the family, the site and the design review constraints.

OF WHICH ASSOCIATIONS ARE YOU A MEMBER?
I belong to the Denver Homebuilders Association and the Southern Nevada Home Builder Association.

WHAT ARE THE NAMES AND POSITIONS OF YOUR STAFF MEMBERS?
Bliss Holland is our business manager. Michael Palmer and Garry Dorrance are project managers. Gregg Blakesley, Tracey Padilla, Fred Salas, Michael Knight, Kevin Lutgen and Daniel Hayes are members of our drafting staff.

WHAT ARE YOUR PERSONAL INDULGENCES?
I have a penchant for interior design and I enjoy collecting art by local artists. I have two rare French mid-1800's vintage mantel clocks and various bronze animal statuaries. I also have 52 lamps in my house of various sizes and styles, as I don't really like ceiling lights. I have four cats, Jilly, Laira, Luna and Mougly. I have a big home filled with an eclectic mix of interesting traditional and antique Victorian furniture, so there are lots of places to just sit around. I also enjoy driving my powerful, well-styled Chrysler sport sedan.

JVL ASSOCIATES INC. ARCHITECTURE AND DESIGN
LAYNE BENNETT
8687 West 108th Avenue
Westminster, CO 80021
303.922.4185
f: 303.922.4694
www.jvlassoc.com

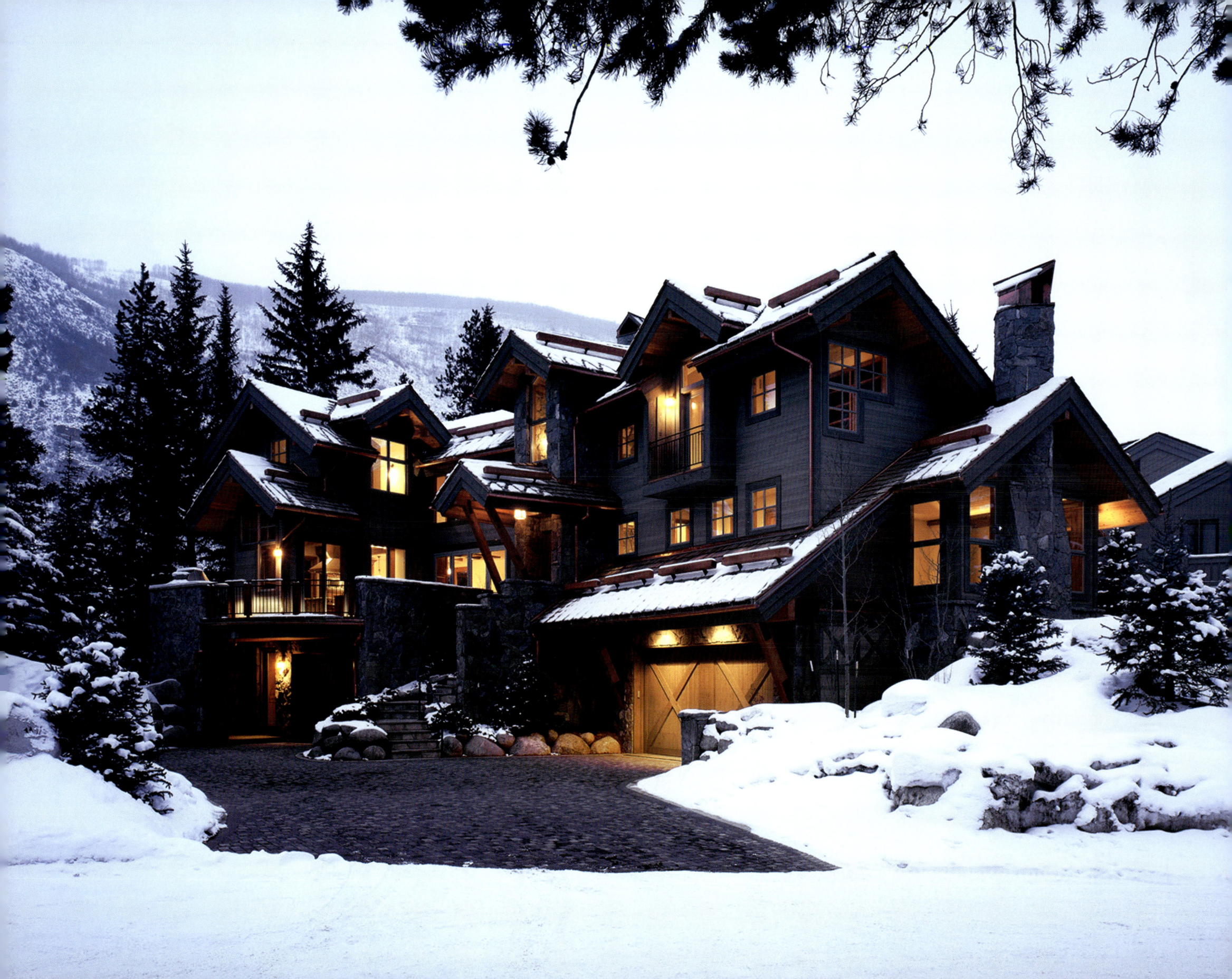

KYLE H. WEBB
KH WEBB ARCHITECTS P.C.

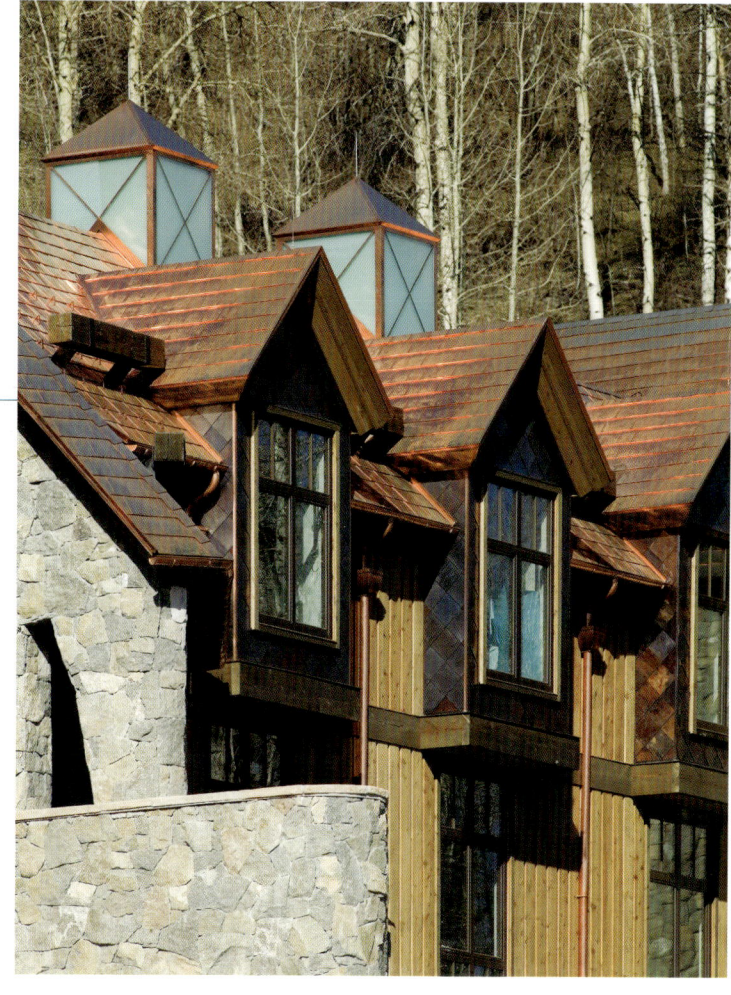

Kyle Webb has been designing masterful architecture in Vail for over 17 years. As the founder of K.H. Webb Architects, his projects are not built on prefabricated architectural designs. His team couples their technical resourcefulness with a shared penchant for things both traditional and new, allowing continued diversity in their designs. In all of the firm's work, subtle and clever accents dripping with detail add a unique architectural flavor that his clients truly feel reflects his or her signature style.

Kyle purposely keeps his team of architects small so they can operate collectively in a professional studio environment where their clients are always regarded as members of their team. Establishing a dialogue early on with their clients ensures the faithful translation of each client's personal needs, desires and vision. Kyle stresses that each client takes on the role of "designer/partner" throughout the process and this is continued throughout every project.

Working with clients as "designer/partner" inevitably allows Kyle to maintain diversity in his work, while ensuring a precise project with no surprises. "We really spend a lot of upfront time getting to know our clients and understanding exactly what they need and want before we draw anything," Kyle explained. Such fine architectural tailoring, smart spatial design and consistent quality have become true hallmarks of K.H. Webb.

The team has designed or collaborated on everything from furniture pieces, bridges and a climbing wall, to bars and wine cellars and residential spaces from 1,000 to 31,000 square feet. Kyle's work has been published regionally and nationally in magazines such as *Vail Valley Magazine*, *Architecture & Design of the West*, *Mountain Horizons*, *Builder/Architect*, *SKI Magazine*, *US Today*, *Peaks Magazine* and *Wine Spectator*. For such work, Kyle as been recognized as much an artist as he is an architect.

ABOVE:
The Falconer House in Beaver Creeks is a home of clean historical allusions on the exterior and contemporary interior detailing.
Photograph by Dann Coffey

FACING PAGE:
The Hornsilver Residence represents the unadorned, yet true, mountain aesthetic that is one of the multitude of stylistic capabilities of KH Webb.
Photograph by Dennis Jones/Dreamcatcher Imaging

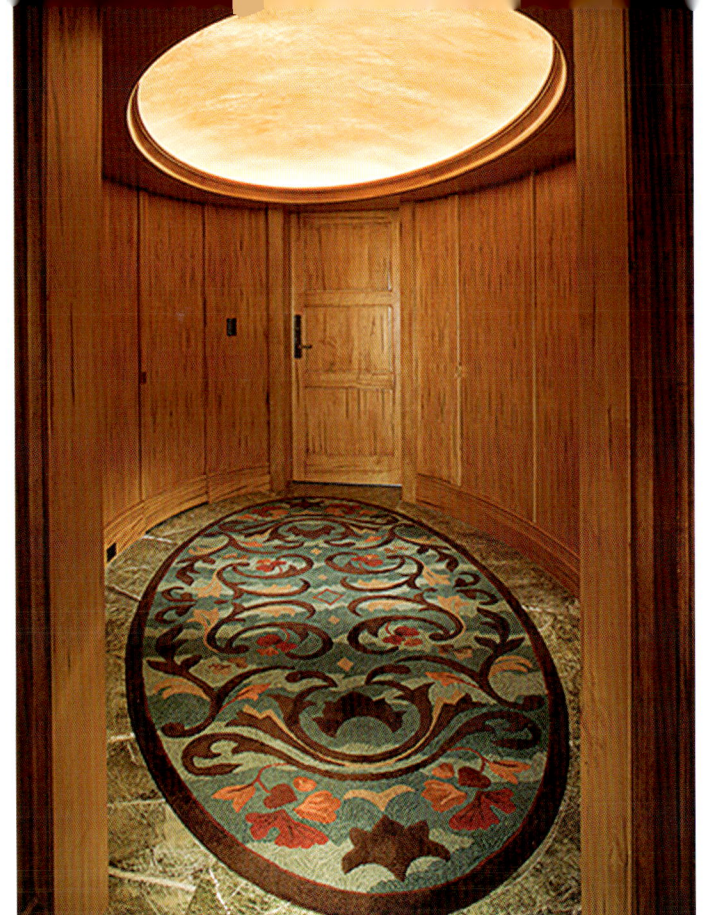
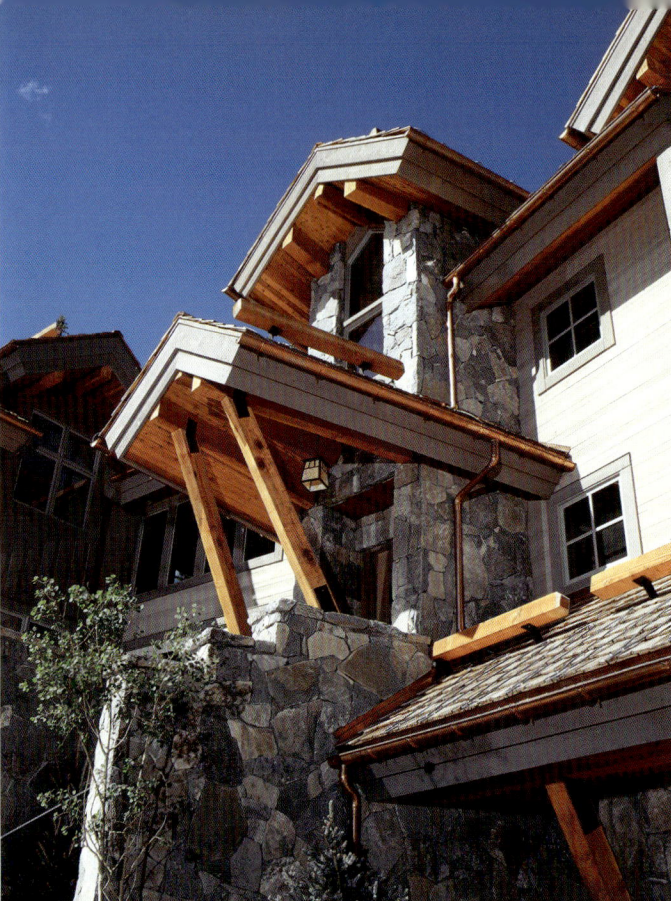

KH Webb's designs will undoubtedly continue to reflect a process of continuous refinement as they strive toward well-conceived and wonderfully articulated architecture that, above all, expresses a tremendous respect and flair for thoughtful design.

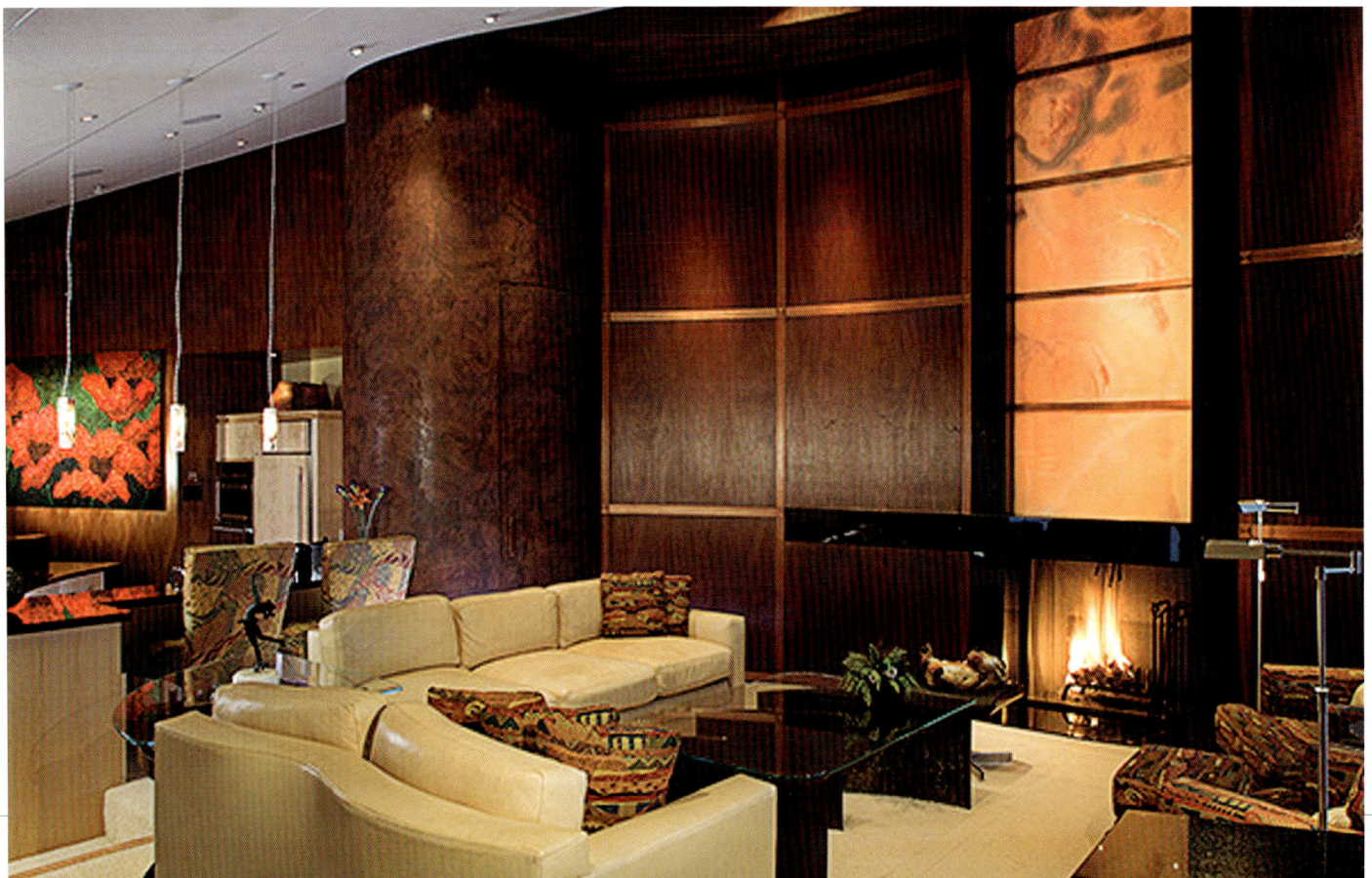

TOP LEFT:
The elliptical foyer of an interior renovation conceals a mud room, entry closet and guest bedroom behind silverleaf maple paneled walls.
Photograph by Dann Coffey

TOP RIGHT:
An entry detail of the Hornsilver Residence.
Photograph by Dann Coffey

BOTTOM:
A penthouse interior renovation in Vail focuses on a back lighted onyx and granite fireplace with a mahogany paneling surround.
Photograph by Dann Coffey

FACING PAGE:
The Venetian plaster cylinder between mahogany paneled walls in this architectural interior conceals a curved glass door that creates a two-bedroom suite.
Photograph by Dann Coffey

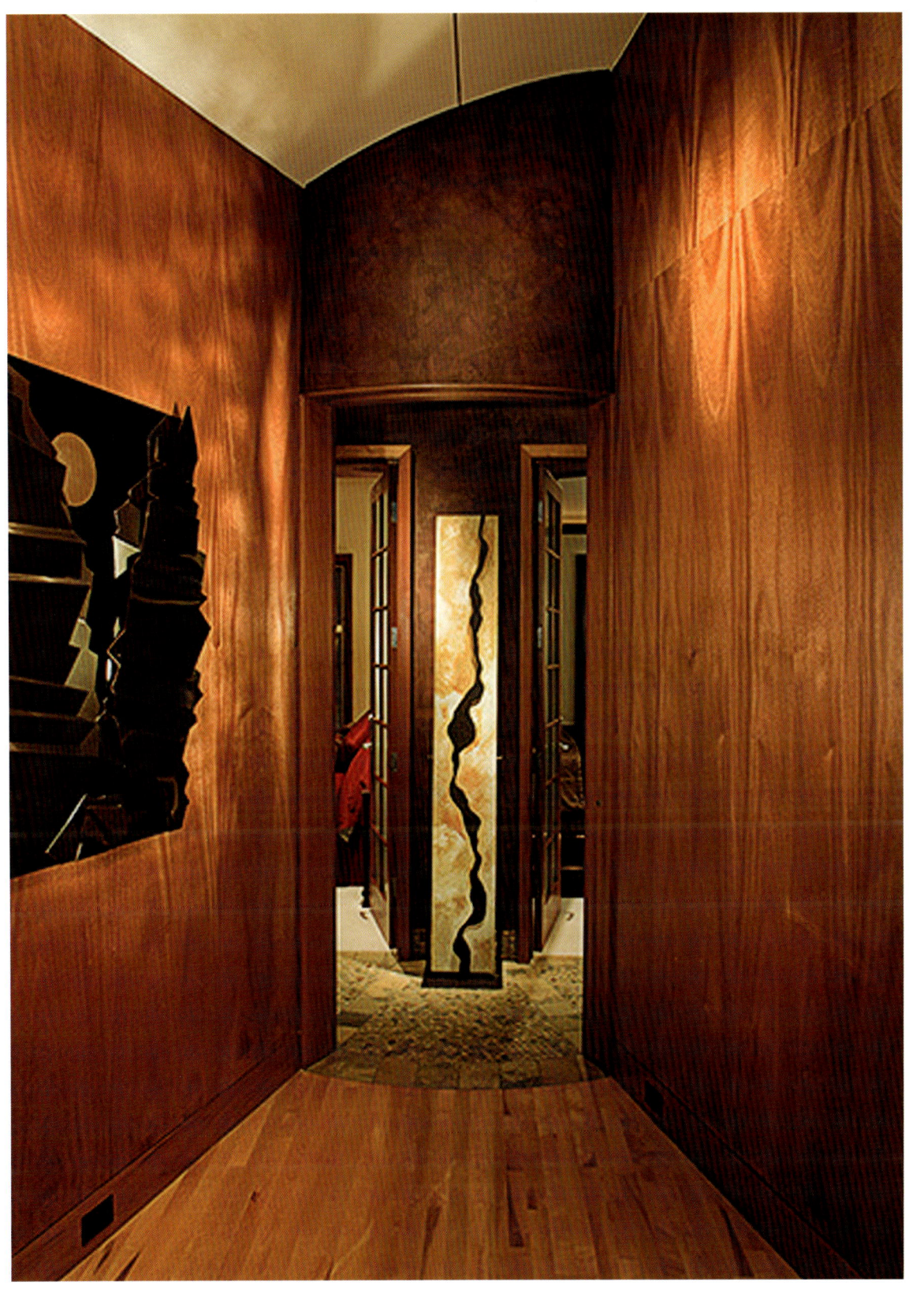

Q&A more about kyle...

WHAT IS THE BEST PART OF BEING AN ARCHITECT?
This is a non-stop, always changing profession. That is what makes it exciting and energizing on a constant basis and challenges us to seek out the unique and personalized solutions for our clients.

WHAT PHILOSOPHY HAVE YOU STUCK WITH FOR YEARS THAT STILL WORKS FOR YOU TODAY?
Our firm purposely stays small so we can give clients the undivided attention they need. This enables us to strive to understand what our clients need and want from the beginning of the process, so it is immensely gratifying when their dreams finally come to fruition.

HAVE YOU BEEN PUBLISHED IN ANY NATIONAL OR REGIONAL PUBLICATIONS?
We have never made any great efforts to seek out publications, but my work has been featured in *Vail Beaver Creek Magazine*, *Vail Valley Magazine*, *Builder/Architect* magazine, *Wine Spectator* and *The Wall Street Journal* to name a few.

WHAT SEPARATES YOU FROM YOUR COMPETITION?
We live by the motto, "Only so big; only so much," so we can give our clients the individual consideration they deserve.

K.H. WEBB ARCHITECTS P.C.
KYLE H. WEBB, AIA
710 West Lionshead Circle, Suite A
Vail, CO 81657
970.477.2990
f: 970.477.2965
www.khwebb.com

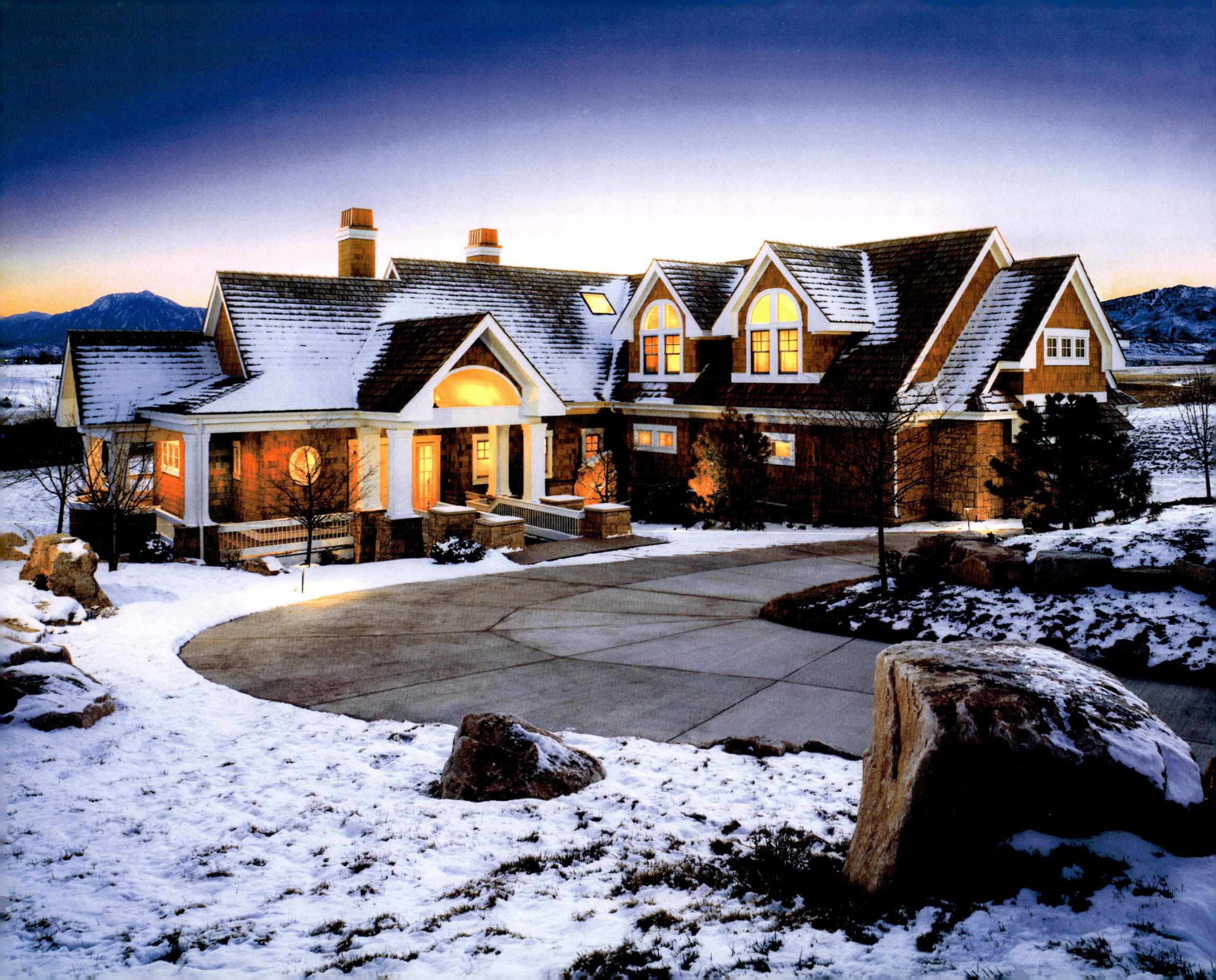

JOHN KNUDSON
JERRY GLOSS
PAUL MAHONY
MARTY BEAUCHAMP

KNUDSON GLOSS ARCHITECTS

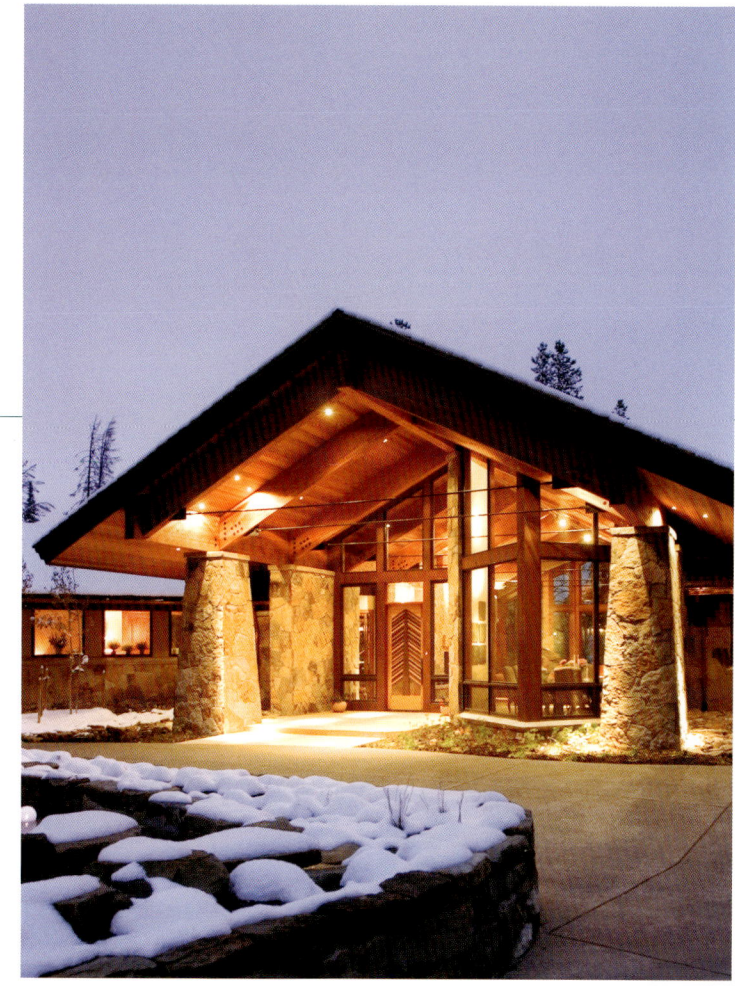

A home should never be static. It should convey a level of excitement and interest, evolving and adapting as the family who lives there grows and changes through the years. That is the guiding design philosophy behind the work of John Knudson and Jerry Gloss, the senior principals of Knudson Gloss Architects (KGA).

Founded in 1977, and one of Boulder's oldest and most esteemed architectural practices, KGA is dedicated to creating custom residences across the country and internationally. Their projects range from small vacation havens to large primary residences in locations from the mountains and plains of Colorado to the beaches of the Bahamas. Understanding the needs of the clients they work for is central to their design process. Through conversational interviews and program preparation, KGA discovers the nuances that enable them to craft a home specifically for their client and their client's lifestyle.

A Colorado native, John Knudson's focus on architecture as a passion and career began early as a high school student and never wavered. He graduated from the University of Colorado with a Bachelors of Architecture. Jerry grew up outside of Baltimore, a great reservoir of architectural styles and heritage. Like John, Jerry's appreciation of architecture as a career developed in high school spurred by a visit to Frank Lloyd Wright's Fallingwater. Jerry graduated from the University of Colorado with a Masters of Architecture before joining John in 1986.

While the work of many architects is easily identifiable by their use of a specific style and material or by the implementation of repeated detailing, that is not the case with KGA. An observant client-to-be noted that each KGA exterior seems to be a one-of-a-kind, and that it's the interior, as functional as it is dramatic, that brands a KGA design.

ABOVE:
This home on Colorado's Front Range was designed to reflect the owner's East Coast heritage. The home is organized along an east-west axis, allowing principle rooms to take advantage of the primary southwest view to the mountains.
Builder: Scottsdale Custom Homes
Photograph by Ron Ruscio

FACING PAGE:
A contemporary, ultra-custom home serves as a family's private Rocky Mountain ski lodge with interior and exterior spaces appearing to flow seamlessly through the large expanses of glass.
Builder: Sweet Homes of Colorado
Photograph by Wayne Thom

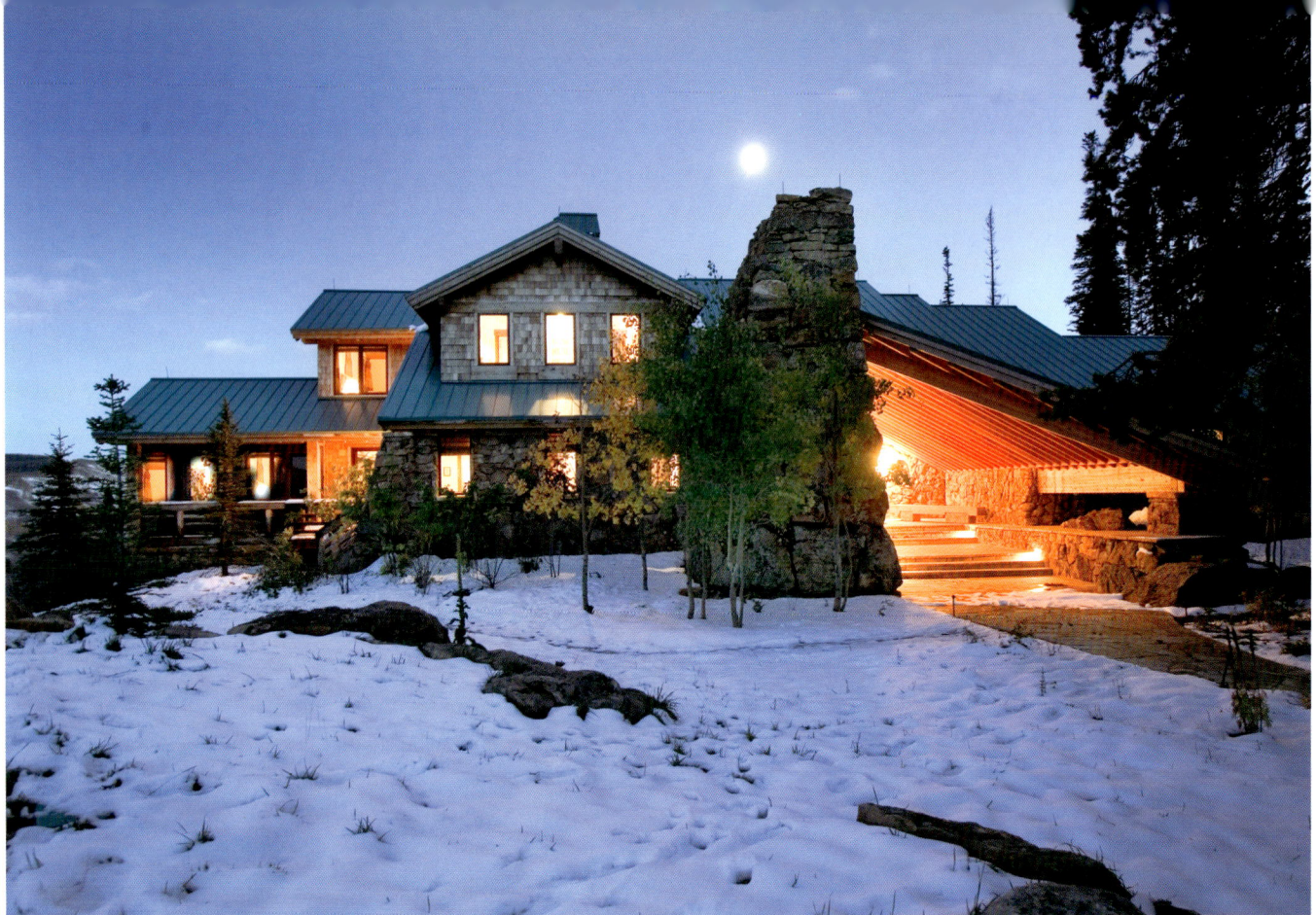

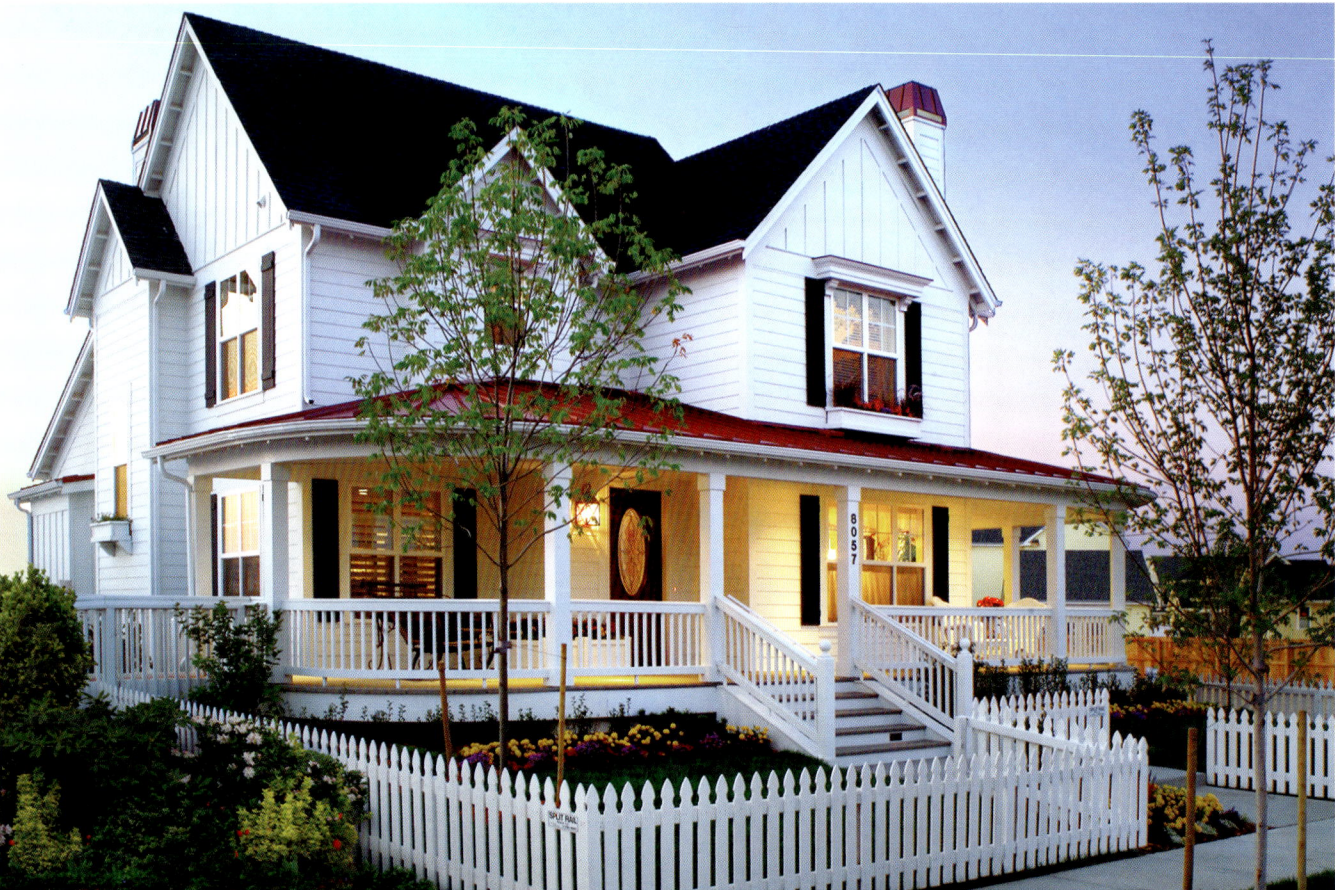

KGA draws from a range of diverse styles that includes contemporary, mountain lodge, and traditional styles such as Prairie, Shingle and Cape Cod. The richness, color, and indigenous qualities of Tuscan, French Rustic, English Cottage, and the quaintness of Norman also make them firm favorites. Each requires an understanding of massing, form, and authentic detailing.

"Clients call us the 'Odd Couple'," John says. "We see things differently. But our different tastes benefit our architecture and our clients. Over the past several years the quality of our collaboration has been increased with the addition of two talented partners, Marty Beauchamp and Paul Mahony. And in the end, it's about the clients and what they desire. It's their home, and KGA works to provide them just that—their home."

TOP LEFT:
Straddling the Continental Divide, this incredible property features panoramic views, massive, battered stone walls, and includes numerous out buildings to support ranch operation.
Builder: Woodstone Homes
Photograph by Wayne Thom

BOTTOM LEFT:
Designed for today's active family, this farmhouse vernacular-inspired home embraces the ideals of the "new urbanism" traditional neighborhood.
Builder: Touchstone Homes
Photograph by Ron Ruscio

FACING PAGE:
The elegant "Old European" character of this home radiates distinction and grace while the spatial arrangement offers ease and comfort for a large family. Masterful use of stone throughout this project coupled with refined detailing gives this estate an unparalleled level of extravagance.
Builder: Bond General Contractors
Photograph by J. Curtis Photography

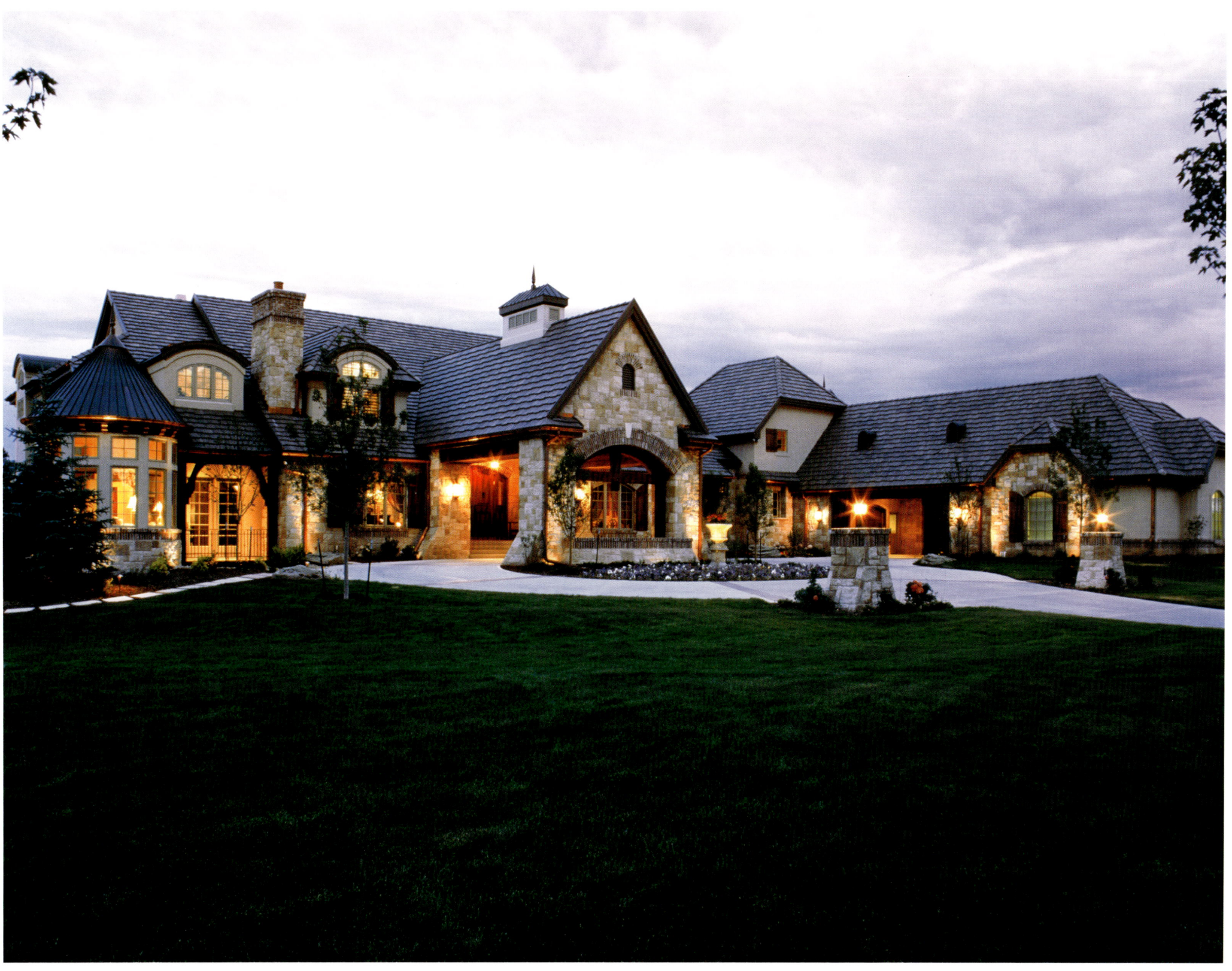

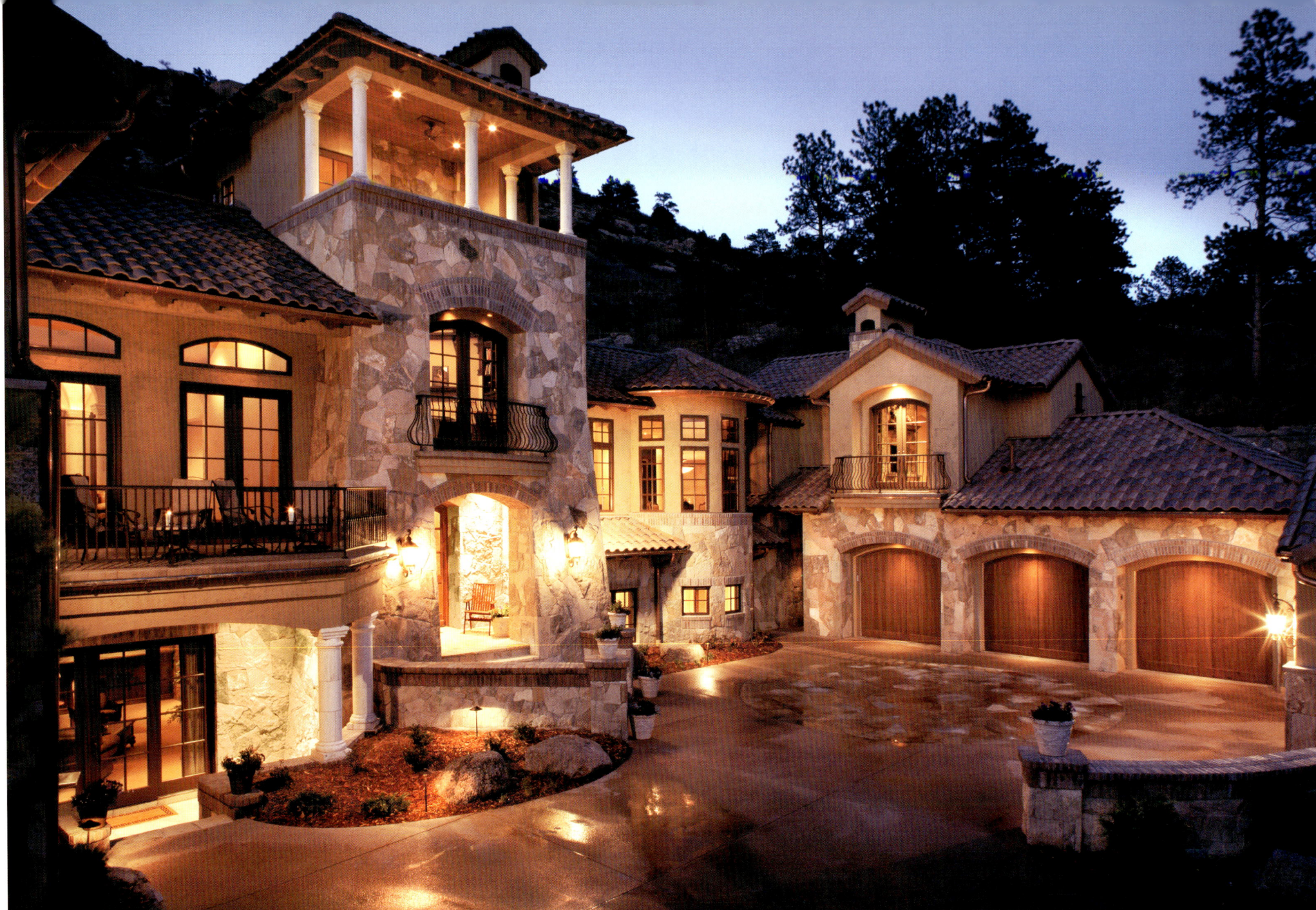

ABOVE:
This site's ridges and ravines played an integral role in the design of this Tuscan hillside custom home.
Builder: Gray Construction
Photograph by Jeff Scroggins

FACING PAGE TOP:
This rear patio just off the dining room is the perfect place for entertaining or just enjoying a quiet evening in the home's outdoor space.
Builder: Gray Construction
Photograph by Jeff Scroggins

FACING PAGE BOTTOM:
Originally built in 1976, this tract home was cleverly redesigned and reworked into a stunning Craftsman-style home.
Builder: Parrish Construction
Photograph by Ken Paul

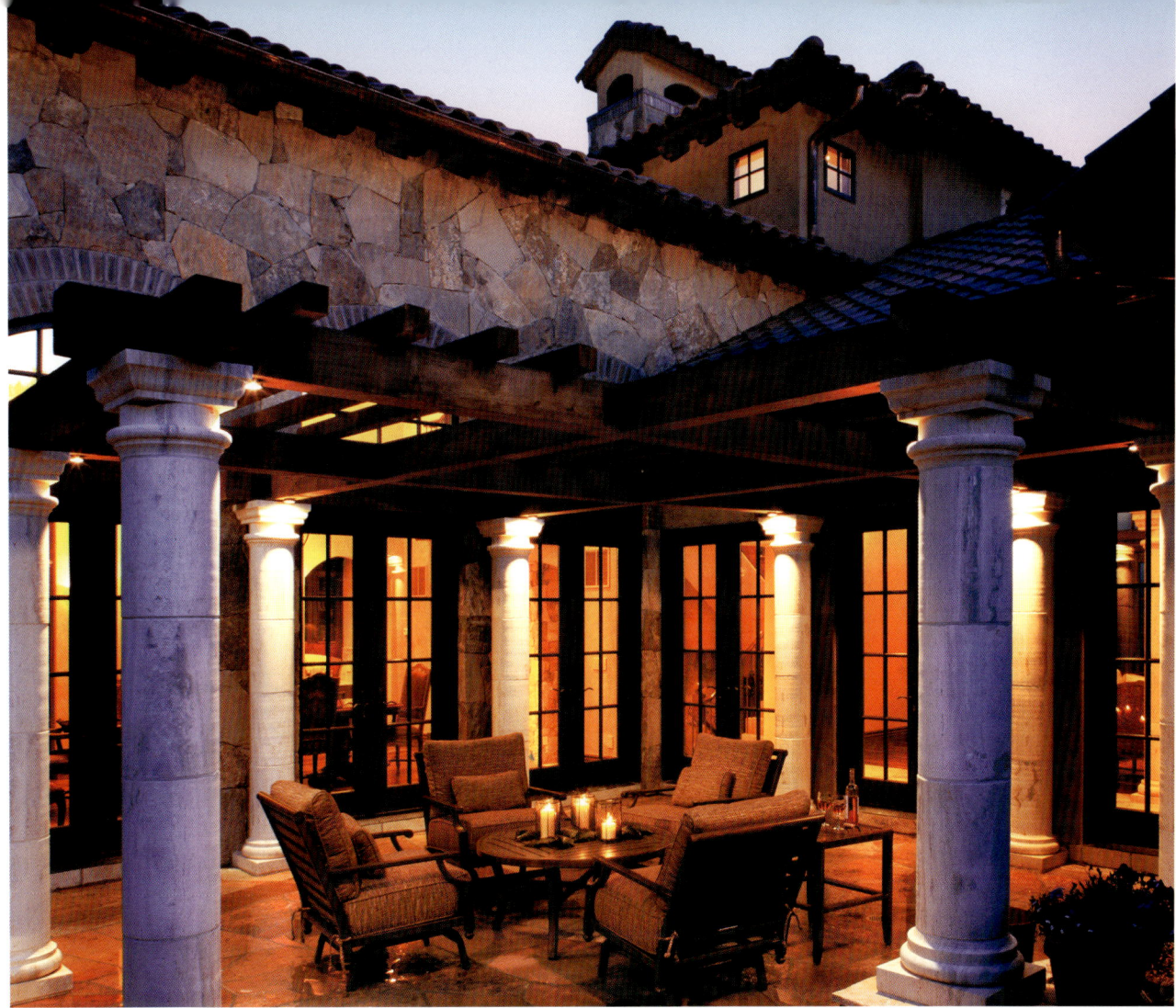

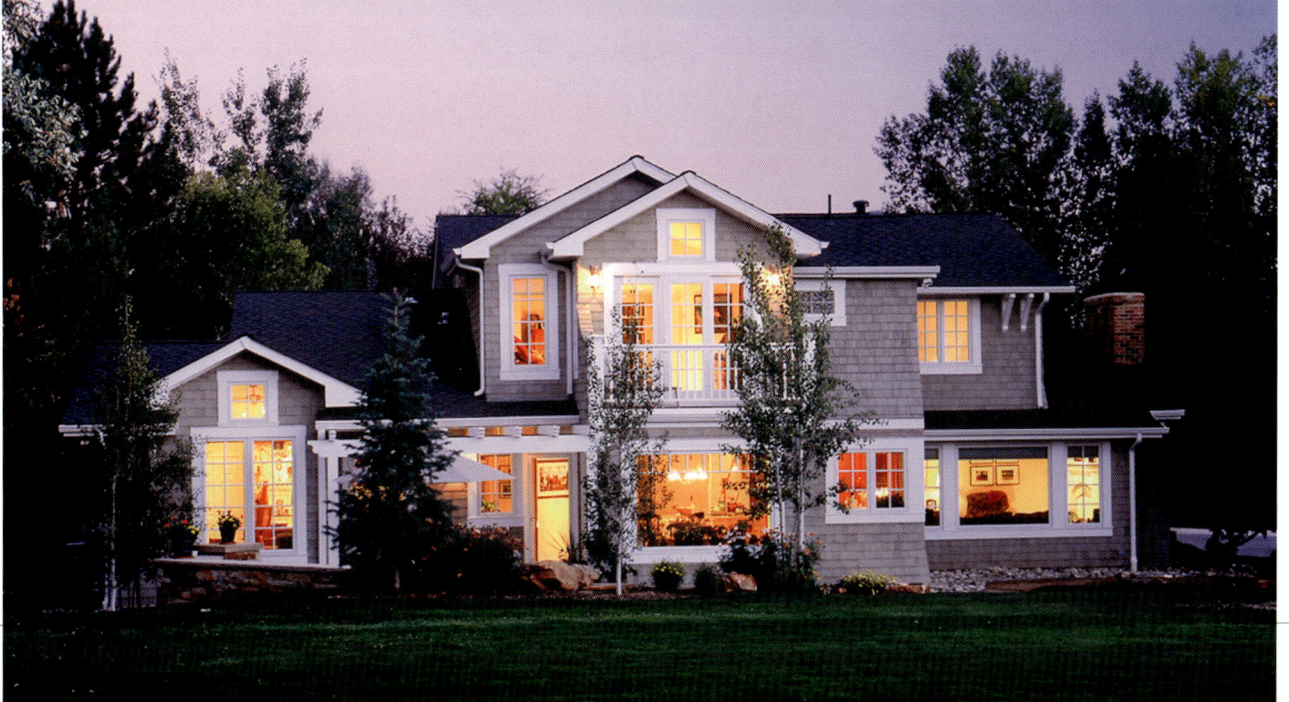

Q&A

more about jerry...

WHAT BOOK HAS HAD THE GREATEST IMPACT ON YOU?
That would be *The Popcorn Report* by Faith Popcorn. It connected me to the understanding of demographics and trends in housing.

WHAT ONE ELEMENT OF STYLE OR PHILOSOPHY HAVE YOU STUCK WITH FOR YEARS THAT STILL WORKS FOR YOU TODAY?
It's all about function. Floor plans and a home's layout must effectively and efficiently serve those who live there, and support them in their lifestyle.

more about john...

WHAT SEPARATES YOU FROM YOUR COMPETITION?
Our ability to design homes based on our clients' desires and our ability to work collaboratively with builders.

MY FRIENDS WOULD TELL YOU I WAS...
A person with a dry sense of humor.

KNUDSON GLOSS ARCHITECTS
JOHN KNUDSON, AIA, FOUNDING AND SENIOR PARTNER
JERRY GLOSS, AIA, SENIOR PARTNER
PAUL MAHONY, AIA, PARTNER
MARTY BEAUCHAMP, PARTNER
4820 Riverbend Road
Boulder, CO 80301
303.442.5882
f: 303.442.5888
www.kgarch.com

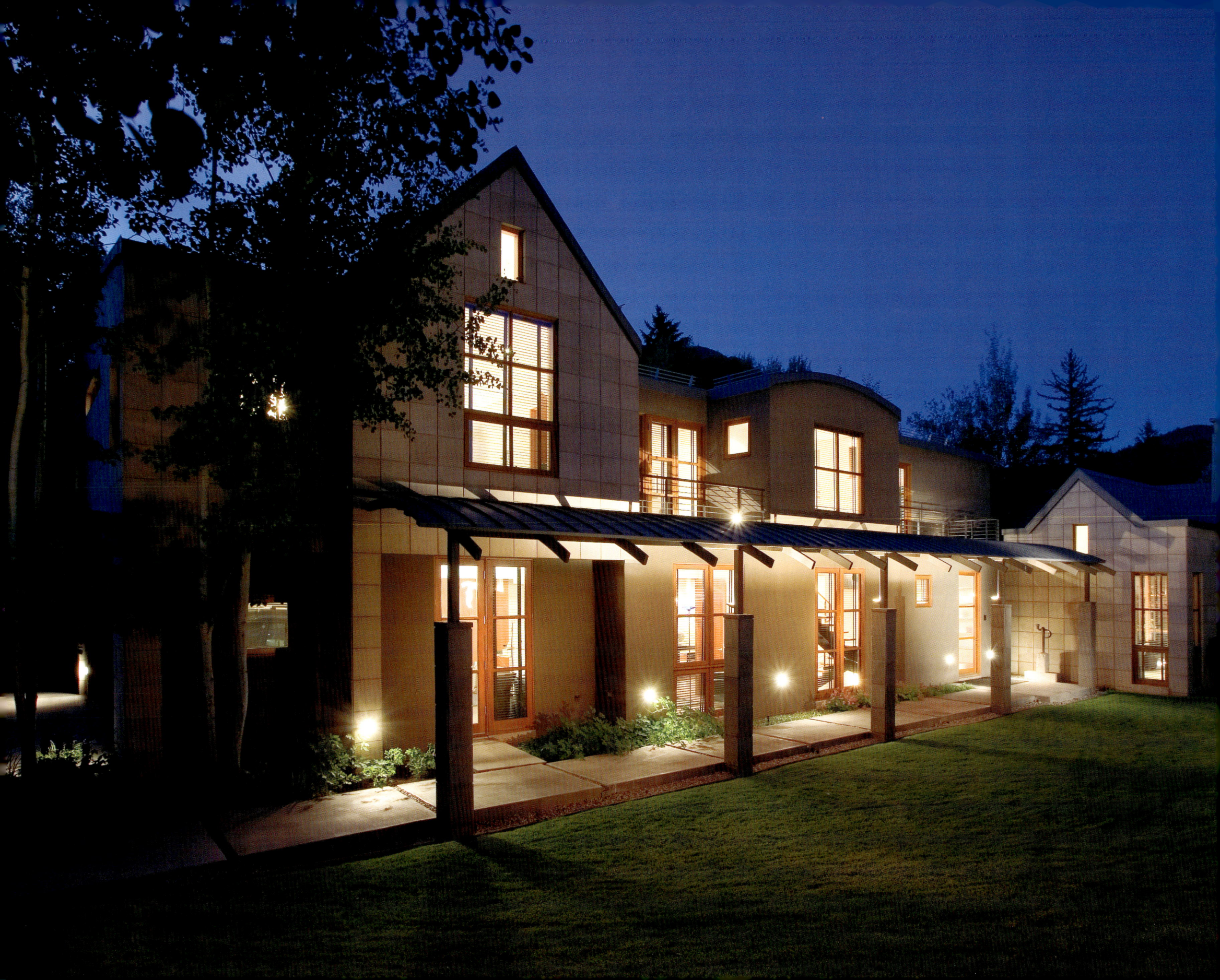

MICHAEL LIPKIN
DAVID WARNER

LIPKIN WARNER DESIGN & PLANNING

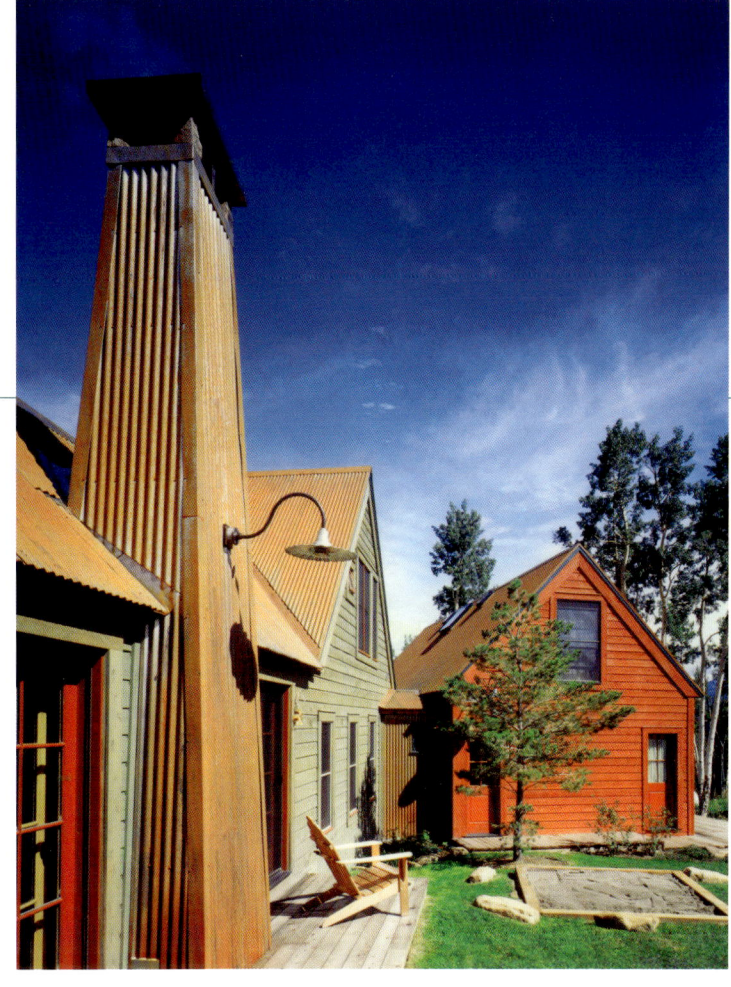

Making a house feel like a home can be as simple as knowing where to place a porch or just the best place to have one's morning coffee. Likewise, one room is better filled with the soft light of an Aspen grove while another might call for the distant views of rugged mountain peaks. To partners Michael Lipkin and David Warner, delving into innumerable questions like these is an essential part of designing a house.

Before a design is molded in any particular way or before any preconceptions are able to settle in, the two carefully bring together ideas from the many facets of the owner and family, the environment and the building's locale. "This is where magic comes from," says David, "it's amazing how often great ideas evolve from something we'd never have though of if we weren't starting with what evolves from our clients and the land."

Lipkin Warner houses take shape while also combining other ideas best described as "notions of hearth and home." These are somewhat universal ideas, which describe the everyday feelings of "being home, at home" Michael likes to point out. They always have some level of expression in a design, such as creating a sense of entry or a feeling of openness; emphasizing the intimacy of a window seat or the warmth of a fireplace. These notions are subtly woven into the fabric of each house, giving the homes a familiar appeal, which comfortably works alongside whatever individual ideas have crafted the overall plan.

Respecting regional variations and historic traditions, which they see in buildings around them, is an important consideration for the two designers. They admire the original Colorado homesteads and the old miners' buildings still found along town streets. They draw inspiration from aspects of these buildings such as lightness of structure and purity of form which have their roots in the early settlers' need for functionality and economy. Michael

ABOVE:
Patio, Nona Mesa residence, San Miguel, Colorado.
Photograph by David Marlow

FACING PAGE:
Entryway, West End residence, Aspen, Colorado.
Photograph by Aspen Architectural Photography

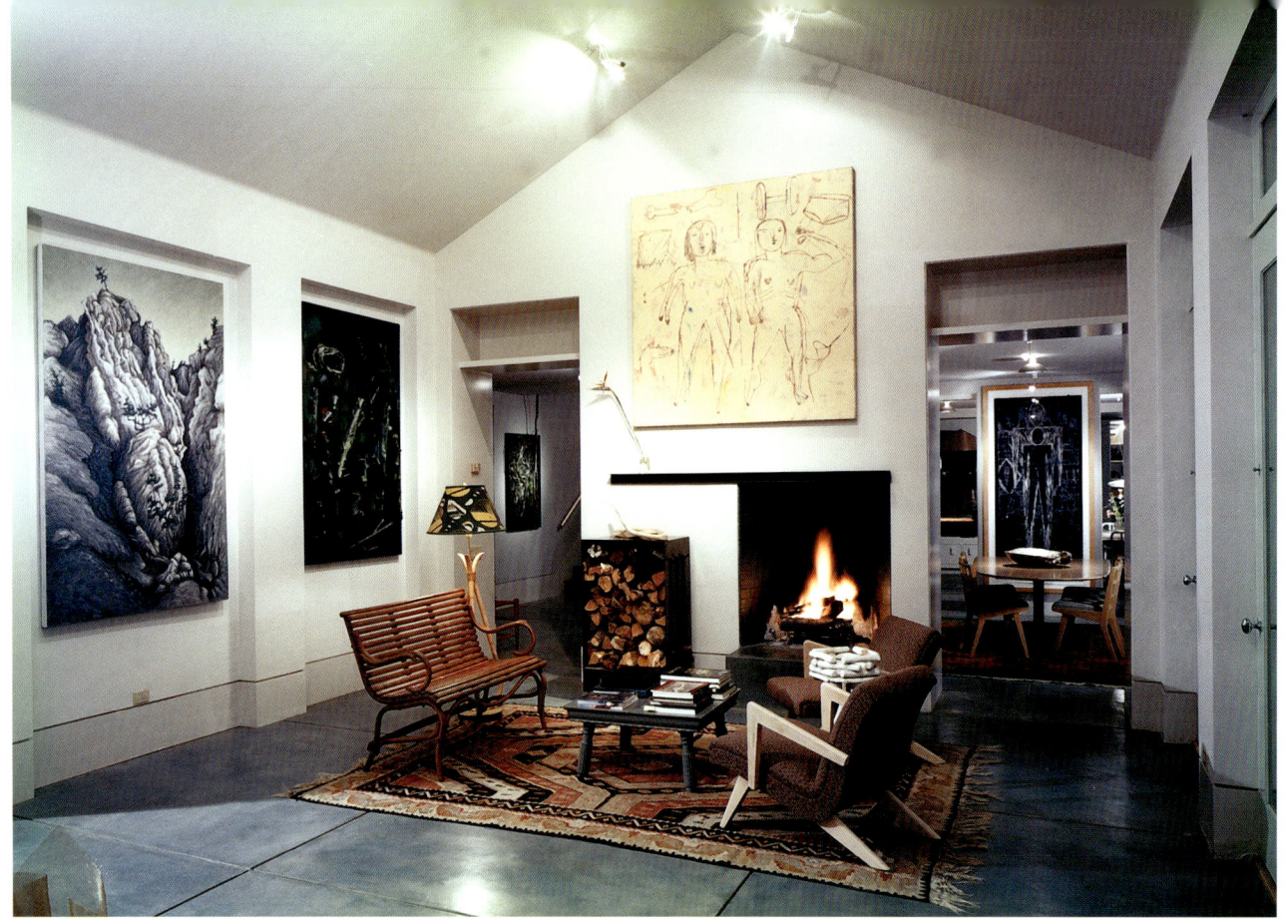

and David believe that economy has multiple implications because, for example, the interior of a barn, which can be the most economical of spaces, can also be the most majestic. In addition, they believe that one should never forget the individual spirit of the early builders who would find expression in such things as a special column bracket or an ornate window bay added to the basics of house, porch and chimney.

Also important in a Lipkin Warner house is the way architectural style integrates with design. Modern or traditional, textured or machined, metal, wood or stone; the many choices for a house can be overwhelming. David believes that in some way, style evolves from the character of each house and its location. To the Lipkin Warner team, it is in this way that the style becomes an outward expression of a house's internal character and not a faddish set of clothes imposed on it for convenience sake.

Never overlooked in a Lipkin Warner house is designing with the landscape. It continually plays an important role from inside, as well as out. In Colorado, the environment can be both rugged and vast; delicate and fragile. Lipkin Warner treats every site with an appropriate level of care, leaving them either as close as possible to their existing state or naturally manicured in a way that respects the original geography. From inside the house, windows are carefully placed to frame specific views and rooms are opened up to porches and terraces. Wings are built around existing features and light is brought in to be reflected by natural materials inside.

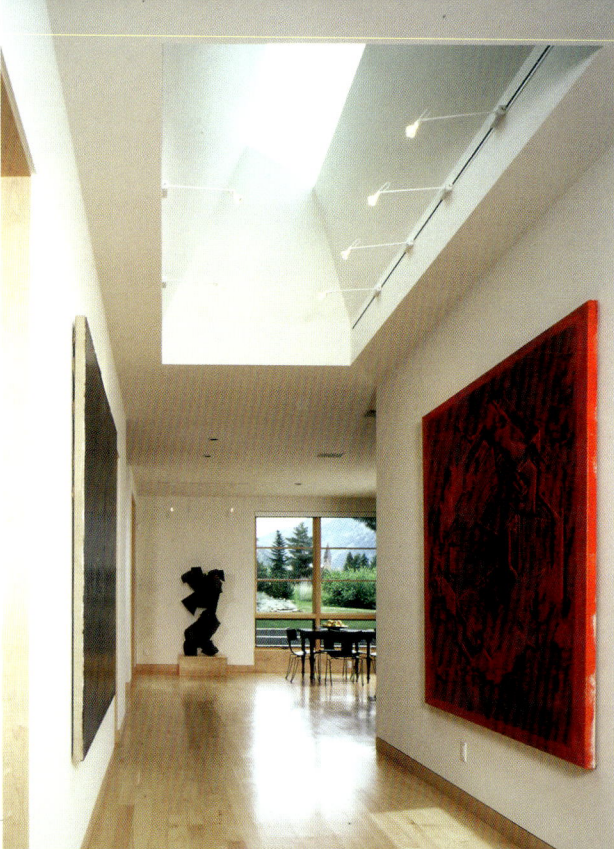
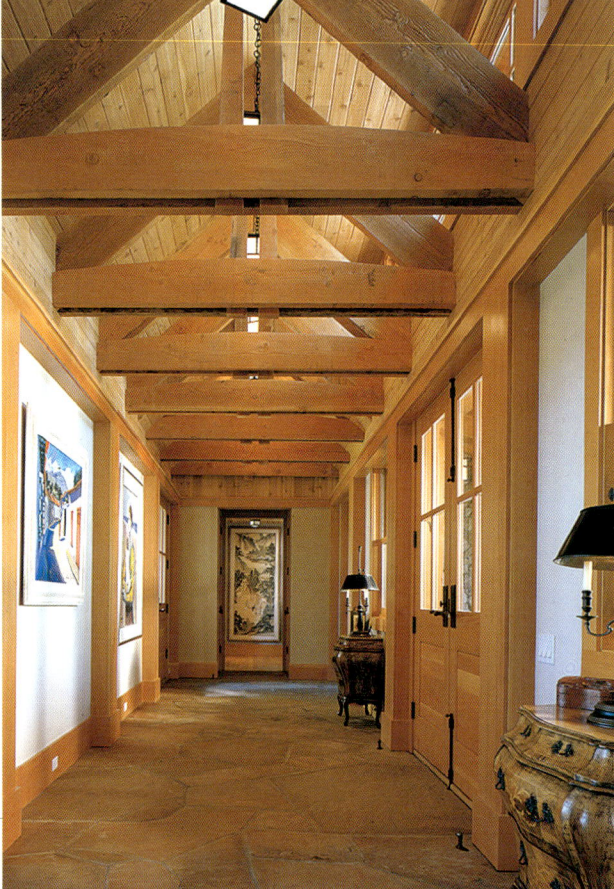

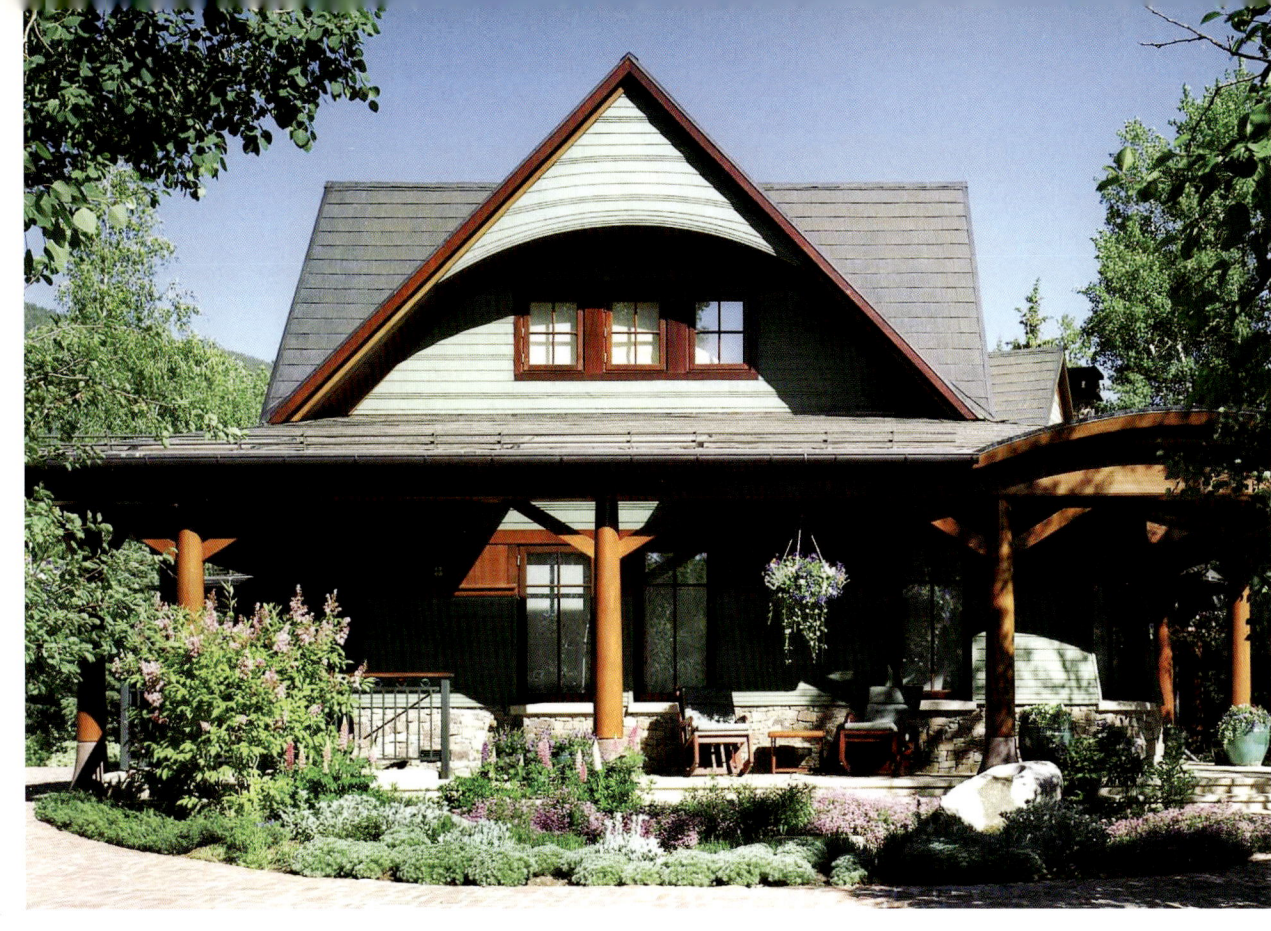

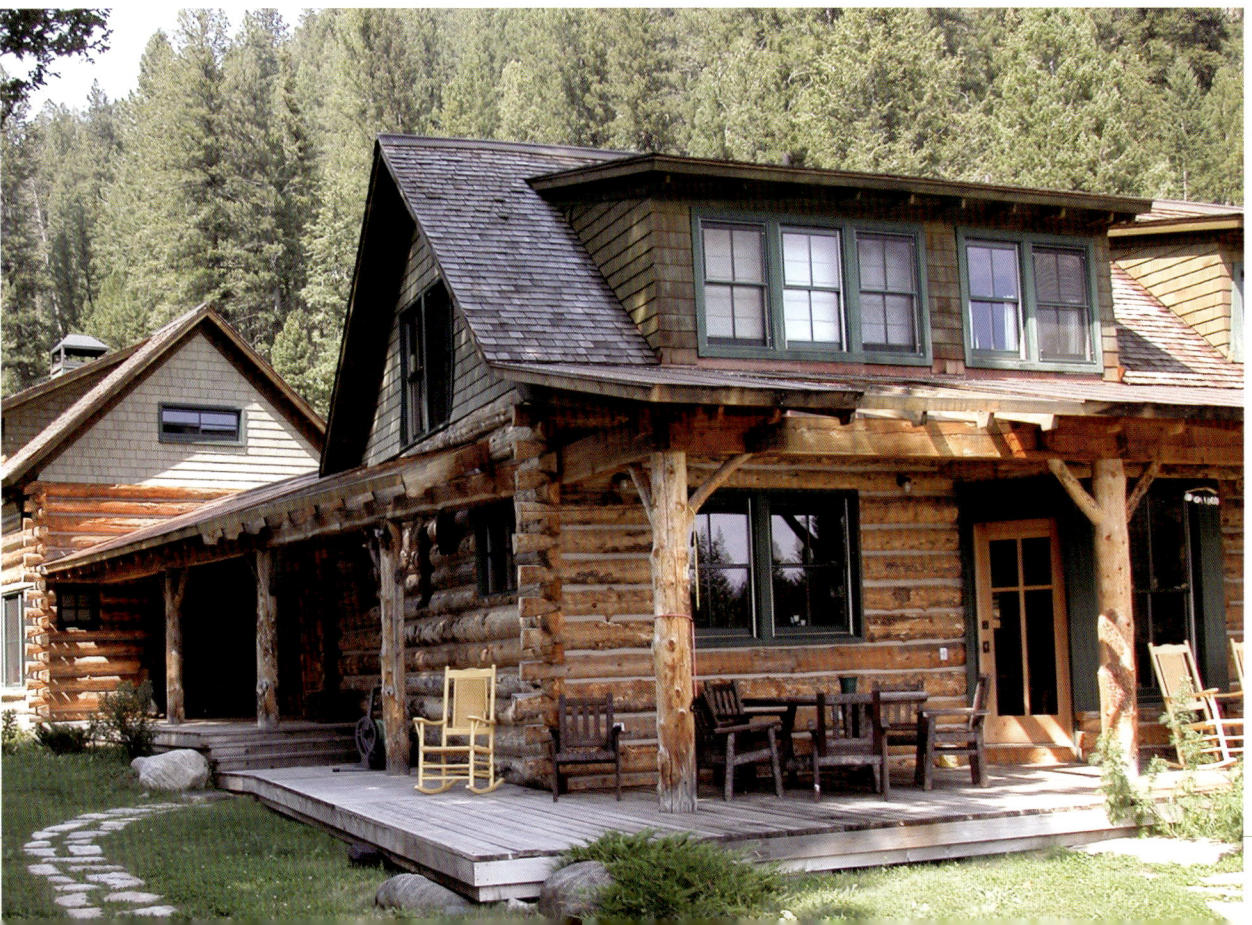

TOP:
Street façade, East End residence, Aspen, Colorado.
Photograph by Wayne Thom

BOTTOM:
Back porch, North Fork residence, Big Sky, Montana.
Photograph by Lipkin Warner

FACING PAGE TOP:
Living room, Castle Creek residence, Aspen, Colorado.
Photograph by David Marlow

FACING PAGE BOTTOM LEFT:
Gallery, Aspen Meadows residence, Aspen, Colorado.
Photograph by Robert Millman

FACING PAGE BOTTOM RIGHT:
Entry gallery, Steamboat residence, Steamboat Springs, Colorado.
Photograph by David Marlow

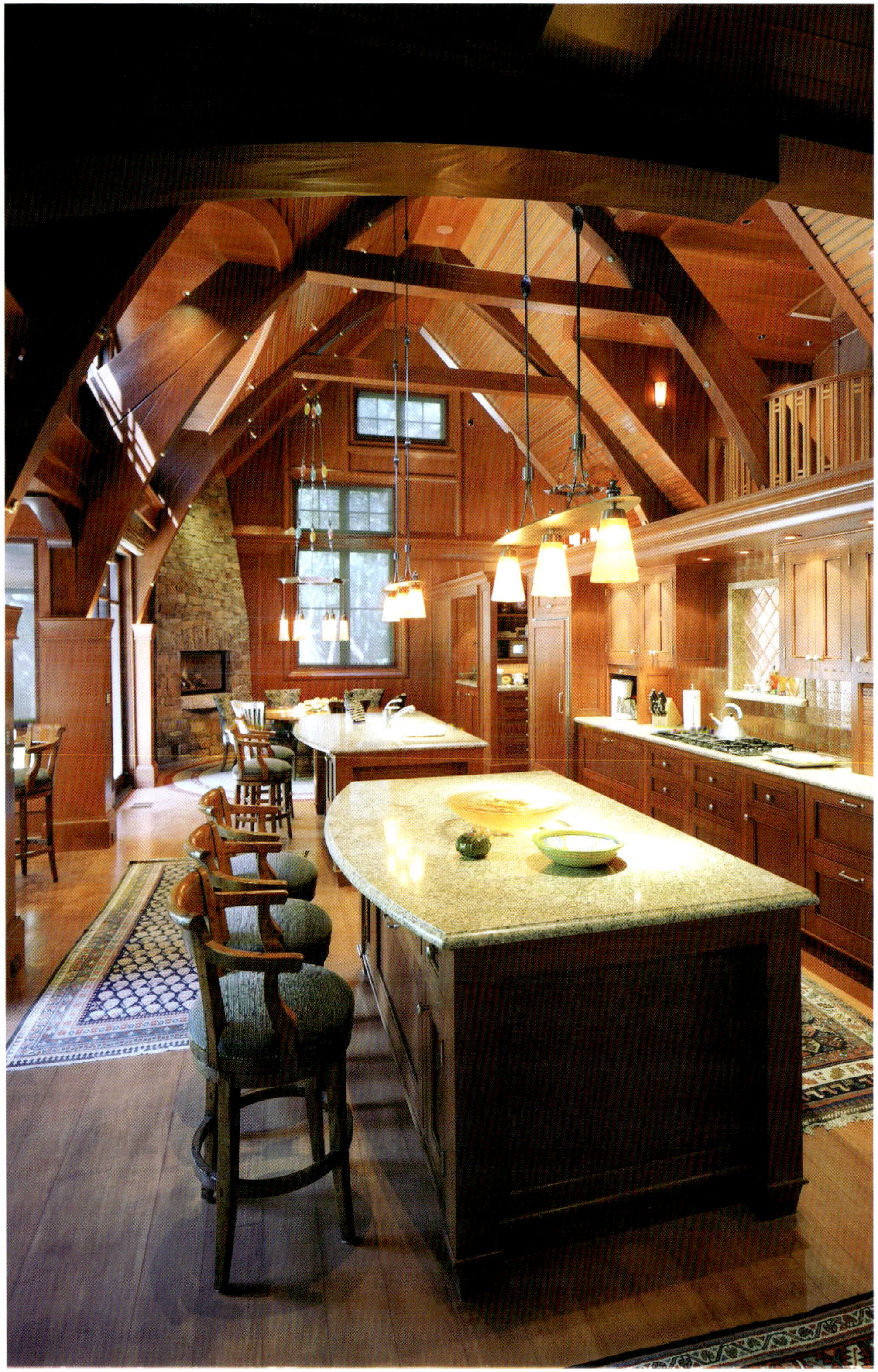

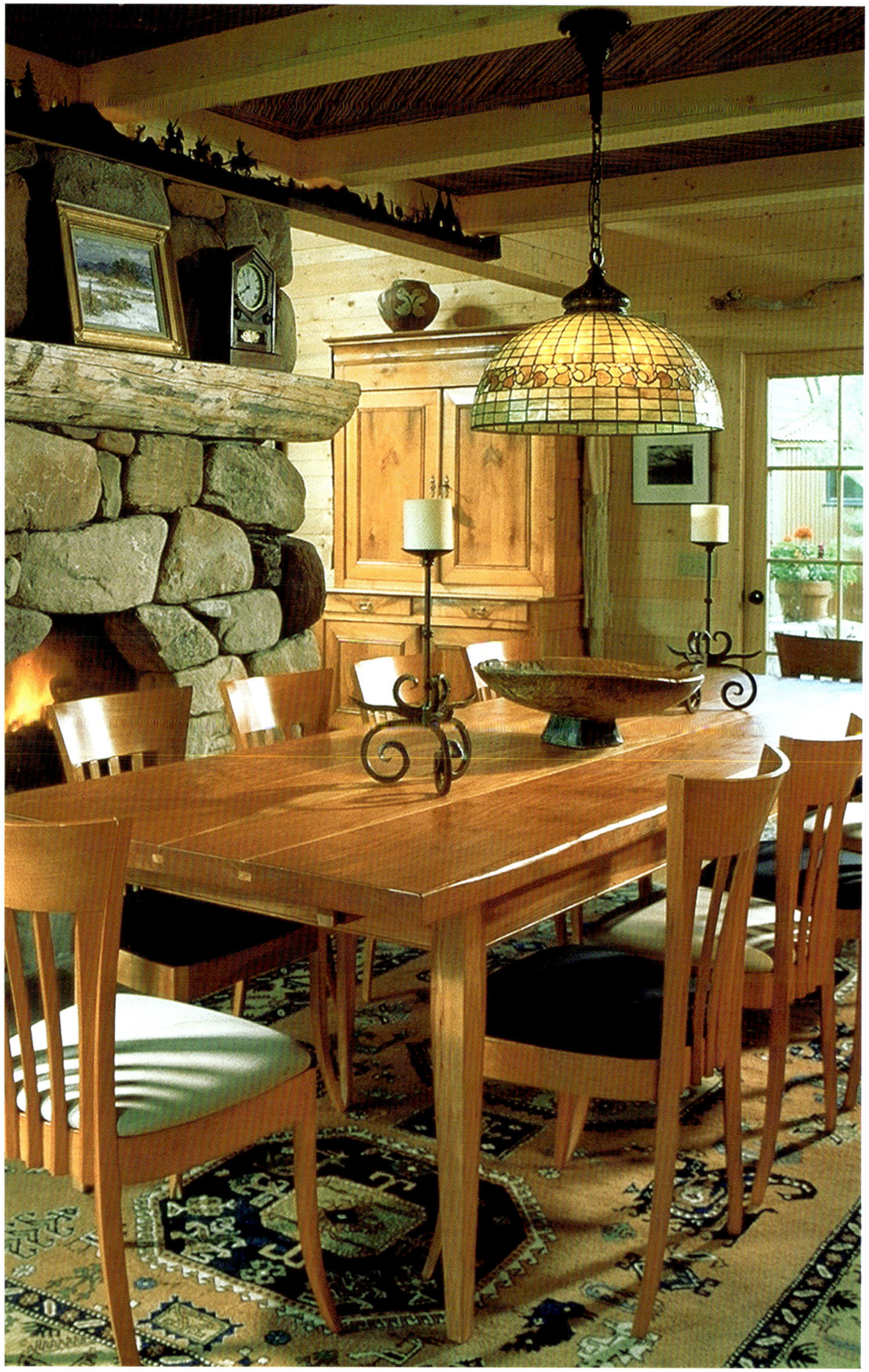

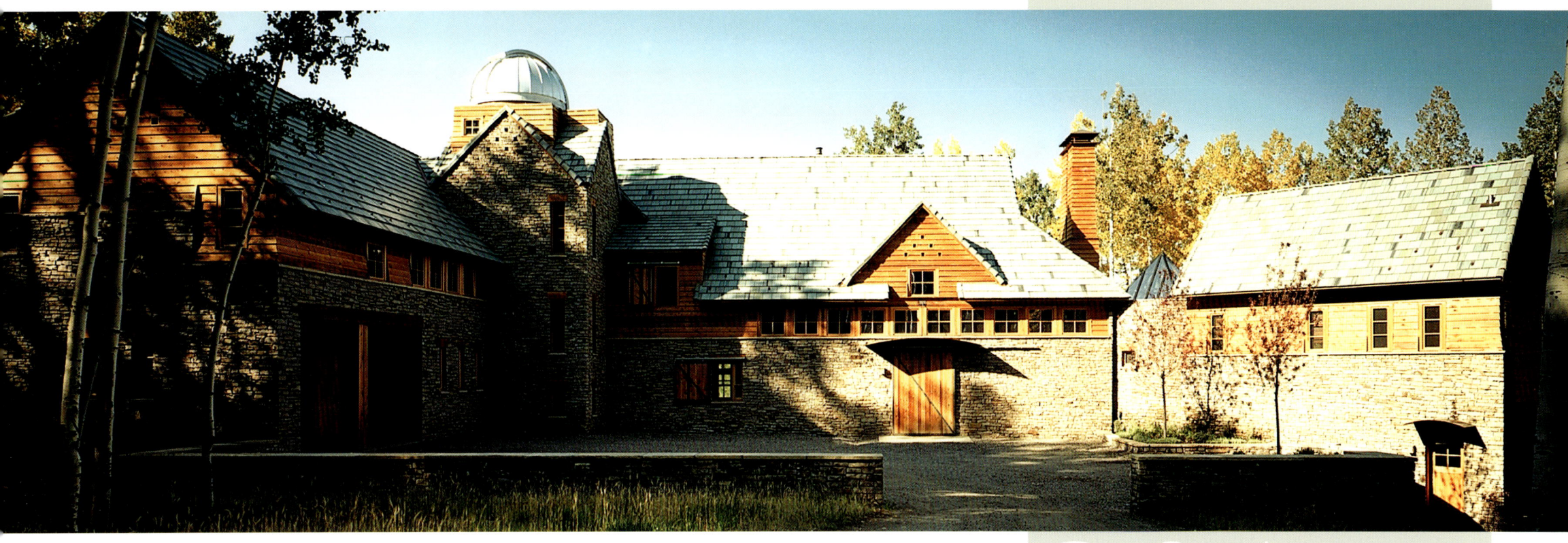

Flowing space inside and out, architectural style, understanding rooms and the way people use them... all of these ideas ultimately complement one another in a complete design. In the end, if one feels "they have the perfect porch to rest on or the best living room for playing board games with their family," the house becomes the endearing and enduring place it's meant to be—home.

FACING PAGE LEFT:
Kitchen, East End residence, Aspen, Colorado.
Photograph by Wayne Thom

FACING PAGE RIGHT:
Dining room, Nona Mesa residence, San Miguel, Colorado.
Photograph by David Marlow

ABOVE:
Entry courtyard, Elk Run residence, Telluride, Colorado.
Photograph by Robert Reck

Q&A more about michael & david...

WHAT IS THE BEST PART OF BEING A DESIGNER?
We love to watch projects evolve and take on their own character.

WHAT'S THE BEST COMPLIMENT YOU HAVE EVER RECEIVED?
Many of our past clients have become our closest friends and that is the best compliment we could ever receive.

HAS YOUR WORK BEEN FEATURED IN ANY PUBLICATIONS?
You can see our work on the pages of *Architectural Digest*, *Metro Home*, *Traditional Home*, *Residential Architecture* and many, many more.

LIPKIN WARNER DESIGN & PLANNING
MICHAEL LIPKIN
DAVID WARNER, AIA
701 East Valley Road, Suite 201
Basalt, CO 81621
970.927.8473
f: 970.925.8487

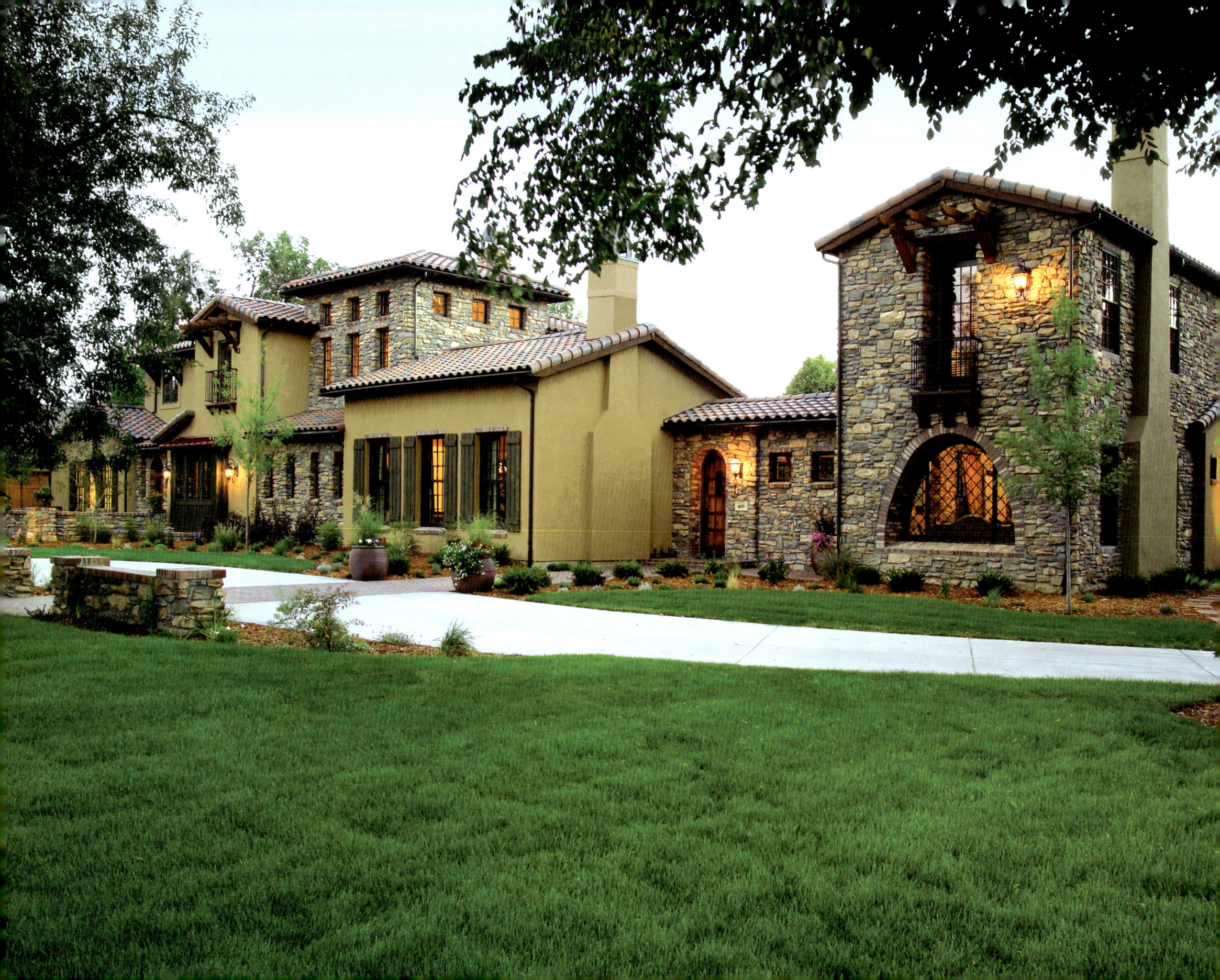

GLEN ZAHORKA

MALIBU HOMES, INC.

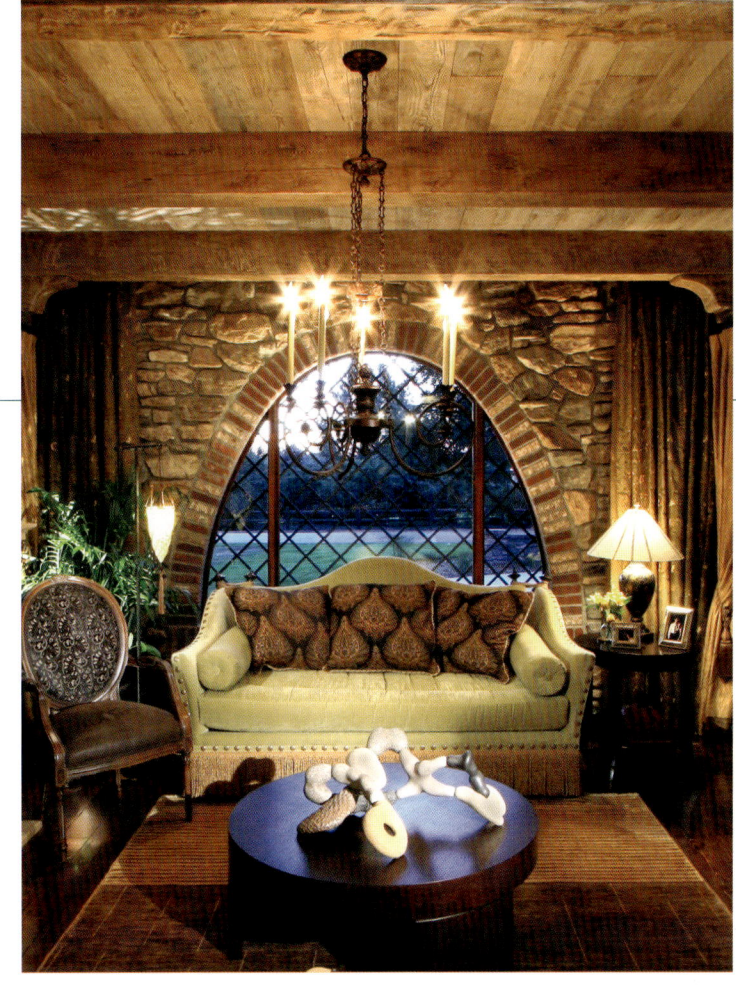

Glen Zahorka built his firm, Malibu Homes, on the philosophy that enduring quality is built on attitude and commitment. He insists on doing everything well and believes the very best designs contribute little unless they are brought to successful completion and quality construction. Glen focuses on creating beautifully-sited signature homes which meld with the natural landscape and are a unique reflection of each client's tastes and interests.

Priding himself on working with his clients from beginning to end, he creates homes that unite his clients' visions with the breathtaking Colorado landscape. Throughout this process, he comes to know his clients so well that he builds lasting relationships with many of them. In fact, the true measure of Malibu Homes' success and reputation is found among their clients who remain friends with Glen and his team long after a home is built.

Glen knew at age five that he wanted to be a builder. He then discovered his passion for custom homes while working college summer breaks for a home builder. Since that time, he has set the standard for superbly designed and constructed homes. His process focuses on persistent attention to detail and the relentless pursuit of flawlessness. He takes special care to become oriented with each and every home, ensuring that the home can obtain the best views and have ample amounts of soft, natural light for the interior.

Glen's great eye for design helps him create the plans for the majority of his spec homes. He even works hands-on with his staff to coordinate color schemes and select hardware, cabinetry, flooring and other finishing touches. He and his team love to use generous amounts of natural materials like stone, wood and stucco to create an Old World ambiance reinforced by historically accurate replications of other details like beams, fireplaces and furniture built ins.

ABOVE:
The use of quality finishes and unique architectural elements help create intimate spaces throughout this home.
Photograph by Ron Ruscio

FACING PAGE:
A 7,500-square-foot rustic Mediterranean home in Old Cherry Hills Village was built to look like it evolved over time.
Photograph by Ron Ruscio

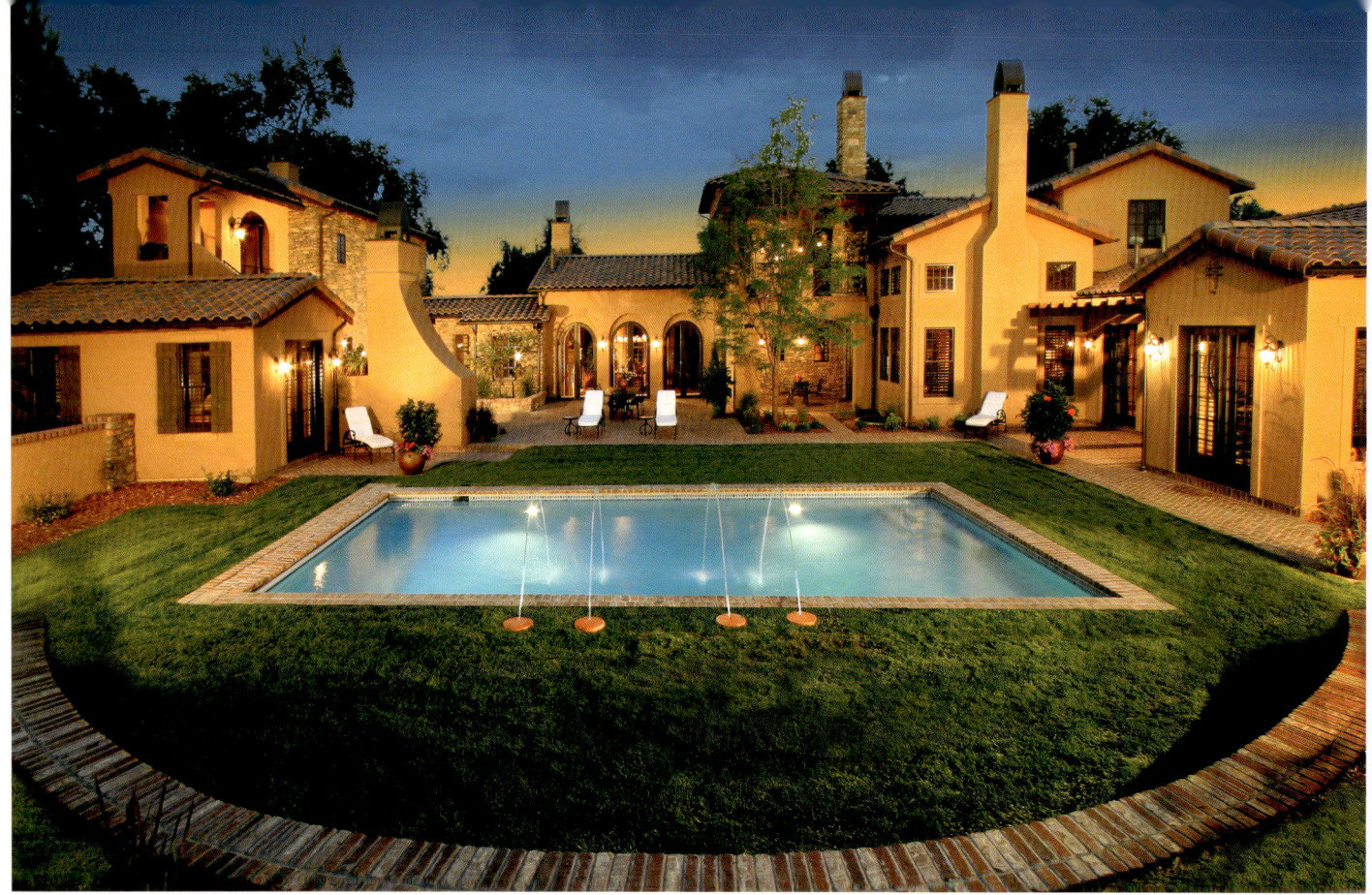

His work has such a reputation for quality that Glen is the man architects come to when they want to build their homes. They choose him not only for his craftsmanship and service, but also for the integrity and trust that they know will be a part of the building process. This process is one that Glen has honed and refined to perfection. "We have never had a client who was disappointed with their finished home," he said. "Our design, execution and results all receive the highest marks."

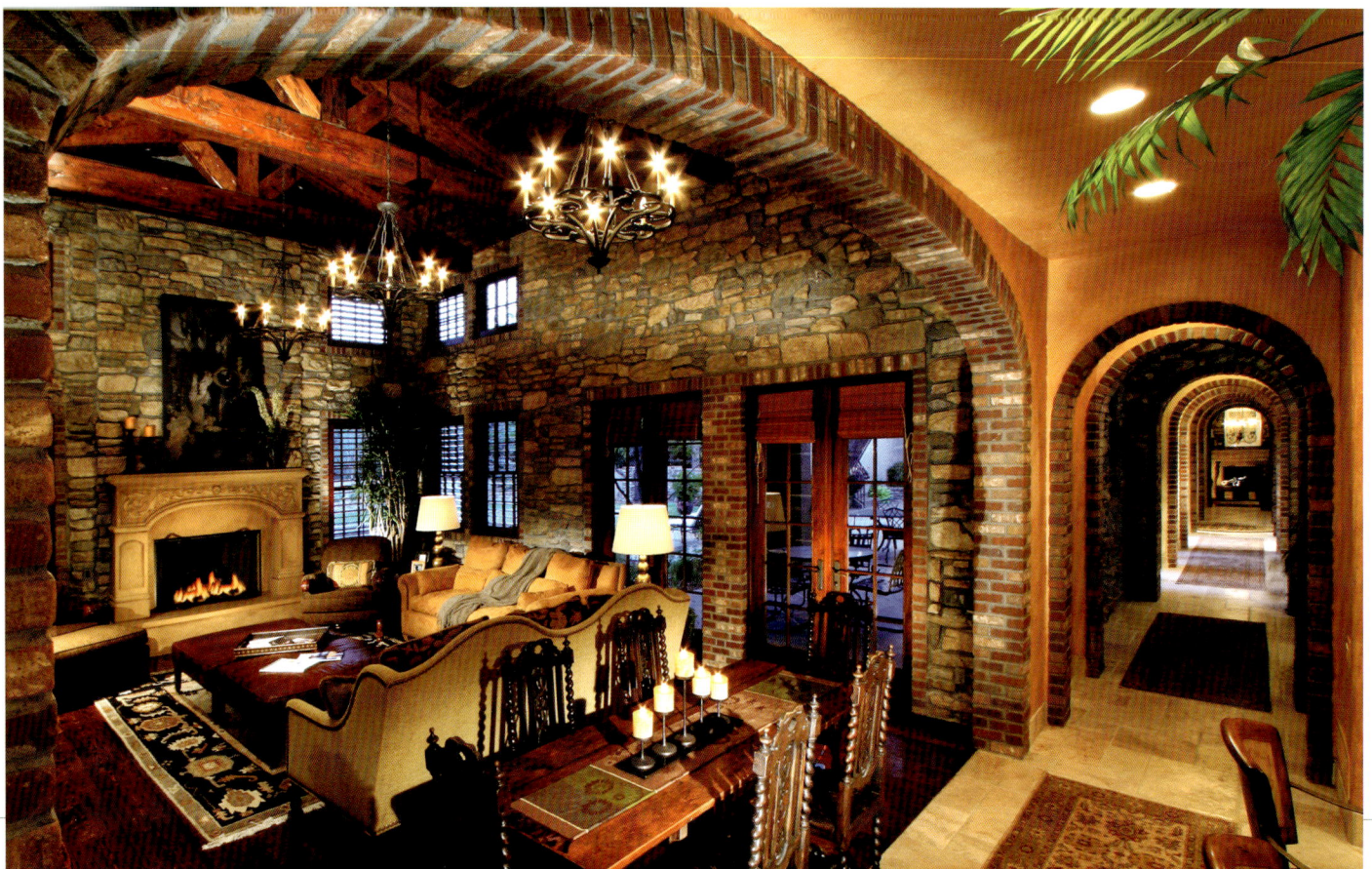

TOP LEFT:
A garden-like courtyard centered around the pool creates a tranquil and private atmosphere.
Photograph by Jeffery Aron

BOTTOM LEFT:
Hatchet-hewn beams, stone lined walls and larch and fir floors combined with tumbled travertine along the hall create the grandeur and detailed craftsmanship of European buildings of the past.
Photograph by Jeffery Aron

FACING PAGE TOP:
The Old World appeal of stone, stucco and tile roofing are beautifully united to create this appealing Greenwood Village home.
Photograph by Dan Ferguson

FACING PAGE BOTTOM:
Quality materials and architectural detail create a kitchen that is an inviting gathering place for family and friends.
Photograph by Dan Ferguson

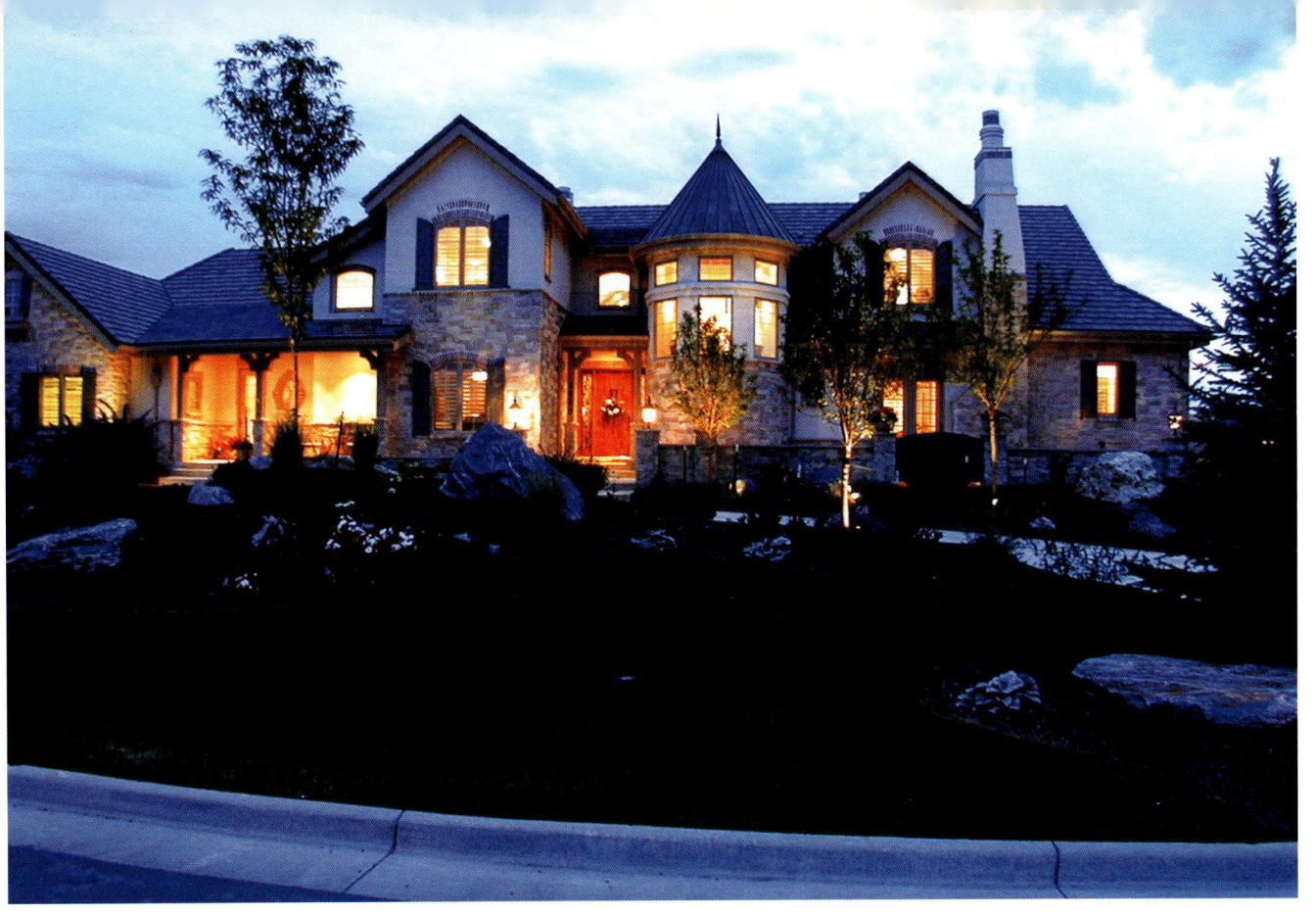

Q&A
more about glen ...

WHAT IS THE MOST UNIQUE HOME YOU'VE BEEN INVOLVED WITH? WHY?
We had the pleasure of building a 7,500-square-foot Country Italian home that turned out to be a masterpiece.

WHAT SEPARATES YOU FROM YOUR COMPETITION?
Our homes are the perfect expressions of our clients' unique personalities.

DESCRIBE YOUR STYLE OR DESIGN PREFERENCES.
The lodges here in Colorado are a great example of timeless architecture. To me the outstanding quality of some of these lodges is intangible; it's the comfort that makes a home a home and I try to bring this to each one of my houses.

HAVE YOU RECEIVED ANY AWARDS?
We received a crowing achievement, the Bar Award for Best Custom Home, in 2006.

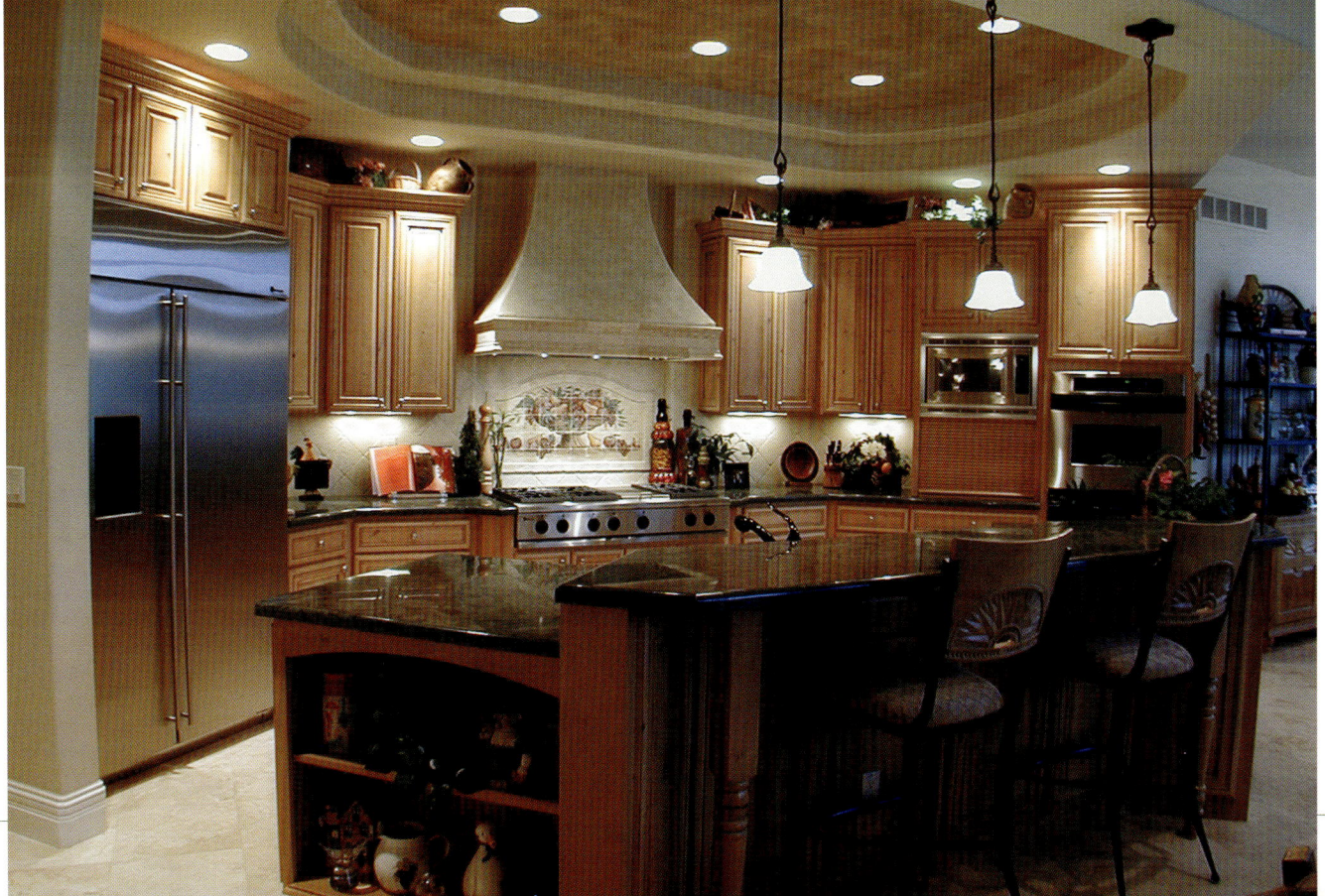

MALIBU HOMES, INC.
GLEN ZAHORKA
12835 East Arapahoe Road, Tower 1, Suite 320
Centennial, CO 80112
303.790.0909
f: 303.790.0404
www.malibuhomescolorado.com

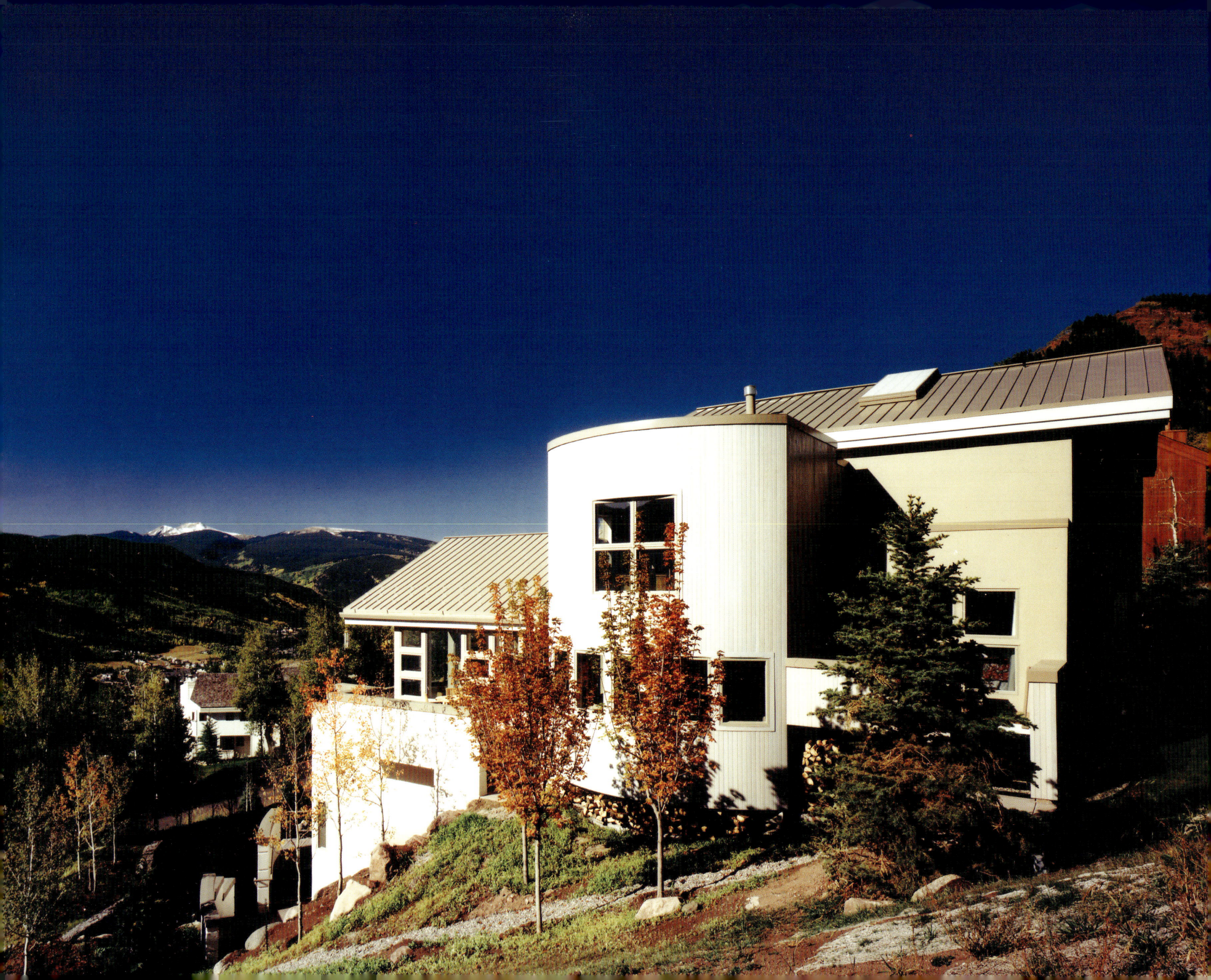

MICHAEL HAZARD
MICHAEL HAZARD ASSOCIATES

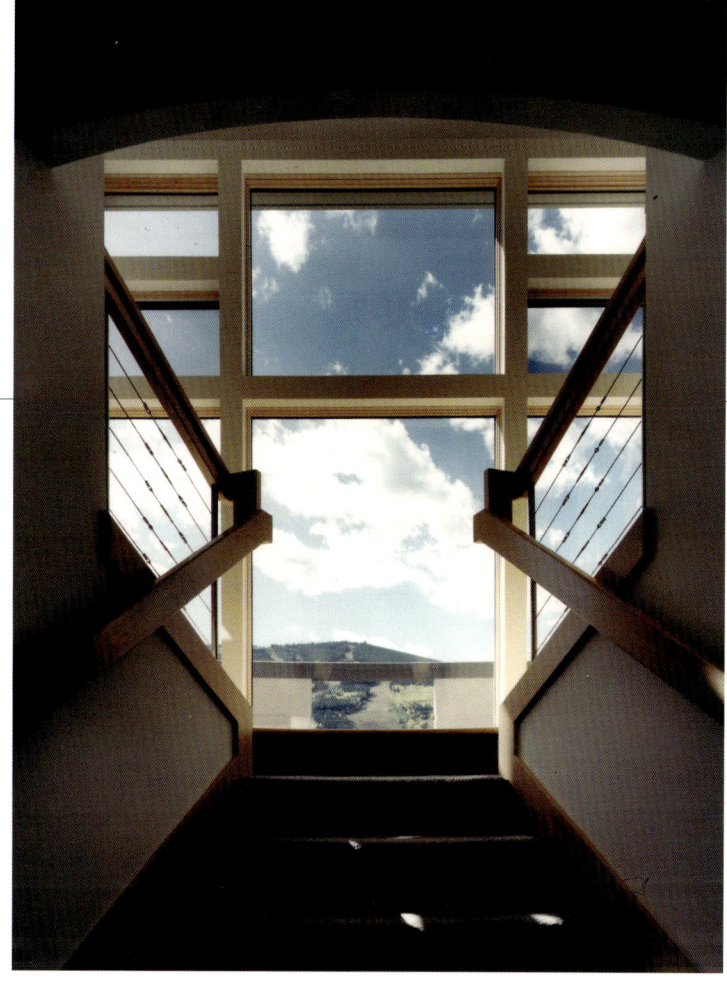

Leaving a challenging career in Chicago after his Bachelor of Architecture study at Notre Dame, Michael Hazard came to Vail in 1982. "I decided that lifestyle was more important than ego," recalls Michael. "And I am forever thankful I made that decision, both for myself and my family."

Designing custom homes in spectacular resort settings has been a lot more fun, according to Michael. Marketing for his practice consists of word-of-mouth–and Michael has been busy since he opened his own studio in 1989. "My time with clients begins with play, moves through work and ends with long-time mutual friendships," Michael notes.

"No doubt, the investment in a new home is serious business, but I try to encourage folks to lighten up and dream. After the rooms and uses are defined in the first hour, I try to discover what puts a smile on clients' faces and makes the design personal."

"Spaces of the imagination" was one of Michael's earliest client requests. Reaching beyond the normal "needs analysis" that is basic to all architecture, Michael points out how architecture is more like language than a drawing. "I like to create spaces that are explored by moving through and around them."

Featured on The Travel Channel's series "Great American Vacation Homes," Michael's design for Ann and Jim Frein's home overlooking Vail Mountain is a fine example. More important to Michael than the completion of the 5,000-square-foot residence is his nearly two decades of friendship with the Frein's since that time. The friendship and trust has flourished through two additions.

ABOVE:
Frein Residence, Vail, Colorado. The main entry stair is positioned at the center of the residence, and upon entering, one must ascend the stairs to the heart of the home. At the top of the stairs, one is immediately met with expansive windows which showcase the breathtaking cross-valley views and ski runs of Vail Mountain.
Photograph by Gordon Schenck

FACING PAGE:
Frein Residence, Vail, Colorado. View, looking southwest towards the New York Mountain Range. The main exterior living spaces are elevated 2½ stories above the entry drive and wrap around the home to rise above the surrounding homes and offer unobstructed, panoramic views.
Photograph by Gordon Schenck

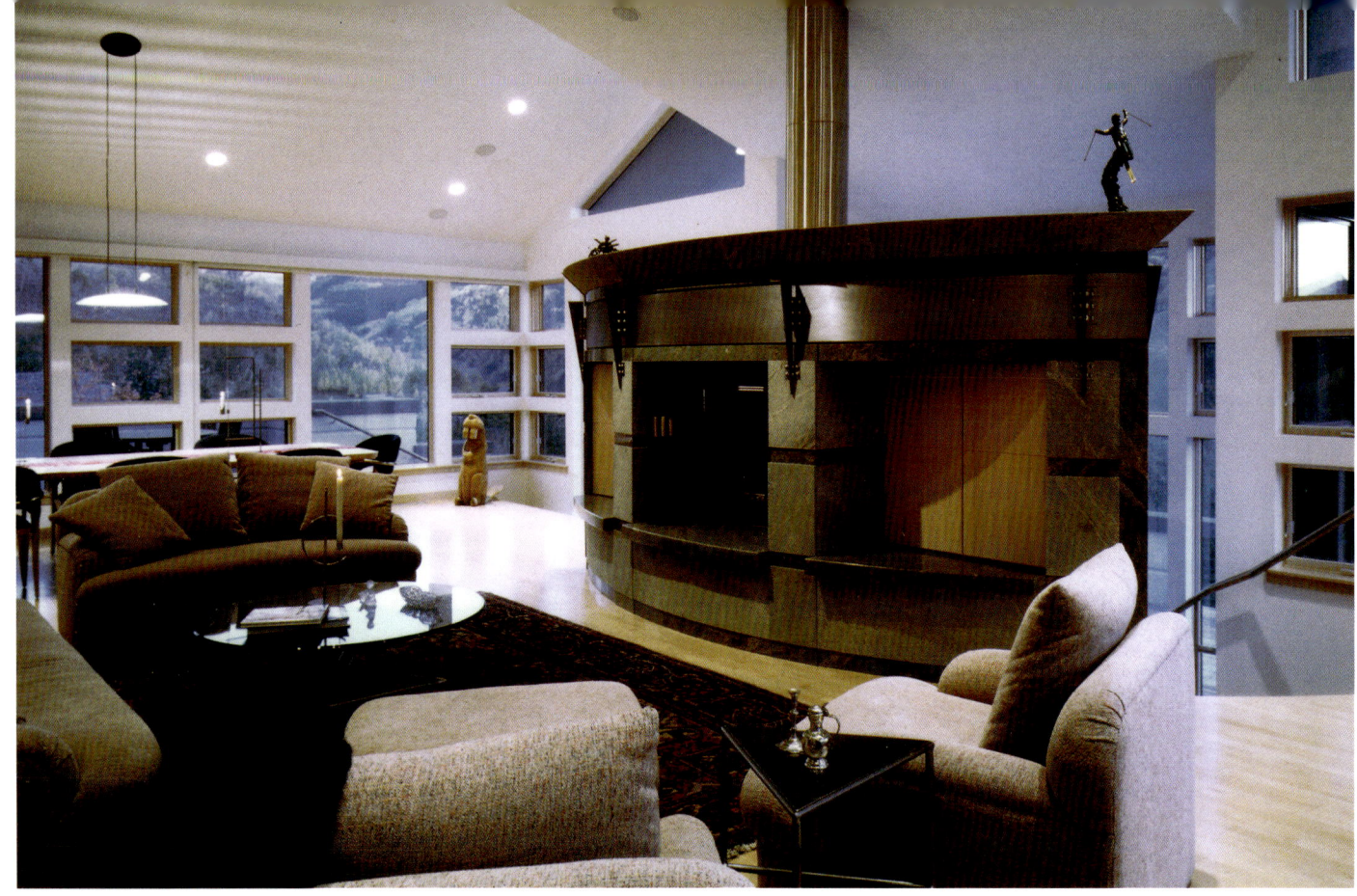

As former president of the local "Chaine des Rotisseurs", a convivial wine appreciation group in Vail, Jim Frein was excited about building his own wine cellar. Giving the wine cellar a prominent place adjacent to the main living area, Michael's design cuts into the hillside, giving the "cellar" all the attributes of a classic cool tasting room, yet it's only steps from breathtaking views of Vail Mountain. It turns out that five of Michael's subsequent clients are also "Chaine" members, all impressed with Michael's originality in capturing tradition.

"The historical form of 'shelter' presents us with infinite variables," notes Michael, "and therein we discover keys to the development of individual character. Traditional. A preferred style that demands close scrutiny. I like to discover how each client defines tradition in the first step to forge distinction between trite duplication and intelligent interpretation." Michael is comfortable working within a community's architectural guidelines while stretching beyond tract-like repetition of empty imagery.

Transparency, in its myriad manifestations, is key in all of Michael's designs. Transparency of form—the roof and walls emphasize the functions that they protect. Intuitive transparency of organization. Transparency of structure that celebrates the strength and counterpoint of a home's "bones." An honest use of materials rather than a meaningless application of them. And, of course, transparency that opens the life inside a home to its magnificent surroundings.

His homes have a freedom inspired by nature, and yet Michael is known for his innovative use of cutting-edge construction techniques and mechanical services. Carefully responding to the form of its terrain, a home may twist playfully to capture the perfect sunset. Sometimes nature is best emphasized through contrast: a crisp architectural edge may juxtapose with the soft lines of a native boulder.

Michael's home designs can be both spectacular and powerfully "quiet," embodying safe refuge. Each new design is passionately different from the rest, antidotes to a mass culture of "McMansions." When a family chooses to work with Michael, they set out on an exploration of what the word "home" means to them. His clients receive much more than a set of drawings locked into the latest trend. With Michael Hazard, they get a home that will live on as part of their particular history.

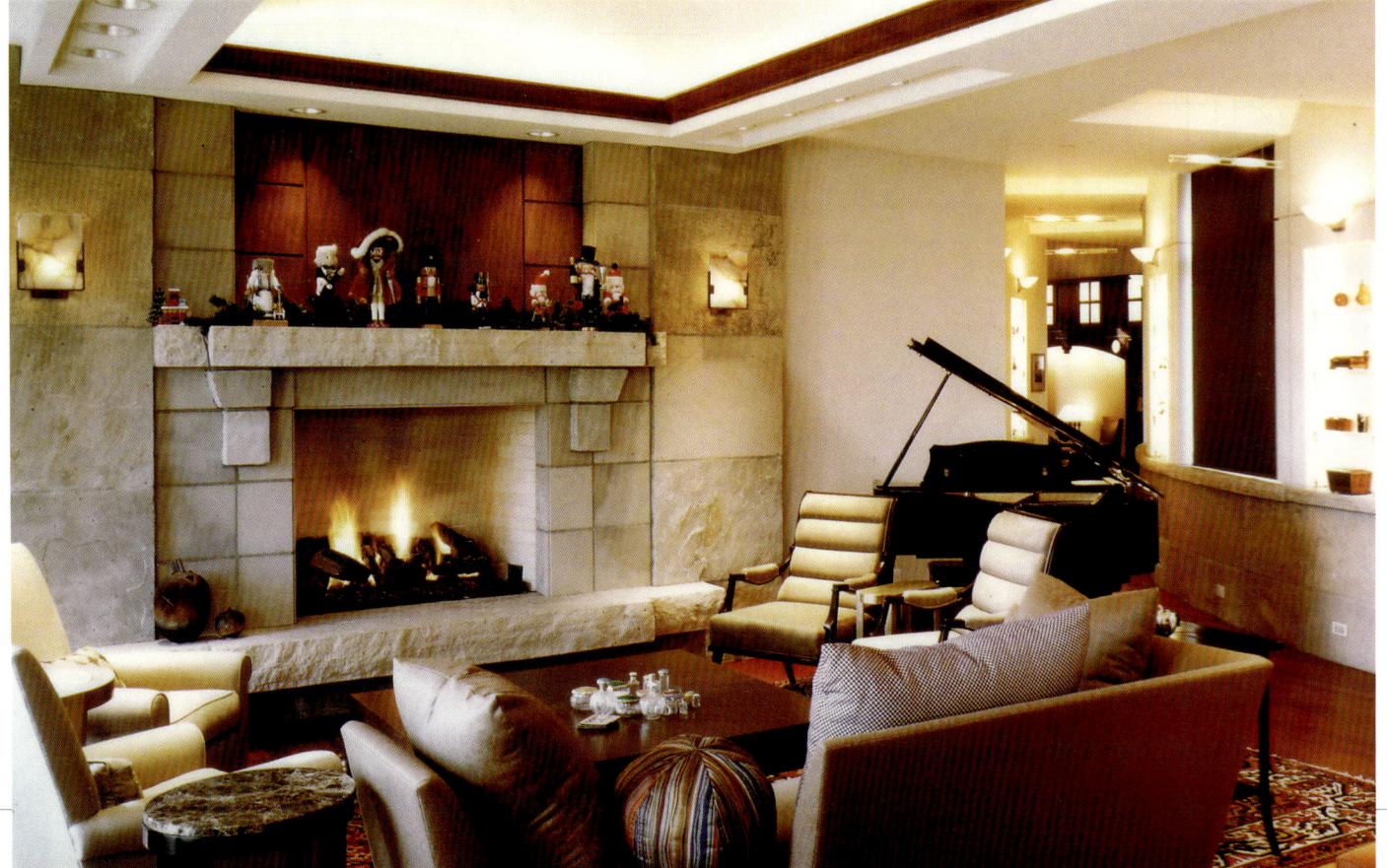

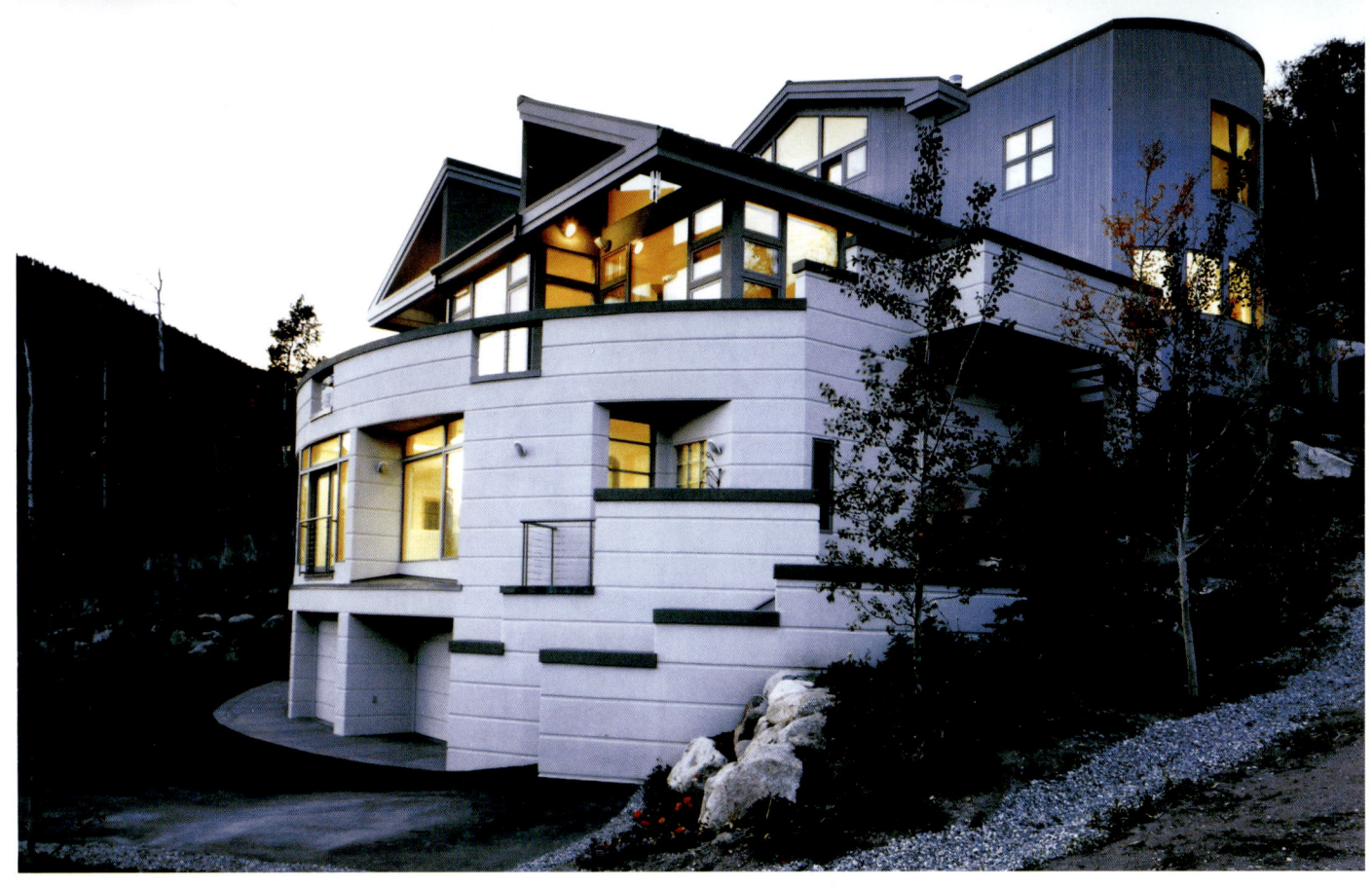

TOP RIGHT:
Frein residence, Vail, Colorado. This twilight view of the south exterior of the home shows how the gently curved, symmetrical base of the home is punctuated with smaller punched openings while the upper portions, housing the main living spaces are treated with large expanses of glass to take in the views.
Photograph by Gordon Schenck

BOTTOM RIGHT:
Private residence, Mountain Star, Colorado. This formal entry court recalls an urban formality, sought by the owners as a response to their former London residence while maintaining its context of the mountains of Colorado with the use of native stone and copper.
Photograph by Dale Nelson Photography

FACING PAGE TOP:
Frein residence, Vail, Colorado. The main living spaces stretch over 40 feet across the south face of the home. The east and west ends of the room accommodate dining and informal seating areas whose focus is directed to the views. The central portion of the room focuses on a granite-clad fireplace/media element.
Photograph by Gordon Schenck

FACING PAGE BOTTOM:
Private residence, Mountain Star, Colorado. This living room was designed with more formal flat and coved ceilings for clients who will make this home their full time residence and deliberately wanted to avoid taller, vaulted ceilings which, to them evoked a vacation home.
Photograph by Dale Nelson Photography

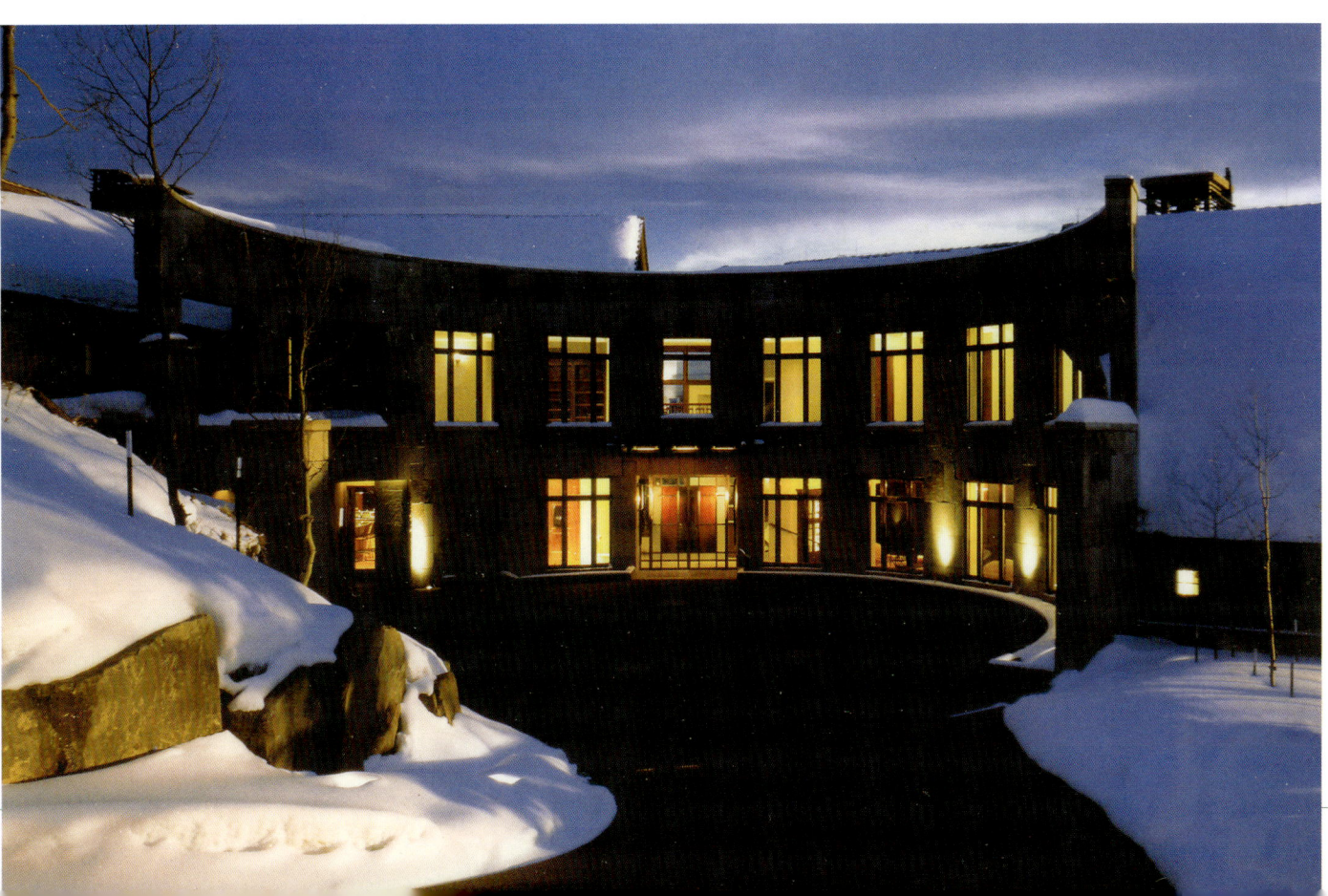

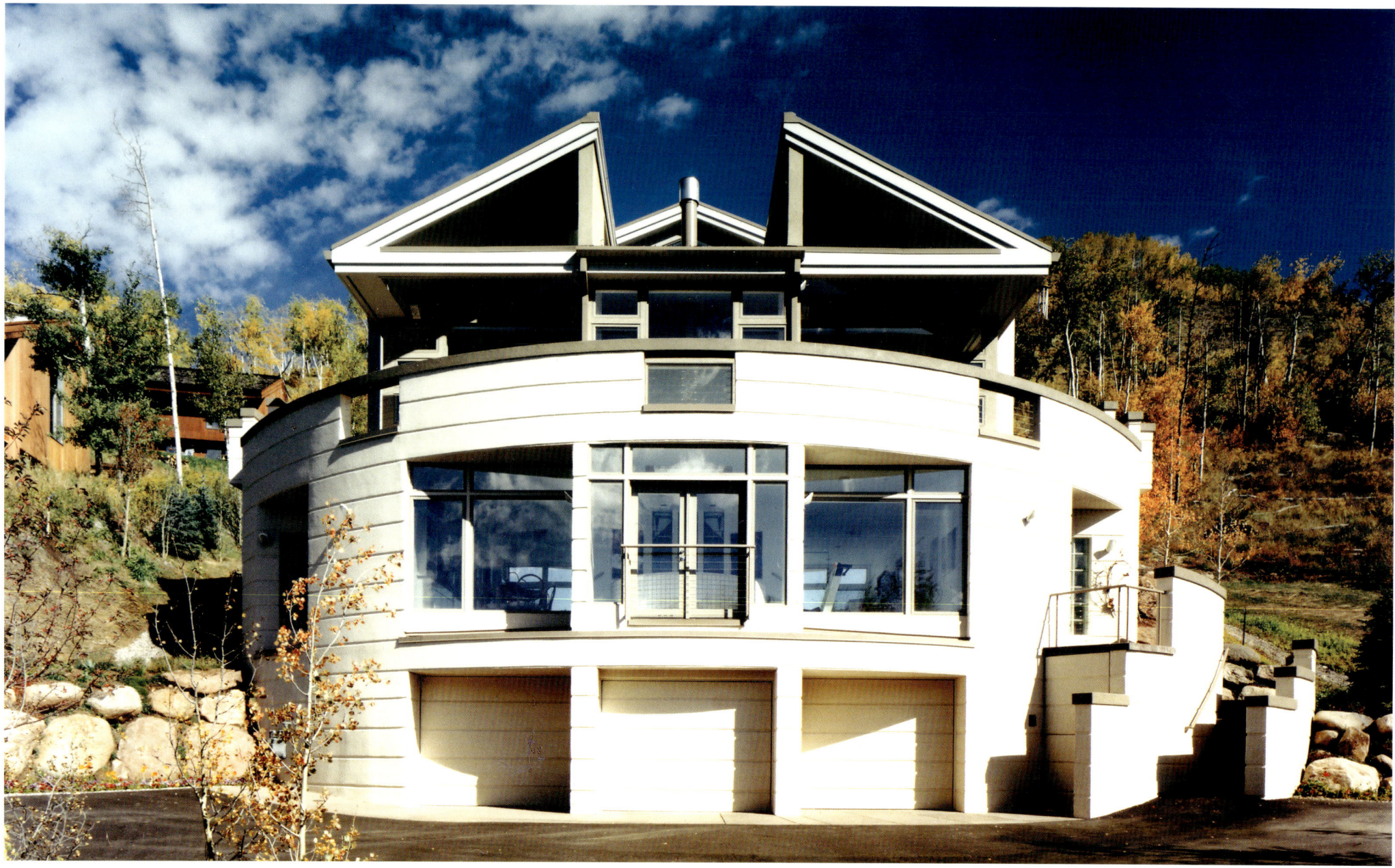

ABOVE:
Frein residence, Vail, Colorado. The guest to this home is ushered up a short exterior flight of stairs to a landing where a hint of the spectacular views can be glimpsed. He is then led through a short hall to the base of the main stairs where the full impact of the view can be appreciated.
Photograph by Gordon Schenck

FACING PAGE:
Private residence, Mountain Star, Colorado. The entry courtyard is at once a response in form to the function of a car's turning radius and a formal counterpart to the exterior facades of the otherwise traditional mountain aesthetic. The custom cut application of the same native buff sandstone, used in random patterns elsewhere, maintains a strong relationship between the home's dual design personalities and the natural outcroppings surrounding the home.
Photograph by Dale Nelson

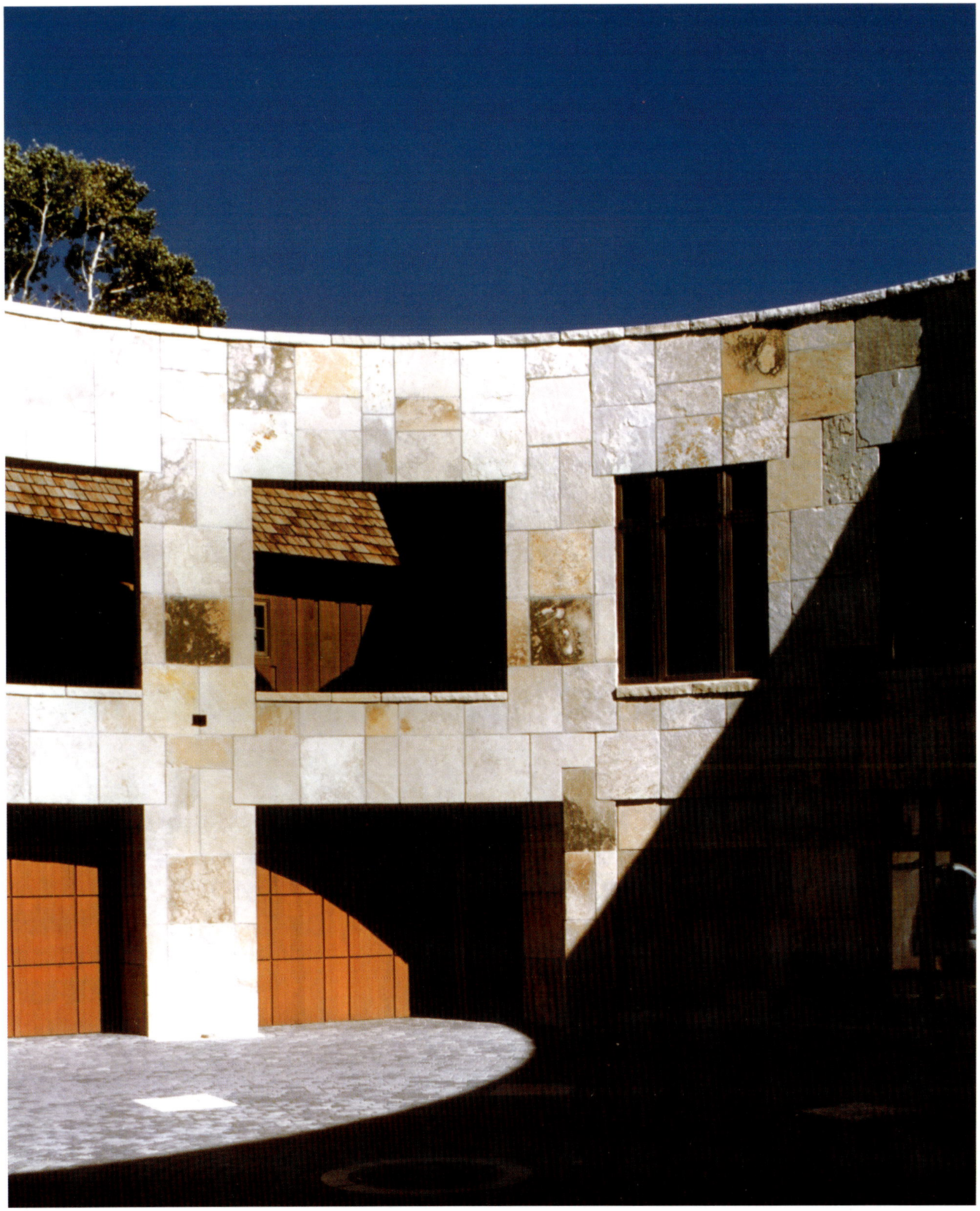

Q&A more about michael...

DESCRIBE YOUR STYLE OR DESIGN PREFERENCES.
I avoid style or fashion in favor of a timeless design that responds to my clients' program first followed by the site: its slope, vegetation historic context and climate. Then I will mold the design as an interpretation of any governing design guidelines.

WHAT IS THE HIGHEST COMPLIMENT YOU'VE RECEIVED PROFESSIONALLY?
At the conclusion of a project, my clients' satisfaction always counts as the most important endorsement of my efforts. Their happiness and enjoyment of their new home says more than any award to me and to new clients. Add an award, from my peers, to the mix and it's a home run!

YOU WOULDN'T KNOW IT, BUT MY FRIENDS WOULD TELL YOU THAT...
I never rest on my prior successes, and approach each new project with a healthy dose of exploration. There are no laurels to rest on, as each new project presents me with a completely new set of circumstances. Although I rely on my methodology in solving new problems, I prefer to wipe the slate clean and strive for a fresh solution so the result is truly custom and unique to each client.

WHAT IS THE BEST PART OF BEING AN ARCHITECT?
The best part of architecture is that it is art married with function which directly and subliminally enhances the quality of people's lives. I really enjoy the process of meeting new clients and molding the interpretations of their experiences to develop their personal environment.

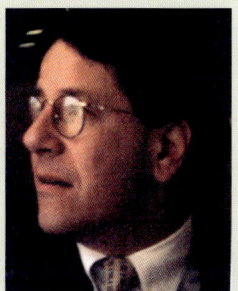

MICHAEL HAZARD ASSOCIATES
MICHAEL A. HAZARD, AIA
P.O. BOX 1068; VAIL, CO 81658   *Mail*
2381 FOX LANE; AVON, CO 81620   *Courier*
970.949.4958
f: 970.949.4838
mha@vail.net

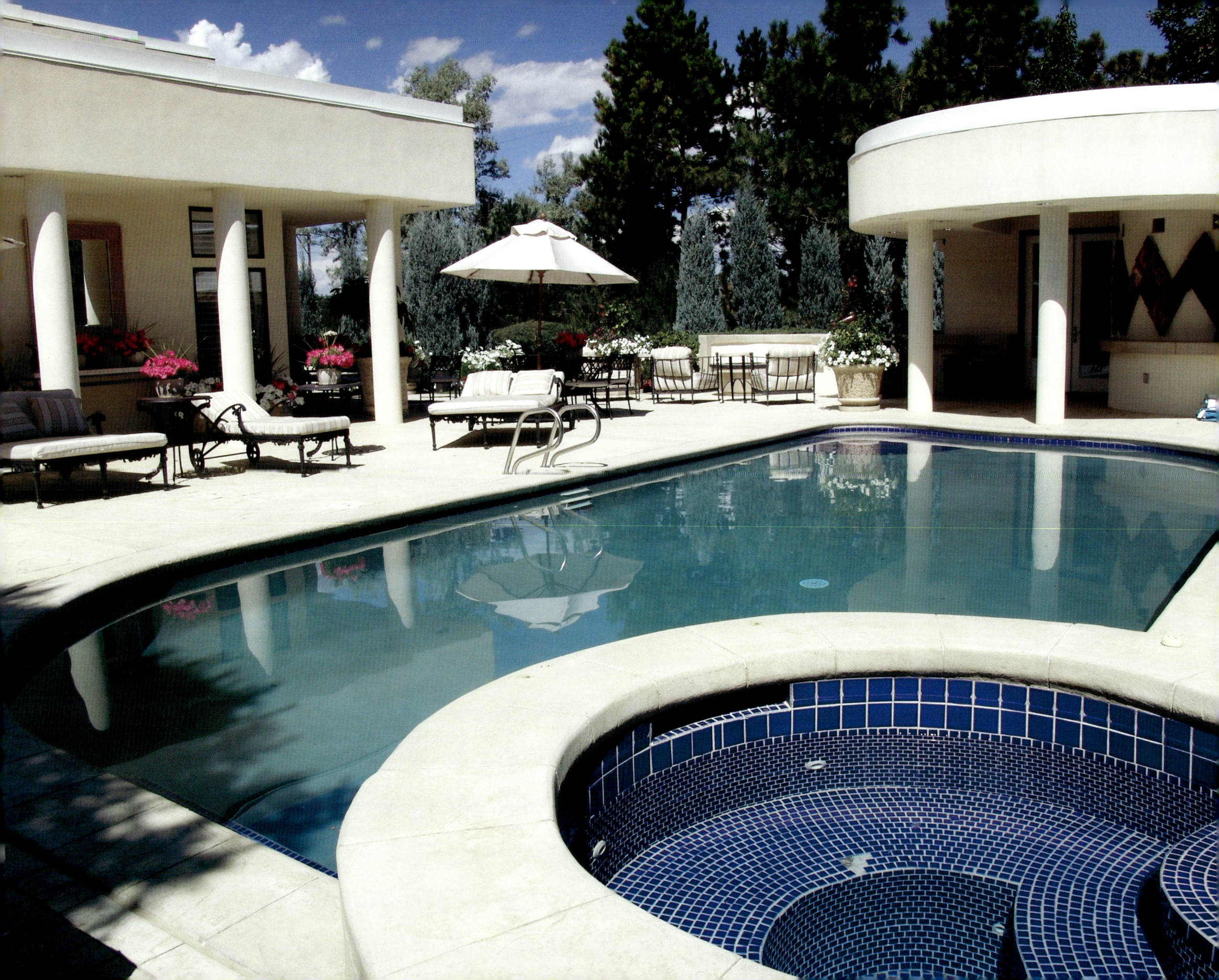

MICHAEL KNORR

MICHAEL KNORR & ASSOCIATES

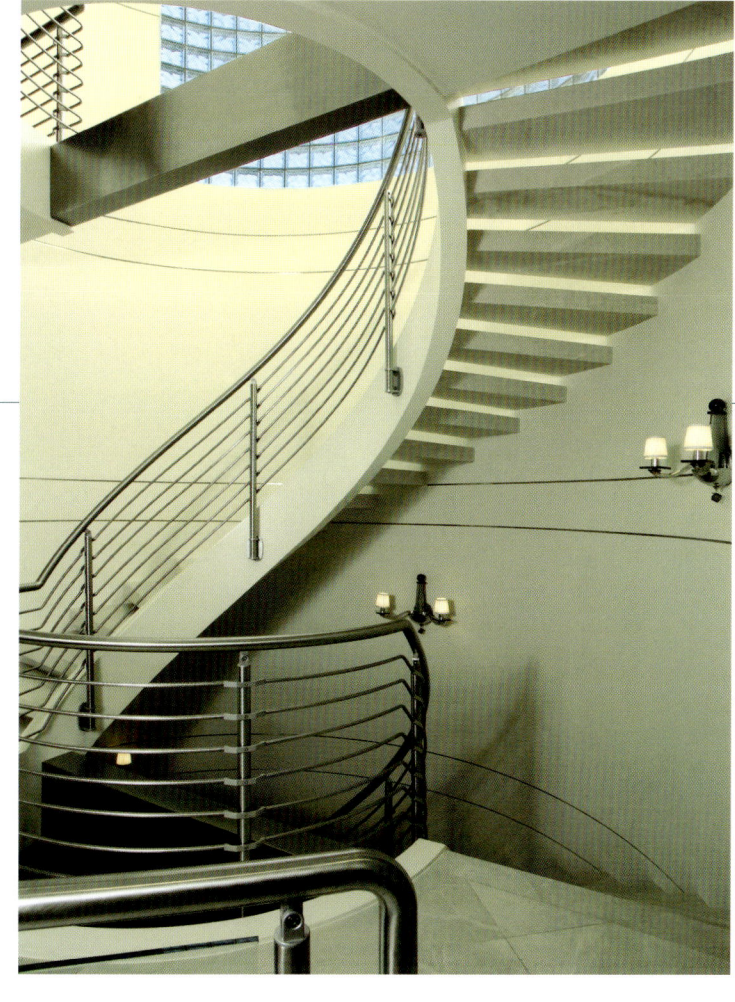

Michael Knorr & Associates was established in Denver 30 years ago after Michael visited Colorado for its skiing and fell in love with everything else. "I love the West and its people being open to new ideas. It's a younger mentality here and an exciting place to be. Colorado is more open to expressive and innovative architecture than many other parts of the country."

People want their home to symbolize their dreams. It should embody what they seek and value in life. A person's dreams are as unique as their personality and their home should express these qualities. Committed to this ideal, Michael Knorr and his team listen carefully to the client. As the first step in the design process they develop a detailed written program tailored to a client's dreams and needs. They have also developed an advanced spreadsheet program which converts room sizes and mechanical considerations into projected square footage. Coupled with a description of every space and the relationship between spaces, this programming process serves as a "checks and balances" system which ensures that the client's creative, practical, and budgetary needs are fulfilled. Understanding the project at this most basic level enables Michael and his client to "get inside the design" before a single line is drawn.

Michael wants his clients to know that their dream home can serve the practical necessities of life and be exciting architecture. While he believes all aspects of a design are important, for Michael it begins with interior space. "Space is what's important. If space is sculpted to have mass, depth, shadow, and light it invites the eye and the mind to explore the environment." He bases each design on the concept that it should evolve from the inside out.

ABOVE:
Flowing spaces and sculptural forms are characteristic of Michael Knorr's architecture.
Photograph by R. Ruscio

FACING PAGE:
The main house and adjacent cabana form a contemporary courtyard around the swimming pool of this Cherry Hills Village residence.
Photograph by R. Munger

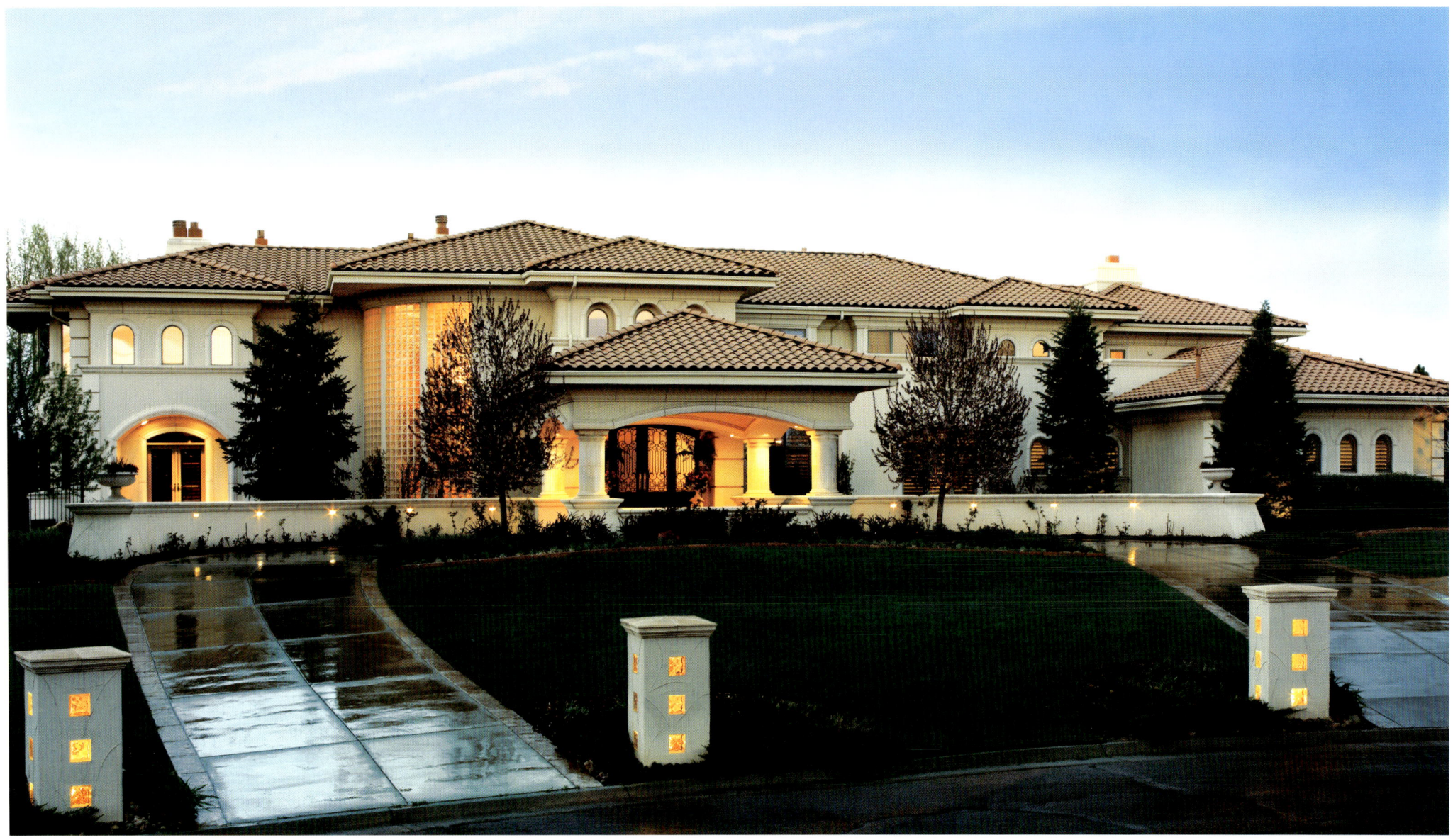

Taking advantage of Colorado's bright, sunny climate, Michael uses light and shadow to accentuate interior and exterior architectural features. Using light as a material, Michael carefully arranges it in subtle and creative ways. His designs capture light, molding it into architectural form to complement and enhance the life within the structure.

A major part of the work of Michael Knorr & Associates is balancing the indoor-to-outdoor relationship of structure to site. His designs typically focus on views and extend living spaces to the outside. Michael treats external spaces as outdoor rooms, sculpting them with the same attention to detail as any room inside the house. After all is done, the partnering of inside and outside spaces and the molding of these spaces into a unified structure create architecture that makes every Michael Knorr design a unique expression for each client.

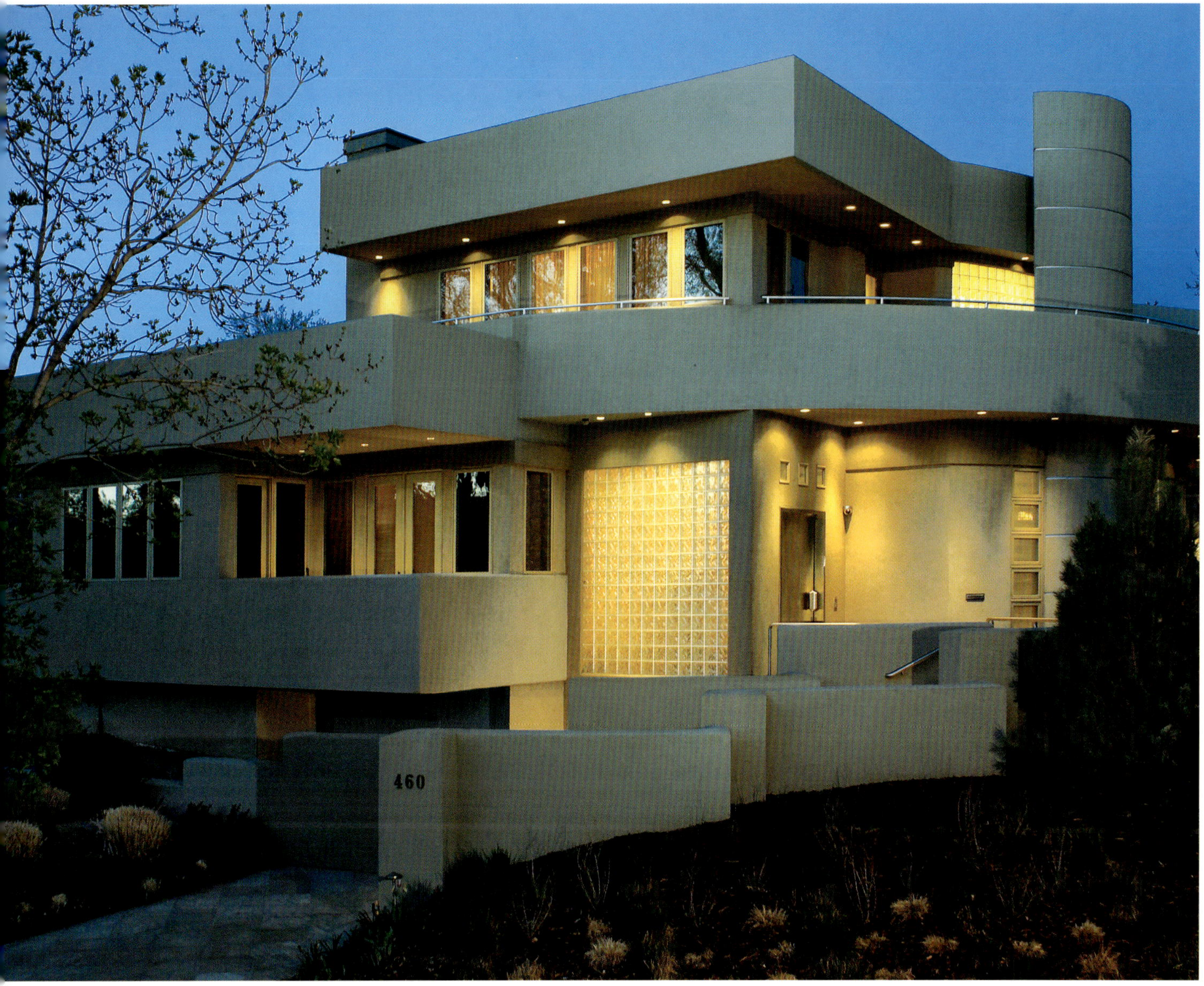

ABOVE:
One of the most striking homes in Denver's Cherry Creek neighborhood plays off the architectural tension of curvilinear and rectilinear geometry.
Photograph by R. Ruscio

FACING PAGE:
The massive *porte cochere* extablishes with authority and grace the classic architectural forms of this suburban estate.
Photograph by R. Ruscio

Q&A more about michael...

WHO HAS HAD THE BIGGEST INFLUENCE ON YOUR CAREER?
Two architects have influenced and inspired my career: Frank Lloyd Wright for his earth-bound, romantic forms and Bruce Goff for his inventiveness.

WHAT IS THE ONE PERSONAL INDULGENCE YOU SPEND THE MOST MONEY ON?
Books—and not just architecture books—books of all kinds. I just finished reading *The Self-Aware Universe* by Amit Goswami.

WHAT DO YOU LIKE THE MOST ABOUT DOING BUSINESS IN COLORADO?
I love that people in the West are open to new ideas and not afraid of the future.

HOW LONG HAVE YOU BEEN AN ARCHITECT?
I decided to become an architect when I was 12 years old and built my first house at the age of 18.

DESCRIBE YOUR STYLE PREFERENCES.
The style is not as important as making sure that the architecture is both comfortable and interesting.

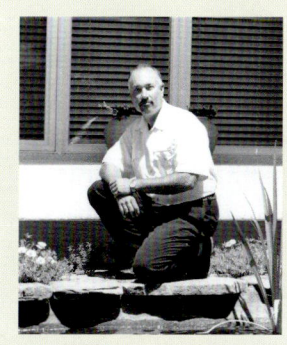

MICHAEL KNORR & ASSOCIATES
MICHAEL KNORR
2131 South Grape Street
Denver, CO 80222
303.744.1887

44 Grand Miramar
Las Vegas, NV 89011
702.233.1947
www.michaelknorr.net

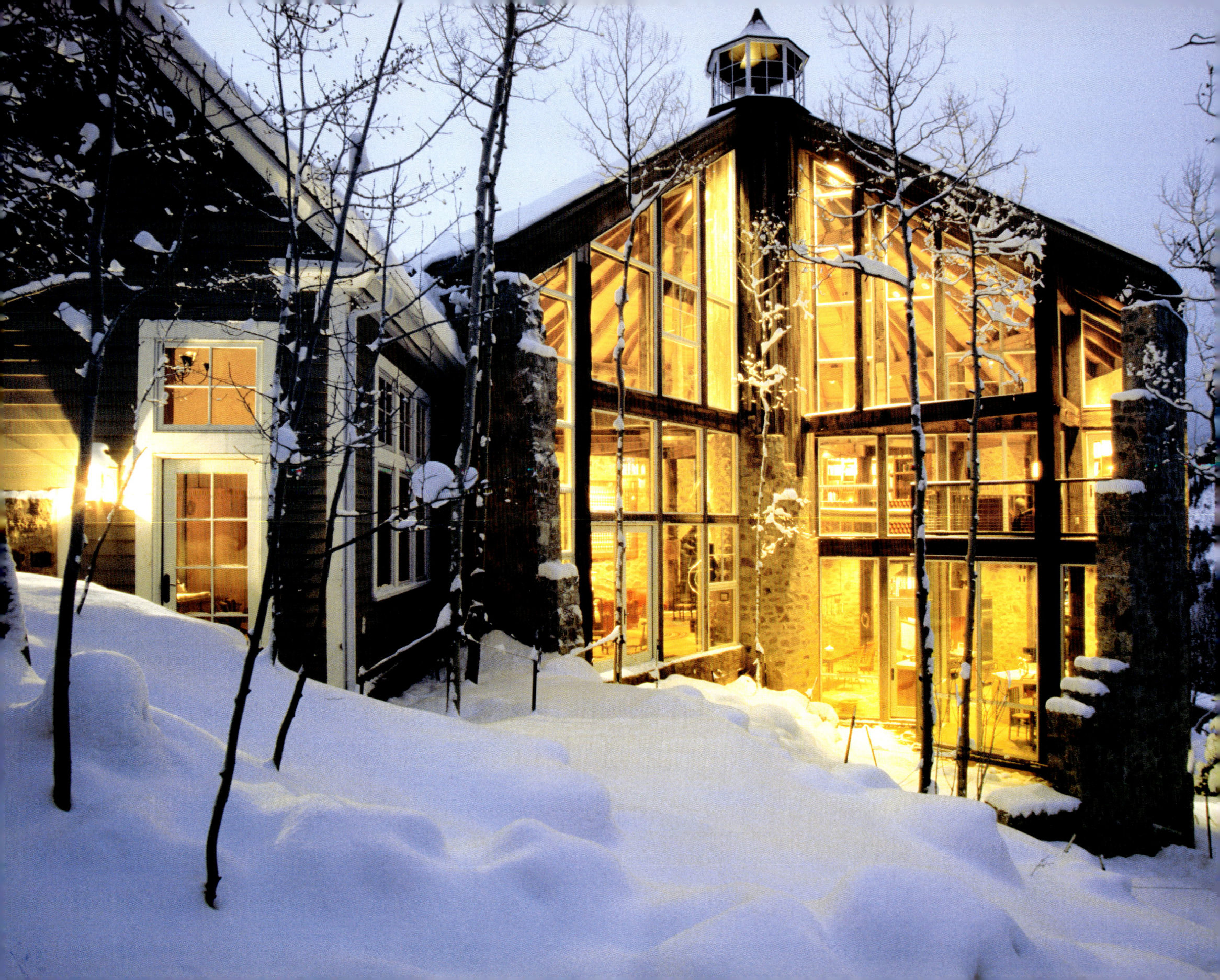

JAMES R. MORTER

MORTER ARCHITECTS

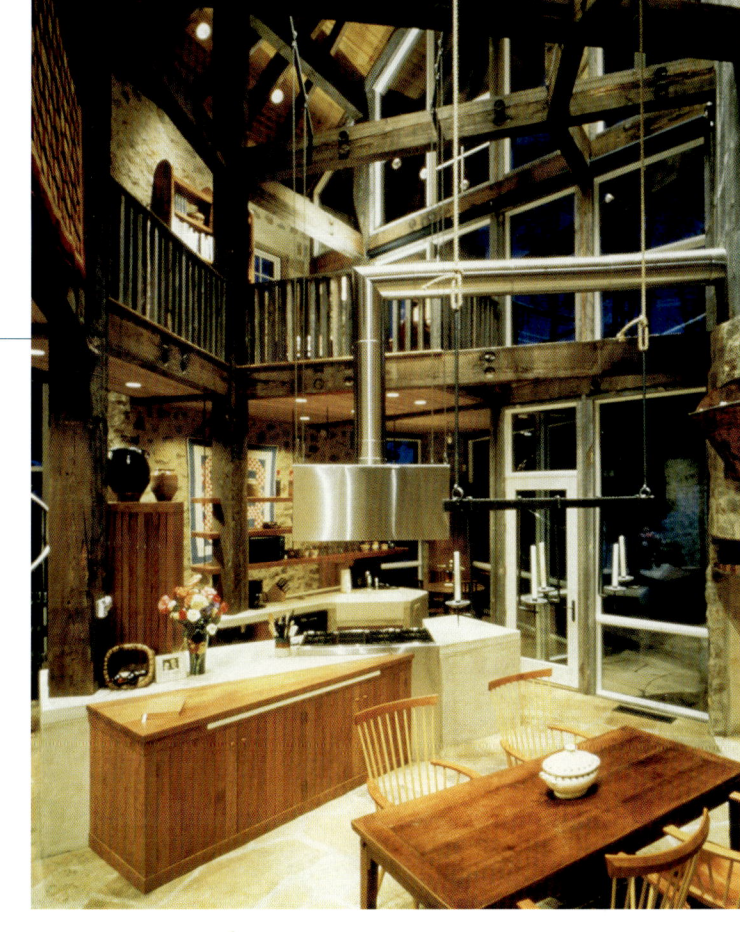

By the time he was a teenager, Jim Morter knew he wanted to be an architect, even though he had never actually met one. His gift for creating architecture, as pieces of well-proportioned and provocative sculpture stems from his Albuquerque childhood, during which he was exposed to indigenous Pueblo-style forms of the Southwest.

Upon graduating from Texas Tech and receiving his degree in architecture, Jim went to work in Honolulu, Hawaii for a few years before signing on with an architectural firm in Denver, Colorado. Soon after, Jim relocated to Vail, Colorado in 1972 to manage its branch office. The opportunity provided two years of experience in mountain architecture after which Jim began his own firm, Morter Architects. Morter Architects is in its third decade as an award-winning firm specializing in the design of custom residences in the Vail Valley, numerous Colorado resort destinations and along the Front Range, as well as throughout the country, Bahamas, and Mexico.

The ever-present open and accessible culture at Morter Architects sets the pace for the client/architect relationship. After an initial meeting to ensure that the project is a good fit for both parties, Jim believes that the initial step in programming the design is spending time at the site, assessing its environmental aspects as well as exploring its access, views and neighboring structures. Before pencil is ever put to paper, Jim finds it imperative to understand his client's desires and needs.

Jim believes in initiating the schematic design process with an intensive one or two day session during which he and a project architect focus solely on the initial design while periodically meeting with the client during that period. This process allows the client to be an integral part of the decision

ABOVE:
The hand-made nature of the residence is reflected in many ways: the cast-in-place concrete kitchen counters and cabinet surrounds; the kitchen shelves suspended by long threaded rods and bolts; the custom-designed vent hood and duct; and the candle chandelier, which is suspended over the dining table by a rope and pulley system.
Photograph by Dann Coffey

FACING PAGE:
Large glazed viewing walls are created by "slicing a piece of pie" from the round structure, providing wonderful views of the home's mountain setting, and also providing access to south-facing outdoor living areas.
Photograph by Dann Coffey

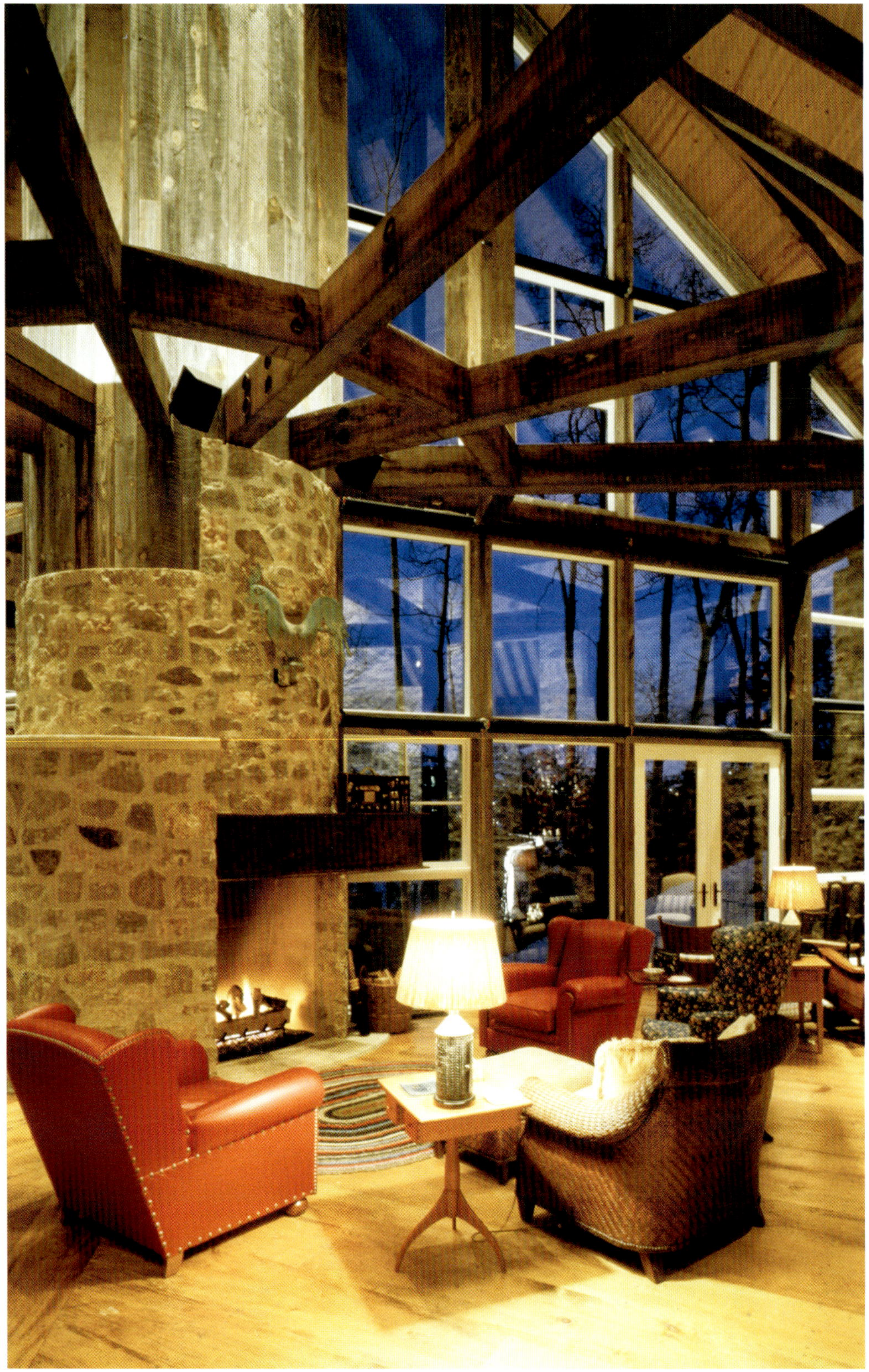

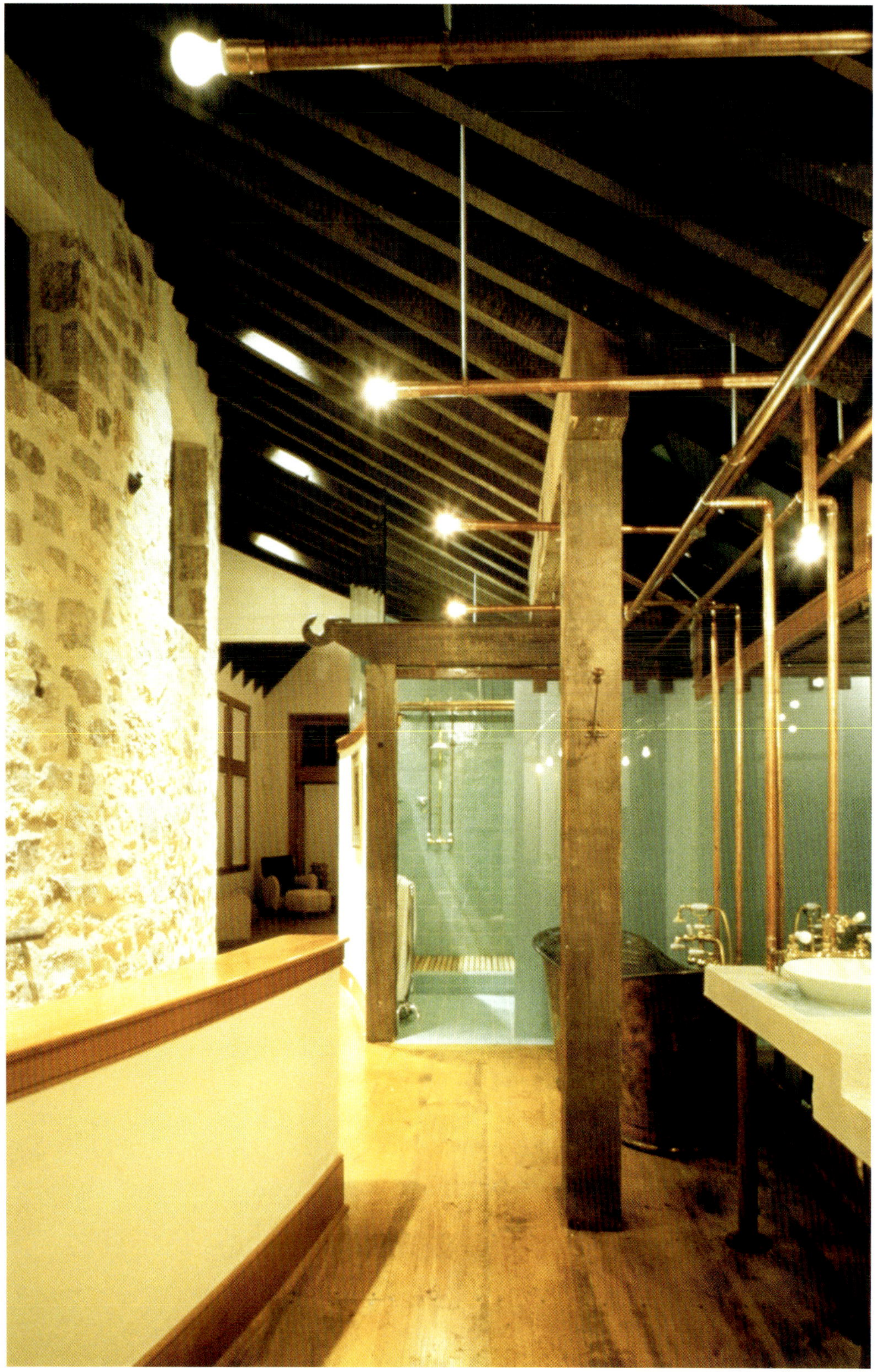

process throughout this preliminary design stage. As a result of this session the clients generally receive preliminary sketches representative of the design intent for their project. This unconventional approach has created some of Morter Architects' most successful projects.

Jim is form-oriented; his architecture defies any formula but typically illustrates the study of solid and void patterns. Morter Architects is known for its innovative use of building materials in its projects. For example, materials such as rusted corrugated metal will be installed alongside traditional finished wood, creating a juxtaposition that plays up the beauty of each element's respective nature.

Morter Architects is renowned for their attention to detail. They define each element of its buildings with a different vocabulary of detailing in addition to teaming with interior designers early in the process to ensure a cohesive language between the architecture and its interior elements. Morter Architects also introduces the builder as early as possible in the process to assure a smooth and efficient experience in the construction of the unique and often unconventional designs.

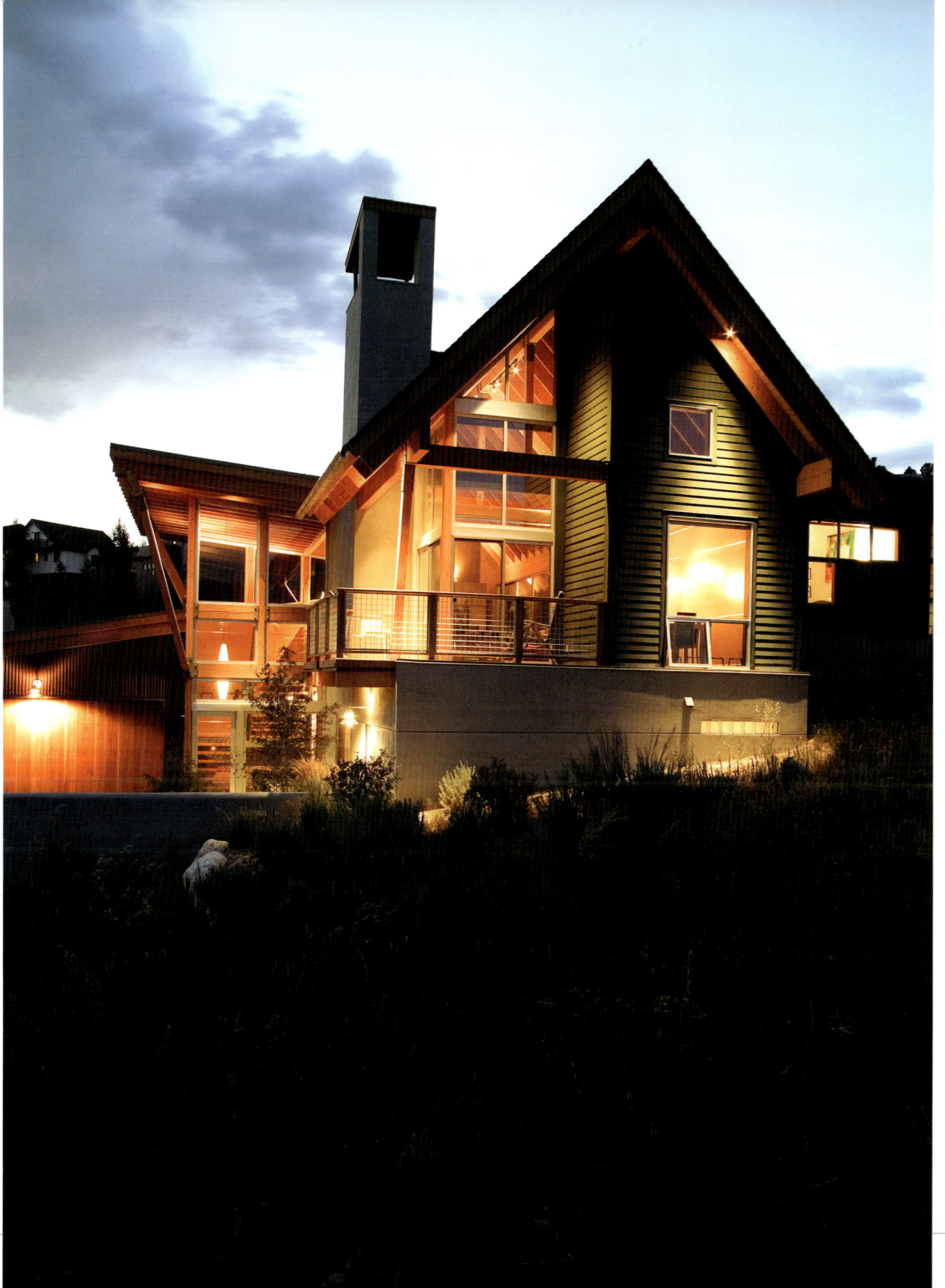

RIGHT:
The beautiful sage-covered site was left undisturbed or was restored for the most part. The two-story glazed form provides a beacon identifying the entry. The base of the home is stucco, providing protection from the months of winter conditions. The clapboard siding is kept well above grade.
Photograph by Dann Coffey

FACING PAGE LEFT:
The circular fireplace form is the centerpiece of the family living spaces. The exposed steel "mantel" is typical of the direct, straightforward detailing found throughout the home. All of the primary living spaces enjoy views of the nearby ski mountain, ski village, and golf course. The structural framing was reclaimed from a warehouse in Oregon, and the wide plank flooring was reclaimed from an industrial structure in New Hampshire.
Photograph by Dann Coffey

FACING PAGE RIGHT:
Intersections of the home's primary forms, in this case the round stone family living form and the Shaker "home" form, are expressed and celebrated. The exposed copper plumbing pipes and electrical conduits were inspired by a men's dormitory in the Shaker community of Hancock, Massachusetts. A steel beam reclaimed from the banks of the Colorado River supports a large panel of frosted glass, which provides privacy to the master shower and toilet area.
Photograph by Dann Coffey

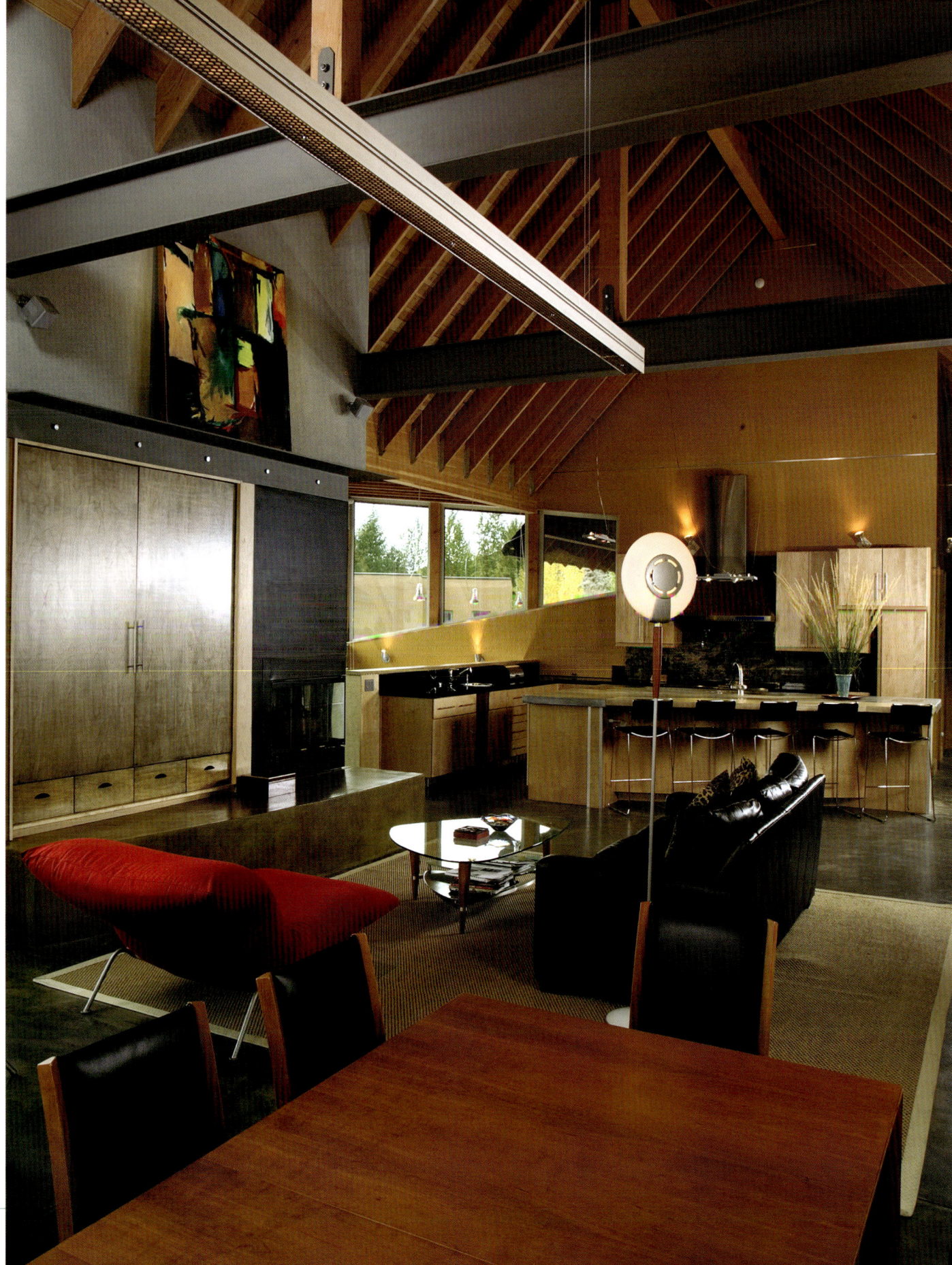

Jim is the sole owner of the firm. He does not distinguish himself as its guru, but is known throughout the firm as a mentor. At the beginning of a new project, Jim allows the opportunity for two or three team members to develop their own schematic designs. Each design is then critiqued by the entire firm before the final design is selected. "I have come to believe that architecture is the highest form of art in that it's not just about creating a beautiful object to look at; it's so much more," Jim says. "It's about environmental issues and people, and it has to function and be earth-friendly and express the purpose of the piece and of those who use it."

LEFT:
Exposed roof structure; stained concrete floor and hearth; lacquered MDF board on the walls; and uncluttered detailing provide an informal, straightforward setting for the primary living spaces. The dining room "chandelier" was fabricated by the owner from a piece of leftover window frame and plastic lens.
Photograph by Dann Coffey

FACING PAGE TOP:
The retaining site wall screens the auto court and garages from the nearby street. The elevated living spaces look over the garage roof and road to a nearby pond and mountain range to the south. Simple gable and shed roof forms create efficient and varied spaces throughout.
Photograph by Dann Coffey

FACING PAGE BOTTOM:
An existing irrigation ditch on the property was transformed into a mountain stream which is a focal point for outdoor living at the rear of the home. The stream is spanned by the master bedroom, which is made up of translucent panels and clear glazing. The stream splashing over the boulders makes for peaceful sleep.
Photograph by Dann Coffey

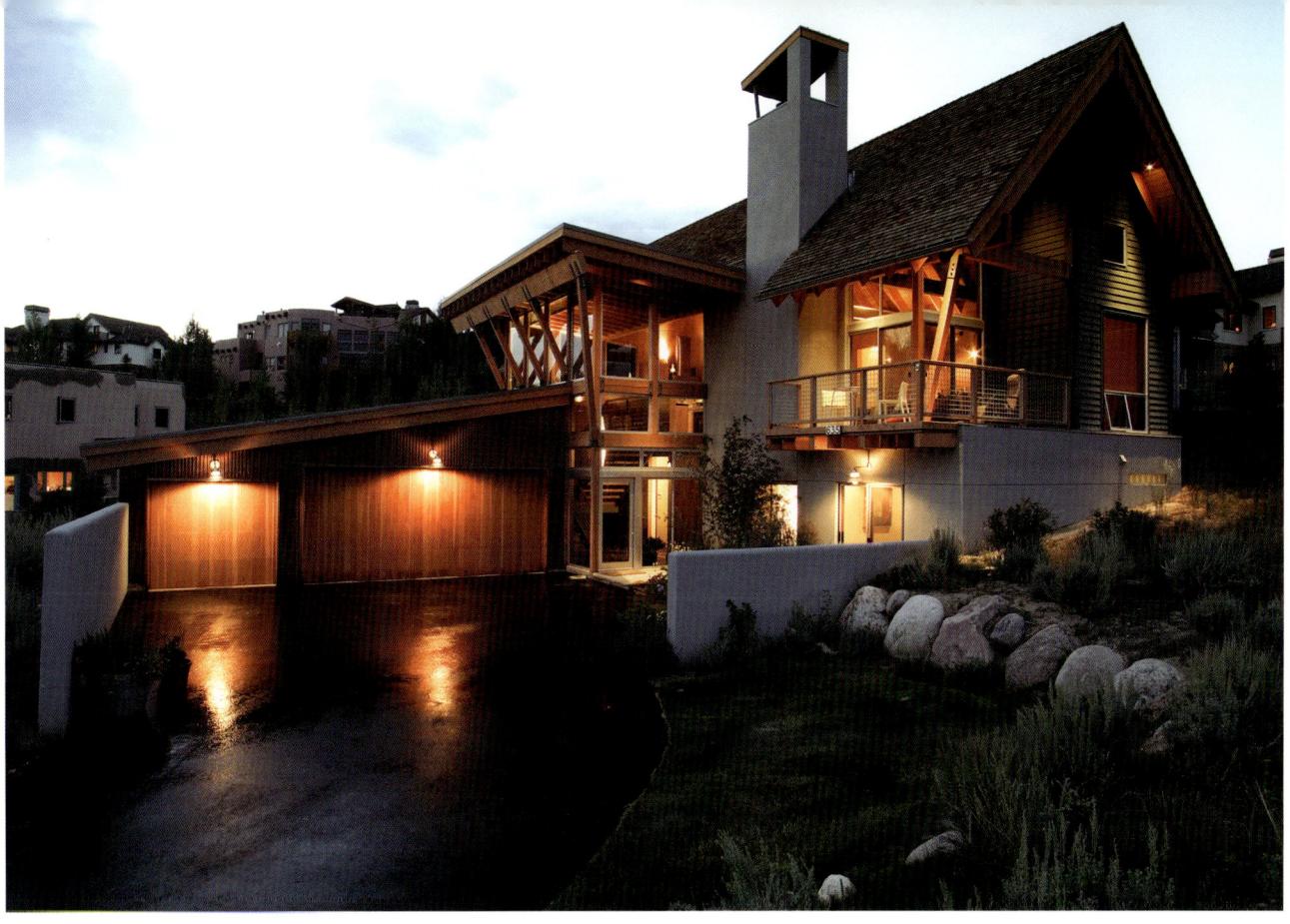

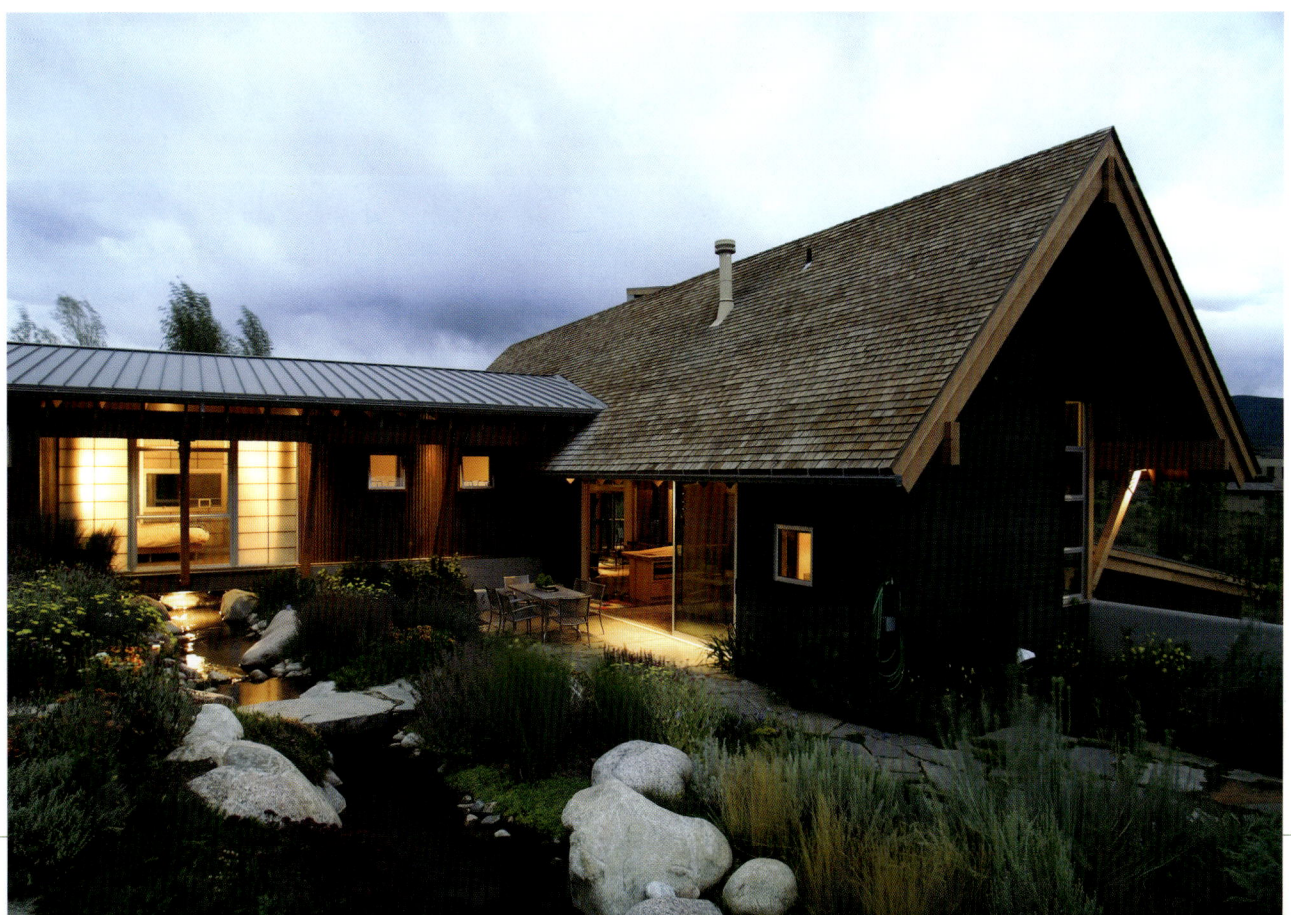

Q&A

more about jim...

ANY AWARDS OR SPECIAL RECOGNITION YOU WOULD LIKE MENTIONED?
My involvement in the Vail community was highlighted by being chosen to design the landmark Gerald R. Ford Amphitheater in 1984, as well as the subsequent renovation in 2000. I am also proud of becoming a part of the AIA College of Fellows in 1993, being chosen as "Architect of the Year" in 1996 by AIA Colorado, and my distinguished alumnus status at Texas Tech University.

WHAT SEPARATES YOU FROM YOUR COMPETITION?
I wear colorful socks. Seriously, my unrelenting striving for high-quality design and detailing and a strong commitment to remaining friends with the client long after the project is completed.

WHAT SIZE IS YOUR COMPANY?
We currently have 11 employees and multiple dogs in the office. I believe in hiring employees who are not afraid to take a project and run with it. Of the three licensed architects and five interns, all can run projects by themselves.

WHAT IS THE BEST PART OF BEING AN ARCHITECT?
Endeavoring to understand peoples' unique personality traits and translating those into architecture.

WHAT IS A SINGLE THING YOU WOULD DO TO BRING A DULL HOUSE TO LIFE?
Introducing more natural light and taking advantage of any exterior connections and views.

NAME ONE THING MOST PEOPLE DON'T KNOW ABOUT YOU.
I own a 16-year-old pot-bellied pig.

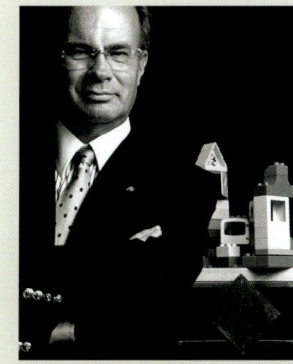

MORTER ARCHITECTS
JAMES R. MORTER, FAIA
2271 North Frontage Road West
Vail, CO 81657
970.476.5105
f: 970.476.0710

AUSTIN OFFICE:
4 Grapewood Court
Austin, TX 78738
512.261.5009
f: 512.261.5387

www.morterarchitects.com

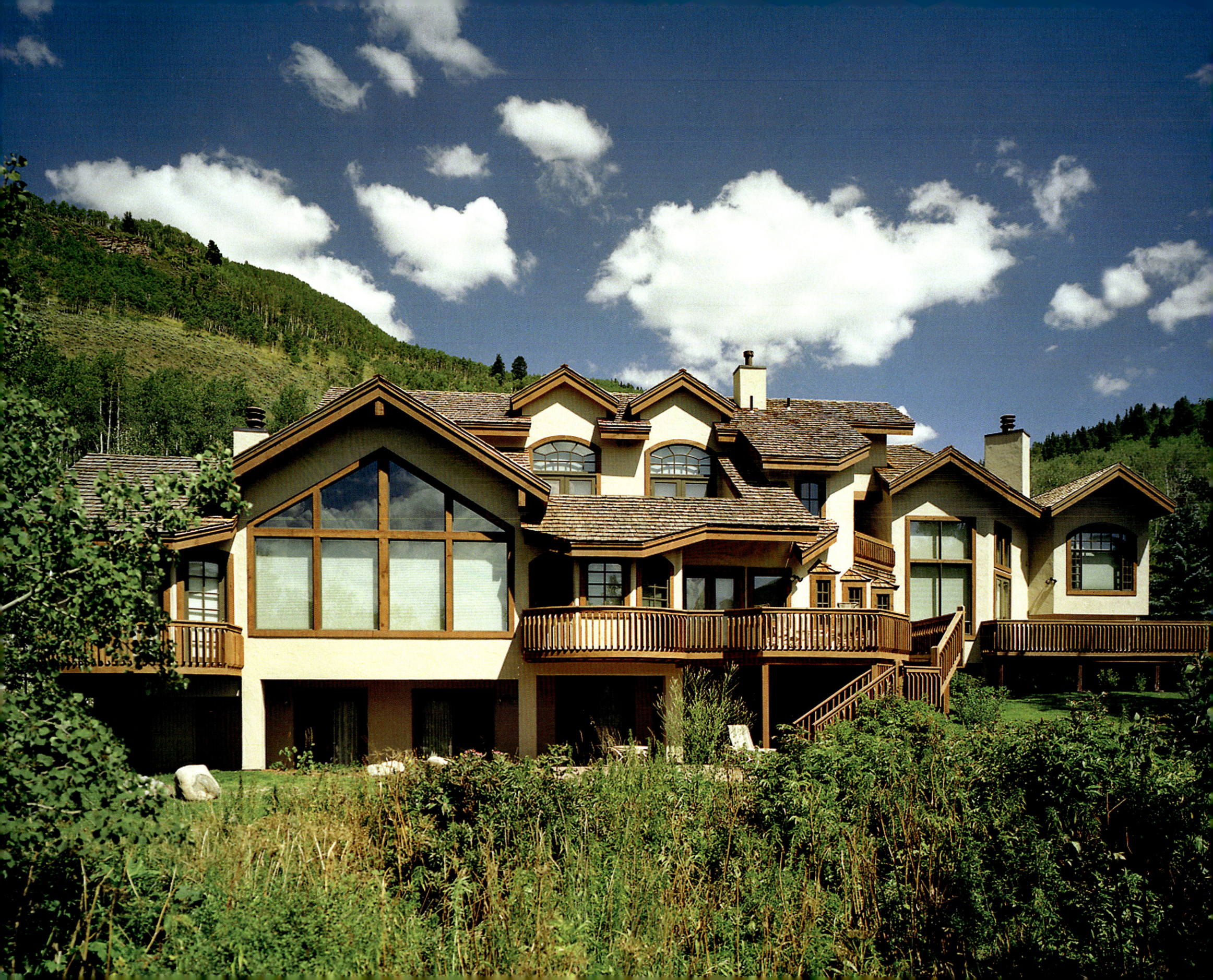

ROLAND KJESBO

NEDBO CONSTRUCTION

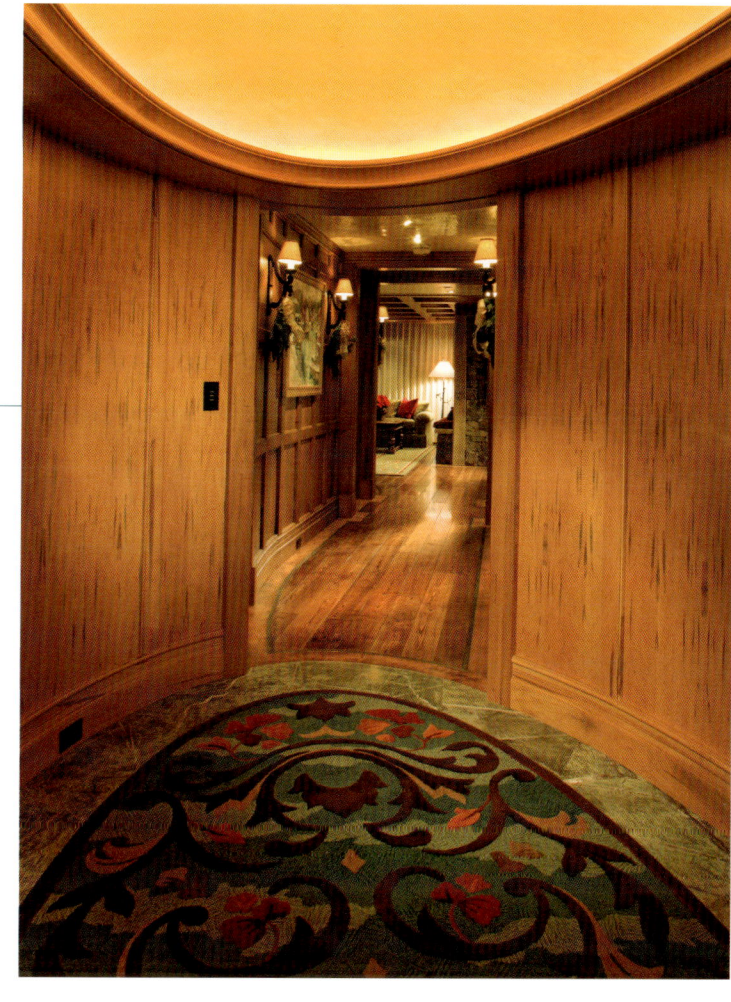

Nedbo Construction is a complete construction service company. Built upon a strong foundation of the technical expertise of their employees, solid management and strong communication, their team of professionals is dedicated to providing a superior finished product. Nedbo Construction offers remodeling, commercial and new construction services.

Averaging over 15 years of experience, Nedbo's superintendents oversee the team, working closely with clients from the initial idea stage until the finest detail at completion. Nedbo is committed to the fulfillment of the client's dream. Creating a new look for the Vail Valley, Nedbo Construction ranks among the premier builders in Vail and Beaver Creek. Outstanding workmanship and quality building techniques merge together to create these exceptional high-end custom homes and commercial properties. Nedbo Construction is dedicated to building the home of their client's dreams with the help of the company's talented and creative subcontractors and the use of only superior quality building materials.

The experts at Nedbo exhibit the area's finest work in construction management; taking new projects from the idea stage to completion and executing the transformation of current homes through complete renovations and remodels. Striving to develop solid working relationships through unfettered communication between owner, architect and designer, the team ensures that each home embodies the uniqueness of the owner's personality. Each Nedbo home is designed and built to reflect the Vail Valley's active lifestyle and the area's scenic beauty. Not only does the company build the homes and buildings in which the community lives and thrives, but it actively supports the community through other efforts such as their active support of the Vail Valley Foundation, Habitat for Humanity, Small Champions, the Vail Recreation District and others.

ABOVE:
A Venetian plastered dome, marble slab flooring and concealed maple doors greet guests in the entryway of this Vail condominium.
Photograph by Dann Coffey

FACING PAGE:
Transformation Complete: renovation of a flat roofed, Southwestern stucco home to a multi-gabled mountain chalet.
Photograph by Dennis Jones, Dreamcatcher Imaging

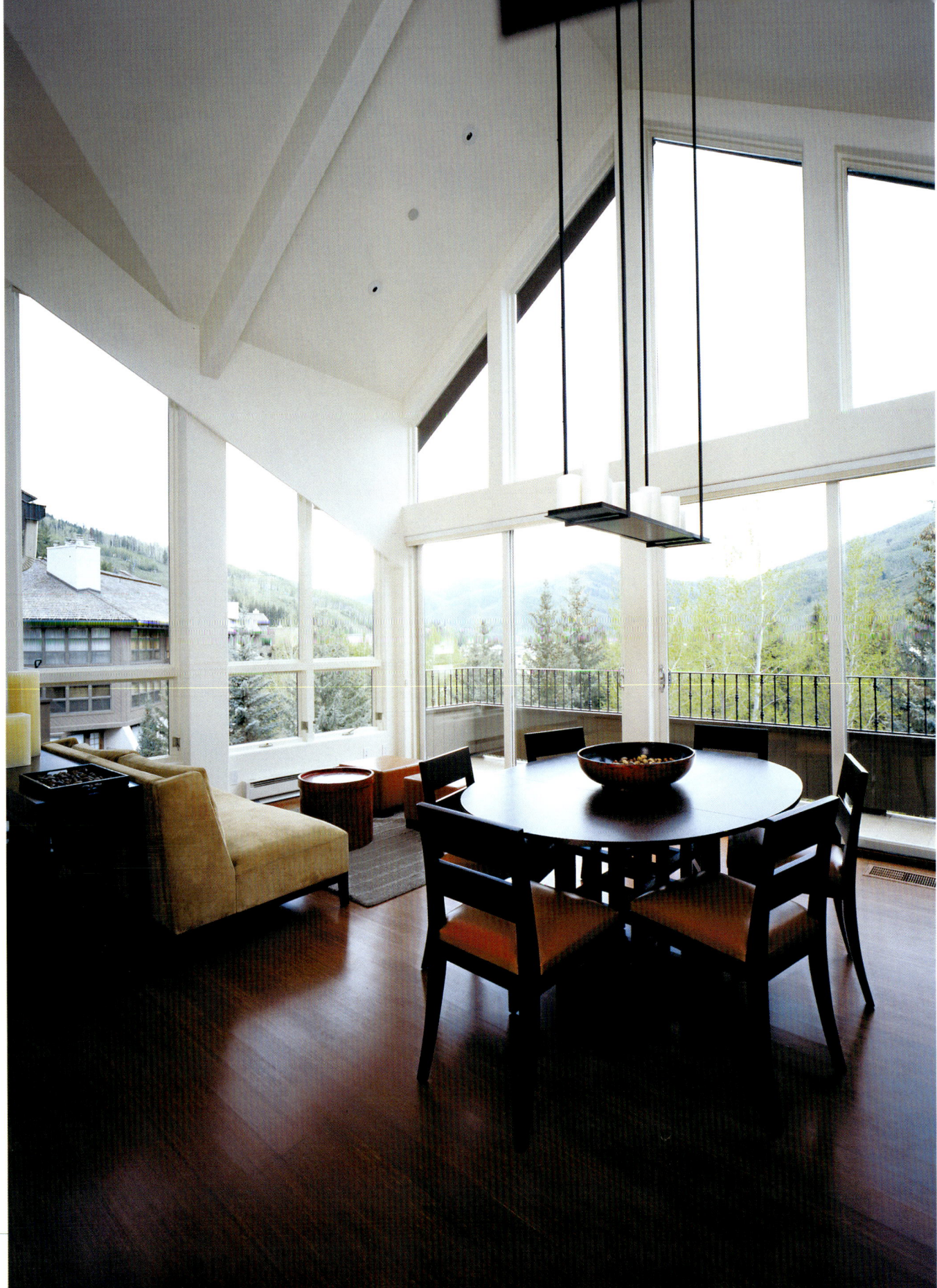

Nedbo opened its doors as Nedbo Construction, Inc., 25 years ago and now employees over 30 Coloradoans. As a testament to their fine work, the company has been featured in the publications *Mountain Living*, *Vail Valley Magazine*, *Vail Valley Golf*, the *Vail Daily* and *Vail Trail*. Nedbo's projects run the full gamut—from residential to commercial. While the company believes that each house is unique and has a full beauty of its own, they also believe it's their job to offer their clients the personal service and attention to detail to make that house a home.

LEFT:
Clean lines and elegant design allow the spectacular view of the Gore Mountain Range to be the main focus.
Photograph by Dennis Jones, Dreamcatcher Imaging

FACING PAGE TOP:
The modern design of poured concrete countertops inlaid with the owner's found objects and hand-dyed bamboo flooring make this condo completely unique to the homeowner.
Photograph by Dennis Jones, Dreamcatcher Imaging

FACING PAGE BOTTOM:
The rustic elegance of the wood coffered ceiling, hand-stenciled Venetian plaster walls and stone fireplace bring warmth and comfort to this condo's kitchen.
Photograph by Dann Coffey

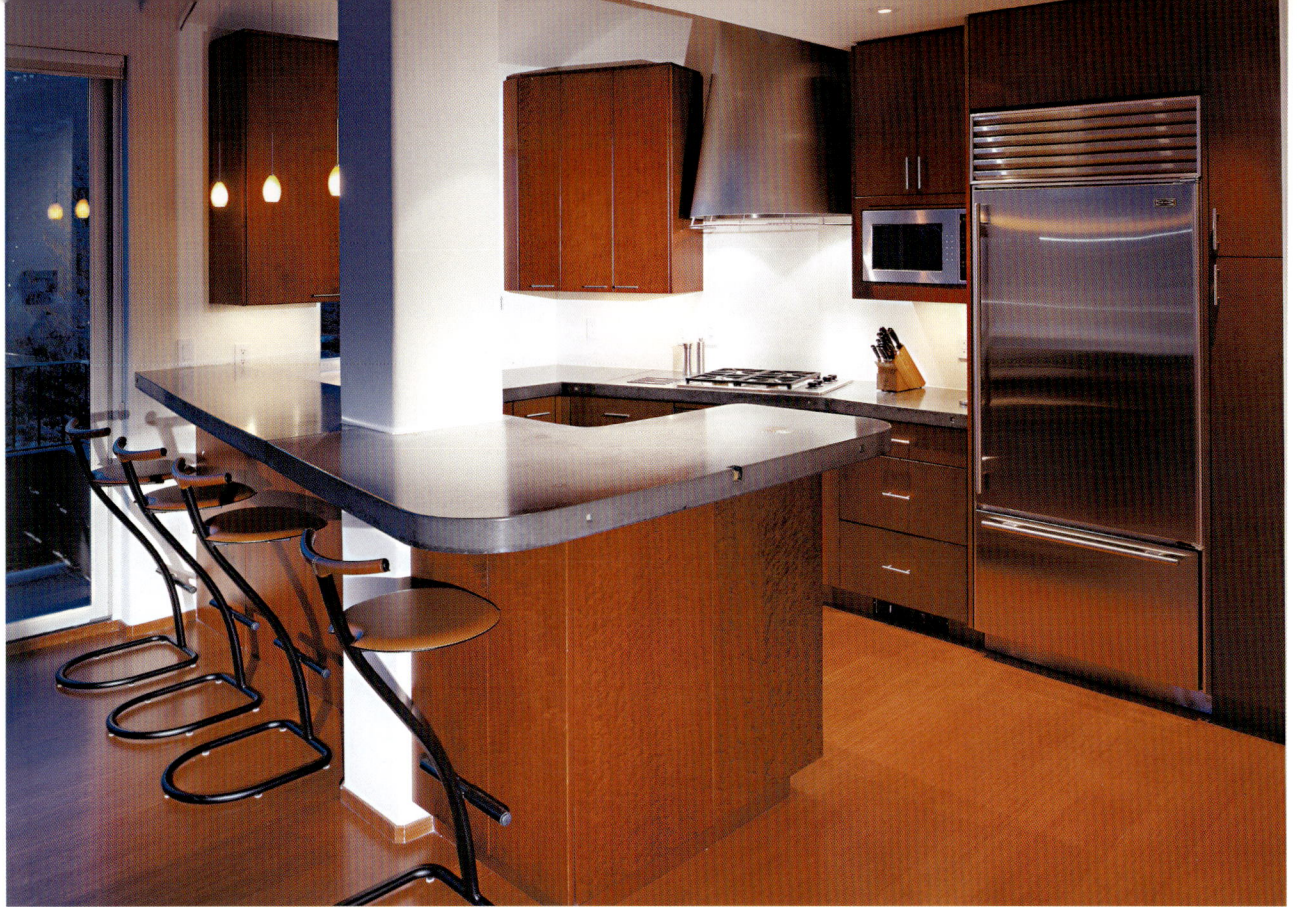

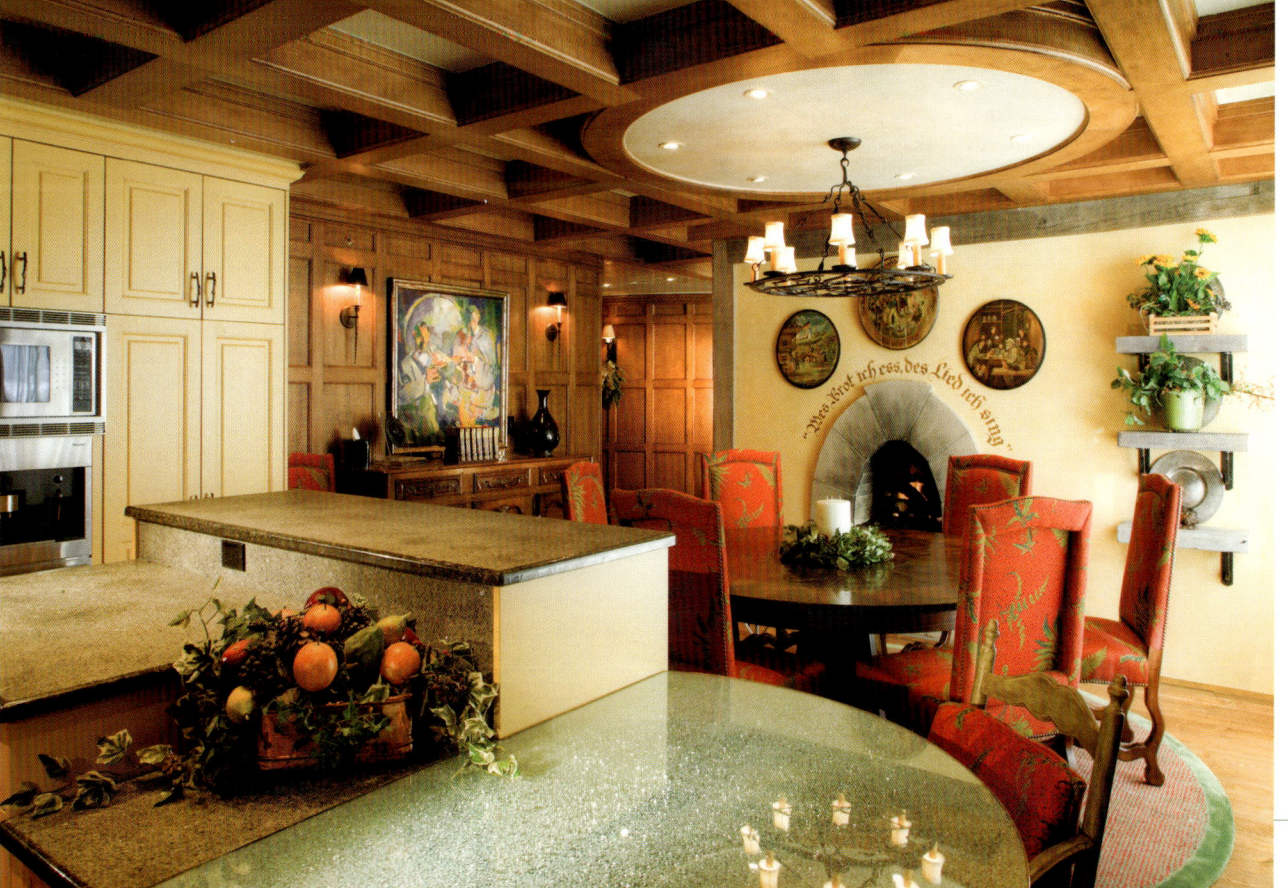

Q & A
more about roland...

WHAT IS THE BEST PART OF BEING A BUILDER?
My team and I feel such an immense sense of satisfaction when we see a client's dream come to fruition.

WHAT IS THE HIGHEST COMPLIMENT YOU'VE EVER RECEIVED PROFESSIONALLY?
I once heard a client exclaim, "It's better than I ever could have imagined!"

WHAT ONE ELEMENT OF STYLE OR PHILOSOPHY HAVE YOU STUCK WITH FOR YEARS THAT STILL WORKS FOR YOU TODAY?
We design and build to fit the client's lifestyle and meld their desires to fit the mountainous environment.

WHAT IS THE MOST DIFFICULT DESIGN OR TECHNIQUE YOU'VE USED IN ONE OF YOUR PROJECTS?
One project we took on required a complete transformation. We renovated a Southwestern, flat-roofed, stucco house into a multi-gabled Bavarian chalet.

WHAT DO YOU LIKE MOST ABOUT DOING BUSINESS IN YOUR LOCALE?
My team and I have the pleasure of working with incredibly talented local craftsmen, architects and designers. Additionally, our international clientele requires us to keep up on all the latest innovations in the building industry.

NEDBO CONSTRUCTION
ROLAND KJESBO
PO BOX 3419
VAIL, CO 81658
970.845.1001
f: 970.845.9979
www.nedbo.com

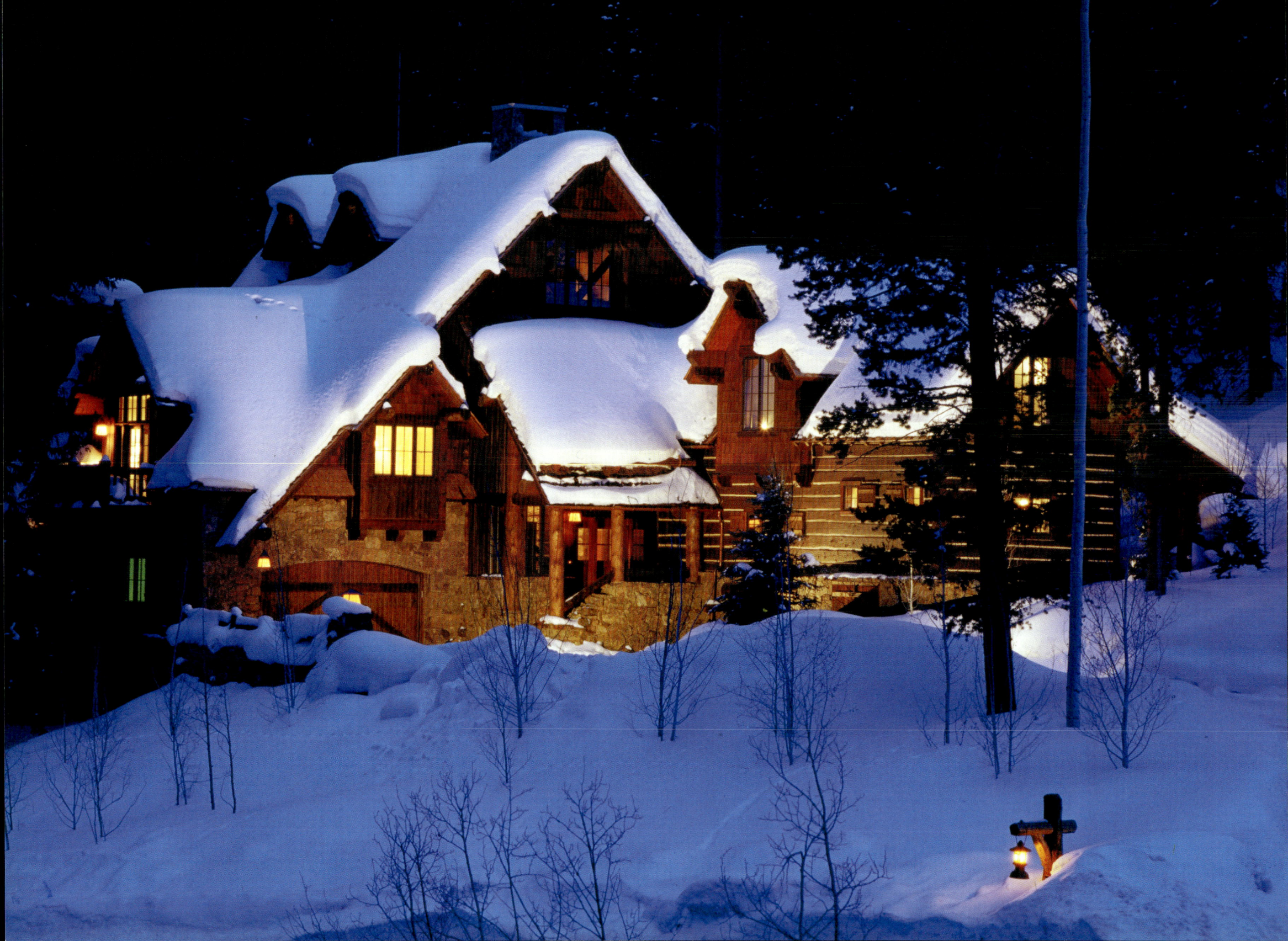

DAVE ARGO

NO NAME ARCHITECTS

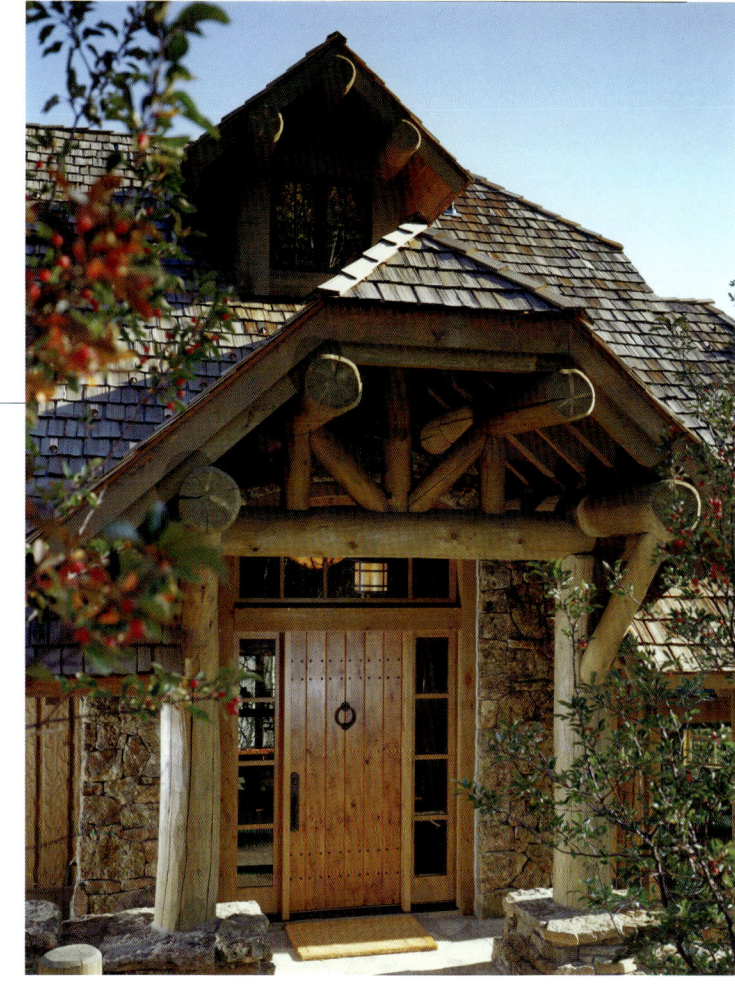

Originally from Kansas, Dave Argo made his way West to Colorado in 1984, attracted to the scenic Rocky Mountains, outdoor recreational opportunities and overall lifestyle. After a year in Denver, a job opportunity at a Vail Valley architecture firm was too enchanting to pass up and he spent nine years refining his architectural skills while working on a wide range of commercial and residential projects in mountain resort communities across the country. It was a weekend drive to Glenwood Springs which brought on a chance sighting of a for-sale sign and the unlikely purchase of a creek side home in No Name (situated between Vail and Aspen) 12 years ago that ultimately led to the founding of No Name Architects.

Since its inception, No Name Architects has remained purposefully small and Dave has specifically chosen to limit his architectural practice to the design of high-end, single-family residences. "Early on, I decided it was important for me to focus on a small number of clients so that I could provide each of them with a very high level of personalized design services. Following my first couple of commissions to design single-family homes, I quickly came to the realization that I really enjoyed working together one-on-one with clients looking to design and build their 'dream home' in the Colorado mountains."

Many of the homes No Name Architects has designed over the past 12 years are used as secondary or vacation homes by the owners and most incorporate very different design characteristics than their primary residence. "Mountain homes typically embrace a somewhat different lifestyle than a 'city home' and often respond more directly to the scenic qualities of the home site. Maximizing the use of windows and patio doors to capture favorable views, providing decks and terraces to expand interior living spaces and bringing sunlight into interior spaces are some of the ways we typically respond to the surrounding mountain environment." He also recognizes that interior living arrangements and lifestyle choices in the mountains are also quite different from people's primary residence; differences that are quite often reflected with open floor plan layouts, an emphasis on a more casual lifestyle and development of a strong relationship between the home and outdoor recreation-based activities.

ABOVE:
Oversized logs, handcrafted into a structural work of art, offer a welcoming atmosphere at the gabled entry to this mountain home.
Photograph by Dann Coffey

FACING PAGE:
Situated along a ski trail at Beaver Creek, this family lodge is nestled into the hillside at the edge of the surrounding forest.
Photograph by Dann Coffey

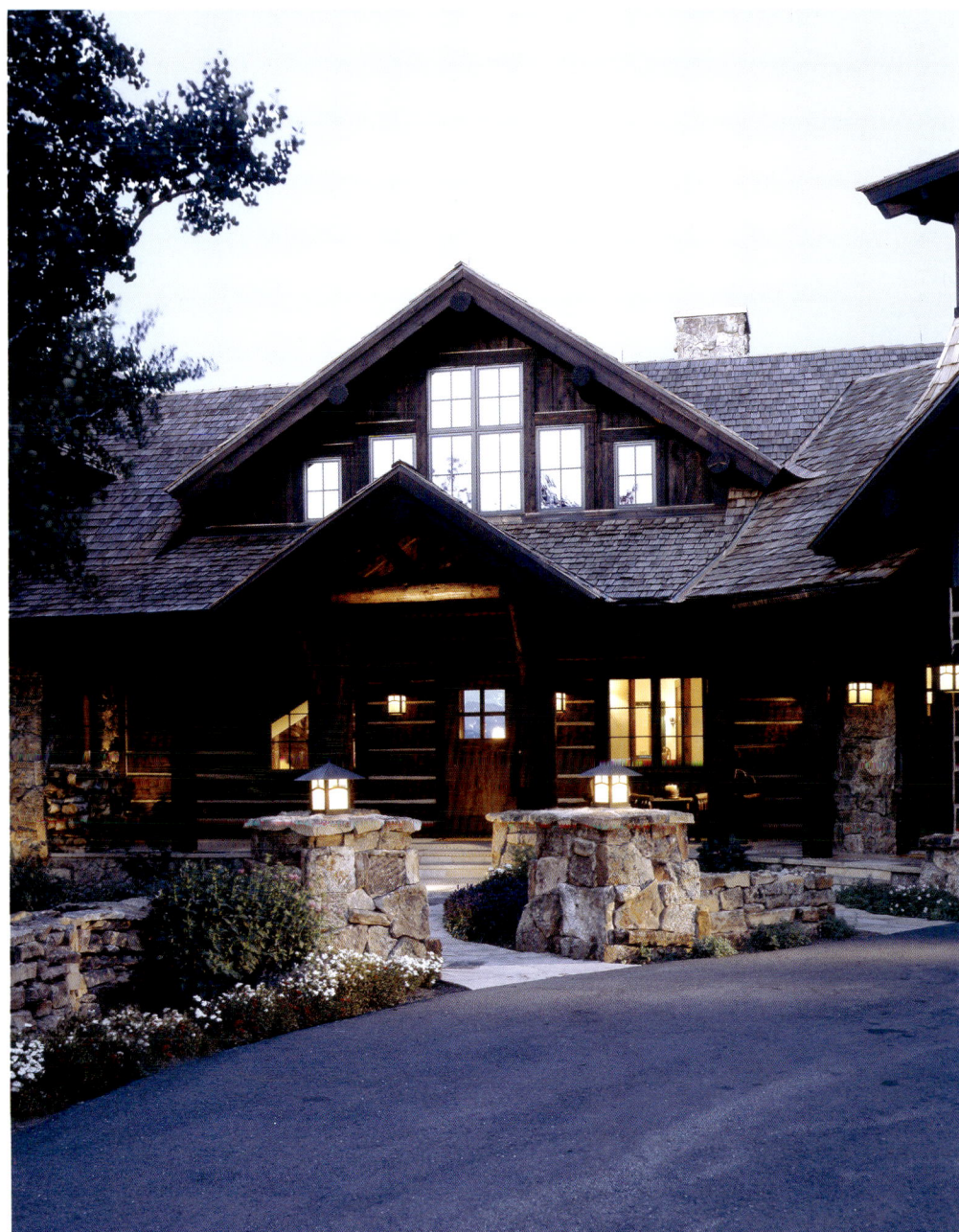
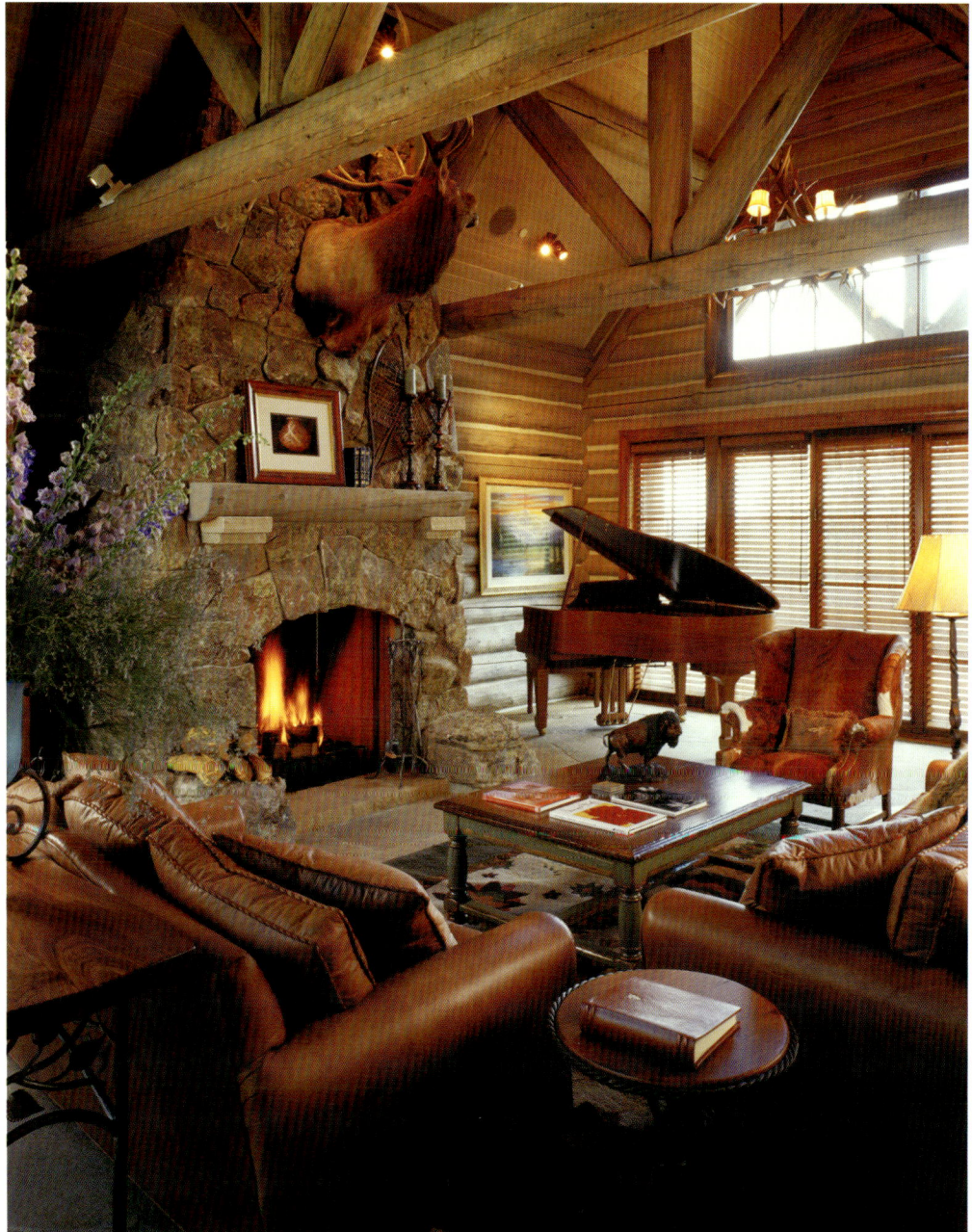

Dave has purposely steered clear of the more traditional model of "growing your business," instead choosing to remain a small design firm, an approach that allows him to devote a large amount of personal attention and involvement to every project designed by No Name Architects. Dave believes that communication with all parties involved—including the client, contractors, other consultants, regulatory agencies and design review boards—is the key to any successful project and he considers effective communication to be one of the firm's greatest strengths.

ABOVE LEFT:
While exhibiting many of the design characteristics found in traditional Colorado ranch houses and outbuildings, this residence also features an energy efficient building envelope.
Photograph by Hatch/Cloos Photography

ABOVE RIGHT:
Handcrafted logs are the focal point of this great room, creating a rustic, and yet, elegant heart of the home.
Photograph by Dann Coffey

FACING PAGE:
The faceted living room of this mountaintop retreat was designed to open itself to long-range views, sunshine and wraparound decks extending living spaces outward.
Photograph by Dann Coffey

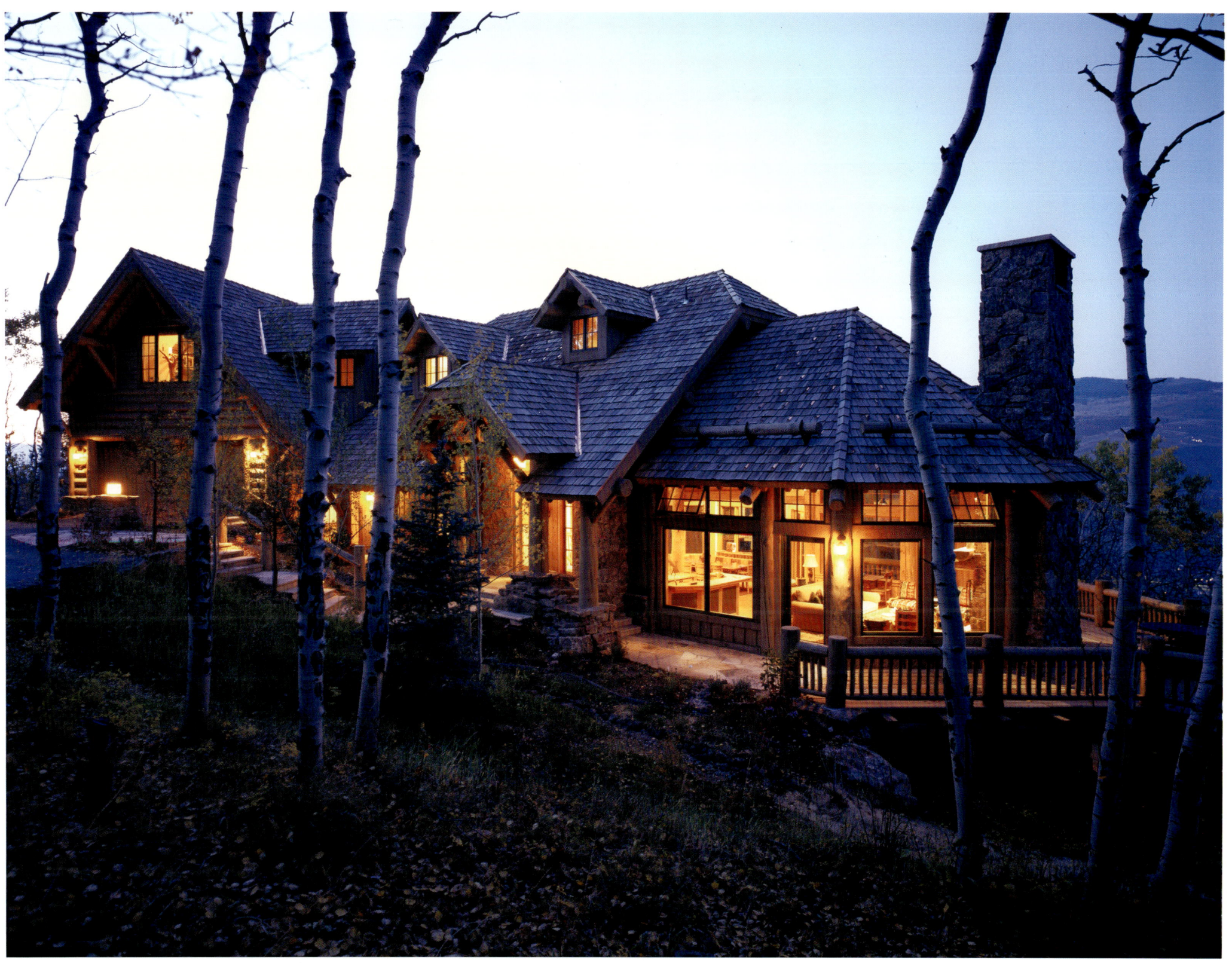

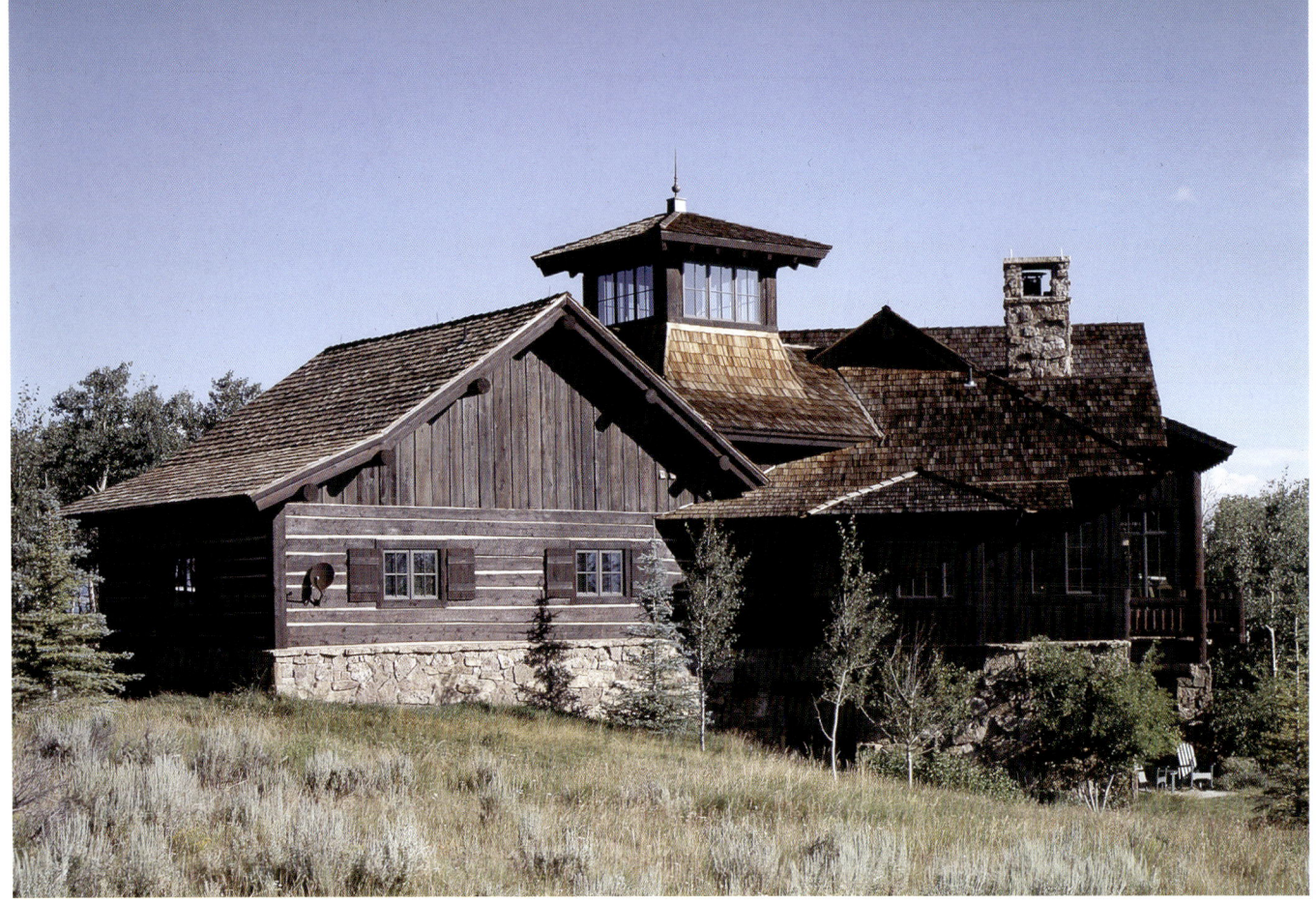

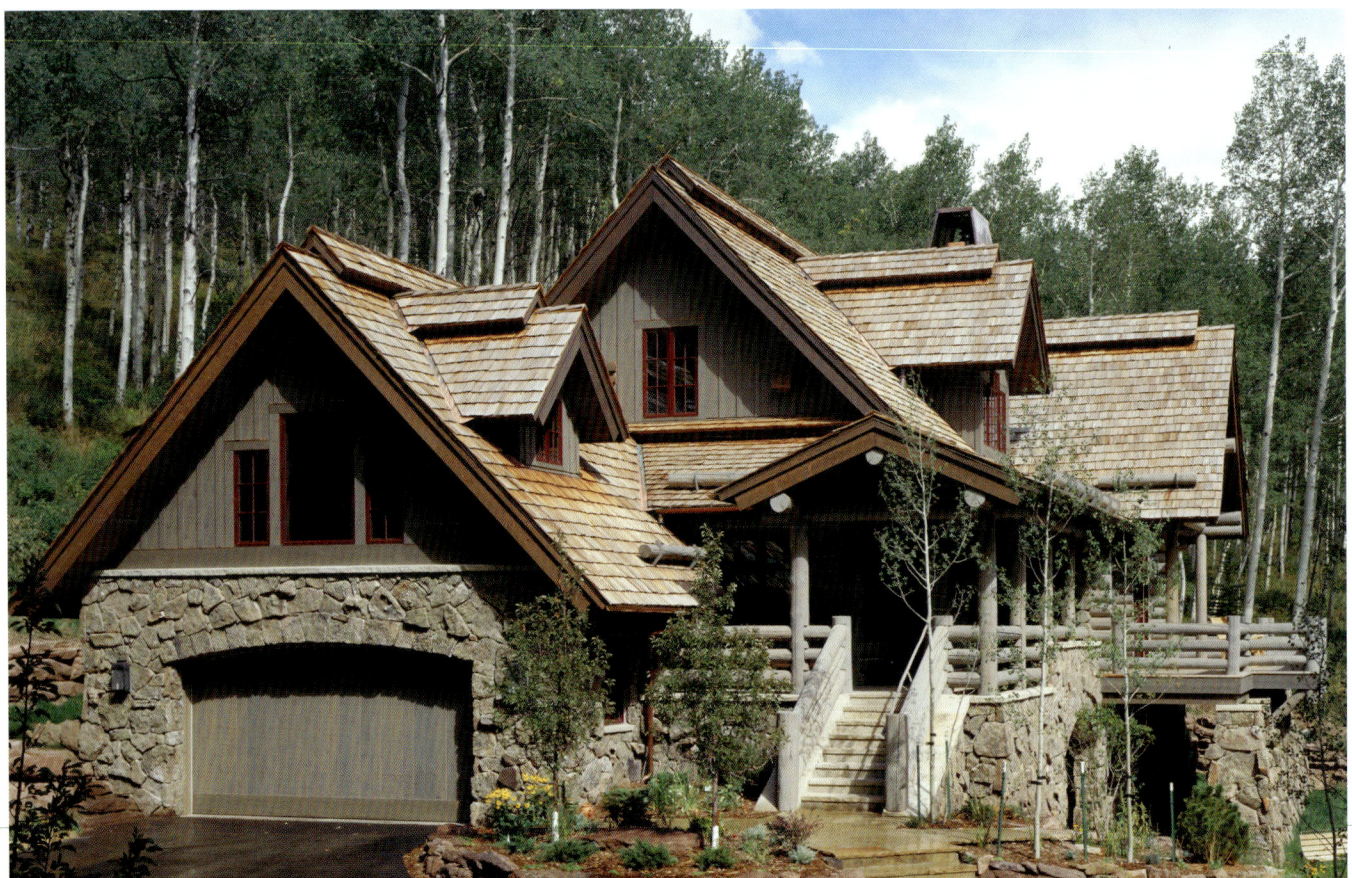

Favoring traditional over contemporary design styles, Dave typically designs homes exhibiting some of the same characteristics, building materials and architectural detailing found in older, indigenous structures of Colorado, including log cabins, lodges, ranches and mining buildings. Often times, these particular designs are influenced by Design Regulations and the design review process adopted by many of the exclusive gated communities now found in the Colorado high country.

Dave believes traditional design styles offer many important lessons, including a respect for nature, the beauty of using natural and indigenous materials and an appropriate sense of scale for buildings located in scenic, natural settings. By combining stone, log and timber materials with contemporary framing techniques, efficient thermal envelopes and state-of-the-art mechanical, heating and lighting systems, it is his goal to create a home that is as functional and comfortable to live within as it is beautiful, well-suited to its surroundings and timeless in appearance.

Although his design solutions from project to project are as individual and unique as his clients, Dave's guiding design process and overall philosophy toward each project is consistent, in order to maintain focus on achieving successful projects and satisfied clients. With a high level of personal attention and involvement in every project, Dave guides his clients through every step of the process with the goal of helping them complete nothing less than their dream home.

TOP LEFT:
Resource efficient materials including stone foundations, hand-hewn log siding, reclaimed barn boards and hand-split cedar shakes blend this home into its environment.
Photograph by Hatch/Cloos Photography

BOTTOM LEFT:
Exterior materials and colors were carefully selected to match this home's surroundings, including a natural gray stain on all log elements, emulating the Aspen forrested hillside.
Photograph by Dann Coffey

FACING PAGE:
Patterned after Forest Service fire look-out stations, this upper level perch features windows on all four sides to capture spectacular mountain vistas in all directions.
Photograph by Dan Davis

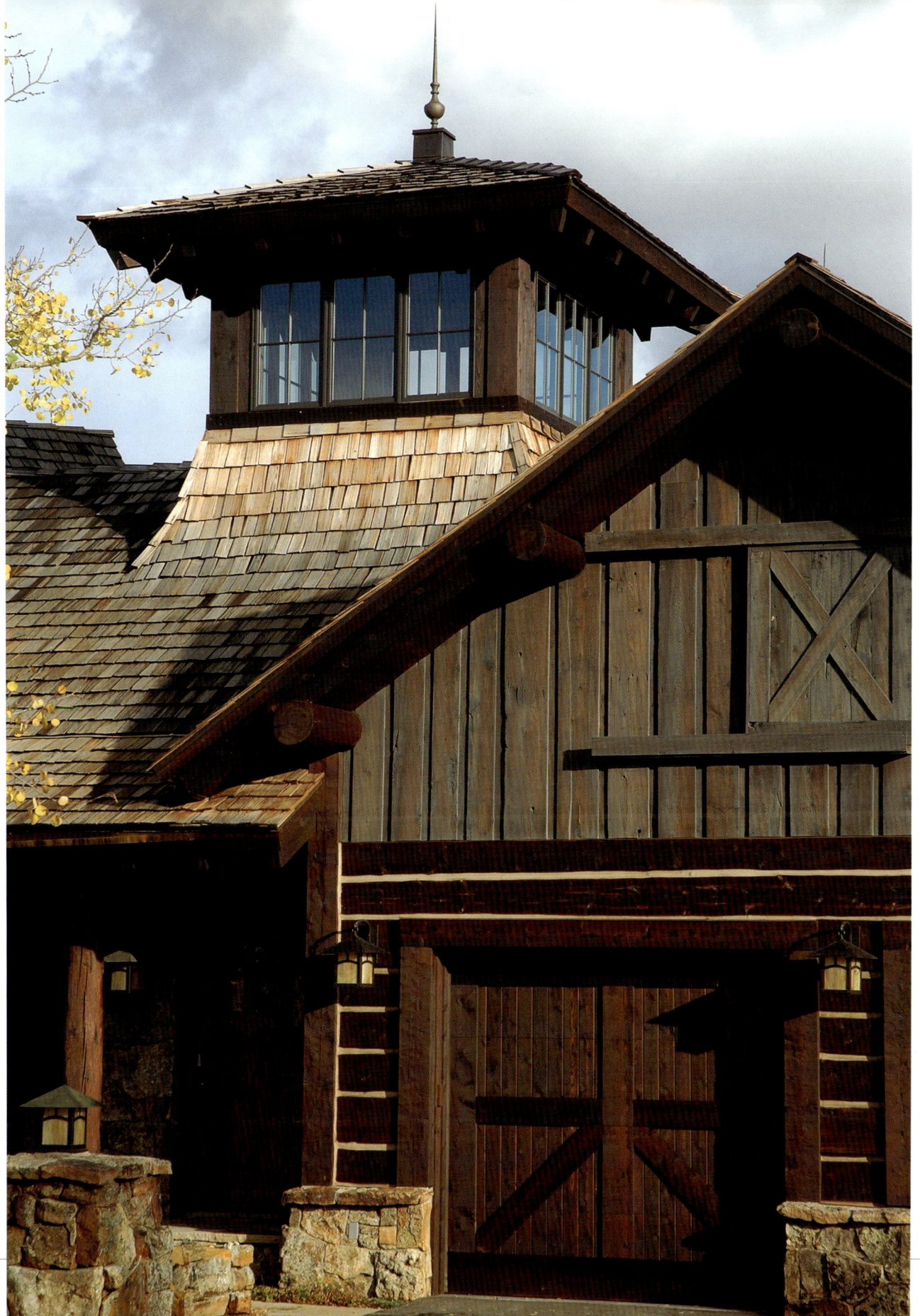

Q&A more about dave...

HAVE YOU BEEN PUBLISHED IN ANY NATIONAL OR REGIONAL PUBLICATIONS? WHICH ONES?
You can see some of my work in *Log Homes Illustrated*, *Log Home Living* and *Cordillera Living* magazine, among others.

WHAT IS THE MOST UNIQUE HOME YOU'VE BEEN INVOLVED WITH? WHY?
The most unique home I have been involved with was probably the family ski lodge located right on the slopes of Beaver Creek, including a great room that truly deserves to be called a "great room." Patterned after the Glacier Park Lodge's lobby, the 35-foot-high vaulted space includes a massive stone fireplace extending all the way up to the peak of the ridgeline. 25-foot-high log posts define the perimeter of the great room, supporting log trusses overhead and framing the overlooking balconies above.

WHAT SEPARATES YOU FROM YOUR COMPETITION?
As a small office principal, I am able to focus all of my personal attention on every single project designed by No Name Architects. The very nature of larger firms precludes the principals from devoting the kind of time to each project that I can. My clients are the recipients of highly personalized professional design services that can be custom-tailored to their own needs, preferences and personal styles.

DESCRIBE YOUR STYLE OR DESIGN PREFERENCES.
Personally, I like buildings that fit into their surroundings and exhibit timeless, rather than trendy characteristics. I think it's important to live in the present, not the past, but I also believe there are intrinsic qualities and characteristics found in some of our historic buildings that simply make people feel "at home." Those intangible elements of design that we sometimes cannot even describe or put our finger on are very desirable qualities for an architect to instill in the places we call "home" and I try to bring those elements into each of the homes I design.

NO NAME ARCHITECTS
DAVID R. ARGO, AIA
121 Hideaway Lane
Glenwood Springs, CO 81601
970.945.6738
www.nonamearchitects.com

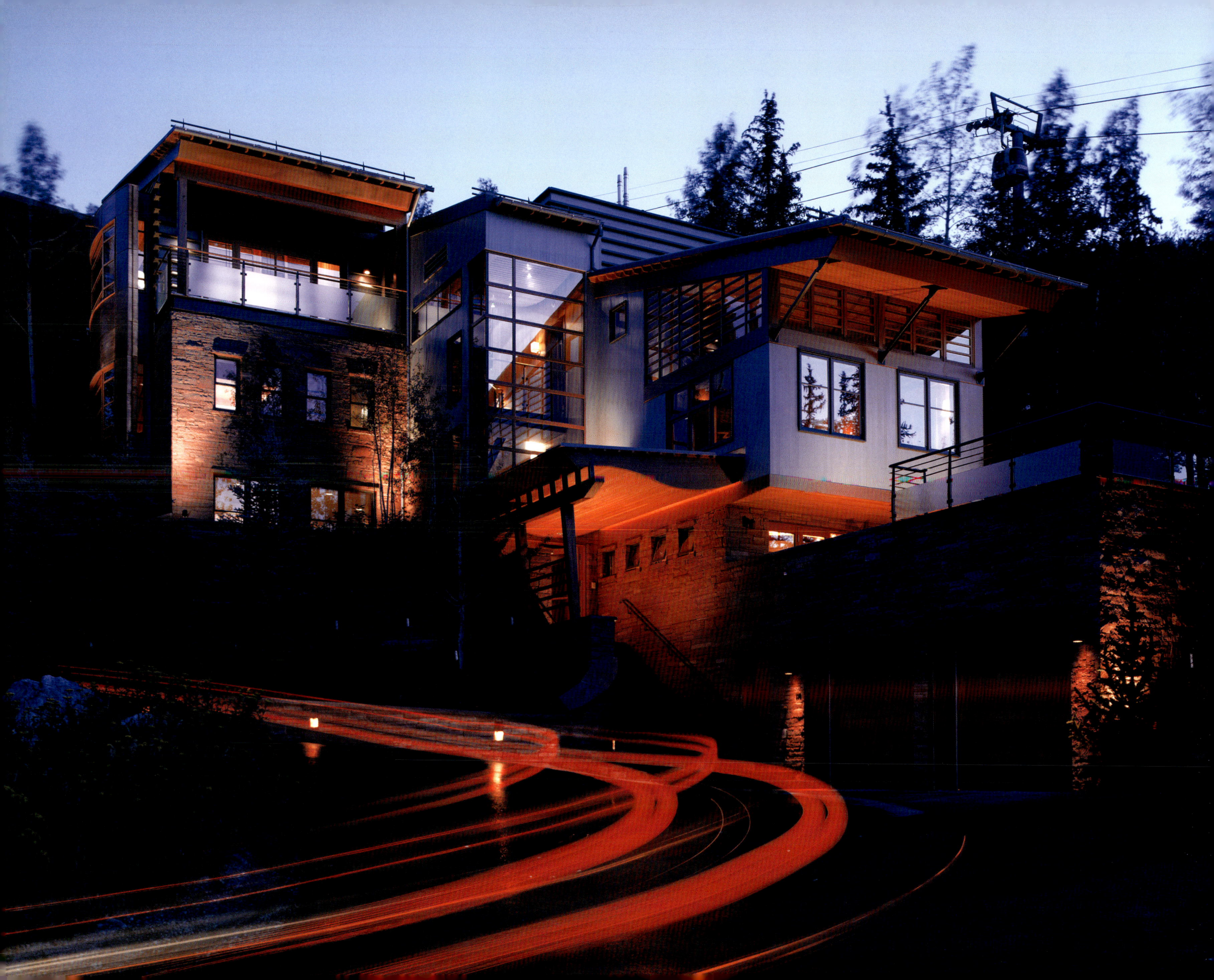

BILL POSS
CHRIS RIDINGS
LES ROSENSTEIN
KIM WEIL
ANDY WISNOSKI

POSS ARCHITECTURE + PLANNING

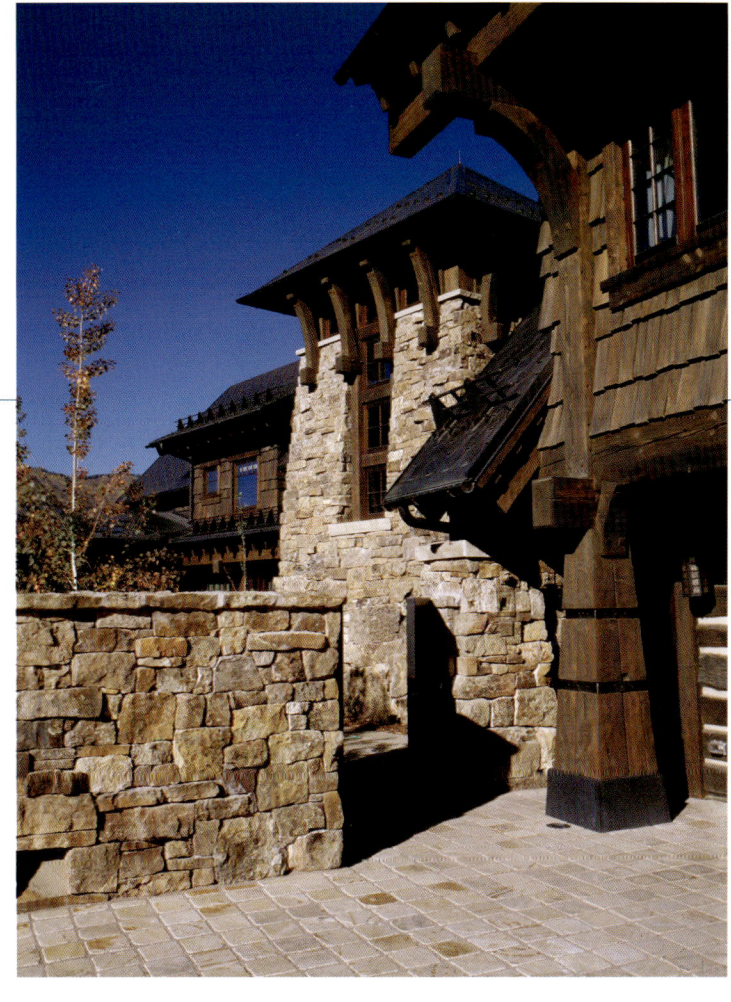

Headed by a team of principals possessing over 100 years of combined experience and varied educational and professional backgrounds, Poss proves that the best architectural firms are those that blend expertise with a diverse body of experience.

Educated at the New York Institute of Technology, Bill practiced architecture in New York and Houston, Texas, before his love of the mountains fueled a move to Aspen, where he founded Poss Architecture + Planning in 1976.

A passionate believer in quality design and client service, he maintains a strong commitment towards integrating a project's architectural design with its regional context and landscape. He also takes great pride in preserving architecture. As a testament to this tightly held belief, he served several years as Chairman of the Aspen Historical Preservation Committee.

A varied practice in styles, Poss Architecture + Planning works mostly on high-end residential homes that range from traditional to contemporary or rustic, but all with a "Colorado mountain influence." And they have traveled all over the country designing these majestic spaces for their clients. They accept only six to eight residential projects a year, limiting the number so that they can provide optimal attention to detail required for complete client satisfaction.

Bill requests that his clients get involved with their projects because as he says, "It's their home not ours." His clients put in their necessary time in the planning and designs of their home and thus in the process reveal to the Poss team who the clients really are at heart and how they live. "It is a discovery process of how they want to live and how the design will evolve," Bill said.

ABOVE:
The tower provides a dynamic feature to the entrance courtyard and accentuates the staircase.
Photograph by Brian Porter

FACING PAGE:
This house sits directly on a ski mountain for easy access and great views.
Photograph by David O. Marlow

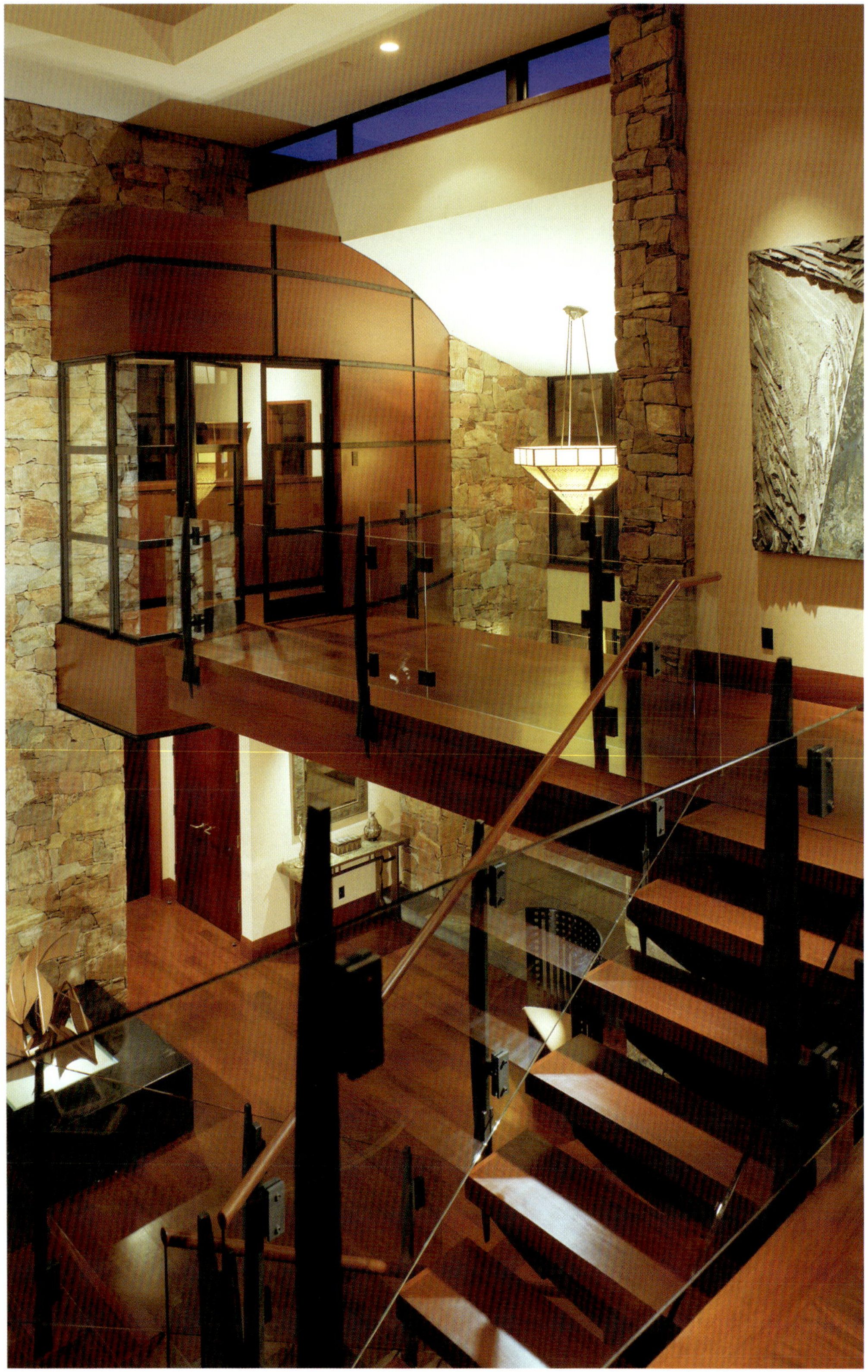

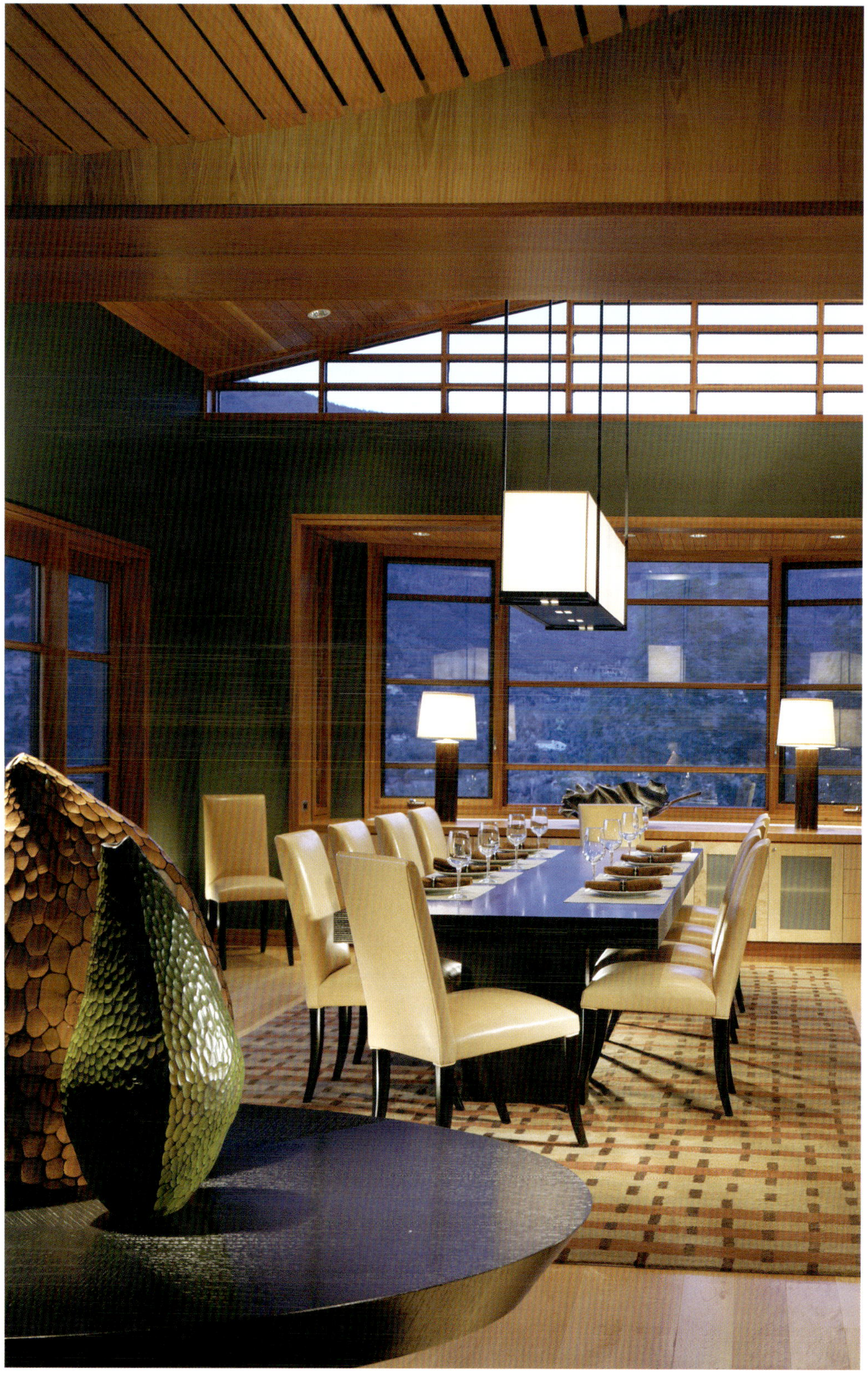

For Bill environment does dictate the aesthetic nature of a design. Some of the ways this philosophy gets incorporated into his homes are through the use of indigenous and reclaimed materials. When working in the mountains and on ranches they enjoy using recycled materials such as logs and timbers. These materials can be garnered from all over the country and sometimes abroad. On one occasion Poss and his team even used some ancient stone flooring (old granite worn over the centuries) recycled from a street in a town in China, the final result gave the client a lot of satisfaction.

Understanding how buildings evolve from their local environment and regional context is essentially the key to making new homes fit in their surroundings. In order to do this successfully the Poss team does a lot of research beforehand to gain an understanding of appropriate influences. An example of this might be seen in their ranch homes. In order to do them successfully you have to examine how they would have evolved historically on their sites utilizing an understanding of the environmental factors that shaped their development and placement of the structures (barns, cabins etc.) that make up a historically correct ranch compound. Poss then infuses these projects with fresh new ideas and materials give the projects an appropriate historical context for today's living. You will still see the charm and character of the old homestead cabins and barns here in these projects, but they now are adapted to meet the needs of modern living.

Another very important aspect of Poss designs is a sense of arrival. The entrance not only introduces you to the interior spaces, but it can connect the house to the site with specific accented views that only working in the mountains provide. When done correctly entrances can be an integral and magical part of a project.

TOP RIGHT:
This house was designed to display the elegance and refinement of a traditional lodge on a sage brush meadow.
Photograph by Joel Eden

BOTTOM RIGHT:
The living area captures the view with windows from floor to ceiling and invites the site into the space flowing continuously from the outside in.
Photograph by David O. Marlow

FACING PAGE LEFT:
The modern wood and natural stone creates an interesting connection for the bridge to the guest suite.
Photograph by David O. Marlow

FACING PAGE RIGHT:
The colors and materials in this room were chosen to provide continuity with the exterior materials and textures.
Photograph by David O. Marlow

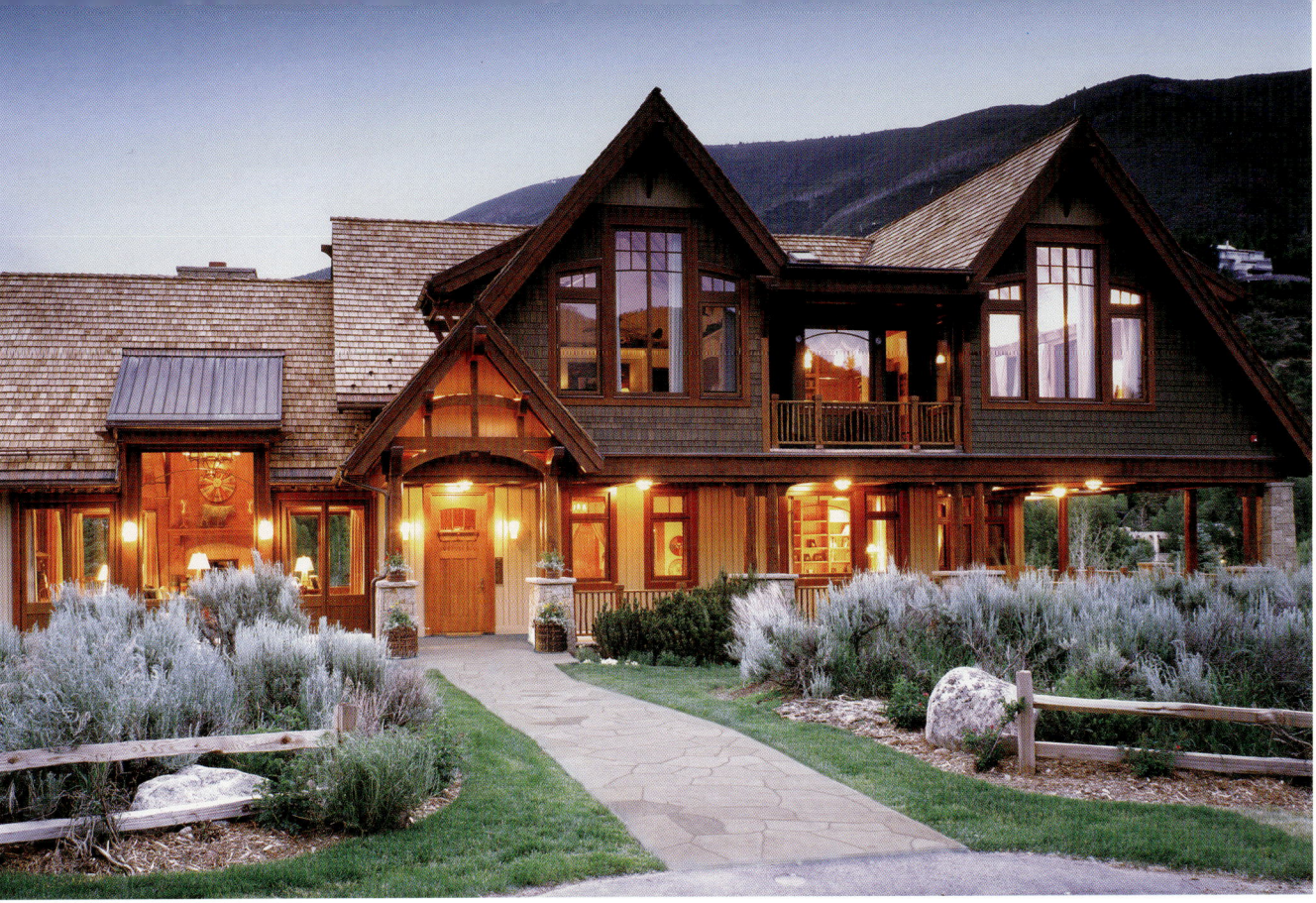

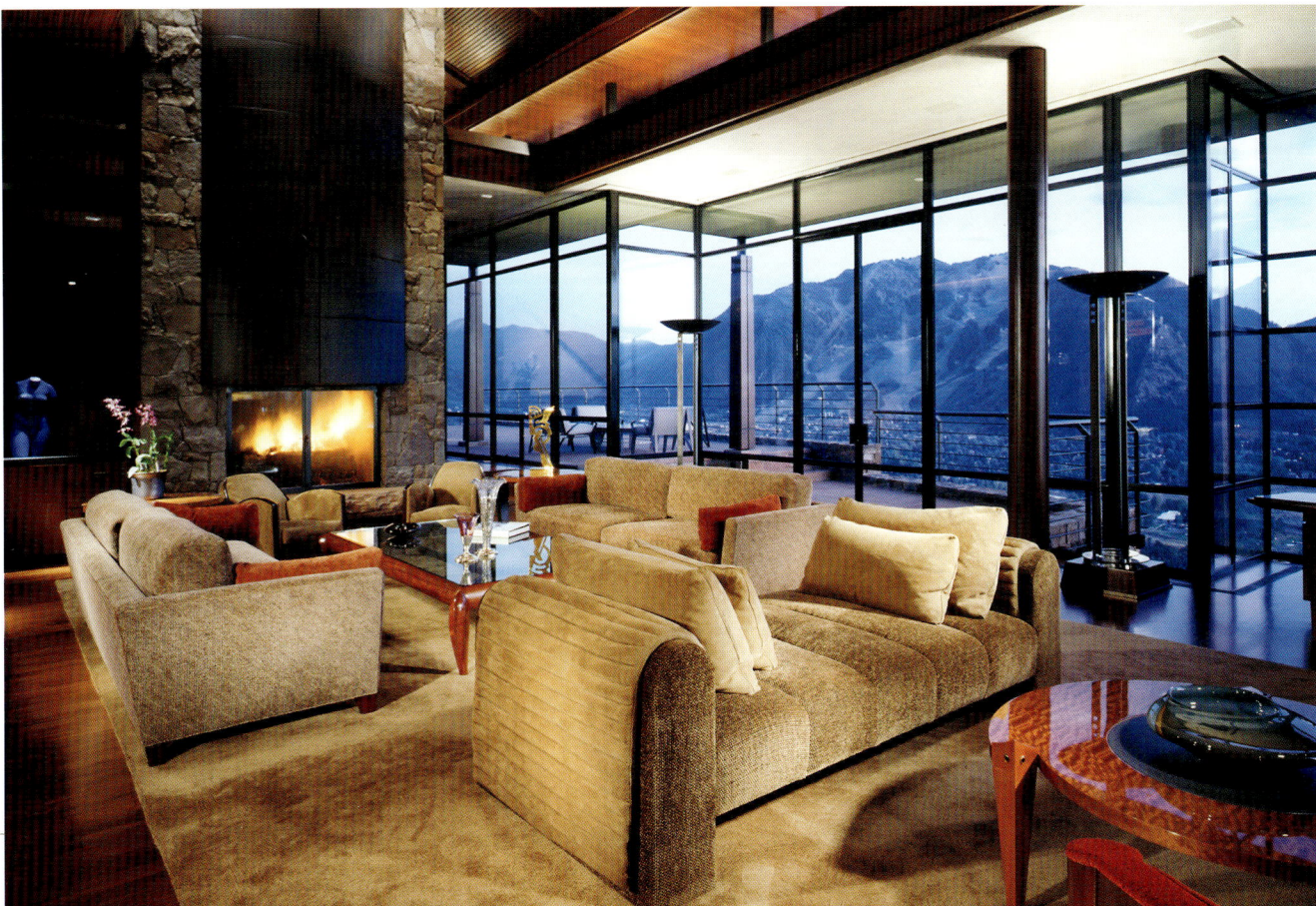

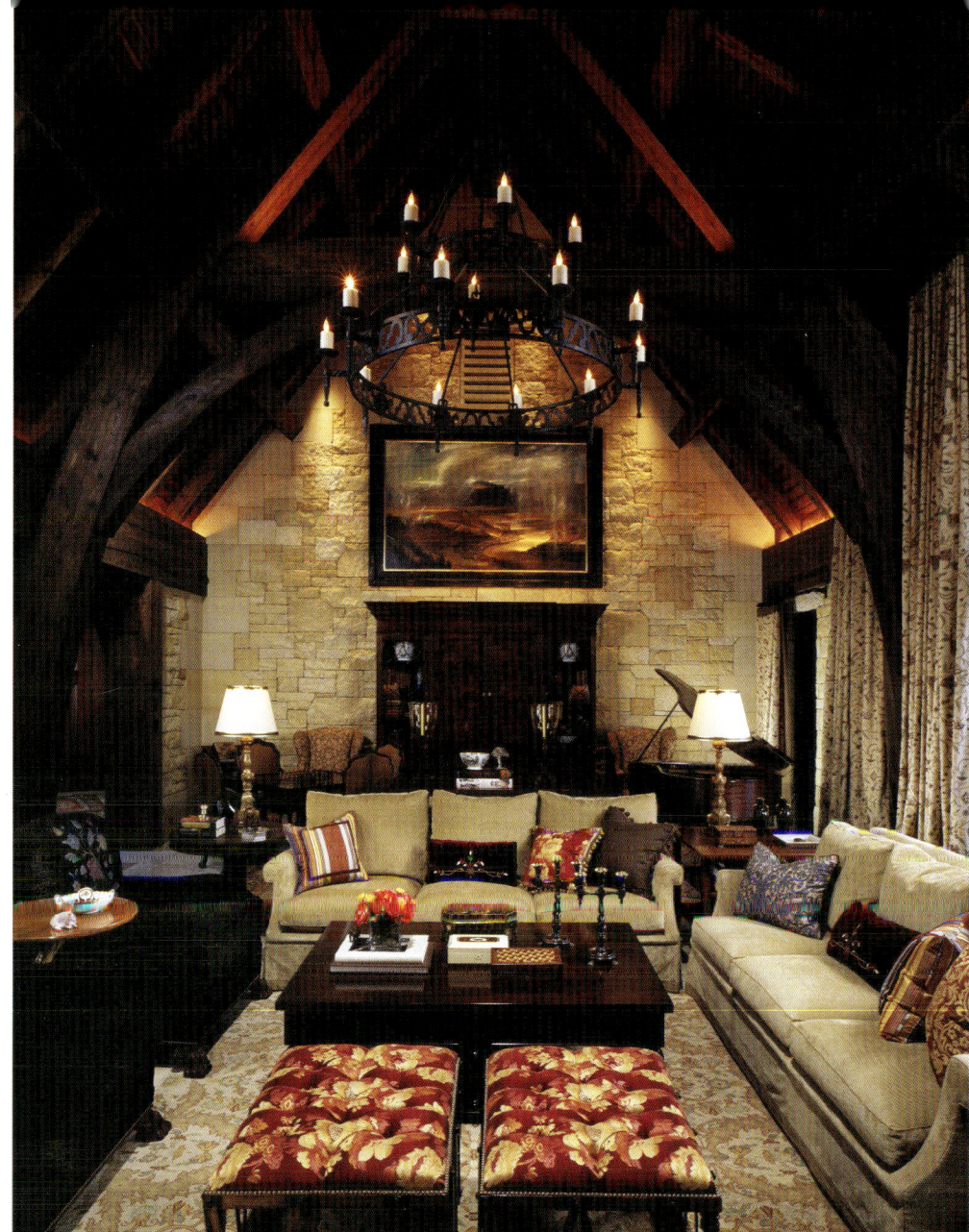

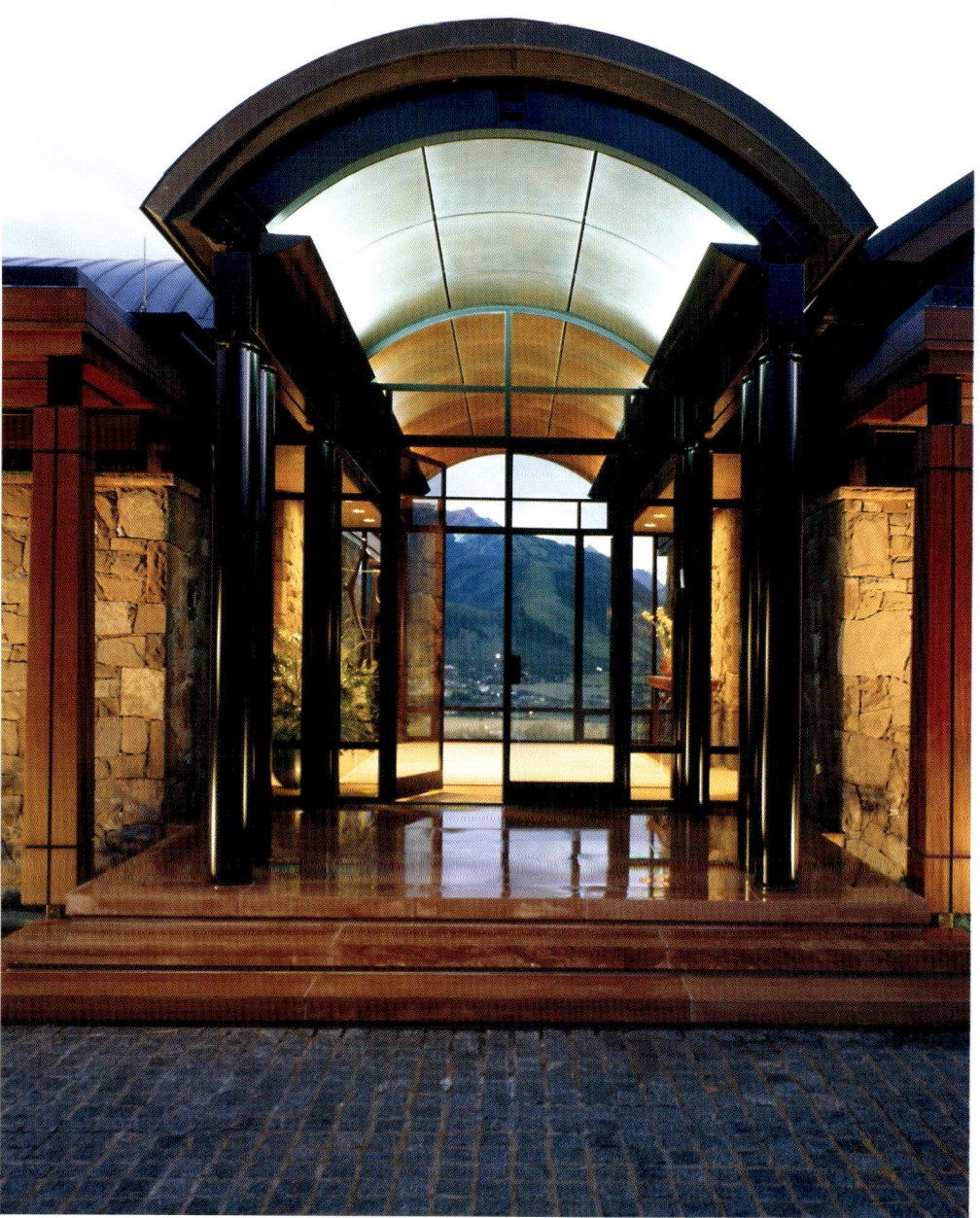

Poss Architecture + Planning understands and embraces the collaborative effort required in creating high-end homes. Usually a group of creative people (architects, landscape architects, interior designers, etc.) are working simultaneously on one project. Therefore, there are many ideas combined together to provide a better project for the client. Having interior designers on staff affords a cohesive vision threaded throughout a project. Sometimes the team's designs and attention to detail extend all the way down to the flatware that client will use for meals on a daily basis. Essentially, their mission is to get involved with the details of a project. Their clients appreciate their efforts and artistry, which always equals a dream home come true.

ABOVE LEFT:
The open truss system, stone walls and mixture of antique and new furniture was used to express a rustic yet elegant style.
Photograph by Pat Sudmeier

ABOVE RIGHT:
The entry frames the mountain view as it draws you into the foyer.
Photograph by David O. Marlow

FACING PAGE TOP:
Like they were built over time, the ranch structures incorporate natural materials of field stone and antique timbers to underscore the vernacular homestead design.
Photograph by Wayne Thom

FACING PAGE BOTTOM:
The pool barn is located off of the main cabin and has a gaming area, bunk rooms and a 55-foot long lap pool for the owner's daily swim.
Photograph by Wayne Thom

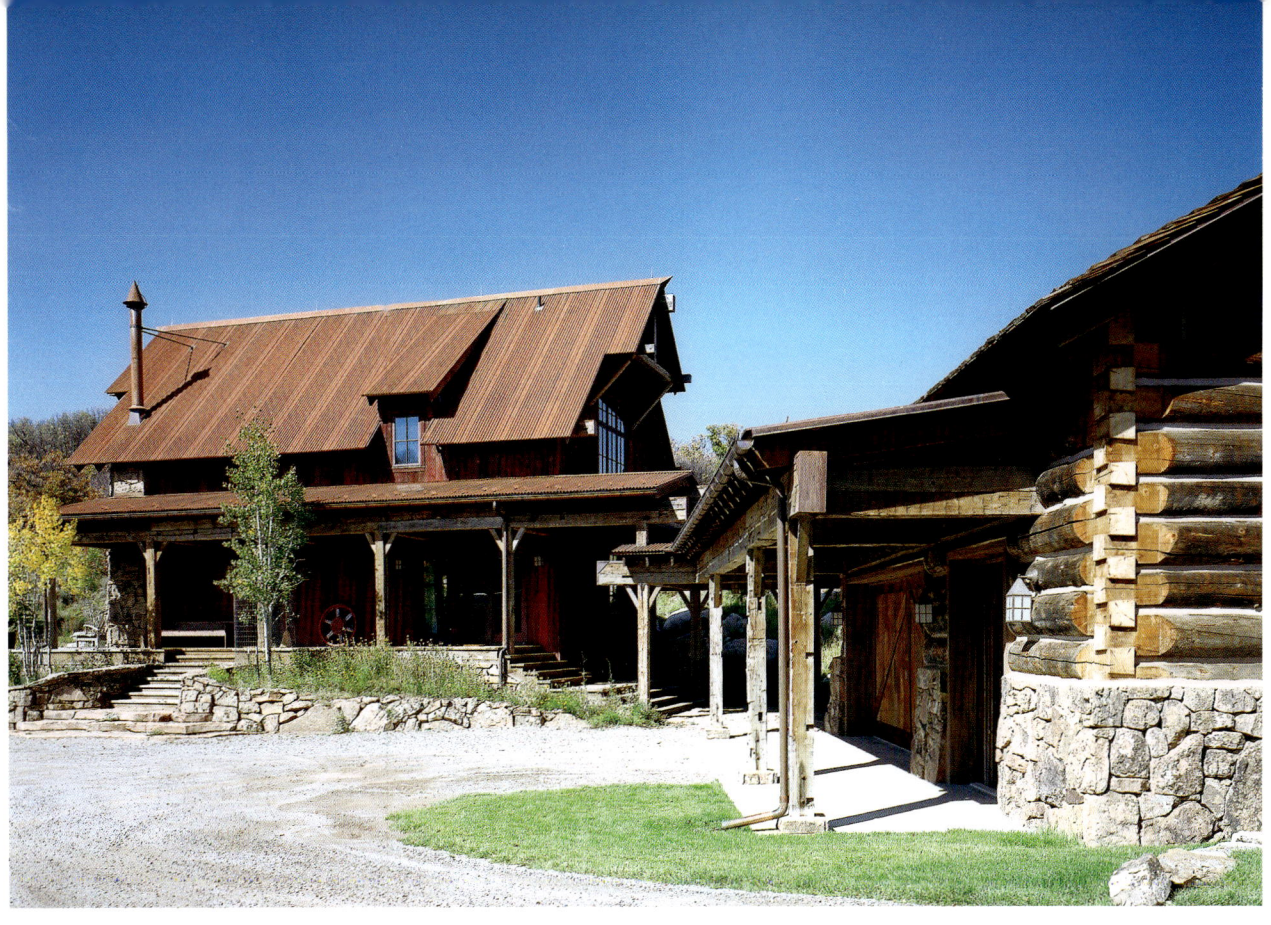

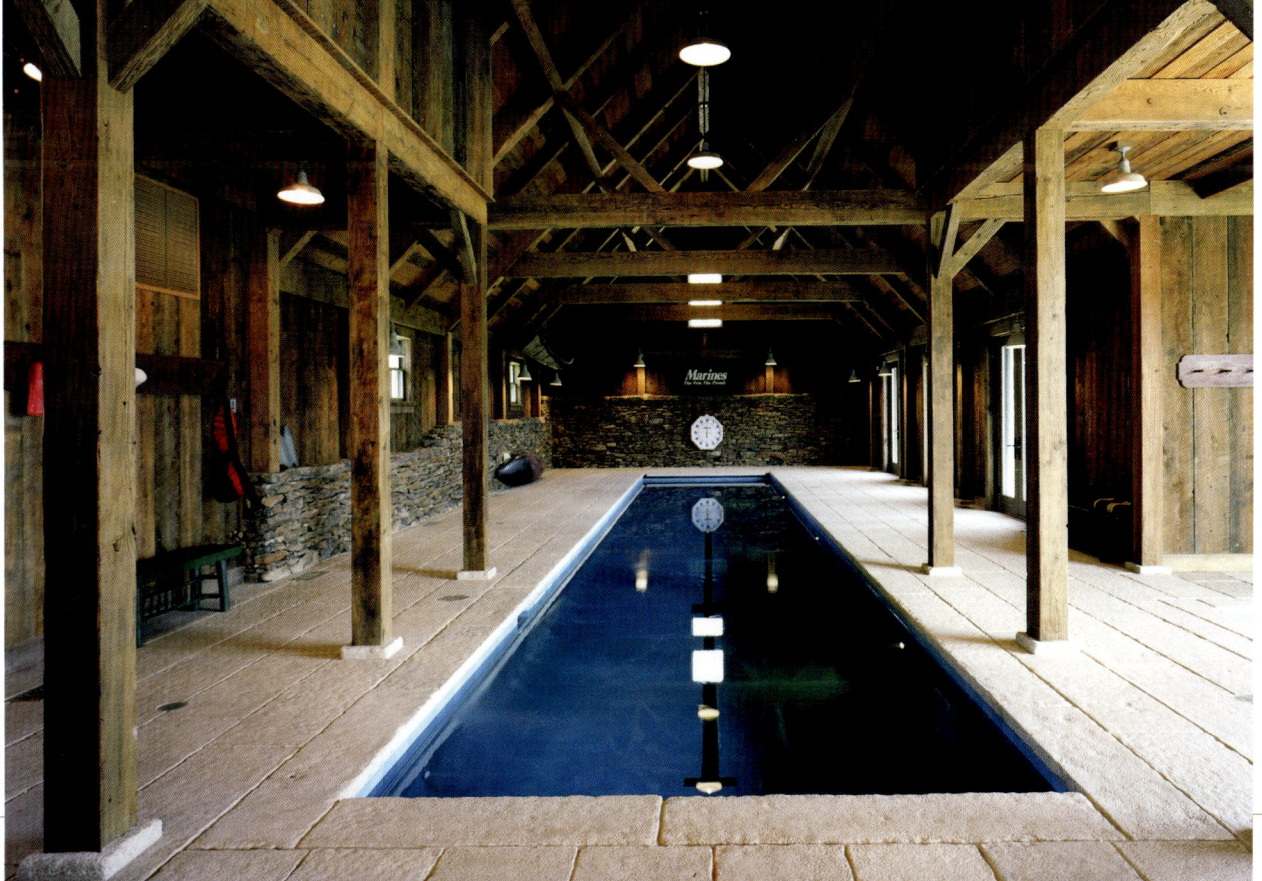

Q&A
more about bill...

WHAT PHILOSOPHY HAVE YOU STUCK WITH FOR YEARS THAT STILL WORKS FOR YOU TODAY?
We design structures that are products of understanding the client.

WHAT DO YOU LIKE MOST ABOUT DOING BUSINESS IN YOUR LOCALE?
The beautiful mountains and views that we get to bask in and work with everyday. This is one of the most beautifully unique places in the world and we're inspired by this beauty on every project.

WHAT IS THE MOST SATISFYING PART OF BEING AN ARCHITECT?
Getting to the end of a project and having a truly satisfied client.

POSS ARCHITECTURE + PLANNING
BILL POSS
CHRIS RIDINGS
LES ROSENSTEIN
KIM WEIL
& ANDY WISNOSKI
605 East Main Street
Aspen, Colorado 81611
970.925.4755
f: 970.920.2950
www.billposs.com

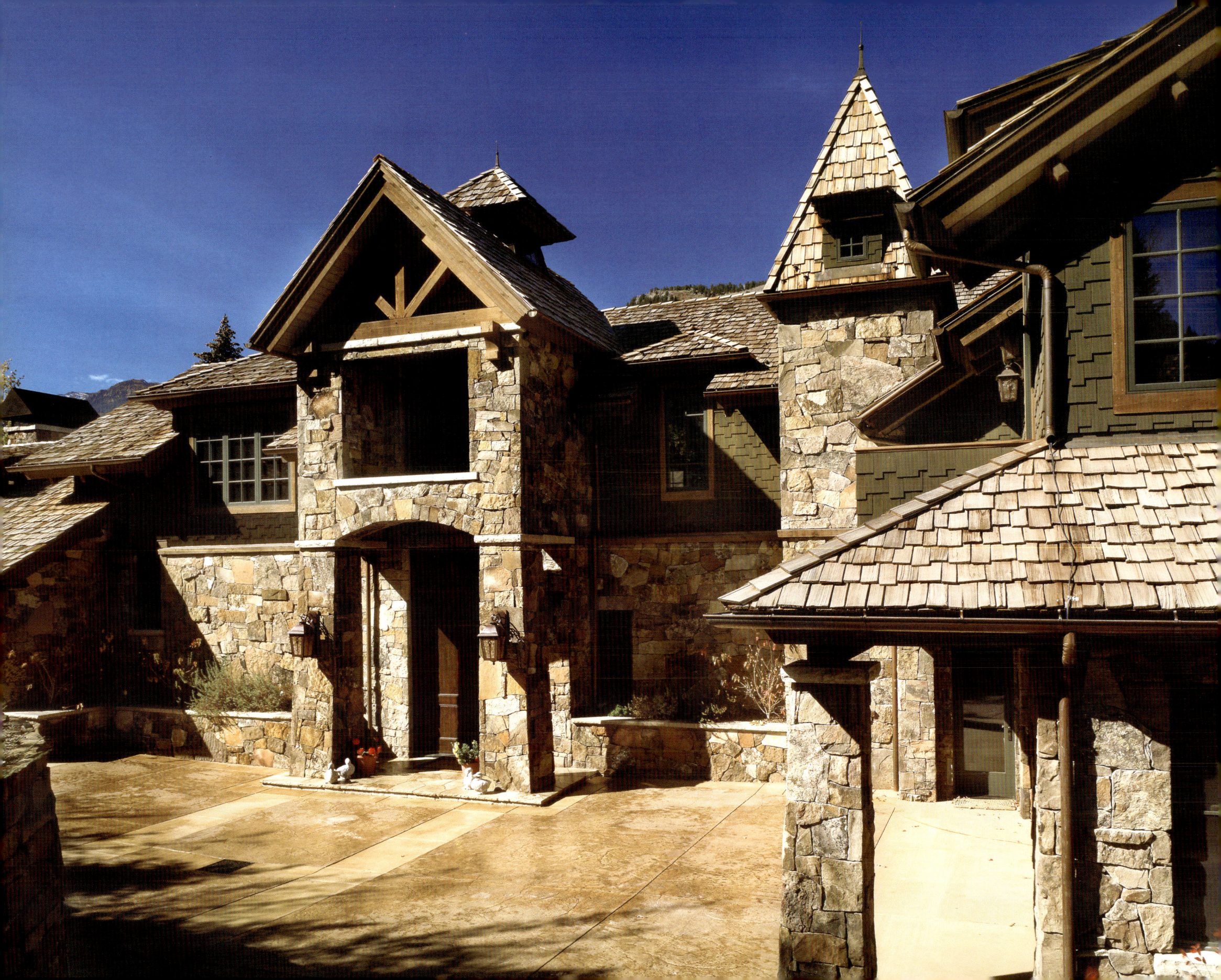

AUGIE RENO
SCOTT SMITH

RENO SMITH ARCHITECTS, LLC

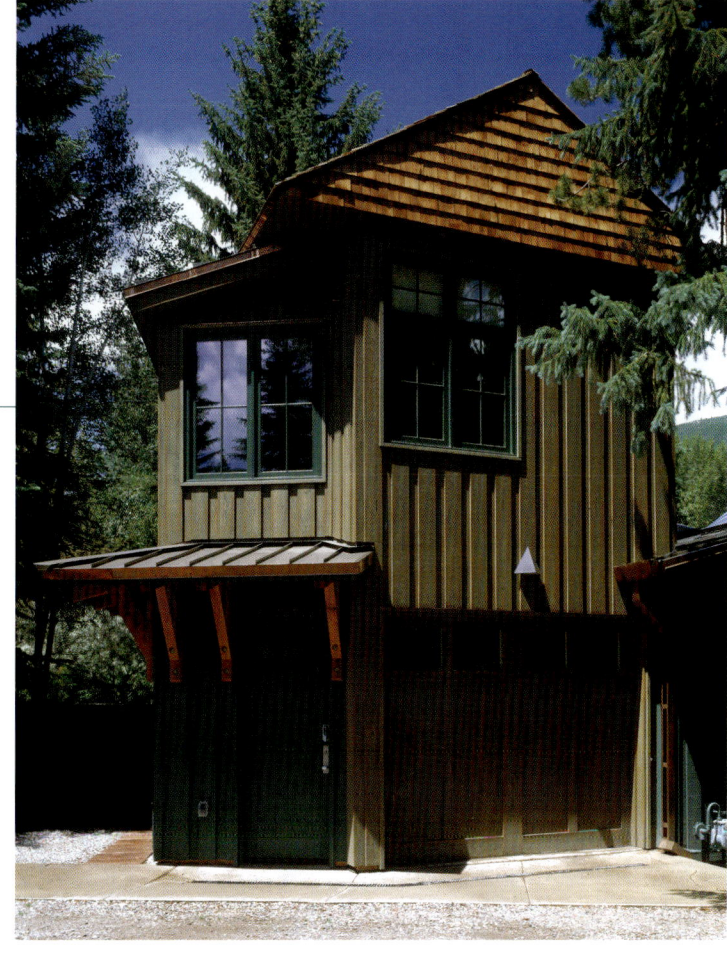

Augie Reno knew he wanted to be an architect long before he attended Western Michigan University on a partial baseball scholarship, transferring to the University of Illinois, Chicago where he completed the five-year professional architecture degree program in four years. After graduation, he expanded his Chicago horizons by answering an ad for a job in Aspen, subsequently founding his architecture firm which currently is celebrating its 25th anniversary. The eight-member Reno-Smith team, including principal Scott Smith, AIA, designs projects ranging from small additions to high-end custom homes of 25,000 square feet, throughout the Roaring Fork Valley and all along Colorado's Western Slope.

Like a maestro blending orchestra sections to create music, Reno-Smith is adept at balancing the rhythms and movements of a building with other key design aspects such as its client's desires and preconceptions, comprehensive planning and site evaluation, and an understanding of myriad and complex zoning issues that often must be navigated. When these elements come together, the result is a fine composition in the physical form of a Reno-Smith custom home.

Reno-Smith's site studies embrace the property in its entirety, assessing adjacent views which may be of another home or of an uninterrupted vista. The study typically is conducted at several different times in a day to gauge the particular effects of sunlight and prevailing winds at certain hours. Reno-Smith's extensive experience, training and research capabilities ensure that such details as how a mountain may or may not obscure the sun or which side of a house will experience a snow buildup will be evaluated for all four seasons.

Augie, who inherited from his father a love for restoring classic cars, and has had more than 100 cars, also customizes cars into hot rods. Like the buildings he designs, he sees cars as pieces of engineered rolling art, as legitimate as his paintings, another of his pursuits.

ABOVE:
Small scale bedroom and garage addition to an eclectic palette of materials, colors and building shapes. Falender Residence, Aspen, Colorado.
Photograph by David O. Marlow

FACING PAGE:
Grand entry and elevator towers of stone stand over the auto courtyard. Maroon Creek Overlook, Aspen, Colorado.
Photograph by David O. Marlow

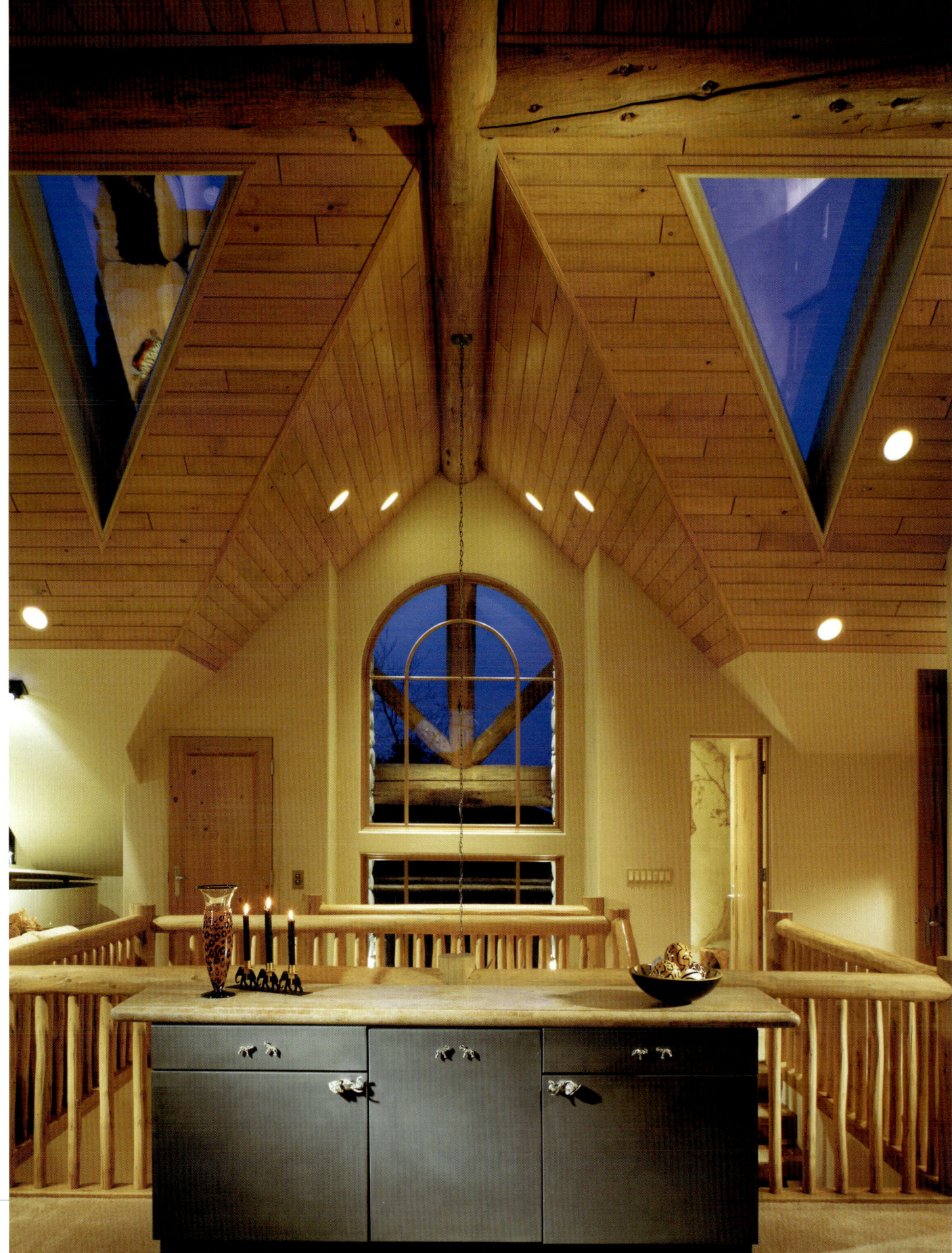

This attention to detail permeates Reno-Smith homes, which often feature indigenous and reclaimed materials that complement the elements and colors of adjacent visible mountains. Stone, durable and sustainable, is used for limited interior areas such as floors, fireplaces or accent walls, and woods such as cedar, pine or oak add warmth and comfort in juxtaposition to cold Colorado winters. The firm's designs typically incorporate intimate areas within more grand spaces. A small sitting room or den serves as a retreat from the activity or emptiness of a much larger place. A common thread is that Reno-Smith clients share a desire for the hallmarks of the mountains, to feel they're in a cabin or lodge with a big roaring fire and spectacular view.

"A lot of the views we design for offer more than mountain landscapes," Augie says. "They're for wildlife, the deer, elk, foxes, wolves and bears. We try to capitalize on that environment so our clients can experience it when they're here."

LEFT:
Juxtaposition of angular forms and openings with curvilinear windows tied together with warm wood and plaster materials. Single family residence, Aspen, Colorado.
Photograph by David O. Marlow

FACING PAGE:
Lodge-like atmosphere for a major living space capturing the warmth of natural materials and breathtaking views. Maroon Creek Overlook, Aspen, Colorado.
Photograph by David O. Marlow

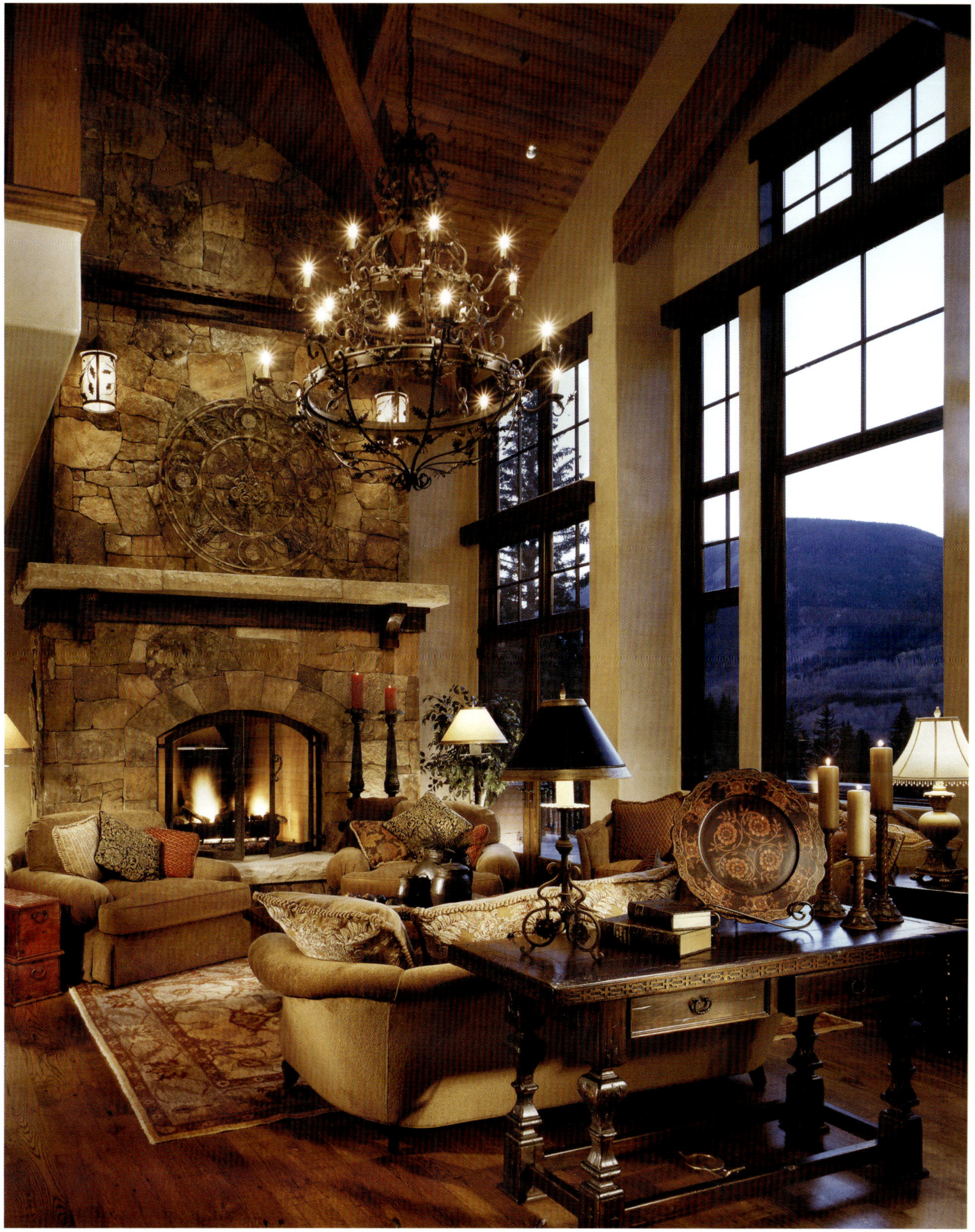

Q&A

more about augie...

WHAT COLOR BEST DESCRIBES YOU?
Red. It's vibrant, alive, on the move, hot and spiritual.

WHAT BOOK ARE YOU READING NOW?
Breaking Ground by Daniel Libeskind.

WHAT IS THE MOST UNIQUE/IMPRESSIVE/BEAUTIFUL HOME YOU'VE BEEN INVOLVED WITH? WHY?
A house we did on the hillside, Red Mountain, in Aspen. It became a village of buildings with different shapes, colors and materials that came out of the hillside.

ANY AWARDS OF SPECIAL RECOGNITION YOU WOULD LIKE MENTIONED?
There are numerous state, regional and local AIA design awards through the years. The most recent came from the City of Aspen for the Annabelle Inn. We were "Business of the Year" in 2001 from the Aspen Chamber Resort Association.

more about scott...

WHAT ELEMENTS OF STYLE OR PHILOSOPHY HAVE YOU STUCK WITH FOR YEARS THAT STILL WORK FOR YOU TODAY?
Commodity, firmness and delight.

WHAT IS A SINGLE THING YOU WOULD DO TO BRING A DULL HOUSE TO LIFE?
I would let in more light.

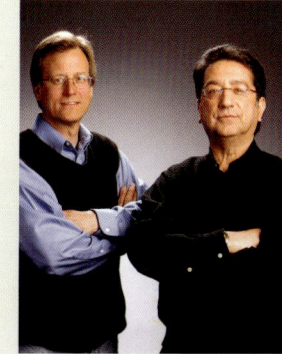

RENO SMITH ARCHITECTS, LLC
AUGUST G. RENO, AIA
SCOTT SMITH, AIA
605 West Main Street.
No. 002
Aspen, CO 81611
970.925.5968
f: 970.925.5993
www.renosmith.com

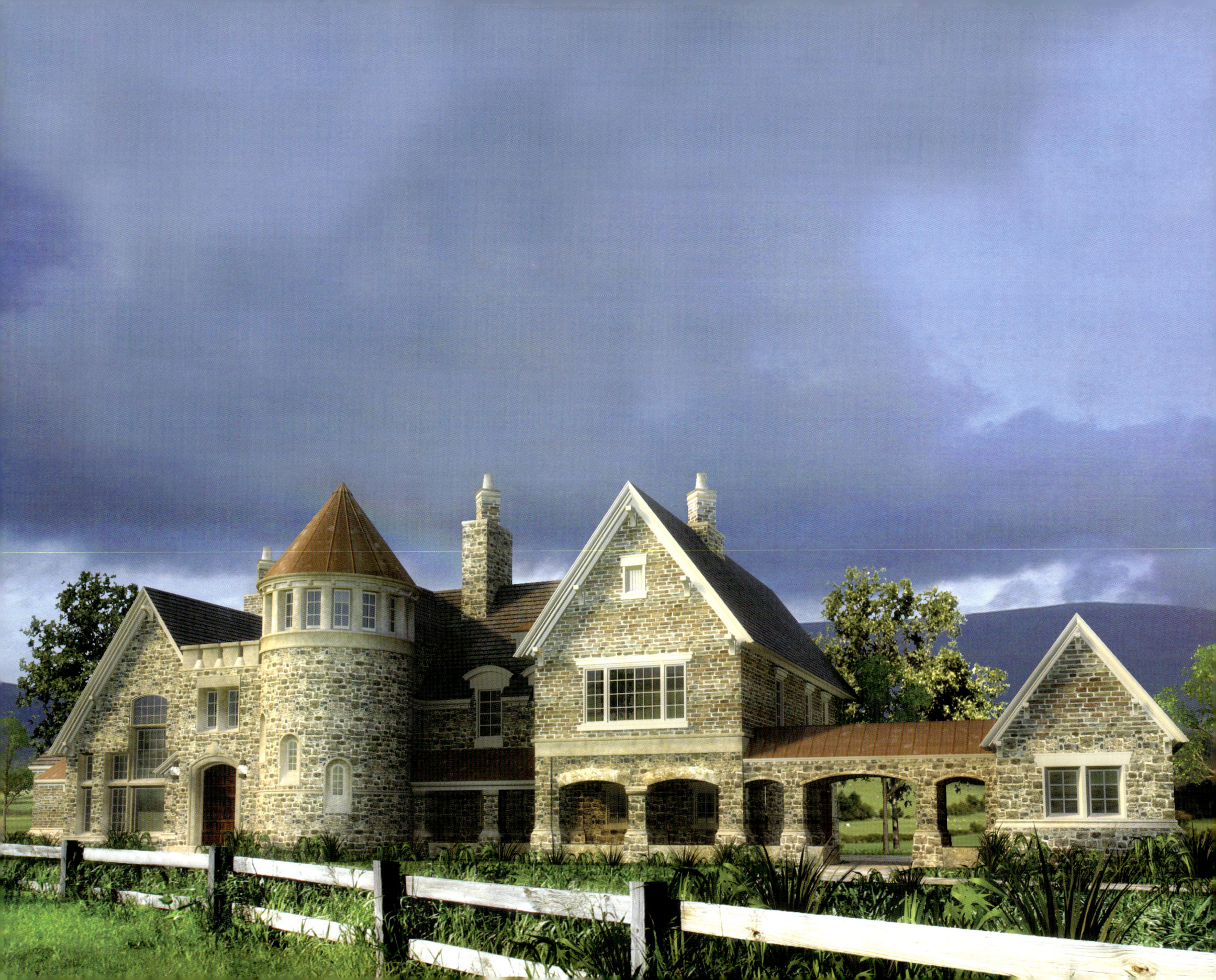

HARVEY ROBERTSON
PAUL MILLER
JEFFREY TERRELL

RMT ARCHITECTS

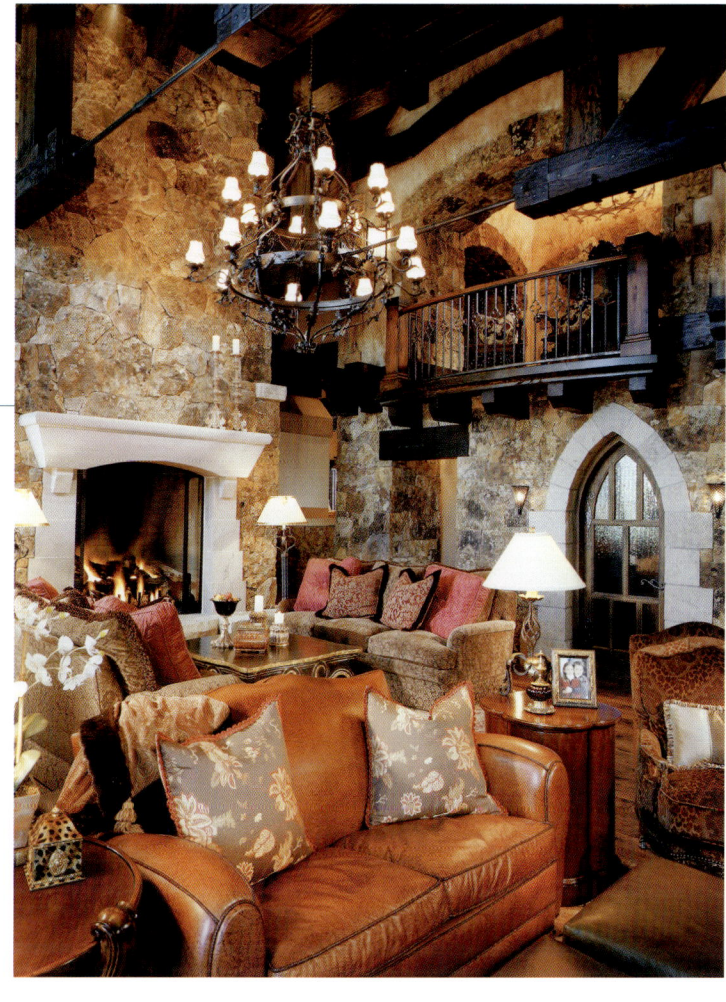

Harvey Robertson, Paul Miller and Jeffrey Terrell are extremely proud and pleased to share their collective and individual experience with their clients through RMT Architects. Their design expertise spans a broad variety of design disciplines as well as 40 years and three continents.

As three equal partners, Harvey, Paul and Jeff make the ultimate team. Jeff and Paul act as the designers and creative sources in the company, meeting with clients for all the initial investigations and conversations and determining design solutions that excite their clients. Although they have very different design styles, they are both committed to the same level of quality in their projects. Like two great chefs working with two different cuisines, they never fail to present an exquisite meal.

Acting as managing partner, Harvey communicates with clients and maintains schedules and budgets. Designing and building a single custom home requires that over six million decisions are made and Harvey is the team member who can orchestrate the complex group of individuals making those decisions. Making large-scale projects happen can often be an art itself and when this is the case, Harvey is the master artist.

RMT has been working for over a decade to define architecture as a worthwhile investment. Harvey, Paul and Jeff have built homes combining their clients' ideas and their own, making their projects truly unique and diverse. From carving a two-ton boulder to form a master bath to constructing an observatory complete with a copper dome and a tunnel connecting the room to the house, this firm has gone to great lengths to raise the architectural bar. RMT has brought in accents to make every project of theirs unique, including a playground slide instead of a traditional staircase and tree trunks instead of traditional columns at the entry of a home.

ABOVE:
A grand wood-burning fireplace sits opposite a balconied watchtower in this Colorado mountain lodge. The wine room resides behind the Gothic arch top doorway.
Photograph by David Marlow

FACING PAGE:
This country estate is inspired by the Scottish Hillside Home tradition, complete with a weathered copper roof adorning the central stair turret.
Photograph by Michael Berg

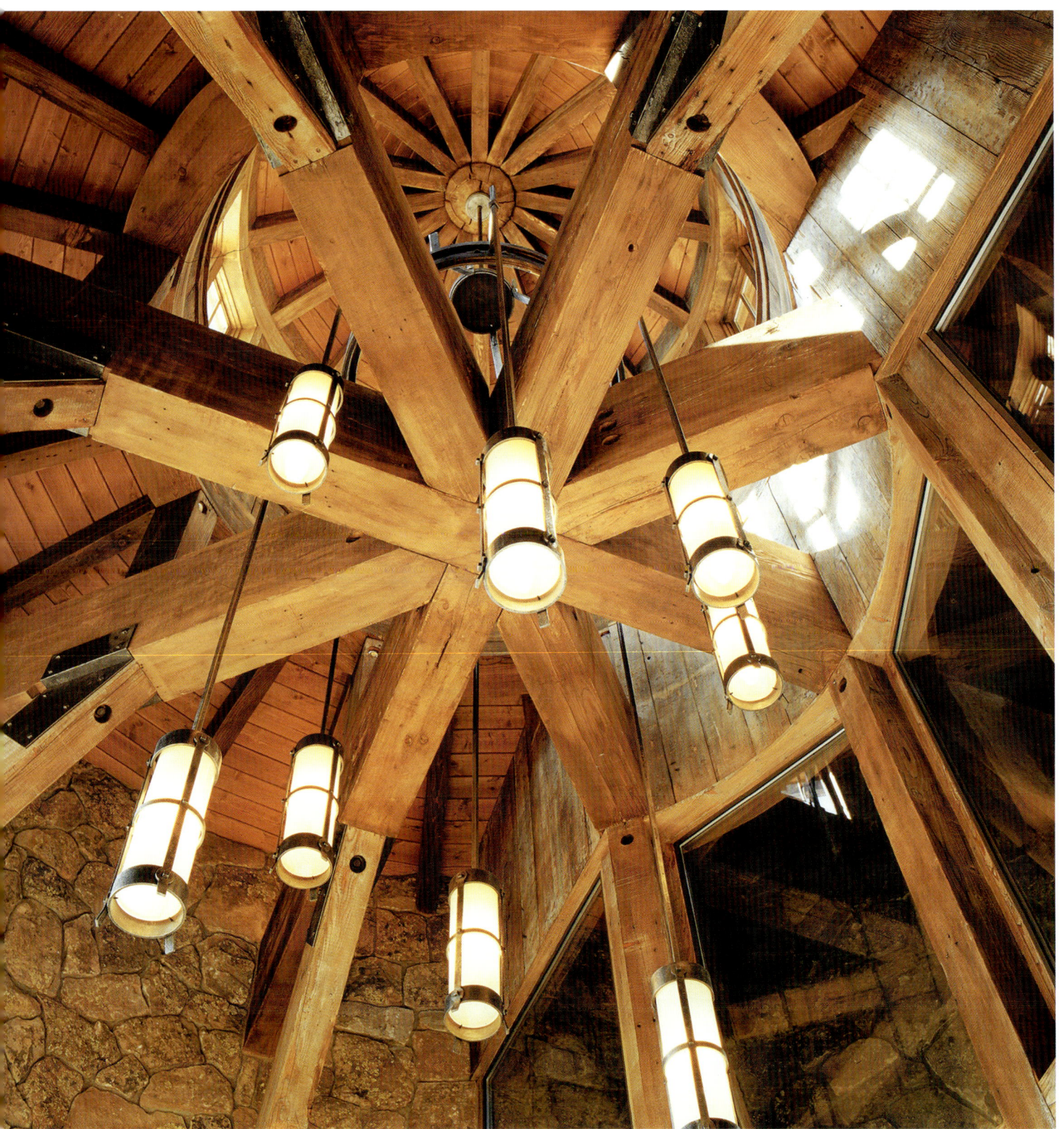

One thing that is made clear by RMT's work is that design is an investment. With architects of their stature on commercial projects, they leave behind a statement. As so often happens with RMT, people visit their clients' corporate properties and tell their friends it's a great place to visit. The firm also tries to translate this idea to their custom homes by catering to their clients and their lifestyles. RMT believes that you cannot measure the peace of mind that comes with living in a place you adore; great design yields an emotional benefit.

The German philosopher Goethe said, "Architecture is frozen music." RMT is always striving to make this statement a reality for their clients.

"Music can move you. It makes you feel emotions for a certain space in time and then you move on, having been within that moment of emotion. It's the same with architecture. I always try to create a similar feeling and atmosphere for my clients. Once you've moved outside of the building, it's like the song ends," explained Jeff.

LEFT:
The ceiling of this circular stair tower is replete with radial custom hewn timbers and staggered light fixtures, creating a sense of depth, space and emotion.
Photograph by Dann Coffey

FACING PAGE LEFT:
This study features two story windows looking out onto the Aspen forest. The stairway leads up to a second level balcony containing floor-to-ceiling bookshelves.
Photograph by David Marlow

FACING PAGE RIGHT:
The powder room for this more contemporary mountain home features a custom stone sink basin made of horizontally laid stone, taking its cues from the local rock formations.
Photograph by Dann Coffey

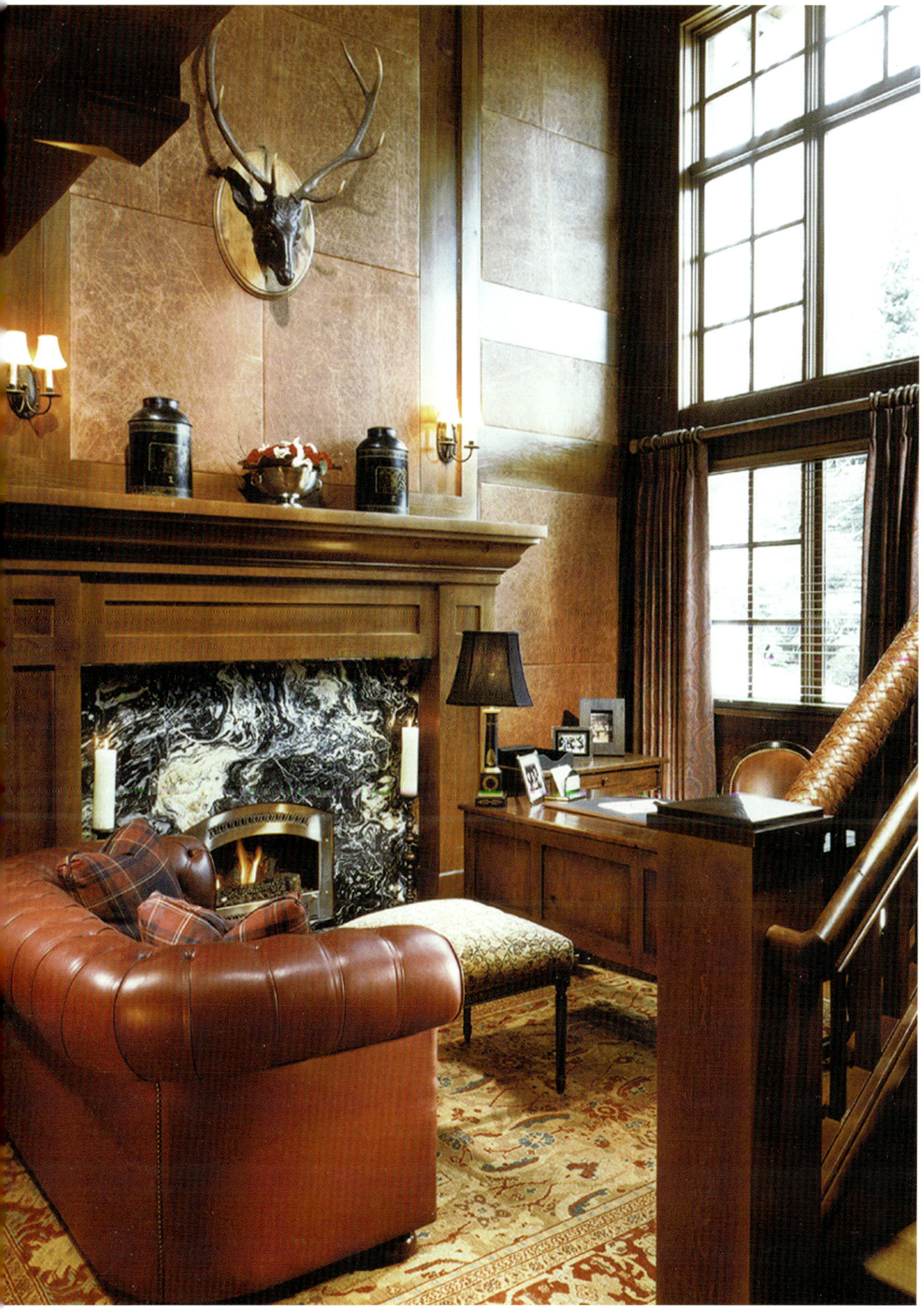

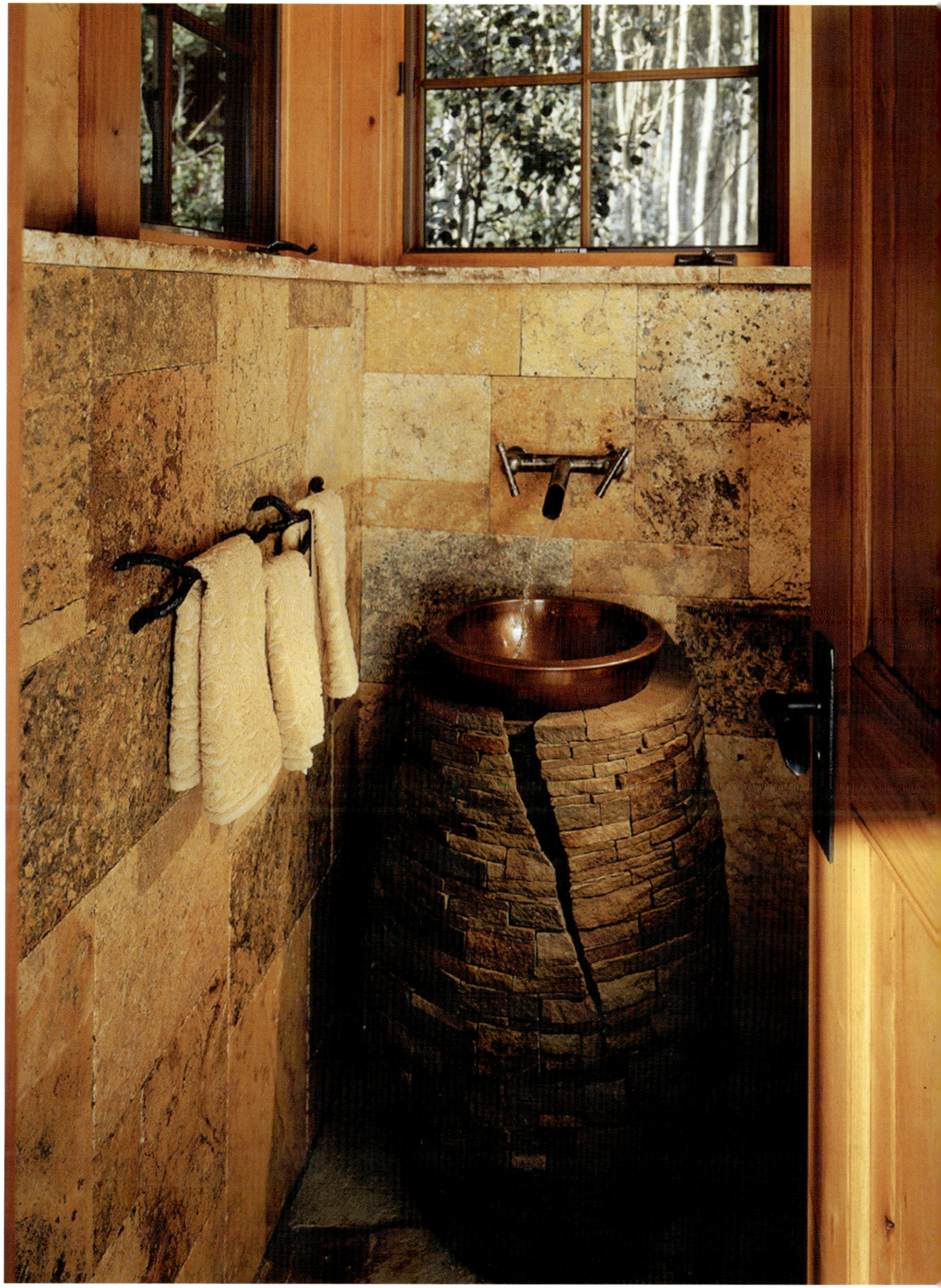

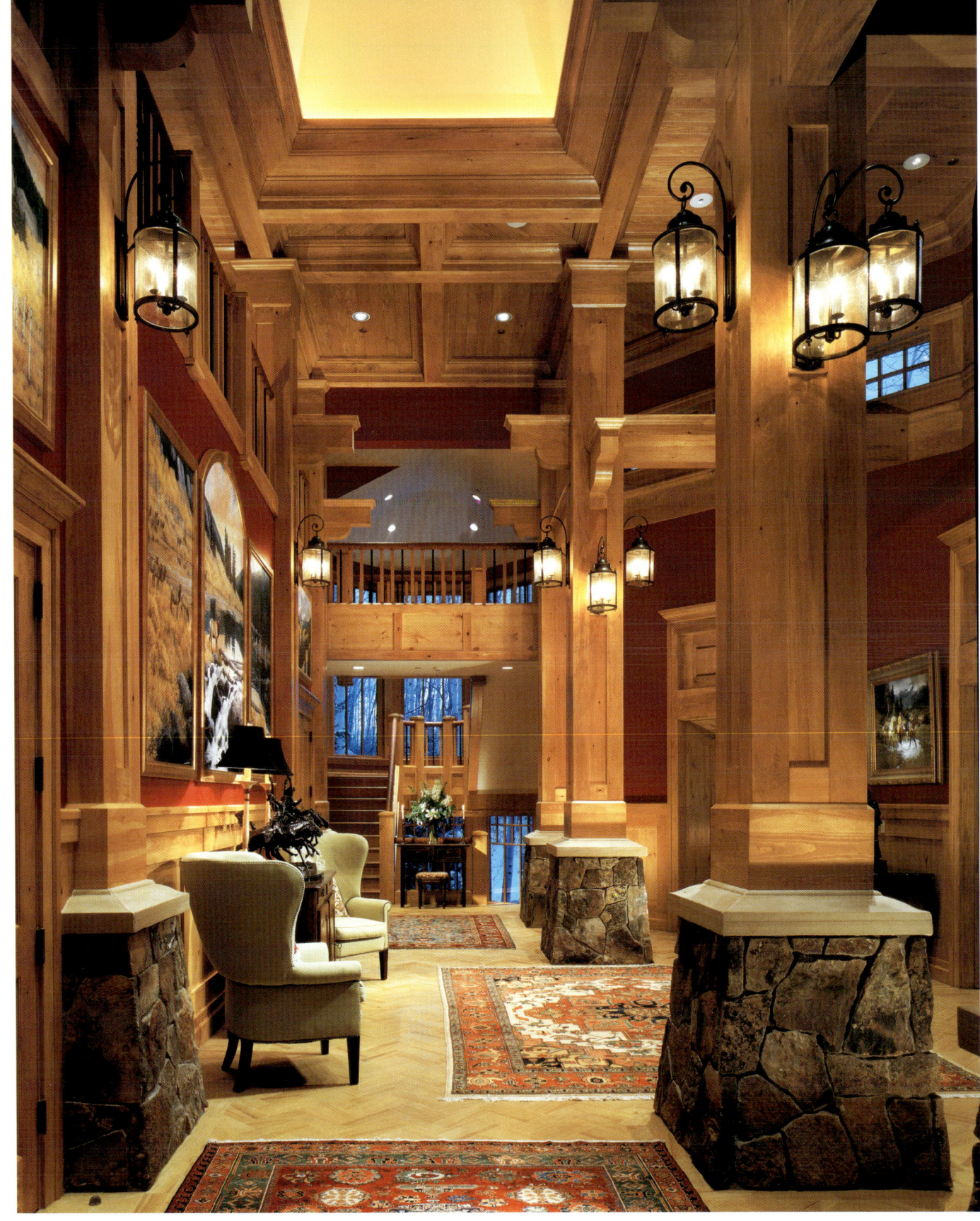

RMT designs their projects keeping in mind their aspirations to create buildings that move people and act as much more than a functional machine meeting technical requirements. Another distinguishing facet of RMT is their belief that the ownership group should share in the intimacies of the design process as a deeply engaged partner. Therefore, dissolving the barrier between the designer's mind and the owner's mind is an extremely important objective in RMT's view. They achieve this by creating a completely open design delivery process.

Consequently, RMT is proud to utilize cutting-edge technologies, enabling the finest communication between one another as well as their clients. Communication and deliberation are greatly enhanced, yielding a dramatic increase in the success of the final product. Whether they're creating a ranch-themed resort, a copper-domed observatory or a small custom home for a family, RMT strives to work with their clients to create a piece of art in which they'll love to live.

LEFT:
The formal entrance hall to this unique mountain home provides a central gathering point for access to the great room, dining room, kitchen, pool, guest wing, and grand stair.
Photograph by David Marlow

FACING PAGE:
Awash in romantic light, this ski-in ski-out home features oversized timbers, and massive amounts of stonework, all of which yield to enormous windows framing the spectacular views.
Photograph by David Marlow

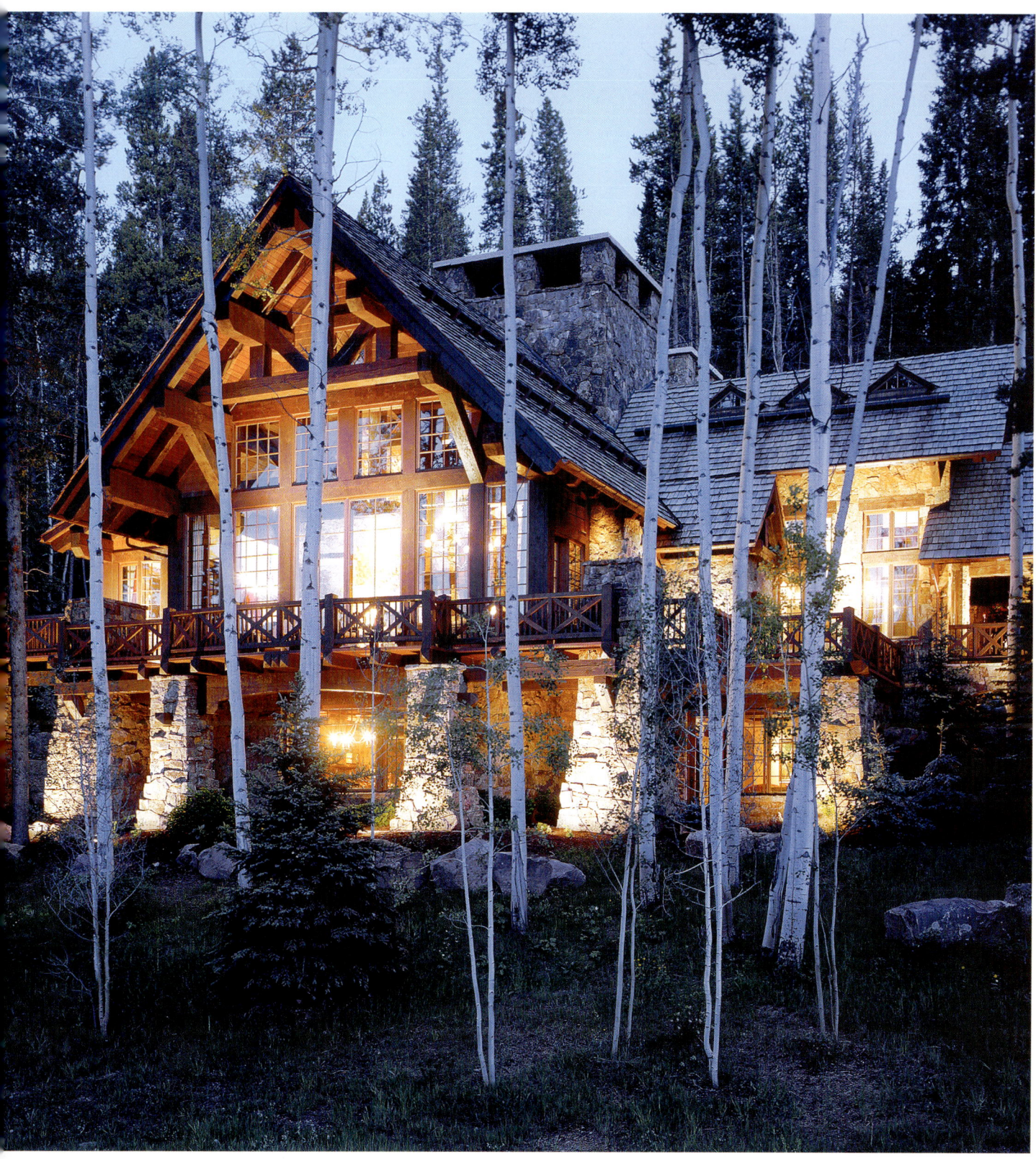

Q&A more about jeff...

WHAT IS THE BEST PART OF BEING AN ARCHITECT?
It is so gratifying to see things which you've imagined in your creative fantasy world one, two or three years earlier ... come to fruition. As a designer, ideas come early in the process and a lot of things happen between that moment when it's on your board and on your mind and when it's finally completed. When the project is complete, it's like seeing an old friend you haven't visited with in a long time.

WHAT PHILOSOPHY HAVE YOU STUCK WITH FOR YEARS THAT STILL WORKS FOR YOU TODAY?
I believe that buildings actually affect people. They move people in ways that are sometimes invisible and subconscious.

WHO HAS HAD THE BIGGEST INFLUENCE ON YOUR CAREER?
Years ago, I worked at a firm in Chicago with my first real mentor and boss Tom Beeby; he was Chairman of Architecture at Yale. Watching him work and listening to him talk about architecture instilled values and ideas in me that I still uphold today.

WHAT IS THE MOST UNIQUE/IMPRESSIVE/BEAUTIFUL HOME YOU'VE BEEN INVOLVED WITH? WHY?
Many of our clients and all of our staff put their heart and soul into every project we work on. We once worked on a project for a couple with two autistic children who wanted a second home on a disciplined budget. We were challenged with coming up with a beautiful design on a steep site while meeting all the local requirements. Now they are living in and loving the home while watching their children grow up.

WHAT DO YOU LIKE MOST ABOUT DOING BUSINESS IN YOUR LOCALE?
We are blessed with amazing clients; people who are willing to do so much off the bell curve. We have the opportunity to do amazing things and work on amazing resort properties.

RMT ARCHITECTS
HARVEY ROBERTSON
PAUL MILLER
JEFFREY TERRELL
PO Box 7630
Avon, CO 81620
970.949.0916
f: 970.949.1017
www.rmtarchitects.com

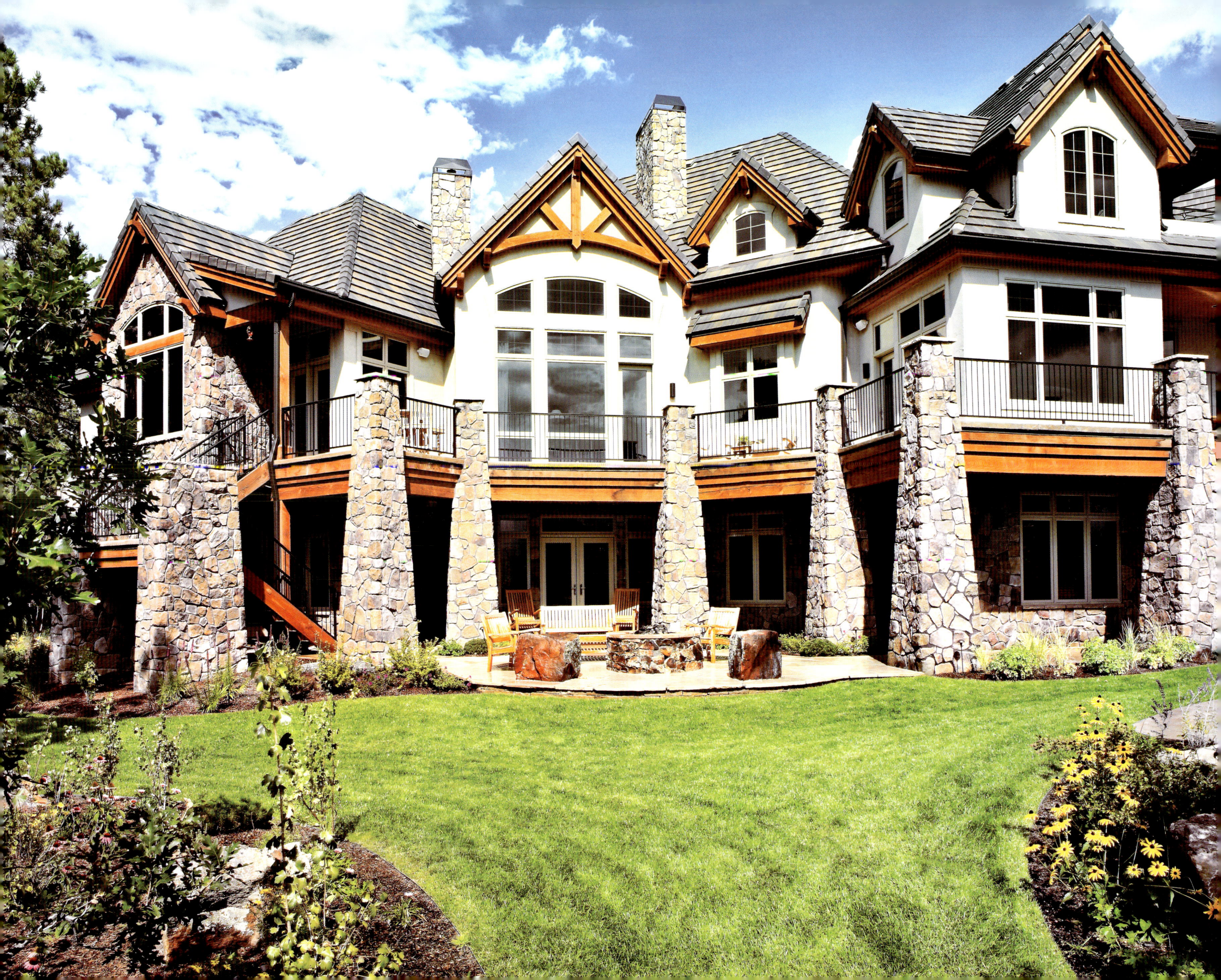

THOMAS W. SATTLER

SATTLER HOMES, INC.

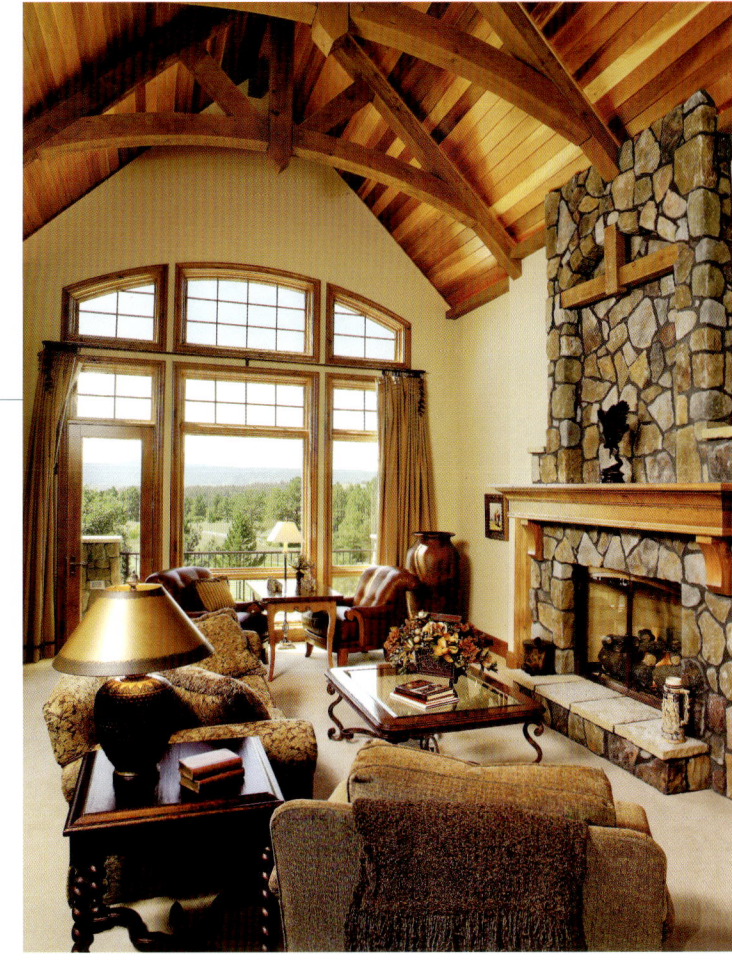

Tom Sattler is a third generation home builder whose company has become widely recognized and distinguished as a leader in the design and building of elegant custom homes. Along the way, he has been guided by the time-honored values of quality and tradition he learned from his grandfather and father in the family home building business in Iowa. A Midwestern upbringing of honesty and integrity still permeates Tom's company, Sattler Homes, Inc., which was founded in 1983.

Whether the design is a spacious golf course home, Tuscan-style mansion or mountainside retreat, each project is one-of-a-kind and built with a carefully orchestrated plan to make the custom home journey an easy one for the client. Sattler Homes establishes a long-term relationship with the customer by listening to them and delivering what they want: the home of their dreams.

While each home is truly unique, Sattler's approach to building remains constant throughout all of his projects because of well-developed organizational systems. Regardless of size, elevation, or finish, through their systems, Sattler Homes attempts to deliver a consistent product, a characteristic which has earned the 25-year-old company the 2003 America's Best Builder Award. Presented annually by *Builder Magazine*, this prestigious award is bestowed upon only four builders each year, recognizing them for business management excellence.

Clients are pleased to learn that the Sattler Homes team is comprised of award-winning architects, interior designers, and contractors who approach each project with the highest standards of excellence. Sensitive to each client's budget, Sattler Homes provides design/build services for a variety of homes: estate custom, custom, semi-custom, and niche production.

ABOVE:
This warm interior boasts a stone fireplace, timber trusses, wood ceilings and windows placed to maximize the views of the golf course and mountains beyond.
Photograph by Ron Ruscio Photography

FACING PAGE:
The client's desire to have a home reminiscent of old Colorado is achieved in this Beaver Creek style.
Photograph by Ron Ruscio Photography

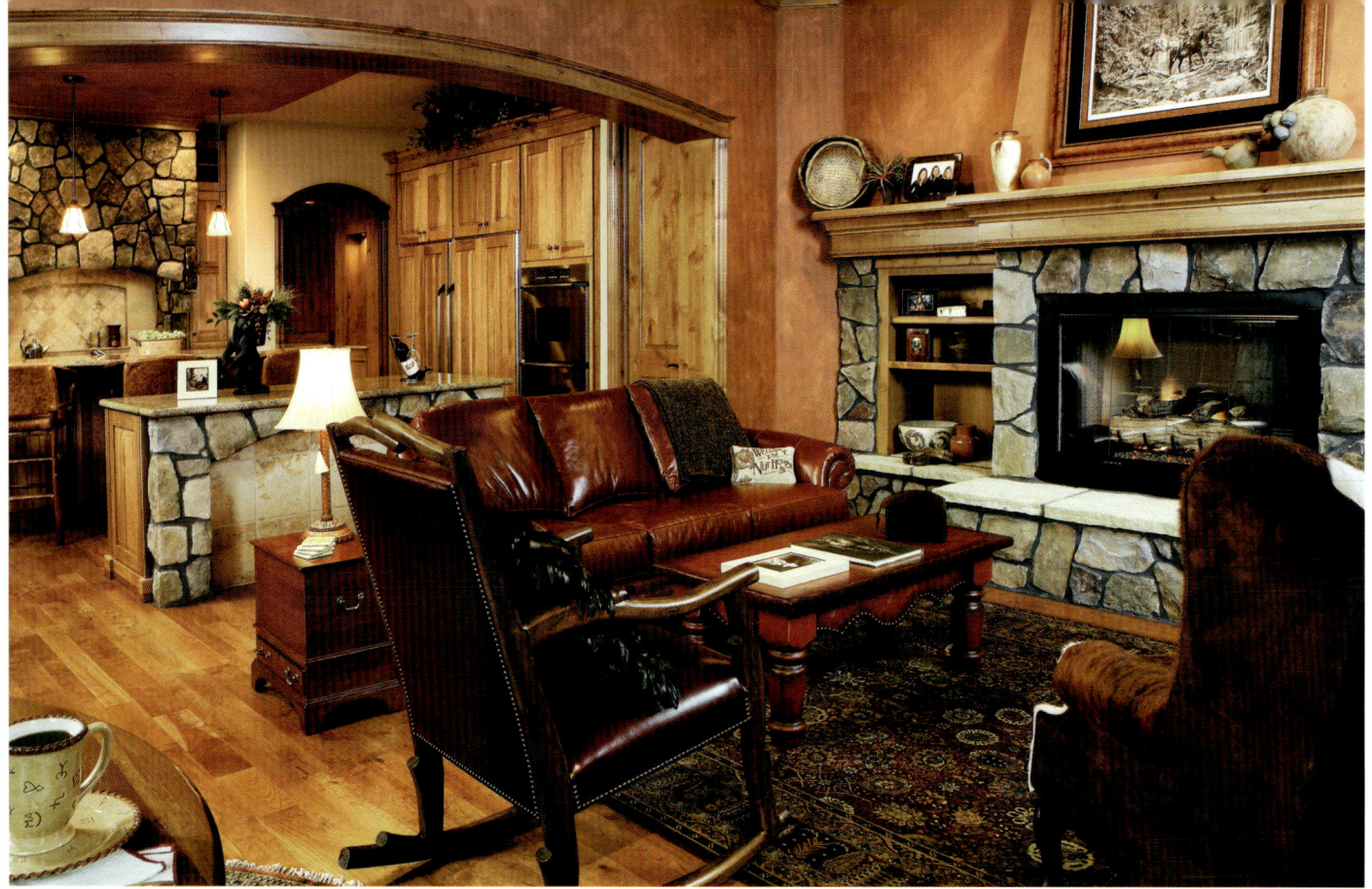

In addition to building exquisite homes, Tom's desire to maintain his personal and professional values in creating quality homes carries over into his involvement with various industry associations including the Home Builders Association of Metro Denver. He is also a National Director of its parent organization, The National Association of Home Builders.

Tom's passion is helping others and his contributions are perhaps best known outside home building circles for designing and creating several "Show Homes for Hope" volunteer events which brought the home building industry together to create an unparalleled show home that highlighted the industry's finest offerings. The proceeds from public ticket sales were donated to local charities. Similarly, Tom has served as co-chair of the 2006 Habitat for Humanity Blitz Build which is also bringing the home building industry together and has committed to aiding lower income families.

Tom attributes his success to dedication, hard work and the support of his team. He expounds, "If honesty and integrity are the most important aspects of your business, and if you take pride in your work, you will create homes prized for their craftsmanship."

TOP LEFT:
The home's use of stone throughout the hearth room and kitchen encourages relaxed and casual entertaining.
Photograph by Ron Ruscio Photography

BOTTOM LEFT:
This "Seasons Room" captures the beauty of the adjacent lake allowing the owners to enjoy Colorado's extraordinary weather just by sliding back the glass walls.
Photograph by Ron Ruscio Photography

FACING PAGE:
A masterful architectural design nestled this mountain home into the cliffs and granite rock overlooking the breathtaking lake below.
Photograph by Ron Ruscio Photography

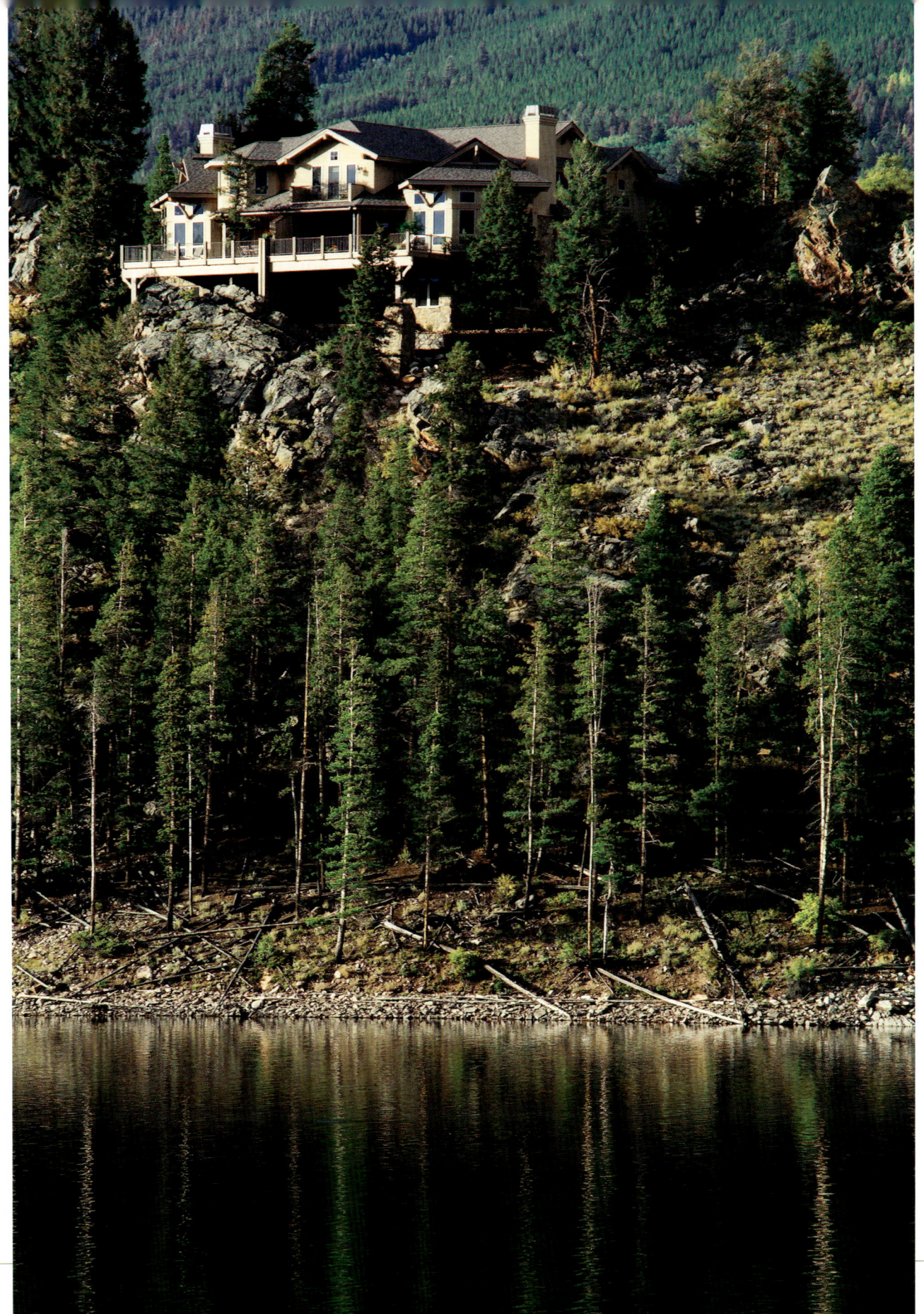

Q&A
more about tom...

FOR WHAT ARE YOUR COLORADO HOMES KNOWN?
Using natural materials such as timber and stone, our homes reflect Colorado's beautiful earth tones.

WHERE DID YOU GROW UP?
I was raised in Iowa by a family of home builders and still refer to my home state as the "mother ship" because several of my siblings are still involved in the business.

WHO IS YOUR RIGHT-HAND MAN?
Vice president of operations, Ed Rogers assists me in leading our small but talented company.

WHAT IS THE SATTLER APPROACH TO DESIGN?
With harmony as the goal, every element is well-planned, from energy-efficiency to lighting and home theatre technology.

SATTLER HOMES, INC.
THOMAS W. SATTLER
5990 Greenwood Plaza Boulevard
Suite 102, Building 2
Greenwood Village, CO 80111
303.771.5995
f: 303.771.3907
www.sattlerhomescolorado.com

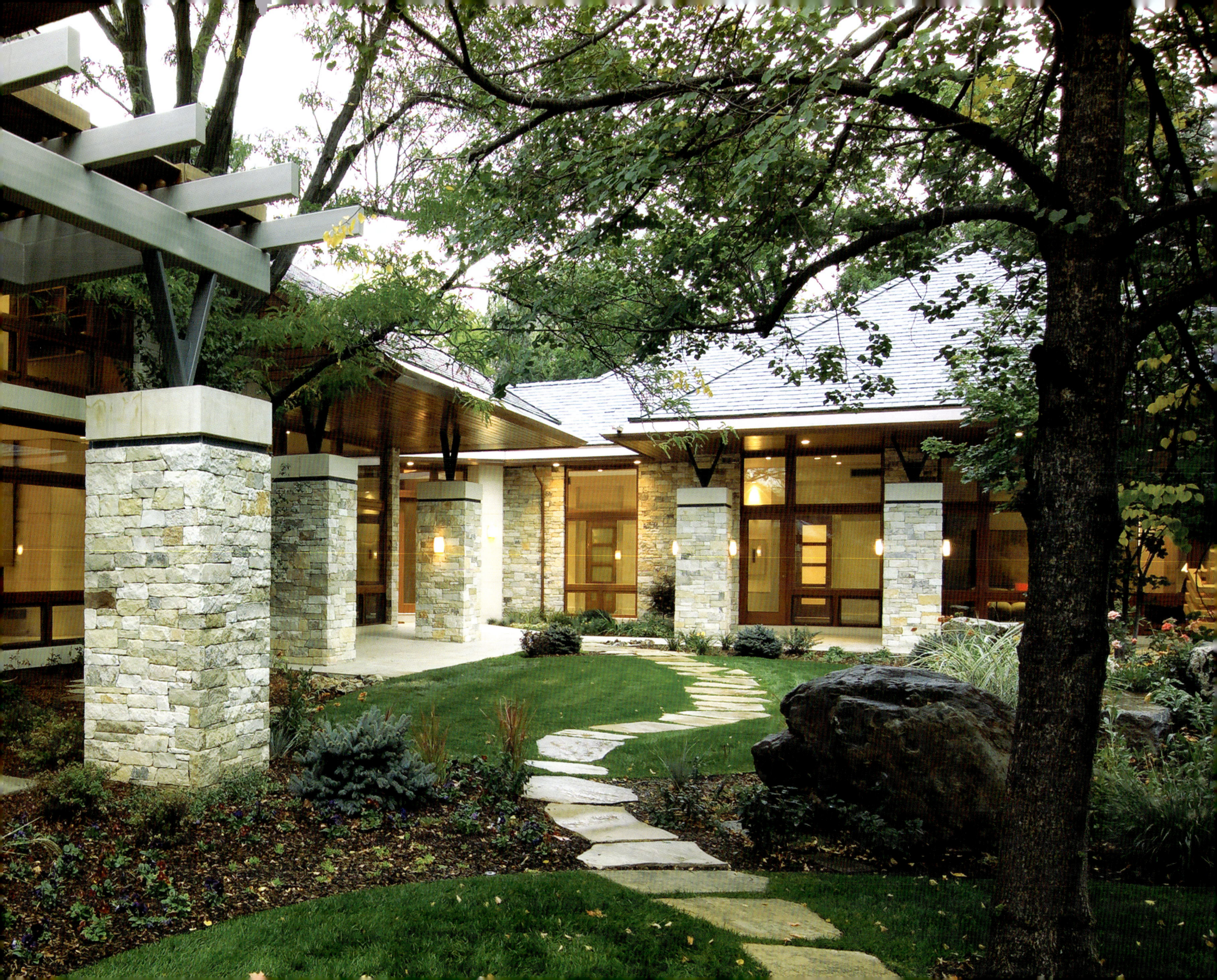

SEARS BARRETT

SEARS BARRETT ARCHITECTS

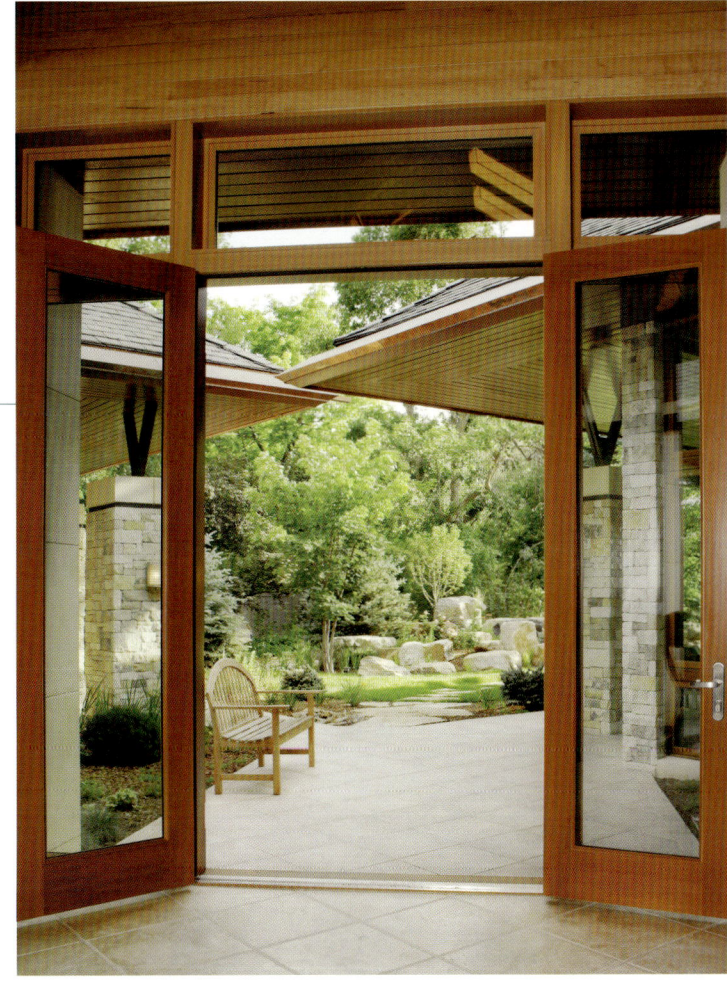

Sears Barrett began his architectural career working as a Vista volunteer in the poorest neighborhoods in Denver. Similar to legal aid, the Community Design Center offered free architectural services to neighborhood organizations focused on improving their facilities. This led to a leadership position at Denver Free University where he coordinated the educational program of the nation's largest community-based free school.

An interest in construction and a fascination with solar design inspired the next chapter in Sears' career. In 1978 he founded one of the first design-build firms specializing in Passive Solar design. "I loved the physical satisfaction of the building process–you can step back at the end of the day and see the walls you have framed." After completing a number of earth integrated, passive solar homes Sears was asked to join the staff of The Solar Energy Institute (now known as The National Renewable Energy Institute). As one of five architects on staff, Sears was responsible for conceiving and managing research programs on the performance of passive solar designs. Following the Arab oil embargo of the early 80s, the federal government placed great importance on conservation and alternative energies. "We felt like we were vanguard, out to change the fundamental assumptions about how to build."

In 1984 Sears decided to return to his primary love of design. His goal was to fuse the lessons learned at the solar institute with elegant, site sensitive residential design. For over 20 years his firm has built a reputation for designs that demonstrate creativity, an artful use of materials, and a fine sense of proportion. "We have done projects in every conceivable architectural language and truly enjoy the mix. Whatever architectural style our clients favor, our goal is to understand the elements and do it well."

ABOVE:
Upon entry the first experience is of openness to the lush garden. Two main roofs of the home float above just inches apart.
Photograph by Ron Ruscio

FACING PAGE:
The owners' goals were to build a contemporary home that provided a blend of refinement, warmth and textural interest through the use of rich materials. Hand-shaped Texas limestone coupled with slate roofs and Douglas fir windows lend a timeless sense of quality.
Photograph by Ron Ruscio

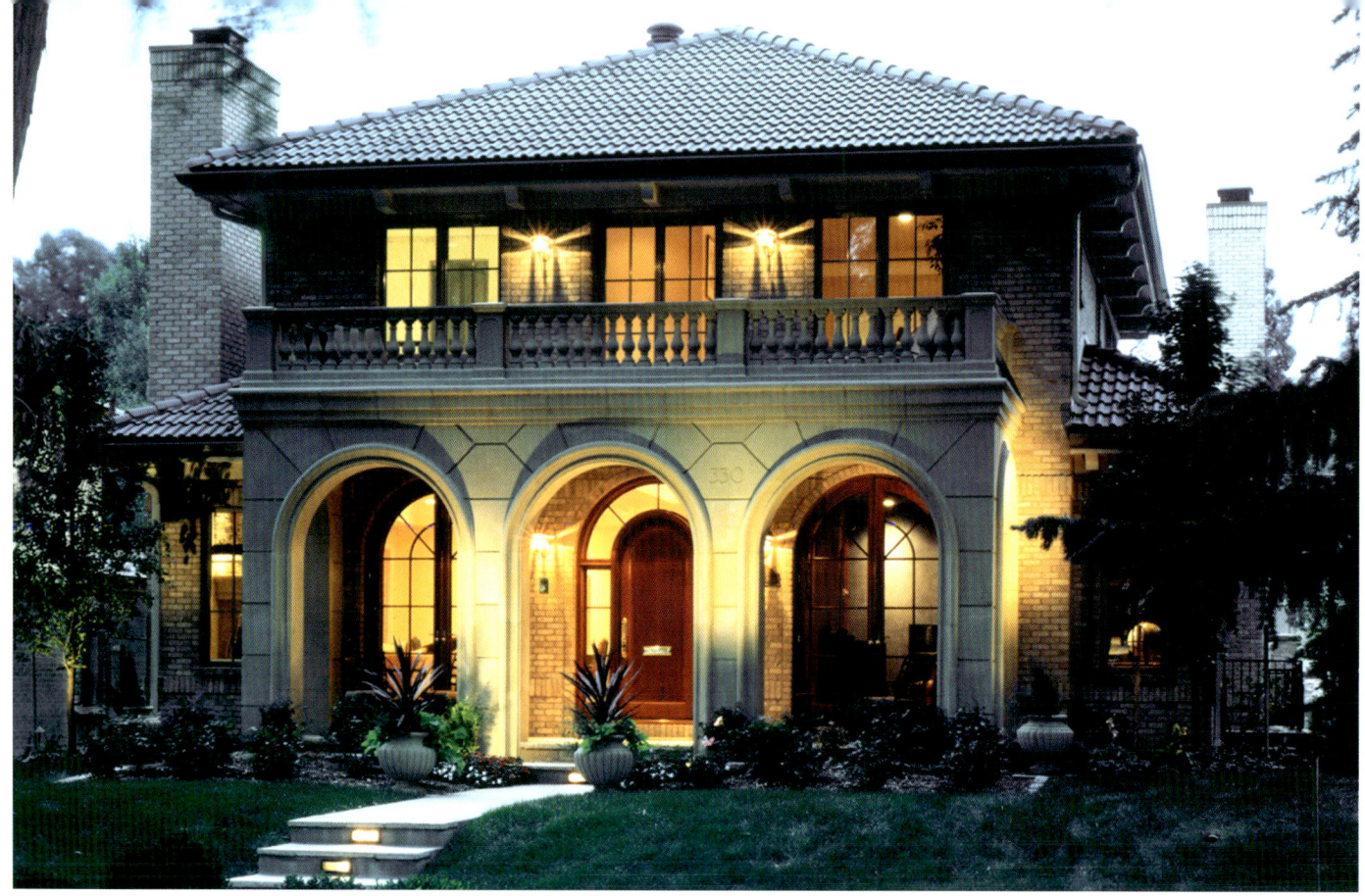

What is most exciting to Barrett is the increasing interest among his clients in conservation and sustainability. "We have always applied passive solar design principles to our work when the site allowed. Now we have many clients who are looking for that unique blend of sustainability and elegant design."

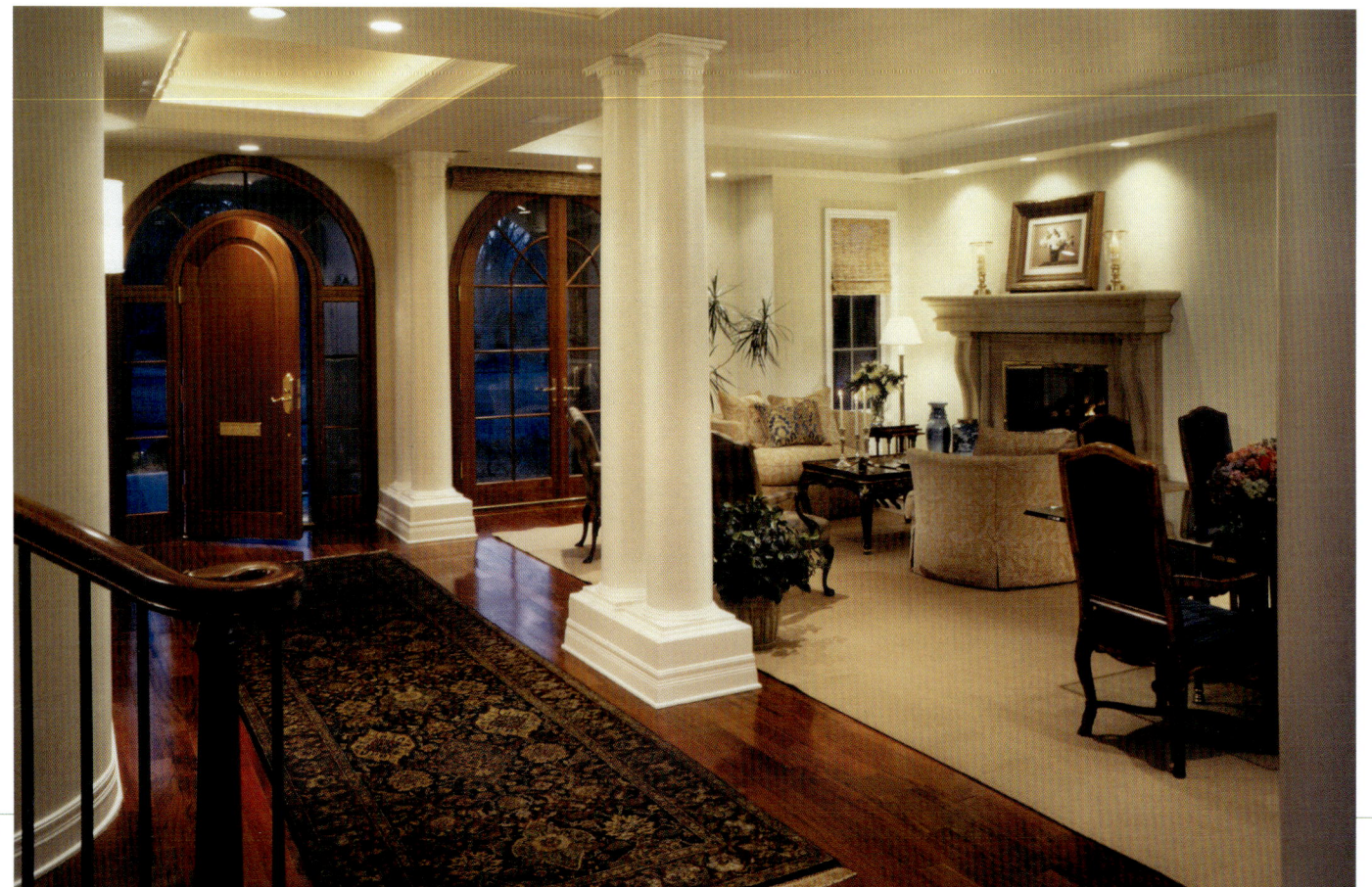

TOP LEFT:
This in-town home, framed by 80-year-old elms, was designed to feel like it was built at the same time as its 80-year-old neighbors. A highly detailed, cast stone loggia and custom mahogany French doors provide a sense of quality and refinement that make it a welcome addition to the neighborhood.
Photograph by Sears Barrett

BOTTOM LEFT:
The extensive use of crown moldings, a cut limestone fireplace surround, Brazilian Cherrywood flooring and a carefully designed lighting scheme all contribute to this refined interior.
Photograph by Sears Barrett

FACING PAGE:
Intricate timber framing above a massive stone base introduces the architectural language that continues through the interior of this post and beam residence.
Photograph by Sears Barrett

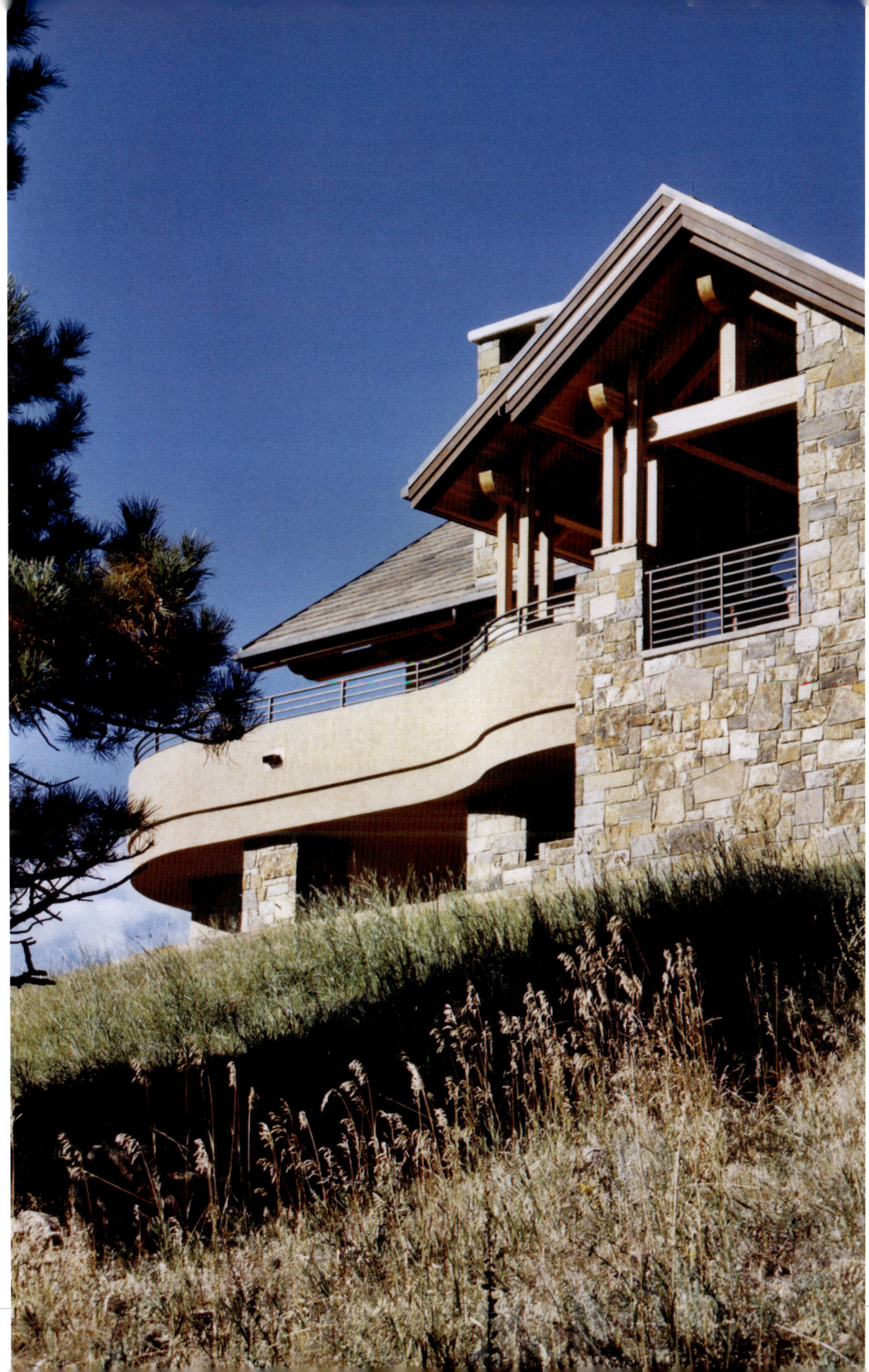

Q&A
more about sears...

WHAT ONE PHILOSOPHY HAVE YOU STUCK WITH FOR YEARS THAT STILL WORKS FOR YOU TODAY?
The guiding principle of our work is to achieve a sense of delight. It is derived from a unique blend of the quality of light, the use of materials and the sense of sculptural space. We think of it as achieving a great fit. There is a unique sense of serenity when a design truly enhances the landscape. On another level the success of a design can be measured by how well the spaces inspire those who dwell within. The final measure of "fit" may ultimately be how lightly this new dwelling treads upon our fragile planet.

HAVE YOU USED UNIQUE TECHNOLOGY IN ANY OF YOUR PROJECTS?
We are currently working on a number of designs that employ a high level of solar utilization with recycled building materials. One product we are very excited about is called Cempo, which is a building block comprised of recycled polystyrene and concrete. It is a highly insulated wall system that provides thermal mass and requires no harvesting of trees.

WHAT DO YOU LIKE MOST ABOUT DOING BUSINESS IN YOUR LOCALE?
I cannot imagine a better place to do residential design than Colorado. On one level we have a broad range of settings from fine old downtown neighborhoods to rapturously beautiful mountain sites. We have a climate second to none with more days of sunshine than almost anywhere in the United States. In Colorado we are free from the pressure to conform to a long-standing tradition of architectural style. I love the West, anything is possible.

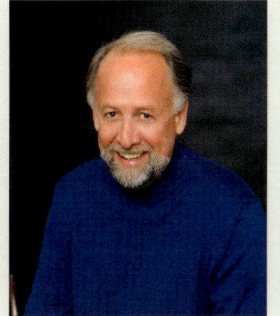

SEARS BARRETT ARCHITECTS
SEARS BARRETT
7901 East Belleview Avenue, Suite 250
Englewood, CO 80111
303.804.0688
f: 303.804.0619
www.searsbarrett.com

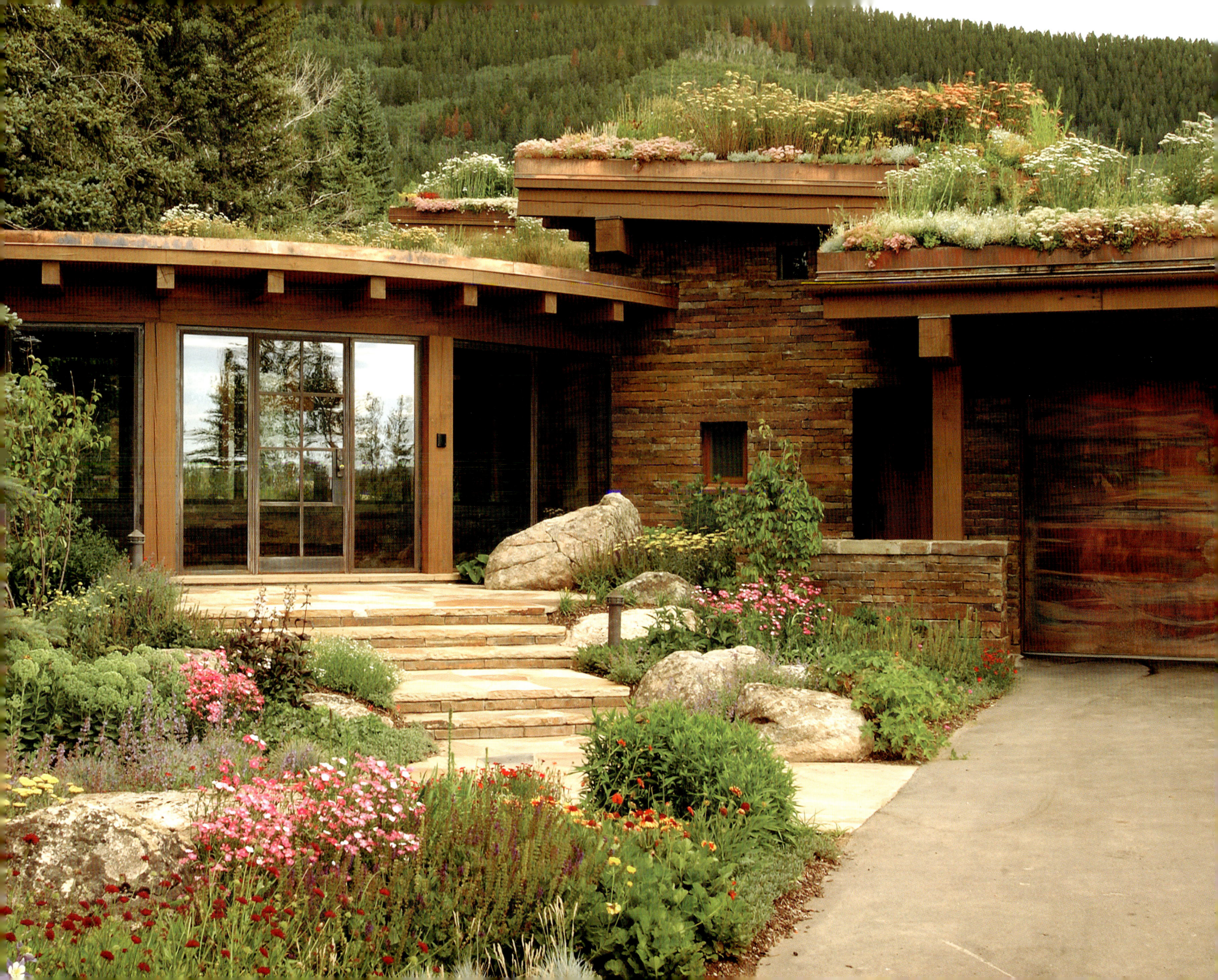

DOUGLAS MILLER DECHANT
SHEPHERD RESOURCES INC/AIA

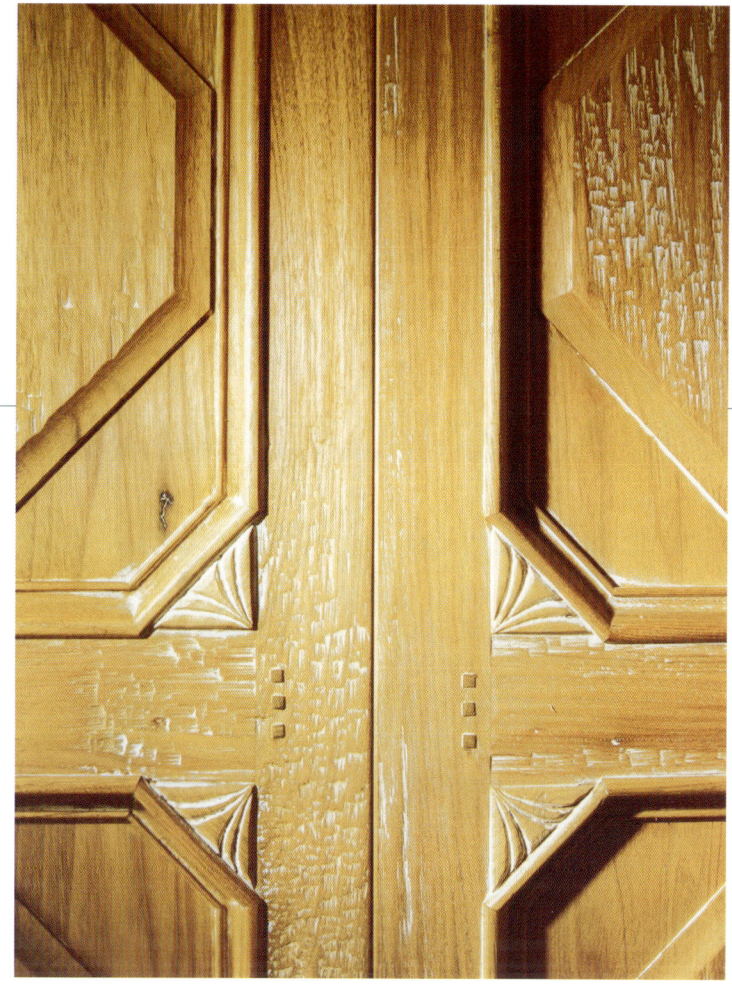

Douglas DeChant is an architect creating "sculptures that are homes" with the passion of an artist. He and his associates take notice of the architectural language emerging from the natural patterns of the land and setting. Together with careful listening to the clients' needs and desires, a vision for the home begins to evolve. This team believes that each commission is an invitation to enter the client's personal life with honor and respect, to create rich, dynamic environments, and to be always aware of the significance of the endeavor.

This 'brainy, spiritual' approach to design has earned praise in publications such as *Luxury Living, Vail Valley Magazine, Architecture & Design of the West*, and in books, *French by Design* and *Rustic Revisited*. DeChant's practice has also received design awards from the American Institute of Architects, the Rocky Mountain Masonry Institute, the Eagle Valley Home Builders Association and others.

This architect is fortunate to have discovered his calling at an early age. DeChant trained at Illinois Institute of Technology's School of Architecture, and among others, has been influenced by school founder and modernist Ludwig Mies van der Rohe of Germany's Bauhaus. He founded Douglas Miller DeChant Architects/Shepherd Resources, Inc/AIA in 1989 with a desire to "place my priority on scale, space, paths, layers and listening to the site, and to fully understand and engage natural light in the setting." He now heads a cohesive 12-person studio focused upon listening and exploring.

The studio DeChant shares with his associates is a dynamic, open environment, the result of this active, gregarious group's desire for collaboration and community. Strength of character and attitude prevail in this inspiring setting along the Eagle River, in the heart of the mountains. They enjoy their design sessions together and support each other in pursuit of the practice's goals. From this central location, they also enjoy their national reach, creating fine homes, resort and golf properties as unique opportunities arise.

ABOVE:
Designing furniture, doors and other personal interior elements completes the vision.
Photograph by Darren Edwards

FACING PAGE:
The architecture becomes integral with the setting in this rich, organic entry to the home.
Photograph by Andrew Wellman

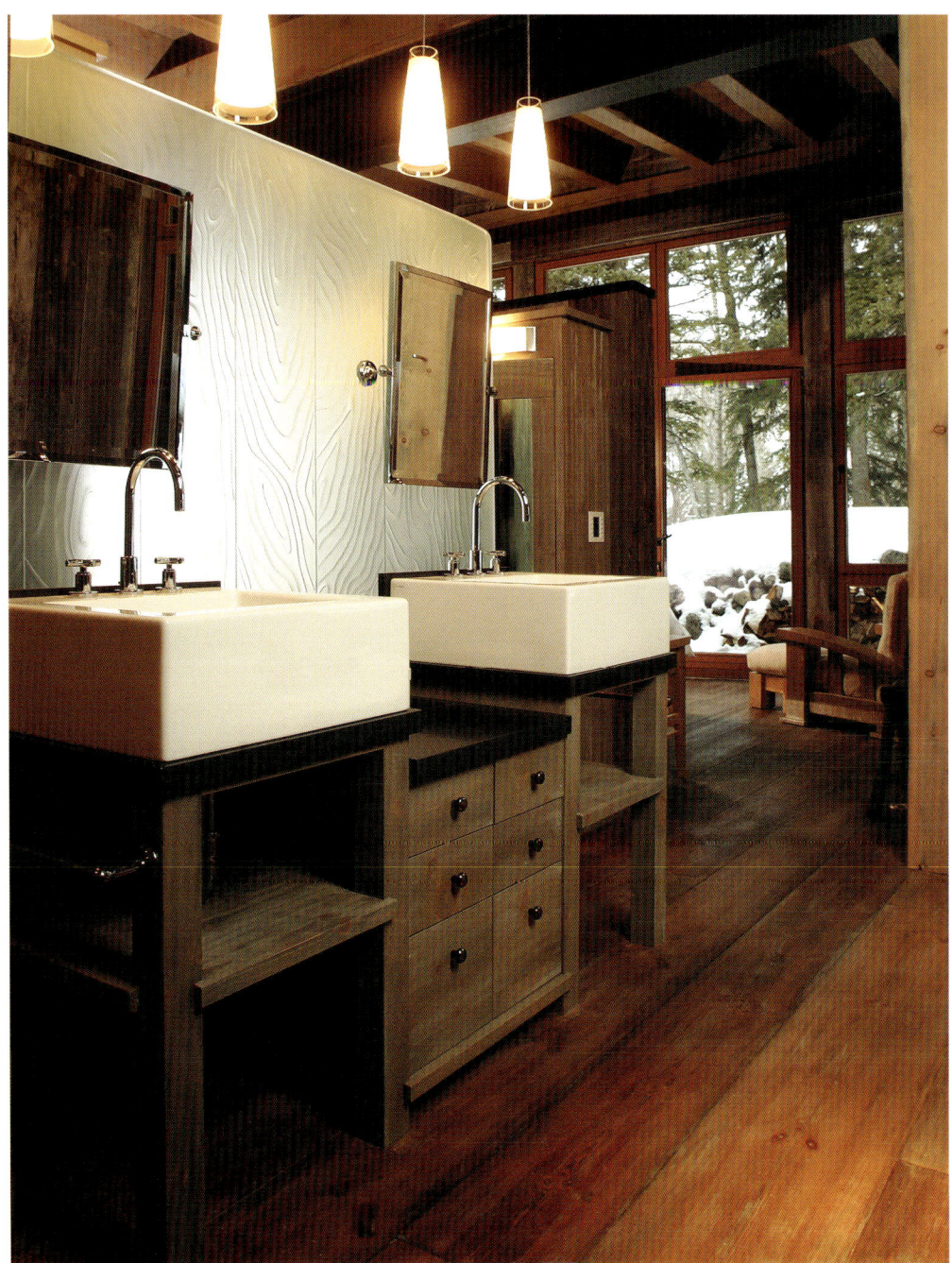
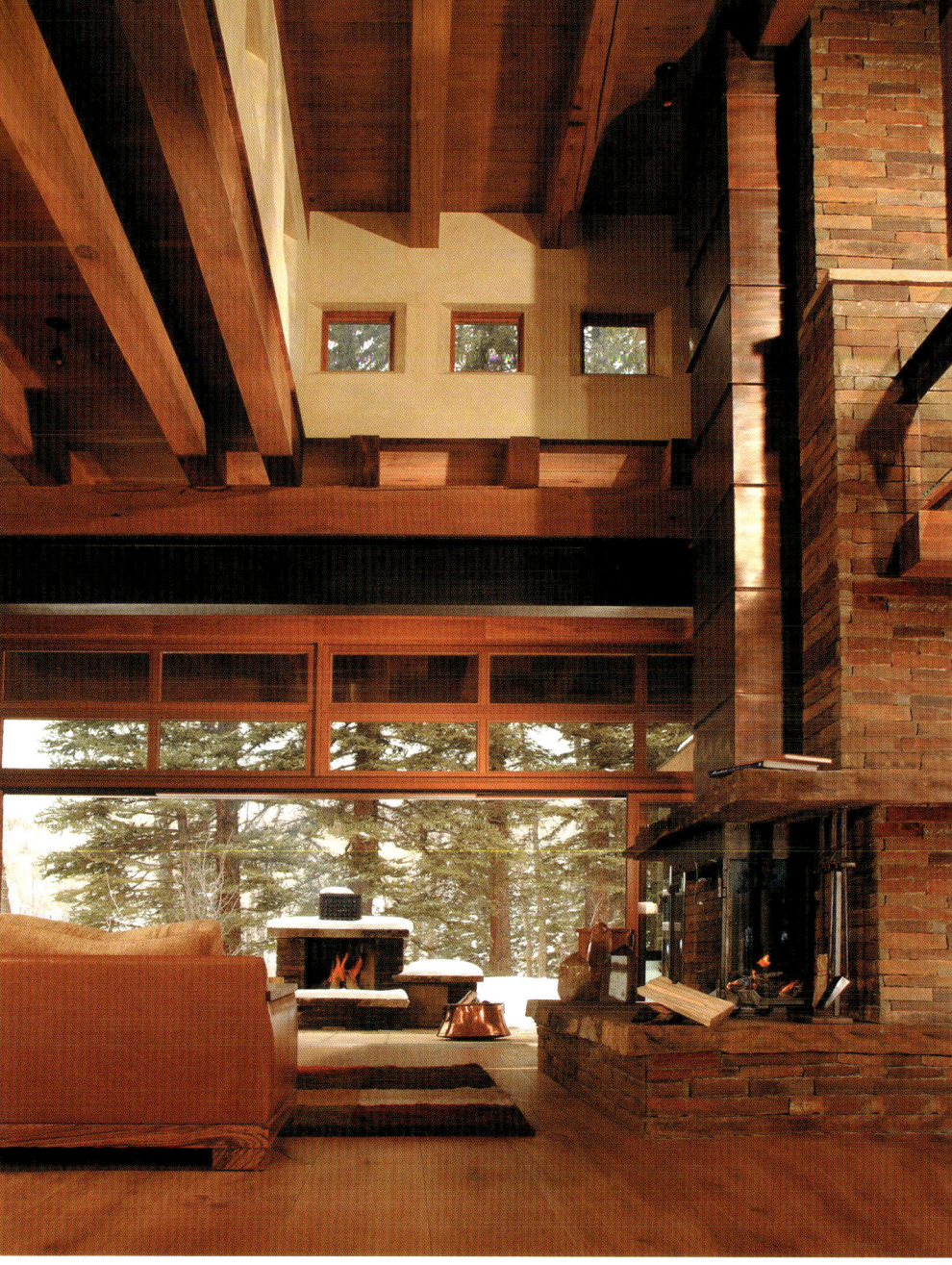

ABOVE LEFT:
A sheet of embossed glass separates this master bath from the closet and dressing area.
Photograph by Andrew Wellman

ABOVE RIGHT:
With the entire wall open to the terrace and exterior fireplace beyond, this living room embraces the forest setting.
Photograph by Andrew Wellman

FACING PAGE:
Intimacy, space, shelter and light prevail in this terrace environment.
Photograph by Andrew Wellman

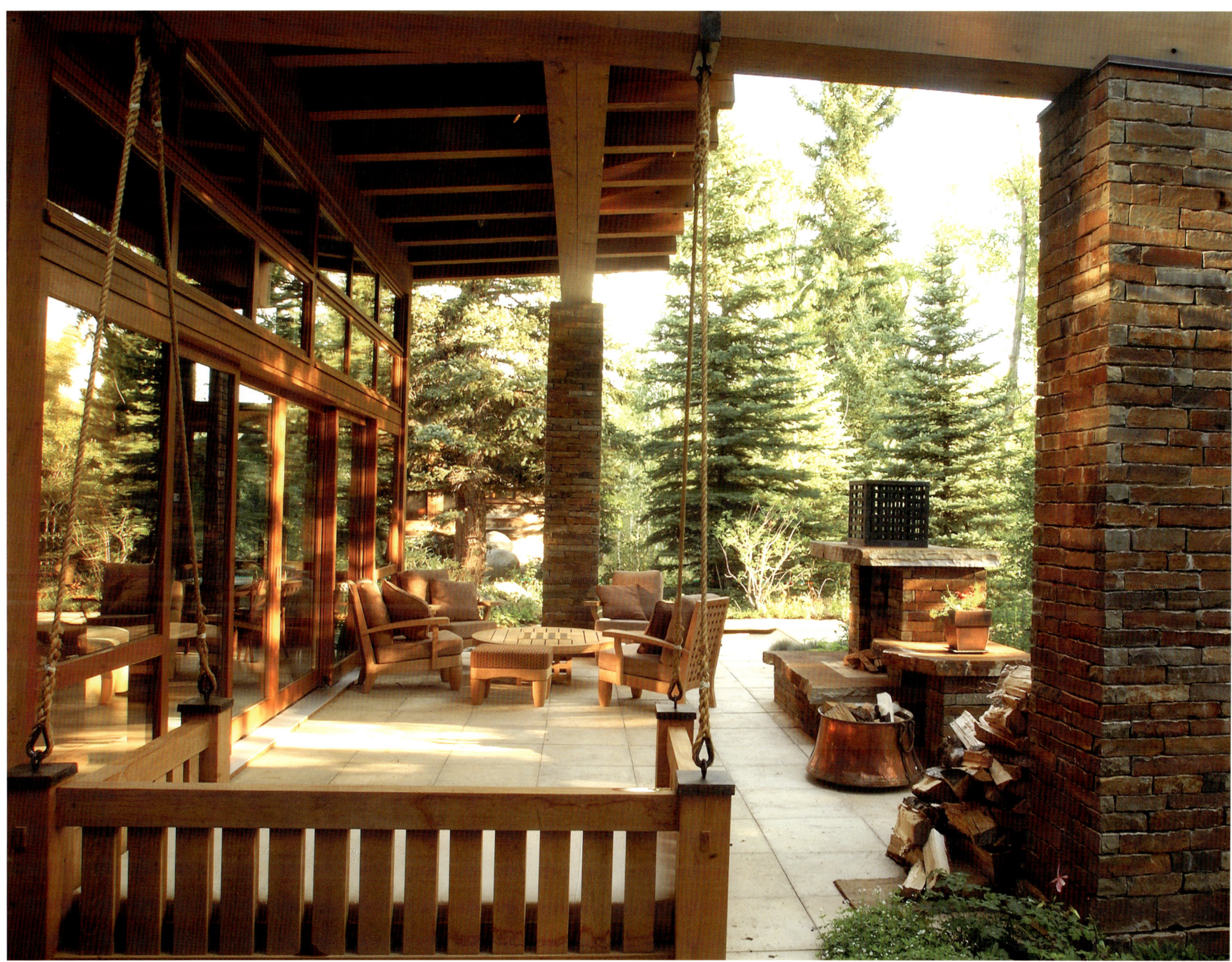

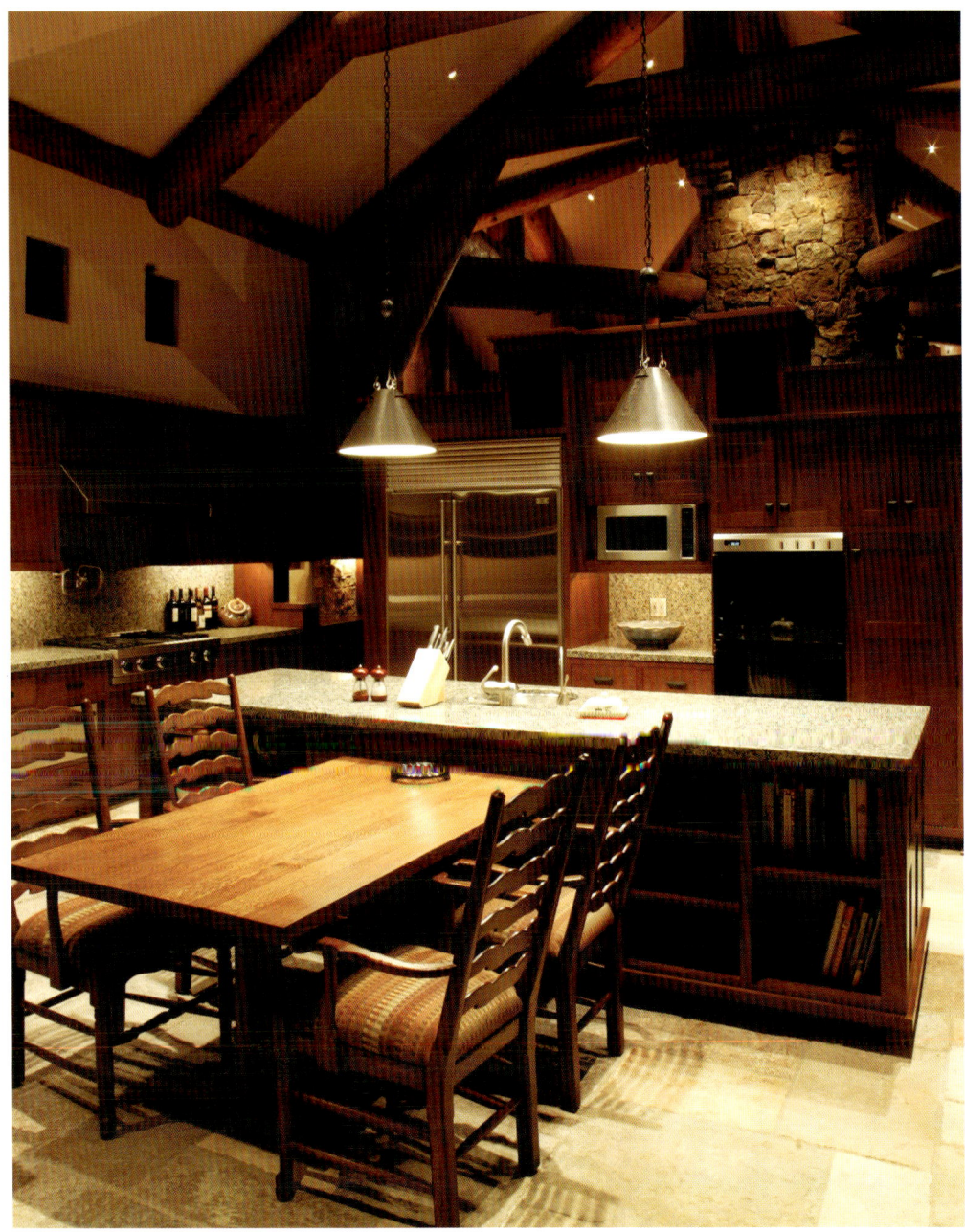
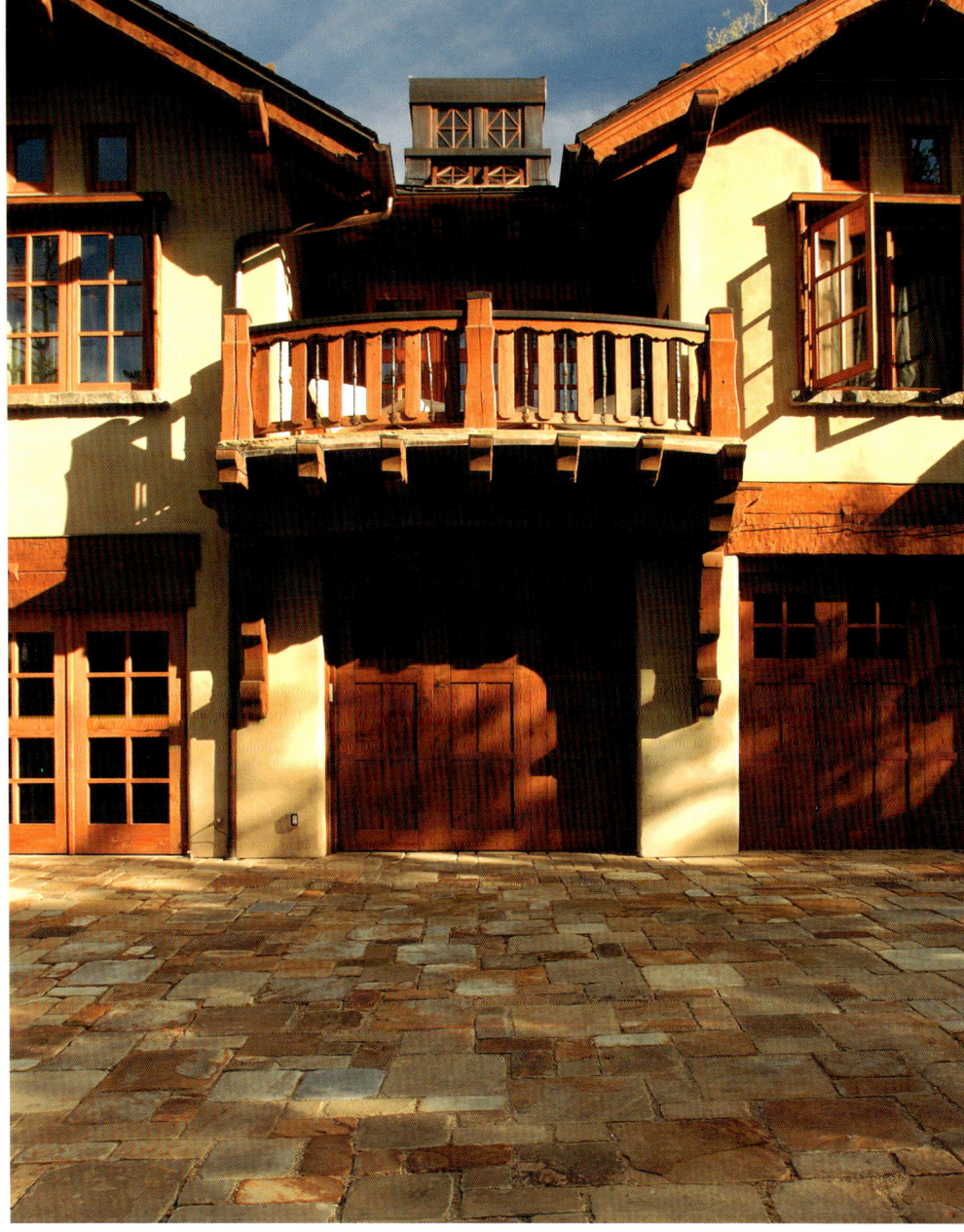

ABOVE LEFT:
The kitchen volume created by the log structure reaches over the cabinets to living spaces beyond.
Photograph by Darren Edwards

ABOVE RIGHT:
Balance, symmetry and rich materials of sandstone, reclaimed Douglas Fir, stucco and copper gather late afternoon light.
Photograph by Andrew Wellman

FACING PAGE:
Massive logs, copper and glass rest securely, yet lightly upon a substantial stone foundation, defining an intimate exterior space.
Photograph by Darren Edwards

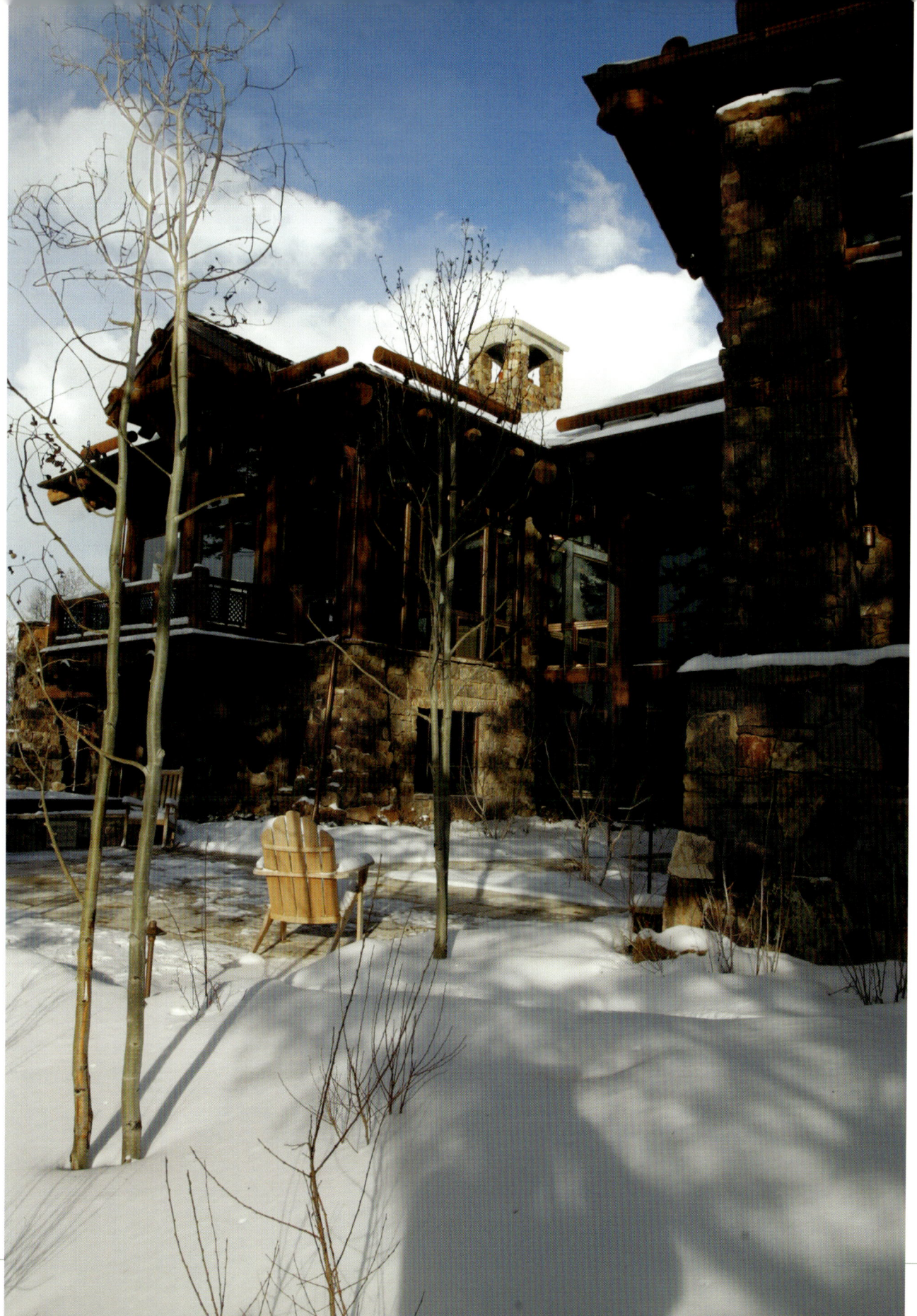

Q&A

more about douglas...

WHAT PERSONAL INDULGENCE DO YOU SPEND THE MOST MONEY ON?
My family; they deserve it.

WHAT IS THE BEST PART OF BEING AN ARCHITECT/BUILDER?
An architect has the privilege of being a visionary and the responsibility of affecting lives.

WHAT IS THE MOST UNIQUE/IMPRESSIVE/BEAUTIFUL HOME YOU'VE BEEN INVOLVED WITH? WHY?
Each home has been unique and beautiful, and each client relationship has been gratifying and fulfilling in unique ways. Each new project is my current favorite.

WHAT DO YOU LIKE MOST ABOUT DOING BUSINESS IN YOUR LOCALE?
While we work nationally, much of our design in the immediate area is in response to our clients' desires for retreat and personal restoration.

SHEPHERD RESOURCES INC./AIA
DOUGLAS MILLER DeCHANT, AIA
PO Box 1624
Avon, CO 81620
970.949.3302
f: 970.949.5121
www.sriarchitect.com

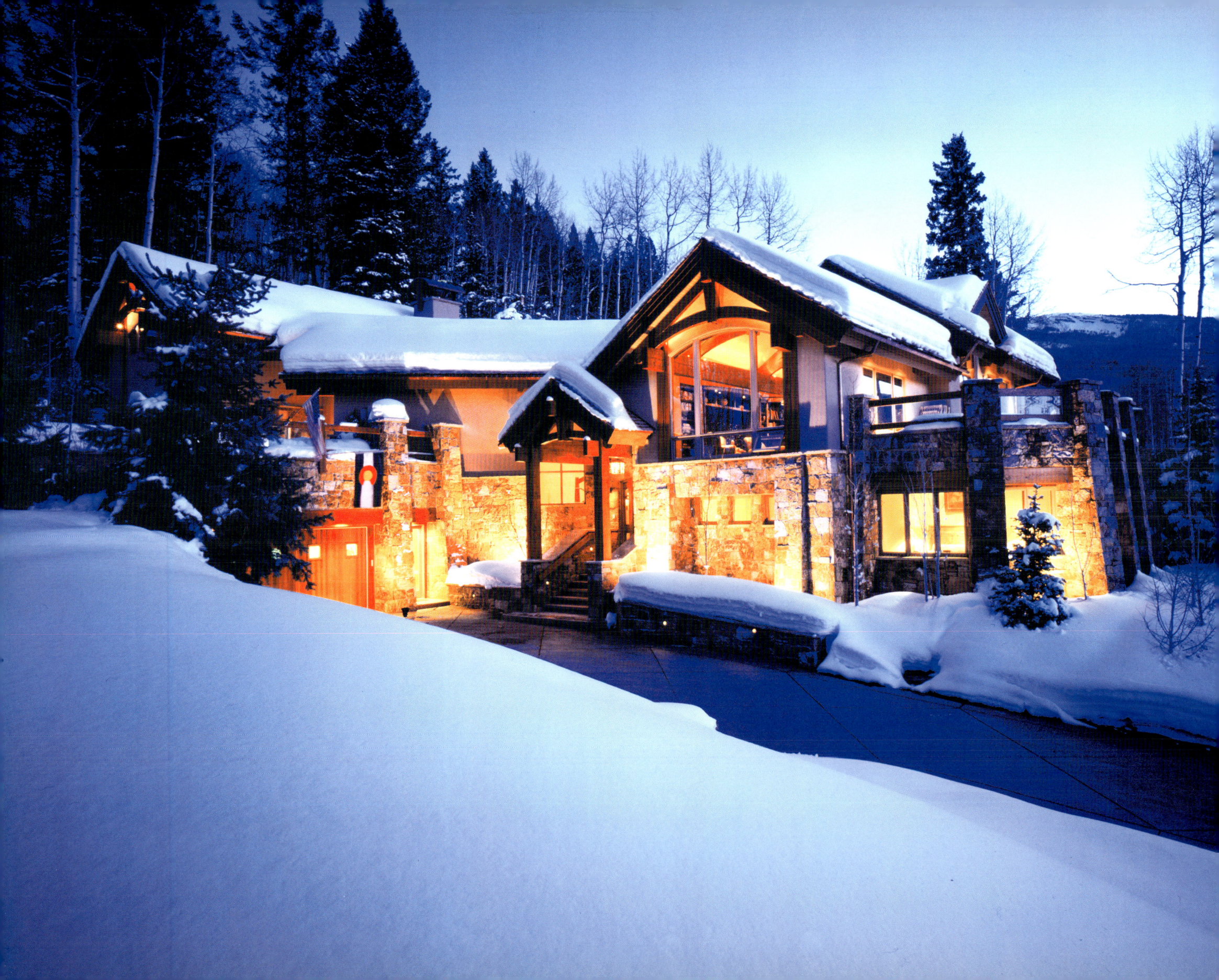

T. MICHAEL MANCHESTER

T. MICHAEL MANCHESTER & ASSOCIATES, INC.

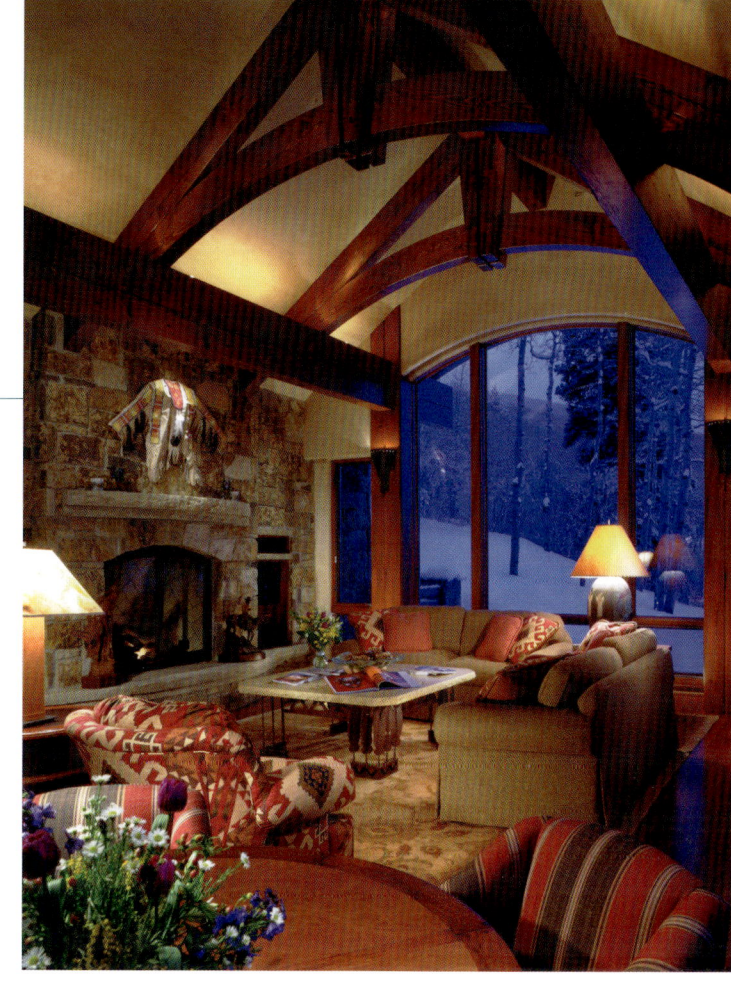

Unlike those who came to Colorado to ski and decided to stay, Michael Manchester knew what he was coming for all along.

Having studied architecture since the age of 12 when he purchased his first drawing board, triangle and T-square, Michael directed his attention to the architectural world and the unique facets of it which surrounded him. While working towards his five-year degree at Arizona State University, he had the unique opportunity to enter a solar energy program in which he spent three years training in architectural solar technology.

In 1984 and on Valentine's Day, no less, he opened T. Michael Manchester & Associates, Inc. His first office was originally located in Aspen and was relocated to Snowmass Village in 1993. The firm's primary focus is custom high-end residential architecture.

Presently, Michael's firm consists of a team of four to five. He prefers a medium-sized firm as it allows him to stay aggressively involved in every project—having a good time with his clients on both a professional and personal level. He enjoys meeting with clients, turning their dreams into reality and solving the problems that translate their ideas into high quality architecture.

Michael works adeptly to avoid developing a particular architectural character as the firm's "style." He believes that architecture's final solution or eventual style is about the owners and the site. Michael combines materials and details with appropriate spatial relationships to create functionality and beauty. He strives to create the intangible "space" that enlivens the human spirit.

The character of Michael's homes may be as varied as Southwestern to Contemporary. He enjoys the diversity and the challenges his commissions present. He has utilized old materials in homes that create character such as using the beams from the original Great Salt Lake Bridge covered in

ABOVE:
Living room in The Pines.
Photograph by David Marlow

FACING PAGE:
Entry view of The Pines home at the base of the Snowmass Ski Area.
Photograph by David Marlow

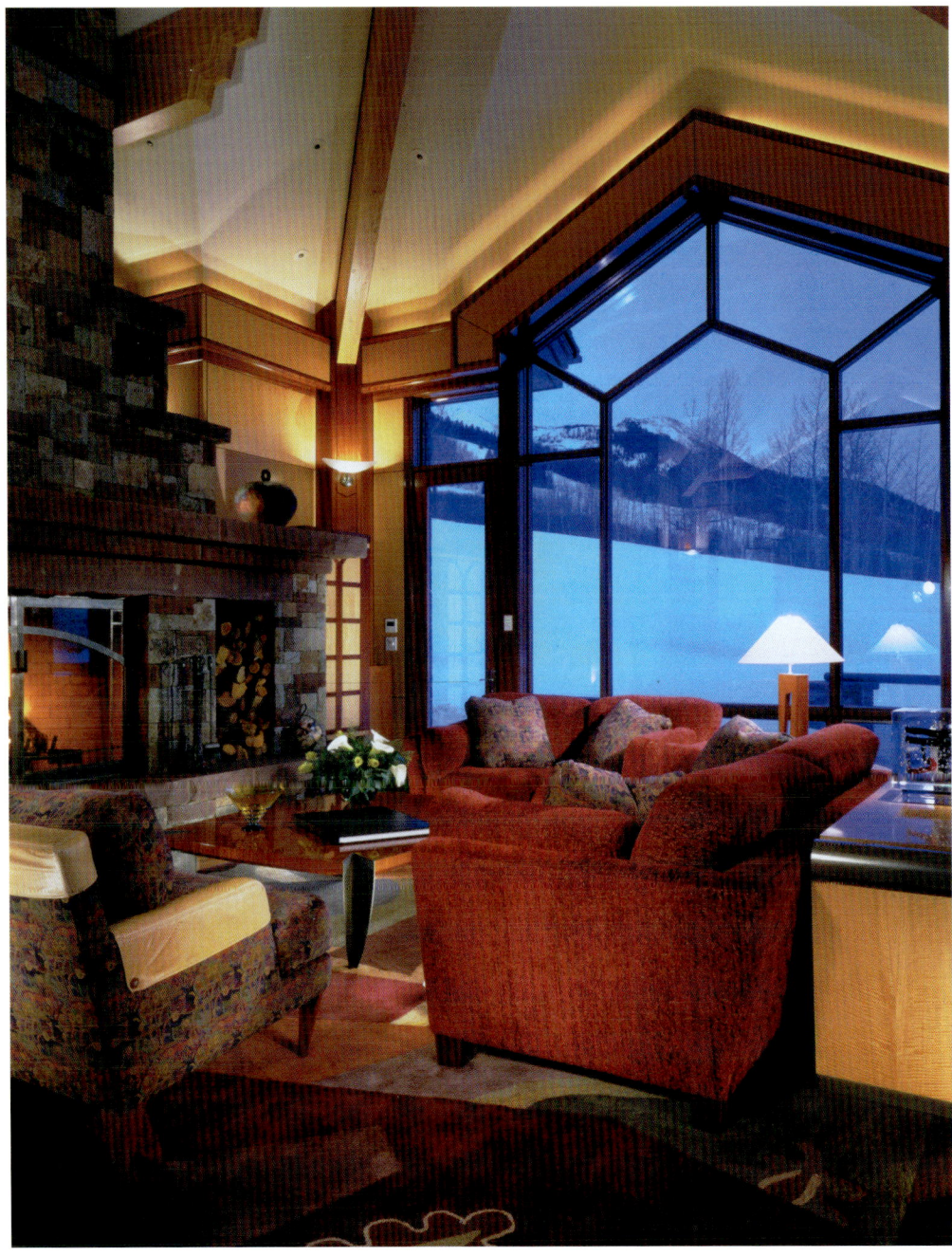
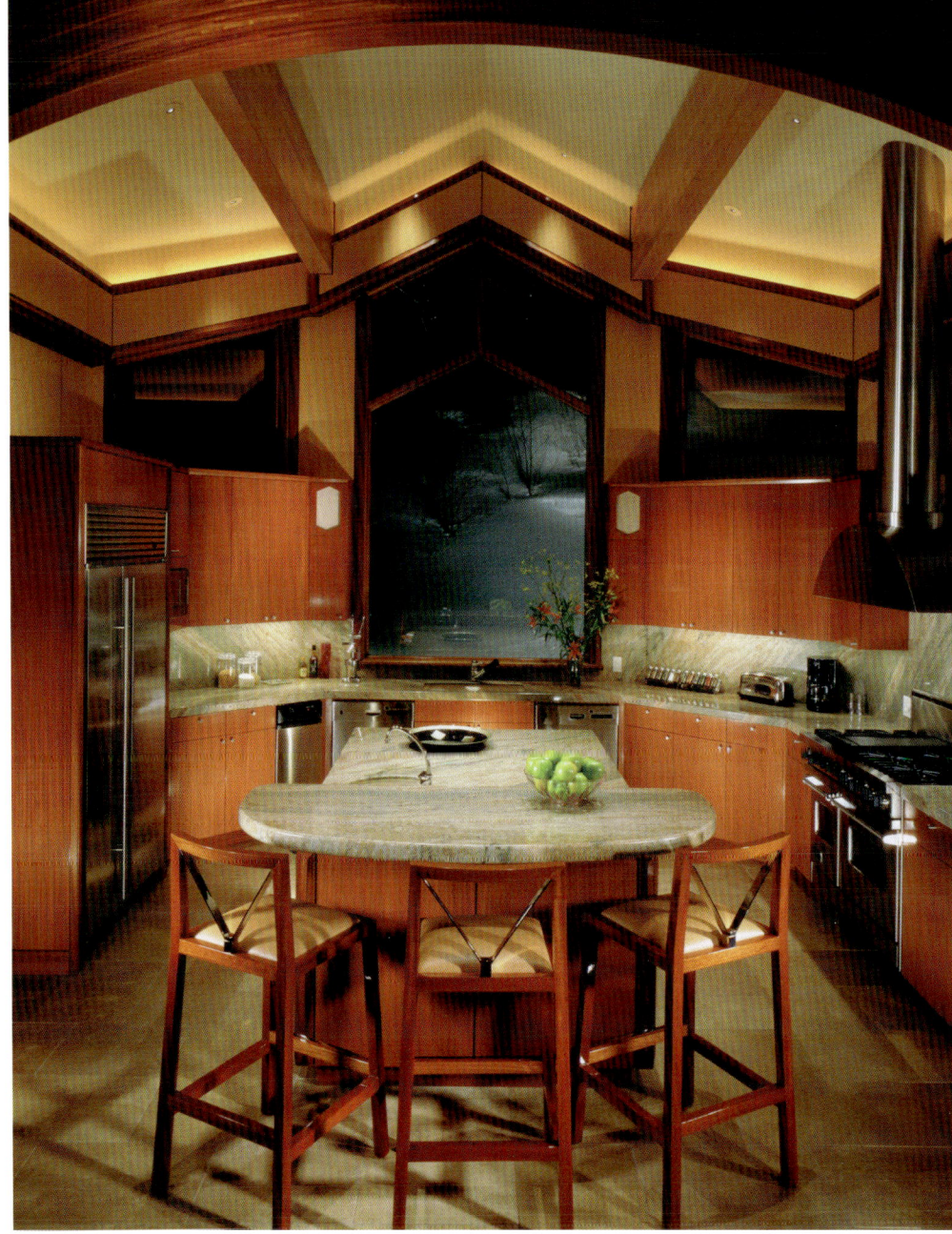

ABOVE LEFT:
The living room at The Divide looking out to the Mountains.
Photograph by David Marlow

ABOVE RIGHT:
The kitchen at The Divide.
Photograph by David Marlow

FACING PAGE:
The entry view of The Divide house.
Photograph by David Marlow

latilla to bring in incredible texture. In more contemporary homes, glass handrails are used where there are trimless window edges, as well as cleaner types of materials.

Michael is especially attracted to the notion of mixing a little contemporary form with the mountain character of Colorado. By using traditional mountain materials like heavy timber and rough stone work mixed with beautiful hardwoods, he achieves a more refined, modern character that fits well in the mountains. The natural environment dictates much of his design. Michael strives to sensitively locate the home to capture the views with overhangs to protect from the climate and appropriate insulation in respect for Mother Nature.

T. Michael Manchester & Associates, Inc. creates architecture mainly within Snowmass Village where many of the homes are for part-time residents. They find and appreciate that these homes are frequently the nucleus of the family; everyone comes to visit in a fun place to go skiing and hiking and to experience the opportunities offered within the mountains. The modern family as a whole can be together here more than anywhere else. In response, the firm spends time to build for capacity but in ways that are still enjoyable for only two. Living rooms, dining rooms and kitchens are made to be enjoyed by two or several family members without any disconnection.

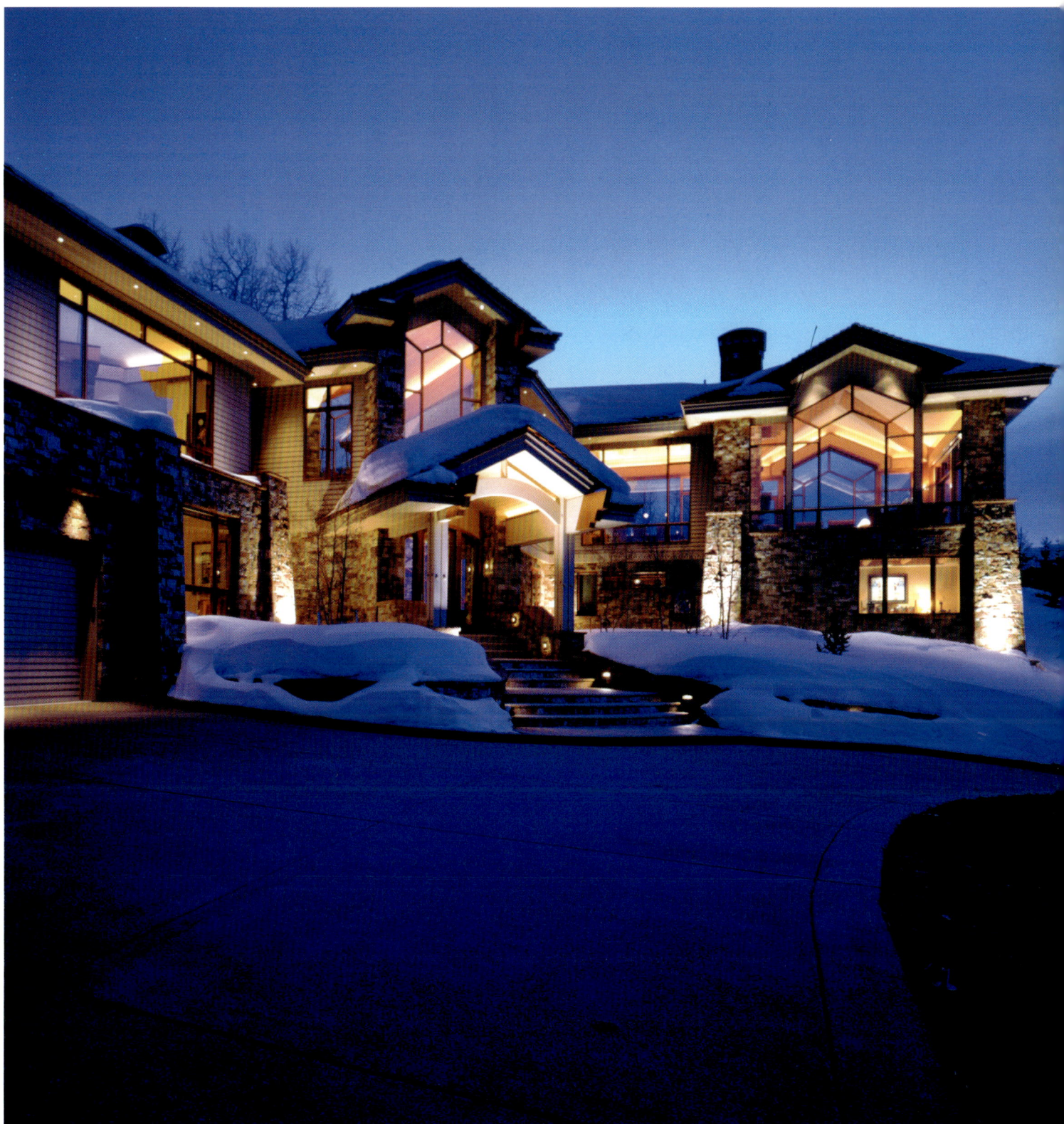

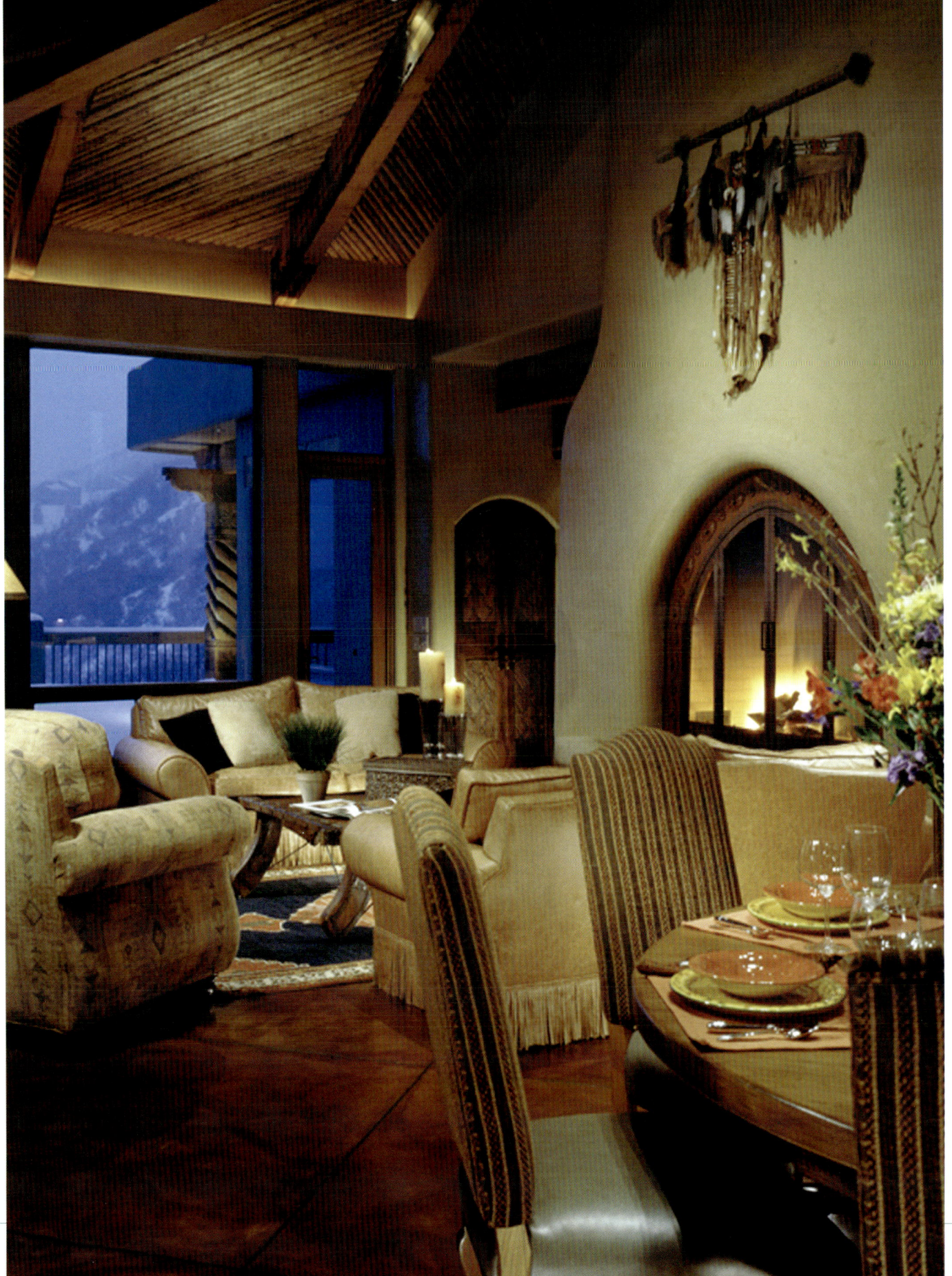

Windows are Michael's strong suit. He believes they are the connection to the beauty and energy of the environment in which they live. "When people spend lots of money on a piece of land, they've invested in a piece of art. The house should capture that piece of art and embrace its splendor. It's all about windows," says the architect. For Michael, integrating the windows into the architecture is one of the most exciting challenges of the entire process.

Most important to Michael Manchester is the belief that architecture should be functional. His grasp of architecture and design is influenced and grounded by the beauty around him. "Seeing the mountains, the sunsets, the wildlife and the trees is how the human spirit connects to the environment. It makes living in the mountains so special and architecture should enhance that connection. That is my goal."

LEFT:
The Keefe living room.
Photograph by David Marlow

FACING PAGE TOP:
The Keefe residence.
Photograph by Bill Boineau

FACING PAGE BOTTOM:
The Keefe kitchen.
Photograph by David Marlow

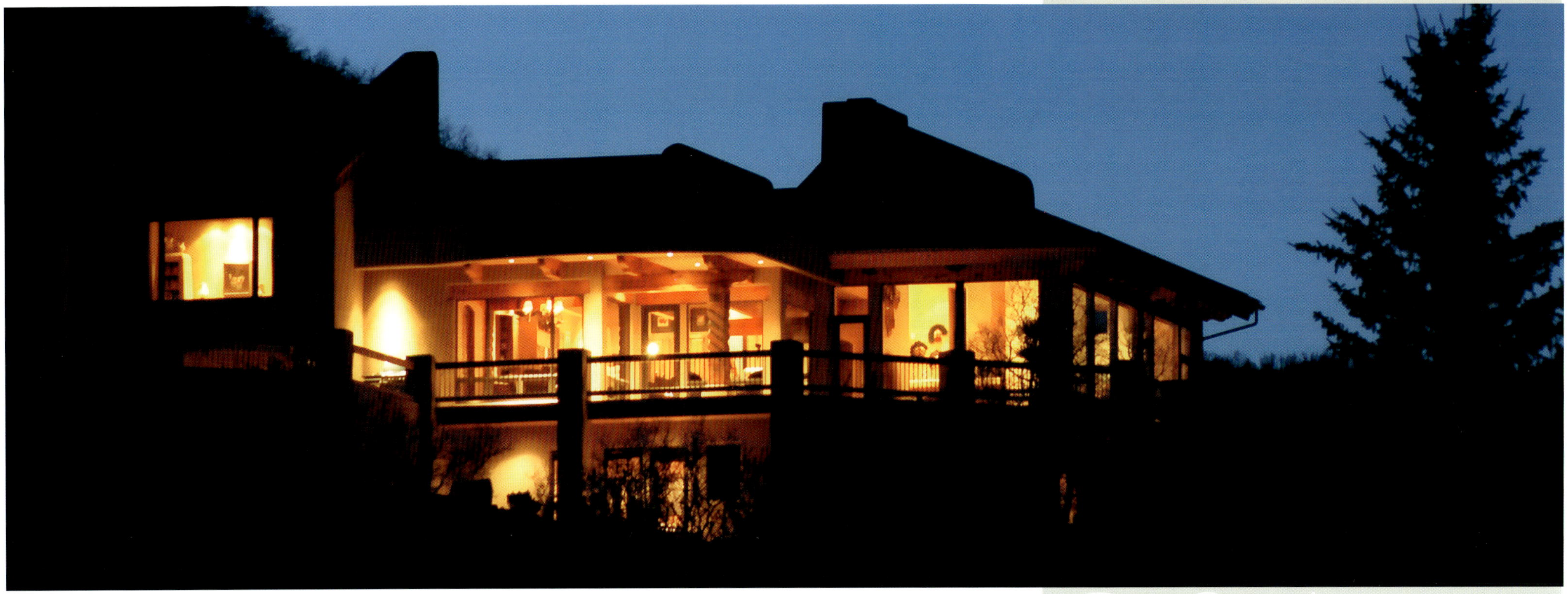

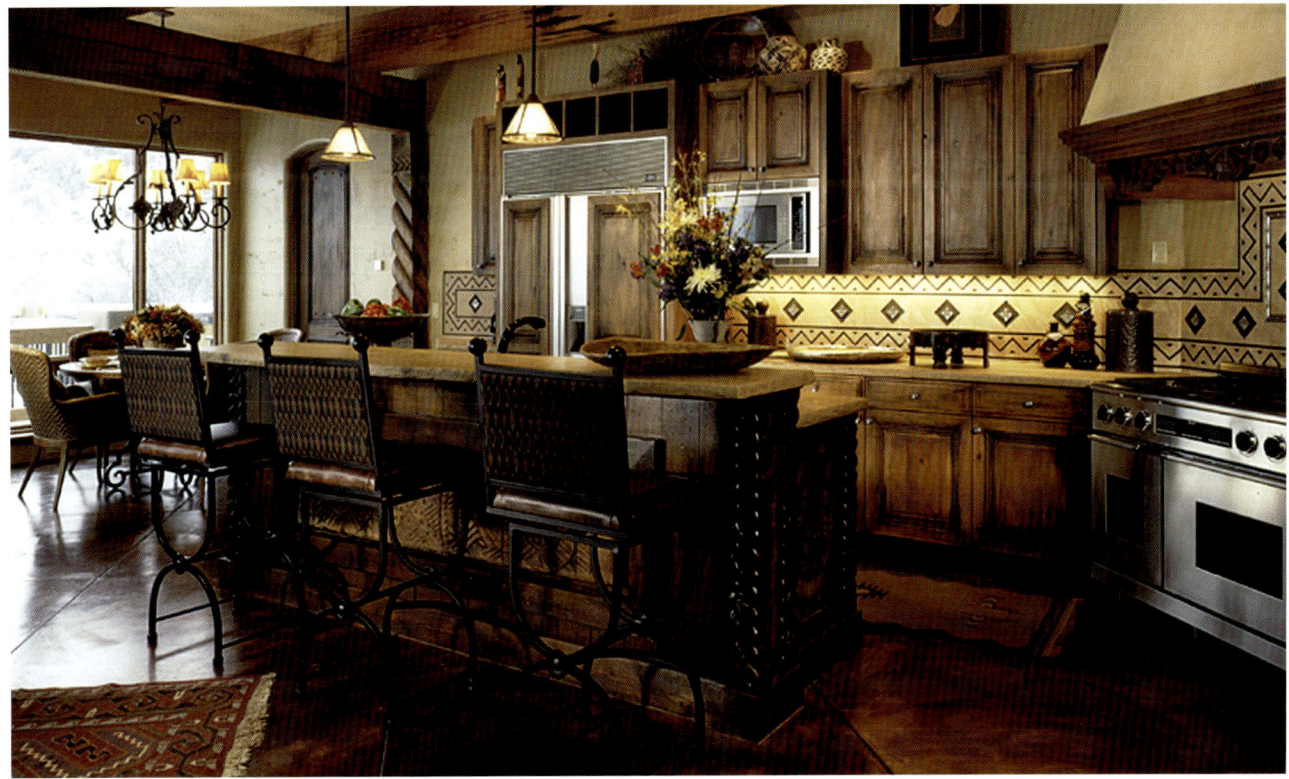

more about michael...

WHAT PERSONAL INDULGENCES DO YOU SPEND THE MOST MONEY ON?
Toys! Mostly bicycles and golf clubs.

WHAT IS THE BEST PART OF BEING AN ARCHITECT?
Mostly it is about the interaction with the clients and helping them achieve their dreams.

WHAT IS THE SINGLE THING YOU WOULD DO TO BRING A DULL HOUSE TO LIFE?
In a physical sense it has to be light, but more importantly it is the people and laughter.

T. MICHAEL MANCHESTER & ASSOCIATES
T. MICHAEL MANCHESTER
PO Box 6573
25 Lower Woodbridge Road
Snowmass Village, CO 81615
970.923.4411
f: 970.923.4414
www.tmmarchitects.com

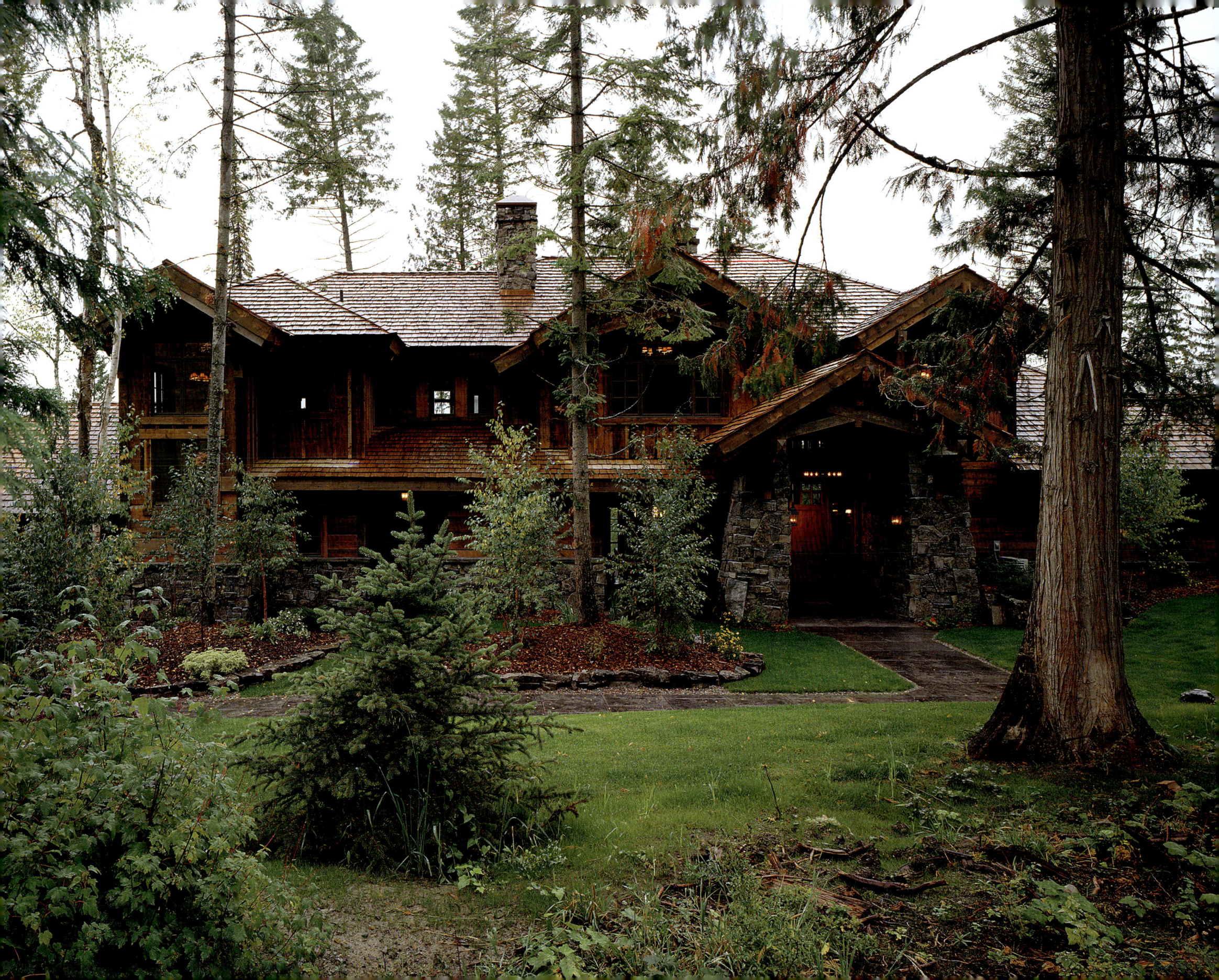

KAREN KEATING
& PAUL DEARDORFF

TKP ARCHITECTS, PC

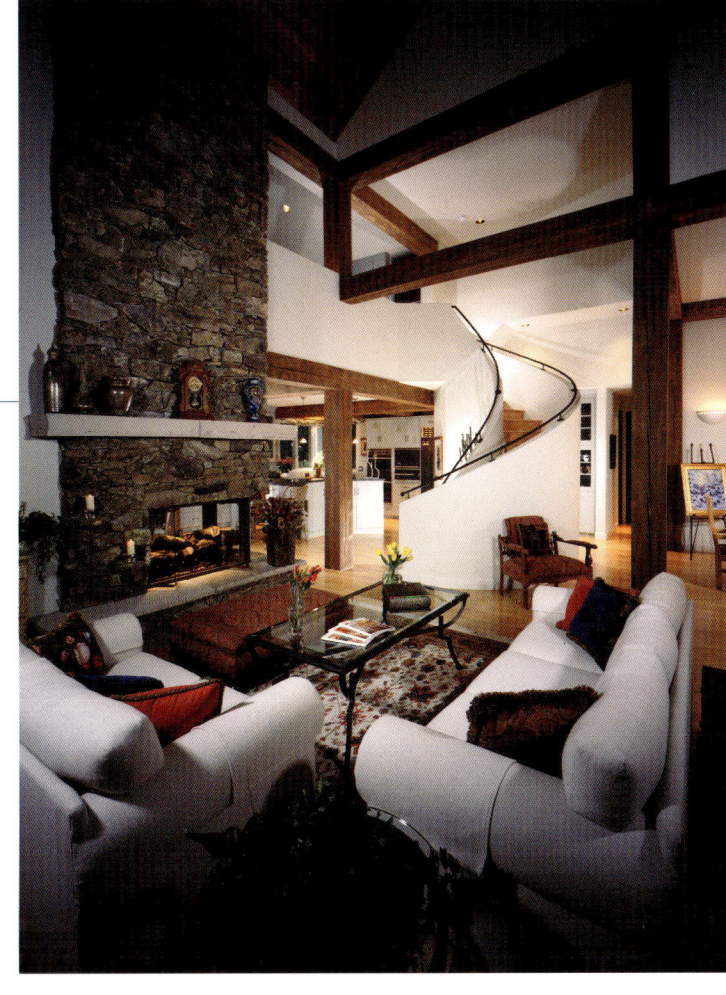

Karen Keating and Paul Deardorff pride themselves on understanding how people live. For more than 20 years, their architectural firm has been designing high-end, award-winning, custom and builder homes for the West's most discriminating clients. TKP possesses an unparalleled ability to listen, and a willingness to approach a project with meticulous detail and study. Their team-oriented style including clients, builders, subcontractors and consultants combined with their talent and experience working with contemporary and historical styles, make them one of the most sought-after firms around.

Karen and Paul have been working together for 17 years and enjoy both their professional and personal relationship; as a married couple, they work together, listen together and design together. When working with clients to design their dream homes, they bring sensibility and sensitivity to the table to meet the needs of individuals, couples and families, as each of them have been, at one time or another, all of these. They approach their projects with a client focused non-egotistical style centered on creativity, good communication and cooperation.

Each home designed by TKP is a reflection of their clients' personality and passions. The sensitive and talented architects, designers, and project managers at TKP Architects excel at interpreting client needs, concerns and tastes, distilling them into a home that will positively affect the lives of those who live there. The opportunity to create wonderful living memories for their clients' families and children provides the impetus to create the quality homes that they are known for. They listen to their clients with an open mind, always giving their best advice while respecting their clients' choices and individual interests.

ABOVE:
Contemporary forms and open flowing spaces are counter pointed with rustic stone and timber for a comfortable, eclectic feel in this Colorado Mountain home.
Photograph by Ken Paul

FACING PAGE:
Reclaimed siding and timber from a historic gold mine, rustic stone and shingles allow this Montana home to nestle seamlessly into the woods overlooking Whitefish Lake.
Photograph by Roger Wade

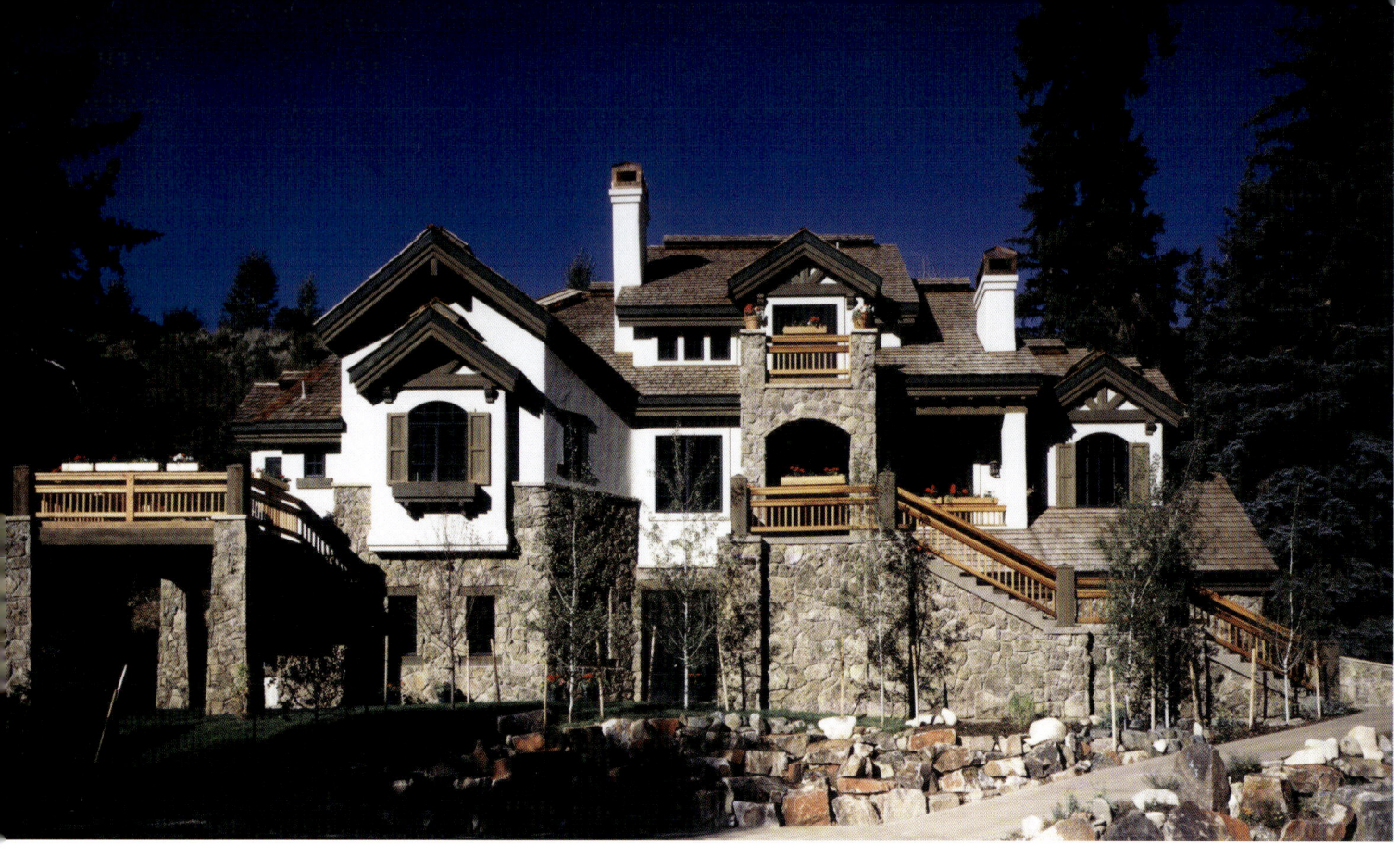

Both Karen and Paul are highly respected in their profession. Karen has acted as a speaker in seminars for architectural associations and is the author and presenter of an acclaimed seminar on communication skills for home-building professionals. She is also co-author of a highly successful full-day seminar on reading and understanding architectural construction drawings. Paul's unique spatial and aesthetic design abilities have been showcased in TKP's most technically complex and beautiful homes. He is responsible for managing TKP's architectural staff, maintaining design quality and furthering their reputation for livable, compelling home designs.

Though each TKP home is unique, all evoke a sense of place, style and comfort that makes them highly livable and timeless. Each home is the result of a "lifestyle approach" to design and reflects individual client tastes and interests. With nearly 40 years of architectural design experience between them, Karen and Paul's approach to design stresses constant communication between architect, builder, and homeowner, from project concept to completion. Both are motivated by a sincere desire to translate the homeowner's lifestyle and dreams into a dream home that showcases the unique personality of each client.

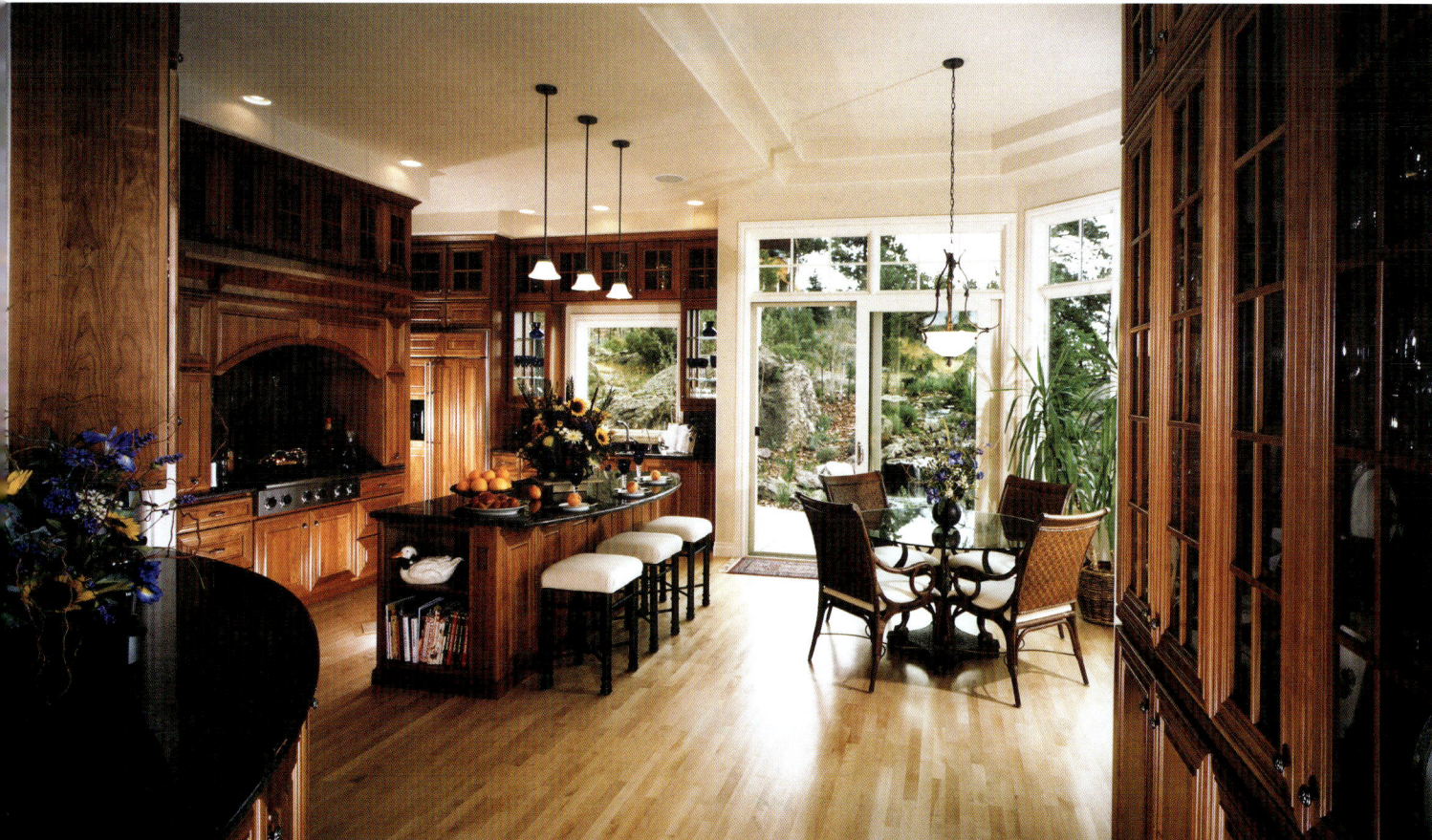

TOP LEFT:
Only 4,200-square-feet of space on all three levels, this Beaver Creek home makes the best use of its challenging site to capture views of the ski slopes, and show off the street presence of a much larger home.
Photograph by J. Curtis

BOTTOM LEFT:
This kitchen and nook open onto a patio next to a waterfall. Creative use of glass in the beautiful cherry cabinets allow for windows through the cabinets next to the sink.
Photograph by Ken Paul

FACING PAGE TOP:
The serene and inviting entry court on this Colorado mountain home tantalizes visitors with just a glimpse of the spectacular Arapaho Range views waiting inside.
Photograph by Ken Paul

FACING PAGE BOTTOM:
Rhythm, texture, light and spatial composition soothe the soul and calm the spirit in this carefully composed interior.
Photograph by Ken Paul

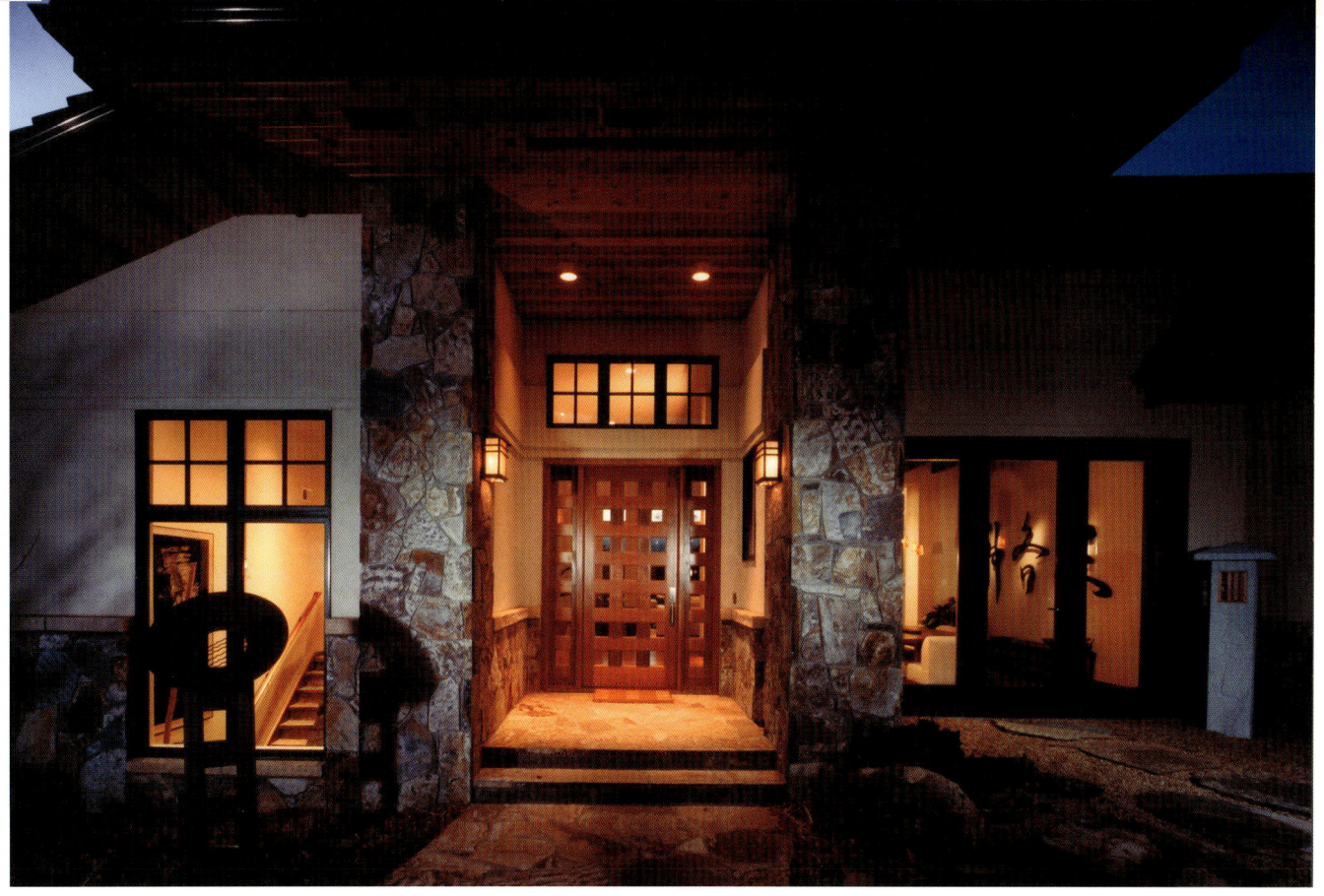

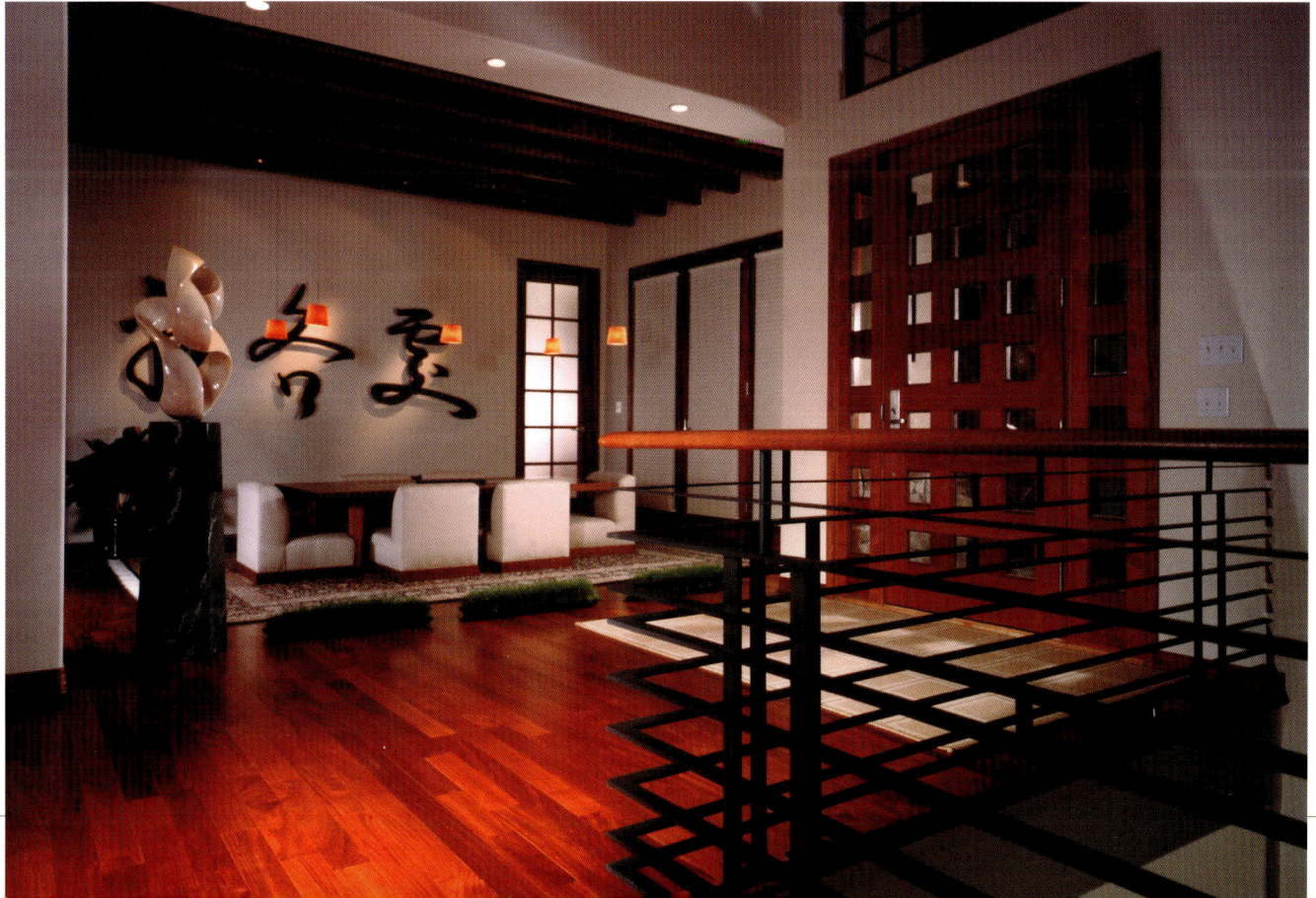

Q&A
more about karen & paul...

WHAT PERSONAL INDULGENCE DO YOU SPEND THE MOST MONEY ON?
Things that enrich our lives with beauty like travel, good food and orchids.

WHAT'S THE BEST COMPLIMENT YOU HAVE EVER RECEIVED?
A client once told us, "You took the time to listen and designed something that is not only beautiful, it is exactly what we wanted! Our new home is going to be a family gathering place, and the time and attention you put into the design will help it serve as a magnet."

WHO HAS HAD THE BIGGEST INFLUENCE ON YOUR CAREERS?
Frank Lloyd Wright, Professors Hank Kowaleski and Wendy McClure, our families, clients, and dreams... but most of all, we have been inspired by one another.

WHAT DO YOU LIKE MOST ABOUT DOING BUSINESS IN COLORADO?
The opportunity to design with nature and the satisfaction of working with some of the most beautiful and challenging land in the country. The people in our town of Golden are warm and friendly and the mountains and mesa are beautiful. It still feels like a small town here.

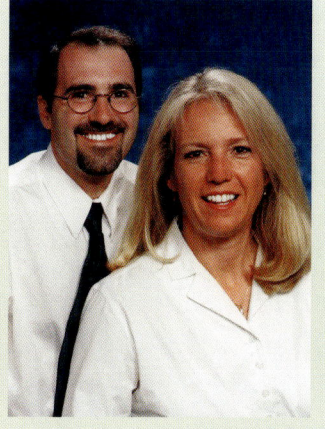

TKP ARCHITECTS, PC
PAUL DEARDORFF
KAREN KEATING, AIA
1509 Washington Avenue
Golden, CO 80401
303.278.8840
f: 303.279.4354
www.keating-partnership.com

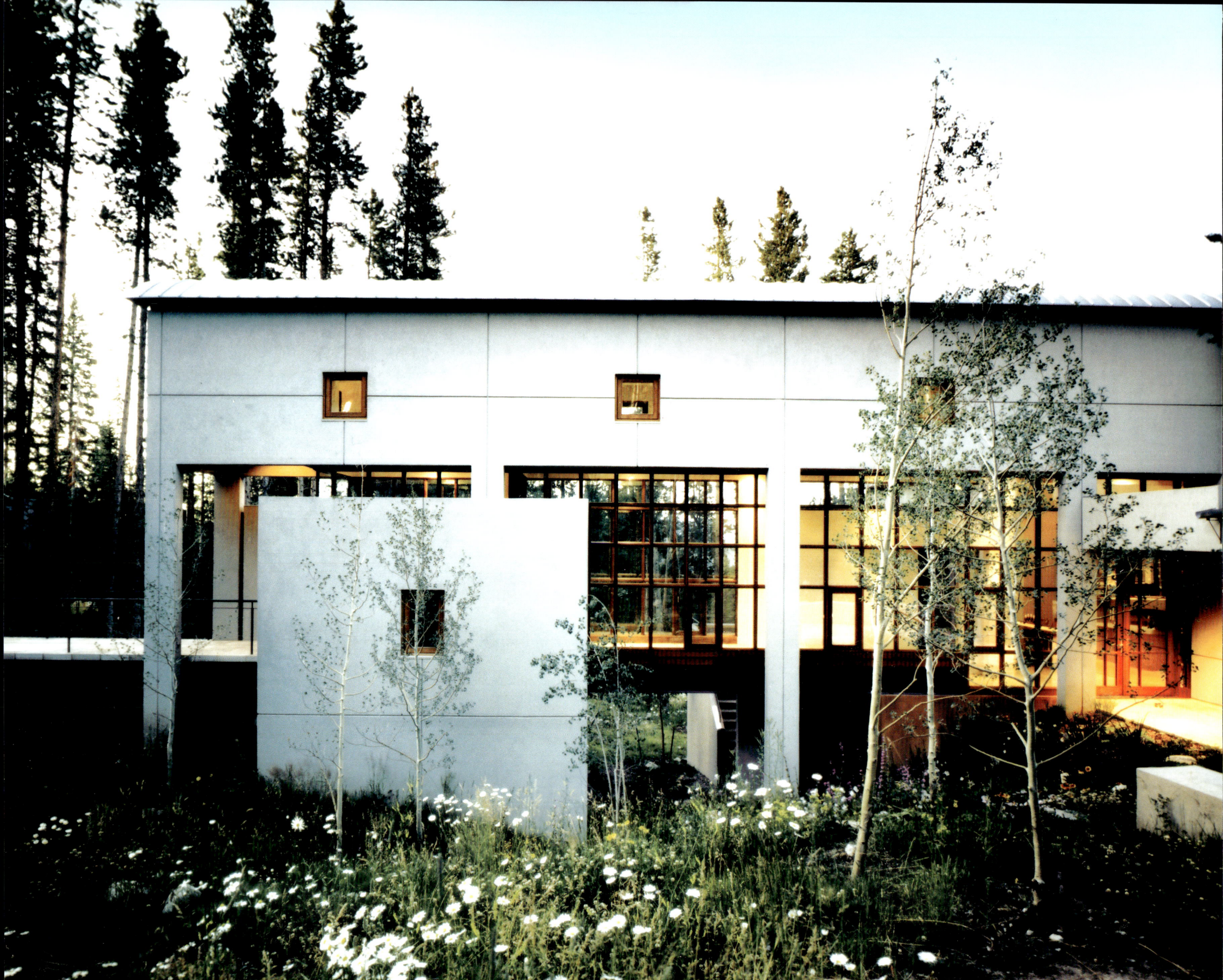

MICHAEL ERNEMANN

THE ERNEMANN GROUP ARCHITECTS

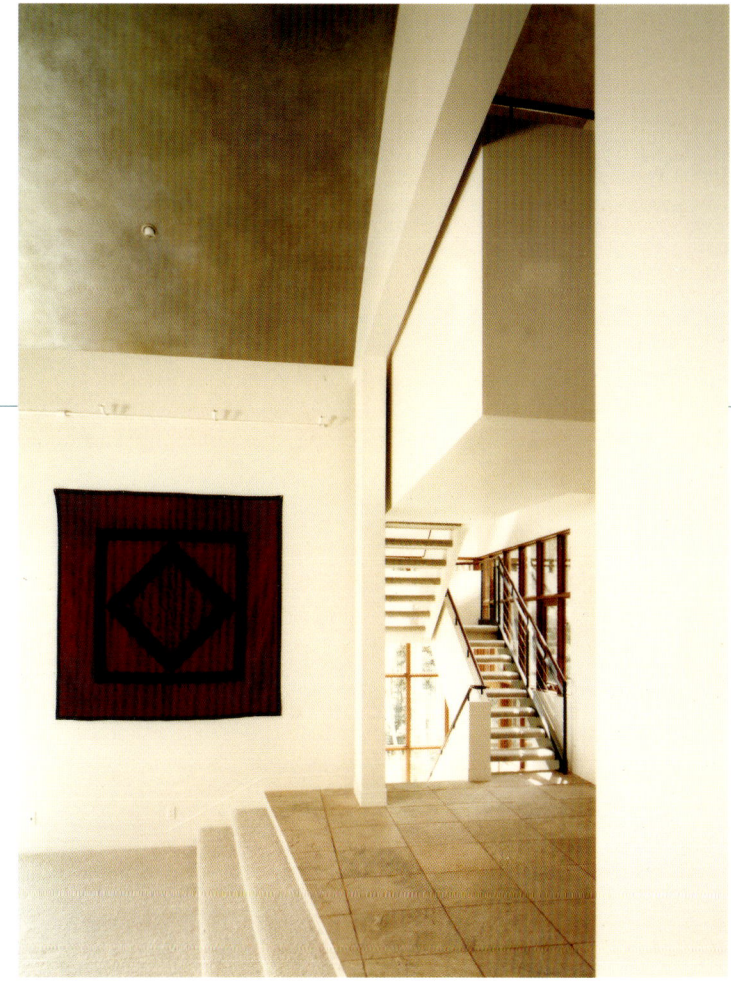

There are qualities about Colorado, tangible and intangible, that draw a person to it. The same can be said of architecture. These qualities continued to beckon Michael Ernemann back to the mountains of Colorado and have continued to inspire his architecture during a career that has spanned more than three decades in Aspen.

After having earned his architecture degree from the University of Michigan, Ernemann joined The Architects Collaborative, a large international firm in Cambridge, Massachusetts, renowned for its modernist design in the Bauhaus tradition. It was a wonderful, career-shaping experience in which he learned the collaborative design process firsthand.

Following his three year internship in Cambridge, Ernemann relocated to Aspen. Just a short year later he moved back to Massachusetts. However, it only took two weeks to realize "West really was best." The main force behind this change of heart was that an opportunity to be far more expressive in designing houses lay in the mountains. Design back East seemed to be constrained by the influences of traditional building form and rectilinear lots, whereas Aspen held much greater freedom. He relished the opportunity to respond in an harmonious way to beautiful settings and it became clear once removed from it that he must return.

In 1973, he opened his own firm for the first time, before briefly leaving Colorado again in 1975 for graduate studies at Stanford. Upon receiving his Masters Degree in Environmental-Economic Planning in 1977, he was once again compelled to return to Colorado where he felt at home and comfortable.

ABOVE:
Like a symphony, occupants experience several movements as they transition through this masterfully planned retreat.
Photograph by Robert Reck

FACING PAGE:
Woven within its environment, grids of mahogany framed windows on either side of the home engage viewers to reconnect with the magic of the great outdoors. Designed to be a beautiful object within a natural setting, the home was designed in a modernist sense yet exudes great warmth and timelessness.
Photograph by Robert Reck

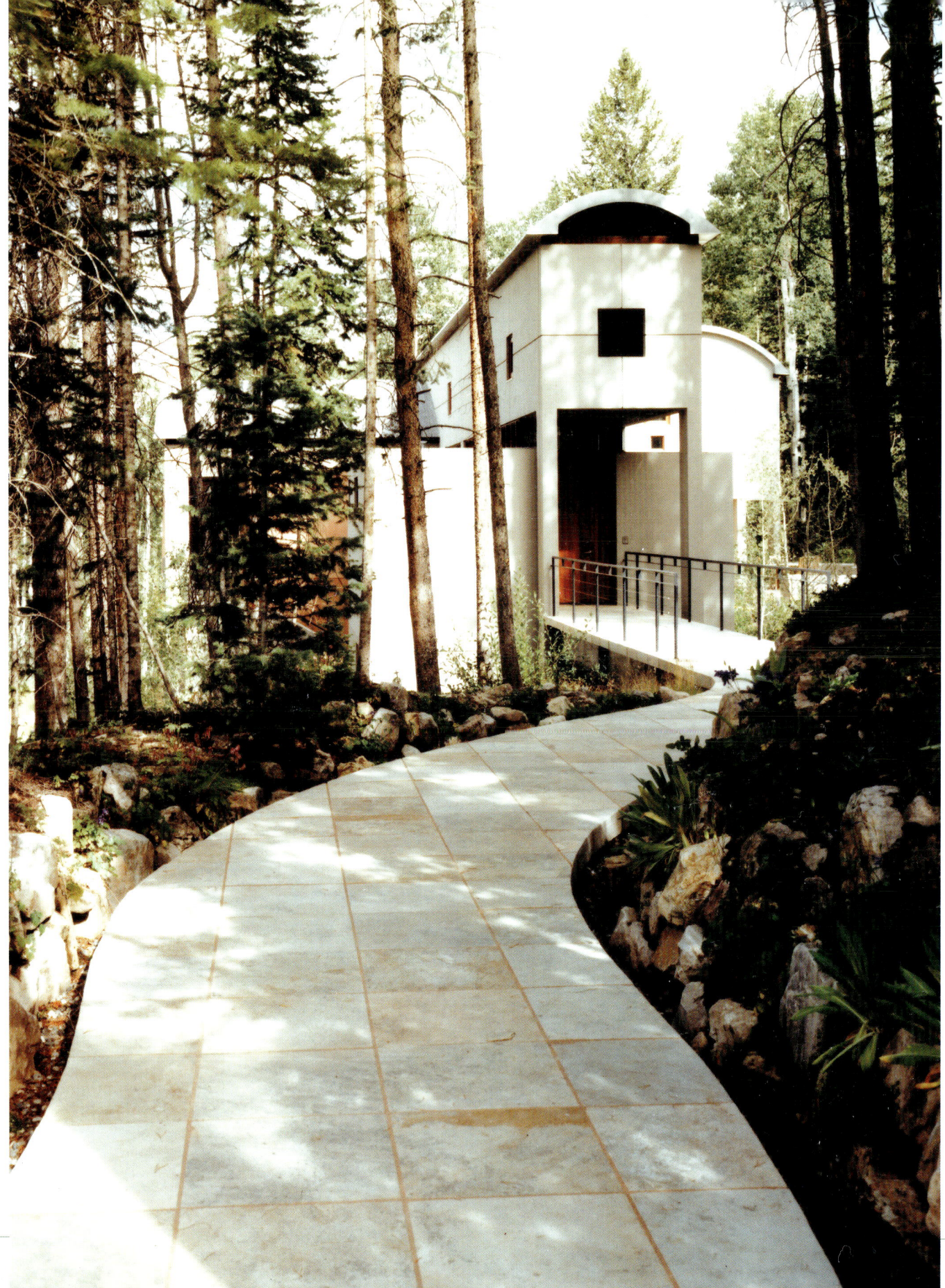

Today The Ernemann Group Architects, founded in 1978, is comprised of a team of four architects and a small support staff. Their design process is collaborative. The input of everyone in the office is encouraged and embraced, because, as Ernemann says, "many sources of ideas can add enormously to producing meaningful design." Ideas inspire new ideas which are built upon over and over until design schemes are developed which achieve the ultimate goals that are set in place for each project. Such goals include the concepts of beauty, harmony, livability, intimacy, sanctuary, humor, transparency, sensitivity, simplicity, joy and magic. At the end of the process, however, each design solution, although unique, is responsive to its particular owner and the setting in which it is to be placed. It is a process that, as Ernemann says, "invariably leads to design solutions that well exceed expectations and, at the same time, enables us to enjoy that which we do immensely."

"Architecture lasts a long time, and therefore, its roots should be thoughtfully derived from precedent and well-planted with introspection and ample adventure." Michael Ernemann believes that in architecture one must respect the past while continually striving to shape the future, and The Ernemann Group does that, both architecturally and imaginatively.

The firm has worked on a broad range of commercial, residential and resort projects in a variety of environments throughout the United States and Canada.

LEFT:
Beginning at the detached garage, a walkway paved with native Colorado buff sandstone initiates the directional spine of the structure and draws visitors into a dialogue with the land. Continuity in flooring and plentitude of windows ensure a seamless transition of outdoor and indoor living space.
Photograph by Robert Reck

FACING PAGE TOP:
Situated at an elevation of 9,100 feet near Aspen, Colorado, this 4,400-square-foot vacation home with 600-square-foot garage boasts panoramic views from nearly every room in the house.
Photograph by Robert Reck

FACING PAGE BOTTOM:
The main living area features a vaulted ceiling—painted to mimic rusted metal—which has an amazing effect at night. To promote conversation, the dining room table is strategically placed in an intimate corner of the wide open space.
Photograph by Robert Reck

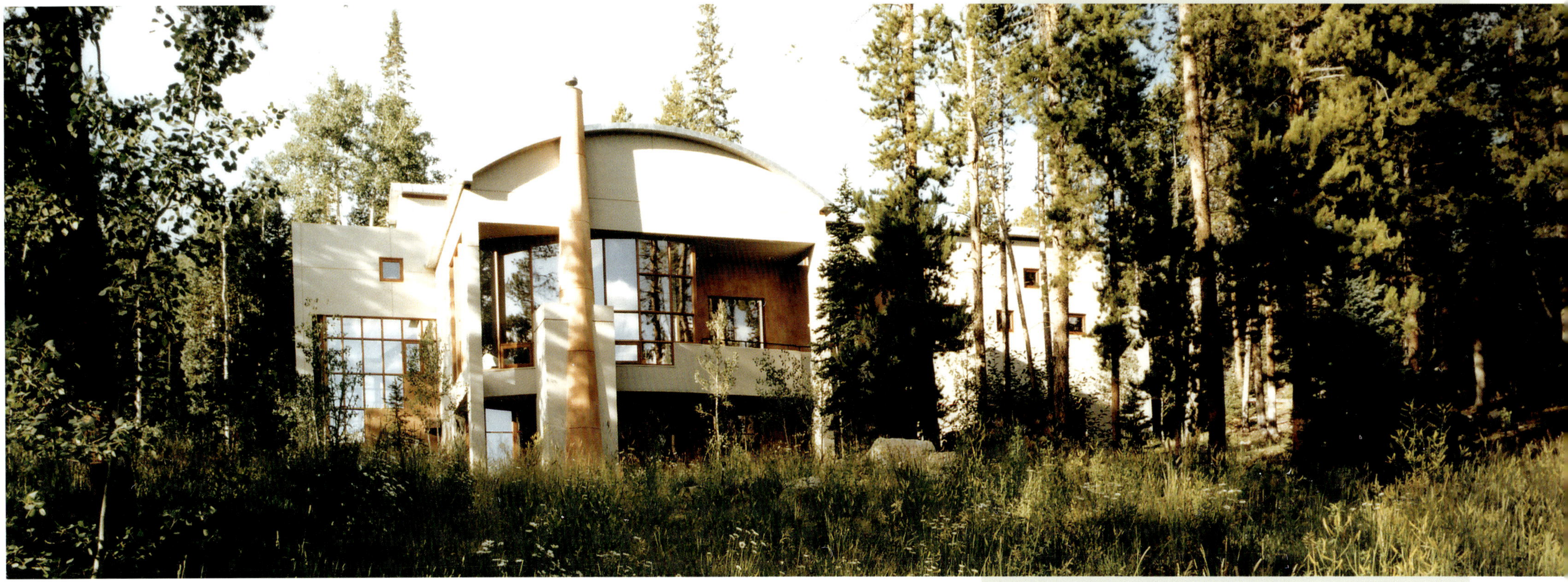

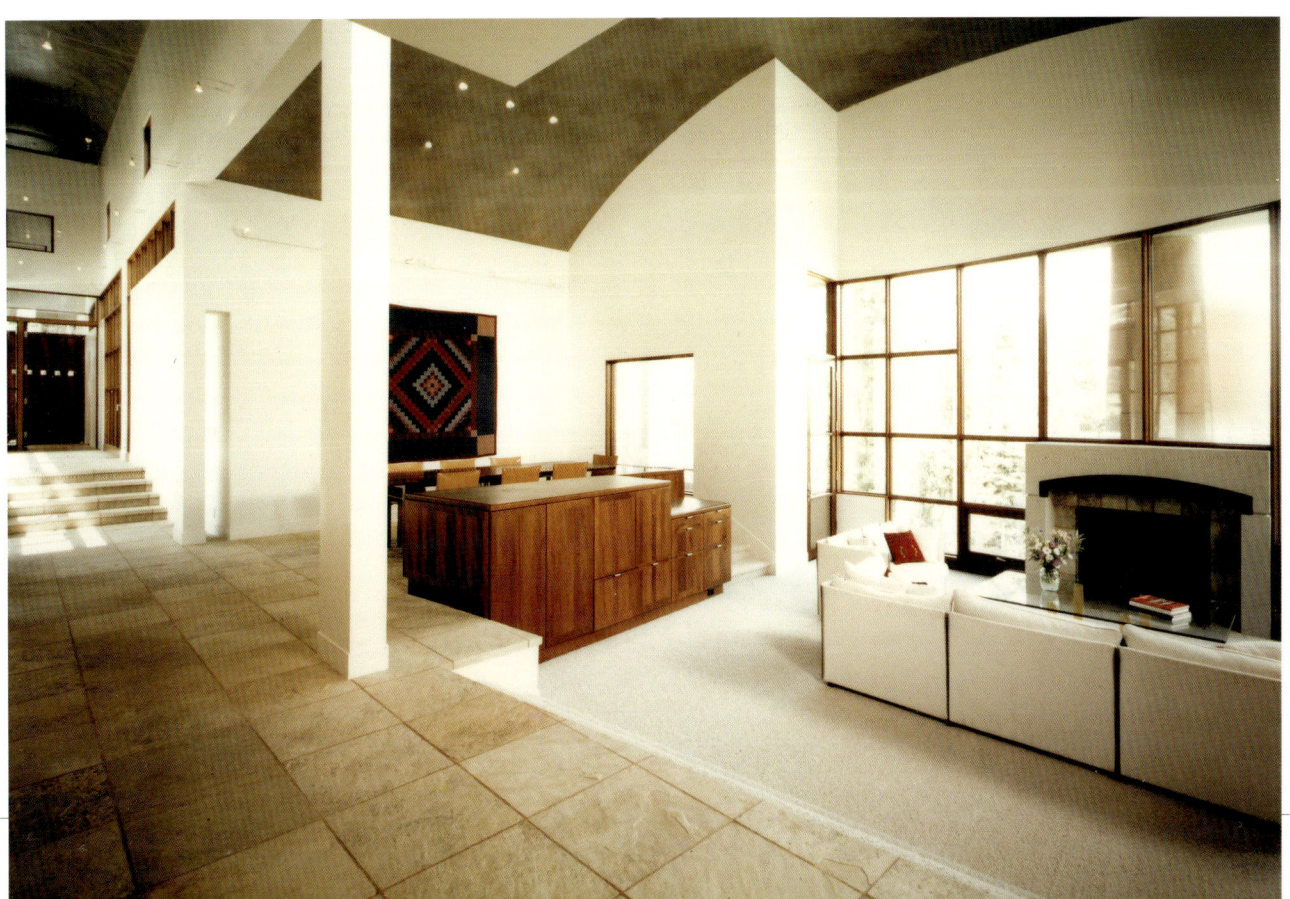

THE ERNEMANN GROUP ARCHITECTS
MICHAEL ERNEMANN
720 East Durant Avenue
Aspen, CO 81611
970.925.2266
www.tegarchitects.com

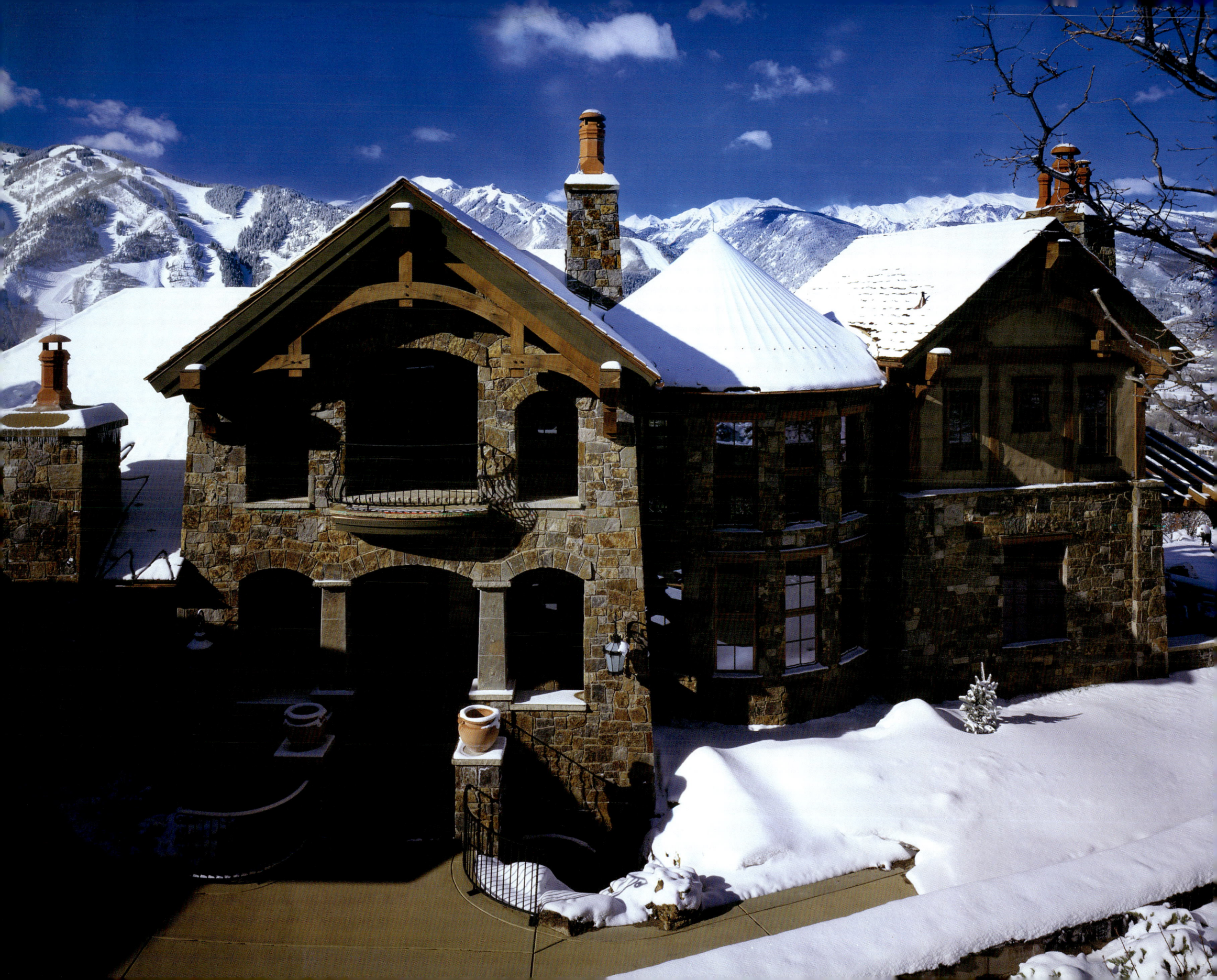

RICHARD WODEHOUSE & MICHAEL AUGELLO

WODEHOUSE AUGELLO BUILDERS

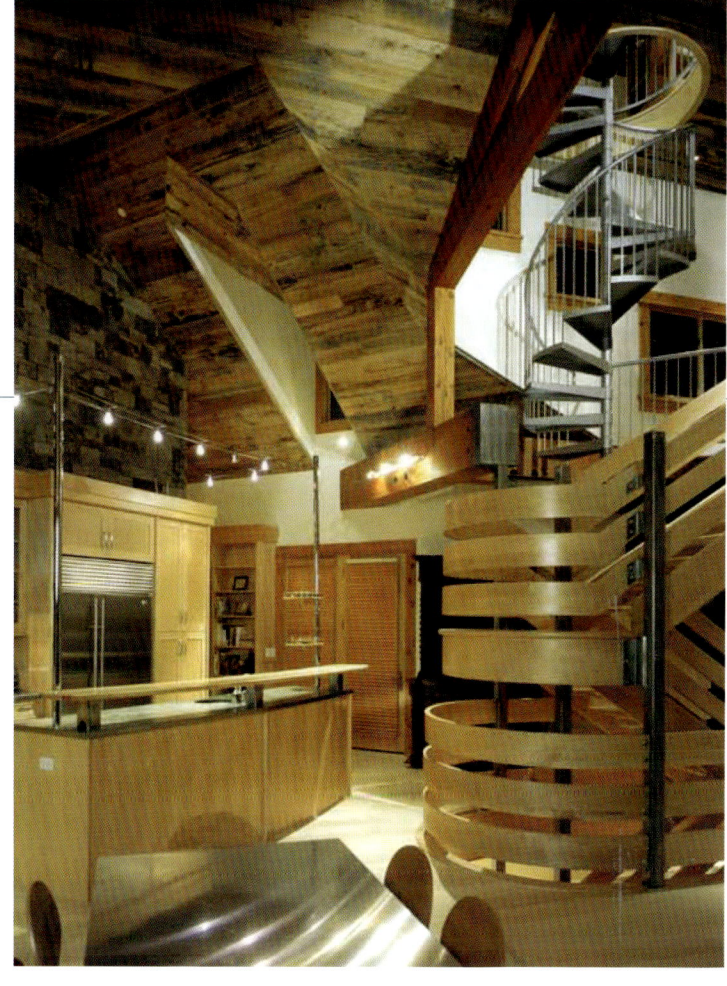

Richard Wodehouse says many of the homes his firm builds can be described as single family resorts, so dynamic and comfortable that clients don't need to take a vacation. As a leading Green builder in the high Rockies, Wodehouse-Augello has a mission to create luxurious homes that respect their surroundings and the environment as a whole. Founded originally in 1975 in San Diego, California, and then in 1990 in Telluride, Wodehouse Builders expanded in 1998 with the addition of longtime New York builder Mike Augello, creating a partnership.

A look at the stunning Rockies of Telluride and Aspen, Colorado makes it easy to see why building Green is so relevant there. For WA, Green equates with quality, a part of the consciousness of taking responsibility and acknowledging that the result of their actions is contributing to the well being of the planet. Among its awards, the company received a 2000 Builder of the Year award from the Colorado Association of Homebuilders, and is often recognized as a leader in building homes that are stunning on the outside, and have a Green heart.

Richard has two decades of experience in Green building, and advocates its practice in the pages of major home magazines. Mike, who began his career as a residential carpenter in the Hudson Valley, was involved with active solar and timber frame construction in the 1970s, and has worked on hundreds of historic renovation/preservation projects. Both he and Richard have been invited to speak about Green building at national conferences and other venues.

The Rockies have proven to be an exceptional fit for Green building, WA believes, often prompting its clients to be concerned with costs. This is why WA promotes an integrated design approach in which all the parties participate from the start to include Green building techniques and products.

ABOVE:
Telluride.
Photograph by Ron Semrod

FACING PAGE:
Red Mountain, Aspen.
Photograph by Jim Laybourn

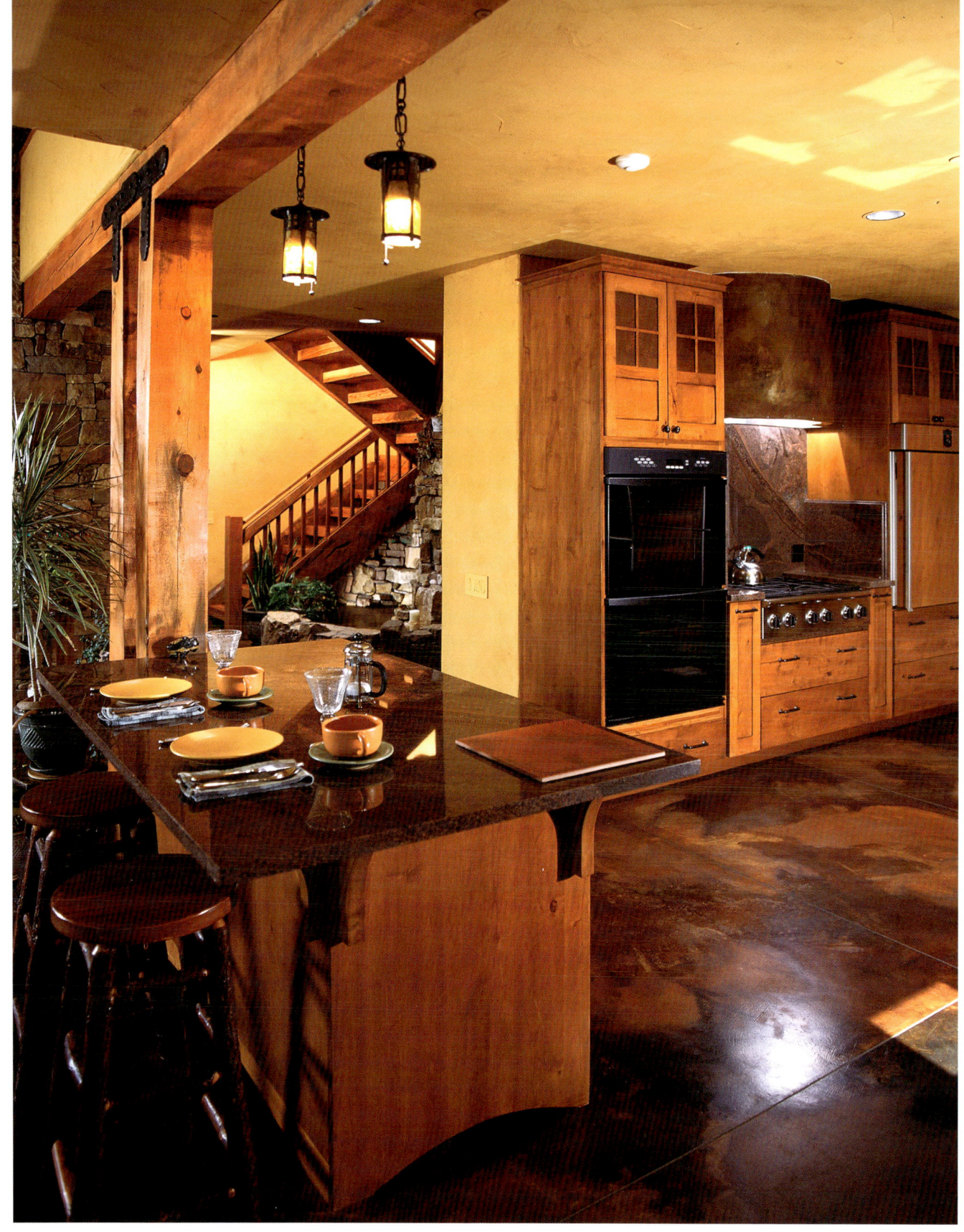

In this way, savings from one area, such as reduced heating/cooling equipment sizing, balance the added cost of another material such as more efficient windows.

WA is proud to work with some of the most prestigious architects in the field, and is well-connected to the communities in which it works. By working with architects and engineers from the start, small adjustments such as proper window orientation, taking advantage of passive solar gain, can result in a home that requires little heating even in the dead of winter. The savings in energy are significant and the natural rhythms of the home are in tune with the environment.

WA's subtle touches lend character and ambiance to its homes. Even the building site itself is carefully handled in an environmentally responsible manner using materials that have the least embodied energy and create the least amount of landfill waste. This careful attention ensures that everyone involved, from carpenters to project managers, has pride in what they are doing.

After clients relax into their new mini-resorts to enjoy the alpenglow, WA maintains a relationship with the home through their unique Home Care Team. The team monitors the home—especially important for second homes—and performs seasonal maintenance, manages upkeep, builds expansions for all the visitors and adds new enhancements as requested.

"We want our owners to feel that they can rely on us to stay with them in the future, long after they have moved in," Richard says. "We don't want them to have to look through the yellow pages to call someone new when they have future work to do on their home."

LEFT:
Brown Ranch, Telluride.
Photograph by Ron Semrod

FACING PAG TOP:
Maroon Creek, Aspen.
Photograph by Steve Mundinger

FACING PAG BOTTOM:
Wilson Peak, Telluride.
Photograph by Ron Semrod

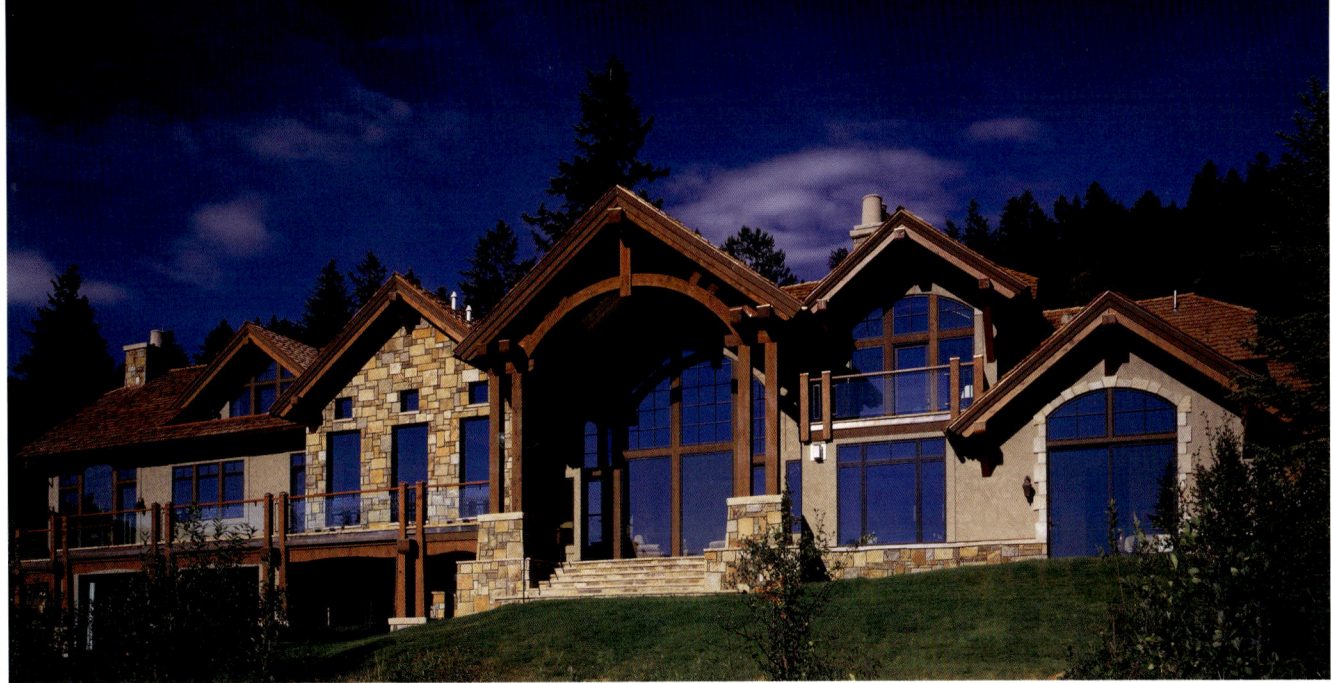

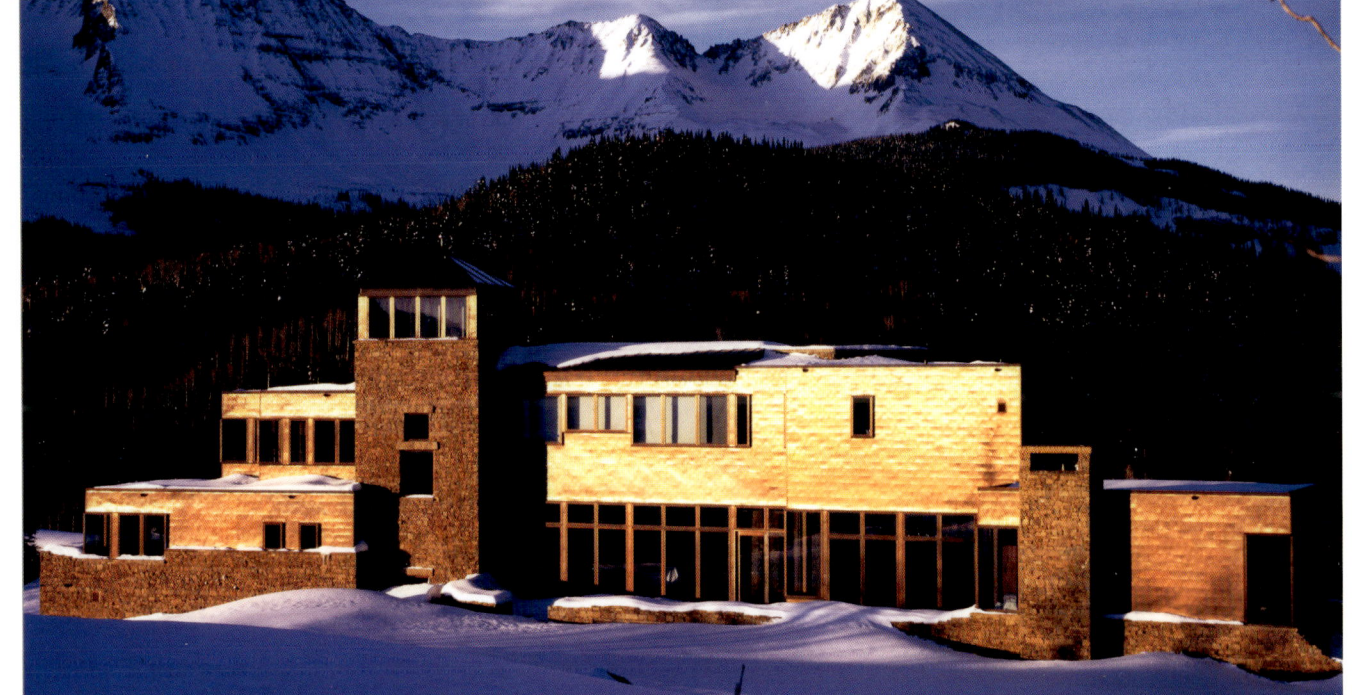

Q&A

more about richard...

NAME SOMETHING MOST PEOPLE DON'T KNOW ABOUT YOU.
I grew up on a hacienda, in southern Chile.

WHO HAS HAD THE MOST INFLUENCE ON YOUR CAREER?
Rob Wellington Quigley, FAIA, an architect in San Diego, California.

WHAT IS THE MOST UNIQUE OR IMPRESSIVE HOME YOU'VE BEEN INVOLVED WITH?
The 12,000-square-foot Frazer homestead in Telluride, Colorado, (shown bottom left), built on a ridge top at an elevation of 13,000-feet. All exterior and interior stone work was generated in the excavation of the foundation. The exterior is copper, glass and stone. Glazing was "tuned" for each elevation to optimize energy conservation.

WHAT IS THE HIGHEST COMPLIMENT YOU'VE RECEIVED PROFESSIONALLY?
Working with people who are dedicated and enjoy the Green building process. And working in a dynamic building team.

more about mike...

NAME ONE THING MOST PEOPLE DON'T KNOW ABOUT YOU?
I've studied the science of restoration, as well as the bureaucracy involved in getting the projects "certified" to receive tax credits. I was one of only five consultants in New York State who was recommended by the State Department of Parks, which oversaw the certification of historic rehab projects.

ANY AWARDS OR SPECIAL RECOGNITION YOU WOULD LIKE MENTIONED?
We were named "Builder of the Year" in 2000 by the Colorado Association of Homebuilders.

WHAT DO YOU LIKE ABOUT DOING BUSINESS IN YOUR LOCALE?
Living and working in paradise. Our clients are envious because they only visit and we live here.

WODEHOUSE-AUGELLO BUILDERS
ASPEN AND TELLURIDE
Richard Wodehouse
Michael Augello
307 L ABC
Aspen, CO 81611
970.728.3525
f: 970.920.9779
www.wodehousebuilders.com

TELLURIDE
200 San Miguel Drive, 2nd floor
Telluride, CO 81435

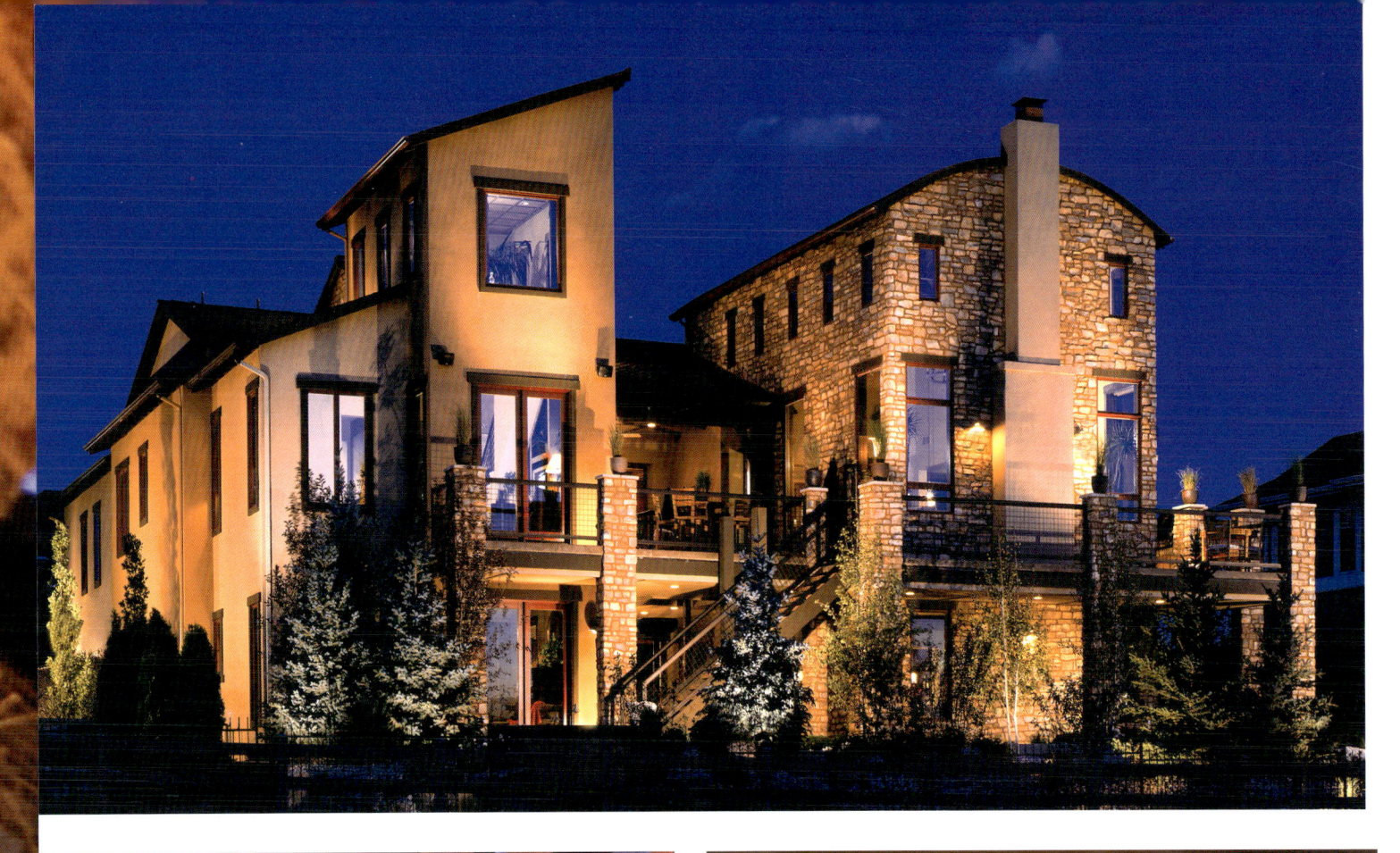

"Regardless of location or type of home, the passion and style we bring to each design is what keeps our clients with us. We can incorporate creative ideas developed in a custom project and integrate elements in a production home—giving it an edge not likely seen in that marketplace. At the same time, we can use creative concepts that are highly successful in a production home with the added benefit of a higher budget afforded in a custom home giving that homeowner luxurious style and function."

A graduate from California Poly Technical State University in San Luis Obispo, Mike is a California native who now makes his home in Colorado. He brings with him a California flair to his designs and his blending of indoor and outdoor space have earned his firm countless awards throughout the United States.

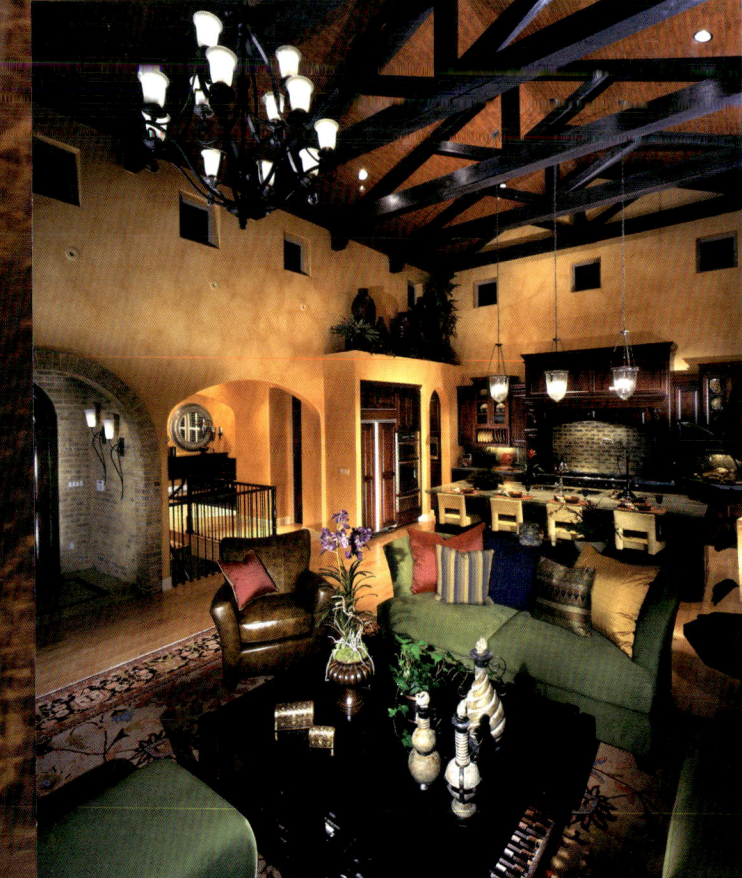

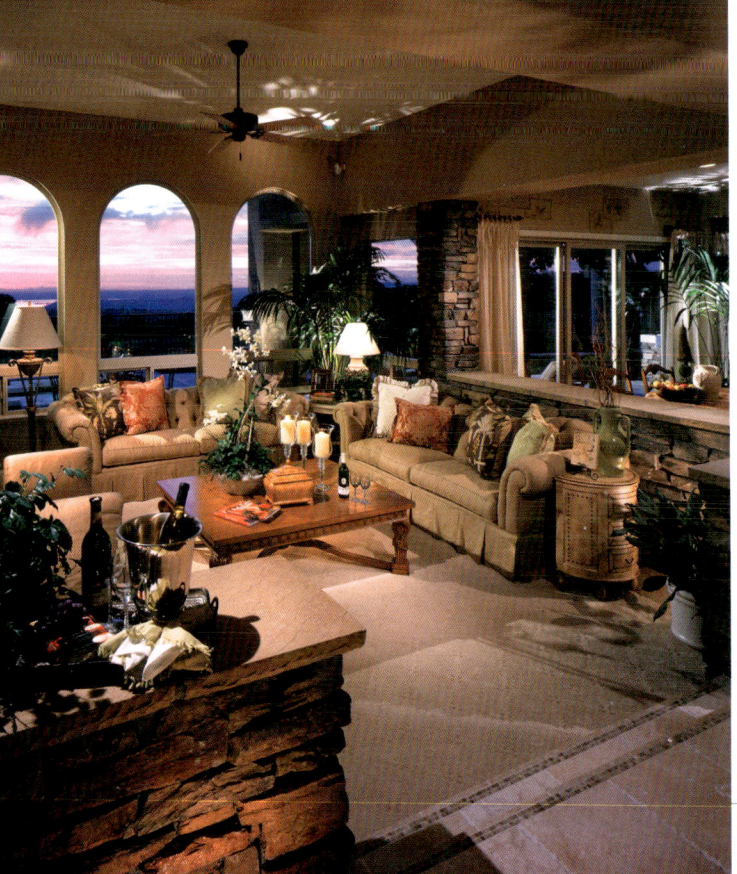

TOP LEFT:
Rear façade of Parade Home 2004 "Eureka," Erie Colorado. Grand Award: "Judges Best Overall" and "People's Choice Award."
Photograph by Aronphoto.com

BOTTOM LEFT:
Grand Hall of Avanzare, Stapleton, Colorado.
Photograph by Aronphoto.com

BOTTOM RIGHT:
Tesoro at Serrano great room, El Dorado Hills, California.
Photograph by Ericfigge.com

FACING PAGE TOP:
Great room connected to strong gallery, organizing the floor plan with the use of rhythm and order, Old Cherry Hills Villa.
Photograph by Aronphoto.com

FACING PAGE BOTTOM:
Entry tower at "Eureka," blending of exterior and interior materials with rustic Colorado details.
Photograph by Aronphoto.com

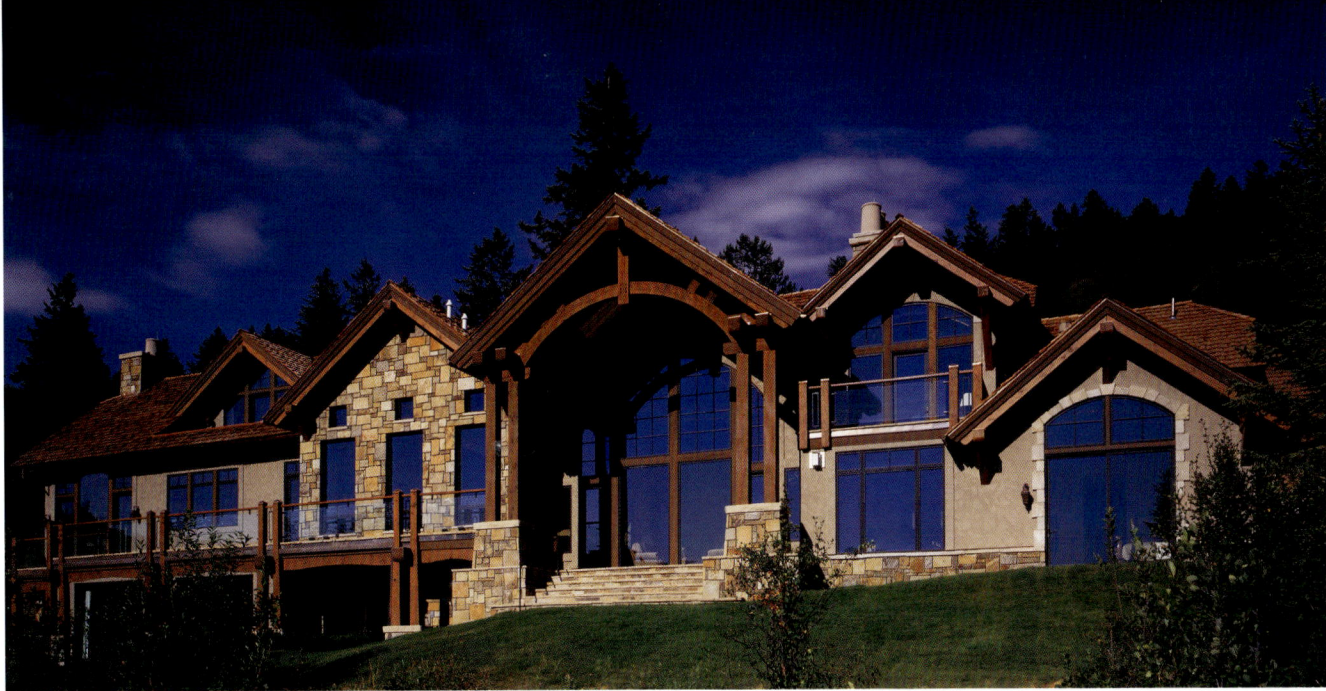

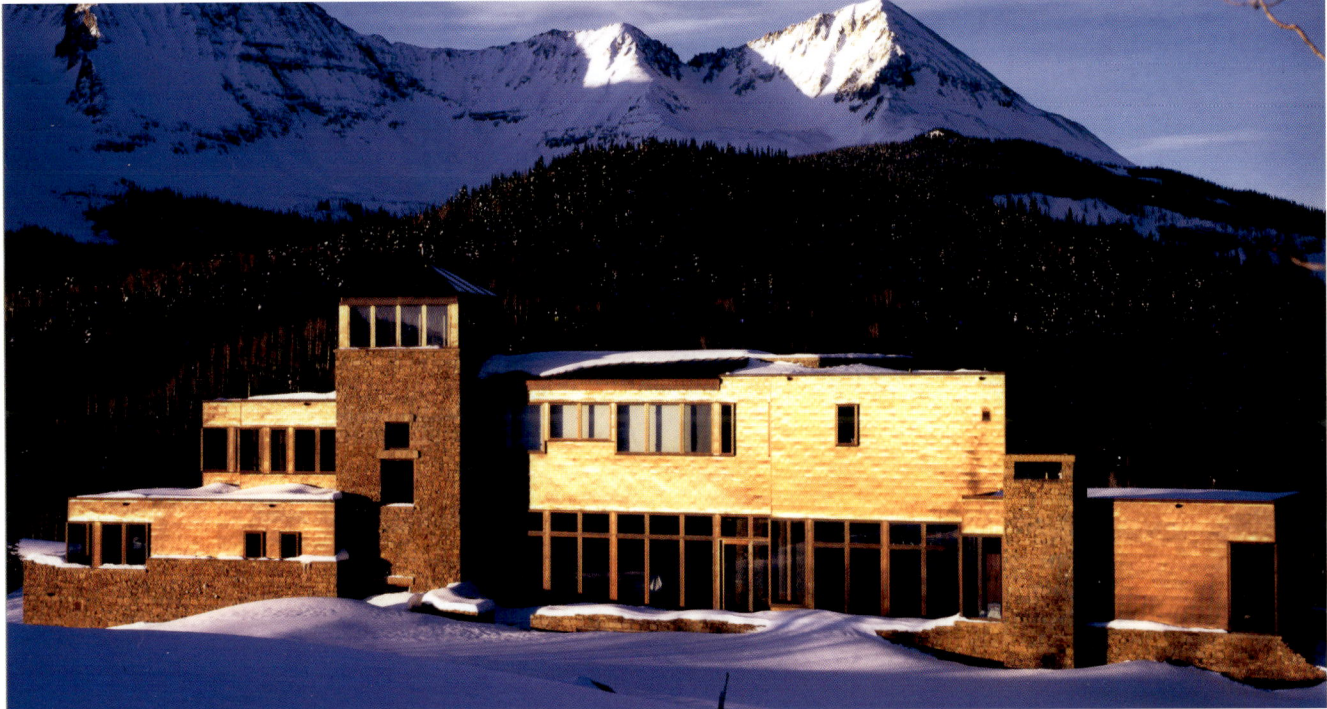

Q&A

more about richard...

NAME SOMETHING MOST PEOPLE DON'T KNOW ABOUT YOU.
I grew up on a hacienda, in southern Chile.

WHO HAS HAD THE MOST INFLUENCE ON YOUR CAREER?
Rob Wellington Quigley, FAIA, an architect in San Diego, California.

WHAT IS THE MOST UNIQUE OR IMPRESSIVE HOME YOU'VE BEEN INVOLVED WITH?
The 12,000-square-foot Frazer homestead in Telluride, Colorado, (shown bottom left), built on a ridge top at an elevation of 13,000-feet. All exterior and interior stone work was generated in the excavation of the foundation. The exterior is copper, glass and stone. Glazing was "tuned" for each elevation to optimize energy conservation.

WHAT IS THE HIGHEST COMPLIMENT YOU'VE RECEIVED PROFESSIONALLY?
Working with people who are dedicated and enjoy the Green building process. And working in a dynamic building team.

more about mike...

NAME ONE THING MOST PEOPLE DON'T KNOW ABOUT YOU?
I've studied the science of restoration, as well as the bureaucracy involved in getting the projects "certified" to receive tax credits. I was one of only five consultants in New York State who was recommended by the State Department of Parks, which oversaw the certification of historic rehab projects.

ANY AWARDS OR SPECIAL RECOGNITION YOU WOULD LIKE MENTIONED?
We were named "Builder of the Year" in 2000 by the Colorado Association of Homebuilders.

WHAT DO YOU LIKE ABOUT DOING BUSINESS IN YOUR LOCALE?
Living and working in paradise. Our clients are envious because they only visit and we live here.

WODEHOUSE-AUGELLO BUILDERS

ASPEN AND TELLURIDE

Richard Wodehouse

Michael Augello

307 L ABC

Aspen, CO 81611

970.728.3525

f: 970.920.9779

www.wodehousebuilders.com

TELLURIDE

200 San Miguel Drive, 2nd floor

Telluride, CO 81435

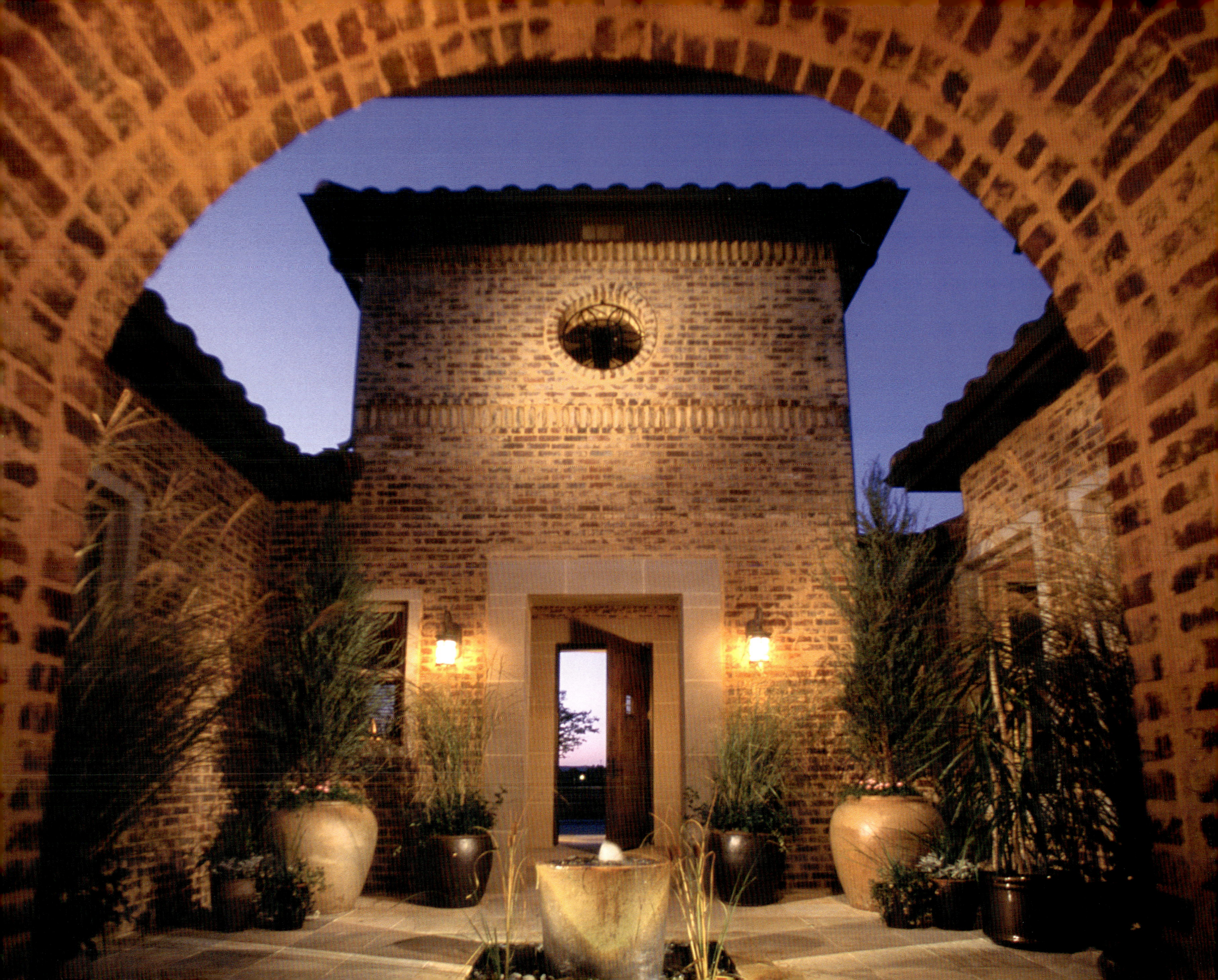

MICHAEL WOODLEY

WOODLEY ARCHITECTURAL GROUP

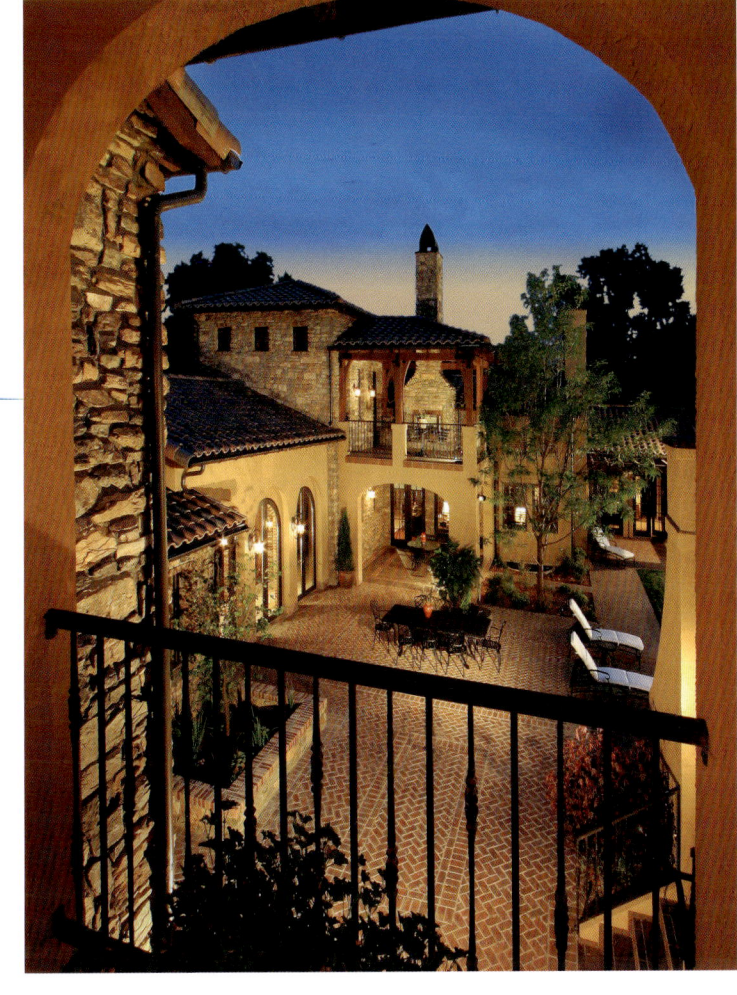

Prior to establishing Woodley Architectural Group, Mike Woodley was with one of the Nation's leading home builders. For over 10 years he was responsible for overseeing their architecture, land planning, graphics and merchandising in the United States, Europe and Mexico. In 1998, Mike started Woodley Architectural Group in California.

Before long, he garnered the reputation of delivering innovative designs with the responsiveness to its clients that can be rare in larger organizations. Woodley Architecture soon expanded and now has offices located in Littleton, Colorado and Costa Mesa, California. Aggressive marketing is not the tool for obtaining new business; rather a stellar reputation and past experience with clients are what keep their project lists ever growing.

Mike's portfolio includes all price ranges and housing types. He is frequently sought out to design for the "Parade of Homes," custom homes showcasing the very best in the building industry. The innovative designs created by Mike and his team, have been recognized as "Best of Show" or "People's Choice" often setting a benchmark for upcoming trends and establishing Mike as a premier custom home designer.

Mike is just as proud and excited about designing for the more "attainable" projects requiring highly creative and functional solutions. His passion and creativity give a distinctive edge over other homes competing in the marketplace. In 2004, Mike was asked to provide the architecture for the military housing on Pearl Harbor for the Navy. Today Mike is commissioned to do custom homes on other islands as well as resort housing in Mexico.

With designs that can be found throughout the United States, Mike's travels have allowed him to bring design trends from other regions and cultures.

ABOVE:
Entry tower and court of "Avanzare"–Stapleton, Colorado–Bar Award's "Home of the Year."
Photograph by Aronphoto.com

FACING PAGE:
Capturing Old World charm "Old Cherry Hills Villa" rear courtyard. Winner of the National Gold Award–"Best Custom Home", located in Cherry Hills, Colorado.
Photograph by Aronphoto.com

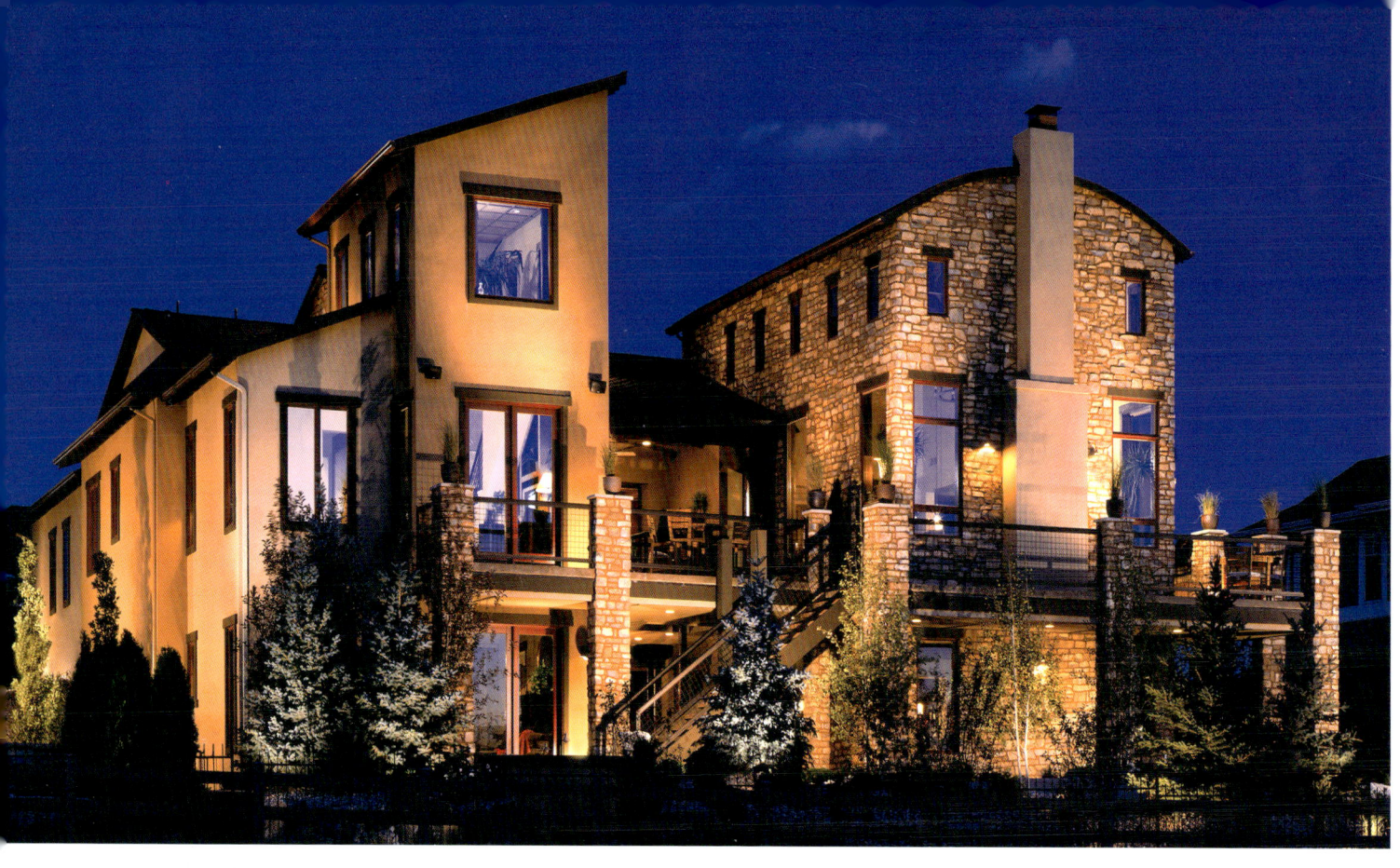

"Regardless of location or type of home, the passion and style we bring to each design is what keeps our clients with us. We can incorporate creative ideas developed in a custom project and integrate elements in a production home—giving it an edge not likely seen in that marketplace. At the same time, we can use creative concepts that are highly successful in a production home with the added benefit of a higher budget afforded in a custom home giving that homeowner luxurious style and function."

A graduate from California Poly Technical State University in San Luis Obispo, Mike is a California native who now makes his home in Colorado. He brings with him a California flair to his designs and his blending of indoor and outdoor space have earned his firm countless awards throughout the United States.

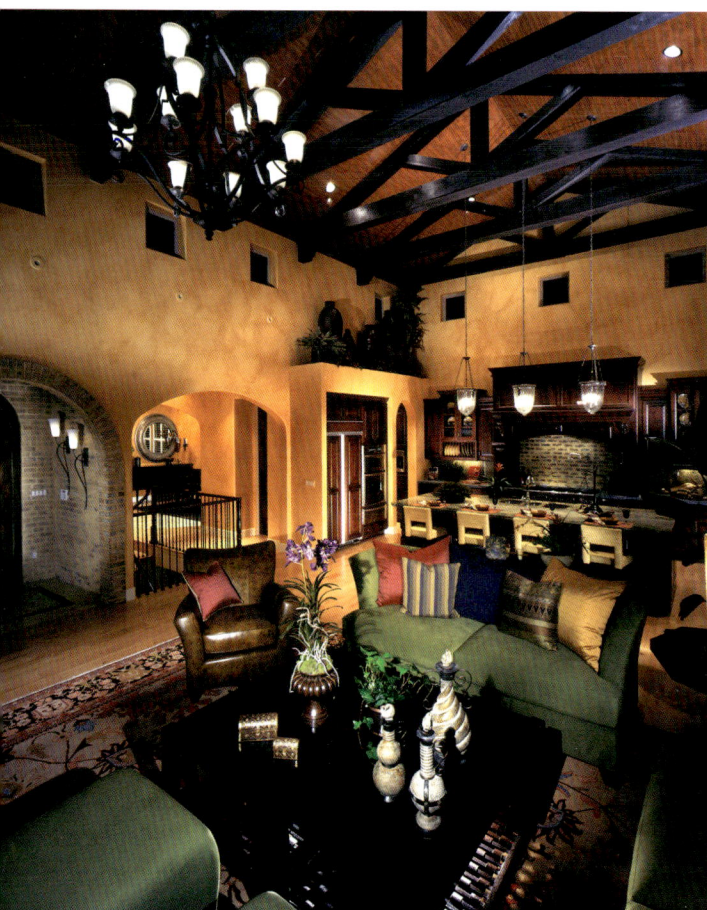

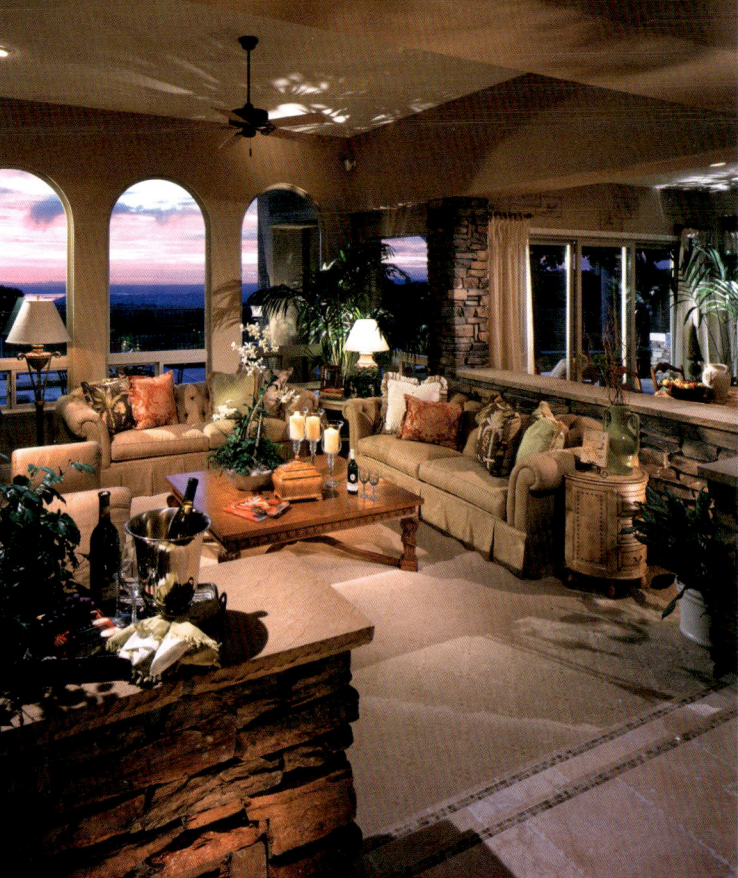

TOP LEFT:
Rear façade of Parade Home 2004 "Eureka," Erie Colorado. Grand Award: "Judges Best Overall" and "People's Choice Award."
Photograph by Aronphoto.com

BOTTOM LEFT:
Grand Hall of Avanzare, Stapleton, Colorado.
Photograph by Aronphoto.com

BOTTOM RIGHT:
Tesoro at Serrano great room, El Dorado Hills, California.
Photograph by Ericfigge.com

FACING PAGE TOP:
Great room connected to strong gallery, organizing the floor plan with the use of rhythm and order, Old Cherry Hills Villa.
Photograph by Aronphoto.com

FACING PAGE BOTTOM:
Entry tower at "Eureka," blending of exterior and interior materials with rustic Colorado details.
Photograph by Aronphoto.com

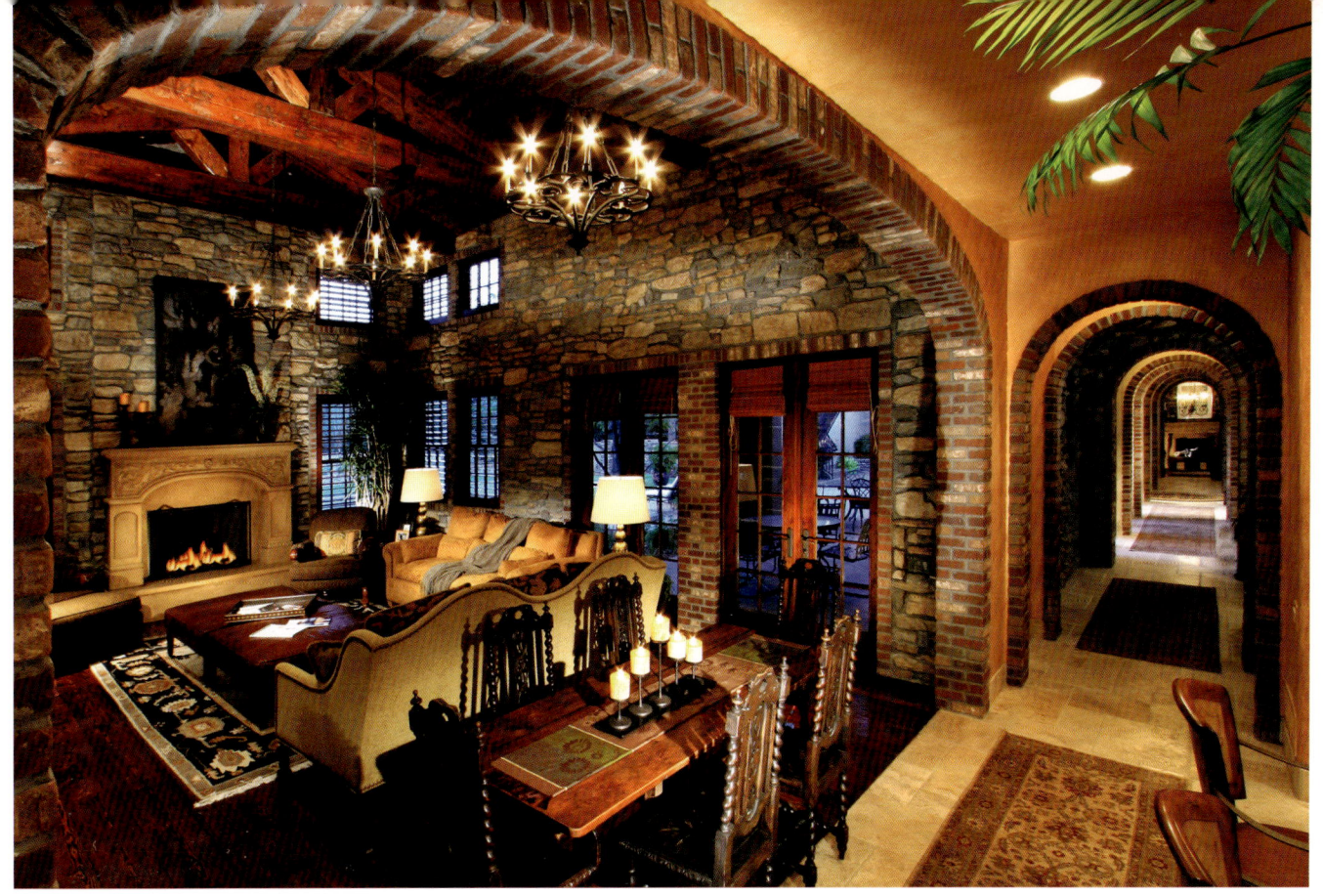

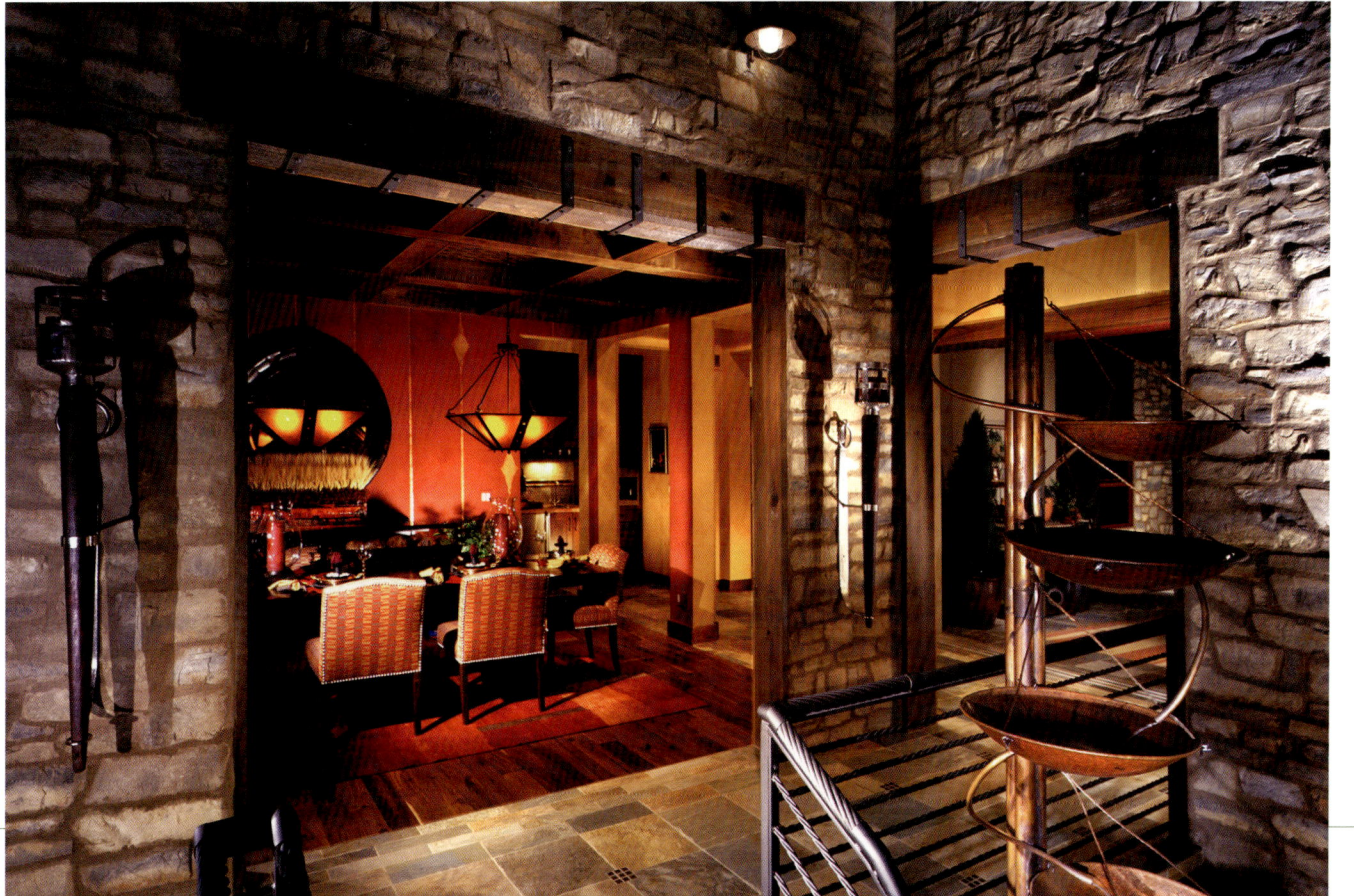

Q&A more about mike...

WHAT ONE ELEMENT OF STYLE OR PHILOSOPHY HAVE YOU STUCK WITH FOR YEARS THAT STILL WORKS FOR YOU?
Treat people the way you would want to be treated.

WHAT IS THE MOST UNIQUE/IMPRESSIVE/BEAUTIFUL HOME WHERE YOU'VE HAD INVOLVEMENT?
I love the diversity of our projects. From multi-million dollar custom homes in the Rockies to military housing in Pearl Harbor. We work on attached projects (condos up to 30 units per acre) to a single home on a 35-acre site.

NAME ONE THING MOST PEOPLE DON'T KNOW ABOUT YOU.
I am a southern California native who grew up surfing and playing hockey. I continue to play hockey and am now coaching a high school team, surfing has been traded for skiing.

ANY ASSOCIATIONS, ACCREDITATIONS OR MEMBERSHIPS YOU WANT MENTIONED?
I am a member of the A.I.A., N.A.H.B. and B.I.A. and am frequently invited to be a featured speaker at P.C.B.C., N.A.H.B., and A.I.A. functions. I have also judged at major design competitions throughout the country.

ANY AWARDS OR SPECIAL RECOGNITION YOU WOULD LIKE MENTIONED?
Woodley Architectural Group has received wide spread industry recognition, winning well over 100 design awards, including Mame, Bar, Sam, Elan, and the highly coveted Gold Nugget and The Nationals-Gold.

WHAT SEPARATES YOU FROM YOUR COMPETITION?
As a principal architect, I still spend most of my time "on the boards" designing, which is very uncommon for a firm with the volume of work we produce.

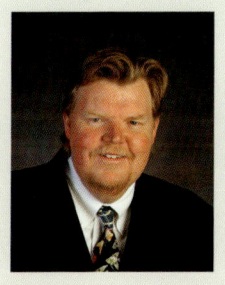

WOODLEY ARCHITECTURAL GROUP
MIKE WOODLEY, AIA
9137 South Ridgeline Boulevard, Suite 120
Highlands Ranch, CO 80129
303.683.7231
f: 303.683.2922
www.woodleyarchitecture.com

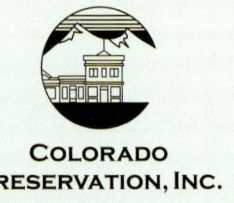

COLORADO PRESERVATION, INC
MARK RODMAN
333 West Colfax Avenue, Suite 300
Denver, CO 80204
303.893.4260
f: 303.893.4333
www.coloradopreservation.org

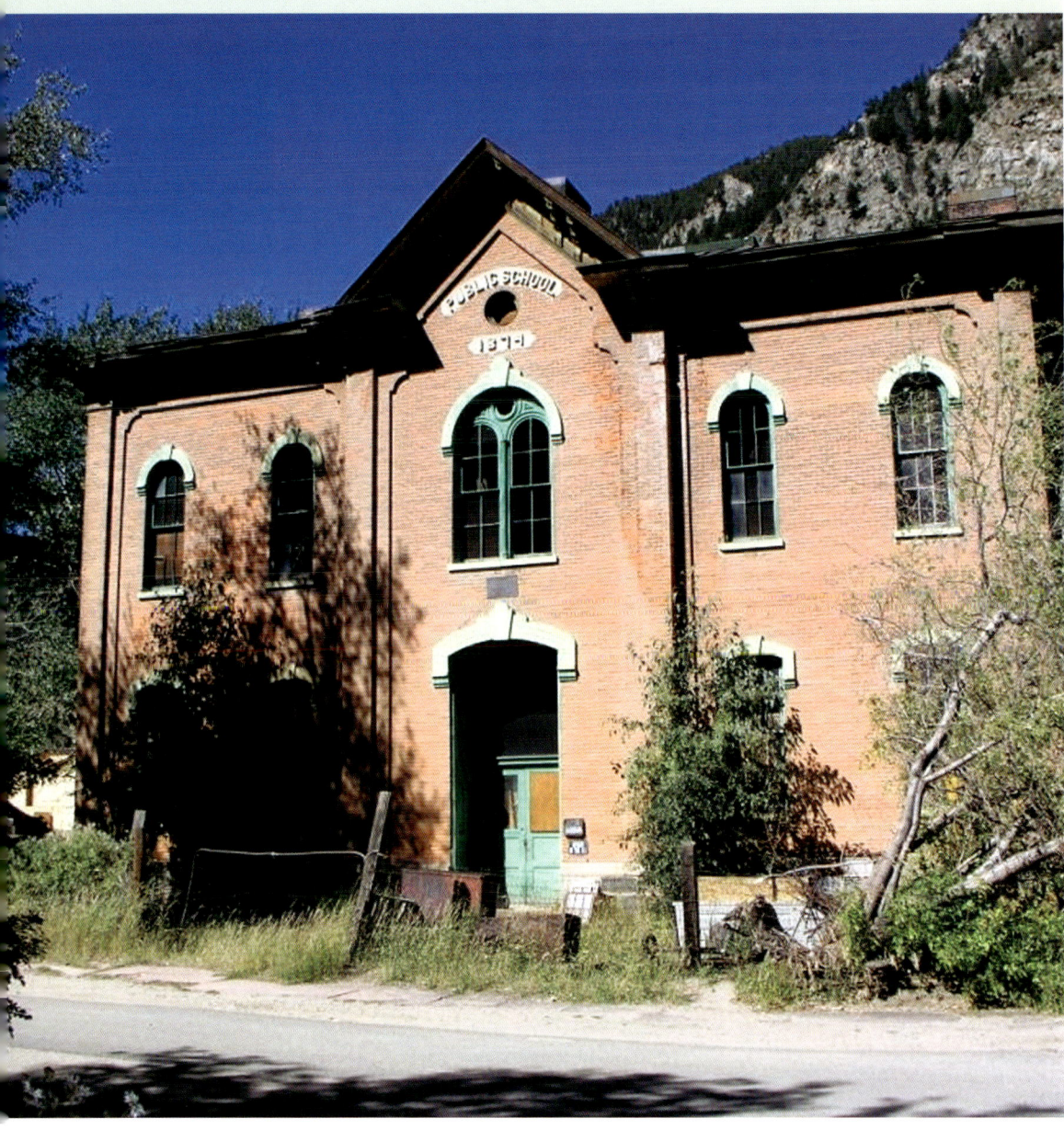

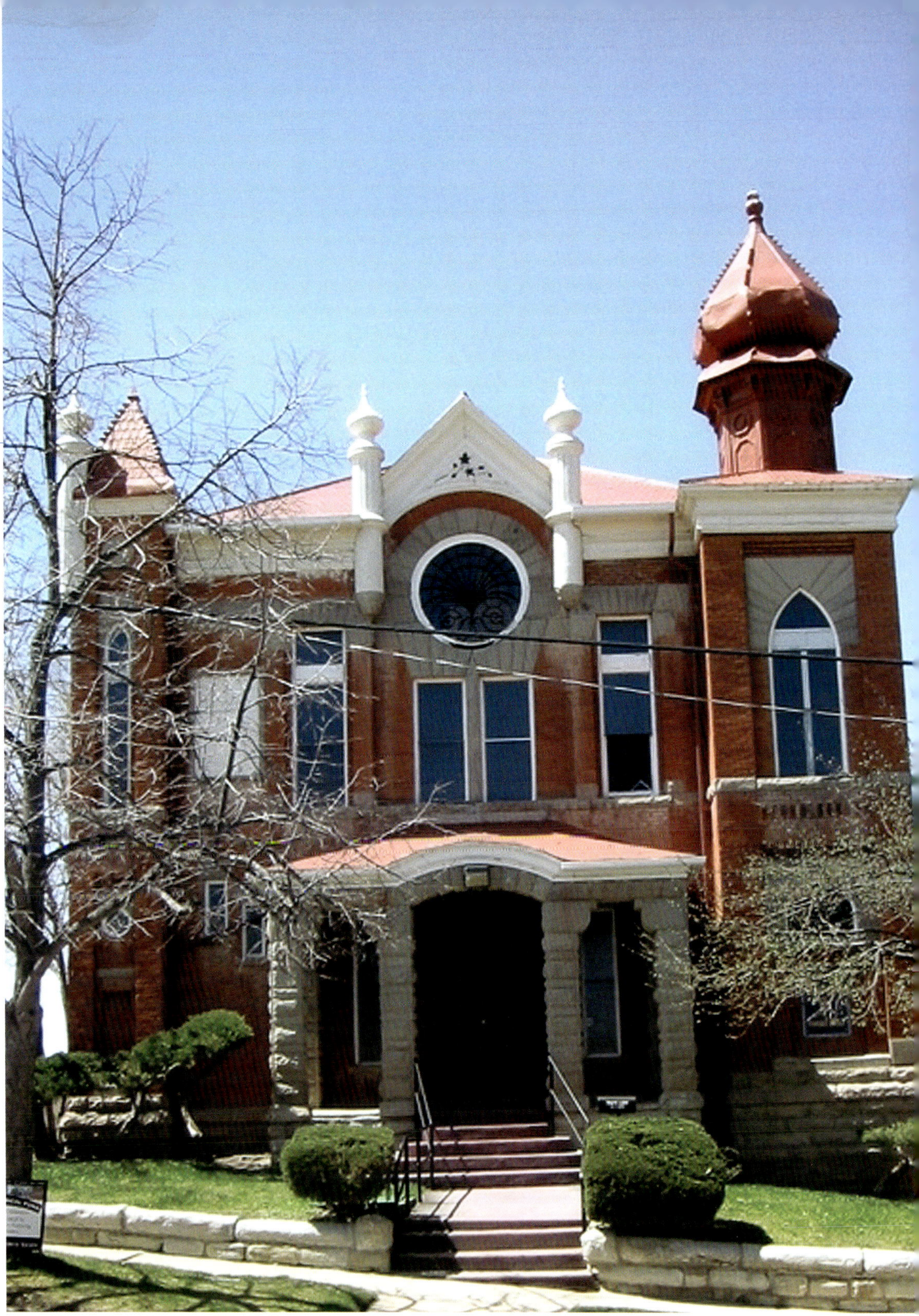

ABOVE:
The 1874 Georgetown School awaits rehabilitation for an adaptive use.
Photograph by Deon Wolfenbarger, Three Gables

ABOVE:
Colorado's oldest synagogue in continuous use was constructed in 1889 in Trinidad.
Photograph by Belinda Zink, Zink & Associates

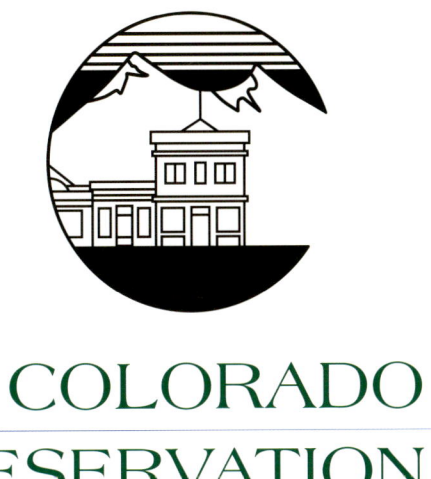

COLORADO PRESERVATION

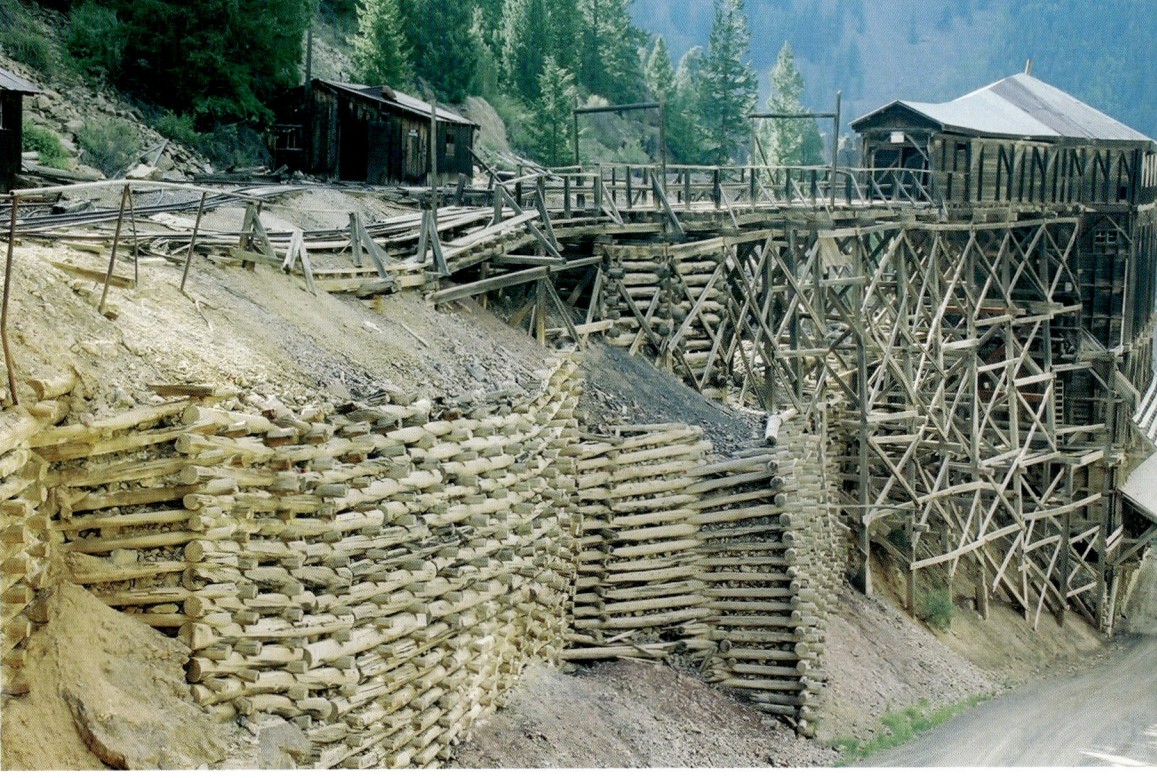

ABOVE:
The Commodore Mine District in Creede is one of Colorado's most scenic historic mining districts.
Photograph by Ed Raines, Geo-Historical Studies

Throughout the mountains and plains are reminders of Colorado's rich heritage. From picturesque schools to ornate synagogues, magnificent mining structures to grand homes, Colorado abounds in historic places. Historic preservation protects the character of these places: Colorado's history and heritage. Colorado Preservation, Inc., a non-profit organization, builds a future for historic places—strengthening communities, developing tourism, conserving resources and promoting economic vitality.

Colorado Preservation, Inc.'s Endangered Places Program provides technical assistance to organizations and individuals working to save and protect structures, sites and landscapes important to Colorado's heritage. Colorado's Most Endangered Places List is published annually to build awareness and assistance for threatened historic resources. Sites such as the 1874 Georgetown School, the 1889 Temple Aaron in Trinidad and Creede's Commodore Mine District constructed in the early 20th century are being preserved through the efforts of Colorado Preservation, Inc. and its local, state and national partners. In 2003, The Redstone Castle, which represents the rise of the late 19th and early 20th century industrial entrepreneur, was seized by the Internal Revenue Service in association with a securities fraud scheme. Through partnerships with the IRS and other historic preservation organizations, a historic preservation easement was negotiated to protect the property from alteration or demolition and provides just one more shining example of how Colorado Preservation, Inc. is building a future for historic places.

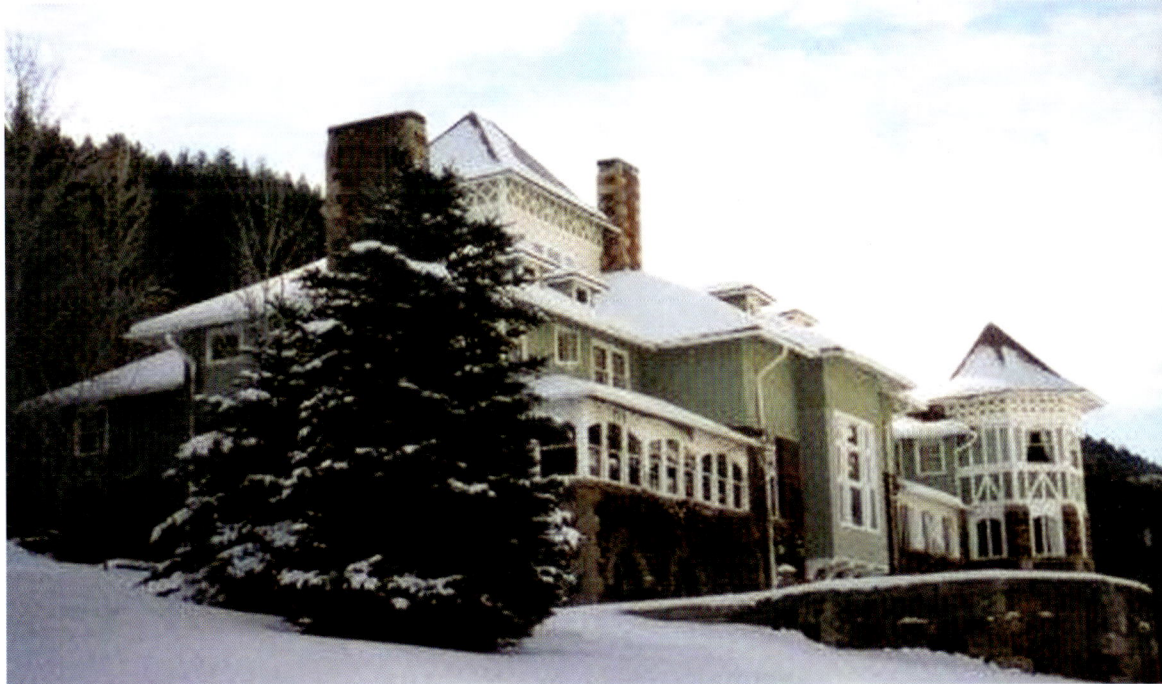

ABOVE:
The 1902 Redstone Castle, now protected by a preservation easement, overlooks the Crystal River Valley of the White River National Forest and the historic town of Redstone.
Photograph by Lawrence Walsh, Colorado Preservation, Inc.

PUBLISHING TEAM

Brian G. Carabet, Publisher
John A. Shand, Publisher
Steve Darocy, Executive Publisher
Elizabeth Fischer, Regional Publisher
Tom Fischer, Regional Publisher

Michele Cunningham-Scott, Art Director
Mary Elizabeth Acree, Graphic Designer
Emily Kattan, Graphic Designer
Ron Ruscio, Contributing Photographer

Elizabeth Gionta, Senior Editor
Aaron Barker, Editor
Sarah Toler, Editor
Rosalie Wilson, Editor
Karen Mitchell, Editor

Kristy Randall, Senior Production Coordinator
Laura Greenwood, Production Coordinator
Jennifer Lenhart, Traffic Coordinator
Carol Kendall, Project Management
Beverly Smith, Project Management

PANACHE PARTNERS, LLC
CORPORATE OFFICE
13747 Montfort Drive
Suite 100
Dallas, TX 75240
972.661.9884
www.panache.com

COLORADO OFFICE
303.799.4244

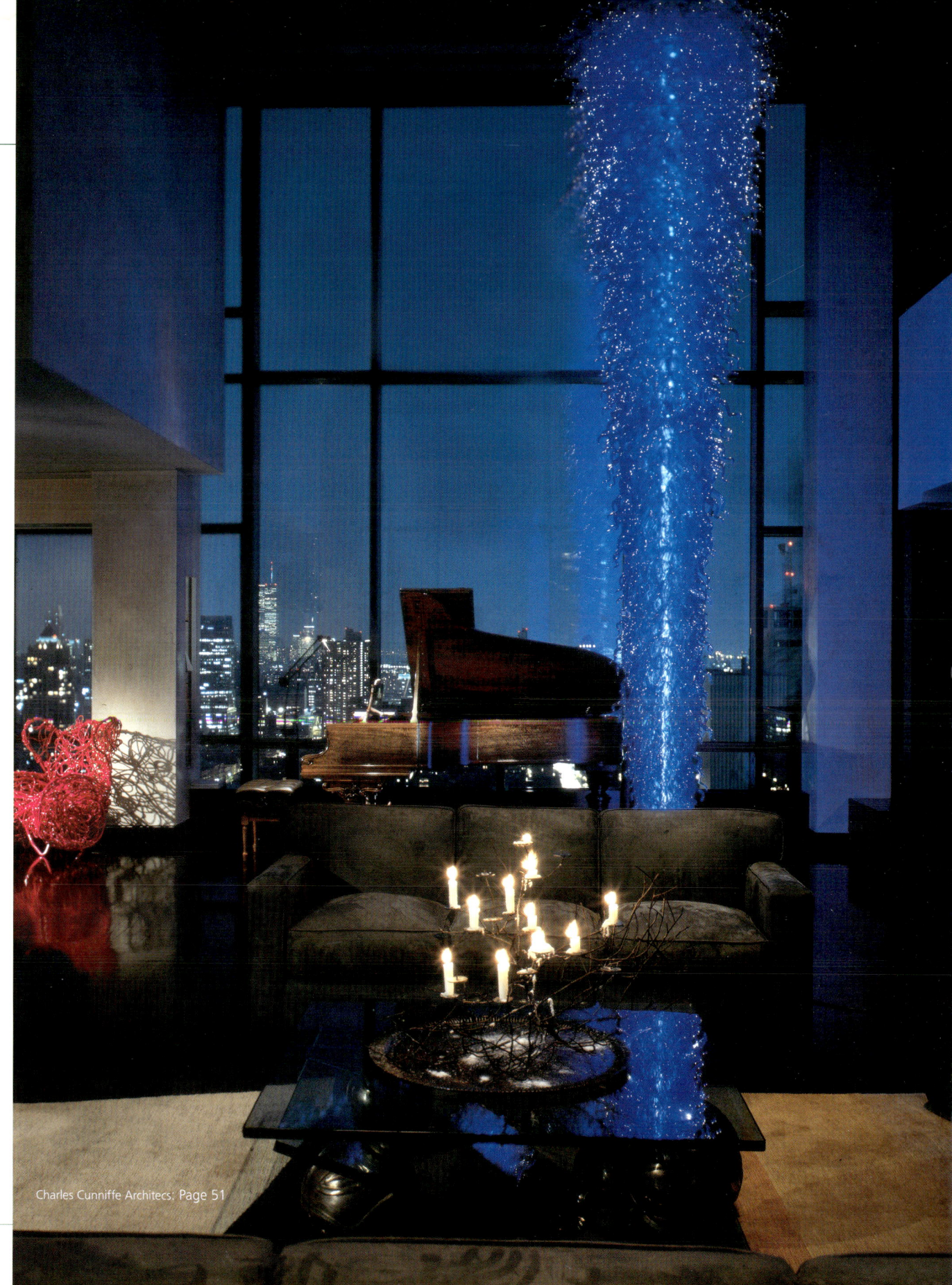

Charles Cunniffe Architects: Page 51